The GALE
ENCYCLOPEDIA of
PSYCHOLOGY

The GALE
ENCYCLOPEDIA of
PSYCHOLOGY

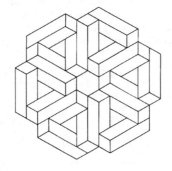

SUSAN GALL, EXECUTIVE EDITOR

Bernard Beins and Alan J. Feldman, Contributing Editors

GALE

DETROIT   NEW YORK   TORONTO   LONDON

Gale Encyclopedia of Psychology

Susan Gall, *Executive Editor*
Bernard Beins, *Contributing Editor*
Alan J. Feldman, *Editor*

Gale Research Staff

Robyn V. Young, *Coordinating Editor*
Mary Beth Trimper, *Production Director*
Evi Seoud, *Production Manager*
Shanna Heilveil, *Production Assistant*
Cynthia Baldwin, *Production Design Manager*
Mary Krzewinski, *Art Director*

ISBN 0-7876-0372-4
Printed in the United States of America
10 9 8 7 6 5 4 3

Library of Congress Cataloging-in-Publication Data

Gale encyclopedia of psychology / Bernard Beins, contributing editor :
  Alan Feldman, editor : Susan Gall, executive editor.
       p.   cm.
  Includes bibliographical references and index.
    ISBN 0-7876-0372-4 (alk. paper)
    1. Psychology--Encyclopedias.   I. Beins, Bernard.   II. Feldman, Alan.
  III. Gall, Susan B.
  BF31.G35   1996
  150' 3--dc20   96-9775
                                                             CIP

Executive Editor
Susan Gall

Contributing Editors
Bernard Beins, Ithaca College, Ithaca, New York
Alan J. Feldman, Perth Amboy High School, Perth Amboy, New Jersey

Managing Editor
Timothy L. Gall

Editorial Advisors and Reviewers
Andrea Canter, Ph.D., Psychologist, Minneapolis Public Schools
Karen Carey, Ph.D., Department of Psychology, California State University, Fresno
Douglas Detterman, Ph.D., Department of Psychology, Case Western Reserve University
Patti Harrison, Ph.D., Department of Educational and School Psychology, University of Alabama
Lynda C. Tirhi, Librarian, Nimitz High School, Irving, Texas

Cordelia R. Heaney, Student Editorial Advisor

Contributors
Bernard Beins
James Calland
Dianne Daeg de Mott
Alan Feldman
Susan Gall
Jim Henry
Mary Anne Klasen
Patricia Martin
Nancy Moore
Cindy Washabaugh
Rosalie Wieder

ORGANIZATION OF THE ENCYCLOPEDIA

The *Gale Encyclopedia of Psychology* includes nearly 500 entries on topics covering key concepts in psychology. It has been designed with ease of use and ready reference in mind.

- Entries are alphabetically arranged in a single sequence.
- Length of entries ranges from brief explanations of a concept in one or two paragraphs to longer, more detailed entries on more complex theories and concepts.
- A brief definition of the entry term appears in italics and precedes the body of the entry.
- Illustrations accompany many of the entries to enhance the reader's understanding of the subject covered.

- Further reading sections are included to point readers to other helpful sources.
- *See also* references are provided at the end of entries to point readers to related entries.
- Cross-references placed throughout the encyclopedia direct readers to entries that include subjects without their own entries.
- The Appendix includes a glossary of terms and a bibliography of references for further study.
- Two indexes complete the work. The first is an index of terms organized by psychology subfield. The second is a comprehensive general index to guide readers to the people and concepts covered in the book.

CONTENTS

ILLUSTRATION CREDITS

Archives of the History of American Psychology, University of Akron: **Alfred Binet, Jerome S. Bruner, Mary Whiton Calkins, James McKeen Cattell, Charles Robert Darwin, René Descartes, John Dewey, Hermann Ebbinghaus, Erik Erikson, Anna Freud, Sigmund Freud, Sir Francis Galton, Arnold Gesell, William James, Carl Jung, Wolfgang Köhler, Christine Ladd-Franklin, Ivan Pavlov, Jean Piaget, Philippe Pinel, B. F. Skinner, Lewis Terman, Margaret Floy Washburn, Robert Yerkes;** Bettmann Archive: **Adolescence, Anger, Anorexia nervosa, Body image, Competition, Deoxyribonucleic acid, Hostility, Nervous system, Right-brain hemisphere; Sleep, Split-Brain Technique, Sports Psychology, Suicide, Synapse;** *Century Dictionary:* **Phrenology;** Courtesy of Martin and Bibi Clarke: **Down syndrome;** Courtesy of the Clarke family: **Family size;** Corel Corporation: **Affect, Aging, Alienation, Attachment, Cognitive Development Theory, Combat Neurosis, Conflict resolution, Creativity, Dementia, Developmental psy**chology, **Emotion, Environment, Equilibrium sense, Gestalt psychology, Handedness, Heredity, Heterosexuality, Identity, Infancy, Interpersonal attraction, Mental health, Mood, Motivation, Personality, Phobia, Play, School phobia, Self-actualization, Self-concept, Sex identity, Social psychology;** EPD Photos: **Addiction, Alcohol dependence and abuse, Contrast effect, Daydreams, Drugs, Dyslexia, Educational psychology, Figure-ground perception, Gifted children; Learning theory;** *FDA Consumer:* **Hearing, Nature/ nurture controversy, Rehabilitation;** Rorschach technique; *Harper's Encyclopedia of the United States, 1912:* **Benjamin Rush;** Courtesy of U.S. Congressman Norman Y. Mineta: **Racism;** Courtesy of Scott and Jodi Schumann: **Twins;** TechPool: **Alzheimer's disease, Aphasia, Autonomic nervous system, Birth, Brain, Central nervous system, Electroencephalograph, Endocrine glands, Hypothalamus, Neuron, Signal detection theory; Vision.**

FOREWORD

Psychology has been one of the most popular undergraduate majors in the United States for more than three decades. At the secondary school level, the popularity of psychology courses has also soared during this period; however, high school courses were initially very different from college courses. High school students, struggling to deal with changes in their bodies, their minds, and their relationships, were offered courses that tended to focus on "adjustment," and to be assigned to teachers trained in other fields—for example, social studies or health. By contrast, college level courses focus on scientific psychology with a strong emphasis on topics such as the biological bases of behavior, perception, memory, and learning.

Since the late 1970s, a number of developments have reduced the gap between high school and college level introductory psychology courses. First, as high school psychology courses multiplied, and the American Psychological Association (APA) became increasingly concerned about the "psychology" being taught at the precollege level, it created the Committee on Psychology in the Secondary Schools (CPSS), whose function is to keep APA informed about trends in high school psychology and to be a resource to high school psychology teachers. Second, the National Science Foundation, as part of its program to improve science education in the secondary schools, funded several training programs for high school psychology teachers.

In 1980, the CPSS contacted the Educational Testing Service, the organization that develops and administers the Scholastic Assessment Test (SAT), and recommended that an Advanced Placement Examination be developed in psychology, with the goal of encouraging secondary schools to offer psychology courses that were equivalent to the college level courses. The Educational Testing Service responded positively to this initiative and after considerable preparation, the first Advanced Placement examination in psychology was offered in 1991. The success of the AP Psychology program has been enormous, with the number of students taking the examination multiplying by the thousands every year.

With this increase in interest in psychology by high school students has come a corresponding demand for reference materials appropriate for high school students. This volume—*Gale Encyclopedia of Psychology*—will be an excellent resource for future students preparing for the AP Psychology examination or simply taking college level psychology courses. The volume opens not just with entries on the classic concepts that might have found their way into early high school psychology course—for example, **ability** and **abnormal psychology**—but also the more rigorously scientific concepts—such as **absolute threshold, action potential,** and **adaptation**—that can be found on the Advanced Placement exam.

In the 1990s, the field of psychology and the introductory psychology course have witnessed an increasing emphasis on cognitive psychology as well as biological psychology (especially neuropsychology). This emphasis is well-reflected in *Gale Encyclopedia of Psychology,* where readers can learn about such topics as **aphasia, neurotransmitters, information processing,** and the **split brain.**

In addition to defining and explaining key psychological concepts (such as **affect, biofeedback,** and **catharsis**), and describing major psychological theories (such as **behaviorism, cognitive development theory**), *Gale Encyclopedia of Psychology* has biographical profiles of some of the most important figures in the history of psychology, including Clifford Beers, Erik Erikson, Sigmund Freud, Sir Francis Galton, Christine Ladd-Franklin, and Jean Piaget. Many colleges require that students concentrating in psychology take a course in "History of Psychology." This attention to important contributors to the field is another valuable component of *GEP.*

The *Gale Encyclopedia of Psychology* is full of useful information for anyone who is interested in psychology, but will be particularly helpful to high school students seeking an understanding of the concepts of academic psychology as employed by experts in the field.

The key names, theories, and concepts are all here, well-defined, and well explained.

Kathleen Malley-Morrison,
Boston University

Kathleen Malley-Morrison is a tenured professor of psychology at Boston University, where she has specialized in family psychology and the teaching of psychology. She was a member of the American Psychological Association's Committee on Psychology in the Secondary Schools for three years, and chairperson of the committee for her last year. Malley-Morrison was Project Director for two National Science Foundation grants for conducting summer workshops for high school psychology teachers. She was also on the Educational Testing Service Advisory Committee that developed the AP Psychology Program and was the first AP Psychology Exam chief reader. Malley-Morrison has published several papers on the teaching of psychology and was co-author of an introductory psychology textbook.

PREFACE

The development of *Gale Encyclopedia of Psychology (GEP)* was directed by two well-respected teachers in the field of psychology. Bernard Beins, who teaches psychology at Ithaca College in Ithaca, New York, contributes to academic psychology in a number of ways. In 1996, he completed a term as secretary of the Society for the Teaching of Psychology. The Society is a division (Division II) of the American Psychological Association, and honored Dr. Beins by making him a fellow. Assisting Dr. Beins in the design of *GEP* was Alan J. Feldman, high school teacher of psychology at Perth Amboy High School in New Jersey. Mr. Feldman was named High School Psychology Teacher of the Year in 1993; in addition to this recognition for teaching excellence, he has been instrumental in helping to shape the teaching of psychology at the high school level. When he is not in front of a class of high school students, Mr. Feldman presents workshops for high school teachers on curriculum development, and the Advanced Placement test in Psychology. In addition, he has helped prepare review courses for students, and has been involved in grading the AP exams.

From a master list prepared by the editors, the editorial advisors reviewed and selected over 450 terms for inclusion in *GEP*. The advisors, representing high schools and colleges across the country, brought the perspective of the target audience for *GEP*—high school students, teachers, librarians, and social service professionals.

Terms reflect the range of subfields encompassed by the field of psychology—from profiles of notable individuals and organizations to essays on key concepts and theories. An index by subfield will help users find topics of interest in Abnormal, Cognitive, Developmental and Social psychology; Behavior, Biographical and Organization profiles, Biological science, History of psychology, Methodology and statistics, Perception, and Personality.

The editors acknowledge with gratitude the support and guidance provided by staff editors at Gale Research: David Salamie, who planted the seed of the idea; Robyn Young (assisted capably by Kyung Lim Kalasky), who edited the entries and kept the project moving forward; Christine Jeryan, who supervised the development process and provided wisdom, support, and encouragement whenever needed; Shanna Heilveil and Evi Seoud, who took the finished product and turned it into a bound volume. To the staff of Eastword Publications Development—Debby Baron, Janet Fenn, Matthew Markovich, and Brian Rajewski—we express our gratitude.

Susan Gall
Executive Editor

Ability

Knowledge or skill, including the potential to acquire knowledge or skills and those already acquired.

The capacity to learn, commonly known as aptitude, and the demonstration of skills and knowledge already learned, called achievement, are among the factors used to evaluate **intelligence**. When evaluating or comparing subjects, two kinds of abilities are considered: verbal ability, including reading comprehension, ability to converse, vocabulary, and the use of language; and problem-solving ability, which includes a person's capacity to make good decisions given a set of circumstances.

Relatively straightforward tests of ability are often used by employers to determine an applicant's skills. For example, a person applying for a job as a word processor may be given a keyboarding test, while a bus-driving applicant would be given a driving test. Tests to evaluate more complex abilities, such as leadership, **motivation**, and social skills tend to be less precise.

Developed around the turn of the twentieth century, formal tests used by psychologists and educators to measure aptitude and achievement remain controversial. Intelligence, or IQ, tests are faulted for ignoring cultural or social biases, particularly with regard to schoolchildren, and critics contend such standardized measures cannot adequately predict a person's future performance.

See also Achievement Tests; Scholastic Assessment Test; Stanford-Binet Intelligence Scales; Vocational Aptitude Test.

Further Reading

Atkinson, Rita L.; Richard C. Atkinson; Edward E. Smith; and Ernest R. Hilgard. *Introduction to Psychology.* 9th ed. San Diego: Harcourt Brace Jovanovich, 1987.

Zimbardo, Philip G. *Psychology and Life.* 12th ed. Glenview, IL: Scott, Foresman, 1988.

Abnormal Psychology

The subfield of psychology concerned with the study of abnormal behavior.

Abnormal behavior is defined as behavior which is considered to be maladaptive or deviant by the social culture in which it occurs. Though disagreement exists regarding which particular behaviors can be classified as abnormal, **psychologists** have defined several criteria for purposes of classification. One is that the behavior occurs infrequently and thus deviates from statistical norms. Another is that the behavior deviates from social norms of acceptable behavior. A third is that the behavior is maladaptive, that it has adverse affects on the individual or on the individual's social group. Lastly, abnormality may be defined based on the subjective feelings of misery, **depression,** or **anxiety** of an individual rather than any behavior he exhibits.

The *Diagnostic and Statistical Manual of Mental Disorders*, **4th edition (***DSM-IV***)** is a classification system of abnormal behaviors which aids psychologists and other mental health professionals in diagnosing and treating mental disorders. *DSM-IV* includes the major categories of abnormal behavior which are anxiety disorders, such as **obsessive-compulsive disorders** and **phobias;** affective disorders, which are disturbances of mood such as **depression;** schizophrenic disorders, which are characterized by major disturbances in personality and distortion of reality; and various **personality disorders.**

While psychologists use similar criteria to diagnose abnormal behavior, their perspectives in understanding and treating related disorders vary greatly. For instance, a psychologist with a psychoanalytic approach would explain depression as a reaction to loss, worsened by **anger** turned inward. A behavioral psychologist would assume a lack of positive reinforcement to be a significant cause in the disease. A cognitive theorist would focus on the negative thought patterns and **attitudes** of an individual in contributing to his depression. And a psychologist with a biological perspective would consider a chemical imbalance in the **nervous system** of a depressed individual to be responsible for his disorder. Many studies have shown that a number of these factors may come into play in the life of an individual suffering from a mental disorder characterized by abnormal behavior.

See also Behavior Disorder; Schizophrenia.

Further Reading

Oldham, John M. *The New Personality Self-Portrait.* New York: Bantam, 1995.

Personality Disorders and the Five-Factor Model of Personality. Washington, DC: American Psychological Association, 1994.

Absolute Threshold

The minimal amount of energy necessary to stimulate the sensory receptors.

The method of testing for the absolute threshold is similar for different sensory systems. Thus, the tester can briefly present a light or a sound (or any other kind of stimulus) at different, low intensities until the observer is unable to detect the presence of the stimulus. In such a task, the person may undergo thousands of trials before the researcher can determine the threshold.

While the absolute threshold is a useful concept, it does not exist in reality. That is, on one occasion, an individual might be unable to detect a certain faint light but on a subsequent occasion, may detect it. In addition, scientists cannot determine with absolute certainty how much energy is present in a light because of limits to the physics of measurement. As a result, psychologists often define the threshold as the lowest intensity that a person can detect 50 percent of the time.

A number of different factors can influence the absolute threshold, including the observer's motivations and expectations, and whether the person is adapted to the stimulus. Scientists have discovered that cognitive processes can influence the measurement of the threshold and that it is not as simple as once understood. Psychologists have also studied how different two stimuli have to be in order to be noticed as not being the same. Such an approach involves what are called difference thresholds.

Further Reading

Galantner, E. "Contemporary Psychophysics." In *New Directions in Psychology*, edited by R. Brown. New York: Holt, Rinehart & Winston, 1962.

Achievement Motivation. See **Motivation**.

Achievement Tests

Standardized tests, administered to groups of students, intended to measure how well they have learned information in various academic subjects.

Spelling tests, timed arithmetic tests, and map quizzes are all examples of achievement tests. Each measures how well students can demonstrate their knowledge of a particular academic subject or skill. Achievement tests on a small scale like these are administered frequently in schools. Less frequently, students

EXAMPLES OF ABSOLUTE THRESHOLDS	
Sense	**Example of threshold**
Vision	The amount of light present if someone held up a single candle 30 mi (48 km) away from us, if our eyes were used to the dark. If a person in front of you held up a candle and began backing up at the rate of one foot (30 cm) per second, that person would have to back up for 44 hours before the flame became invisible.
Hearing	The ticking of a watch in a quiet environment at 20 ft (6 m).
Taste	One drop of quinine sulfate (a bitter substance) in 250 gal (946 l) of water. Quinine is one of the components of tonic water.
Smell	One drop of perfume in a six-room house. This value will change depending on the type of substance we are smelling.
Touch	The force exerted by dropping the wing of a bee onto your cheek from a distance of one centimeter (0.5 in). This value will vary considerably depending on the part of the body involved.

are given more inclusive achievement tests that cover a broader spectrum of information and skills. For instance, many states now require acceptable scores on "proficiency" tests at various grade levels before advancement is allowed. Admission to colleges and graduate studies depends on achievement tests such as the **Scholastic Assessment Test (SAT),** which attempts to measure both aptitude and achievement, the Graduate Record Exam (GRE), the Law School Admissions Test (LSAT), and the Medical College Admissions Test (MCAT). The Iowa Test of Basic Skills (ITBS) and the California Achievement Test (CAT) are examples of achievement tests given to many elementary school students around the United States.

Useful achievement tests must be both reliable and valid. Reliable tests are consistent and reproducible. That is, a student taking a similar test, or the same test at a different time, must respond with a similar performance. Valid tests measure achievement on the subject they are intended to measure. For example, a test intended to measure achievement in arithmetic—but filled with difficult vocabulary—may not measure arithmetic achievement at all. The students who score well on such a test may be those who have good vocabularies or above-average reading ability in addition to appropriate arithmetic skills. Students who fail may have achieved the same arithmetic skills, but did not know how to demonstrate them. Such tests would not be considered valid. In order for reliable comparisons to be made, all standardized tests, including achievement tests, must be given under similar conditions and with similar time limitations and scoring procedures. The difficulty of maintaining consistency in these administration procedures makes the reliability of such tests questionable, critics contend.

Many researchers point to another problem with achievement tests. Because it is difficult to distinguish in test form the difference between aptitude—innate ability—and achievement—learned knowledge or skills—the results of tests that purport to measure achievement alone are necessarily invalid to some degree. Also, some children attain knowledge through their experiences, which may assist them in tests of academic achievement. The presence of cultural biases in achievement tests is a frequent topic of discussion among educators, psychologists, and the public at large. Political pressure to produce high scores and the linking of achievement to public funds for schools have also become part of the achievement-test controversy.

Yet further skepticism about achievement test results comes from critics who contend that teachers frequently plan their lessons and teaching techniques to foster success on such tests. This "teaching to the test" technique used by some teachers makes comparisons with other curricula difficult; thus, test scores resulting from the dif-

ferent methods become questionable as well. **Test anxiety** may also create unreliable results. Students who experience excessive anxiety when taking tests may perform below their level of achievement. For them, achievement tests may prove little more than their aversion to test-taking.

Further Reading

Houts, Paul L., ed. *The Myth of Measurability.* New York: Hart Publishing Co., 1977.

Wallace, Betty, and William Graves. *Poisoned Apple: The Bell-Curve Crisis and How Schools Create Mediocrity and Failure.* New York: St. Martin's Press, 1995.

Acquired Immune Deficiency Syndrome (AIDS)

A progressive, degenerative disease involving several major organ systems, including the immune system and central nervous system. Uniformly fatal, it is associated with human immunodeficiency virus (HIV), a viral infection that progressively weakens the immune system.

Since Acquired Immune Deficiency Syndrome (AIDS) manifests itself in a number of different diseases and conditions, it has been difficult to arrive at a formal definition. In an attempt to standardize the definition of AIDS, the Centers for Disease Control in 1992 included among its diagnostic criteria a count of 200 or fewer CD4T lymphocyte cells per cubic ml of blood (a sign of severe immune system suppression). AIDS was first recognized in 1981 as a cluster of symptoms in homosexual men in New York City and San Francisco. Eventually, similar symptoms were found among intravenous drug users, hemophiliacs, and other recipients of blood transfusions. In 1984, the human immunodeficiency virus (HIV) was isolated and subsequently determined as the probable cause of AIDS.

HIV is transmitted through sexual intercourse, contact with infected blood and blood products, and the **birth** process. However, casual social contact—even if close and prolonged—has not been found to spread HIV. The greatest number of HIV cases are sexually transmitted, through both homosexual and heterosexual intercourse. Screening of donated blood and blood products since 1985 has drastically reduced the risk of transfusion-related HIV. Children may be infected *in utero* or by exposure to blood and vaginal secretions during childbirth. The child of an infected mother has a 25 to 35 percent chance of acquiring the virus.

Persons infected with HIV initially show no symptoms. Within three to six weeks after infection they may exhibit flu-like symptoms that last up to three weeks and resolve spontaneously. According to long-term studies, all or almost all persons infected with HIV eventually become ill with full-blown AIDS, although the incubation period varies from less than a year to as long as 15 years. AIDS is considered full-blown when the immune system is seriously suppressed. At this point, the patient becomes vulnerable to opportunistic infections and diseases that are able to attack because of reduced immune system defenses. These include candiasis, pneumocystis carinii pneumonia (PCP), herpes and other viral infections, toxoplasmosis, and tuberculosis. AIDS also weakens the body's defenses against carcinomas, and conditions such as lymphoma and Kaposi's sarcoma are common complications of the disease. AIDS also attacks the nervous system. Neurological disorders such as encephalitis and **dementia** occur in over two-thirds of AIDS patients. HIV/AIDS patients are also prone to blood abnormalities, respiratory infections, and gastrointestinal problems, including diarrhea, which is partly responsible for the weight loss that occurs in the course of the disease.

Comforting a person with AIDS or any other fatal illness is challenging for friends, family, and others around him. Isolation is one of the most difficult aspects of this disease, often resulting from misinformation and fear about how the disease is spread. There is no scientific evidence that AIDS is spread through casual contact, and there is no reason to avoid gestures of friendship and comfort, such as a personal visit, a hug, or holding the patient's hand.

According to the World Health Organization, an estimated five to ten million people worldwide are infected with HIV. The highest incidence of AIDS is in major cities in Asia, Africa, and the United States. In the United States alone, there are thought to be over one million infected with HIV, and over 250,000 cases of full-blown AIDS have been reported. AIDS has become a leading cause of death in men and women under the age of 45 and children under the age of five. Originally thought of as a "gay men's disease," in 1993 AIDS was the nation's fourth leading cause of death in women between the ages of 15 and 44.

HIV is usually diagnosed through a test called ELISA (enzyme-linked immunosorbent assay), which screens the blood for HIV antibodies. If the test is posi-

PEOPLE WITH AIDS IN THE UNITED STATES, 1995		
Characteristic	Cases Reported by Number	Cases Reported by Percent of Total
Men	428,480	85.5%
Women	72,828	14.5%
Age group (yrs)		
0 to 4	5,432	1.1%
5 to 12	1,385	0.3%
13 to 19	2,300	0.5%
20 to 29	91,054	18.2%
30 to 39	227,754	45.5%
40 to 49	122,569	24.4%
50 to 59	36,640	7.3%
Over 60	14,176	2.8%
Vital status		
Living	189,929	37.9%
Deceased	311,381	62.1%

Source: Centers for Disease Control, U.S. Department of Health and Human Services.

tive, a more specific test, the Western blot assay, is administered. Most patients will test positive for HIV one to three months after being infected, and 95 percent will test positive after five months. There is no effective vaccine against the HIV virus, and no known cure for AIDS, but antiviral drugs have been effective in slowing the progression of the disease, particularly the suppression of the immune system. One of the earliest of these medications to be effective was azidothymidine (AZT), which inhibits viral **DNA** polymerase.

The best method of containing the AIDS epidemic is education and prevention. Much of the anti-AIDS effort both in the United States and globally has been directed toward promoting safer sex practices, including abstinence (especially among young people) and the use of latex condoms, which greatly reduce the chance of infection. The threat of HIV among intravenous drug users has been addressed by programs offering education, rehabilitation, and the free dispension of sterile needles. Modification of sexual behavior among homosexuals has been successful in reducing the incidence of new HIV infections among the gay population. However, risk-related behavior is increasing among young homosexuals under the mistaken belief that the threat of AIDS applies mostly to older gay men. Risky sexual behavior has also remained widespread among heterosexual teenagers in the 1990s, especially among African-American and Hispanic males.

Further Reading

Anonymous. *It Happened to Nancy.* New York: Avon Books, 1994.
Foster, Carol, et al., eds. *AIDS.* Wylie, TX: Information Plus, 1992.
Siegel, Larry. *AIDS, The Drug and Alcohol Connection.* Center City, MN: Hazelden, 1989.
A Conversation With Magic. Lucky Duck Productions, 1992. Videorecording.

Action Potential

A momentary electrical event occurring through the membrane of a nerve cell fiber in response to a stimulus, forming a nerve impulse.

An action potential is transmitted along a **nerve** fiber as a wave of changing electrical charge. This wave travels at a speed that ranges from about five feet per second to about 350 feet per second, depending on various properties of the nerve fiber involved and other factors.

An action potential occurs in about one millisecond. During an action potential, there is a change in voltage across the nerve cell membrane of about 120 millivolts, and the negative electrical charge inside the resting nerve cell is reversed to a positive electrical charge. This change in voltage and reversal of electrical charge results from the movement of sodium ions, which carry a positive charge, into the nerve cell fiber. This is followed by the movement of potassium ions, which also carry a positive charge, out of the nerve cell fiber, allowing the nerve cell to return to its resting state. The temporarily increased permeability of the nerve cell fiber membrane, first to sodium ions and then to potassium ions, is caused by a chemical transmitter substance.

Further Reading

Adams, Raymond. *Principles of Neurology.* New York: McGraw-Hill, 1993.

Adaptation

Behavior that enables an organism to function effectively in its environment.

Adaptive behavior is crucial to the process of natural selection, enabling those organisms or species best suited to a particular **environment** to survive. Ethologists, who study the behavior of animals in their natural habitats from an evolutionary perspective, have documented two main types of adaptive behavior. "Closed programs" are transmitted from one generation to the next relatively unchanged, while "open genetic programs" involve greater degrees of environmental influence.

Adaptation occurs in individual organisms as well as in species. Sensory adaptation consists of physical changes that occur in response to the presence or cessation of stimuli. Examples include the adjustment our eyes make when we go from broad daylight into a darkened theater, or the way in which cold water becomes more comfortable after an initial plunge. Once a steady level of stimulation (such as light, sound, or odor) is established, we no longer notice it. However, any abrupt changes require further adaptation.

The adrenalin-produced reaction to environmental dangers called the "fight or flight" syndrome (including rapid breathing, increased heart rate, and sweating) can also be considered a form of adaptation, as can the psychological responses involved in classical and **operant conditioning,** which involve learned behaviors motivated by either positive **reinforcement** or fear of **punishment**.

Further Reading

Lorenz, Konrad. *The Foundations of Ethology.* New York: Springer-Verlag, 1981.

Addiction/Addictive Personality

A wide spectrum of complex behaviors that ranges from patterns of behavior to physical addiction.

Addiction has come to refer to a wide and complex range of behaviors. In addition to familiar addictions, such as alcohol dependence, drug dependence, and smoking, addictive behavior has also been associated with food, exercise, work, and even relationships with others (codependency). Some experts describe the spectrum of behaviors designated as addictive in terms of five interrelated concepts: patterns, habits, compulsions, impulse control disorders, and physical addiction. Compulsions differ from patterns and habits in that they originate for the purpose of relieving **anxiety**. Impulse control disorders, such as overeating, constitute a specific type of compulsive behavior that provides short-term gratification but is harmful in the long run. In contrast to these various types of potentially addictive behavior, physical addiction involves dependence on a habit-forming substance characterized by tolerance and well-defined physiological withdrawal symptoms.

In spite of the variety of activities that can be considered addictive, people who engage in them tend to have certain **attitudes** and types of behavior in common. An addiction is generally associated with relieving anxiety or blocking out other types of uncomfortable feelings. To a greater or lesser extent, people engaged in addictive behavior tend to plan their lives around it; in extreme cases they will do almost anything to obtain the substance or engage in the behavior. The addiction makes them neglect other areas of their lives. They are commonly secretive about it, either out of shame or to protect their access to a substance. When confronted, they generally deny that they have a problem, although privately they regret their addictive behavior, which in many cases they have tried without success to discontinue. They tend to rationalize engaging in the behavior and tell themselves they can stop whenever they want. They may also blame others for their addiction and often experience frequent and uncontrollable **mood** swings.

Substance abuse and dependence (substance-related disorders) are among the psychological disorders in the list of major clinical syndromes (Axis I) found in the **American Psychiatric Association's** *Diagnostic and Statistical Manual of Mental Disorders*. Alcohol, which is classified as a depressant, is probably the most frequently abused psychoactive substance. Alcohol abuse and dependence affects over 20 million Americans—about 13 percent of the adult population. An alcoholic has been defined as a person whose drinking impairs his

CAFFEINE AND NICOTINE

Two popular stimulants that most people do not consider "drugs" are caffeine and nicotine. However, caffeine, which speeds up thought processes and can produce anxiety and even tremors in high doses, is addictive; its withdrawal symptoms include headaches, fatigue, craving, and shakiness. Nicotine, the psychostimulant in tobacco, has a powerful effect on the autonomic nervous system. While some claim that nicotine addiction is more psychological than physical, it is associated with definite withdrawal symptoms, including cravings, restlessness, irritability, and weight gain.

or her life adjustment, affecting health, personal relationships, and/or work. Alcohol dependence, sometimes called alcoholism, is about five times more common in men than women, although alcohol abuse by women and by teenagers of both sexes is growing.

When blood alcohol level reaches 0.1 percent, a person is considered to be intoxicated. Judgment and other rational processes are impaired, as well as motor coordination, speech, and vision. Alcohol abuse typically progresses through a series of stages from social drinking to chronic alcoholism. Danger signs that indicate the probable onset of a drinking problem include the frequent desire to drink, increased alcohol consumption, memory lapses ("blanks"), and morning drinking. Among the most acute reactions to alcohol are four conditions referred to as alcoholic psychoses: alcohol idiosyncratic intoxication (an acute reaction in persons with an abnormally low tolerance for alcohol); alcohol withdrawal delirium (delirium tremens); **hallucination**s; and Korsakoff's psychosis, an irreversible **brain** disorder involving severe **memory** loss.

Aside from alcohol, other psychoactive substances most frequently associated with abuse and dependence are barbiturates (which, like alcohol, are depressants); narcotics (opium and its derivatives, including heroin); stimulants (amphetamines and cocaine); antianxiety drugs (tranquilizers such as Librium and Valium); and psychedelics and hallucinogens (marijuana, mescaline, psilocybin, LSD, and PCP). While drug abuse and dependence can occur at any age, they are most frequent in adolescence and early adulthood.

The causes of substance abuse are multiple. Some people are at high risk for dependence due to genetic or physiological factors. Researchers have found the sons of alcoholics to be twice as prone to alcoholism as other people. Among pairs of identical twins, if one is an alcoholic, there is a 60 percent chance that the other will be also. In spite of an apparent inherited tendency toward alcoholism, the fact that the majority of people with alcoholic parents do not become alcoholics themselves demonstrates the influence of psychosocial factors, including **personality** factors and a variety of environmental stressors, such as occupational or marital problems.

Variations in the incidence of alcoholism among different ethnic groups show that social learning also plays a role in addiction. Parental influence, especially in terms of **modeling** the use of alcohol and other drugs, has a strong influence on the behavior of children and adolescents, as does peer behavior. Although positive experiences with one drug may lead to experimentation with another, the "stepping stone" theory of drug use—for example, using marijuana leads to the use of hard drugs—is highly speculative as the majority of marijuana smokers do not go on to use other drugs. Only heavy marijuana use has been linked to the use of other drugs.

Not all addictive behavior involves the use of drugs or alcohol. One such potentially life-threatening type of behavior is compulsive overeating associated with **obesity.** While obesity is viewed as a physiological condition in some cases, it is commonly linked to a long-standing pattern of overeating and an addictive relationship to food that can generally be traced to personality factors in combination with learned responses. Another type of non-drug-related addictive behavior is compulsive gambling. While about half of all persons engage in some

form of gambling at some point in their lives, compulsive gamblers carry this activity to the extent that it disrupts their lives psychologically and financially.

Addictions are difficult to treat. Addictive behavior often involves long-term psychological problems or ongoing stressors in a person's life. Rates of initial "cure" followed by relapse are very high, and many consider recovery to be an ongoing, lifelong process. Physical addictions alter a person's brain chemistry in ways that make it difficult to be exposed to the addictive substance again without lapsing back into addiction; abstinence is generally necessary for recovery from substance dependency. People addicted to a type of activity—such as compulsive spending or eating—from which it is impossible to abstain entirely must learn to understand and alter their behaviors.

The first step in the recovery process is admitting that there is a problem and seeking help. Biological intervention may be necessary, including medication to treat withdrawal symptoms and treatment for malnutrition. (Many heroin addicts are given methadone, a synthetic opiate that is addictive but less harmful than heroin). There are many kinds of psychological intervention available, offered in forms ranging from counseling to inpatient programs. Among the most effective are **group therapy**; environmental intervention (which deals with negative factors in an addict's social environment); **behavior therapy**, including aversive conditioning; and 12-step programs based on the approach pioneered by Alcoholics Anonymous.

See also Codependence.

Further Reading
Cohen, Irving A. *Addiction: The High-Low Trap.* Santa Fe, NM: Health Press, 1995.

Engel, Joel. *Addicted: In Their Own Words. Kids Talk About Drugs.* New York: Tom Doherty Associates, 1990.

Porterfield, Kay Marie. *Focus on Addictions: A Reference Handbook.* Santa Barbara: ABC-CLIO, 1992.

Adjustment Disorders

The development of significant emotional or behavioral symptoms in response to an identifiable event that precipitated significant psychological or social stress.

Adjustment disorders are maladpative, or unhealthy, responses to stressful or psychologically distressing life events, such as the end of a romantic relationship or being terminated from a job.

The **American Psychiatric Association** has identified and categorized several varieties of adjustment disorders, depending on accompanying symptoms and their duration. These subtypes include adjustment disorder with depressed **mood**, with **anxiety**, with anxiety and depressed mood, and with disturbances of conduct. The disorders can additionally be classified as acute or chronic. It is thought that adjustment disorders are fairly common; recent figures estimate that 5 to 20 percent of persons seeking outpatient psychological treatment suffer from one of these disorders. Psychiatrists rigidly define the time frames in which these disorders can occur to differentiate them from other types of responses to stressful events, such as **post-traumatic stress disorder** and acute **stress** disorder. Adjustment disorders must occur within three months of the stressful event and can, by definition, last no longer than six months.

Symptoms of these various adjustment disorders include a decrease in performance at work or school, and withdrawal from social relationships. These disorders can lead to **suicide** or suicidal thinking and can complicate the course of other diseases when, for instance, a sufferer loses interest in taking medication as prescribed or adhering to difficult diets or exercise regimens.

Adjustment disorders can occur at any stage of life. In early **adolescence**, individuals with adjustment disorders tend to be angry, aggressive, and defiant. Temper tantrums are common and are usually well out of balance with the event that caused them. Other adolescents with adjustment disorders may, alternately, become passive and withdrawn, and older teens often experience intense anxiety or **depression**. They may experience what psychologists call "depersonalization," a state in which a person feels he or she can observe their body interacting with others, but feels nothing.

Many psychological theorists and researchers consider adjustment disorders in adolescents as a stage in establishing an **identity**. Adolescents may develop adjustment disorders as part of a **defense mechanism** meant to break their feelings of dependence on their parents. This sort of psychological maneuver may precipitate problems in families as adolescents begin seeking individuals outside the family as replacements for their parents. This can be particularly destructive when these feelings of dependence are transferred to involvement with gangs or **cults**.

Further Reading

Diagnostic and Statistical Manual of Mental Disorders. 4th ed. Washington, D.C.: American Psychiatric Association, 1994.

Nicholi, Armand, ed. *The New Harvard Guide to Psychiatry.* Cambridge, MA: Harvard University Press, 1988.

"The Not-so Maddening Crowd: Crowding Stress Leads to Coping Behavior in Primates." *Discover* (February 1994): 14.

Shanok, Rebecca. "Coping with Crisis." *Parents Magazine* (October 1991): 169.

Adler, Alfred (1870–1937)

Psychiatrist known for his theory of individual psychology and for his pioneering work with children and families.

Alfred Adler was born in a suburb of Vienna, Austria, in 1870. After graduating from the University of Vienna medical school in 1895, he at first practiced ophthalmology but later switched to psychiatry. In 1902, Adler joined the discussion group that later became the Vienna Psychoanalytic Society. **Sigmund Freud** was also a member. Adler eventually became president and editor of its journal. After 1907, however, Adler's growing disagreement with Freud's theories, especially with their heavy emphasis on the role of **sexuality** in **personality** formation, alienated him from the ranks of Freudians.

In 1911, Adler and his followers left the Psychoanalytic Society to form their own group, The Society of Individual Psychology, and developed the system of individual psychology, a holistic, humanistic, therapeutic approach. Adlerian psychology views the individual as primarily a social rather than a sexual being and places more emphasis on choices and values than Freudian psychology. Adler saw the individual striving toward perfection and overcoming feelings of inferiority (a concept later popularized as the **"inferiority complex"**). After serving in military hospitals during World War I, Adler became interested in child psychology. He established a network of public child guidance clinics in the Vienna school system, offering what was probably the very first family counseling. There were 28 of these facilities in operation until the Nazis ordered them closed in 1934. Adlerian parent study groups still meet throughout the United States and Canada.

In 1926 Adler began dividing his time between Vienna and the United States. He was appointed visiting lecturer at Columbia University in New York in 1927. In 1932 he became a lecturer at the Long Island College of Medicine and emigrated to the United States with his wife. Adler died suddenly in 1937 in Aberdeen, Scotland, while on a lecture tour. There are more than 100 professional Adlerian organizations and 34 training institutes in the United States, Canada, and Europe.

Further Reading

Adler, Alfred. *Co-operation Between the Sexes: Writings on Women and Men, Love and Marriage, and Sexuality.* New York: Norton, 1982.

———. *The Individual Psychology of Alfred Adler: A Systematic Presentation in Selections From His Writings.* New York: Harper & Row, 1964.

Groups of adolescents often dress alike and spend time together as a group. While adolescents may struggle against authority figures, they often submit willing to the demands of peer pressure.

Adolescence

Transitional period of human life between the onset of sexual maturity that marks the end of childhood, and full adulthood.

In Western culture, adolescence typically occurs during the years from about age 12 to about age 21, although individuals develop in different ways, at different rates, and at different ages. Adolescence is a time of physiological, psychological, and social turbulence. Sometimes treated as, and expected to act as, children, and sometimes treated as, and expected to act as, adults, adolescents are often subject to an inconsistent set of behavioral standards that further complicates an already tentative interactive relationship between them and their rapidly expanding worlds.

Physiologically, adolescence is dominated by the **maturation** of the reproductive system and the resulting appearance of secondary sex characteristics. During adolescence, females reach menarche (begin to menstruate) and develop breasts. Males begin to produce viable spermatozoa and grow beards. Pubic hair appears in both sexes. Virtually every part of the body undergoes some change during adolescence, with most increasing in size.

In growth spurts, on average, females gain about four inches in height and about 35 pounds in weight during adolescence, while males gain about nine inches in height and about 55 pounds in weight. In both sexes, the body itself changes in shape and proportion. The popular impression that females mature earlier than males rests largely on the observation that, on average, females tend to attain adult height and weight about two years earlier than males.

Psychologically, adolescence is normally a time of significant inner turmoil and stress. During this period, an individual slowly forms a more or less comprehensive system of mature values, and greatly enlarges the critical capacity for responsible self-direction required to live by those values. A major psychological consequence of the physiological changes of the adolescent is the paramount need to control and to direct new and relatively powerful sexual urges in appropriate ways. This is difficult to accomplish, especially in the absence of a fully formed value system and responsible self-direction, and its necessity is the source of considerable adolescent **conflict**. Other psychological conflicts arise in the forms of issues of self-image, independence, and the alternating appeal of looking backward to childhood and forward to adulthood, both of which, unlike adolescence, represent fairly well-defined and secure roles. The physiological changes of adolescence may contribute in part to some serious psychological disorders, such as **schizophrenia.** Others, such as drug or alcohol abuse and **anorexia nervosa,** are caused, at least in part, by the psychological stress of adolescence. The psychological dynamics of adolescence are complex, but a satisfactory resolution of the unique problems that occur at this time of life is necessary for a healthy future psychological development to be possible.

Socially, adolescence is a period during which the kinds of physiological changes and psychological conflicts described above occasionally result in behaviors that, from the point of view of adults, shift radically and vary widely, or are plainly self-contradictory. In a normal adolescent, elation may be closely followed by **depression,** or unassailable self-confidence may be almost immediately replaced by overwhelming self-doubt. The same adolescent who struggles intensely and incessantly in rebellion against parents and other authority figures might acquiesce instantly to the demands of peer pressure. At the same time, several important social functions may be served by adolescent peer groups. Beyond simply presenting an opportunity to learn how to deal with other people, peer groups can provide a therapeutic and evaluative **role playing** atmosphere in which adolescents are free to discuss many of their mutual concerns.

One of the most unfortunate social aspects of adolescence is the view of it shared by many, if not most, adults. With the possible exception of old age, no other period of human life is held in such low regard, and this view surely has a negative effect on adolescents themselves. The prolonged adolescence that exists in Western societies is becoming longer still, as the average age of reproductive **maturity** becomes lower and full adulthood is often postponed by attendance at college. So, in a sense, adolescence is a function of affluence. Primitive societies generally have no concept of adolescence. In these societies, upon reaching sexual maturity, children—who have already been taught most of the skills necessary to live as adults—are initiated directly into adulthood via relatively short rites of passage. In Western societies, the problems of adolescence are intensified by a lack of tangible learning experiences and growth opportunities for children that frequently leaves them unprepared to make the many important decisions required of them as their worlds suddenly and dramatically expand at the beginning of adolescence.

Fundamentally, adolescence is a natural quest for independent **identity.** It involves a number of difficult and stressful tasks, such as breaking close emotional ties to parents and forging new ones with other people, understanding and establishing healthy and loving relationships as a sexual being, making choices about career orientation and life goals, and learning to accept the reality and profound implications of personal responsibility. It is a time of anxiety, experimentation, rebellion, and essential **adaptation.** Adolescence is a perilous but unavoidable and ultimately survivable storm in every person's journey to adulthood.

See also Child Development; Sexuality.

Further Reading

Erikson, Erik. *Identity, Youth, and Crisis.* New York: W. W. Norton, 1968.
Stress, Risk, and Resilience in Children and Adolescence. New York: Cambridge University Press, 1994.

Adoption

Act or process by which individuals who are not biologically related as parent(s) and child become established, usually legally and socially, as parent(s) and child.

Adoption, in various forms, is an institution in many cultures, and has been practiced for thousands of years. The primary purpose of adoption in ancient cultures was to ensure the continuity of male lineage in a given family for economic, political, or religious reasons. In these circumstances, the adopted individual was almost always male, and very often an adult. While the adoption of adults is still generally permitted, the great majority of modern adoption cases involves infants and children of either sex, and adoption is now widely regarded as an aspect of societal responsibility to care for the young.

In most countries, adoption is a legal proceeding. Adoption statutes became widespread in the United States beginning in the middle of the 19th century, and a number of adoption agencies were formed at that time to assist in the adoption process. Generally, adoption laws require that the consent of the biological parent(s) or guardian of the infant or child (and of the child, if above a certain age, usually about 13) be obtained, that the suitability of the prospective adoptive parent(s) and home be determined, and that a probationary period of residence with the prospective adoptive parent(s) be completed. When the adoption process is concluded, all parties assume the rights and responsibilities of their nonadoptive counterparts. Adoption laws are intended to establish normal parent-child relationships, and they reflect the accepted view in psychology and other fields that a stable family life is very important in the healthy development of children.

In the past, access to specific, official adoption information was often denied to adopted individuals and their biological parent(s). In recent years, however, because of

Facial expressions are an important component of a person's affect.

vidual's affect fluctuates according to his or her emotional state. What is considered a normal range of affect, called the *broad effect*, varies from culture to culture, and even within a culture. Certain individuals may gesture prolifically while talking, and display dramatic facial expressions in reaction to social situations or other stimuli. Others may show little outward response to social **environment**s, expressing only a narrow range of emotions to the outside world.

Persons with **psychological disorders** may display variations in their affect. A *restricted* or *constricted affect* describes a mild restriction in the range or intensity of display of feelings. As the reduction in display of emotion becomes more severe, the term *blunted affect* may be applied. The absence of any exhibition of emotions is described as *flat affect*; in this case, the voice is monotone, the face is expressionless, and the body is immobile. Extreme variations in expressions of feelings is termed *labile affect*. When the outward display of emotion is out of context for the situation, such as laughter while describing **pain** or sadness, the affect is described as inappropriate.

See also Mood.

Further Reading

Moore, Bert S. and Alice M. Isen, eds. *Affect and Social Behavior.* New York: Cambridge University Press, 1990.

Thayer, S. *The Origin of Everyday Moods.* New York Oxford University Press, 1995.

Affective Disorders. See **Bipolar Disorder; Depression; Mania**.

a growing interest among these persons in identifying and locating biological relatives, such information is gradually becoming more available, and a number of agencies have been formed to assist in these searches. Also in recent years, adoption across racial and cultural lines has become increasingly common and controversial.

Further Reading

Hibbs, Euthymia, ed. *Adoption.* Madison, CT: International Universities Press, 1991.

Affect

A psychological term for an observable expression of emotion.

A person's affect is the expression of **emotion** or feelings that he or she displays to others. Affect includes facial expressions, hand gestures, tone of voice, and other signs of emotion such as laughing or weeping. An indi-

Affiliation

The need to form attachments to other people for support, guidance, and protection.

The need to form attachments with others is termed affiliation. Attachment is one of 20 psychological needs measured by the Thematic Apperception Test, a projective **personality** test developed at Harvard University in 1935 by Henry Murray. Subjects look at a series of up to 20 pictures of people in a variety of recognizable settings and construct a story about what is happening in each one. The need for affiliation (referred to as "n Aff") is scored when a test-taker's response to one of the pictures demonstrates concern over "establishing, maintaining, or restoring a positive affective relationship with another person." In the hierarchy of needs outlined by **Abraham Maslow**, the need for affiliation (or "belongingness") appears midway between the most basic physical needs and the highest-level need for **self-actualization**.

Anxiety has been observed to strengthen one's need for affiliation. In addition, females generally show a higher need for affiliation than males. Traditionally, affiliation has been negatively correlated with achievement. While achievement centers on one's personal self-improvement, affiliation focuses on concern for others, even to the extent of deliberately suppressing competitive tendencies or accomplishments that may make others less comfortable.

Further Reading

Harvey, Terri L., Ann L. Orbuch, and John H. Weber, eds. *Attributions, Accounts, and Close Relationships.* New York: Springer-Verlag, 1992.

Meinhold, Patricia. *Child Psychology: Development and Behavior Analysis.* Dubuque, IA: Kendall/Hunt, 1993.

Aggression

Any act that is intended to cause pain, suffering, or damage to another person.

Aggressive behavior is often used to claim status, precedent, or access to an object or territory. While aggression is primarily thought of as physical, verbal attacks aimed at causing psychological harm also constitute aggression. In addition, fantasies involving hurting others can also be considered aggressive. The key component in aggression is that it is deliberate—accidental injuries are not forms of aggression.

Theories about the nature and causes of aggression vary widely in their emphases. Those with a biological orientation are based on the idea that aggression is an innate human instinct or drive. **Sigmund Freud** explained aggression in terms of a death wish or instinct (Thanatos) that is turned outward toward others in a process called displacement. Aggressive impulses that are not channeled toward a specific person or group may be expressed indirectly through safe, socially acceptable activities such as sports, a process referred to in psychoanalytic theory as **catharsis**. Biological theories of aggression have also been advanced by ethologists, researchers who study the behavior of animals in their natural **environment**s. Several have advanced views about aggression in humans based on their observations of animal behavior. The view of aggression as an innate instinct common to both humans and animals was popularized in three widely read books of the 1960s—*On Aggression* by Konrad Lorenz, *The Territorial Imperative* by Robert Ardrey, and *The Naked Ape* by Desmond Morris. Like Freud's Thanatos, the aggressive instinct postulated by these authors builds up spontaneously—with or without outside provocation—until it is likely to be dis-

charged with minimal or no provocation from outside stimuli.

Today, instinct theories of aggression are largely discredited in favor of other explanations. One is the frustration-aggression hypothesis first set forth in the 1930s by John Dollard, Neal Miller, and several colleagues. This theory proposes that aggression, rather than occurring spontaneously for no reason, is a response to the frustration of some goal-directed behavior by an outside source. Goals may include such basic needs as food, water, sleep, sex, love, and recognition. Contributions to frustration-aggression research in the 1960s by Leonard Berkowitz further established that an environmental stimulus must produce not just frustration but **anger** in order for aggression to follow, and that the anger can be the result of stimuli other than frustrating situations (such as verbal abuse).

In contrast to instinct theories, **social learning theory** focuses on aggression as a learned behavior. This approach stresses the roles that social influences, such as models and **reinforcement**, play in the acquisition of aggressive behavior. The work of **Albert Bandura**, a prominent researcher in the area of social learning, has demonstrated that aggressive behavior is learned through a combination of **modeling** and reinforcement. Children are influenced by observing aggressive behavior in their parents and peers, and in cultural forms such as movies, **television**, and comic books. While research has shown that the behavior of live models has a more powerful effect than that of characters on screen, film and television are still pervasive influences on behavior. Quantitative studies have found that network television averages 10 violent acts per hour, while on-screen deaths in movies such as *Robocop* and *Die Hard* range from 80 to 264. Some have argued that this type of **violence** does not cause violence in society and may even have a beneficial cathartic effect. However, correlations have been found between the viewing of violence and increased interpersonal aggression, both in childhood and, later, in **adolescence**. In addition to its modeling function, viewing violence can elicit aggressive behavior by increasing the viewer's arousal, desensitizing viewers to violence, reducing restraints on aggressive behavior, and distorting views about **conflict resolution**.

As Bandura's research demonstrates, what is crucial in the modeling of violence—both live and on screen—is seeing not only that aggressive behavior occurs, but also that it works. If the violent parent, playmate, or superhero is rewarded rather than punished for violent behavior, that behavior is much more likely to serve as a positive model: a child will more readily imitate a model who is being rewarded for an act than one who is being punished. In this way, the child can learn without actually being rewarded or punished himself—a concept known as vicarious learning.

The findings of social learning theory address not only the acquisition, but also the instigation of aggression. Once one has learned aggressive behavior, what environmental circumstances will activate it? The most obvious are adverse events, including not only frustration of desires but also verbal and physical assaults. Modeling, which is important in the learning of aggression, can play a role in instigating it as well. Seeing other people act in an aggressive manner, especially if they are not punished for it, can remove inhibitions against acting aggressively oneself. If the modeled behavior is rewarded, the reward can act vicariously as an incentive for aggression in the observer. In addition, modeled aggression may serve as a source of emotional **arousal**.

Some aggression is motivated by reward: aggressive behavior can be a means of obtaining what one wants. Another motive for aggression is, paradoxically, obedience. People have committed many violent acts at the bidding of another, in both military and civilian life. Other possible motivating factors include stressors in one's physical environment, such as crowding, noise, and temperature, and the delusions resulting from mental illness. In addition to the acquisition and instigation of aggression, various types of reinforcement, both direct and vicarious, help determine whether aggression is maintained or discontinued.

Researchers have attempted to learn whether certain childhood characteristics are predictors of aggression in adults. Traits found to have connections with aggressive behavior in adulthood include maternal deprivation, lack of identification with one's father, **pyromania**, cruelty to animals, and parental abuse. A 22-year longitudinal study found patterns of aggression to be established by the age of eight—the aggressive behavior of both boys and girls at this age was a strong predictor of their future aggression as adults. Other factors cited in the same study include the father's upward social mobility, the child's degree of identification with parents, and preference for violent television programs.

Further Reading

Aggression and Peacefulness in Humans and Other Primates. New York: Oxford University Press, 1992.

Aggressive Behavior: Current Perspectives. New York: Plenum Press, 1994.

Bandura, Albert. *Aggression: A Social Learning Analysis.* New York: Prentice-Hall, 1973.

Of Mice and Women: Aspects of Female Aggression. New York: Academic Press, 1992.

Age has had no influence on this shopkeeper's working hours. Short-term memory may deteriorate with aging, but scientists have shown that other mental capabilities remain vigorous, and may even continue to improve.

Aging

The process by which the human body changes and matures over time, especially the means by which dying cells are not replaced in sufficient numbers to maintain current levels of function; the process by which human behavior alters with time.

Psychological studies of aging populations began in earnest in the late nineteenth century when psychologists found that mental abilities deteriorated with age. These abilities included **memory** and the types of mental performance measured in **IQ tests**. In some individuals, verbal abilities were shown to deteriorate with advanced age, although at a slower rate than other skills; with others, verbal abilities, especially vocabulary, may increase with age. Such data have often been corroborated in tests with chimpanzees, where younger animals perform better in tests of memory and other such areas of mental functioning. For decades, then, it was assumed that the physical deterioration of the body, so evident in the elderly, was surely matched by a similar decline in the mind.

Recent studies, however, have begun to cast doubt on these assumptions. One area where current research has disproved a long-held belief about the aging of the mind is in the death of neurons, formally thought to necessarily lead to diminished mental functioning. It is now known that the **brain** has far more neurons than it could ever use, and that as they die their functions are taken over by nearby neurons. Scientists have recently proven that while abilities like short-term memory and performing certain specific tasks within a time constraint often deteriorate after mid-life, other areas of mental activity, such as wisdom and judgment, become more acute and powerful. Still other studies have shown that brains in older subjects are capable of performing many tasks as quickly and efficiently as brains in younger subjects, although the tasks are performed using different areas of the brain. For instance, research conducted at the Georgia Institute of Technology studied typing speeds in accomplished typists of college age and another group in their sixties. Common sense suggests that the older typists would perform less well because of decreased hand-eye coordination and slower reaction time. Surprisingly, both groups typed at the same speed. Researchers explained the results by pointing out that the assumptions about dexterity and response time were correct, but that the older typists had made clever, efficient adjustments, such as making fewer finger movements and to read ahead in the text, to compensate for their deficiency in those areas.

Fifty seems to be a crucial age in determining the brain's pattern of aging. Once a person has passed that age, brain functioning and mental ability are thought to be determined by essentially three factors: mental habits, chronic disease, and the mind's flexibility.

The elderly populations of many Western countries are the fastest growing segment of the population. In the United States, it is estimated are that by the year 2030 there will be 50 million persons over age 65. Among the elderly, the fastest growing population is people over 85. Such demographic data will continue to focus attention on the process of aging and the psychological problems faced by the elderly. Perhaps the most common psychological disorder often associated with aging is **depression**. According to the National Institute of Mental Health, depression among the elderly range from 10 to 65 percent. **Suicide** rates among the elderly have been increasing at alarming rates. A study conducted by the federal government found that between 1980 and 1986, suicides by persons aged 65 and older increased 23 percent among white men, 42 percent among black men, and 17 percent among white women.

Further Reading

Cadoff, Jennifer. "Feel Your Best at Every Age." *McCall's* (February 1994): 128.

Kahn, Ada, and Jan Fawcett, eds. *The Encyclopedia of Mental Health*. New York: Facts on File, 1993.

Schrof, Joannie M. "Brain Power." *U.S. News and World Report* (28 November 1994): 88+.

White, Kristin. "How the Mind Ages: Aging: Getting It Right." *Psychology Today* (November/December 1993): 38+.

Alcohol Dependence and Abuse

The abuse of alcohol in any of its various forms, exhibited by repeated episodes of excessive drinking often to the point of physical illness during which increasing amounts of alcohol must be consumed to achieve the desired effects.

The **American Psychiatric Association** has ranked alcohol dependence and abuse into three categories. People in the first category can be described as what society normally thinks of as "alcoholics." These individuals consume alcohol regularly, usually daily, in large amounts. The second group of drinkers are those who consume alcohol regularly and heavily, but, unlike the first group, have the control to confine their excessive drinking to times when there are fewer social consequences, such as the weekend. The third category of drinkers defined by the APA are individuals who endure long periods of sobriety before going on a binge of alcohol consumption that can last a night, a weekend, a week, or longer. People belonging in the latter two categories often resist seeking help for the condition because, due to the control they are able to exercise over their intake, they are able to maintain a normal daily schedule and function well at work or at school.

Other psychologists categorize alcohol dependence and abuse into "species." There are several species currently recognized by some in the medical community, including *alpha*, a minor, controllable dependence; *beta*, a dependence that has brought on physical complaints; *epsilon*, a dependence that occurs in sprees or binges; *gamma*, a severe biological dependence; and *delta*, an advanced form of *gamma* where the drinker has great difficulty going 24 to 48 hours without getting drunk. It should be noted, however, that many psychologists dispute these particular subdivisions on the grounds that the original data behind their creation has been shown to be flawed.

Alcohol dependence and abuse in adolescents and persons under 30 years of age is often accompanied by abuse of other substances, including marijuana, cocaine, amphetamines and nicotine, the primary drug in ciga-

Patterns of alcohol abuse typically begin in adolescence for young men, and after about age 25 for women.

rettes. These conditions may also be accompanied by **depression**, but current thinking is unclear as to whether depression is a symptom or a cause of alcohol dependence and abuse. **Heredity** appears to play a major role in the contraction of this disorder, with recent discoveries of genes said to carry a predisposition to them. Studies of adopted children who are genetically related to alcohol abusers but raised in families free of the condition suggest that **environment** plays a smaller role in its onset than heredity. Recent studies suggest that between 10 to 12 percent of the adult population of the United States suffers from some form of alcohol abuse or dependence.

Alcohol dependence and abuse typically appear in males and females at different ages. Males are more likely to begin heavy drinking as teenagers, while females are more likely to begin drinking in their mid- to late-twenties. In males, the disease is likely to progress rapidly, whereas in females it can often take years for debilitating symptoms to develop. According to the U.S. Department of Health and Human Services, 14 percent of males aged 18 to 29 report symptoms of alcohol dependence, and 20 percent revealed that their drinking has brought about negative consequences in their lives. As age progresses, these figures drop steadily. In females aged 18 to 29, similar statistics demonstrated that 5 to 6 percent admit to symptoms of dependence and that this number stays essentially the same until age 49, at which point it plummets to one percent. Females reporting negative consequences of drinking, however, begins at 12 percent but drops to statistical insignificance after age 60.

A key physiological component of alcohol dependence is what is referred to as neurological **adaptation**, or, more commonly, tolerance, whereby the **brain** adapts itself to the level of alcohol contained in the body and in the bloodstream. This process occurs over time as the drinker drinks more regularly while increasing intake in order to achieve the desired affect. In some cases, however, high levels of tolerance to alcohol is an inborn physical trait, independent of drinking history.

There is considerable debate as to the exact nature of alcoholism (the biological disease) and alcohol dependence and abuse (the psychological disorders). The disease model, which have been embraced by physicians and Alcoholics Anonymous for over fifty years, is undergoing reexamination, particularly for its view that total abstinence is the only method for recovery. Many psychologists now believe that some victims of alcohol dependence and abuse can safely return to controlled drinking without plunging back into self-destructive binges. Experiments have been conducted, for instance, that indicate the consumption of a few drinks after a lengthy period of abstinence can lessen the resolve to remain totally abstinent, but that a devastating return to abusive drinking is not the inevitable result. In fact, some psychologists contend that the binge drinking that occurs after initially "falling off the wagon" is less a result of the return of alcohol to the body than to the feelings of uselessness and self-pity that typically accompany such a failure to keep a promise to oneself.

Although it may be premature to suggest that a paradigm shift has occurred in the psychological community regarding alcohol dependence and abuse, many researchers do in fact believe that the disease model, requiring total, lifelong abstinence, no longer adequately addresses the wide variety of disorders related to excessive, harmful intake of alcohol. It is important to note, however, that the human body has no physical requirement for alcohol and that persons with a history of uncontrollable drinking should be very careful in experimenting with alcohol after having achieved a hard-won abstinence. Other factors to keep in mind are problems alcohol can cause to the fetuses of pregnant women, a condition known as fetal alcohol syndrome (FAS). Some researchers believe that children born with FAS are prone to learning disabilities, behavior problems, and cognitive deficits, although others feel the evidence is insufficient to establish a reliable link between these problems and FAS. Alcohol also has a negative affect on human organs, especially the liver, and a lifetime of drinking can cause terminal illnesses of the liver, stomach, and brain. Finally, drunk driving is a tremendous problem in the United States, as are violent crimes committed by people who are under the influence of alcohol.

See also Addiction/Addictive Personality.

Further Reading

Barlow, David H. and V. Mark Durand, eds. *Abnormal Psychology*. Pacific Grove, CA: Brooks/Cole, 1995.

Knapp, Caroline. "My Passion for Liquor." *New Woman* (August 1995): 80-83.

Noble, Ernest P. "Moderate Drinking Is Not for People in Recovery." *Addiction Letter* (September 1995): 1-2.

Sheed, Wilfrid. "Down in the Valley." *Psychology Today* (November 1995): 26-28.

Szpir, Michael. "Alcoholism, Personality, and Dopamine." *American Scientist* (September 1995): 425-26.

Alcoholism

Psychologists prefer to use the terms "alcohol dependence" or "alcohol abuse," because the term "alcoholism" is usually thought of as a physical disease rather than a psychological condition.

See also Alcohol Dependence and Abuse.

Alienation

The state of being emotionally separated from others and from one's own feelings.

Alienation is a powerful feeling of isolation and loneliness, and stems from a variety of causes. Alienation may occur in response to certain events or situations in society or in one's personal life. Examples of events that may lead to an individual's feeling of alienation include the loss of a charismatic group leader, or the discovery that a person who served as a role model has serious shortcomings. Examples of personal events are a death in the family, a job change, divorce, or leaving home for the first time. Although most people may find that such occurrences trigger temporary feelings of disillusionment or loneliness, a small percentage will be unable to overcome these events, and will feel hopelessly adrift and alone.

Many sociologists have observed and commented upon an increase in this feeling of alienation among young people since the 1960s. They attribute this alienation to a variety of societal conditions: the rapid changes in society during this period, the increase in alcohol and drug abuse, **violence** in the media, or the lack of communal values in the culture at large. Some sociologists observe that individuals become alienated when they perceive government, employment, or educational institutions as cold and impersonal, unresponsive to those who need their services. Entire groups may experience alienation—for example, ethnic minorities or residents of inner city neighborhoods who feel the opportunities and advantages of mainstream society are beyond their reach.

Feeling separated from society is not the only way sa person experiences alienation: sometimes the individual feels alienation as disharmony with his or her true self. This condition develops when a person accepts societal expectations (to take over a family business, for example) that are counter to the person's true goals, feelings, or desires (perhaps to be a teacher). He may appear to be successful in the role others expect him to assume, but his true wish is hidden, leaving him feeling deeply conflicted and alone.

In the workplace, jobs have become increasingly specialized since the 1700s and the Industrial Revolution. Workers may see little connection between the tasks they perform and the final product or service, and may thus feel intense loneliness while in the midst of a busy work environment. In the 1840s, American writer and philosopher Henry David Thoreau (1817–1862) observed that "the mass of men lead lives of quiet desperation. What is called resignation is confirmed desperation." Thoreau dealt with his own feelings of alienation by retreating to a solitary, simple life on the banks of Walden Pond in rural Massachusetts. He felt less isolated there—even though he lived in solitude—than when he lived in a town, surrounded by people. When living in town, his feelings of alienation confronted him daily, since his activities did not reflect his true feelings and desires.

Alienation is expressed differently by different people. Some become withdrawn and lethargic; others may react with **hostility** and violence; still others may become disoriented, rejecting traditional values and behavior by adopting an outlandish appearance and erratic behavior patterns. As society undergoes rapid changes, and traditional values and behavioral standards are challenged, some people find little they can believe in and so have difficulty constructing a reality in which they can find a place for themselves. It is for this reason that social and cultural beliefs play such an important role in bringing about or averting a feeling of alienation.

Psychologists help people cope with feelings of alienation by developing exercises or designing specific tasks to help the person become more engaged in society. For example, by identifying the alienated individual's true feelings, the psychologist may suggest a volunteer activity or a job change to bring the individual into contact with society in a way that has meaning for him or her.

Some have proposed treating the epidemic of alienation among America's young people by fostering social solutions rather than individual solutions. One such social solution is the idea of communitarianism, a movement begun early in the 1990s by Amitai Etzioni, a

A person experiencing feelings of alienation may feel isolated and alone even when surrounded by crowds of people.

sociology professor from George Washington University in Washington, D.C. Etzioni became a popular speaker and writer in the mid-1990s with the publication of his book, *The Spirit of Community*. Etzioni advocates a return to community values to replace the rampant alienation of contemporary culture, education to reinforce shared societal morals focusing on family values, and strictly enforcing anti-crime measures. This movement has met serious criticism, however; civil libertarian groups are concerned about communitarian beliefs that certain rights can and should be restricted for the good of the community.

Further Reading

D'Antonio, Michael. "I or We." *Mother Jones* (May-June 1994): 20+.

Foster, Hal. "Cult of Despair." *New York Times* (30 December 1994): A3.

Guinness, Alma, ed. *ABCs of the Human Mind.* Pleasantville, NY: Reader's Digest Association, 1990.

Jackson, Richard. "Alone in the Crowd: Breaking the Isolation of Childhood." *School Library Journal* (November 1995): 24.

Upton, Julia. "A Generation of Refugees." *The Catholic World* (September-October 1995): 204+.

Alzheimer's Disease

An irreversible, progressive condition in which nerve cells in the brain degenerate, and the size of the brain decreases.

Alzheimer's disease is the most common degenerative **brain** disorder, although onset of the disease is rare before the age of 60. After that age, the incidence of Alzheimer's disease increases steadily, and more than one-quarter of all individuals above the age of 85 have this disease. In addition, Alzheimer's disease is the cause of about three-quarters of all cases of **dementia** in individuals above the age of 65. General interest in, and research focusing on the cause and treatment of this condition have grown in recent years because the number of elderly persons in the population is increasing.

The cause of Alzheimer's disease is not known, but several theories of causality have been advanced. These theories propose genetic, environmental, viral, immunological, biochemical, and other causes for the disease. The specific features of Alzheimer's disease vary from individual to individual, but the general course of the disease is fairly consistent in most cases. The symptoms of the disease tend to be more severe at night. The first stage of Alzheimer's disease is usually forgetfulness, accom-

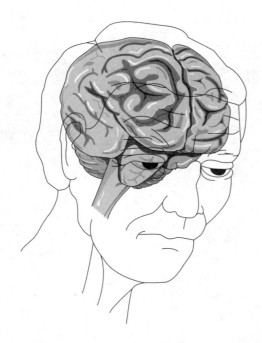

Although its cause is not known, researchers have observed changes in brain chemistry and brain cell deterioration in patients with Alzheimer's Disease.

panied by some **anxiety** and mild **depression.** This usually develops into a more serious loss of **memory,** especially of recent events, moderate spatial and temporal disorientation, loss of **ability** to concentrate, **aphasia,** and increased anxiety. This set of symptoms is usually followed by profound spatial and temporal disorientation, **delusions, hallucinations,** incontinence, general physical decline, and death.

Further Reading

Edwards, Allen. *When Memory Fails.* New York: Plenum, 1994.

Gregg, Daphna. *Alzheimer's Disease.* Booston: Harvard Medical School Health Publications, 1994.

Ambivalence

Generally, the concurrent existence, in an individual, of contrasting, opposing, or contradictory feelings, emotions, or attitudes regarding a person, object, or idea.

Amivalence is experiencing contrasting or contradictory feelings in response to a situation or circumstance. In this sense, it is not at all unusual for some ambivalence to be present in the experience of normal individuals. On the other hand, ambivalence can be pathological, either in terms of its cause or its effect. In psychoanalytical theory, the term ambivalence is more narrowly defined as the coexistence, in an individual, of feelings of love and hate toward the same person. Some psychologists and psychiatrists prefer to restrict the use of the term still further, and define it as the coexistence, in a schizophrenic individual, of intense sexual and destructive wishes directed toward a family member. The term ambivalence is also used in reference to a condition in which an individual is simultaneously drawn or impelled toward two mutually exclusive or antagonistic goals.

Further Reading

Weigert, Andrew. *Mixed Emotions.* Albany: SUNY Press, 1991.

American Psychiatric Association

A national medical society whose approximately 38,000 members—physician and medical students—specialize in the diagnosis and treatment of mental and emotional disorders.

The oldest medical specialty society in the United States, the American Psychiatric Association was founded in October 1844, when thirteen physicians who specialized in the treatment of mental and emotional disorders met in Philadelphia and founded the Association of Medical Superintendents of American Institutions for the Insane. (It is interesting to note that this forerunner of the American Psychiatric Association preceded the American Medical Association, which was founded in 1847.) The goals of the physicians meeting in Philadelphia were to communicate professionally, cooperate in the collection of data, and improve the treatment of the mentally ill.

The American Psychiatric Association's objectives are still designed to advance care for people with mental illnesses: to improve treatment, **rehabilitation,** and care of the mentally ill and emotionally disturbed; to promote research, professional education in **psychiatry** and allied fields, and the prevention of psychiatric disabilities; to advance the standards of psychiatric services and facilities; to foster cooperation among those concerned with the medical, psychological, social and legal aspects of **mental health;** to share psychiatric knowledge with other practitioners of medicine, scientists, and the public; and to promote the best interests of patients and others actually or potentially using mental health services.

The American Psychiatric Association supports psychiatrists and their service to patients through publications such as the *American Journal of Psychiatry,* the oldest specialty journal in the United States, and the *Psy-*

chiatric News, the Association's official newsletter, as well as numerous books, journals and reports. The Association's annual meeting attracts more than 15,000 attendees and features hundreds of sessions and presenters. Additionally, the Association schedules more than 200 meetings each year among its councils, committees, and task forces to advance the cause of mental health. The American Psychiatric Association also offers a comprehensive continuing medical education program to its members. The *Diagnostic and Statistical Manual of Mental Disorders (DSM-IV),* an authoritative reference work, is published by American Psychiatric Association.

See also Diagnostic and Statistical Manual of Mental Disorders.

Further Information

American Psychiatric Association
 Address: 1400 K Street, NW,
 Washington, D.C. 20005
 Telephone: 202-682-6000.

American Psychological Association (APA)

The American Psychological Association (APA) was founded in July 1892, and by the 1990s, it was both the world's largest association of psychologists and the major organization representing psychology in the United States. APA has 77,000 members from around the world; 47,000 students and high school teachers are affiliate members. APA sponsors approximately 50 specialty divisions.

The program of the APA is organized in four directorates, namely Science, Practice, Public Interest, and Education, all of which contribute to the goal of seeking ways to increase human wellness through an understanding of behavior. The Science Directorate promotes the exchange of ideas and research findings through conventions, conferences, publications, and traveling museum exhibits. It also helps psychologists locate and obtain research funding. The Practice Directorate promotes the practice of psychology and the availability of psychological care. It lobbies both federal and state legislatures on issues such as health care reform, regulatory activities such as state licensure, and public service such as the pro bono services provided through the Disaster Response Network. The Public Interest Directorate supports the application of psychology to the advancement of human welfare through program and policy development, conference planning, and support of research, training, and advocacy in areas such as minority affairs, women's issues, and lesbian and gay concerns. The Education Direc-

torate serves to advance psychology in its work with educational institutions, professional agencies, and programs and initiatives in education.

APA publishes books as well as more than 24 scientific and professional journals and newsletters, including *APA Monitor* and *American Psychologist.* Since 1970, *PsychINFO,* a worldwide computer database, has provided references in psychology and related behavioral and social sciences. The week-long APA annual convention is the world's largest meeting of psychologists. More than 15,000 psychologists attend, and have opportunities to attend the presentation of more than 3,000 papers, lectures, and symposia.

See also American Psychological Society (APS); National Association for Mental Health; National Institute of Mental Health.

Further Information

American Psychological Association
 Address: 1200 Seventeenth Street NW,
 Washington, D.C. 20036
 Telephone: 202-336-5500

American Psychological Society (APS)

Organization devoted to academic, applied, and science-oriented psychology.

The American Psychological Society was founded in 1988 to represent the interests of academic, applied, and science-oriented psychology and psychologists. The formation of APS originated from the Assembly for Scientific and Applied Psychology (ASAP), a group that attempted to reform the **American Psychological Association (APA)** to give the scientists greater representation and autonomy. As of early 1996, the APS had nearly 16,000 members.

Headquartered in Washington, D.C., APS prides itself on its strong, committed leadership and minimal bureaucracy. It publishes two bimonthly journals, *Psychological Science* and *Current Directions in Psychological Science,* and produces a monthly newsletter. The APS holds annual conventions and actively lobbies Congress for funds to support scientifically-oriented research projects in psychology. In 1991, it initiated a national behavioral science research agenda known as the Human Capital Initiative (HCI). The goal of HCI is to apply the knowledge gained from scientific psychology to address such social ills as illiteracy, substance abuse, violence, as well as mental and physical health.

Further Information

American Psychological Society
    Address: 1010 Vermont Avenue, Suite 1100,
    Washington, D.C. 20005
    Telephone: 202-783-2077

Americans with Disabilities Act (ADA)

U.S. federal legislation (PL 101-336; 42 U.S.C. 12101) enacted in 1990 and designed to prohibit certain forms of discrimination against individuals with disabilities.

In 1990, approximately 40 million Americans could be classified as having one or more physical or mental disabilities. The Americans with Disabilities Act (ADA) was enacted to legally address the widespread and serious social problem of discrimination against these individuals in employment, housing, public accommodations, education, transportation, communication, public service, and other areas. In addition to establishing enforceable standards in reference to discrimination against individuals with disabilities and ensuring that the federal government enforces those standards, the intent of this legislation was to provide a clear national mandate for the elimination of discrimination against individuals with disabilities and to allow these individuals into the economic and social mainstream of American life.

See also Disability.

Further Reading

Bowe, Frank. *Equal Rights for Americans with Disabilities.* New York: Franklin Watts, 1992.

Ames Room

Specially constructed space that demonstrates aspects of visual perception.

People make sense out of visual scenes by relying on various cues. The Ames Room is a specially constructed space that demonstrates the power of these cues. Normally, people use monocular depth cues such as relative size and height in the visual plane as indicators of depth. If two people of similar size stand a distance part, the one closer to the viewer appears larger. Similarly, the person farther away appears higher in the visual plane.

An Ames Room is constructed to look like a normal room. In reality, the floor slants up on one side and, at the same time, slopes up from front to back. Finally, the back wall is slanted so that one side is closer to the viewer than the other. The figure below shows a top view of the shape of the room and the spot from which the viewer looks at the scene.

If one person stands at the back right corner of the room (Person B), and another person at the left corner (Person A), Person A should appear somewhat smaller than Person B because Person A is farther from the viewer. However, because the room is constructed so that the back wall looks normal, the viewer has no depth cues and Person A appears unusually small, while Person B appears very large. If a person moves from one corner to the other, he gives the illusion of shrinking or growing as he moves. That is, the cues that people normally use for size are so powerful that viewers see things that could not possibly be true.

Amnesia

A partial or total loss of memory.

There are numerous causes of amnesia, including stroke, injury to the **brain**, surgery, alcoholism, encephalitis, and **electroconvulsive therapy**. Contrary to the popular notion of amnesia–in which a person suffers a severe blow to the head, for example, and cannot recall his or her past life and experiences–the principal symptom of amnesia is the inability to retain new information, beginning at the point at which the amnesia began. The capacity to recall past experiences may vary, depending on the severity of the amnesia.

There are two types of amnesia: retrograde and anterograde. Retrograde amnesia refers to the loss of **memory** of one's past, and can vary from person to person. Some retain virtually full recall of things that happened prior to the onset of amnesia; others forget only their recent past, and still others lose all memory of their past lives. Anterograde amnesia refers to the inability to recall events or facts introduced since the amnesia began.

Amnesiacs often appear perfectly normal. Motor skills such as tying laces and bows and bike riding are retained, as is the **ability** to read and comprehend the meaning of words. Because of this phenomenon, researchers have suggested that there is more than one area of the brain used to store memory. General knowledge and perceptual skills may be stored in a memory separate from the one used to store personal facts.

The most famous study of amnesia involves a patient called H.M., who in 1953 underwent brain surgery designed to treat his **epilepsy**. Following the surgery, he could recall all the events of his past life up until three weeks before the operation. However, H.M. could no longer function normally because he had lost the ability to learn new facts and associations. For example, he could not recognize his doctor from day to day or hour to hour.

Childhood amnesia, a term coined by **Anna Freud** in the late 1940s, refers to the fact that most people cannot recall childhood experiences during the first three to five years of life. It has been suggested that this type of amnesia occurs because children and adults organize memories in different ways based on their brain's physical development. Others believe children begin remembering facts and events once they have accumulated enough experience to be able to relate experiences to each other.

Further Reading

Atkinson, Rita L.; Richard C. Atkinson; Edward E. Smith; and Ernest R. Hilgard. *Introduction to Psychology.* 9th ed. San Diego: Harcourt Brace Jovanovich, 1987.

Bolles, Edmund Blair. *Remembering and Forgetting: An Inquiry into the Nature of Memory.* New York: Walker and Co., 1988.

Zimbardo, Philip G. *Psychology and Life.* 12th ed. Glenview, IL: Scott, Foresman, 1989.

Anaclitic Depression. See **Depression**.

Anal Stage. See **Psychosexual Development**.

Anger

One of the primordial emotions, including fear, grief, pain, and joy.

Anger is usually caused by the frustration of attempts to attain a goal, or by hostile or disturbing actions such as insults, injuries, or threats that do not come from a feared source. The sources of anger are different for people at different periods in their lives. The most common cause of anger in infants, for example, is restraint of activity. Children commonly become angry due to restrictive rules or demands, lack of **attention**, or failure to accomplish a task. As children reach adolescence and adulthood, the primary sources of anger shift from physical constraints and frustrations to social ones. In adults, the basis of anger include disapproval, deprivation, exploitation, manipulation, betrayal, and humiliation, and the responses to it become less physical and more social with age. The tantrums, fighting, and screaming typical of childhood give way to more verbal and indirect expressions such as swearing and sarcasm. Physical **violence** does occur in adults, but in most situations it is avoided in deference to social pressures.

Like fear, anger is a basic emotion that provides a primitive mechanism for physical survival. The physio-

This protester's facial expression and body language reveal both his feelings and the physiological changes that accompany them, including increased heart rate and blood pressure, rapid breathing, and muscle tension.

logical changes that accompany anger and **fear** are very similar and include increased heart rate and blood pressure, rapid breathing, and muscle tension. However, anger produces more muscle tension, higher blood pressure, and a lower heart rate, while fear induces rapid breathing. Unlike the adrenalin-produced "fight or flight" response that characterizes fear, anger is attributed to the secretion of both adrenalin and another hormone, noradrenalin. Other physical signs of anger include scowling, teeth grinding, glaring, clenched fists, chills and shuddering, twitching, choking, flushing or paling, and numbness.

People use a number of **defense mechanisms** to deal with anger. They may practice denial, refusing to recognize that they are angry. Such repressed anger often finds another outlet, such as a physical symptom. Another way of circumventing anger is through passive **aggression**, in which anger is expressed covertly in a way that prevents retaliation. Both sarcasm and chronic lateness are forms of passive aggression. In the classroom, a passive aggressive student will display behavior that is subtly uncooperative or disrespectful but which provides no concrete basis for disciplinary action. Passive aggressive acts may even appear in the guise of a service or favor, when in fact the sentiments expressed are those of **hostility** rather than altruism. Some of the more extreme defenses against anger are paranoia, in which anger is essentially projected onto others, and bigotry, in which such a projection is targeted at members of a specific racial, religious, or ethnic group.

Further Reading

Carter, William Lee. *The Angry Teenager.* Nashville: Thomas Nelson, 1995.

Dentemaro, Christine. *Straight Talk About Anger.* New York: Facts on File, 1995.

Ellis, Albert. *Anger: How to Live With and Without It.* New York: Citadel Press, 1977.

Letting Go of Anger: The 10 Most Common Anger Styles and What To Do About Them. Oakland, CA: New Harbinger Publications, 1995.

Licata, Renora. *Everything You Need to Know About Anger.* New York: Rosen Publishing Group, 1994.

Luhn, Rebecca R. *Managing Anger: Methods for a Happier and Healthier Life.* Los Altos, CA: Crisp Publications, 1992.

Anonymity

A condition in which the identity of an individual is not known to others.

Research has provided considerable evidence that in conditions of anonymity many, if not most, individuals tend to act in significantly more immoral ways than they do in normal circumstances where their identities are known. Anonymity seems to be conceptually related to deindividuation, a condition in which an individual's sense of personal identity is temporarily lost. Deindividuation occurs, for example, as a part of the dynamics of mob behavior.

Further Reading

Kappeler, Susanne. *The Will to Violence: The Politics of Personal Behavior.* New York: Teachers College Press, 1995.

Anorexia Nervosa

An eating disorder where preoccupation with dieting and thinness leads to excessive weight loss while the individual contin-ues to feel fat and fails to acknowledge that the weight loss or thinness is a problem.

Symptoms of anorexia nervosa include significant weight loss, continuation of weight loss despite thinness, persistent feeling of being fat even after weight loss, exaggerated fear of gaining weight, loss of menstrual periods, preoccupation with food, calories, nutrition and/or cooking, dieting in secret, compulsive exercising, **sleep disorders,** and a pattern of binging and purging. The condition also has psychosexual effects. The sexual development of anorexic adolescents is arrested, while adults who have the disease generally lose interest in sex. While the term *anorexia* literally means "loss of appetite," anorexics generally do feel hunger but still refuse to eat.

The great majority of anorexics (about 95 percent) are women. Risk factors for the disorder may include a history of alcoholism and/or **depression,** early onset of **puberty,** tallness, perfectionism, low self-esteem, and certain illnesses such as juvenile diabetes. Psychosocial factors associated with the disease are over-controlling parents, an upwardly mobile family, and a culture that places excessive value on female thinness. Emotionally, anorexia often involves issues of control; the typical anoretic is often a strong-willed adolescent whose aversion to food is a misdirected way of exercising autonomy to compensate for a lack of control in other areas of his or her life.

Medical consequences of anorexia may include infertility, osteoporosis, lower body temperatures, lower blood pressure, slower pulse, a weakened heart, lanugo (growth of fine body hair), bluish hands and feet, constipation, slowed metabolism and reflexes, loss of muscle mass, and kidney and heart failure. Anorexics also have been found to have abnormal levels of several **neurotransmitters,** which can, in turn, contribute further to depression. People suffering from anorexia often must be hospitalized for secondary medical effects of the condition. Sometimes the victim must be force-fed in order to be kept alive. Due to medical complications as well as emotional distress caused by the disorder, anorexia nervosa is one of the few mental disorders that can be fatal. The **American Psychiatric Association** estimates that mortality rates for anorexia may be as high as 5 to 18 percent.

According to the National Association of Anorexia Nervosa and Associated Disorders (ANAD), anorexia nervosa and its related disorders, **bulimia** and binge eating disorder, afflict an estimated seven million women and one million men in the United States. The peak times of onset are ages 12 to 13 and age 17. The American Anorexia and Bulimia Association (AABA) calculates that

Singer Karen Carpenter, whose death at age 32 was related to anorexia nervosa, celebrates here with her brother on his birthday. The two formed the singing duo, The Carpenters.

KAREN CARPENTER (1950–1983)

Karen Carpenter died on February, 4, 1983, from complications of anorexia nervosa. Her death was caused by cardiotoxicity—cardiac arrest caused by an overdose of the over-the-counter medication, ipecac. Carpenter took increasing amounts of ipecac after eating to induce vomiting. Her death marked a tragic end to an eight-year struggle to overcome anorexia nervosa.

Friends say Karen became obsessed with her weight after a concert reviewer referred to her "chubbiness" in the early 1970s. When her weight dropped to 85 pounds, she was hospitalized for seven weeks; during her stay, she conquered her addiction to laxatives.

The Carpenters—known for their breezy hits, such as "We've Only Just Begun"—sold over 80 million records and won three Grammy Awards. Karen Carpenter died one month before her 33rd birthday.

as many as 1 percent of teenage girls become anoretic and 10 percent of those may die as a result.

In order to reduce the risks of eating disorders, cultural ideals connecting thinness and beauty to self-worth and happiness must change so that children establish healthier **attitudes** and eating behaviors, and learn to value themselves and others for intrinsic qualities, rather than extrinsic ones focusing on appearance. Treatment and cure for anorexia are possible through skilled psychiatric intervention which includes medical evaluation, psychotherapy for the individual and family group, nutritional counseling, and possibly medication and/or hospitalization. With treatment and the passage of time, about 70 percent of anorexics eventually recover and are able to maintain a normal body weight.

The American Anorexia and Bulimia Association is the principal and oldest national non-profit organization working for the prevention, treatment, and cure of eating disorders. Its mission is inclusive of sufferers, their families, and friends. The AABA publishes a quarterly newsletter reviewing developments in research and programming. It also organizes a referral network which includes educational programs and public information materials, professional services and outpatient programs, patient and parent support groups, and training of recovered patients as support group facilitators.

See also Body Image; Bulimia nervosa.

Further Information

American Anorexia and Bulimia Association (AABA)
  Address: 418 E. 78th Street,
  New York, New York 10021
  Telephone: 212-734-1114
American Dietetic Association (ADA)
  NCDC-Eating Disorders
  Address: 216 W. Jackson Blvd.,
  Chicago, Illinois 60606
  Telephone: 800-366-1655
National Anoretic Aid Society
  Address: 445 E. Dublin-Granville Road,
  Worthington, Ohio 43229
  Telephone: 614-436-1112
National Association of Anorexia Nervosa and
  Associated Disorders (ANAD)
  Address: Box 7, Highland Park, Illinois 60035
  Telephone: 708-831-3438

Further Reading

Epling, W. Rank. *Solving the Anorexia Puzzle.* Toronto: Hogrefe and Hubers, 1991.
Maloney, Michael. *Straight Talk About Eating Disorders.* New York : Facts on File, 1991.

Anti-Social Personality. See **Conduct Disorder**.

Anxiety

An unpleasant emotional state characterized by apprehension, worry, and fear.

Stimulated by real or imagined dangers, anxiety afflicts people of all ages and social backgrounds. When it occurs in unrealistic situations or with unusual intensity, it can disrupt or disable normal life. Some researchers believe anxiety is synonymous with **fear**, occurring in varying degrees and in situations in which people feel threatened by some danger. Others describe anxiety as an unpleasant emotion caused by unidentifiable dangers or dangers that, in reality, pose no threat. Unlike fear, which is caused by realistic, known dangers, anxiety can be more difficult to identify and to alleviate.

Rather than attempting to formulate a strict definition of anxiety, most psychologists simply make the distinction between normal anxiety and neurotic anxiety. Normal (sometimes called objective) anxiety occurs when people react appropriately to the situation causing the anxiety. For example, most people feel anxious on the first day at a new job for any number of reasons. They are uncertain how they will be received by co-workers, they may be unfamiliar with their duties, or they may be unsure they made the correct decision in taking the job. Despite these feelings and any accompanying physiological responses, they carry on and eventually adapt. In contrast, neurotic anxiety is characterized by disproportionately intense feelings that interfere with a person's ability to carry out normal or desired activities. Many people experience stage fright—the fear of speaking in public in front of large groups of people. There is little, if any, real danger posed by either situation, yet each can stimulate intense feelings of anxiety that can affect or derail a person's desires or obligations. **Sigmund Freud** described neurotic anxiety as a danger signal. In his **id-ego-super-ego** scheme of human behavior, anxiety occurs when unconscious sexual or aggressive tendencies conflict with physical or moral limitations.

Anxiety disorders are common occurrences that afflict millions of people. All of them include such physiological responses as a change in heart rate, trembling, dizziness, and tension, which may range widely in severity and origin. People who experience generalized anxiety disorder and **panic** disorders usually do not recognize a specific reason for their anxiety. **Phobias** and **obsessive-compulsive disorder**s occur as people react to specific situations or stimuli. Generalized anxiety disorder is characterized by pervasive feelings of worry and tension, often coupled with fatigue, rapid heart rate, impaired sleep, and other physiological symptoms. Any kind of stress can trigger inappropriate, intense responses, and panic attacks can result. People suffering from generalized anxiety experience "free-floating" fears, that is, no specific event or situation triggers the response. People keep themselves on guard to ward against unknown dangers.

It is believed that generalized anxiety disorder is, at least to some extent, inherited, or is caused by chemical imbalances in the body. Depending on the severity of the symptoms and the responsiveness of the patient, treatment may vary. Often, drugs in the benzodiazepine family (Valium, Librium, and Xanax) are prescribed. These drugs combat generalized anxiety by relaxing the **central nervous system**, thus reducing tension and relaxing muscles. They can cause drowsiness, making them an appropriate treatment for insomnia. In proper dosages, they can relieve anxiety without negatively affecting thought processes or alertness.

Controlling or eliminating the physical symptoms of anxiety without medication is another method of treatment. For example, practiced breathing techniques can slow the heart rate. Access to fresh air can ease sweating. Effective control of such symptoms can be useful in controlling the anxiety itself. **Psychotherapy** is another method of treating generalized anxiety disorder and is used in conjunction with drug therapy or in cases where medication proves ineffective. While there is no definitive cause for the disorder, communicating their feelings to a sympathetic therapist helps some people reduce their anxiety.

Further Reading

Atkinson, Rita L.; Richard C. Atkinson; Edward E. Smith; and Ernest R. Hilgard. *Introduction to Psychology.* 9th ed. San Diego: Harcourt Brace Jovanovich, 1987.

Goodwin, Donald W. *Anxiety.* New York: Oxford University Press, 1986.

Zimbardo, Philip G. *Psychology and Life.* 12th ed. Glenview, IL: Scott, Foresman, 1988.

Anxiety Disorder. See **Anxiety**.

Apgar Score

An indication of a newborn infant's overall medical condition.

The Apgar Score is the sum of numerical results from tests performed on newborn infants. The tests were devised in 1953 by pediatrician Virginia Apgar (1909–1974). The primary purpose of the Apgar series of tests is to determine as soon as possible after birth whether an infant requires any medical attention, and to determine whether transfer to a neonatal (newborn infant) intensive care unit is necessary. The test is administered one minute after birth and again four minutes later. The newborn in-

APGAR SCORING SYSTEM			
Factor	0 points	1 point	2 points
Heart rate	No heartbeat	Under 100 beats per minute	Over 100 beats per minute
Respiration	Not breathing	Irregular, with weak cry	Regular, with strong cry
Muscle tone	Limp, no movement	Limited movement of the limbs	Active movement of the limbs
Color	Completely blue, pale	Pink body with blue hands and feet	All pink
Reflexes	No response to being poked in the nose	Grimace when poked	Cry, cough, or sneeze when poked

fant's condition is evaluated in five categories: heart rate, breathing, muscle tone, color, and reflexes. Each category is given a score between zero and two, with the highest possible test score totaling ten (a score of 10 is rare, see chart). Heart rate is assessed as either under or over 100 beats per minute. Respiration is evaluated according to regularity and strength of the newborn's cry. Muscle tone categories range from limp to active movement. Color—an indicator of blood supply—is determined by how pink the infant is (completely blue or pale; pink body with blue extremities; or completely pink). Reflexes are measured by the baby's response to being poked and range from no response to vigorous cry, cough, or sneeze. An infant with an Apgar score of eight to ten is considered to be in excellent health. A score of five to seven shows mild problems, while a total below five indicates that medical intervention is needed immediately.

Aphasia

A condition, caused by neurological damage or disease, in which a person's previous capacity to understand or express language is impaired. The ability to speak, listen, read, or write may be affected depending on the type of aphasia involved.

In contrast to neurological problems that affect the physical **ability** to speak or perform other linguistic functions, aphasia involves the mental ability to manipulate speech sounds, vocabulary, grammar, and meaning. There are several different types of aphasia. Each has different symptoms and is caused by damage to a different part of the **brain**.

The great majority of aphasias are caused by damage to the left hemisphere of the brain, which is the dominant **language** hemisphere for approximately 95 percent of right-handed people and 60 to 70 percent of left-handed people. Two areas in the left hemisphere—Broca's area and Wernicke's area—and the pathways connecting them are especially important to linguistic ability, and damage to these areas is the most common cause of aphasia. Broca's area, located in the frontal lobe of the left hemisphere, is named for the 19th-century French physician Paul Broca (1824–1880), an early pioneer in the study of lateralization (the specialized functioning of the right and left sides of the brain). Aphasia resulting from damage to this area, called Broca's aphasia, is characterized by slow, labored, "telegraphic" speech, from which common grammatical function words, such as prepositions and articles, are missing ("I went doctor"). In general, however, comprehension of spoken and written language is relatively unaffected.

Wernicke's area, in the upper rear part of the left temporal lobe, is named for Carl Wernicke (1848–1905), who first described it in 1874. Aphasia associated with this area—called Wernicke's aphasia—differs dramatically from Broca's aphasia. While speech in Broca's aphasia is overly concise, in Wernicke's aphasia it is filled with an abundance of words (logorrhea), but they are words which fail to convey the speaker's meaning. Even though their pitch and rhythm sound normal, many of the words are used incorrectly or are made-up words with no meaning (aphasic jargon). Besides their speech difficulties, persons with Wernicke's aphasia also have trouble comprehending language, repeating speech, naming objects, reading, and writing. An interesting exception to their comprehension impairment is their ability to respond readily to direct commands that involve bodily movement, such as "Close your eyes."

Certain types of aphasia—called disconnection aphasias—are caused by damage to the connections of

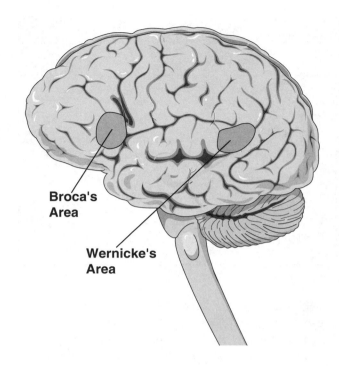

Broca's Area

Wernicke's Area

A main cause of aphasia is damage to the left hemisphere of the brain. When Broca's area of the brain is damaged, slow, telegraphic speech results. When Wernicke's area is damaged, the result is loss of comprehension and inappropriate use of words.

Broca's or Wernicke's areas to each other or to other parts of the brain. Conduction aphasia results from damage to the fiber bundles connecting the two language areas and is characterized by fluent but somewhat meaningless speech and an inability to repeat phrases correctly. In transcortical sensory aphasia, the connections between Wernicke's area and the rest of the brain are severed, but the area itself is left intact. Persons with this condition have trouble understanding language and expressing their thoughts but can repeat speech without any trouble. Another type of aphasia, word deafness, occurs when auditory information is prevented from reaching Wernicke's area. Persons affected by word deafness can hear sounds of all kinds and understand written language, but spoken language is incomprehensible to them, since the auditory signals cannot reach the part of the brain that decodes them.

Most types of aphasia are accompanied by some difficulty in naming objects. However, when this problem is the only symptom, the condition is called anomic aphasia. Persons with anomic aphasia can comprehend and repeat the speech of others and express themselves fairly well, although they are unable to find some of the words they need. However, they do poorly when asked to name specific objects. Anomic aphasia is caused by left hemisphere damage that does not affect either Broca's or Wer-

nicke's area. It commonly occurs after a head injury and also in **Alzheimer's disease**. Global aphasia is caused by widespread damage to the dominant cerebral hemisphere, either left or right. This condition is characterized by an almost total loss of all types of verbal ability—speech, comprehension, reading, and writing.

It is possible for people suffering from aphasia following a stroke or head injury to recover some of their language abilities with the aid of a speech therapist. However, there is little chance of recovery from severe cases of aphasia.

See also Left-Brain Hemisphere; Right-Brain Hemisphere.

Further Reading

Browning, Elizabeth. *I Can't See What You're Saying.* New York: Coward, McCann & Geoghegan, 1973.

Hughes, Kathy. *God Isn't Finished With Me Yet.* Nashville: Winston-Derek, 1990.

Howard, David. *Aphasia Therapy: Historical and Contemporary Issues.* Hillsdale, NJ: Erlbaum, 1987.

Applied Psychology

The area of psychology in which basic theory and research are applied to the actual problems faced by individuals on a daily basis.

Applied psychology can be best understood by comparing it to the area of **psychology** known as basic psychology, which is concerned with answering questions about behavior through psychological theory and research. Applied psychology utilizes this knowledge to actively intervene in the treatment of individuals with mental or emotional disorders, and is also employed in business, education, and government.

Approximately two-thirds of American psychologists work in applied fields. Many are involved in clinical or **counseling psychology**, diagnosing and treating individuals with various problems of **adjustment**. Approximately one-third of the psychologists in practice in the United States today are clinical psychologists, and most people are referred to them for treatment of a wide range of problems, including developmental, medical, and rehabilitative as well as psychiatric. These professionals use a wide range of therapies, ranging from Freudian **psychoanalysis** to Rogerian **client-centered therapy** to newer cognitive approaches. Clinical psychologists may go into private practice, either alone or in groups, or work in hospitals or clinics. They may also practice in a variety of other settings, including community mental-health centers, university medical schools, centers for the mentally and physically handicapped, prisons, state institutions and hospitals, judicial courts, and probation offices. A subfield within **clinical psychology** is community psychology, which investigates environmental factors that contribute to mental and emotional disorders. Health psychologists deal with the psychological aspects of physical illness, investigating the connections between the mind and a person's physical condition.

Applied psychology also includes the areas of school and **educational psychology**. School psychologists are state certified and work in public school settings, often with children who have learning, behavioral, and emotional problems. They perform individualized **assessment**s of each child, consult with his or her parents, and advise the school system on methods to best facilitate the child's education. Educational psychologists, by comparison, study the process of education itself; how people learn and which educational methods and materials are most successful. Applied research in this field focuses on how to improve teaching, solve learning problems, and measure learning **ability** and progress. Educational psychologists may devise **achievement tests,** evaluate teaching methods, develop learning aids and curricula, and investigate how children of various ages learn. They often serve as researchers and educators at teacher training institutions, in university psychology departments, and on the staffs of educational research organizations. Educational psychologists also work in government agencies, business, and the military.

Applied psychology has many applications in business and industry. Organizational and industrial psychologists are concerned with the relationships between people and their jobs. They study and advise employers in such areas as employee morale, job-related **stress**, job enrichment, leadership qualities, and the effects of flex time in productivity. Personnel psychologists screen job applicants, assess job performance, and recommend employees for promotion. Consumer psychologists study the preferences and buying habits of consumers as well as their responses to advertising, often working together with advertising copywriters, public relations experts, and statisticians. They are employed not only by business but also by government agencies such as the Food and Drug Administration and the Federal Trade Commission.

Engineering psychology applies information about human behavior to the design of machines, tools, jobs, and work environments to provide the best possible match with the abilities and limitations of the human beings who will use them. It is part of a broader area known as human-factors engineering (also called ergonomics) that has links to anatomy, anthropometry, environmental medicine, and toxicology. One very specific work **environment** that provides the arena for another specialization is the military. Military psychologists applying psychological research to the operations of the armed forces are involved in personnel selection, testing, and training; evaluating morale; analyzing job performance; studying social interaction among troops; and exploring the dynamics of combat situations. Psychology has also contributed to the exploration of space in areas including the selection and training of astronauts; the study of alterations in work-rest cycles; the design of space vehicles, space suits, and equipment used in space; and research on the operational problems of space flight.

A relatively new specialty is **forensic psychology**, which involves the application of psychology to law enforcement and the judicial system. While some forensic psychologists perform research in academic settings, others work in police departments, participating in officer training and assisting in criminal investigations. Forensic psychologists may help create personality profiles of criminals; formulate principles for jury selection; hypnotize victims, eyewitnesses or defendants to enhance their memories; or study the problems involved in eyewitness testimony. Yet another emerging area is program evaluation, whose practitioners evaluate the effectiveness and cost efficiency of government programs for the Congressional Budget Office, the General Accounting Office, and other government offices and agencies.

Like psychologists engaged in research, the majority of those who practice applied psychology hold Ph.D. degrees in the field. Doctoral programs generally require completion of a four- to six-year program offered by a university psychology department. The course of study includes a broad overview (including courses in such areas as **statistics**, **personality** theory, and **psychotherapy**), as well as specialization in a particular subfield and completion of a practicum, internship, and dissertation. Some clinical psychologists hold a Psychology Doctorate (Psy.D.), a degree that was introduced at the University of Illinois in 1968 and is geared exclusively toward the training of clinicians rather than researchers. Offered at universities and at independent, "free-standing" professional schools of psychology, the Psy.D. program stresses course work in applied methods of assessment and intervention and eliminates the dissertation requirement.

Further Reading

Beck, Robert C. *Applying Psychology: Critical and Creative Thinking.* 3rd ed. Englewood Cliffs, NJ: Prentice-Hall, 1992.

Wise, Paula Sachs. *The Use of Assessment Techniques by Applied Psychologists.* Belmont, CA: Wadsworth Publishing Co., 1989.

Aptitude Tests. See **Vocational Aptitude Testing**

Archetype

A central concept in the theory of personality developed by Swiss psychiatrist Carl Jung.

Archetypes are primordial images and symbols found in the collective unconscious, which—in contrast to the personal unconscious—gathers together and passes on the experiences of previous generations, preserving traces of humanity's evolutionary development over time.

Carl Jung began to evolve his theory of archetypes around 1910 while working with patients at the Burghölzli Mental Hospital. Noting the presence of universal symbols from religion and mythology in the **dreams** and fantasies of uneducated patients, who would have had no conscious way of learning them, he concluded that these images belonged to a part of the **unconscious** not derived from personal experience. Jung proposed that universal images and ideas can be passed from generation to generation like biological traits, and he formulated the concept of the collective unconscious, whose contents become conscious when called forth by appropriate experiences in one's life. In formulating his ideas about archetypes, Jung supplemented his clinical observations with a comprehensive study of myths and symbols that later included investigations into the religions and mythologies of preliterate peoples in Africa and the southwestern United States.

Jungian archetypes are like prototypes or molds that each person fills in differently depending on his or her individual experience. For example, although the term "mother" has certain universal connotations that come to mind for most people, the details of this archetype will be different for everyone. For Jung, archetypes were more than a theoretical construct—his interest in them was primarily therapeutic. He claimed that his patients improved when they understood the ways in which their difficulties were related to archetypes. There is no limit to the number of possible archetypes: they are as varied as human experience itself. Many take the form of persons, such as the hero, the child, the trickster, the demon, and the earth mother. Others are expressed as forces of nature (sun, moon, wind, fire) or animals. They may also occur as situations, events (birth, rebirth, death), or places.

Jung considered four archetypes, in particular, important enough to form separate systems within the **personality**. These include the persona, the anima and animus, the shadow, and the self. The persona is a person's public image, the self he or she shows to others ("persona" is derived from the Latin word for mask). The persona is necessary for survival, as everyone must play certain roles, both socially and professionally, to get along in society. However, management of the persona can cause emotional difficulties. A common problem occurs when a person comes to identify too strongly with the persona that he or she has created, a condition that Jung called inflation. Victims of this problem are often highly successful, accomplished people who have become so preoccupied with projecting a certain image—often for professional advancement—that their lives become empty and alienated.

The anima and animus are the opposite of the persona—they represent a person's innermost self. They are also distinguished by gender: the anima is a man's feminine side, and the animus is a woman's masculine side. Jung theorized that in order for persons of both sexes to understand and respond to each other, each sex had to incorporate and be able to express elements of the other, a belief that foreshadowed both the feminist and men's movements in the United States by over half a century. The shadow is associated with a person's animal instincts, the "dark side" that is outside the control of the conscious personality. However, it is also potentially a source of spontaneity, creativity, and insight. In contrast to the anima and animus, the shadow is involved in one's relationships to persons of the same sex. Perhaps the most important archetype is that of the Self, which organizes and unites the entire personality. However, rather than combining all the other archetypes or aspects of personality, the Self has a dynamic all its own, which governs both inner harmony and harmony with the external world. It is closely related to the ability of human beings to reach their highest potential, a process that Jung called individuation, which he considered every person's ultimate goal.

Further Reading

Hall, Calvin S. and Vernon J. Nordby. *A Primer of Jungian Psychology.* New York: Mentor, 1973.

Hopcke, Robert. *A Guided Tour of the Collected Works of C. G. Jung.* Shambhala; distributed in the U.S. by Random House, 1989.

Arousal

An increase in the level of an individual's readiness for activity.

Generally, arousal describes a state of readiness. When aroused, an individual experiences a heightened readiness for activity that may involve sensory alertness, glandular secretion, muscular tension, or other features. Specifically, arousal is an increase in cortical activity in response to stimulation from sensory receptors believed to be mediated by the reticular formation and other lower brain structures.

Further Reading

Thayer, Robert. *The Biophysiology of Mood and Arousal.* New York: Oxford University Press, 1989.

Artificial Intelligence

Computer-based technology intended to replicate the complicated processes of human cognition, including such complex tasks as reasoning, and machine learning, whereby a man-made device actually incorporates its experiences into new endeavors, learning from its mistakes and engaging in creative problem solving.

The study of artificial intelligence, referred to as AI, has accelerated in recent years as advancements in computer technology have made it possible to create more and more sophisticated machines and software programs. The field of AI is dominated by computer scientists, but it has important ramifications for psychologists as well because in creating machines that replicate human thought, much is learned about the processes the human **brain** uses to "think."

Creating a machine to think highlights the complexities and subtleties of the human mind. For instance, creating a machine to recognize objects in photographs would seem, at first thought, rather simple. Yet, when humans look at a photograph, they do so with expectations about the limitations of the media. We fill in the missing third dimension and account for other missing or inconsistent images with our sense of what the real world looks like. To program a computer to make those kinds of assumptions would be a gargantuan task. Consider, for instance, all the information such a computer would need to understand that the array of images all pressed up against a flat surface actually represent the three-dimensional world. The human mind is capable of decoding such an image almost instantaneously.

This process of simulating human thought has led to the development of new ideas in information processing. Among these new concepts are fuzzy logic, whereby a computer is programmed to think in broader terms than either/or and yes/no; expert systems, a group of programming rules that describe a reasoning process allowing computers to adapt and learn; data mining, detecting patterns in stimuli and drawing conclusions from them; genetic algorithm, a program that provides for random mutation for the machine to improve itself; and several others.

Recent applications of AI technology include machines that track financial investments, assist doctors in diagnoses and in looking for adverse interactions in patients on multiple medications, and spotting credit card fraud. An Australian scientist working in Japan is attempting to create a silicon brain using newly developed quantum resistors. Reported in a 1995 article in *Business Week*, Hugo de Garis is leading a team of scientists to create a computing system capable of reproducing itself. As *Business Week* reports, the project will attempt to "not only coax silicon circuits into giving birth to innate intelligence but imbue them with the power to design themselves—to control their own destiny by spawning new generations of ever improving brains at electronic speeds." This type of technology is called evolvable hardware.

Other recent advances in AI have been the creation of artificial neural systems (ANS) which has been described as "an artificial-intelligence tool that attempts to simulate the physical process upon which intuition is based—that is, by simulating the process of adaptive biological learning." ANS, essentially, is a network of computers that are grouped together in ways similar to the brain's configuration of biological processing lobes.

Even considering all of these advancements, many people are skeptical that a machine will ever replicate human cognition. Marvin Minsky, a scientist at the Massachusetts Institute of Technology, states that the hardest thing of all in the creation of artificial intelligence is building a machine with common sense.

Further Reading

Anthes, Gary H. "Great Expectations: Award Winning AI Scientist Raj Reddy . . ." *Computer World* (3 April 1995): 82.

Chartrand, Sabra. "A Split in Thinking among Keepers of Artificial Intelligence." *New York Times* (18 July 1993).

Port, Otis. "Computers That Think Are Almost Here." *Business Week* (17 July 1995): 68-73.

Wright, Robert. "Can Machines Think?" *Time* (25 March 1996): 50-58.

Assessment, Psychological

The assessment of personality variables.

Psychological assessment is used for a variety of purposes, ranging from screening job applicants to providing data for research projects. Most assessment methods fall into one of three categories: observational methods, **personality** inventories, or projective techniques.

Observational assessment is carried out by a trained professional either in the subject's natural setting (such as a classroom), an experimental setting, or during an interview. Interviews may be either structured with a standard agenda, or unstructured, allowing the subject to determine much of what is discussed and in what order.

Impressions gained from interviews are often recorded using **rating scale**s listing different personality traits.

Personality inventories consist of questionnaires on which people report their feelings or reactions in certain situations. They may assess a particular trait, such as anxiety, or a group of traits. One of the oldest and best known personality inventories is the Minnesota Multiphasic Personality Inventory (MMPI), a series of 550 questions used to assess a number of personality traits and psychological disturbances. The MMPI is scored by comparing the subject's answers to those of people known to have the traits or disturbances in question. While initially designed to aid in the diagnosis of serious personality disorders, the MMPI is now widely used for persons with less severe problems, as enough data has been collected from this population to allow for reliable interpretation of test results. One problem with personality inventories is that people may try to skew their answers in the direction they think will help them obtain their objective in taking the test, whether it is being hired for a job or being admitted to a therapy program. Validity scales and other methods are commonly used to help determine whether an individual has answered the test items carefully and honestly.

A projective test gives the subject a greater opportunity for imaginative freedom of expression than does a personality inventory, where the questions are fixed beforehand. Projective tests present individuals with ambiguous situations which they must interpret, thus projecting their own personalities onto those situations. The best known projective test is the Rorschach, or inkblot, test first devised by the Swiss psychologist Hermann Rorschach in the 1920s. The test subject describes his or her reactions to elaborate inkblots presented on a series of ten cards. Responses are interpreted with attention to three factors: what parts or parts of each inkblot the subject responds to; what aspects of the inkblot are stressed (color, shape, etc.); and content (what the inkblot represents to the subject). Another widely used projective test is the Thematic Apperception Test (TAT), developed at Harvard University in the 1930s. In this test, the subject is shown a series of pictures, each of which can be interpreted in a variety of ways, and asked to construct a story based on each one. Responses tend to reflect a person's problems, motives, preoccupations, and interpersonal skills. Projective tests require skilled, trained examiners, and the reliability of these tests is difficult to establish due to their subjective nature. Assessments may vary widely among different examiners. Scoring systems for particular traits have been fairly reliable when used with the Thematic Apperception Test.

See also Rorschach Technique.

Further Reading

Handbook of Psychological Assessment. New York: Wiley, 1990.

Personality and Ability: The Personality Assessment System. Lanham, MD: University Press of America, 1994.

Wise, Paula Sachs. *The Use of Assessment Techniques by Applied Psychologists.* Belmont, CA: Wadsworth Publishing Co., 1989.

Assimilation

An aspect of adaptation proposed by French psychologist Jean Piaget.

In the **cognitive development** theory of **Jean Piaget**, assimilation is one of two complementary activities involved in **adaptation**, the process of learning from and adjusting to one's **environment**. Assimilation consists of taking in new information and incorporating it into existing ways of thinking about the world. Conversely, accommodation is the process of changing one's existing ideas to adapt to new information. When an infant first learns to drink milk from a cup, for example, she tries to assimilate the new experience (the cup) into her existing way of ingesting milk (sucking). When she finds that this doesn't work, she then changes her way of drinking milk by accommodating her actions to the cup. The dual process of accommodation and assimilation leads to the formation and alteration of schemas, generalizations about the world which are formed from past experience and used to guide a person through new experiences. According to Piaget, cognitive development involves the constant search for a balance between assimilation and accommodation, which he referred to as equilibration.

In the context of **personality**, the term "assimilation" has been used by Gordon Allport (1897–1967) to describe the tendency to fit information into one's own attitudes or expectations. In the study of **attitudes and attitude change**, it means adopting the attitudes of people with whom we identify strongly.

Further Reading

Allport, G. *Pattern and Growth in Personality.* New York: Holt, Rinehart, and Winston, 1961.

Piaget, Jean, and Bärbel Inhelder. *The Psychology of the Child.* New York: Basic Books, 1969.

Associationism

The view that mental processes can be explained in terms of the association of ideas.

Advanced primarily by a succession of 18th- and 19th-century British philosophers, associationism anticipated developments in the modern field of psychology in a variety of ways. In its original empiricist context, it was a reaction against the Platonic philosophy of innate ideas that determined, rather than derived from, experience. Instead, the associationists proposed that ideas originated in experience, entering the mind through the senses and undergoing certain associative operations.

The philosopher John Locke (1632–1704) introduced the term "association of ideas" in the fourth edition of his *Essay Concerning Human Understanding* (1700), where he described it as detrimental to rational thought. George Berkeley (1685–1753), an Irish bishop, applied associationist principles to visual **depth perception**, arguing that the capacity to see things in three dimensions is the result of learning, not of innate **ability**. The British physician David Hartley (1705–1757) also dealt with the biological implications of associationism, formulating a neurophysiological theory about the transmission of ideas and also describing physical activity in terms of association (a concept that anticipated subsequent principles of **conditioning**). Hartley also developed a comprehensive theory of associationism that encompassed **memory**, **imagination**, **dreams**, and morality. The Scottish philosopher David Hume (1711–1776) proposed the principles of similarity and contiguity, asserting that ideas that are similar or experienced simultaneously (or in rapid succession) become associated with each other.

James and John Stuart Mill (father and son philosophers) continued to examine associationism into the 19th century. The elder Mill proposed a mechanistic theory that linked ideas together in "compounds," especially through the principle of contiguity. The younger Mill, whose defining metaphor for the association of ideas was "mental chemistry," differed from his father in claiming that the mind played an active rather than a passive role in forming associations. He also suggested that a whole idea may amount to more than the sum of its parts, a concept similar to that later advocated by psychologists of the Gestalt school. Other 19th-century figures known for associationist ideas were Thomas Browne, who proposed several secondary laws of association, and Alexander Bain (1818–1903), who formulated a comprehensive psychological system based on association.

Aside from similarity and contiguity, other governing principles have been proposed to explain how ideas become associated with each other. These include temporal contiguity (ideas or sensations formed close together in time), repetition (ideas that occur together repeatedly), recency (associations formed recently are the easiest to remember), and vividness (the most vivid experiences form the strongest associative bonds). In the 20th century, the clearest heir to associationism is **behaviorism**, whose principles of conditioning are based on the association of responses to stimuli (and on one's association of those stimuli with positive or negative **reinforcement**). Also, like associationism, behaviorism emphasizes the effects of environment (nurture) over innate characteristics (nature). Association appears in other modern contexts as well: the **free association** of ideas is a basic technique in the theory and practice of **psychoanalysis**, and association plays a prominent role in more recent cognitive theories of memory and learning.

Further Reading

Locke, John. *An Essay Concerning Human Understanding*. Buffalo: Prometheus Books, 1995.

Russell, Bertrand. *A History of Western Philosophy*. New York: Simon and Schuster, 1945.

Schultz, D. P. *A History of Modern Psychology*. 3rd ed. New York: Academic Press, 1981.

Attachment

The psychological connectedness between a parent and child.

Newborn infants are completely dependent on adults for all of their needs. They also depend on their primary caregiver to provide them with physical contact and emotional reassurance, needs crucial for attachment. The success of this earliest of relationships can affect people for the rest of their lives. Children who achieve sufficient levels of attachment to their caregivers are likely to be socially adept, emotionally secure, and self-reliant as adults. Children who do not achieve a sufficient level of attachment, or who were smothered by an overattaching parent, are likely to be socially tenuous, dependent on others, and suffer emotional difficulties.

Early behaviorist psychologists theorized that the need for attachment arose from an infant's physical needs for food and warmth, both of which were provided by the mother. They believed that a baby's preference for the mother was the result of **conditioning**. Research in the 1950s, however, cast these theories into doubt. One of the most famous research studies in this area was done by Harry Harlow. He placed infant monkeys in a cage with two surrogate mother dolls: one made of wire holding a bottle of milk and the other made of soft cloth. According to the behaviorist view, the monkey should have developed an attachment to the wire mother because she was the source of food. But the infant monkeys developed attachments to the cloth mothers, suggesting that the need for comfort and warmth are more important, or more psychologically ingrained, than the **need** for food.

This Peruvian mother meets her infant's need for physical contact and emotional security by carrying him on her back. Children whose attachment needs are met during the early years of life are more likely to be self-reliant and confident adults.

Later experiments with monkeys also revealed the effects secure attachments had on infants. In one experiment, strange foreign objects were introduced to a cage with an infant monkey. When alone, the monkey would react with **fear**. When the cloth mother was present, however, the infant would first retreat to the mother in fear, but then, having been reassured, it would begin to explore the foreign object. Human infants, too, are much more likely to react with fear to unknowns if a mother is not in the vicinity. With a mother present, however, an infant is much more exploratory—even if the mother is not within sight but nearby.

John Bowlby, in his 1980 book *Attachment and Loss*, was one of the first to map out the stages of attachment. Bowlby suggested that from **birth** until about the age of three months, babies are in the initial pre-attachment phase. Here, infants simply need to be held and demonstrate no preference for who does the holding. The next

phase, attachment-in-the-making phase, takes place from 3 to 4 months and is marked by an infant's emerging preference to be held by familiar figures, although it is important to note that the figure does not necessarily have to be the mother. The final stage of attachment Bowlby theorized is the clear-cut attachment phase. Beginning at about six months, this phase features an infant's clear insistence on its mother or its primary caregiver.

Mary Ainsworth, a prominent researcher in attachment and an associate of Bowlby's, has devised a test to measure the type and degree of attachment a child feels for his mother. The test, called the Ainsworth Strange Situation test, involves a mother leading her child into a strange room, which the child is free to explore with the mother present. A stranger then enters the room and the mother leaves. If the infant becomes distressed, the stranger will try and console her. The mother then returns and the stranger leaves. In another scenario, the mother leaves again after the stranger returns. Finally, the mother returns for good and the stranger leaves. Based on the infants' response to their mothers' return, children are labeled "securely attached," "avoidant" or "ambivalent."

Psychologists believe that the main purpose of attachment is to help children begin to explore the world. As the above studies show, if presented with a strange situation, an infant will either avoid or engage in exploration, chiefly dependent upon whether an attachment figure is present. Additionally, it has been shown that lack of attachment in early life can have a negative impact on exploratory propensity in later life. In 1971, researchers separated a group of monkeys from their mothers for six days and then analyzed their behaviors two years later in comparison to a control group that had not undergone separation. The group that had been separated was observed to be far more reticent in exploratory behaviors than the control group. Still other studies indicate that cognitive functioning in children is enhanced among "securely attached" (according to the Ainsworth scale) infants.

Further Reading

Ainsworth, M., M. Blehar, E. Walters, and S. Wall. *Patterns of Attachment: A Psychological Study of the Strange Situation.* Hillsdale, NJ: Erlbaum, 1978.

Thompson, Andrea. "The Affection Factor." *Working Mother* (April 1995): 63.

Wise, Nicole. "What's in Passion?" *Parenting* (May 1993): 131.

Attention

Selective concentration or focus on a particular stimulus.

Attention describes the focusing of perceptive awareness on a particular stimulus or set of stimuli that results in the relative exclusion of other stimuli and is often accompanied by an increase in the readiness to receive and to respond to the stimulus or set of stimuli involved. A state of attention may be produced initially in many ways, including as a conscious, intentional decision, as a normal function of social interaction, or as a reaction to an unexpected event. In any case, attention is a fundamental component of learning. There is evidence that very young human infants have an innate **ability** and inclination to attend to, however briefly, particular instances of auditory or visual stimulation. Children often demonstrate the effects of their attention in the form of apparent misperceptions. For example, the relative size of objects near the center of a child's visual stimulus field is regularly overestimated by the child. In human adults, generally, attention seems to be directly related to the novelty, incongruity, complexity, or personal significance of the situation. As situations become increasingly familiar or similar to situations previously experienced by an individual, the actions of that individual become increasingly routine, and the individual becomes less attentive. There are distinct and measurable neurological and physiological, bioelectric and biochemical aspects and correlates of attention, and the capacity to achieve or to maintain a state of attention may be limited by a number of mental or physical dysfunctions.

In psychology, the term "attention span" is used technically and specifically to mean the number of separate stimulus elements, or the amount of stimulus material, that can be perceived and remembered after a brief presentation. In popular usage, the term attention span is used to mean the amount of time that can be continuously spent in a state of attention.

Further Reading

Hans, James. *The Mysteries of Attention.* Albany: SUNY Press, 1993.

Attention Deficit Disorder (ADD)

A behavioral syndrome in children.

Attention Deficit Disorder is a behavioral syndrome in children characterized by **attention** problems, such as inability to concentrate, difficulty in completing tasks, and being easily distracted, combined with impulsiveness and other characteristics of **hyperactivity.**

See also Attention Deficit Hyperactivity Disorder (ADHD).

Attention Deficit Hyperactivity Disorder (ADHD)

A disorder originating approximately 50 percent of the time in children younger than age four, characterized by inattention, impulsivity, and hyperactivity.

Studies indicate that three to five percent of all children exhibit signs of attention deficit hyperactivity disorder (ADHD), and that ADHD is diagnosed six to nine times more often in males than females. Biologically, it is thought that abnormalities in the nervous system contribute to the onset of ADHD. Behaviorally, a chaotic home **environment** and occurrences of **child abuse** may be contributing factors to the disorder. It is also believed that ADHD is hereditary to a certain degree, and studies suggest that immediate relatives disproportionately suffer from related disorders, including alcoholism. Approximately one-third of children with ADHD will retain certain aspects of the disorder through adulthood.

Children and adults experience the symptoms of ADHD in most areas of their life. It affects their performance in school or at work, depending on their age, and it affects them socially. In some cases, however, ADHD sufferers experience the disorder in only one arena, such as a child who may be hyperactive only in school, or an adult who finds it impossible to concentrate during meetings or while socializing with friends after work. Particularly stressful situations, or those requiring the sufferer to concentrate for prolonged periods of time often will exacerbate a symptom or a series of symptoms. In this way, ADHD has a circular, building affect whereby **attention**-requiring situations magnify the disorder, making the sufferer attempt to concentrate even harder, which, again, makes further concentration even more difficult.

Of the three main symptoms of ADHD, impulsivity is characterized by abandoning tasks before they are completed and poor organizational skills. Sufferers will often appear not to understand instructions as they haphazardly attempt to finish a project or job. They may exhibit impulsivity by thinking they have fully understood a series of instructions for a given task and begin with fervor, only to realize, perhaps when it is too late, that in reality they did not fully listen to or understand what they were being told. With family members, ADHD sufferers are often abrupt, interrupting people regularly. They also tend to be accident prone and can at times seem to cause one chaotic scene after another as they make their way through a given day.

In social situations, ADHD sufferers may exhibit impulsivity in numerous ways. One common manifestation of this particular symptom is excessive, seemingly thoughtless, risk-taking. Among young children with

ADHD, for instance, they will be the first in the group to attempt a dangerous stunt, such as jumping from a high perch or running across a busy street, often doing so with little or no consideration of the danger involved. Young sufferers will also often find it difficult to await their turn when playing games.

Children with ADHD exhibit **hyperactivity** and in-attentiveness in that they find it difficult to complete assignments on time and are regularly thrown out of sync by their inability to organize their time. They find it difficult to remain seated for long periods, often fidgeting in their chairs, creating games for themselves, and playing excessively with an inanimate object, such as a rubber band, a stapler, or crayons. These children will often interrupt teachers and are often reprimanded for excessive chattiness with other students.

In very young children, ADHD is most obviously displayed through excessive movements; they appear to be constantly running from one frenzied activity to the next. Adolescents usually appear restless and irritable and, like all sufferers, have tremendous difficulty remaining still. While many of these symptoms appear normal, it is important to note that even very young toddlers are capable of remaining still and concentrating on a given task or event, such as watching television or being read to.

ADHD can lead to other serious difficulties in life, including low self-esteem, moodiness, frequent bursts of **anger,** and difficulty dealing with normal frustrations. People with the disorder are also habitual academic underachievers and tend to receive poorer education. The **American Psychiatric Association (APA)** states that a substantial proportion of children diagnosed with ADHD are also likely to be affected with other related disorders, including **anxiety** disorders and communication disorders.

Further Reading

Diagnostic and Statistical Manual of Mental Disorders. 3rd & 4th eds. 1994. Washington, D.C.: American Psychiatric Association.

Graham, Janis. "Pay Attention!" *Parenting* (September 1995): 118-24.

Williams, Laurie C. "Understanding ADHD." *Essence* (July 1995): 102-04.

Attitudes and Attitude Change

An attitude is a predisposition to respond cognitively, emotionally, or behaviorally to a particular object, person, or situation in a particular way.

Attitudes have three main components: cognitive, affective, and behavioral. The cognitive component concerns one's beliefs; the affective component involves feelings and evaluations; and the behavioral component consists of ways of acting toward the attitude object. The cognitive aspects of attitude are generally measured by surveys, interviews, and other reporting methods, while the affective components are more easily assessed by monitoring physiological signs such as heart rate. Behavior, on the other hand, may be assessed by direct observation.

Behavior does not always conform to a person's feelings and beliefs. Behavior which reflects a given attitude may be suppressed because of a competing attitude, or in deference to the views of others who disagree with it. A classic theory that addresses inconsistencies in behavior and attitudes is Leon Festinger's theory of **cognitive dissonance**, which is based on the principle that people prefer their cognitions, or beliefs, to be consistent with each other and with their own behavior. Inconsistency, or dissonance, among their own ideas makes people uneasy enough to alter these ideas so that they will agree with each other. For example, smokers forced to deal with the opposing thoughts "I smoke" and "smoking is dangerous" are likely to alter one of them by deciding to quit smoking, discount the evidence of its dangers, or adopt the view that smoking will not harm them personally. Test subjects in hundreds of experiments have reduced cognitive dissonance by changing their attitudes. An alternative explanation of attitude change is provided by Daryl Bem's self-perception theory, which asserts that people adjust their attitudes to match their own previous behavior.

Attitudes are formed in different ways. Children acquire many of their attitudes by **modeling** their parents' attitudes. Classical **conditioning** using pleasurable stimuli is another method of attitude formation and one widely used by advertisers who pair a product with catchy music, soothing colors, or attractive people. **Operant conditioning,** which utilizes rewards, is a mode of attitude formation often employed by parents and teachers. Attitudes are also formed through direct experience. It is known, in fact, that the more exposure one has toward a given object, whether it is a song, clothing style, beverage, or politician, the more positive one's attitude is likely to be.

One of the most common types of communication, *persuasion,* is a discourse aimed at changing people's attitudes. Its success depends on several factors. The first of these is the source, or communicator, of a message. To be effective, a communicator must have credibility based on his or her perceived knowledge of the topic, and also be considered trustworthy. The greater the perceived similarity between communicator and audience, the greater the communicator's effectiveness. This is the principle behind politicians' perennial attempts to portray themselves in a folksy, "down home" manner to their constituency. This practice has come to include distinguishing and distancing themselves from "Washington insiders" who are perceived by the majority of the electorate as being different from themselves.

In analyzing the effectiveness of the persuasive message itself, the method by which the message is presented is at least as important as its content. Factors influencing the persuasiveness of a message include whether it presents one or both sides of an argument; whether it states an implicit or explicit conclusion; whether or not it provokes **fear;** and whether it presents its strongest arguments first or last. If the same communicator were to present an identical message to two different groups, the number of people whose attitudes were changed would still vary because audience variables such as age, sex, and **intelligence** also affect attitude change. Many studies have found women to be more susceptible to persuasion than men, but contrasting theories have been advanced to account for this phenomenon. Some have attributed it to the superior verbal skills of females which may increase their **ability** to understand and process verbal arguments. Others argue that it is culturally determined by the greater pressure women feel to conform to others' opinions and expectations.

The effect of intelligence on attitude change is inconclusive. On one hand, it has been hypothesized that the greater one's intelligence, the more willing one is to consider differing points of view. On the other hand, people with superior intelligence may be less easily persuaded because they are more likely to detect weaknesses in another person's argument. There is, however, evidence of a direct link between self-esteem and attitude change. People with low self-esteem are often not attentive enough to absorb persuasive messages, while those with high self-esteem are too sure of their own opinions to be easily persuaded to change them. The most easily persuaded individuals tend to be those with moderate levels of self-esteem, who are likely to pay a reasonable amount of attention to what those around them say and remain open enough to let it change their minds.

The medium of persuasion also influences attitude change ("the medium is the message"). Face-to-face communication is usually more effective than mass communication, for example, although the effectiveness of any one component of communication always involves the interaction of all of them. The effects of persuasion may take different forms. Sometimes they are evident right away; at other times they may be delayed (the so-called "sleeper effect"). In addition, people may often change their attitudes only to revert over time to their original opinions, especially if their **environment** supports the initial opinion.

The information-processing model of persuasion, developed by psychologist William McGuire, focuses on a chronological sequence of steps that are necessary for successful persuasion to take place. In order to change listeners' attitudes, one must first capture their attention, and the listeners must comprehend the message. They must then yield to the argument, and retain it until there is an opportunity for action—the final step in attitude change.

Further Reading

Chapman, Elwood N. *Attitude: Your Most Priceless Possession.* 2nd ed. Los Altos, CA: Crisp Publications, 1990.

Eiser, J. Richard *Social Psychology: Attitudes, Cognition, and Social Behaviour.* New York: Cambridge University Press, 1986.

Zimbardo, Philip G. *The Psychology of Attitude Change and Social Influence.* Philadelphia: Temple University Press, 1991.

Attribution

The thought processes people undertake to explain their own behavior and that of others.

Besides impression formation, the other key area focused on in the study of **social perception** is attribution. The most fundamental observation a person may make about another's behavior is whether it is due to internal or external causes (is the behavior determined by the person's own characteristics or by the situation in which it occurs?). This decision is based on a combination of three factors. *Consensus* refers to whether other people exhibit similar behavior; *consistency* relates to whether the behavior occurs repeatedly; and *distinctiveness* is concerned with whether the behavior occurs in similar situations.

Certain cognitive biases tend to influence whether people attribute behavior to internal or external causes. When the behavior of others is being observed, knowledge of the external factors influencing that behavior is limited, which often leads the observer to attribute it to internal factors, a tendency known as the fundamental attribution error. However, people are aware of numerous external factors that play a role in their own behavior. This fact, combined with a natural desire to think well of one's self, produces actor-observer bias, a tendency to attribute behavior—especially when inappropriate or unsuccessful—to external factors.

Further Reading

Harvey, Terri L., Ann L. Orbuch, and John H. Weber, eds. *Attributions, Accounts, and Close Relationships.* New York: Springer-Verlag, 1992.

Inglehart, Marita Rosc. *Reactions to Critical Life Events: A Social Psychological Analysis.* New York: Praeger, 1991.

Weary, Gifford. *Attribution.* New York: Springer-Verlag, 1989.

Authoritarian Personality

A personality pattern described in detail in the 1950 book of the same name that grew out of a study of anti-Semitism.

Theodor Adorno (1903–1969) led a team of researchers at the University of California, Berkeley, to determine whether there was a correlation between anti-Semitism and certain **personality traits**. While the original goal had been the identification of an "anti-Semitic" personality, the scope was widened, first from anti-Semitic to "Fascist" then to "authoritarian," when the study found that people prejudiced against one ethnic or racial group were likely to be prejudiced against others as well.

A major determining factor in the formation of the authoritarian personality was found to be a pattern of strict and rigid parenting, in which obedience is instilled through physical **punishment** and harsh verbal discipline. Little parental praise or affection is shown, independence is discouraged, and the child's behavior is expected to meet a set standard. Significantly, such parents instill in children not only obedience to themselves but also a deeply entrenched sense of social hierarchy which entails obedience to all persons of higher status. When they reach adulthood, people with this personality structure discharge the hostility accumulated by their harsh upbringing against those whom they perceive to be of lower status by forming negative stereotypes of them and discriminating against or overtly persecuting them. It is also thought that they may be projecting their own weaknesses and fears onto the groups they denigrate as inferior. Other traits associated with this personality type include dependence on authority and rigid rules, **conformity** to group values, admiration of powerful figures, compulsiveness, concreteness, and intolerance of ambiguity.

Further Reading

Eiser, J. Richard *Social Psychology: Attitudes, Cognition, and Social Behaviour.* New York: Cambridge University Press, 1986.

Stone, William F., Gerda Lederer, and Richard Christie, eds. *Strength and Weakness: the Authoritarian Personality Today.* New York: Springer-Verlag, 1993.

Autism

A severe psychological disorder that first appears in early childhood and is characterized by impaired social interaction and language development, and other behavioral problems.

First described by Dr. Leo Kanner in 1943, autism is a severe psychological disorder that affects an estimated four children in 10,000. Autism manifests itself in early childhood. The autistic child is impaired socially, in language development, and exhibits other behavioral problems. This disorder is also known as infantile or childhood autism and Kanner's autism.

The occurrence of autism is four times higher in boys than girls. It is now believed that some of the "wild" or "feral" children found living outdoors on their own may have been autistic children abandoned by their parents. The most famous of these was Victor, the "wild boy of Aveyron," discovered in 1799 at the age of approximately 11. Although he remained almost totally unable to speak, Victor showed great improvements in socialization and cognitive ability after working for several years with Jean-Marc-Gaspard Itard, a physician and teacher of the deaf.

Contrary to earlier beliefs, autism is not thought to have psychological origins, such as inadequate parenting. Several possible causes of autism have been proposed, including phenylketonuria (an inherited metabolic disease), exposure to rubella or certain chemicals *in utero*, and hereditary predisposition. There is no accurate test for autism, although CT scans of autistic children sometimes reveal abnormalities in the ventricles of the **brain**. Autism is usually diagnosed in children between the ages of two and three years based on clinical observation and parental reports. Until this point, manifestations of the disorder are difficult to detect, and in some cases an autistic child will develop normally for the first year or two of life. However, a break usually occurs before the age of two and a half, when speech development (if it has begun) stops and social responses fail to develop.

Children and adults with autism demonstrate a marked impairment in social interaction. Generally, it first appears in children as an inability to form a close attachment to their parents. As infants, they may refuse to cuddle and may react to physical contact by stiffening their bodies and attempting to slide away. Often, autistic children do not develop other feelings that commonly accompany emotional attachments, such as grief, sadness, guilt, or shame, and when older, they are generally impervious to being left with strangers. There is also a lack of interest in or a failure to form peer relationships, and the ordinary desire to share experiences and interests with others tends to be lacking. Autistic children lack interest and skill in games and other typical kinds of reciprocal child's play, including imitative play. Standard nonverbal behaviors that support social interactions—eye contact, facial expressions, and body language—are generally not used appropriately.

Language difficulties are the single symptom that most often leads parents to seek diagnosis and help for autistic children. The development of spoken language is either delayed or totally absent in children with autism. Those who can speak still have trouble listening to others and initiating or carrying on a conversation. The speech of autistic persons often lacks normal grammatical structures and is also nonstandard in terms of such characteristics as pitch, speed, rhythm, or stress on syllables. Echolalia (echoing other people's voices or voices heard on television) is also common.

Besides social and language impairments, the other major symptom of autism is the presence of repetitive, ritualized patterns of behavior. These may be repeated physical movements, such as rocking, swaying, flapping one's arms, or clapping. Autistic behavior may also take such forms as arranging objects in specific patterns or quantities, mimicking a particular action, or performing a routine activity exactly the same way every day. Other behavioral characteristics associated with autism are a preoccupation with a single interest (often one for which a large number of facts may be collected); resistance to trivial changes in routine; fascination with a moving object (such as revolving doors) or a particular part of an object; and a strong attachment to an inanimate object. Persons with autism may exhibit oversensitivity to certain stimuli (such as light or touch), unusual pickiness in eating, inappropriate **fear** and/or fearlessness, and self-injuring behavior, such as head banging. As many as 25 percent of autistic children develop epileptic seizures later in life, often in adolescence, although this particular symptom appears only in those who are mentally retarded.

Three-fourths of autistic children are mentally retarded, and 60 percent have IQ scores below 50. However, many demonstrate skill in music, mathematics, long-term memorization of trivial data, and specialized tasks such as assembling jigsaw puzzles. Autistic children with IQ scores of 70 and above have the best prognosis for living and working independently as adults, although only one in six children with autism becomes a well-adjusted adult, with another one out of six achieving a fair degree of adjustment. Even those autistic adults who function relatively well will still experience difficulty with social interaction and communication, and highly restricted interests and activities. Besides IQ, other predictors of future adjustment for autistic children are their degree of language development, the overall severity of their symptoms, and the types of treatment they receive. While **psychotherapy** has not been of value in treating persons with autism, **behavior modification**, medication, and dietary recommendations have been proven effective in controlling specific symptoms. Special education programs are able to improve the social interaction of autistic children and enhance their academic skills. Developmental work that includes parents has been found to be especially helpful.

Further Information

Autism Society of America
(formerly National Society for Autistic Children)
Address: 7910 Woodmont Avenue, Suite 650
Bethesda, MD 20814-3015
Telephone: 301-657-0881; 800-3328-8476

Further Reading

Autism: Nature, Diagnosis, and Treatment. New York: Guilford Press, 1989.

Cunninghame, Karen. *Autism: A World Apart.* Fanlight Productions, 1988.

Frith, Uta. *Autism: Explaining the Enigma.* Basil Blackwell, 1989.

Jordan, Rita. *Understanding and Teaching Children with Autism.* New York: Wiley, 1995.

Autoeroticism

Manual stimulation (usually self-stimulation) of the genital organs with the intention, typically, of producing sexual arousal and orgasm.

Autoeroticism is the scientific term used to describe masturbation, the stimulation of the genital organs to achieve orgasm. Although masturbation was widely condemned in most premodern societies, and has been the subject of remarkable and persistent superstitions and extreme taboos, there is evidence that contemporary attitudes toward masturbation are becoming increasingly tolerant of this behavior. Studies in the United States and Europe indicate that about 90 percent of adolescent and adult males and about 80 percent of adolescent and adult females have engaged in masturbation. While masturbation is usually a private, solitary activity, it is often accompanied by fantasies of sexual activity that involve another person. Relatively few individuals consistently prefer masturbation to sexual activity that involves another person. It has been shown that masturbation is not physically harmful, and the psychological significance of masturbation depends on how it is regarded by the individual.

Further Reading

Marcus, Irwin M., and John J. Francis, eds. *Masturbation: From Infancy to Senescence.* New York: International Universities Press, 1975.

Autonomic Nervous System

The nervous system responsible for regulating automatic bodily processes, such as breathing and heart rate. The autonomic sys-

tem also involves the processes of metabolism, or the storage and expenditure of energy.

The **nervous system** consists of two main structures, the **central nervous system** (the **brain** and the spinal cord) and the peripheral nervous system (the sense organs and the **nerve**s linking the sense organs, muscles, and glands to the central nervous system). The structures of the peripheral nervous system are further subdivided into the autonomic nervous system (automatic bodily processes) and the somatic nervous system.

The part of the autonomic nervous system that controls the storage of energy (called anabolism) is the parasympathetic division. Parasympathetic (or anabolic) activities involve bodily functions that occur in normal, nonstressful situations. For example, after eating, the digestive process begins, whereby nutrients are taken from the food and stored in the body. The flow of blood increases to the stomach and intestines while at the same time the heart rate decreases and saliva is secreted. The parasympathetic division also mediates sexual **arousal**, even though most parasympathetic functions lead to lower overt arousal levels. Sexual climax is controlled by the sympathetic division.

In general, sympathetic processes reverse parasympathetic responses. The sympathetic division is activated when the body mobilizes for defense or in response to stress. Such processes use energy stored during anabolism; this use of energy is referred to as catabolism. In defensive situations, the heart rate increases, the lungs expand to hold more oxygen, the pupils dilate, and blood flows to the muscles.

While the autonomic nervous system normally functions quite appropriately, abnormalities can appear. In **anxiety** disorders, for example, certain somatic (bodily) symptoms such as muscular tension, hyperventilation, increased heart rate, and high blood pressure are increased, posing the body for attack. This physiological response can lead to such additional maladies as headaches and digestive problems. At times, parasympathetic responses occur simultaneously. In extreme stressful situations, for example, an individual may experience involuntary discharge of the bladder and bowels. Some research has also indicated deficiencies in autonomic arousal processes in psychiatric patients prior to schizophrenic breakdown.

For decades, scientists believed that autonomic processes were not amenable to voluntary control. In recent years, however, people with heart problems have learned to modify heart rates and headache sufferers have learned to modify blood flow to relieve pain through **biofeedback** techniques.

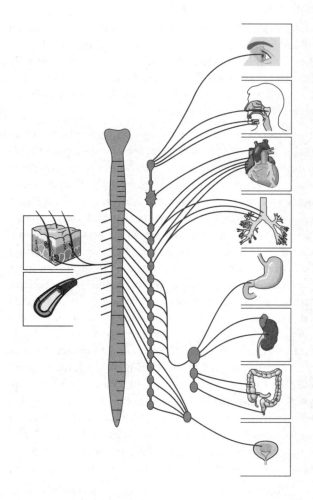

The sympathetic nervous system, one part of the autonomic nervous system, mobilizes the body for action.

Further Reading

Biofeedback and Behavioral Medicine. New York: Aldine Pub. Co., published annually since 1981.

Avoidance Learning

An individual's response to avoid an unpleasant or stressful situation; also known as escape learning.

Avoidance learning is the process by which an individual learns a behavior or response to avoid a stressful or unpleasant situation. The behavior is to avoid, or to remove oneself from, the situation. Researchers have found avoidance behavior challenging to explain, since the **reinforcement** for the behavior is to not experience the negative reinforcer, or **punishment**. In other words, the reinforcement is the absence of punishment. To explain this, psychologists have proposed two stages of learning: in stage one, the learner experiences **classical condition-**

ing; a warning, or stimulus paired with a punishment. The learner develops a **fear** response when he experiences the stimulus. In stage two, the learner experiences **operant conditioning;** whereby he realizes that an action response to the stimulus eliminates the stressful outcome.

In a common laboratory experiment conducted to demonstrate avoidance learning, a rat is placed in a confined space with an electrified floor. A warning signal is given, followed by an electric current passing through the floor. To avoid being shocked, the rat must find an escape, such as a pole to climb or a barrier to jump over onto a nonelectric floor. At first, the rat responds only when the shock begins, but as the pattern is repeated, the rat learns to avoid the shock by responding to the warning signal. An example of avoidance learning in humans is the situation when a person avoids a yard where there is a barking dog. This learning is particularly strong in individuals who have been attacked by a dog.

See also Drive Reduction Theory; Stress.

Further Reading

Archer, Trevor, and Lars-Gvran Nilsson. *Aversion, Avoidance, and Anxiety: Perspective on Aversively Motivated Behavior.* Hillsdale, NJ: L. Erlbaum Associates, 1989.

Ruben, Douglas H. *Avoidance Syndrome: Doing Things Out of Fear.* St. Louis, MO: W.H. Green, 1993.

B

Bandura, Albert (1925–)

American psychologist whose work is concentrated in the area of social learning theory.

Albert Bandura was born in the province of Alberta, Canada, and received his B.A. from the University of British Columbia. He earned his M.A. and Ph.D. in clinical psychology at the University of Iowa, focusing on social learning theories in his studies with Kenneth Spence and Robert Sears. Graduating in 1952, Bandura completed a one-year internship at the Wichita Guidance Center before accepting an appointment to the department of psychology at Stanford University, where he has remained throughout his career. In opposition to more radical behaviorists, Bandura considers cognitive factors as causal agents in human behavior. His area of research, social cognitive theory, is concerned with the interaction between **cognition, behavior,** and the **environment.**

Much of Bandura's work has focused on the acquisition and modification of **personality** traits in children, particularly as they are affected by observational learning, or **modeling,** which, he argues, plays a highly significant role in the determination of subsequent behavior. While it is common knowledge that children learn by imitating others, little formal research was done on this subject before Neal Miller and John Dollard published *Social Learning and Imitation* in 1941. Bandura has been the single figure most responsible for building a solid empirical foundation for the concept of learning through modeling, or imitation. His work, focusing particularly on the nature of **aggression**, suggests that modeling plays a highly significant role in determining thoughts, feelings, and behavior. Bandura claims that practically anything that can be learned by direct experience can also be learned by modeling. Moreover, learning by modeling will occur although neither the observer nor the model is rewarded for performing a particular action, in contrast to the behaviorist learning methods of **Ivan Pavlov** and **B.F. Skinner,** with their focus on learning through con-ditioning and **reinforcement.** However, it has been demonstrated that **punishment** and reward can have an effect on the modeling situation. A child will more readily imitate a model who is being rewarded for an act than one who is being punished. Thus, the child can learn without actually being rewarded or punished himself—a concept known as *vicarious learning.* Similarly, Bandura has shown that when a model is exposed to stimuli intended to have a conditioning effect, a person who simply observes this process, even without participating in it directly, will tend to become conditioned by the stimuli as well.

Based on his research, Bandura has developed modeling as a therapeutic device. The patient is encouraged to modify his or her behavior by identifying with and imitating the behavior of the therapist. Although modeling was first studied in relation to children, it has been found to be effective in treating **phobias** in adults as well. The patient watches a model in contact with a feared object, at first under relatively non-threatening conditions. The patient is encouraged to perform the same actions as the model, and the situation is gradually made more threatening until the patient is able to confront the feared object or experience on his or her own.

Bandura has also focused on the human capacity for symbolization, which can be considered a type of inverse modeling. Using their symbolic capacities, people construct *internal* models of the world which provide an arena for planning, problem-solving, and reflection and can even facilitate communication with others. Another area of social cognition theory explored by Bandura is self-regulatory activity, or the ways in which internal standards affect motivation and actions. He has studied the effects of beliefs people have about themselves on their thoughts, choices, motivation levels, perseverance, and susceptibility to **stress** and **depression.** Bandura is the author of many books, including *Adolescent Aggression* (1959), *Social Learning and Personality* (1963), *Principles of Behavior Modification* (1969), *Aggression*

(1973), *Social Learning Theory* (1977), and *Social Foundations of Thought and Action* (1985).

Further Reading
Decker, Philip J. *Behavior Modeling Training.* New York: Praeger, 1985.

Beers, Clifford (1876–1943)

American reformer and founder of the mental hygiene movement.

Clifford Whittingham Beers was born in New Haven, Connecticut, studied at Yale University, and began a professional career in the insurance industry. In 1900 he was institutionalized for a mental breakdown after a **suicide** attempt and diagnosed as manic-depressive. Confined to both public and private institutions over a three-year period, Beers found the treatment of mental patients inhumane and ineffective. When his efforts to complain directly to hospital administrators were ignored, Beers smuggled letters out to state officials, and his efforts met with some success. By 1903 Beers was able to return to his career, but continued to work on behalf of reforming the treatment of the mentally ill.

In 1908 Beers published *A Mind That Found Itself,* a popular autobiographical study of his confinement and recovery, which was praised by the prominent psychologist and philosopher **William James.** After the publication of this work, and with the general support of the medical community, Beers became a leading figure in the movement to reform the treatment of, and attitudes toward, mental illness. In the same year his book was published, Beers founded the Connecticut Society for Mental Hygiene (a name suggested by the psychologist **Adolf Meyer,** another supporter of Beers's efforts). This organization lobbied for improved treatment of mental patients and heightened public awareness of mental illness. In 1909, Beers organized the National Committee for Mental Hygiene and served as its secretary until 1939. He also helped establish the American Foundation for Mental Hygiene in 1928.

Beers's influence eventually spread beyond the United States. In 1918 he helped Clarence M. Hincks found a mental hygiene society in Canada, the Canadian National Committee for Mental Hygiene. Beers was active in organizing the International Congress on Mental Health in 1930, and three years later received an award for his achievements in the mental health field from the National Institute of Social Science. Beers's autobiography remained popular and influential, having gone into 26 printings by the time of his death in 1943.

Behavior Disorder

A very general term used to classify virtually any behavior pattern that is abnormal or aberrant.

The term behavior disorder is an imprecise term used to describe any behavior pattern that is abnormal or aberrant enough to indicate a need for psychological counseling or therapy. The term behavior disorder is sometimes used as a synonym for the older term neurosis.

See also Psychological Disorder.

Behavior Modification

The use of positive reinforcement to adjust an individual's motivation and change behavior.

Based on **operant conditioning,** behavior modification is one technique used in **behavior therapy.** In behavior modification, specific consequences are designated for specific behaviors. The desired behavior is matched with a positive **reinforcement** or reward, and the behavior the person is seeking to change or eliminate has no such reward. Often used with children, the goal of behavior modification is to link **attention** and positive reinforcement to the desired behaviors, and to eliminate attention or reinforcement for negative behaviors.

Further Reading
Bandura, Albert. *Principles of Behavior Modification.* New York: Holt, Rinehart, and Winston, 1969.
Blackham, Garth J. *Modification of Child and Adolescent Behavior.* 3rd ed. Belmont, CA: Wadsworth Pub. Co., 1980.
DeVito, Paul, and Ralph Hyatt. "What Constitutes 'Appropriate Punishment'?" *USA Today* (March 1995): 89+.
Sutherland, Valerie, et al., "Quality Behavior for Quality Organizations." *Leadership and Organization Development Journal* (June 1995): 10+.

Behavior Therapy

A term describing a variety of therapeutic methods that approach emotional and behavioral problems as the result of learned behaviors that can be changed.

The use of classical and **operant conditioning** to alter human behavior, which was pioneered in the late 1950s and early 1960s, grew out of discoveries earlier in the century by such prominent behaviorists as **Ivan Pavlov, John B. Watson**, and **B. F. Skinner**. By the 1970s behavioral therapy was widely used as an alternative to psychodynamic and other traditional types of treatment. Unlike other approaches, behavior-oriented therapies focused on observable behaviors rather than **unconscious** conflicts or analytical insights, and on the present rather than the past. Adopting the behaviorist emphasis on learning as the primary basis for both normal and abnormal behaviors, behavioral therapists viewed their clients' problems in terms of learned maladaptive thoughts and/or behaviors that could be replaced by new, more appropriate behaviors.

Behavior therapy has encompassed a number of different approaches. Some have been based on Skinnerian operant conditioning (changing behavior by changing the response to it). This type of treatment is usually associated with the term "behavior modification." Others have derived their treatment methods from the principles of **classical conditioning** pioneered by such figures as Pavlov, C. L. Hull, and N. E. Miller. Among the clinicians responsible for adapting classical conditioning to therapeutic purposes, the most notable has been Joseph Wolpe. Most recently, interests in the field of behavioral therapy have shifted from an exclusive focus on observable behavior to include the ways in which **cognition**s mediate between human behavior and social environment. The resulting treatment method is known as **cognitive behavior therapy**. Two well known forms of cognitive behavior therapy are rational-emotive therapy (RET), developed by Albert Ellis, and the cognitive therapy of Aaron Beck, often used to treat persons suffering from **depression** and **anxiety** disorders.

As an initial step in many types of behavioral therapy, the client monitors his or her own behavior carefully, often keeping a written record. The client and therapist establish a set of specific goals that will result in gradual behavior change. The therapist's role is often similar to that of a coach or teacher who gives the client "homework assignments" and provides advice and encouragement. Therapists continuously monitor and evaluate the course of the treatment itself, making any necessary adjustments to increase its effectiveness.

A number of specific techniques are commonly used in behavioral therapy. Human behavior is routinely motivated and rewarded by positive **reinforcement**, and a more specialized version of this phenomenon, called systematic positive reinforcement, is used by behavior-oriented therapists. Rules are established that specify particular behaviors that are to be reinforced and a reward system is set up. With children, this sometimes takes the form of tokens that may be accumulated and later exchanged for certain privileges. Just as providing reinforcement strengthens behaviors, withholding it weakens them. Eradicating undesirable behavior by deliberately withholding reinforcement is another popular treatment method called **extinction**. For example, a child who habitually shouts to attract attention may be ignored unless he or she speaks in a conversational tone.

Aversive conditioning employs the principles of classical conditioning to lessen the appeal of a behavior that is difficult to change because it is either very habitual or temporarily rewarding. The client is exposed to an unpleasant stimulus while engaged in or thinking about the behavior in question. Eventually the behavior itself becomes associated with unpleasant rather than pleasant feelings. One treatment method used with alcoholics is the administration of a nausea-inducing drug together with an alcoholic beverage to produce an aversion to the taste and smell of alcohol by having it become associated with nausea. In counterconditioning, a maladaptive response is weakened by the strengthening of a response that is incompatible with it. A well-known type of counterconditioning is systematic **desensitization**, which counteracts the anxiety connected with a particular behavior or situation by inducing a relaxed response to it instead. This method is often used in the treatment of people who are afraid of flying. **Modeling**, another treatment method, is based on the human tendency to learn through observation and **imitation**. A desired behavior is performed by another person while the client watches. In some cases, the client practices the behavior together with a model (often the therapist).

Further Reading

Ammerman, Robert T., and Michel Hersen, eds. *Handbook of Behavior Therapy with Children and Adults: A Developmental and Longitudinal Perspective.* New York: Allyn and Bacon, 1993.

Craighead, Linda W. *Cognitive and Behavioral Interventions: An Empirical Approach to Mental Health Problems.* Boston: Allyn and Bacon, 1994.

Kanfer, Frederick H., and Arnold P. Goldstein, eds. *Helping People Change: A Textbook of Methods.* 4th ed. New York: Pergamon Press, 1991.

O'Leary, K. Daniel, and G. Terence Wilson. *Behavior Therapy: Application and Outcome.* Englewood Cliffs, NJ: Prentice-Hall, 1975.

Wolpe, Joseph. *The Practice of Behavior Therapy.* Tarrytown, NY: Pergamon Press, 1990.

Behavioral Neuroscience. See **Physiological Psychology**.

Behaviorism

A mode of psychological study that considers only objective and measurable elements of observed behavior and discounts as inappropriate for study such abstract factors as will, feeling, and imagination.

Edward Thorndike initially proposed that humans and animals acquire behaviors through the association of stimuli and responses. He advanced two laws of learning to explain why behaviors occur the way they do. The **Law of Effect** specifies that any time a behavior is followed by a pleasant outcome, that behavior is likely to recur. The Law of Exercise states that the more a stimulus is connected with a response, the stronger the link is between the two. **Ivan Pavlov**'s groundbreaking work on **classical conditioning** also provided a mechanistic, observable way to study behavior. Although most psychologists agree that neither Thorndike nor Pavlov were behaviorists in the strictest sense, their work paved the way for the emergence of behaviorism.

John B. Watson (1878–1958) further expanded the concepts of behaviorism and became its chief advocate. He concluded that humans, like other animals, were complex machines governed not by thought or will, but by neural "wiring" that could only be altered by conditioning. In fact, Watson went so far as to claim that no direct relationship existed between thought and neural activity and that thought was merely the aftereffect of peripheral events, such as muscle movements or glandular secretions. Therefore, according to Watson, what occurs in the "mind" is completely irrelevant to psychology because, not only is it hidden from observation, it does not relate directly to behavior. Most psychologists accepted Watson's perspective, which dominated psychology from the first decade of the twentieth century until the 1960s, although they often disagreed with his extreme stance regarding the nonexistence of mental processes.

B. F. Skinner is credited with popularizing behaviorism. He rejected the mentalistic traditions developed by the earlier behaviorists and contended that all behavior is controlled by external factors. Skinner established the role of **reinforcement** in controlling behavior and asserted that only **environment**al factors influence behavior. His controversial works, *Walden Two* (1948) and *Beyond Freedom and Dignity* (1971), presented his behavioral ideas to the nonscientific public.

Beginning in the 1960s, psychologists became convinced that behavioral theory could not adequately characterize the complexity of behavior. At this point, many people also began looking with skepticism on the mechanistic rules of behavioral engineering.

Psychologists had rejected the notion of mental concepts because they were seen as unscientific. With the development of computers, it was clear that machines, which were controlled by physical laws, could perform many of the same tasks that humans could. As a result, psychologists became more accepting of mental processes as being consistent with scientific study. Gradually, psychologists concluded that new approaches to the study of behavior were appropriate. Behaviorism was not shown to be incorrect, rather, it was merely shown to be less useful than other approaches.

Further Reading

Blackham, Garth J. *Modification of Child and Adolescent Behavior.* 3rd ed. Belmont, CA: Wadsworth Pub. Co., 1980.

Contemporary Behavior Therapy: Conceptual and Empirical Foundations. New York: Guilford Press, 1982.

Craighead, Linda W. *Cognitive and Behavioral Interventions: An Empirical Approach to Mental Health Problems.* Boston: Allyn and Bacon, 1994.

Kanfer, Frederick H., and Arnold P. Goldstein, eds. *Helping People Change: A Textbook of Methods.* 4th ed. New York: Pergamon Press, 1991.

O'Leary, K. Daniel, and G. Terence Wilson. *Behavior Therapy: Application and Outcome.* Englewood Cliffs, NJ: Prentice-Hall, 1975.

Stern, Richard. *The Practice of Behavioural and Cognitive Psychotherapy.* New York: Cambridge University Press, 1991.

Bender-Gestalt Test

Diagnostic assessment test to identify learning disability, neurological disorders, and developmental delay.

The complete name of this test is Bender Visual Motor Gestalt Test. It is a test used with all age groups to help identify possible learning disabilities, neurological disorders, **mental retardation,** or developmental delay. Test results also provide information about specific abilities, including motor coordination, **memory,** and organization. The test-taker is given a series of nine designs, each on a separate card, and asked to reproduce them on a blank sheet of paper. There is no time limit. The test is scored by professionals who consider a variety of factors, including form, shape, pattern, and orientation on the page.

See also Learning Disability.

Further Reading

Lacks, Patricia. *Bender Gestalt Screening for Brain Dysfunction.* New York: Wiley, 1984.

Bestiality. See **Paraphilia**.

Bettelheim, Bruno (1903–1990)

Austrian born American psychologist known for his treatment of emotionally disturbed children, particularly autistic children.

Bruno Bettelheim was born in Vienna in 1903. He was trained as a psychoanalyst, receiving his Ph.D. from the University of Vienna in 1938. In the same year, the Nazis conquered Austria and Bettelheim was interned in the Dachau and Buchenwald concentration camps. He was released in 1939 and emigrated to the United States, where he first became a research associate of the Progressive Education Association at the University of Chicago, and then an associate professor at Rockford College from 1942 to 1944.

In 1943, Bettelheim gained widespread recognition for his article, "Individual and Mass Behavior in Extreme Situations," a study of human adaptability based on his concentration camp experiences. In 1944, he was granted a dual appointment by the University of Chicago as assistant professor and head of the Sonia Shankman Orthogenic School, a residential treatment center for 6 to 14-year-old children with severe emotional problems. Here he successfully treated many children unresponsive to previous therapy, using the technique—which has been both lauded and criticized—of unconditionally accepting their behavior. Bettelheim was also concerned with the emotional lives and upbringing of normal children, and with applying psychoanalytic principles to social problems.

In three decades as an author of works for both scholarly and popular audiences, Bettelheim covered a broad range of topics. *Love Is Not Enough* (1950), *Truants from Life* (1954), and *The Empty Fortress* (1967) are based on his work at the Orthogenic School. *The Informed Heart* (1960) deals with Bettelheim's concentration camp experiences. *Children of the Dream* (1969) analyzes communal childrearing methods on an Israeli kibbutz and their implications for American family life. *The Uses of Enchantment* (1976) argues for the importance of fairy tales in a child's development. Bettelheim's later books include *On Learning to Read: The Child's First Fascination with Meaning* (1981) and *Freud and Man's Soul* (1982). A full professor at the University of Chicago from 1952, Bettelheim retired from both teaching and directorship of the Orthogenic School in 1973. Following the death of his wife in 1984 and after suffering a stroke in 1987, Bettelheim committed **suicide** in 1990.

See also Adaptation; Autism.

Further Reading

Sutton, Nina. *Bettelheim, A Life and a Legacy.* New York: Basic Books, 1996.

Binet, Alfred (1857–1911)

French psychologist. Founder of experimental psychology in France and a pioneer in intelligence testing.

Alfred Binet was born in Nice, France, in 1857. After studying both law and medicine in Paris, he earned a doctorate in natural science. Binet's psychological training—

Alfred Binet

ing—mostly at Jean-Martin Charcot's neurological clinic at the Salpetriere Hospital—was in the area of **abnormal psychology,** particularly hysteria, and he published books on **hypnosis** (*Le magnetisme animal,* with C.S. Fere in 1886) and suggestibility (*La suggestibilite,* 1900). From 1895 until his death in 1911, Binet served as director of France's first psychological laboratory at the Sorbonne of the University of Paris. Also in 1895, he established the journal *L'Annee psychologique.* Binet had been interested in the psychology of—and individual differences in—**intelligence** since the 1880s and published articles on **emotion, memory, attention,** and problem solving. In 1899 he set up a special laboratory where he devised a series of tests which he used to evaluate the intellectual development of his two daughters. His 1903 book, *L'Etude experimentale de l'intelligence,* was based on his studies of them.

In 1905, Binet and Theodore Simon created the first intelligence test to aid the French government in establishing a program to provide special education for mentally retarded children. In 1908 they revised the test, expanding it from a single scale of measurement to a battery of tests for children in different age groups, with the focus now shifted from identifying retardation to the general measurement of intelligence. A further test revision in 1911 introduced the concept of **mental age.** In 1916, the American psychologist **Lewis Terman** used the 1908 Binet-Simon scale as the basis for the **Stanford-Binet Intelligence Scale,** the best-known and most researched intelligence test in the United States. Binet co-authored *Les enfants anormaux (Abnormal Children)* (1907) with Simon and published *Les idees modernes sur les enfants (Modern Ideas on Children)* in 1909. He died in Paris in 1911.

See also Intelligence Quotient, I.Q. test; Mental Retardation.

Further Reading
Wolf, Theta Holmes. *Alfred Binet.* Chicago: University of Chicago Press, 1973.

Binocular Depth Cues

Properties of the visual system that facilitate depth perception by the nature of messages that are sent to the brain.

Binocular depth cues are based on the simple fact that a person's eyes are located in different places. One cue, binocular disparity, refers to the fact that different optical images are produced on the retinas of both eyes when viewing an object. By processing information about the degree of disparity between the images it receives, the **brain** produces the impression of a single object that has depth in addition to height and width.

The second cue, called binocular convergence, is based on the fact that in order to project images on the retinas, the two eyes must rotate inward toward each other. The closer the perceived object is, the more they must rotate, so the brain uses the information it receives about the degree of rotation as a cue to interpret the distance of the perceived objects. Yet another cue to **depth perception** is called binocular accommodation, a term that refers to the fact that the lens of the eye changes shape when it brings an image into focus on the retina. The muscular activity necessary for this accommodation acts

BINOCULAR DISPARITY DEMONSTRATION

This simple experiment demonstrates binocular disparity. Hold a pencil about 12 inches (30 cm) from your face. With one eye closed, align the pencil with the edge of a doorway, window, or other vertical line in the room. Close that eye, open the other, and observe the position of the pencil: it will have jumped. Binocular disparity describes this phenomenon of different images of the pencil in each eye.

as a signal for the brain to generate perception of depth and distance.

See also Vision.

Further Reading
Bennett, Jill. *Sight.* Morristown, NJ: Silver Burdett, 1986.
Chalkley, Thomas. *Your Eyes.* 3rd ed. Springfield, IL: C.C. Thomas, 1995.
Elkins, James. *The Object Stares Back: On the Nature of Seeing.* New York: Simon & Schuster, 1996.

Biofeedback

A technique that allows individuals to monitor their own physiological processes so they can learn to control them.

Biofeedback originated with the field of psychophysiology, which measures physiological responses as a way of studying human behavior. Types of behavior that may be studied in this way range from basic emotional responses to higher cognitive functions. Today, biofeedback is also associated with behavioral medicine, which combines behavioral and biomedical science in both clinical and research settings. In biofeedback training, the monitoring of physiological responses is performed for therapeutic instead of (or in addition to) investigative purposes. Biofeedback has been applied with success to a variety of clinical problems, ranging from migraine headaches to hypertension.

The technique provides people with continuous information about physiological processes of which they are normally unaware, such as blood pressure or heart rate. Through special equipment, these processes are recorded, and the information is relayed back to the person through a changing tone or meter reading. With practice, people learn strategies that enable them to achieve voluntary control over the processes involved. For example, persons trying to control their blood pressure levels may see a light flash whenever the pressure drops below a certain level. They may then try to remember and analyze what their thoughts or emotions were at that moment and deliberately repeat them to keep the pressure level low. Initially, they may simply be asked to try and keep the light flashing for as long as possible and given verbal **reinforcement** for their efforts.

The biofeedback training may continue for several days or weeks, with the subjects trying to keep the light flashing for longer periods in subsequent sessions. Eventually they will need to produce the desired response without electronic feedback, a goal which can be accomplished through various methods. They may practice the learned response at the end of the training session or at home between sessions. There can also be random trials without feedback during the sessions. An alternate strategy is the gradual and systematic removal of the feedback signal during the training sessions over a period of time. After the initial training is completed, subjects may return to the biofeedback facility to assess their retention of the skills they have learned or for additional training.

Biofeedback training has been used in treating a number of different clinical problems. Monitoring of patients' heart rates has been used with some success to help people suffering from heartbeat irregularities, including premature ventricular contractions (PVCs) and tachycardia, while hypertensive individuals have been able to control high blood pressure through the use of biofeedback. Clinicians have been particularly successful in their use of neuromuscular feedback to treat complaints arising from tension in specific muscles or muscle groups. Tension headaches have been alleviated through the reduction of frontalis (forehead) tension, and relaxation of the face and neck muscles has been helpful to stutterers. Feedback from muscle groups has been helpful in the rehabilitation of stroke patients and other persons with neuromuscular disorders such as foot drop. These patients may be unable to relax or contract muscles at will, and biofeedback can make them aware of small, otherwise imperceptible changes in the desired direction and allow them to repeat and eventually increase such changes.

In addition to its alleviation of physical complaints, neuromuscular biofeedback has been an effective tool in the treatment of chronic **anxiety**, even when it has resisted **psychotherapy** and medication. By learning deep muscle relaxation, anxious patients, including those suffering from related conditions such as insomnia, have seen a reduction in their symptoms. Even for patients who have been able to achieve relaxation through other means, such as meditation or progressive relaxation, biofeedback can be a valuable supplementary technique that offers special advantages, such as allowing a therapist to track closely the points at which a patient tenses up and try to learn what thoughts are associated with the tension. Biofeedback-induced relaxation of forehead muscles has also been effective in treating asthma.

Another type of biofeedback involves the monitoring of **brain** activity through **electroencephalographs (EEGs)**. A reduction of seizures in epileptics has been reported through biofeedback techniques involving EEG activity near the sensorimotor cortex, known as sensory motor rhythm. Brain wave activity has also been of interest in connection with alpha waves, which are thought to characterize a desirable state of relaxed alertness. Patients have been taught to increase their alpha rhythms in three or four 30-minute conditioning sessions.

Further Reading

Andreassi, John L. *Psychophysiology: Human Behavior and Physiological Response.* New York: Oxford University Press, 1980.

Beatty, J., and H. Legewie, eds. *Biofeedback and Behavior.* New York: Plenum Press, 1977.

Bipolar Disorder

A condition (traditionally called manic depression) in which a person alternates between the two emotional extremes of depression and mania (an elated, euphoric mood).

Bipolar disorder is classified among affective disorders in the **American Psychiatric Association**'s *Diagnostic and Statistical Manual of Mental Disorders*. The National Institute of Mental Health (NIMH) estimates that about one in one hundred people will develop the disorder, which affects some two million Americans. While this condition occurs equally in both males and females and in every ethnic and racial groups, it is more common among well-educated, middle- and upper-income persons. Those suffering from untreated bipolar disorder will generally experience an average of four **depression/mania** episodes in a ten-year period. However, some people go through four or more **mood** swings a month, while others may only experience a mood swing every five years. The onset of bipolar disorder usually occurs in the teens or early twenties.

Of all types of depressive illness, bipolar disorder is the one that is most likely to have biological origins, specifically an imbalance in the **brain**'s chemistry. Genetic factors play an important role in the disease. In one study, one-fourth of the children who had one manic-depressive parent became manic-depressive themselves, and three-fourths of those with two manic-depressive parents developed the disorder. The likelihood of bipolar disorder being shared by identical **twins** is also exceptionally high. Manic depression has also been associated with the "biological clock" that synchronizes body rhythms and external events.

The depressed state of a person suffering from bipolar disorder resembles major depression. It is characterized by feelings of sadness, apathy, and loss of energy. Other possible symptoms include sleep disturbances; significant changes in appetite or weight; languid movements; feelings of worthlessness or inappropriate guilt; lack of concentration; and preoccupation with death or **suicide**. When they shift to a manic state, people with bipolar disorder become elated and overly talkative, speaking loudly and rapidly and abruptly switching from one topic to another. Plunging into many work, social, or academic activities at once, they are in constant motion and are hyperactive. They also demonstrate grandiosity—an exaggerated sense of their own powers, which leads them to believe they can do things beyond the power of ordinary persons. Other common symptoms include excessive and/or promiscuous sexual behavior and out-of-control shopping sprees in which large amounts of money are spent on unnecessary items. People in a manic phase typically become irritable or angry when others try to tone down their ideas or behavior, or when they have difficulty carrying out all the activities they have begun. **Mania** may also be accompanied by **delusions** and **hallucinations**.

Mania creates enormous turmoil in the lives of its victims, many of whom turn to drugs or alcohol as a way of coping with the **anxiety** generated by their condition—61 percent of persons with bipolar disorder have substance abuse or dependency problems. In addition, 15 percent of those who fail to receive adequate treatment for bipolar disorder commit suicide. The disease may be misdiagnosed as **schizophrenia**, unipolar depression, a personality disorder, or drug or alcohol dependence. Individuals commonly suffer from it for as long as seven to ten years without being diagnosed or treated.

However, effective treatment is available. Lithium, which stabilizes the brain chemicals involved in mood swings, is used to treat both the mania and depression of bipolar disorder. This drug, which is taken by millions of people throughout the world, halts symptoms of mania in 70 percent of those who take it, usually working within one to three weeks—sometimes within hours. Antipsychotic drugs or benzodiazepines (tranquilizers) may initially be needed to treat cases of full-blown mania until lithium can take effect. Persons taking lithium must have their blood levels, as well as kidney and thyroid functions, monitored regularly, as there is a relatively narrow gap between toxic and therapeutic levels of the drug. Since lithium also has the ability to prevent future manic episodes, it is recommended as maintenance therapy even after manic-depressive symptoms subside. Some persons resist remaining on medication, however, either because they fear of becoming dependent on the drug or because they are reluctant to give up the "highs" or alleged creativity of the manic state. However, psychiatrists have reported instances in which lithium was not as effective after being discontinued as it had been initially.

Many great artists, writers, musicians, and other people prominent in both creative and other fields have suffered from bipolar disorder, including composers Robert Schumann and Gustav Mahler, painter Vincent van Gogh, writers Virginia Woolf and Sylvia Plath, and actresses Patty Duke and Kristy McNichol. The NIMH reports that 38 percent of all Pulitzer Prize–winning poets have had the symptoms of bipolar disorder.

Further Reading

Duke, Patty. *Call Me Anna.* New York: Bantam, 1987.

Jamison, Kay. *Touched with Fire: Manic-Depressive Illness and the Artistic Temperament.* New York: Free Press, 1993.

....

Birth

In humans, the process of delivering a child from the uterus, usually by passage through the birth canal at the end of pregnancy, normally after a gestation period of about 267 days; also called parturition, or labor.

Childbearing is often viewed as the transition to adult female **sexuality.** Birth labor is divided into several stages. During the latent phase (Stage 0), which lasts from several hours to as long as three days, uterine contractions (either regular or irregular) are present, but the cervix has not dilated more than three or four centimeters. The mucus plug may be passed at this stage. The first stage of labor begins with uterine contractions accompanied by mild pain at intervals of about 10 to 20 minutes and sensations of discomfort in the small of the back which eventually become stronger and spread to the entire abdominal area. The cervix, or neck of the uterus, dilates rapidly from three or four centimeters until its opening is large enough to allow the passage of the child (10 centimeters). By the end of the first stage (although sometimes much earlier), the sac containing the amniotic fluid which surrounds the child breaks. The first stage can take up to 12 hours with first-time mothers, although it may be very rapid in women who have had several children. It can last many hours in obstructed labor, where the baby is unusually large or badly angled.

The second stage of labor begins with the complete dilation and effacement (thinning) of the cervix and ends when the baby is born. At this stage, the contractions are increasingly frequent and intense, ultimately recurring at intervals of two to three minutes and lasting about a minute. The mother begins contracting her abdominal muscles voluntarily ("bearing down"), and the baby is expelled, usually head first, by a combination of this voluntary contraction and the involuntary contractions of the uterine muscles. The physician aids in the delivery by guiding the infant's head and shoulders out of the birth canal. About 2 to 3 percent of babies are born feet first (breech babies). Obstetrical forceps may be applied during the second stage of labor to speed delivery in order to ease either maternal exhaustion or infant distress. Other medical techniques utilized include the episiotomy, a surgical incision along the back of the vagina to enlarge the opening. (This procedure is now performed less frequently than it was in the past.)

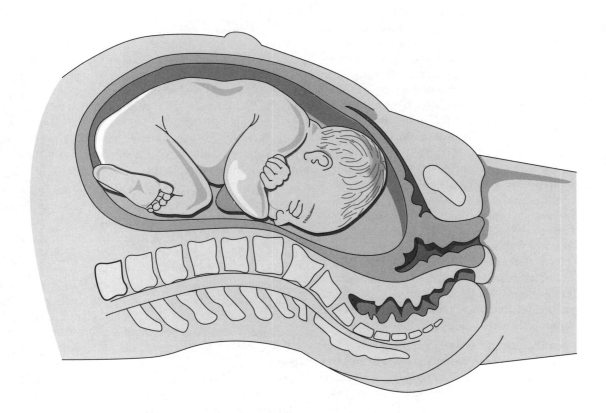

Normal position of infant at birth.

When the baby is born, mucus and blood are removed from the nose and mouth by means of suctioning. The umbilical cord is clamped and cut, and the child is given to the mother to hold. The infant's physical condition is then assessed by the **Apgar score,** which evaluates the overall level of health based on heart rate, skin color, muscular activity and respiratory effort, and response to stimuli. During the third stage of labor, which occurs within the first hour after the child is born, placental material, or afterbirth, is expelled through the birth canal by strong uterine contractions called afterbirth pains. These contractions also help the uterus to return to its normal size. The doctor examines the placenta and amniotic sac to confirm that all tissue has been expelled from the uterus, as serious complications may result if fragments remain inside, especially hemorrhaging. If parts of the placenta or sac are missing, the doctor removes them by hand. Finally, the episiotomy (if one has been performed) is sutured with absorbable stitches. The total duration of labor averages about 13 hours for first deliveries and about eight hours for subsequent deliveries, although there are large individual variances from these figures.

The pain of the birth process can be relieved by drugs, but many of these drugs also have the effect of slowing uterine contractions or depressing the respiratory system of the child. Drugs are either not used—or used with special care—in the case of **twins** or premature infants. Moderate doses of narcotic analgesics may be given to the mother, which are metabolized quickly and nearly absent by the time of delivery. Local anesthetics similar to Novocaine may be administered to provide pain relief in the cervical and vaginal areas, offering more localized relief with fewer side effects than narcotics. Methods of childbirth have been developed in which the use of drugs is kept to a minimum.

The natural childbirth movement begun by Fernand Lamaze, which advocates birth without drugs or medical intervention, departed from the practices of the 1940s and 1950s, when the administration of drugs and medical procedures such as episiotomies were standard obstetrical procedure. Natural childbirth methods use nonmedical relaxation techniques for pain control and allow for more active participation in labor by the mother and a lay coach, usually the husband. They typically include prenatal classes for the mother and coach. Women who use the Lamaze method are taught to perform three activities simultaneously during contractions: breathing in a special pattern, chanting a nonsense phrase coordinated with the rhythm of her breathing, and staring intently at an object.

The home delivery movement, which became popular in the United States during the 1970s, gave way to the established of birthing centers (in or affiliated with hospitals) staffed by nurse-midwives and obstetricians in an attempt to duplicate the family-centered, drug-free experience of home birth but without the risks posed by the absence of medical professionals. The natural childbirth movement has also focused on easing the birth experience for the infant. In *Birth Without Violence,* the physician Frederick Leboyer described modern hospital birth as "torture of the innocent" and proposed measures to make the transition to life outside the womb a more gentle one for the newborn. These measures include dim lights and a quiet atmosphere in the delivery room, postponing cutting of the umbilical cord, and bathing the infant in lukewarm water. Psychologists Otto Rank and R.D. Laing have elaborated on the idea of **birth trauma** as a factor in adult mental and emotional problems, and Leonard Orr developed rebirthing in the 1970s as a holistic healing technique for eliminating negative beliefs that influence an adult's behavior and **attitudes.**

Occasionally, complicating factors that can affect the mother, the child, or both are encountered in the birth process. These factors include, for example, poor health, anatomical abnormalities, prematurity, and unusual orientation of the child in the uterus, such as breech presentation, in which the child moves through the birth canal head last, and (rarely) transverse presentation, in which the child is positioned sideways. In some women, the pelvic space is too small for spontaneous birth of a baby, and the delivery of the child is accomplished through a surgical opening made in the mother's abdominal wall and uterus, in a procedure called a cesarean section. For a healthy mother and child, the risks of childbirth are extremely low. Premature labor, which occurs in about one pregnancy out of 20, is the primary danger to mother and child during the last trimester of pregnancy and the major cause of newborn death. About 40 to 50 percent of mothers—especially first-time mothers—experience mild postpartum **depression,** thought to be caused by a combination of biochemical factors and adjustment to the pressures and demands of parenthood. A smaller percentage—between 5 and 10 percent—become severely depressed. Postpartum depression usually lasts up to 90 days.

Further Reading

Ellis Jeffrey W., ed. *Miracle of Birth.* New York: Beekman House, 1989.

Hotchner, Tracy. *Pregnancy and Childbirth: The Complete Guide for a New Life.* 2nd ed. New York: Avon, 1990

Martin, Margaret. *The Illustrated Book of Pregnancy and Childbirth.* New York: Facts on File, 1991.

Nathaniels, Peter. *Life Before Birth and a Time to Be Born.* Ithaca, NY: Promethean Press, 1992.

Birth Order

A chronological sequence of the birth of children in a family.

Research has indicated that there is a correlation between **birth** order and other aspects of life. For example, first-born children, when compared to their siblings, tend to score slightly higher on **intelligence** tests and to attain a slightly higher socioeconomic status. Some psychologists believe that birth order is a significant factor in the development of **personality**.

The psychologist **Alfred Adler** pioneered in the study of relationships between birth order and personality. As part of his view that patients need to be understood in the context of their family environments, Adler hypothesized that a child's position in the family is associated with certain problems that are responded to in similar ways by other children in the same birth position. Adler stressed that it was not the numerical birth position itself that mattered but rather the situation that tended to accompany that position, and the child's reaction to it. Thus, for example, first-born children, when compared to their siblings, tend to have a greater chance of developing feelings of inferiority as their focal position in the family structure is altered by the birth of a sibling. Later-born children, on the other hand, tend to have stronger social skills, having had to deal with siblings throughout their lives, as opposed to first-borns, who have their parents to themselves initially and thus have their first socialization experiences with adults only. Later-borns, having had to compromise more at home, are better equipped to develop the flexibility that can make their subsequent relationships more successful. It has also been posited that birth order influences one's choice of a marriage partner. The "duplication hypothesis" advanced by Walter Toman (1976) states that people seek to duplicate their sibling relationships in marriage, a duplication that includes birth order.

More specific research on the effects of birth order has generally focused on five ordinal birth positions: first-born, second-born, middle, last, and only-born child in a family. Studies have consistently linked first-born children and academic achievement. The number of first-born National Merit Scholarship winners was found to equal the number of second- and third-borns combined. Separate studies have found high academic achievement levels among first-borns in both urban ghettoes in the United States and at British universities. First-born children are generally responsible, assertive, and task-oriented, often rising to leadership positions as adults. They are more frequently mentioned in *Who's Who* publications than individuals in any other birth position and are overrepresented among members of Congress and U.S. presidents. Studies have also found that first-born students are especially vulnerable to **stress** and tend to seek the approval of others. Adler found that there were more first-borns than later-borns among problem children.

Second-born and/or middle children tend to feel inferior to the older child or children, since they do not realize that their lower level of achievement is a function of age. They often try to succeed in areas not excelled in by their elder siblings. Middle-born children have shown a relatively high level of success in team sports, and both they and last-borns have been found to be better adjusted emotionally if from large families. Studies have also found middle children to be sensitive to injustice and likely to have aesthetic interests. Generally trusting, accepting, and other-centered, they tend to maintain relationships successfully.

The last-born child, who is never dethroned as the "baby" of the family, often exhibit a strong sense of security and noncompetitiveness. They are, as a group, the most successful socially and have the highest self-esteem levels of all the birth positions. One study found last-borns more likely than first-borns or only children to join a fraternity or sorority. Like youngest children, only children are never displaced as the youngest in the family. With only adult models to emulate within the family, only children are achievement-oriented and most likely to attain academic success and attend college. However, studies show that only children have the most problems with close relationships and the lowest need for **affiliation.** They are also the most likely to be referred for help with psychiatric disorders.

Further Reading

Forer, Lucille. *The Birth Order Factor.* New York: D. McKay Co., 1976.

Birth Trauma

In psychoanalysis, birth provides the first experience of anxiety in an individual's life.

In psychoanalytical theory, birth trauma is the first major occasion of great **anxiety** in the life of an individual experienced at **birth** as the infant moves from the gentle comfort of the womb into a new **environment** full of harsh and unfamiliar stimuli. While most psychoanalytical psychologists assign a moderate degree of importance to the birth trauma in terms of its effects, some believe that the birth trauma is the prototypical basis of all later anxiety neuroses. The universality of the birth experience presents obvious difficulties in the precise determination of the nature and effects of the birth trauma. The term birth trauma may also mean any physical injury to an infant that occurs during birth.

Further Reading

Hotchner, Tracy. *Pregnancy and Childbirth: The Complete Guide for a New Life.* 2nd ed. New York: Avon, 1990

Martin, Margaret. *The Illustrated Book of Pregnancy and Childbirth.* New York: Facts on File, 1991.

Body Image

The subjective conception of one's own body, based largely on evaluative judgments about how one is perceived by others.

Body image is usually of physical appearance, but may also be of body functions or other features. It is linked to internal sensations, emotional experiences, fantasies, feedback from others, and is a basic part of a person's **self-concept.** Self-perceptions of physical inferiority can have a strong effect on all areas of one's life. They may lead to avoidance of social or sexual activities or result in eating disorders.

The perceived correspondence of one's physical characteristics to cultural standards plays a crucial role in the formation of body image. In the South Pacific island of Tonga, for example, corpulence is considered a sign of wealth and elevated social status, but would be termed **obesity** in Western societies, particularly in the United States where the slim and firm athletic form is idealized. Deference to cultural standards and concepts can be very damaging, as few people attain an "ideal body," no matter how it is defined, and those who depart drastically from it can suffer a sharply reduced sense of self-worth.

Body image is of interest to psychologists primarily in terms of whether or not it is in reasonable agreement with reality. A seriously distorted or inappropriate body image is characteristic of a number of mental disorders, such as **anorexia nervosa,** of which it is a classic symptom and major diagnostic criterion. The anorexic, most likely an adolescence female, perceives herself as "fat" even when she is emaciated. A distorted sense of body image may comprise a disorder in itself, known as body dysmorphic disorder, or dysmorphophobia. People affected by this condition generally become preoccupied with a specific body part or physical feature and exhibits signs of **anxiety** or **depression.** Commonly, the victim mentally magnifies a slight flaw into a major defect, sometimes erroneously believing it the sign of a serious disease, such as cancer, and may resort to plastic surgery to relieve their distress over their appearance.

It has been proposed that a healthy body image is one that does not diverge too widely from prevailing cultural standards but leaves room to allow for a person's individuality and uniqueness. As people age, they revise their views of the ideal body so that they can continue to feel reasonably attractive at each stage of their lives.

These models have the idealized slender female body, one that most women find impossible to achieve. When the individual—often a young woman—cannot resolve her body image with her ideal, mental disorders such as anorexia nervosa may develop.

See also Anorexia Nervosa; Bulimia Nervosa.

Further Reading

Brown, Marie Scott. *Normal Development of Body Image.* New York: Wiley, 1977.

Brain

The master control center of the body, the brain is a part of the central nervous system and consists of a mass of grayish-pink jelly-like nerve tissues with many surface ridges and grooves. Located in the cranium or skull at the upper end of the spinal cord, the brain serves to control and coordinate the mental and physical actions of the body.

The brain is composed of three primary divisions, the forebrain, midbrain, and hindbrain, and divided into the left and right hemispheres. The adult brain weighs a little more than three pounds (1.35 kg) and controls such multiple functions as receiving sensory messages, movement, using **language,** regulating involuntary body processes, producing **emotions,** thinking, and remembering.

The forebrain is the largest and most complicated of the brain structures and is responsible for most types of complex mental activity and behavior. It is involved in a huge array of responses including initiating movements, receiving sensations, emoting, thinking, talking, creating, and imagining. The forebrain consists of two main divisions: the diencephalon and the cerebrum. The diencephalon is composed of the **thalamus** and **hypothalamus,** both involved in basic drives, sensation, and emotion. The thalamus, often referred to as the "sensory relay" because it receives neural input—**pain,** visual, and other sensory signals—from all senses but smell. The hypothalamus relays hunger, thirst, and sex drives, and is also the site of a person's "internal clock" that regulates biological rhythms according to a cycle of roughly 24 hours. The cerebrum is the larger part of the forebrain. Its parts, which are covered by the cerebral cortex, include the corpus callosum, striatum, septum, hippocampus, and amygdala. The latter two structures, central to **memory** and emotion, are part of the limbic system, along with the septum and parts of the cortex, thalamus, and hypothalamus. The cortex is convoluted and divided into four lobes or areas.

The midbrain, or mesencephalon, is the small area near the lower middle of the brain. Its three sections are the tectum, which contains auditory and visual relay stations; the tegmentum, containing the reticular formation, a long column of nerve cells, called neurons, extending down into the hindbrain which serve to alert the forebrain to incoming sensory information; and the crus cerebri, a descending group of fibers. Portions of the midbrain have been shown to control smooth and reflexive movements, and it is important in the regulation of **attention, sleep,** and **arousal.**

The hindbrain (rhombencephalon), which is basically a continuation of the spinal cord, is the part of the brain that receives incoming messages first. Lying beneath the cerebral hemispheres, it consists of three structures: the cerebellum, the medulla, and the pons, which control vital functions of the **autonomic nervous system** such as breathing, blood pressure, and heart rate. The cerebellum, a large convoluted structure attached to the back surface of the brain stem, receives information from hundreds of thousands of sensory receptors in the eyes, ears, skin, muscles and joints, and uses the information to regulate coordination, balance, and movement, especially finely coordinated movements, such as threading a needle or tracking a moving target. The medulla, situated just above the spinal cord, controls heartbeat and breathing and contains the reticular formation which extends

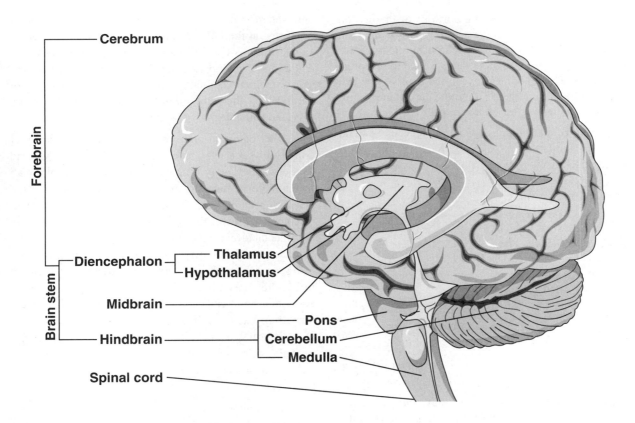

Cerebrum

Forebrain

Diencephalon — Thalamus
Hypothalamus

Brain stem

Midbrain

Hindbrain

Pons
Cerebellum
Medulla

Spinal cord

The control center of the human body, the brain, is composed of the forebrain, the midbrain, and the hindbrain.

into and through the pons. The pons, a band of nerve fibers connecting the midbrain, medulla (hindbrain), and cerebrum, controls sleep and dreaming. Because of their shape and position at the base of the brain, the pons and medulla are often referred to as the brain stem.

The cortex, or outer covering of the cerebrum, performs many important functions. Although its convoluted folds enable it to fit into a compact area, it actually has a surface of one to two square feet. It is much larger in humans than in most other species and is involved with the processing of sensory information, control of voluntary movements, complex mental activity, and other sophisticated aspects of human thought and behavior. The ridges and valleys of the cerebral cortex divide it into four lobes: the frontal, parietal, occipital, and temporal. The cortex also has functional divisions independent of these spatial ones. These include the motor and sensory cortex, and the association cortex, which performs tasks such as associating words and images. Association occurs in all lobes of the brain, and damage to different lobes produces dramatically different kinds of impairment in dealing with spoken and written language.

Modern science has revealed dramatic findings about the specialized functions of the right and left hemi-spheres of the brain. Some of the best known research has focused on "split-brain" patients who had the corpus callosum (which connects the two hemispheres) severed to control severe **epilepsy,** a procedure that drastically affected the ways in which they perceived and responded to their external **environment.** Based on studies of these patients, it was found that certain activities are "lateralized," or performed more efficiently by one hemisphere than the other. For example, logic and language capacity are generally concentrated in the left hemisphere, while spatial, artistic, and musical abilities are stronger in the right. However, lateralization is not uniform, notably in the case of left-handed people, of whom about a third have language functions controlled by either the right hemisphere or both.

The human brain consists of one hundred billion to one trillion neurons and an even greater number of support cells called glia. Until recently, scientists thought that the only function of glial cells—whose name means "glue"—was to hold the neurons together, but current research suggests that glia play a more active role in facilitating communication. The neurons, which consist of three elements—**dendrite**s, cell body, and axon—send nerve impulses from cell to cell along pathways which receive, process, store and retrieve information. The dendrites are the message-receiving portions of the neuron and the axons are the message-sending part of the cell. Both are branching fibers that reach out in many extensions to join the neuron to other neurons and to receptors and effectors. The junction between the axon of one cell and the dendrite of another is a minute gap eighteen millionths of an inch wide called a **synapse.**

See also Brain Disorders; Central Nervous System; Left-Brain Hemisphere; Reflexes; Right-Brain Hemisphere; Senses; Split-Brain Technique.

Further Reading

Asimov, Isaac. *The Human Brain: Its Capacities and Functions.* New York: Penguin, 1994.

Mind and Brain: Readings from Scientific American Magazine. New York: W.H. Freeman, 1993.

Smith, Anthony. *The Mind.* New York: Viking Press, 1984.

Brain Disorders

Any of the various disorders associated with the human brain, including stroke, trauma, and tumors.

It has recently been reported that neurology, the study of the brain, is the fastest growing specialty in the life sciences. With this growth has come a wealth of new information about the origins of and treatments for some of the more prevalent brain disorders. There are many varieties of brain disorders that affect humans, including **Alzheimer's disease**, **Parkinson's disease, epilepsy**, and other disorders that are more generally thought of as being "behavioral" rather than biological. These types of disorders that could be termed disorders of the brain in a broad sense include **depression, schizophrenia,** and **bipolar disorder**. Beyond these, however, are several other types of disorders of the brain, including stroke, trauma, brain tumors, and developmental disorders such as muscular dystrophy and cerebral palsy.

Strokes are the third leading cause of death in the United States and are one of the leading causes of disability among older adults. According to the most recent statistics, a staggering 1,200 people suffer from strokes each day in this country. "Stroke" is technically a lay term; when physicians speak of strokes, they are referring to thromboses, hemorrhages or embolisms. Basically, the term stroke refers to the loss of blood to a part of the brain and the resulting tissue damage. Because of the variables involved, strokes are often not correctly diagnosed. Often, especially with very mild events, a patient will attribute odd sensations to something else. The effects of a stroke may vary, based on its origins and the area of the brain that was deprived of blood. Generally speaking, if tissue damage occurred in the right brain

hemisphere, the victim may experience some degree of paralysis on the left side of the body, a distortion of vision, especially the ability to perceive depth and distance, and a loss of memory. If the tissue affected is on the left side of the brain, patients may experience some degree of paralysis on the right side of the body, minor memory loss, and some degree of language loss.

Other common brain disorders include the array of conditions caused by head trauma. Injuries to the head can, obviously, vary tremendously, but such injuries all result in biochemical abnormalities in the brain. After the head has been injured in some way, a tremendous amount of chemicals travel through the brain, which often have detrimental effects on brain cells, including paralysis and behavioral and cognitive losses. Recent medical advances have uncovered some drugs and treatments that can offset this after-effect of trauma, and physicians now know that brain cells can be replaced in adults, a procedure that was thought impossible only a decade ago. Doctors now have the ability to procure accurate images of the brain from magnetic resonance imaging (MRI) machines, allowing them to pinpoint damaged areas for treatment.

The incidence of brain tumors has increased in recent years, although it is not certain if this trend is simply a result of better diagnostic technology, such as MRIs. Nonetheless, treatments devised thus far have generally been less than stellar. Researchers have found that certain genes inside tumors are capable of creating resistance to drugs being used to destroy the tumor. Often, if drug treatment of brain tumors is ineffective, surgery is required to remove the tumor, which can further damage the brain.

Developmental neurologic disorders of the brain include well-known brain diseases such as Alzheimer's, Parkinson's, muscular dystrophy, and cerebral palsy. Most of these disorders are now known to be inheritable, passed from one generation to another genetically. Recent research has isolated the gene that causes strains of Alzheimer's, Huntington's disease, and several other muscular disorders. Cerebral palsy, a devastating developmental neurologic disorder involving severe muscle and coordination deterioration, has been attributed to stroke in newborn infants.

In 1995, the National Institutes of Health (NIH) spent the following studying brain disorders: Alzheimer's disease, $305 million; stroke, $116 million; multiple sclerosis, $80 million; Parkinson's disease, $72 million; epilepsy, $55 million; and head injury, $51 million. As a way of comparison, NIH spent $199 million studying arthritis in 1995.

Further Reading

"Cognitive Impairment to Dementia." *The Lancet* (25 February 1995): 465.

"Combating Disorders of the Brain." *New York Times* (30 August 1994).

Connaughton, P. Noel. "Decade of the Brain: A Midpoint Status Report." *Patient Care* (15 July 1995).

Guiness, Alma E., ed. *The Reader's Digest ABCs of the Human Mind.* Pleasantville, NY: Reader's Digest Association, 1990.

Mattson, Sarah N. "MRI and Prenatal Alcohol Exposure: Images Provide Insight into FAS." *Alcohol Health and Research World* (Winter 1994): 49.

Brain Stem. See **Brain**.

Brainwashing

A systematic, coercive effort to alter an individual's beliefs and attitudes, usually by physical and/or psychological means; also referred to as "thought control."

Brainwashing has been used predominantly in reference to severe programs of political indoctrination, although it is used occasionally in connection with certain religious, especially cultic, practices. Brainwashing works primarily by making the victim's existing beliefs and **attitudes** nonfunctional and replacing them with new ones that will be useful in the **environment** created by the captor.

Basically, the techniques of brainwashing involve the complete removal of personal freedom, independence, and decision-making prerogatives; the radical disruption of existing routine behavior; the total isolation from, and destruction of loyalties to, former friends and associates; the absolute obedience to authority in all matters; intense physical abuse and threats of injury, death, and permanent imprisonment; and the constant presentation of the new beliefs as the only correct and acceptable alternative to continuing an unenlightened life. These techniques are intended to induce in the victim a state of childlike trust in, and dependency on, the captor. Confessions of imagined past crimes are often part of the brainwashing process, with the victim admitting to trivial or absurd shortcomings and errors, and sometimes implicating others falsely. Other captives who have already been brainwashed may be used to reinforce the process, criticizing the victim and supporting the captors and their value system. Once the process begins to take hold, threats and **punishment**s are replaced by rewards. The victim is allowed increased physical comfort and given psychological **reinforcement** in the form of approval and friendship. All efforts are directed toward cementing his or her new **identity,** based on the new set values and beliefs provided by the captor.

The study of the techniques and effects of brainwashing grew markedly in the 1950s, after a number of U.S. soldiers appeared to have become indoctrinated when taken prisoner during the Korean War. They confessed to imagined crimes, including the waging of germ warfare, and refused to be repatriated when the war ended. Studies of these prisoners of war and of individuals who had undergone ideological conversion in Chinese prisons during the same period revealed connections between the radical changes in attitude caused by brainwashing and existing knowledge about attitude and identity formation and change in ordinary circumstances. While some brainwashed individuals may actually be released and allowed to return home, researchers have expressed doubts about whether the process can be completely effective or really last for a prolonged period. Its short-term and long-term effectiveness in actually altering an individual's beliefs—both within the brainwashing environment and removed from that environment—vary from individual to individual, depending on personality characteristics and many other factors. Intense effort and complete control over the victim are required, and must be exercised over a period of years. Consequently, many of the brainwashing efforts made during the Korean War were ineffective, with the prisoners either resisting change or merely becoming confused instead of indoctrinated. In addition, certain attitudes on the part of prisoners proved particularly resistant to change. Due to these limitations, many psychologists believe it would be impossible to brainwash large populations, even with the use of mass media.

A classic literary example of brainwashing is found in George Orwell's novel, *1984.* The protagonist, Winston Smith, is subjected to isolation, humiliation, physical deprivation and violence, and constant threats of further violence. He is also forced to make false confessions which include implicating and denouncing others. His captors express their intent to "squeeze you empty and fill you with ourselves." Their ultimate success in forcing Smith to adapt to whatever beliefs they choose is most memorably demonstrated in his final capitulation to the view that two plus two equals five.

See also Cults.

Further Reading

Hyde, Margaret. *Brainwashing and Other Forms of Thought Control.* New York: McGraw-Hill, 1977.

Brief Reactive Psychosis

An uncommon acute mental disorder precipitated by an event that causes intense psychological stress.

Episodes that are classified as brief reactive psychoses may last more than two hours but less than one month. Typical triggering events can be the death of a spouse or other loved one, combat trauma, financial disaster, or any other major event involving psychosocial **stress.** Brief reactive psychosis has a sudden onset, typically in late **adolescence** and early adulthood, and is characterized by **delusions, hallucinations,** incoherent speech, disorganized or catatonic behavior, and possibly aggressive or suicidal impulses. Although episodes of brief reactive psychosis occur in a short period of time, the degree of cognitive impairment during these episodes may be very severe, and often individuals with this condition must be prevented from acting in dangerously inappropriate or self-destructive ways. Complete recovery usually follows, however, and the patient is restored to his or her prior level of functioning.

Bruner, Jerome S. (1915–)

American psychologist and educator whose principal areas of study are in the fields of cognitive psychology and language development.

Jerome S. Bruner was born in New York City and educated at Duke University. During World War II, Bruner worked on the subject of propaganda and popular **attitudes** for U.S. Army intelligence at General Dwight D. Eisenhower's headquarters in France. He obtained his Ph.D. from Harvard University in 1947, after which he became a member of the faculty, serving as professor of psychology, as well as cofounder and director of the Center for Cognitive Studies. In 1972 Bruner left Harvard to teach for several years at Oxford University. He returned to Harvard as a visiting professor in 1979 and two years later joined the faculty of the new School for Social Research in New York City. Bruner's early work in **cognitive psychology** focused on the sequences of decisions made by subjects as part of their problem-solving strategies in experimental situations.

Beginning in the 1940s, Bruner, together with his colleague Leo Postman, did important work on the ways in which **needs, motivations,** and expectations (or "mental sets") affect **perception.** Their approach, sometimes referred to as the "New Look," contrasted a functional perspective with the prevailing "formal" one that treated perception as a self-sufficient process to be considered separately from the world around it. When Bruner and

Jerome S. Bruner

Postman showed young children toys and plain blocks of equal height, the children, expecting toys to be larger than blocks, thought the toys were taller. The toys also seemed to increase in size when the researchers made them unavailable. In further experiments involving mental sets, the two scientists used an instrument called a tachistoscope to show their subjects brief views of playing cards, including some nonstandard cards, such as a red ace of spades. As long as the subjects were not alerted to the presence of the abnormal cards, almost none saw them.

Bruner's work in cognitive psychology led to an interest in the cognitive development of children and related issues of education, and in the 1960s he developed a theory of cognitive growth. Bruner's theories, which approach development from a different angle than those of **Jean Piaget,** focus on the environmental and experiential factors influencing each individual's specific development pattern. His argument that human intellectual **ability** develops in stages from infancy to adulthood through step-by-step progress in how the mind is used has influenced experimental psychologists and educators throughout the world. Bruner is particularly interested in **language** and other representations of human thought. In one of his best-known papers, Bruner defines three modes of representing, or "symbolizing," human thought. The *enactive* mode involves human motor capacities and includes activities such as using tools. The *iconic* mode pertains to sensory capacities. Finally, the *symbolic* mode involves reasoning, and is exemplified by language, which plays a central role in Bruner's theories of **cognition** and development. He has called it "a means, not only for representing experience, but also for transforming it."

Bruner's view that the student should become an active participant in the educational process has been widely accepted. In *The Process of Education* (1960) he asserts that, given the appropriate teaching method, every child can successfully study any subject at any stage of his or her intellectual development. Bruner's later work involves the study of the pre-speech developmental processes and linguistic communication skills in children. *The Relevance of Education* (1971) applied his theories to infant development. Bruner was appointed a visiting member of the Institute for Advanced Study at Princeton University. In 1963, he received the Distinguished Scientific Award from the **American Psychological Association,** and in 1965 he served as its president. Bruner's expertise in the field of education led to his appointment to the President's Advisory Panel of Education, and he has also advised agencies of the United Nations. Bruner's books include *A Study of Thinking* (1956), *On Knowing: Essays For the Left Hand* (1962), *On Knowing* (1964), *Toward a Theory of Instruction* (1966), *Processes of Cognitive Growth* (1968), *Beyond the Information Given* (1973), and *Child's Talk* (1983).

See also Child Development; Cognitive Development Theory; Developmental Psychology.

Further Reading
Bruner, Jerome S. *In Search of Mind: Essays in Autobiography.* New York: Harper & Row, 1983.

Bulimia Nervosa

An eating disorder in which a person indulges in recurrent episodes of binge eating, followed by purging through self-induced vomiting or by the use of laxatives and/or diuretics in order to prevent weight gain.

The symptoms of bulimia nervosa include eating uncontrollably (binging) and then purging by dieting, fasting, exercising, vomiting, or abusing laxatives or diuretics. A binge involves a large amount of food, for example, several boxes of cookies, a loaf of bread, a half gallon of ice cream, and a bucket of fried chicken, eaten in a short and well-defined time period. Specific behaviors associated with bulimia include: 1) eating high-calorie "junk food" (candy bars, cookies, ice cream, etc.); 2) eating surreptitiously; 3) eating until stopped by a stomach ache, drowsiness, or external interruption; 4) a tendency to go on "crash diets"; and 5) weight that varies over a 10-pound (4.5 kg) range. Although all of these behaviors are not present in all bulimics, the presence of at least three makes it likely that an individual is suffering from the disorder. In general, binging episodes occur at least twice a week, and may take place two or more times a day.

Unlike anorexics, bulimics may be close to normal weight or overweight (within 15 percent of normal standards) and do not suffer from amenorrhea or lose interest in sex. Bulimics feel out of control, realize that their eating patterns are abnormal, and experience intense feelings of guilt and shame over their binging. Their preoccupation with body weight and secretive eating behaviors may combine with **depression** or **mood** swings. Possible warning signals of bulimia may include irregular periods, dental problems, swollen cheeks, heartburn, bloating, and alcohol or drug abuse.

The American Anorexia/Bulimia Association estimates that up to 5 percent of college-age women are bulimic and more than 90 percent of all bulimics are women. The onset of the disorder commonly occurs in the late teens or early twenties and can begin after a period of dieting or weight loss. Risk factors for the disorder involve a pattern of excessive dieting in an attempt to weigh less, a history of depression or alcoholism, low self-esteem, obese parents or siblings, and a history of **anorexia nervosa.** It has also been suggested that bulimia may have physiological causes, including a defective satiety mechanism.

In order to reduce the risks of developing an eating disorder, cultural **attitudes** associating thinness and beauty with personal worth and happiness must change to reflect a greater emphasis on developing healthier attitudes and eating behaviors in early childhood. Individuals must learn to value themselves and others for intrinsic rather than extrinsic qualities such as appearance.

Although bulimia is seldom life-threatening, it is a serious illness with severe medical consequences, including abdominal pain, vomiting blood, electrolyte imbalance possibly leading to weakness or cardiac arrest, muscle weakness, and intestinal damage. Bulimics and anorexics rarely cure themselves and the longer the behavior continues, the more difficult it is to help the individual change. The most effective treatment involves a team approach consisting of medical evaluation, individual and/or group **psychotherapy,** nutritional counseling, anti-depressant medication, and possible hospitalization. Psychotherapy generally consists of investigating the patient's **unconscious** motivations for binging in combination with **behavior modification** techniques to help cope with the disease. Commonly recommended medications include diphenylhydantoin (Dilantin), an anticonvulsant, and tricyclic antidepressants. Even with treatment, only about one-third of bulimics appear to recover while another third show some improvement in their eating behavior. The remaining third do not respond to treatment and 10 to 20 percent of these people eventually die of the disease.

See also Anorexia Nervosa; Body Image.

Further Information

American Anorexia/Bulimia Association (AABA)
    Address: 418 E. 76th St.,
    New York, New York 10021
    Telephone: 212-734-1114
American Dietetic Association (ADA)
    NCND-Eating Disorders
    Address: 216 W. Jackson Blvd.,
    Chicago, Illinois 60606
    Telephone: 800-366-1655
National Anorexic Aid Society
    Address: 445 E. Dublin-Granville Rd.,
    Worthington, Ohio 43229
    Telephone: 614-436-1112
National Association of Anorexia Nervosa and Associated Disorders (ANAD)
    Address: Box 7, Highland Park, Illinois 60035
    Telephone: 708-831-3438

Bystander Effect

The effect of the presence of others on an individual's perception of and response to a situation.

The term bystander effect, or bystander apathy, was first employed by psychologists in the early 1960s. The 1964 murder of New Yorker Kitty Genovese provides an illustration of this phenomenon. Genovese, who was being savagely attacked outside her apartment building, screamed for help for over 30 minutes. Although 40 neighbors heard Genovese's desperate cries, no one came to her aid or even called the police. Researchers have explained several components of the bystander effect. First, witnesses must perceive the situation as an emergency. When others are present, not taking action or behaving as if nothing were wrong, all observers tend to view the situation as a nonemergency. Psychologists describe this as *pluralistic ignorance*, in which the behavior of the group causes each individual to be lulled into inaction. In the case of Genovese's murder, her neighbors were not hearing her cries for help as a group. Each person, isolated in his or her own apartment, heard the disturbance and had no way of knowing the reactions of others who were hearing Genovese's screams. However, each person could believe that someone else was taking action, and therefore the responsibility for response fell to that other person. Psychologists call this reaction *diffusion of responsibility*.

Experiments have been developed to demonstrate the components of the bystander effect. In one experiment designed to test the power of pluralistic ignorance, male subjects were given appointments for an interview. As they wait in an outer room, smoke begins to pour through a ventilation duct. Researchers observed the subjects through a one-way mirror for three minutes. Seventy-five percent of the subjects who were alone in the waiting room reported the smoke within two minutes, while 13 percent of those tested in groups reported the smoke. Those who did not report the smoke explained that, since others in the room did not seem to be concerned, the smoke must have been air conditioning vapors or steam. This experiment illustrates that bystanders can contribute significantly to an individual's interpretation of a situation.

Further Reading

Latani, Bibb. The *Unresponsive Bystander: Why Doesn't He Help?* New York: Appleton-Century Crofts, 1970.

Palma, Giuseppe. *Apathy and Participation: Mass Politics in Western Societies.* New York: Free Press, 1970.

C

Calkins, Mary Whiton (1863–1930)

American psychologist and philosopher who became the first woman president of both the American Psychological Association (1905) and the American Philosophical Association (1918).

The eldest of five children born to Reverend Wolcott Calkins, a strong-willed, intellectually gifted evangelical minister, and Charlotte Grosvenor Whiton, a daughter of an established New England Puritan family, Mary Whiton Calkins grew up in a close-knit family that valued education. As her mother's mental and physical health began to deteriorate, Calkins took on increased responsibilities for her younger siblings as well as her mother.

After earning a B.A. from Smith College with a concentration in the classics, Calkins began teaching Greek at Wellesley College in 1887. In 1888, she was offered the new position of instructor in psychology there, which was contingent upon a year's training in the discipline. Consistent with university policy toward women in 1890, Calkins was granted special permission to attend classes in psychology and philosophy at Harvard University and in laboratory psychology at Clark University in Worcester, but was denied admission to their graduate studies programs. She was also denied permission to attend regular Harvard seminars until faculty members **William James** and Josiah Royce (1855–1916), as well as Calkins's father, intervened on her behalf. After she was enrolled in James's seminar, four men enrolled in the class dropped it in protest. Attendance at James's seminar led to individual study with him, and within a year Calkins had published a paper on **association,** suggesting a modification to James's recently published *Principles of Psychology.* Her paper was enthusiastically received by her mentor, who referred to it when he later revised his book.

Returning to Wellesley in the fall of 1891, Calkins established the first psychology laboratory at a women's college in the United States with help from Edmund San-

Mary Whiton Calkins

ford, a faculty member at Clark, with whom she collaborated on an experimental study of **dreams** published in the *American Journal of Psychology.* In 1893, seeking further laboratory training, Calkins returned to Harvard to work with James's protégé, Hugo Münsterberg (1863–1916), investigating the factors influencing **memory.** During the course of this work, Calkins originated the "paired associates" technique, a method of testing memory by presenting test subjects with paired numbers and colors. Her findings revealed that numbers paired with bright colors were retained better than those associated with neutral colors. However, the prime factor influencing memory was frequency of exposure. The results of this research were published as a supplement to *Psychological Review* in 1896.

In 1895, Calkins requested and took an examination equivalent to the official Ph.D. exam. Her performance was praised by James as "the most brilliant examination for the Ph.D. that we have had at Harvard," surpassing that of his junior colleague, George Santayana (1863–1952). Nevertheless, Calkins was still denied admission to candidacy for the degree. With the creation of Radcliffe College in April 1902, Calkins was one of the first four women to be offered the Ph.D., but she refused it in protest.

Calkins taught at Wellesley College until her retirement in 1929, and had published four books and more than 100 papers in psychology and philosophy. In 1901, she published a well-received *Introduction to Psychology* and spent the early 1900s developing a psychology of the self that anticipated later theories of **personality.** In 1909, Columbia University awarded Calkins a honorary Doctor of Letters (Litt.D.) and in 1910, Smith College granted her the Doctor of Laws (LL.D.). Calkins died in 1930.

Further Reading

Scarborough, Elizabeth and Laurel Furumoto. *Untold Lives: The First Generation of American Women Psychologists*, 17-51. New York: Columbia University Press, 1987.

Catharsis

The release of repressed psychic energy.

The term catharsis originated from the Greek word *katharsis,* meaning to purge, or purgation. In psychology, the term was first employed by **Sigmund Freud**'s colleague Josef Breuer (1842–1925), who developed a "cathartic" treatment for persons suffering from hysterical symptoms through the use of **hypnosis.** While under hypnosis, Breuer's patients were able to recall traumatic experiences, and through the process of expressing the original emotions that had been repressed and forgotten, they were relieved of their symptoms. Catharsis was also central to Freud's concept of **psychoanalysis,** but he replaced hypnosis with **free association**.

In other schools of **psychotherapy,** catharsis refers to the therapeutic release of **emotions** and tensions, although not necessarily **unconscious** ones such as Freud emphasized. Certain types of therapy in particular, such as psychodrama and primal scream therapy, have stressed the healing potential of cathartic experiences.

See also Repression.

Further Reading

Jenson, Jean C. *Reclaiming Your Life: A Step-by-Step Guide to Using Regression Therapy to Overcome the Effects of Childhood Abuse.* New York: Dutton, 1995.

Cathexis

In classic psychoanalysis, the investment of psychic energy in a person or object connected with the gratification of instincts.

The English word for cathexis—which replaces the German besetzung—is derived from the Greek word for "I occupy." Through the process of cathexis, which **Sigmund Freud** saw as analogous to the channeling of an electrical charge, the psychic energy of the **id** is bound to a selection of objects. An infant's earliest cathected objects are his mother's breast, his own mouth, and the process of sucking.

When a cathected object becomes a source of conflict, as parents do during the Oedipal stage, anti-cathexes redirect all thoughts about the object to the **unconscious** level in order to relieve **anxiety**. Thus, cathexes originate in the id, while anti-cathexes are formed by the **ego** and the **superego**.

Freud believed that most personality processes are regulated by cathexes and anti-cathexes. He considered anti-cathexes as an internal form of frustration, paralleling the external frustration of **instinct**s that one encounters from environmental factors over which one has no control. In the case of anti-cathexis, this frustration is provided internally by one's own psychic mechanisms. However, it cannot occur until one has experienced external frustration, generally in the form of parental discipline. Having been subjected to external controls, one becomes able to develop inner ones.

Cathexes are involved in the **repression** of memories, which can be recalled either by weakening the anti-cathexis or strengthening the cathexis. Either process is difficult and may be facilitated by the use of special techniques, including **hypnosis, free association**, and the interpretation of dreams.

Further Reading

Freud, Sigmund. *The Standard Edition of the Complete Psychological Works of Sigmund Freud.* London: Hogarth Press, 1962.

Firestone, Robert. *Psychological Defenses in Everyday Life.* New York: Human Sciences Press, 1989.

Goleman, Daniel. *Vital Lies, Simple Truths: the Psychology of Self-Deception.* New York : Simon and Schuster, 1985.

Hall, Calvin S. *A Primer of Freudian Psychology.* New York: Harper and Row, 1982.

Cattell, James McKeen (1860–1944)

American pioneer in psychological research techniques and founder of a psychological testing company.

James McKeen Cattell developed an approach to psychological research that continues to dominate the field of psychology today. During psychology's early years, most research focused on the sensory responses of single individuals studied in depth because Wilhelm Wundt (1832–1920), the first experimental psychologist, favored this approach. As Cattell's ideas developed, his perspective diverged greatly from Wundt's, and Cattell developed techniques that allowed him to study groups of people and the individual differences among them.

Cattell's career was quite varied. He traveled to the University of Göttingen to study with the philosopher Rudolf Hermann Lotze (1817–1881) and later with Wundt at Leipzig. Following that, he returned home to the United States and worked with G. Stanley Hall (1844–1924), one of America's most famous psychologists. Apparently, Cattell's relationship with Hall was less than positive, and Cattell did not complete his doctoral work at that time. When he was with Hall, however, Cattell developed an interest in studying psychological processes.

Subsequently, he returned to Leipzig and earned his doctorate with Wundt, although his correspondence with his parents revealed that Cattell did not hold Wundt in high esteem as a scientist. According to some, those letters also depict Cattell as arrogant, self-confident, and disrespectful of others. While in Germany, Cattell improved on existing psychological instrumentation and invented new ways to study psychological processes.

After leaving Germany, Cattell taught briefly in the United States, then traveled to England and worked with Sir Francis Galton (1822–1911). Cattell was highly impressed with Galton's use of statistics and quantification of research, and he also supported some of Galton's other ideas, such as the importance of individual differences and the application of scientific knowledge to create a eugenics movement.

Ultimately, Cattell adopted the practice of testing a large number of research subjects and using statistics to understand his results. Cattell coined the term "mental test" and devoted a significant amount of time trying to develop a useful **intelligence test**. He recorded the results of simple tasks (e.g., the speed of a person's response to a simple sound, the ability to detect slight differences in weights of stimuli, and simple **memory** for letters of the alphabet), hoping to find a correlation between sensory response and academic performance, or

James McKeen Cattell

intelligence. He was disappointed to find that, not only did sensory performance fail to relate to academic success, the different sensory measures did not even correlate with one another. As a result, he abandoned such an approach to mental testing.

Even though Cattell's research on intelligence was unsuccessful, he nonetheless exerted a dramatic influence on other American psychologists. During his career at Columbia University, more students earned doctorates in psychology with him than with any other psychologist. Cattell also affected psychology in the United States in other ways. For example, he founded the journal *Psychological Review* with another prominent psychologist, J. Mark Baldwin (1861–1934), then resurrected the financially troubled journal *Science,* which he acquired from Alexander Graham Bell. Cattell also helped start the American Association for the Advancement of Science, one of the premier scientific organizations in America today. He also published *Scientific Monthly* and *School and Society.* Not surprisingly, as his editing and publishing increased, his research diminished.

Cattell left the academic world in 1917 when Columbia University dismissed him because of his unpopular opposition to sending draftees into battle in the first World War. He sued the University for libel and won $40,000 in court, but he did not return to the institution.

Instead, he attempted further application of psychological testing when he founded the Psychological Corporation, a company organized to promote commercial psychological tests. His entrepreneurial abilities failed him in this endeavor, however; the company earned only about $50 during its first two years. After he left, the organization began to prosper, and today, the Psychological Corporation is a flourishing business. Cattell continued his work as a spokesperson for applied psychology until his death.

Further Reading

Benjamin, L. T., Jr. *A History of Psychology: Original Sources and Contemporary Research.* New York: McGraw-Hill, 1988.

Schultz, D. P., and S.E. Schultz. *A History of Modern Psychology.* 6th ed. Fort Worth, TX: Harcourt Brace College Publishers, 1996.

Central Nervous System

In humans, that portion of the nervous system that lies within the brain and spinal cord; it receives impulses from nerve cells throughout the body, regulates bodily functions, and directs behavior.

The central nervous system contains billions of **nerve** cells, called neurons, and a greater number of support cells, or glia. Until recently, scientists thought that the only function of glial cells—whose name means "glue"—was to hold the neurons together, but current research suggests a more active role in facilitating communication. The neurons, which consist of three elements—**dendrite**s, cell body, and axon—send electrical impulses from cell to cell along pathways which receive, process, store, and retrieve information. The dendrites are the message-receiving portions of the neuron and the axons are the message-sending part of the cell. Both are branching fibers that reach out in many extensions to join the neuron to other neurons. The junction between the axon of one cell and the dendrite of another is a minute gap, eighteen millionths of an inch wide, which is called a **synapse.**

The spinal cord is a long bundle of neural tissue continuous with the **brain** that occupies the interior canal of the spinal column and functions as the primary communication link between the brain and the rest of the body. It is the origin of 31 bilateral pairs of spinal **nerve**s which radiate outward from the central nervous system through openings between adjacent vertebrae. The spinal cord receives signals from the peripheral senses and relays them to the brain. Its sensory neurons, which send sense data to the brain, are called afferent, or receptor, neurons; motor

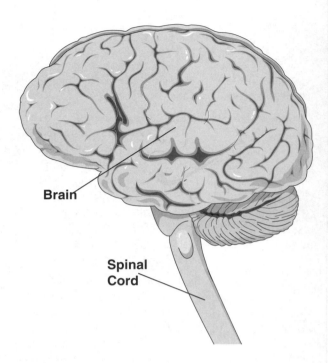

The central nervous system is made up of the brain and spinal cord.

neurons, which receive motor commands from the brain, are called efferent, or **effector**, neurons.

The brain is a mass of neural tissue that occupies the cranial cavity of the skull and functions as the center of instinctive, emotional, and cognitive processes. Twelve pairs of cranial **nerve**s enter the brain directly. It is composed of three primary divisions: the forebrain, midbrain, and hindbrain, which are divided into the left and right hemispheres and control multiple functions such as receiving sensory messages, movement, **language,** regulating involuntary body processes, producing **emotion**s, thinking, and **memory.** The first division, the forebrain, is the largest and most complicated of the brain structures and is responsible for most types of complex mental activity and behavior. It is involved in a huge array of responses, including initiating movements, receiving sensations, emoting, thinking, talking, creating, and imagining. The forebrain consists of two main divisions: the diencephalon and the cerebrum. The cerebrum is the larger part of the forebrain. Its parts, which are covered by the cerebral cortex, include the corpus callosum, striatum, septum, hippocampus, and amygdala.

The midbrain, or mesencephalon, is the small area near the lower middle of the brain. Its three sections are the tectum, tegmentum, and crus cerebri. Portions of the midbrain have been shown to control smooth and reflexive movements, and it is important in the regulation of **attention, sleep,** and **arousal.** The hindbrain (rhombencephalon), which is basically a continuation of the spinal cord, is the part of the brain that receives incoming messages first. Lying beneath the cerebral hemispheres, it consists of three structures: the cerebellum, the medulla, and the pons, which control such vital functions of the **autonomic nervous system** as breathing, blood pressure, and heart rate. The cerebellum, a large convoluted structure attached to the back surface of the brain stem, receives information from hundreds of thousands of sensory receptors in the eyes, ears, skin, muscles, and joints, and uses the information to regulate coordination, balance, and movement, especially finely coordinated movements such as threading a needle or tracking a moving target. The medulla, situated just above the spinal cord, controls heartbeat and breathing and contains the reticular formation which extends into and through the pons. The pons, a band of nerve fibers connecting the midbrain, medulla (hindbrain) and cerebrum, controls sleep and dreaming. The pons and medulla, because of their shape and position at the base of the brain, are often referred to as the brainstem.

Further Reading
Changeux, Jean-Pierre. *Neuronal Man.* New York: Pantheon Books, 1985.

Cerebellum. See **Brain**.

Cerebral Cortex. See **Brain**.

Character

General term in psychology used to describe behavior motivations and personality traits that make each person an individual.

Character is most often used in reference to a set of basic innate, developed, and acquired **motivation**s that shape an individual's behavior. There qualities of an individual's motivation are shaped during all stages of childhood. By late adolescence, around age 17, the traits that make up individual's character are normally integrated into a unique and distinctive whole. The term character is sometimes used as roughly synonymous with the term **personality**, although such usage does little to reduce the imprecision of either term. Some psychologists believe that differences in character among individuals largely reflect affective, or emotional, differences, that are the result of biochemical or other organic variations. Many psychologists claim that character, to some extent, is a function of experience. These psychologists, generally, believe that, as the early behavior of an individual directed toward a primary, instinctive goal is modified by environmental circumstances, the motivational

system of the individual is also modified, and the character of the individual is affected. There is some dispute among psychologists about whether, or to what extent, character may be controlled by conscious or rational decisions, and about whether, or to what extent, character may be dominated by **unconscious** or irrational forces. At the same time, there is widespread agreement among psychologists that, while much research remains to be done to delineate the genetic, instinctive, organic, cognitive, and other aspects of character, the development of a reasonably stable and harmonious character is an essential part of a psychologically healthy existence.

Further Reading
Kupperman, Joel. *Character.* New York: Oxford University Press, 1991.

Chemotherapy

Any medical treatment that is based primarily on the use of chemicals.

In the field of psychology, chemotherapy is defined as the use of drugs for psychotherapeutic treatment of behavioral or mental disorders. Many psychologists, including psychotherapists, believe that abnormal psychological conditions are ultimately caused by biochemical factors, and that the most effective methods of treatment of these conditions involve the use of chemicals. Other psychotherapists rely on the use of **drugs** to produce a more quiescent or receptive state in their patients, thereby increasing the effectiveness of more traditional types of psychotherapeutic techniques. In any case, chemotherapy is generally considered to be a useful part of **psychotherapy**.

Further Reading
Chemotherapy & You: a Guide to Self-help During Treatment. Bethesda, MD: U.S. Dept. of Health and Human Services, Public Health Service, National Institutes of Health, National Cancer Institute, 1985.

Child Abuse

The act of harming children by neglect, violence, sexual attack, or by inflicting psychological or emotional distress.

For much of history, children have been considered the property of parents and the family system was rarely, if ever, intervened upon by society. If a mother or father routinely abused their children it went unnoticed, or if noticed, merely ignored. It was largely considered a parent's prerogative to do whatever he or she wanted with

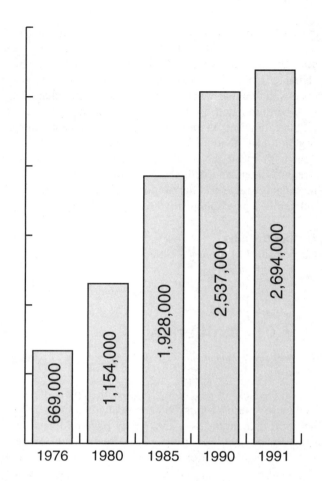

669,000 — 1976
1,154,000 — 1980
1,928,000 — 1985
2,537,000 — 1990
2,694,000 — 1991

Child abuse cases reported in the United States, 1976–91. The increase has been attributed to the stresses of modern society, including single parenthood, poverty, and alcohol and drug abuse. Some experts feel that the increase is also due, in part, to increases in reporting child abuse cases to authorities.

their child. Over the past several decades, however, the issue and, seemingly, the prevalence of child abuse has become widespread. There is debate among psychologists today about the number of child abuse cases. Some wonder if the increase is due to more incidences of abuse or if increased awareness among the public encourages more reporting. The first detailed account of the abuse of children was published in 1962 by Harry Hemke in an article titled "The Battered Child Syndrome," and since then there have been numerous articles and books published on this subject.

Over the years, child abuse has been divided into several categories, or types, although many psychologists dispute the usefulness of doing so. In compiling statistics on abuse, the United States Department of Health and Human Services (HHS) considers four categories of abuse: neglect, physical abuse, sexual abuse, and emotional maltreatment. Obviously, these categories are not mutually exclusive (that is, any given child can experi-

ence one or all, and all types of abuse are forms of "emotional maltreatment").

Statistically, it is difficult to find reliable national figures for cases of child abuse because each state keeps its own records and has its own definitions of what constitutes abuse. Nonetheless, several organizations do compile national estimates of abuse and neglect, and one of the most commonly cited is the National Committee for the Prevention of Child Abuse, headquartered in Chicago. In its figures compiled for 1995, the agency found approximately 993,000 substantiated claims of child maltreatment—a 4.2% increase since 1994. Of these, 54% were categorized as neglect; 25% as physical abuse; 11% as sexual abuse; 3% as emotional maltreatment; and 6% as other. These figures represent substantiated cases, meaning they have been investigated by child protection services and have been found valid. Overall, reports of abuse numbered 3.12 million. In 1995, 1,215 children died from abuse and neglect. Of these, 85% were under five years old and 45% were under the age of one. These statistics, like any statistics on child abuse, must be considered incomplete, since not all cases of abuse are reported. There is still strong social and familial pressure to avoid the issue when abuse is seen, although this has been changing over the last several years.

Child abuse occurs throughout society, despite myths about its prevalence among lower-income populations. A correlation has also been found between child abuse and parental use of alcohol or other **drugs**. Several studies conducted during the 1970s confirmed that nearly 70% of substantiated cases of abuse were related to alcohol. Most abusers are likely to have been abused themselves and generally resort to **violence** as a way to cope with life stressors. Their abusive actions can be seen as subconscious reactions to an array of stressful aspects of parenting, including disappointment in the gender or appearance of a child; a jealous reaction to the attention a child diverts from themselves; an attempt by the abuser to hurt the other parent; or a reaction against the child for failing to meet unrealistic expectations.

Pedophiles, or sexual abusers of children, occur across all economic and cultural groups. Psychologically, however, they share certain traits. Pedophiles often have a history of being abused themselves, and abusing other children seems to be triggered by increased life stressors, such as marital problems, job layoffs, or abuse of drugs.

Over the last several years, there has been what many consider to be an epidemic in reportings of child sexual abuse. As reported in *The CQ Researcher* in 1993, "Almost overnight, the national consciousness has been jolted into confronting a disturbing possibility: **Incest** and child molestation may be far more common than previously thought." This increased reporting of sexual abuse has become a highly contentious topic among the psychological community and in the media as well. Many find the reports a reflection of a sexually disturbed society, while others believe that increased reporting is the result of sensationalist media accounts, celebrity pronouncements about their own abuse, and over-zealous therapists who too readily suggest to patients that episodes of sexual abuse may lay at the heart of their other problems.

Another disturbing trend has been an increase in reports of ritual abuse, or Satanic Ritual Abuse (SRA), in which, it is alleged, children are systematically and repeatedly tortured by friends and family members in elaborate Satanic ceremonies often involving human sacrifice and ritual **rape**. Writing in *The Journal of Psychohistory* in 1994, psychoanalyst David Lotto reported that at a recent convention of the **American Psychological Association**, 800 therapists reported that they were currently treating cases of ritual abuse. A 1988 study conducted by University of New Hampshire researcher David Finkelhor found that as many as 13% of child abuse allegations occurring at day care centers involved ritual abuse. Another report followed the cases of 24 ritual abuse trials and found that 23 people had been convicted of some kind of abuse. Looking at this phenomena critically, however, it is important to point out, as was done by an FBI investigator at a 1991 conference of the American Psychological Association, that in several years of intensive investigation by local and federal law enforcement, there has never been any evidence of a network of Satanic child abusers. Victims often report the existence of elaborate underground sacrificial alters where their abuse occurred, and yet no trace has ever been found of such a construction.

Putting aside the current controversy over the prevalence of child sexual abuse in this country, it is safe to say that no one would dispute that sexual abuse does in fact occur, and that its affects are devastating. Sexual abuse is a frequently cited cause, for instance, of **dissociative identity disorder**. Sexual abuse, like severe physical and emotional abuse, can lead to other psychological disorders as well, such as **depression**, **mood** disorders, **anxiety** and **panic** disorders, and substance abuse.

Further Reading

"Child Sexual Abuse: Does the Nation Face an Epidemic Or a Wave of Hysteria?" *The CQ Researcher* (15 January 1993).

Cockburn, Alexander. "Out of the Mouths of Babes: Child Abuse and the Abuse of Adults." *The Nation* (12 February 1990): 190.

Interview with National Committee for the Prevention of Child Abuse, April 17, 1996.

Lotto, David. "On Witches and Witch Hunts: Ritual and Satanic Cult Abuse." *Journal of Psychohistory* (Spring 1994): 373.

Lowry, Richard. "How Many Battered Children?" *National Review* (12 April 1993): 46.

Smith, Timothy. "You Don't Have to Molest That Child." Pamphlet published by the National Committee for the Prevention of Child Abuse, 1987.

Terry, Sara. "Children Are Falling Victim to a New Kind of Sexual Offender: Other Children." *Rolling Stone* (31 October 1991): 68.

Child Development

The study of the sequential physical, cognitive, emotional, and social changes a child undergoes between birth and adolescence or adulthood.

The first detailed scientific study of child development was probably **Charles Darwin**'s *Biographical Sketch of an Infant* (1877), based on a log he had kept on the development of his eldest child. In this work, Darwin advanced the hypothesis that each individual's development from birth to adulthood parallels or recapitulates the phylogenetic development of the human species as a whole (he had made a similar observation about the development of the fetus). Darwin's ideas influenced the early study of child development, also known as the child study movement.

In the United States, the most famous figure associated with Darwin's evolutionary approach was G. Stanley Hall, who was labeled "the father of child psychology in America." The development of **intelligence** testing around World War I directed attention to the intellectual development of children, especially those considered either gifted or mentally retarded. As the century progressed, emphasis shifted from the study of children as a source of scientific knowledge to a more altruistic endeavor aimed at improving their welfare. From **Sigmund Freud** and **Jean Piaget** to Benjamin Spock and T. Berry Brazelton, child development has been studied and written about to better understanding of children in order to promote their well being during the various stages of childhood, and to help them mature into healthy adults.

Freud developed many theories about the enormous influence of childhood experiences on adult behavior and also proposed a five-stage chronological model of childhood **psychosexual development.** The oral stage (**birth to 1.5 years**), in which primary gratification is through sucking, is followed by the anal stage (1.5 to 3 years), in which control of elimination is a primary concern. Next comes the phallic stage (3 to 7 years), during which a child experiences and resolves the Oedipal crisis and assumes his or her sexual identity. During the latency stage (ages 7 to 12) sexuality is dormant, and the primary love objects are people outside the home. With the genital stage, which begins at age 12 and lasts into adulthood, instinctual sexual drives increase and parental attachments are dissolved.

Arnold Gesell was among the first psychologists to undertake a thorough quantitative study of normal human development from birth through **adolescence**. Based on his work at Yale's Child Development Clinic and his own Institute, Gesell produced reports that had a widespread influence on both parents and educators, and created the Gesell Development Schedules, which are still used today to assess motor and language development, adaptive behavior, and personal-social behavior in children between four weeks and six years of age.

Probably the most famous theory of child development is the cognitive development model pioneered by the Swiss psychologist Jean Piaget. Piaget divided child development between birth and late adolescence into four stages of increasingly complex and abstract thought, each qualitatively different from the ones preceding it but still dependent on them. The first, or sensorimotor, stage (birth to approximately 2 years) is a time of nonverbal, experimental basic learning when infants experience the world primarily through their senses and gradually gain mastery of their own bodies and external objects. The preoperational stage (ages 2 to 6 years) involves the association of objects with words and the ability to solve more complex problems, although the child's focus at this stage remains egocentric, a term that refers to the inability to consider things from another person's perspective. The third, or concrete operations, stage (6 to 11 years of age) is a period during which categorizing activities and the earliest logical operations occur. The fourth, or formal operations, stage (ages 12 and higher) is characterized by the gradual emergence of a mature **ability** to reason and deal with abstract relationships.

Another well-known development theory structured in stages is the one proposed by neo-Freudian **Erik Erikson** in *Childhood and Society* (1950). While Erikson's eight-stage theory encompasses the entire human life span, much of it is centered on childhood and adolescence. Each developmental stage in Erikson's scheme is concerned with a central conflict: trust versus mistrust in infancy; autonomy versus doubt and shame in early childhood; initiative versus guilt in the preschool period; and industry versus inferiority during the early school years. The goals of the first four stages create the foundation for the successful negotiation of the fifth stage, in which the adolescent must form a stable identity and achieve a sense of self.

Lawrence Kohlberg's work on the development of moral reasoning approaches childhood from a different perspective. After studying the different ways in which children aged 7 through adolescence respond to moral dilemmas, Kohlberg determined that there are universal stages in **moral development,** which, like the cognitive stages delineated by Piaget, differ from each other qualitatively. Children from the ages of 7 through about 10 act on the preconventional level, which involves deferring to adults and obeying rules based on the immediate prospect of **punishment** or reward. At around age 10, they progress to the conventional level, where their behavior is guided by the opinions of other people and the desire to conform. During adolescence, children become capable of postconventional morality, which entails the ability to formulate abstract moral principles and act on motives that transcend self-interest and even social norms that conflict with one's personal sense of justice.

LANDMARK PUBLICATIONS ON CHILD DEVELOPMENT

1877 Charles Darwin's *Biographical Sketch of an Infant,* observations on development of his eldest child.

1880 G. Stanley Hall, the "father of child psychology in America," publishes *The Contents of Children's Minds.*

1914 John Broadus Watson publishes his most important work *Behavior—An Introduction to Comparative Psychology.*

1926 Jean Piaget publishes *The Child's Conception of the World,* followed ten years later by *The Origin of Intelligence in Children.*

1934 Arnold Gesell publishes *An Atlas of Infant Behavior,* followed by *Child in the Culture of Today* (1943), *The Child from Five to Ten* (1946), and *Child Development* (1949).

1946 Benjamin Spock publishes *The Common Sense Book of Baby and Child Care.*

1950 Erik Erikson publishes *Childhood and Society.*

In recent years, researchers in child development have focused increasingly on the developmental patterns and needs of minorities and women. Carol Gilligan, Kohlberg's colleague at Harvard University, found fault with Kohlberg's exclusive focus on white males in his initial research, and in her own study, *In a Different Voice,* Gilligan differentiates between male and female moral development. In contrast to the male problem-solving approach to moral dilemmas based on an "ethic of justice," she describes a female "ethic of care" that is based on **empathy** and involves the **perception** of moral dilemmas in terms of conflicting responsibilities rather than competing rights.

Further Reading

Bee, Helen L. *The Developing Child.* 5th ed. New York: Harper & Row, 1989.

Dworetzky, John. *Introduction to Child Development.* 5th ed. Minneapolis: West Publishing Co., 1993

Meinhold, Patricia. *Child Psychology: Development and Behavior Analysis.* Dubuque, IA: Kendall/Hunt Publishing Co., 1993.

Owens, Karen. *The World of the Child.* New York: Holt, Rinehart, and Winston, 1987.

Papalia, Diane E. *A Child's World: Infancy through Adolescence.* 5th ed. New York : McGraw-Hill, 1990.

Child Psychiatrist

A licensed physician specializing in the diagnosis and treatment of mental disorders and other psychological, emotional, behavioral and developmental problems affecting children, adolescents and their families.

The child psychiatrist performs a comprehensive diagnostic examination to evaluate a given problem focusing on its genetic, developmental, emotional, cognitive, educational, family, peer, and social components. The child psychiatrist then designs a treatment plan including these components and discusses the recommendations with the child and family. Approaches may involve individual, group or family **psychotherapy**; medication; or consultation with professionals from schools, juvenile courts, social agencies, or other community organizations.

Training for child psychiatrists requires four years of medical school, one year of hospital medical training (internship), a minimum of two years of approved residency training in general adult psychiatry, and two years of training in child psychiatric work in an approved residency program. Upon completion of the child psychiatry residency and the passing of an examination in general psychiatry administered by the American Board of Psychiatry and Neurology, the child psychiatrist is eligible for certification in the subspecialty of child and adolescent psychiatry. Child psychiatrists trained in a specific method of treating people with emotional problems (called **psychoanalysis**) are called child psychoanalysts. This method, taught in psychoanalytic institutes, was created by **Sigmund Freud** and includes the study of unconscious **motivation** and dream analysis.

Child Psychologist

A person who studies both the covert (thoughts, perceptions and feelings) and overt behavior (observable actions) of children during the period from conception to the end of adolescence and uses behavioral principles in scientific research or in applied settings for the treatment of emotional problems.

A child psychologist is a health professional who is not trained as a physician, but who specializes in diagnosing and treating children and adolescents with social, emotional, psychological, behavioral and developmental problems. Such therapists have an advanced degree such as a Ph.D. (Doctor of Philosophy), a Psy.D. (Doctor of Psychology), or an Ed.D (Doctor of Education). This training usually involves four years of graduate education plus a year of internship and research studies in such specialized areas as **mental health** and therapy, **perception,** physiology, **child development,** learning or teaching.

Clinical child psychologists may work either in private practice or at a hospital, mental institution, or social service agency. They administer testing (**intelligence** tests, projective or **personality** tests, developmental screening tests and diagnostic assessment tests) and provide counseling services, but do not assess physical or neurological causes of mental problems or prescribe medications.

Child Psychology

A component of developmental psychology, which is the study of human development and the factors that shape behavior throughout life. Child psychology focuses specifically on development and changes in children's behavior. Because behavioral changes occur almost continually during childhood, the subject of child psychology constitutes a large part of developmental psychology.

Numerous issues are addressed in the study of child psychology, with three most often involved in debate. The first is referred to as the **nature-nurture controversy** and focuses on the question of how important genetic inheritance is in defining our characteristics (nature), and how important our environmental experiences are (nurture). Another question is that of passivity vs. activity in the child. That is, whether the child is the passive recipient of information imposed upon him by his **environment** or whether he actively pursues knowledge and manipulates objects in his environment to learn and grow. A third point of contention among child psychologists is the nature of development itself. While some psychologists believe that a child's development occurs as a continuous progression, others argue that development is explained more realistically as a discontinuous process involving a series of stages or steps toward **maturity,** with periods of levelling off, or plateaus, occurring between stages. **Jean Piaget** is notable for his significant impact in this field through research and study of these and other issues.

The **child psychologist** uses various research techniques to study the developmental process. Two of the most important are the longitudinal method (see longitudinal study), which is the study of an individual or process over a period of time, and the cross-sectional method (see **cross-sectional study**), which is the study of groups of individuals or processes at a particular point in time.

Child psychologists study children at various stages of life, from neonatal (newborn) through **adolescence** and focus on various areas of development, including motor development (movements involving muscle action), sensory perception (see **senses**), cognitive development (see **cognition**), language development (see **language**), social development, and emotional development (see **emotion**). They may address such questions as "How does the newborn use its vision to explore the world?", "How do parental styles of discipline contribute to a child's sense of independence and social maturity?", and "What factors influence aggressive behavior in a child?"

See also Developmental Psychology.

....

Chomsky, Noam (1928–)

American linguist whose theory of transformational or generative grammar has had a profound influence on the fields of both linguistics and psychology.

Noam Chomsky was born in Philadelphia and educated at the University of Pennsylvania, where he received his B.A. (1949), M.A. (1951), and Ph.D. (1955). In 1955, he was appointed to the faculty of the Massachusetts Institute of Technology (MIT), where he has served as professor of foreign languages and linguistics. He has also taught courses and lectured at many universities throughout the world, including Oxford University. Besides his work in the field of psycholinguistics, Chom-

sky is also well known as a leftist activist and social critic. He was an outspoken opponent of the Vietnam War and has remained critical of media coverage of politics. Although Chomsky's work is primarily of interest to linguistics scholars, several of his theories have had popular applications in **psychology.**

Chomsky was a pioneer in the field of psycholinguistics, which, beginning in the 1950s, helped establish a new relationship between linguistics and psychology. While Chomsky argued that linguistics should be understood as a part of **cognitive psychology,** in his first book, *Syntactic Structures* (1957), he opposed the traditional learning theory basis of **language acquisition.** In doing so, his expressed a view that differed from the behaviorist view of the mind as a *tabula rasa;* his theories were also diametrically opposed to the verbal learning theory of **B. F. Skinner**, the foremost proponent of **behaviorism.** In Chomsky's view, certain aspects of linguistic knowledge and **ability** are the product of a universal innate ability, or "language acquisition device" (LAD), that enables each normal child to construct a systematic grammar and generate phrases. This theory claims to account for the fact that children acquire language skills more rapidly than other abilities, usually mastering most of the basic rules by the age of four. As evidence that an inherent ability exists to recognize underlying syntactical relationships within a sentence, Chomsky cites the fact that children readily understand transformations of a given sentence into different forms—such as declarative and interrogative—and can easily transform sentences of their own. Applying this principle to adult mastery of language, Chomsky has devised the now-famous nonsense sentence, "Colorless green ideas sleep furiously." Although the sentence has no coherent meaning, English speakers regard it as still more nonsensical if the syntax, as well as the meaning, is deprived of underlying logic, as in "Ideas furiously green colorless sleep." (The same idea underlies Lewis Carroll's well-known poem "Jabberwocky" from his *Alice in Wonderland.)* Chomsky's approach is also referred to as "generative" because of the idea that rules generate the seemingly infinite variety of orders and sentences existing in all languages. Chomsky argues that the underlying logic, or *deep structure*, of all languages is the same and that human mastery of it is genetically determined, not learned. Those aspects of language that humans have to study are termed *surface structures*.

Chomsky's work has been highly controversial, rekindling the age-old debate over whether language exists in the mind before experience. His theories also distinguish between language *competence* (knowledge of rules and structure) and *performance* (how an individual uses language in practice). Besides *Syntactic Structures,* Chomsky's books include *Current Issues in Linguistics*

Theory (1964), *Aspects of the Theory of Syntax* (1965), *Topics in the Theory of Generative Grammar* (1966), *Cartesian Linguistics* (1966), *Language and Mind* (1968), *Reflections on Language* (1975), *Logical Structure of Linguistic* Theory (1975), and *Knowledge of Language* (1986).

Further Reading
D'Agostino, F. *Chomsky's System of Ideas.* Oxford: Oxford University Press, 1986.

Classical/Respondent Conditioning

A theory about how learning occurs, linking a specific stimulus to a behavioral response.

Ivan Pavlov inadvertently discovered the basic principles of classical conditioning, a branch of **psychology** that has fascinated researchers for the past century. While investigating the physiology of digestion, Pavlov noticed that his experimental dogs would salivate when food was not available, and that the appearance of an animal caretaker was sufficient to induce salivation. This chance discovery led to a program of research on the learning of behaviors. Basically, Pavlov noted that in normal circumstances, his dogs would salivate when meat powder was placed in their mouths. This behavior was seen to involve an unconditioned (e.g., unlearned or automatic) response to an unconditioned (e.g., naturally occurring) stimulus. Subsequently, the dogs began to associate the presence of a researcher (the neutral stimulus) with the arrival of food (the meaningful stimulus) by displaying an anticipatory behavior—salivating. At this point, the dog was emitting a learned behavior, which became known as the conditioned response. The term used to describe the emergence of the behavior is acquisition; **extinction** occurs when a behavior disappears because the conditioned stimulus no longer accompanies the unconditioned stimulus.

The research that followed after Pavlov's discovery revealed a similar pattern: an unconditioned (naturally occurring) stimulus led to an unconditioned (automatic or unlearned) response. If the unconditioned stimulus were paired with a conditioned (initially neutral) stimulus, an organism would subsequently emit a conditioned (learned) response that was virtually the same as the unconditioned response.

Psychologists have studied two specific phenomena relevant to conditioning, discrimination and generalization. When an organism discriminates, it responds to a conditioned stimulus but not to a similar, novel stimulus; when it generalizes, it responds to a new, different stimulus as it might have to a conditioned stimulus. As a rule, the greater the similarity between two stimuli, the greater the similarity is in the response. This learning phenomenon has generally been applied to involuntary behaviors such as reflexes rather than voluntary behaviors, which are more amenable to study through operant or instrumental conditioning. Pavlov attempted to expand his ideas to include complex human behavior, which he believed was simply a series of conditioned responses. He developed a theory of abnormal behavior to characterize psychiatric disturbances, with only limited success.

One surprising project Pavlov developed involved using **pain** as a conditioned stimulus. In an experiment, he gave a dog mild electric shocks paired with an unconditioned stimulus (food). Soon, the animal began to salivate when the shock was administered, and Pavlov gradually increased the force of the shock. In the end, the dog appeared to suppress the pain reaction and responded calmly to a shock that would normally produce considerable agitation. This observation has been paralleled to some forms of human behavior, such as **masochism,** the seeking of stimulation that others might find painful.

Further Reading
Classical Conditioning. 3rd ed. Hillsdale, NJ: L. Erlbaum Associates, 1987.
Lieberman, David A. *Learning: Behavior and Cognition.* Belmont, CA: Wadsworth Publishing Co., 1990.

Client-Centered Therapy

An approach to counseling and psychotherapy that places much of the responsibility for the treatment process on the patient, with the therapist taking a non-directive role.

Developed in the 1930s by the American psychologist **Carl Rogers,** client-centered therapy—also known as non-directive or Rogerian therapy—departed from the typically formal, detached role of the therapist common to **psychoanalysis** and other forms of treatment. Rogers believed that therapy should take place in the supportive **environment** created by a close personal relationship between client and therapist. Rogers's introduction of the term "client" rather than "patient" expresses his rejection of the traditionally authoritarian relationship between therapist and client and his view of them as equals. The client determines the general direction of therapy, while the therapist seeks to increase the client's insightful self-understanding through informal clarifying questions.

Rogers believed that the most important factor in successful therapy was not the therapist's skill or training, but rather his or her attitude. Three interrelated attitudes on the part of the therapist are central to the success

KEY TO SUCCESS IN CLIENT-CENTERED THERAPY

Qualities of the therapist

Congruence: therapist's openness to the client

Unconditional positive regard: therapist accepts the client without judgement

Empathy: therapist tries to convey an appreciation and understanding of the client's point of view

Goals of the therapy

Increase self-esteem

Expand openness to life experiences

of client-centered therapy: congruence, unconditional positive regard, and **empathy**. Congruence refers to the therapist's openness and genuineness—the willingness to relate to clients without hiding behind a professional facade. Therapists who function in this way have all their feelings available to them in therapy sessions and may share significant ones with their clients. However, congruence does not mean that therapists disclose their own personal problems to clients in therapy sessions or shift the focus of therapy to themselves in any other way.

Unconditional positive regard means that the therapist accepts the client totally for who he or she is without evaluating or censoring, and without disapproving of particular feelings, actions, or characteristics. The therapist communicates this attitude to the client by a willingness to listen without interrupting, judging, or giving advice. This creates a nonthreatening context in which the client feels free to explore and share painful, hostile, defensive, or abnormal feelings without worrying about personal rejection by the therapist.

The third necessary component of a therapist's attitude is empathy ("accurate empathetic understanding"). The therapist tries to appreciate the client's situation from the client's point of view, showing an emotional understanding of and sensitivity to the client's feelings throughout the therapy session. In other systems of therapy, empathy with the client would be considered a preliminary step enabling the therapeutic work to proceed, but in client-centered therapy, it actually constitutes a major portion of the therapeutic work itself. A primary way of conveying this empathy is by active listening that shows careful and perceptive attention to what the client is saying. In addition to standard techniques, such as eye contact, that are common to any good listener, client-centered therapists employ a special method called reflec-

tion, which consists of paraphrasing and/or summarizing what a client has just said. This technique shows that the therapist is listening carefully and accurately and gives clients an added opportunity to examine their own thoughts and feelings as they hear them repeated by another person. Generally, clients respond by elaborating further on the thoughts they have just expressed.

Two primary goals of client-centered therapy are increased self-esteem and greater openness to experience. Some of the related changes that it seeks to foster in clients include increased correspondence between the client's idealized and actual selves; better self-understanding; decreases in defensiveness, guilt, and insecurity; more positive and comfortable relationships with others; and an increased capacity to experience and express feelings at the moment they occur. Beginning in the 1960s, client-centered therapy became allied with the **human potential movement**. Rogers adopted terms such as "person-centered approach" and "way of being" and began to focus on personal growth and **self-actualization**. He also pioneered the use of **encounter groups**, adapting the **sensitivity training** (T-group) methods developed by Kurt Lewin (1890–1947) and other researchers at the National Training Laboratories in 1950s.

While client-centered therapy is considered one of the major therapeutic approaches, along with psychoanalytic and cognitive-behavioral therapy, Rogers's influence is felt in schools of therapy other than his own, and the concepts and methods he developed are drawn on in an eclectic fashion by many different types of counselors and therapists.

Further Reading

Rogers, Carl. *Client-Centered Therapy.* Boston: Houghton Mifflin, 1951.

———. *On Becoming a Person.* Boston: Houghton Mifflin, 1961.

———. *A Way of Being.* Boston: Houghton Mifflin, 1980.

Clinical Psychology

The application of psychological principles to diagnosing and treating persons with emotional and behavioral problems.

Clinical psychologists apply research findings in the fields of mental and physical health to explain dysfunctional behavior in terms of **normal** processes. The problems they address are diverse and include mental illness, **mental retardation,** marital and family issues, criminal behavior, and chemical dependency. The clinical psychologist may also address less serious problems of **adjustment** similar to those encountered by the counseling psychologist.

Approximately one-third of the psychologists working in the United States today are clinical psychologists. A number of clinical psychologists are in private practice, either alone or in group practice with other mental health professionals. Others may practice in a variety of settings, including community mental-health centers, university medical schools, social work departments, centers for the mentally and physically handicapped, prisons, state institutions and hospitals, juvenile courts, and probation offices. Clinical psychologists use **psychological assessment** and other means to diagnose psychological disorders and may apply **psychotherapy** to treat clients individually or in groups. In the United States, they are governed by a code of professional practice drawn up by the **American Psychological Association.**

Individuals consult clinical psychologists for treatment when their behaviors or **attitudes** are harmful to themselves or others. Many different treatment types and methods are employed by psychologists, depending on the setting in which they work and their theoretical orientation. The major types of therapy include psychodynamic therapies, based on uncovering **unconscious** processes and **motivation**s, of which the most well known is Freudian **psychoanalysis;** phenomenological, or humanistic, therapies (including the Rogerian and Gestalt methods) which view psychotherapy as an encounter between equals, abandoning the traditional doctor-patient relationship; and behavior-oriented therapies geared toward helping clients see their problems as learned behaviors that can be modified without looking for unconscious motivations or hidden meanings. These therapies, derived from the work of **Ivan Pavlov** and **B.F. Skinner**, include methods such as **behavior modification** and **cognitive-behavior therapy,** which may be used to alter not only overt behavior but also the thought patterns that drive it.

The work of the clinical psychologist is often compared with that of the **psychiatrist,** and although there is overlap in what these professionals do, there are also specific distinctions between them. As of 1996, clinical psychologists cannot prescribe drugs to treat **psychological disorders**, and must work in conjunction with a psychiatrist or other M.D. who is authorized to administer controlled substances. However, a movement is underway for prescription privileges for psychologists. The clinical psychologist has extensive training in research methods and in techniques for diagnosing, treating, and preventing various disorders. Most psychologists earn a Ph.D. degree in the field, which requires completion of a four- to six-year program offered by a university psychology department. The course of study includes a broad overview of the field (including courses in such areas as **statistics, personality** theory, and psychotherapy), as well as specialization in a particular subfield and completion of a practicum, internship, and dissertation.

A new training program for psychologists was developed and introduced at the University of Illinois, which offered the first Psychology Doctorate (Psy.D.) in 1968. This degree program is geared exclusively toward the training of clinicians rather than researchers. It stresses course work in applied methods of assessment and intervention and eliminates the dissertation requirement. The number of Psy.D. programs in the United States has grown since 1968, with some programs offered at universities and others at independent, "free-standing" professional schools of psychology.

Assessment plays a prominent role among the functions of clinical psychology. The term "clinical psychology" itself was first used at the end of the nineteenth century in connection with the testing of mentally retarded and physically handicapped children. The discipline soon expanded with the growing interest in the application of assessment techniques to the general population following **Robert Yerkes**'s revision of the **Stanford Binet Intelligence scales** in 1915, creating a widely used point scale for the measurement of human **mental ability.** Clinical psychologists must be familiar with a variety of techniques of assessing patients through interviews, observation, tests, and various forms of **play.** Assessment may be used to compare an individual with others in a reliable way using standardized norms; determine the type and circumstances of symptomatic behaviors; understand how a person functions in a given area (cognition, social skills, emotion); or match a patient to a particular diagnostic category for further treatment.

While the clinical psychologist does not specialize in research, the two disciplines often overlap. With their varied experiences, clinicians are qualified to participate in research on, for example, cost effectiveness in health care, design of facilities, doctor-patient communication, or studies of various treatment methods. Clinical psychologists routinely contribute to the training of mental health professionals and those in other areas of health care, serving on the faculties of universities and independent institutes of psychology, where they teach courses, supervise practicums and internships, and oversee dissertation research. They also carry out administrative appointments which call for them to assist in the planning and implementation of health care services and are represented in international groups such as the World Health Organization.

Further Reading

Bernstein, Douglas A. *Introduction to Clinical Psychology.* New York: McGraw-Hill, 1980.

Lilienfeld, Scott O. *Seeing Both Sides: Classic Controversies in Abnormal Psychology.* Pacific Grove, CA: Brooks/Cole, 1995.

Nietzel, Michael T. *Introduction to Clinical Psychology.* 3rd ed. Englewood Cliffs, NJ: Prentice Hall, 1991.

Cocaine. See **Drugs.**

Codependence

A term used to describe a person who is intimately involved with a person who is abusing or addicted to alcohol or another substance.

The concept of codependence was first developed in relation to alcohol and other substance abuse addictions. The alcoholic or drug abuser was the *dependent,* and the person involved with the dependent person in any intimate way (spouse, lover, child, sibling, etc.) was the codependent. The definition of the term has been expanded to include anyone showing an extreme degree of certain **personality** traits: denial, silent or even cheerful tolerance of unreasonable behavior from others, rigid loyalty to family rules, a need to control others, finding identity through relationships with others, a lack of personal boundaries, and low self-esteem. Some consider it a progressive disease, one which gets worse without treatment until the codependent becomes unable to function successfully in the world. Progressive codependence can lead to **depression**, isolation, self-destructive behavior (such as **bulimia, anorexia,** self-mutilation) or even **suicide**. There is a large self-help movement to help codependents take charge of themselves and heal their lives.

There is some criticism of the "codependence movement" by those who feel it is only a fad that encourages labeling and a weak, dependent, victim mentality that obscures more important underlying truths of oppression. Many critics claim the definition of codependence is too vague and the list of symptoms too long and broad to be meaningful. These critics believe that all families fit the "dysfunctional" label; by diagnosing a person as "codependent," all responsibility for the individual's dissatisfaction, shortcomings, and failures comes to rest on the individual and his or her family. Larger issues of cultural, societal, or institutional responsibility are ignored. However, some proponents of the codependence definition are widening their perspective to look at how society as a whole, as well as separate institutions within society, function in an addictive, dysfunctional, or codependent way.

Further Reading

Beattie, Melody. *Codependent No More: How to Stop Controlling Others and Start Caring for Yourself.* San Francisco: Hazelden/HarperCollins, 1987.

Johnson, Sonia. *Wildfire: Igniting the She/Volution.* Albuquerque, NM: Wildfire Books, 1989.

Katz, Dr. Stan J., and Eimee E. Liu. *The Codependency Conspiracy: How to Break the Recovery Habit and Take Charge of Your Life.* New York: Warner Books, 1991.

Cognition

A general term for the higher mental processes by which people acquire knowledge, solve problems, and plan for the future.

Cognition depends on the **ability** to imagine or represent objects and events that are not physically present at a given moment. Cognitive functions include **attention, perception**, thinking, judging, decision making, problem solving, **memory**, and linguistic ability.

One of the most basic cognitive functions is the ability to conceptualize, or group individual items together as instances of a single concept or category, such as "apple" or "chair." Concepts provide the fundamental framework for thought, allowing people to relate most objects and events they encounter to preexisting categories. People learn concepts by building prototypes to which variations are added and by forming and testing hypotheses about which items belong to a particular category. Most thinking combines concepts in different forms. Examples of different forms concepts take include propositions (proposals or possibilities), mental models (visualizing the physical form an idea might take), schemas (diagrams or maps), scripts (scenarios), and images (physical models of the item). Other fundamental aspects of cognition are reasoning, the process by which people formulate arguments and arrive at conclusions, and problem solving—devising a useful representation of a problem and planning, executing, and evaluating a solution.

Memory—another cognitive function—is crucial to learning, communication, and even to one's sense of identity (as evidenced by the effects of **amnesia**). Short-term memory provides the basis for one's working model of the world and makes possible most other mental functions; long-term memory stores information for longer periods of time. The three basic processes common to both short- and long-term memory are encoding, which deposits information in the memory; storage; and retrieval. Currently, the question of whether short- and long-term memory are qualitatively and biologically distinct is a matter of debate.

The cognitive function that most distinctively sets humans apart from other animals is the ability to communicate through **language**, which involves expressing propositions as sentences and understanding such expressions when we hear or read them. Language also enables the mind to communicate with itself. The interaction between language and thought has been a topic of much speculation. Of historical interest is the work of Benjamin Whorf (1897–1941), the proponent of the idea that the language people use determines the way in which they view the world. As of the late 1990s, most psychologists view the Whorfian hypothesis with skepticism, believing that language and perception interact to influence one another.

Language acquisition is another topic of debate, with some—including psycholinguist **Noam Chomsky**—arguing that all humans have innate language abilities, while behaviorists stress the role of **conditioning** and social learning theorists stress the importance of **imitation** and **reinforcement**.

Since the 1950s, **cognitive psychology**, which focuses on the relationship between cognitive processes and behavior, has occupied a central place in psychological research. The cognitive psychologist studies human perceptions and the ways in which cognitive processes operate on them to produce responses. One of the foremost cognitive psychologists is **Jerome Bruner**, who has done important work on the ways in which needs, motivations, and expectations (or "mental sets") affect perception. In 1960, Bruner and his colleague, George A. Miller, established the Harvard Center for Cognitive Studies, which was influential in the "cognitive revolution" of the following years. In the area of linguistics, the work of Noam Chomsky has rekindled the age-old debate over whether language exists in the mind before experience. Other well-known work in cognitive psychology includes that of D.E. Berlyne on curiosity and information seeking; George Kelly's theory of personal constructs; and investigations by Herman Witkin, Riley Gardner, and George Klein on individual perceptual and cognitive styles.

The development of the modern computer has influenced current ways of thinking about cognition through computer simulation of cognitive processes for research purposes and through the creation of information-processing models. These models portray cognition as a system that receives information, represents it with symbols, and then manipulates the representations in various ways. The senses transmit information from outside stimuli to the **brain**, which applies perceptual processes to interpret it and then decides how to respond to it. The information may simply be stored in the memory or it may be acted on. Acting on it usually affects a person's environment in some way, providing more feedback for the system to process. Major contributions in the area of information processing include D.E. Broadbent's information theory of attention, learning, and memory; and Miller, Galanter, and Pribram's analysis of planning and problem solving.

See also Artificial Intelligence.

Further Reading

Anderson, John R. *Cognitive Psychology and Its Implications.* New York: W.H. Freeman, 1985.

Ashcraft, Mark H. *Human Memory and Cognition.* New York: HarperCollins College Publishers, 1994.

Broadbent, Donald E. *Perception and Communication.* New York: Oxford University Press, 1987.

Halpern, Diane F. *Sex Differences in Cognitive Abilities.* Hillsdale, NJ: L. Erlbaum Associates, 1992.

Cognitive Behavior Therapy

A therapeutic approach designed to alter cognitions—including thoughts, beliefs, and images—as a way of changing behavior.

Cognitive-behavior therapy is an outgrowth of **behavior modification** therapy, from which it borrows several techniques, including detailed record keeping by the client, **modeling**, visualization, and practicing new skills in the real world. In the 1960s, practitioners of behavior therapy found that the success of their treatment depended in part on a patient's cognitive processes and that certain cognitions, such as self-blame, rendered even powerful external modifications ineffective. As a result, interest grew in the use of cognitive skills to address environmental problems.

In *Principles of Behavior Modification* (1969), **Albert Bandura** emphasized the importance of cognitive processes in regulating behavior, pointing out that humans, unlike other species, develop a variety of cognitive reactions to the conditioning processes used in behavior modification. Thus, human behavior is based not only on outside stimuli but also on the subjective judgments people make about their own and others' behavior in reaction to those stimuli. Bandura focused in particular on the formation of distorted cognitions, based on prior experiences, that do not accurately reflect the actual conditions in one's **environment** and may result in inappropriate types of behavior. For example, if people believe they are failures, they will become depressed by a difficult situation instead of coping effectively with it. Cognitive-behavior therapy provides clients with learning experiences designed to change distorted ways of thinking about the world so that they can function more effectively in it. The work of Bandura's student, Michael Mahoney—notably his book *Cognition and Behavior Modification*—has had a seminal influence on cognitive-behavioral therapy. Mahoney also served as an editor of the field's journal, *Cognitive Therapy and Research.*

The various schools or methods of cognitive-behavioral therapy generally address the broad areas of **anxiety** and **stress** reactions, **depression**, and social skills. While their exact techniques vary, their methods have certain characteristics in common. They all focus on the client's present situation, feelings, and problems (the "here-and-now") as opposed to the emphasis of traditional psychoanalytic methods on the client's childhood or other elements of the past. Treatment begins with the identification of self-destructive cognitive patterns that are causing the client's problems. Generally, this is done through detailed self-monitoring by the client, who is often provided with a special recording sheet by the therapist. The client and therapist then agree on which types of cognition need to be changed, and the therapist suggests healthier and more positive alternatives to the client's present ways of thinking about stressful or other problematic situations.

Next, the client is aided in developing the skills needed to substitute old cognitive patterns with the new ones, including accurate assessment of situations, control of negative thoughts and feelings, positive self-talk, awareness of physical **arousal**, and self-evaluation. The client is given the opportunity to practice these skills in imaginary—and sometimes in actual—stressful situations. By actually confronting and handling a problem situation, clients learn not only how to cope but also that they can.

One well-known type of cognitive-behavior therapy is rational-emotive therapy (RET), developed by Albert Ellis, which helps people eliminate self-defeating or problem-causing thoughts, such as "I fail at whatever I try" or "I must be perfect to be a worthwhile person," and replace them with more rational ones. Clients are taught to recognize their own self-defeating thought patterns and shown how these patterns cause problems in their daily lives. Through logic, modeling, and encouragement, they learn to replace such thoughts with alternative ones that are positive and calming—a process called cognitive restructuring. Another cognitively-oriented therapy is that developed by Aaron Beck and known simply as cognitive therapy, which is often used with persons suffering from depression or anxiety disorders. It is based on challenging negative styles of thinking—such as focusing more on failure than on success—and reducing the tendency of depressed people to blame all negative events on their own perceived incompetence by helping them develop more optimistic ways of thinking. Other cognitive-behavior therapies include self-instructional therapy, covert modeling therapy, coping skills training, anxiety management training, stress inoculation training, and various problem-solving therapies.

In the sensorimotor stage, an infant gains mastery of his own body and its place in his environment.

Further Reading

Beck, Aaron. *Cognitive Therapy in Clinical Practice: An Illustrated Casebook.* New York: Routledge, 1989.

Ellis, Albert. *Humanistic Psychotherapy: The Rational-Emotive Approach.* New York: Julian Press, 1973.

Freeman, Arthur M. *The 10 Dumbest Mistakes Smart People Make and How to Avoid Them.* New York: HarperCollins, 1992.

Cognitive Development Theory

First proposed in 1932 by Jean Piaget, the most comprehensive and influential theory of how the ability to think and reason develops from childhood through adolescence to adulthood.

Jean Piaget's theory of cognitive development, originally derived from observations of his own children, outlines four stages of increasingly complex and abstract thought, each one more logically consistent than the ones preceding it. During the first, or sensorimotor, stage (**birth** to approximately two years old), **perception** is closely related to motor activity, such as sucking, shaking, banging, and hitting. Through such activities, infants gradually gain mastery of their own bodies as well as external objects, learning about the properties of objects and about how to manipulate them. At this stage, they also develop a concept of themselves as separate from the external world. The nonverbal, experimental learning of this stage leads ultimately to what Piaget terms "object constancy" or permanence: the sense that objects have a continuing existence outside our immediate sensory experience. This developing concept can be seen in the child's intense interest in games involving objects that are repeatedly made to disappear and reappear, such as games of "peekaboo."

The preoperational stage (ages 2 to 6 years) involves the association of objects with words. Objects can also be seen as representing something else, as when a broom or stick is treated as a horse and "ridden" around the room. Although children can now think in symbolic terms, they do not yet have much **ability** to organize thoughts logically. Certain key concepts such as causality, time, volume, and perspective are still lacking, as is an understanding of "conservation of quantity"—the fact that substances retain the same volume even when shifted into containers of different sizes and shapes. When one of two identical balls of clay is rolled into an elongated shape, a child at the preoperational stage will believe that the longer ball has more clay because his or her thinking is still dictated by visual impressions. At both the preoperational and sensorimotor stages, the child's focus is egocentric (characterized by an inability to consider things from a perspective other than one's own). Other qualities common to this stage are centration (**attention** to only one feature of a situation) and irreversibility (inability to reverse the direction of one's thoughts).

During the third, or concrete operational, stage (6 or 7 to 11 years of age), children become capable of logical operations, but only in relation to concrete objects (as opposed to purely symbolic reasoning, which occurs during the subsequent formal operations stage). At the concrete operational stage, children can understand the conservation of number and amount, enabling them to add, subtract, count, and measure. Conservation of length, mass, area, weight, time, and volume are also mastered, in this specific order. At this stage children begin to categorize, reverse the direction of their thinking, and have an increased understanding of relationships. They also begin to lose their egocentric focus, becoming aware of other perspectives.

The fourth, or formal operations, stage begins in **adolescence** (ages 11 or 12) with the development of the ability to reason about abstract concepts. Adolescents become capable of formulating and testing hypotheses, imagining logical consequences and causality, and dealing with abstract relationships like probability and ratio. At this stage, scientific reasoning becomes possible, as well as speculation about philosophical issues. A net-work of interrelated ideas emerges, and abstract concepts and moral values become as important as concrete objects.

Although much of the research that has been done on cognitive development supports Piaget's observations, it has been found that children do not always reach the different stages at the age levels he specified. In addition, some critics believe that the abilities of preschool children exceed those he described, especially if their responses are not dependent on language. As Piaget himself reworked his theories, he came to view the different stages in a spiral rather than a linear form, with knowledge attained at a prior stage reintegrated in greater complexity at higher levels.

Further Reading

Bruner, Jerome S. *Studies in Cognitive Growth: A Collaboration at the Center for Cognitive Studies.* New York: John Wiley & Sons, 1966.

Ginsburg, Herbert, and Sylvia Opper. *Piaget's Theory of Intellectual Development.* Englewood Cliffs, NJ: Prentice-Hall, 1988.

Piaget, Jean, and Bärbel Inhelder. *The Growth of Logical Thinking from Childhood to Adolescence.* New York: Basic Books, 1958.

Cognitive Dissonance

An influential concept in the study of the relationship between attitudes and behavior.

First proposed by Leon Festinger in 1957, the theory of cognitive dissonance is based on the principle that people prefer their cognitions, or beliefs, to be consistent with each other and with their own behavior.

Inconsistency, or dissonance, among their own ideas makes people uneasy enough to alter these ideas so that they will agree with each other. For example, smokers forced to deal with the opposing thoughts "I smoke" and "smoking is dangerous" are likely to alter one of them by deciding to quit smoking. Alternatively, one can diffuse dissonance by reducing its importance (discounting the evidence against smoking or adopting the view that smoking will not harm you personally); adding new information that gives more weight to one of the dissonant beliefs or appears to reconcile them (deciding that smoking is less dangerous than the stresses it helps alleviate).

In a classic study of cognitive dissonance, subjects were asked to perform a dull task and then to persuade others that this task was interesting and enjoyable. Some were paid one dollar to do this, while others were paid $20, and all of their **attitudes** toward the task were measured at the conclusion of the experiment. The subjects who had been paid one dollar showed a marked improvement in their attitude toward the task, while the more highly paid subjects did not. The designers of the experiment interpreted their results in the following way. Cognitive dissonance was created in all of the subjects by the conflicting facts that the task had been boring and that they were saying it was interesting—their statements and beliefs did not match. However, those who were paid $20 had been given a justification for lying: they could tell themselves that their actions made some kind of sense. However, the actions of the other group made no sense unless they could persuade themselves that the task had indeed been interesting. Thus they acted to reduce the dissonance by changing their original belief.

Children have shown similar responses to experimental situations involving cognitive dissonance. In one case, children were asked not to play with an appealing toy. One experimenter made this request mildly and politely while another one made it in a threatening fashion. Those children who had accommodated the polite request also became less attracted to the toy, since liking the toy and giving it up were conflicting experiences that created dissonance. However, the children who were threatened felt no pressure to change their opinions about the toy since they had a logical reason for giving it up.

Several types of cognitive dissonance have been identified. In post-decision dissonance, a person must decide between two choices, each of which has both positive and negative components (in other contexts, this type of situation is called a multiple approach-avoidance conflict). Forced compliance dissonance occurs when people are forced to act in ways that conflict with their beliefs and can not find any way to justify their actions to themselves. Dissonance also occurs when people are exposed to new information that threatens or changes their current beliefs. Various group situations also generate cognitive dissonance. It occurs when a person must abandon old beliefs or adopt new ones in order to join a group, when members disagree with each other, and when the group as a whole has its central beliefs threatened by an external event or by the receipt of new information.

Festinger proposed that some individuals have a higher tolerance for cognitive dissonance than others. Subsequent researchers have found correlations between various **personality** traits, such as extroversion, and the ability to withstand dissonance.

Further Reading

Festinger, Leon. *A Theory of Cognitive Dissonance.* Stanford, CA: Stanford University Press, 1957.

Cognitive Psychology

An approach to psychology which focuses on the relationship between cognitive or mental processes and behavior.

The cognitive psychologist studies human **perception**s and the ways in which cognitive processes operate to produce responses. Cognitive processes (which may involve language, symbols, or imagery) include perceiving, recognizing, remembering, imagining, conceptualizing, judging, reasoning, and processing information for planning, problem-solving, and other applications. Some cognitive psychologists may study how internal cognitive operations can transform symbols of the external world, others on the interplay between genetics and **environment** in determining individual cognitive development and capabilities. Still other cognitive psychologists may focus their studies on how the mind detects, selects, recognizes, and verbally represents features of a particular stimulus. Among the many specific topics investigated by cognitive psychologists are language acquisition; visual and auditory perception; information storage and retrieval; altered states of **consciousness;** cognitive restructuring (how the mind mediates between conflicting, or dissonant, information); and individual styles of thought and perception.

The challenges of studying human cognition are evident when one considers the work of the mind in processing the simultaneous and sometimes conflicting information presented in daily life, through both internal and external stimuli. For example, an individual may feel hunger pangs, the external heat of the sun, and sensations of bodily movement produced by walking while simultaneously talking, listening to a companion, and recalling past experiences. Although this attention to multiple stimuli is a common phenomenon, complex cognitive processing is clearly required to accomplish it.

At its inception as a discipline in the nineteenth century, psychology focused on mental processes. However, the prevailing structuralist methods, which analyzed consciousness introspectively by breaking it down into sensations, images, and affective states, fell out of favor early in the twentieth century and were superseded by those of the behaviorists, who replaced speculation about inner processes with the study of external, observable phenomena. Although important inroads continued to be made into the study of mental processes—including the work of the Würzburg School, the Gestalt psychologists, the field theory of Kurt Lewin, and **Jean Piaget**'s theories of cognitive development in children—the behaviorist focus remained dominant in the United States through the middle of the twentieth century.

Since the 1950s, cognitive approaches have assumed a central place in psychological research and theorizing.

One of its foremost pioneers is **Jerome Bruner,** who, together with his colleague Leo Postman, did important work on the ways in which **need**s, **motivation**s, and expectations (or "mental sets") affect perception. Bruner's work led him to an interest in the cognitive development of children and related issues of education, and he later developed a theory of cognitive growth. His theories, which approached development from a different angle than—and mostly complement—those of Piaget, focus on the environmental and experiential factors influencing each individual's specific development pattern.

In 1957, Leon Festinger advanced his classic theory of **cognitive dissonance,** which describes how people manage conflicting cognitions about themselves, their behavior, or their environment. Festinger posited that conflict among such cognitions (which he termed dissonance) will make people uncomfortable enough to actually modify one of the conflicting beliefs to bring it into line with the other belief. Thus, for example, the conflicting cognitions "I smoke" and "smoking is bad" will lead a smoker either to alter the first statement by quitting, or the second one by telling himself or herself that smoking is not bad. In 1960, Jerome Bruner and George A. Miller established the Harvard Center for Cognitive Studies, which became influential in the "cognitive revolution." As a result, an increasing number of experimental psychologists abandoned behaviorist studies of rats and mazes for research involving the higher mental processes in human beings. This trend in psychology paralleled advances in several other fields, including neuroscience, mathematics, anthropology, and computer science.

Language became an important area of study for cognitive psychologists. In 1953, the term "psycholinguistics" was coined to designate an emerging area of common interest, the psychology of language, and **Noam Chomsky,** a professor at the Massachusetts Institute of Technology, became its most famous proponent. Chomsky argued that the underlying logic, or deep structure, of all languages is the same and that human mastery of it is genetically determined, not learned. His work has been highly controversial, rekindling the age-old debate over whether language exists in the mind before experience. Other well known studies in cognitive psychology includes that of D.E. Berlyne's work on curiosity and information seeking; George Kelly's theory of personal constructs, and investigations by Herman Witkin, Riley Gardner, and George Klein on individual perceptual and cognitive styles.

The emergence of cybernetics and computer science have been central to contemporary advances in cognitive psychology, including computer simulation of cognitive processes for research purposes and the creation of information-processing models. Herbert Simon and Allen Newell created the first computer simulation of human thought, called Logic Theorist, at Carnegie-Mellon University in 1956, followed by General Problem Solver (GPS) the next year. Other major contributions in this area include D.E. Broadbent's information theory of **attention,** learning, and **memory,** and Miller, Galanter, and Pribram's analysis of planning and problem solving. Despite skepticism that computer-generated "thought" will ever match human cognition, the study of **artificial intelligence** has helped scientists learn more about the human mind. In turn, this type of psychological research is expected to aid in the development of more sophisticated computers in the future through links between the psychological study of cognition and research in electrophysiology and computer science. This subfield of cognitive engineering focuses on the application of knowledge about human thought processes to the design of complex systems for aviation, industry, and other areas.

At one time, the study of cognitive processes was specific to cognitive psychology. As research began to yield information regarding the applicability of these processes to all areas of psychology, the study of cognitive processes was taken up and applied in many other subfields of psychology, such as abnormal and **developmental psychology.** Today, the term "cognitive perspective" or "cognitive approach" is applied in a broader sense to these and other areas of psychology.

See also Abnormal Psychology; Cognitive Behavior Therapy; Cognitive Development Theory; Information-Processing Approach.

Color Vision

The ability to perceive color.

Color vision is a function of the **brain**'s ability to interpret the complex way in which light is reflected off every object in nature. What the human eye sees as color is not a quality of an object itself, nor a quality of the light reflected off the object; it is actually an effect of the stimulation of different parts of the brain's visual system by the varying wavelengths of light.

Each of three types of light receptors called cones, located in the retina of the eye, recognizes certain ranges of wavelengths of light as blue, green, or red. From the cones, color signals pass via neurons along the visual pathway where they are mixed and matched to create the **perception** of the full spectrum of 5 million colors in the world.

Because each person's neurons are unique, each of us sees color somewhat differently. Color blindness, an inherited condition which affects more men than women, has two varieties: monochromats lack all cone receptors and cannot see any color; dichromats lack either red-green or blue-yellow cone receptors and cannot perceive hues in those respective ranges. Another phenomenon, known as color weakness or anomalous trichromat, refers to the situation where a person can perceive a given color, but needs greater intensity of the associated wavelength in order to see it normally.

See also Vision.

Coma

An abnormal state of profound unconsciousness accompanied by the absence of all voluntary behavior and most reflexes.

A coma may be induced by a severe neurological injury—either temporary or permanent—or by other physical trauma. A comatose individual cannot be aroused by even the most intense stimuli, although he or she may show some automatic movements in response to **pain.** Comas often occur just before death in the course of many diseases. The affected **brain** cells may be either near the surface (cerebral cortex) or deeper in the brain (diencephalon or brainstem). Specific conditions that produce comas include cerebral hemorrhage; blood clots in the brain; failure of oxygen supply to the brain; tumors; intracranial infections that cause meningitis or encephalitis; poisoning, especially by carbon monoxide or sedatives; concussion; and disorders involving electrolytes. Comas may also be caused by metabolic abnormalities that impair the functioning of the brain through a sharp drop in the blood sugar level, such as diabetes.

The passage from wakefulness to coma can be rapid and/or gradual. Often, it is preceded by lethargy and then a state resembling light **sleep.** In general, treatment of a coma involves avoiding further damage to the brain by maintaining the patient's respiratory and cardiac functions, and by an intravenous (usually glucose) nutritional supply to the brain.

Combat Neurosis

The preferred term to describe mental disturbances related to the stress of military combat; also known by such alternative terms as combat fatigue syndrome, shell shock, operational or battle fatigue, combat exhaustion, and war neurosis.

Combat neurosis describes any **personality** disturbance that represents a response to the **stress** of war. It is closely related to **post-traumatic stress disorder,** and is often characterized under that term. Symptoms of

A small percentage of military personnel who serve in combat situations develop personality disturbances or disorders.

the disturbance may appear during the battle itself, or may appear days, weeks, months, or even years later. An estimated ten percent of all personnel who fought in World War II experienced symptoms of combat neurosis, known then according to the **American Psychiatric Association** as "gross stress reaction." (The term was applied to personality disturbances resulting from catastrophes other than war as well.) More recently, considerable attention from both the general public and the medical community has focused on the combat neuroses experienced by those who fought during the Vietnam and Persian Gulf Wars. There is no specific set of symptoms that are triggered by war or combat; rather, in most cases, the disturbance begins with feelings of mild **anxiety**.

Symptoms of combat neuroses vary widely. The first signs are typically increased irritability and problems with sleeping. As the disturbance progresses, symptoms include **depression**, bereavement-type reactions (characterized as guilt over having survived when others did not), nightmares, and persistent, terrifying **daydreams**. The inability to concentrate and loss of **memory** are also common. Emotional indifference, withdrawal, lack of **attention** to personal hygiene and appearance, and self-endangering behaviors are also possible signs of combat neurosis. Individuals suffering from combat neurosis often react to these symptoms by abusing alcohol or drugs.

Combat neuroses can be a severe mental disorder and the potential success of treatment varies considerably. Some patients are treated successfully with antidepressant and antianxiety medications. For a small percentage, however, hospitalization may be required.

See also Post-Traumatic Stress Disorder.

Further Reading

Herman, Judith Lewis. *Trauma and Recovery.* New York: Basic Books, 1992.

Porterfield, Kay Marie. *Straight Talk About Post-traumatic Stress Disorder: Coping With the Aftermath of Trauma.* New York: Facts on File, 1996.

Waites, Elizabeth A. *Trauma and Survival: Post-traumatic and Dissociative Disorders in Women.* New York: Norton, 1993.

Comparative Psychology

A subfield of experimental psychology which focuses on the study of animals for the purpose of comparing the behavior of different species.

Studies of animal behavior have taken two main directions in the twentieth century. The type of research most often practiced in the United States has been animal research, involving the study of animals in laboratories and emphasizing the effects of **environment** on behavior. European research, by comparison, has been more closely associated with the area of inquiry known as **ethology,** which concentrates on studying animals in their natural environment and emphasizes the **evolution** of behavioral patterns which are typical of a particular species. Prompting an increase in the study of animal behavior, ethology has laid the groundwork for an understanding of species-typical behavior and also led to progress in relating and contrasting behaviors among different species. Comparative psychology serves a number of functions. It provides information about the genetic relations among different species, furthers understanding of human behavior, tests the limitations of psychological theories, and aids in the conservation of the natural environment.

Compensation

A psychological defense mechanism in which an individual unconsciously develops or overdevelops one area of personality as substitutive behavior to make up for a deficiency or inferiority in another area.

In classic Freudian psychoanalytical theory, the principal function of compensation is to prevent **unconscious** feelings of, or fears of, inadequacy, as well as the impulses associated with those feelings and fears, from reaching **consciousness.** For example, the development of assertive or aggressive behavior may be a compensation for feelings of inferiority about height. Many psychologists and psychiatrists generally agree with this view, and believe that compensation is not an uncommon reaction to feelings of inferiority.

The term compensation is also used in neurophysiology to mean a recovery of function after damage to a neural structure of the central nervous system, in which the neural structure is not regenerated but its function is performed by other tissues.

See also Defense Mechanism; Inferiority Complex.

Competition

An adaptive strategy that pits one person's interests against another's.

Psychologists have long been in disagreement as to whether competition is a learned or a genetic component of human behavior. Perhaps what first comes to mind when thinking of competition is athletics. It would be a mistake, however, not to recognize the effect competition has in the areas of academics, work, and many other areas of contemporary life. This is especially true in the United States, where individual rigor and competition appear to be nationalistic qualities Americans cherish and praise. It has often been suggested that the American capitalist-driven society thrives because of the spirited competition for a limited amount of resources available.

Psychologically speaking, competition has been seen as an inevitable consequence of the psychoanalytic view of human drives and is a natural state of being. According to **Sigmund Freud,** humans are born screaming for **attention** and full of organic drives for fulfillment in various areas. Initially, according to this view, we compete for the attention of our parents—seeking to attract it either from siblings or from the other parent. Thereafter, we are at the mercy of a battle between our base impulses for self-fulfillment and social and cultural mores which prohibit pure indulgence.

Decathlete Dan O'Brien starts the 100-meter race at the Olympic trials. Psychologists disagree as to whether competition is a learned or genetic component of human behavior.

Current work in anthropology has suggested, however, that this view of the role of competition in human behavior may be incorrect. Thomas Hobbes (1588–1679), one of the great philosophers of the seventeenth century, is perhaps best remembered for his characterization of the "natural world," that is, the world before the imposition of the will of humanity, as being "nasty, brutish, and short." This image of the pre-rational world is still widely held, reinforced by **Charles Darwin**'s seminal work, *The Origin of Species,* which established the doctrine of natural selection. This doctrine, which posits that those species best able to adapt to and master the natural environment in which they live will survive, has suggested to many that the struggle for survival is an inherent human trait which determines a person's success. Darwin's theory has even been summarized as "survival of the fittest"—a phrase Darwin himself never used—further highlighting competition's role in success. As it has often been pointed out, however, there is nothing in the concept of natural selection that suggests that

competition is the most successful strategy for "survival of the fittest." Darwin asserted in *The Origin of Species* that the struggles he was describing should be view as metaphors and could easily include dependence and co-operation.

Many studies have been conducted to test the importance placed on competition as opposed to other values, such as cooperation—by various cultures, and generally conclude that Americans uniquely praise competition as natural, inevitable, and desirable. In 1937, the world-renowned anthropologist Margaret Mead published *Cooperation and Competition among Primitive Peoples,* based on her studies of several societies that did not prize competition, and, in fact, seemed at times to place a negative value on it. One such society was the Zuni Indians of Arizona, and they, Mead found, valued cooperation far more than competition. For example, the Zuni held a ritual footrace that anyone could participate in, the winner of which was never publicly acknowledged and, in fact, if one person made a habit of winning the race, that person was prevented from participating in the future. After studying dozens of such cultures, Mead's final conclusion was that competitiveness is a culturally-created aspect of human behavior, and that its prevalence in a particular society is relative to how that society values it.

Further Reading

Boyd, David. "Strategic Behaviour in Contests: Evidence from the 1992 Barcelona Olympic Games." *Applied Economics* (November 1995): 1037.

Clifford, Nancy. "How Competitive Are You?" *Teen Magazine* (September 1995): 56.

Epstein, Joseph. *Ambition: The Secret Passion.* New York: E.P. Dutton, 1980.

Freud, Anna. *The Writings of Anna Freud.* Vol. 6, *Normality and Pathology in Childhood: Assessments of Development.* International Universities Press, 1965.

Kohn, Alfie. *No Contest: The Case Against Competition.* Boston: Houghton Mifflin, 1986.

Mithers, Carol. "The Need to Compete: Why Competition Is Good for You."*Ladies Home Journal* (February 1995): 136.

Concept Learning

Learning ways in which items are categorized and related to each other.

Concept learning has often been studied in experimental situations using artificial concepts (such as "square") whose properties or rules apply equally in every case (all squares must have four equal sides and four right angles). In contrast, real-life, or natural, concepts have characteristic rather than defining features—there is no one feature that every member of such a category must possess.

Natural concepts are often learned through the use of prototypes, highly typical examples to which less typical ones are then matched. For example, a robin would be a prototypical or "good" example of a bird, while a penguin, which is lacking an important defining feature of this category—flight—would not. Similarly, the concept "house" is introduced to children in temperate climates as a squarish structure with four walls, windows, and a chimney. The nontypical example "igloo" may then be added later as an instance that corresponds to some, but not all, of the prototypical characteristics that the children have learned for this concept. The other major method of concept learning is through the trial-and-error method of testing hypotheses. People will guess or assume that a certain item is an instance of a particular concept; they then learn more about the concept when they see whether their hypothesis is correct or not.

People learn simple concepts more readily than complex ones. Certain rules about complexity have been found to predict ease in learning concepts. For example, the easiest concept to learn is one with only a single defining feature. The next easiest is one with multiple features, all of which must be present in every case (the conjunctive classification rule). It is more difficult to master a concept when either one feature or another must be present (the disjunctive rule). People also learn concepts more easily when they are given positive rather than negative examples of a concept (e.g., shown what it is rather than what it is not).

Further Reading

Anderson, Barry F. *Cognitive Psychology: The Study of Knowing, Learning, and Thinking.* San Diego, CA: Academic Press, 1975.

Bourne, Lyle Eugene. *Cognitive Processes.* New York: Prentice-Hall, 1979.

Conditioned Response

In classical conditioning, behavior that is learned in response to a particular stimulus.

Reflexive behaviors occur when an animal encounters a stimulus that naturally leads to a reflex. For example, a loud noise generates a fright response. If an initially neutral stimulus is paired with the noise, that neutral or conditioned stimulus produces a fright response. In classical conditioning, the response to the **conditioned stimulus** is called a conditioned response.

Conditioned responses develop in a process called acquisition, in which the natural or unconditioned stimulus is paired with the conditioned stimulus. Some responses develop more quickly than others; similarly, some responses are stronger than others. The nature of the conditioned response depends on the circumstances in which acquisition occurs. The conditioned response emerges most effectively if the conditioned stimulus appears slightly before the unconditioned stimulus. This process is called "delayed conditioning" because the unconditioned stimulus is delayed relative to the conditioned stimulus. The response is weaker if the conditioned and unconditioned stimuli begin together, and becomes even weaker if the unconditioned stimulus precedes the conditioned stimulus. In general, the conditioned response resembles the unconditioned response (e.g., the normal fright response) very closely. Psychologists have shown, however, that the conditioned response is not identical to the unconditioned response and may be very different.

An animal usually produces a conditioned response to stimuli that resemble the conditioned stimulus, a process called stimulus generalization. Balancing this is a complementary tendency not to respond to anything but the conditioned stimulus itself; the process of ignoring stimuli is called stimulus discrimination. The combination of generalization and discrimination leads to appropriate responses.

Conditioned Stimulus

In classical conditioning, a stimulus leads to a learned response.

In **Ivan Pavlov**'s experimentations with **classical conditioning,** a sound was paired with the placement of meat powder in a dog's mouth, and the powder naturally induced salivation. After the powder and the sound had co-occurred a few times, the dog salivated when the sound occurred, even when the meat powder was not administered. Although most research in classical conditioning has involved reflexive behaviors that are typically involuntary, other nonreflexive behaviors have also been classically conditioned. The effects of the conditioned stimulus can vary widely in different circumstances. For example, if the unconditioned stimulus is more intense, the conditioned stimulus will have a greater effect. On the other hand, if the conditioned stimulus does not always occur when the natural, unconditioned stimulus does, the conditioned stimulus will have less effect. Further, if an animal has associated a particular conditioned stimulus with a certain unconditioned stimulus and a new conditioned stimulus is presented, the animal will typically not develop a response to the new conditioned stimulus. Psychologists refer to this lack of a response to the new stimulus as blocking.

The conditioned stimulus seems to exert its effect by providing information to the animal. If the animal has already gained information through an initial conditioned stimulus, the second one will not be very useful. Similarly, if the potential conditioned stimulus does not always occur with the unconditioned stimulus, the information provided by the conditioned stimulus is less useful to the animal. If the conditioned stimulus occurs without the unconditioned stimulus, **extinction** will occur; that is, the conditioned stimulus will no longer have an effect. The reflex can be conditioned more easily the second time around if the two are again paired. Sometimes, after extinction has taken place, the conditioned stimulus will produce the reflexive behavior without the unconditioned stimulus, a process called spontaneous recovery.

Psychologists have applied knowledge of classical conditioning to human behavior. For example, people with allergies may rely on drugs that have unwanted side effects. Their allergies have been alleviated by pairing a unique odor (the conditioned stimulus) with the drug (the unconditioned stimulus). Over time, presentation of the odor by itself may alleviate the allergic symptoms.

Conditioning

A broad term to describe techniques used by psychologists to study the process of learning.

Psychology has often been defined as the study of behavior. As such, psychologists have developed a diverse array of methods for studying both human and animal activity. Two of the most commonly used techniques are **classical conditioning** and **operant conditioning.** They have been used to study the process of learning, one of the key areas of interest to psychologists in the early days of psychology. Psychologists also attach considerable significance to conditioning because it has been effective in changing human and animal behavior in predictable and desirable ways.

The Russian physiologist **Ivan Pavlov** developed the principles of classical conditioning. In his Nobel Prize-winning research on the digestive processes, he placed meat powder in the mouths of his research animals and recorded their levels of salivation. At one point, he noticed that some of his research animals began to salivate in the absence of food. He reasoned that the presence of the animal caretakers led the animals to anticipate the meat powder, so they began to salivate even without the food.

When classical conditioning occurs, an animal or person initially responds to a naturally occurring stimulus with a natural response (e.g., the food leads to salivation). Then the food is systematically paired with a previously neutral stimulus (e.g., a bell), one that does not lead to any particular response. With repeated pairings, the natural response occurs when the neutral stimulus appears.

Pavlovian (i.e., classical) conditioning influenced psychologists greatly, even though Pavlov himself was skeptical of the work psychologists performed. In the United States, **John Watson**, the first widely known behaviorist, used the principles of classical conditioning in his research. For example, in a widely cited study, Watson tried to develop a classically conditioned phobia in an infant.

Although classical conditioning became the dominant Russian model for the study of **behaviorism,** another form of conditioning took hold in the United States. This version, which became known as operant or instrumental conditioning, initially developed from the ideas of the psychologist **Edward Thorndike.** Thorndike began his psychological research by studying learning in chickens, then in cats. Based on the problem solving of these animals, he developed the **Law of Effect,** which in simple form states that a behavior that has a positive outcome is likely to be repeated. Similarly, his Law of Exercise states that the more a response occurs in a given situation, the more strongly it is linked with that situation, and the more likely it is to be repeated in the future.

Operant conditioning was popularized by the psychologist **B.F. Skinner**. His research and writings influenced not only psychologists but also the general public. Operant conditioning differs from classical conditioning in that, whereas classical conditioning relies on an organism's response to some stimulus in the environment, operant conditioning relies on the organism's initiating an action that is followed by some consequence.

For example, when a hungry person puts money into a vending machine, he or she is rewarded with some product. In psychologists' terms, the behavior is reinforced; in everyday language, the person is satisfied with the outcome. As a result, the next time the person is hungry, he or she is likely to repeat the behavior of putting money into the machine. On the other hand, if the machine malfunctions and the person gets no food, that individual is less likely to repeat the behavior in the future. This refers to **punishment**.

Any time a behavior leads to a positive outcome that is likely to be repeated, psychologists say that behavior has been reinforced. When the behavior leads to a negative outcome, psychologists refer to punishment. Two types of **reinforcement** and punishment have been described: positive and negative.

Positive reinforcement is generally regarded as synonymous with reward: when a behavior appears, something positive results. This leads to a greater likelihood that the behavior will recur. Negative reinforcement involves the termination of an unpleasant situation. Thus, if a person has a headache, taking some kind of pain reliever leads to a satisfying outcome. In the future, when the person has a headache, he or she is likely to take that pain reliever again. In positive and negative reinforcement, some behavior is likely to recur either because something positive results or something unpleasant stops.

Just as reinforcement comes in two versions, punishment takes two forms. Psychologists have identified positive punishment as the presentation of an unpleasant result when an undesired behavior occurs. On the other hand, when something positive is removed, this is called negative punishment. In both forms of punishment, an undesired behavior results in a negative consequence. As a result, the undesired behavior is less likely to recur in the future.

Many people mistakenly equate negative reinforcement with punishment because the word "negative" conjures up the idea of punishment. In reality, a situation involving negative reinforcement involves the removal of a negative stimulus, leading to a more satisfying situation. A situation involving punishment always leads to an unwanted outcome.

Beginning with Watson and Skinner, psychology in the United States adopted a behavioral framework in which researchers began to study people and animals through conditioning. From the 1920s through the 1960s, many psychologists performed conditioning experiments with animals with the idea that what was true for animals would also be true for humans. Psychologists assumed that the principles of conditioning were universal. Although many of the principles of learning and conditioning developed in animal research pertain to human learning and conditioning, psychologists now realize that each species has its own behavioral characteristics. Consequently, although the principles of conditioning may generalize from animals to humans, researchers must consider the differences across species as well.

Further Reading

Mackintosh, N. J. *Conditioning and Associative Learning.* New York: Oxford University Press, 1983.

Walker, James T. *The Psychology of Learning.* Upper Saddle River, NJ: Prentice-Hall, 1996.

Conduct Disorder

A psychiatric category of repetitive and persistent abnormal behavior of children and adolescents that violates the basic rights of others.

Conduct disorder may involve serious aggressive behavior that threatens or results in physical harm to other persons or animals, or nonaggressive behavior that causes property damage or loss. Examples of these behaviors include bullying, cruelty, fighting (especially with a weapon), mugging, vandalism, and arson. There are two subtypes of conduct disorder, childhood-onset and adolescent-onset, based on age at the first appearance of the condition. The childhood-onset type of conduct disorder is more likely to be associated with serious aggressive behavior and has a worse prognosis than the adolescent-onset type, but a significant number of individuals with either type of conduct disorder develop an **antisocial personality** as adults. The incidence of conduct disorder is higher among boys than among girls, higher in urban **environment**s than in suburban and rural environments, and may be generally increasing. Conduct disorder is often associated with lower-than-average **intelligence,** and is one of the most frequently diagnosed conditions in mental health facilities for children.

See also Aggression.

Further Reading

Toth, Michele. *Understanding and Treating Conduct Disorders.* Austin, TX: Pro-Ed, 1990.

Kernberg, Paulina F. *Children with Conduct Disorders: A Psychotherapy Manual.* New York: Basic Books, 1991.

Conflict Resolution

The process of resolving interpersonal, social, professional, or political conflicts.

While conflicts—disagreements resulting from incompatible or opposing needs, drives, wishes, or internal demands—may be harmful to individuals and groups, they can be resolved in ways that benefit all concerned. Organizational research has indicated that it is more effective to manage and resolve conflicts than to sidestep or eliminate them. Similar methods may be used to resolve the various types of interpersonal conflicts (as opposed to intrapersonal conflicts, which involve the mental struggles within an individual over competing choices or courses of action). Conflicts may have several basic resolutions: one of the competing options may be chosen over the other(s); a compromise solution, either proposed beforehand or resolved in the resolution process, may be agreed upon; or the opposing parties may

The resolution of conflict takes many forms—from settling an argument between two children on a playground to mediation of disputes between two nations. One of former U.S. president Jimmy Carter's achievements was the mediation of an agreement between Israel and Egypt.

CAMP DAVID PEACE AGREEMENT

One of the major accomplishments of Jimmy Carter, U.S. president from 1976-1980, was the mediation of a peace agreement between Israel and Egypt. The agreement was signed by the two countries at Camp David, the U.S. presidential retreat, in September 1978. The so-called Camp David Accords were reached largely through Carter's personal skill at facilitating the resolution of conflict between the two nations.

terminate their relationship if they are unable to reach an agreement.

The most common method of managing conflicts that involve more than one person is bargaining, which may be divided into two main types: distributive and integrative. In distributive bargaining, the opposing sides attempt to change each others' preferences through argument or coercion. Communication may be both verbal and nonverbal. Verbal bargaining, or negotiation, usually involves an exchange of offers and counteroffers by the

two sides. It may also include threats or nonverbal intimidation. A resolution based on the superior power of one side is said to be based on coercion. The achievement of a compromise depends upon being able to reach a viable solution—one that provides each party with an outcome that is more acceptable than leaving the conflict unresolved or ending the relationship. Integrative bargaining consists of developing options not present at the outset of negotiations that offer all parties advantages over their existing situations. One common technique in integrative bargaining is log-rolling: introducing supplementary issues as bargaining chips to help resolve the primary conflict. Ideally, bargaining results in a win-win situation, in which each side gains what is most important while conceding on those issues that are less crucial.

Conflicts may also be resolved through norm-following, which relies on the invocation of rules or precedents. Knowledge of general societal norms may be invoked, or the norms may pertain directly to the relationship of the parties involved in the conflict ("the last time we disagreed about which movie to see, I agreed to see *The Terminator* if you would see *Terms of Endearment*") or to comparable experiences in other relationship, either past or present ("my other professors give me extra time on exams"). Another method of resolving conflicts is by introducing superordinate goals that focus the attention of potentially opposed parties (such as rivals for promotion) on their common bonds and goals (setting shared departmental goals for increased productivity) in order to defuse antagonism over a possible source of conflict.

When other methods of conflict resolution fail, third-party intervention by an outside mediator may be effective. A mediator can assist the two sides in clarifying their positions, defuse emotions, and focus on important issues. Mediation can also restore communications that have broken down altogether. Depending on the circumstances, an outside mediator may either impose an agreement on the opposing parties or provide nonbinding suggestions for resolving the conflict. In mediation that is not imposed, the ultimate responsibility for resolving the conflict remains with the opposing parties themselves: the mediator assists them in finding a solution but should retain an active role in the process. Roles played by a mediator include those of courier, interpreter educator, and catalyst.

Whereas conflict resolution at other levels involves interpersonal strategies, the resolution of intrapersonal conflicts—such as a decision between two career choices—consists mostly of assembling the information necessary for the decision and arranging one's priorities. **Psychotherapy** is an important means of resolving intrapersonal conflicts, as conflicts between different **motivations** exert a strong influence on human behavior. Four basic types of conflict have been identified: 1) *approach-approach* conflicts, in which a person must choose between two desirable activities that cannot both be pursued; 2) *avoidance-avoidance* conflicts, in which neither choice in a situation is considered acceptable and one must choose the lesser of two evils; 3) *approach-avoidance* conflicts, where one event or activity has both positive and negative features; and 4) *multiple approach-avoidance* conflicts, which involves two or more alternatives, all of which have both positive and negative features.

Further Reading

Boulding, Kenneth Ewart. *Conflict and Defense: a General Theory.* Lanham, MD: University Press of America, 1988.

Cahn, Dudley, ed. *Conflict in Personal Relationships.* Hillsdale, NJ: L. Erlbaum Associates, 1994.

Fisher, Ronald J. *The Social Psychology of Intergroup and International Conflict Resolution.* New York: Springer-Verlag, 1990.

Conformity

Adaptation of one's behavior or beliefs to match those of the other members of a group.

Conformity occurs in response to unspoken group pressure, as opposed to compliance, which results from overt pressure. Both conformity and compliance are attempts to adhere to social norms—informal agreements about what is and is not appropriate behavior in particular situations. In most cases, conforming to social norms is so natural that people are not even aware they are doing it unless someone calls it to their attention or violates the norms.

Through controlled experiments, researchers have been able to learn some key facts about the nature of conformity. The first classic experiment in conformity was carried out in the 1930s by Muzafer Sherif. It made use of an optical illusion called the autokinetic phenomenon, which refers to the fact that a small stationary point of light in a darkened room will appear to move. However, the amount of movement experienced by different people varies. Sherif found that when several subjects were placed together in a room with a stationary light and each was asked to describe its movement out loud, their answers became increasingly similar as they unconsciously sought to establish a group norm. The power of social norms was demonstrated even more strikingly when the subjects continued to adhere to the norm later when they were retested individually.

Sherif's experiment demonstrates one of the important conditions that produces conformity: ambiguity. There was no clear-cut right answer to the question asked of the subjects, so they were more vulnerable to reliance on a norm. In the 1950s another researcher, Solomon Asch, devised a conformity experiment that eliminated the ambiguity factor. Subjects were asked to match lines of different lengths on two cards, where one answer was obviously the right one. However, each subject was tested in a room full of "planted" peers who deliberately gave the wrong answer in some cases. About three-fourths of the subjects tested knowingly gave an incorrect answer at least once in order to conform to the group.

Asch's experiment revealed other factors—notably unanimity and size of the majority—that influence conformity even when ambiguity is not an issue. Unanimity of opinion is extremely powerful in influencing people to go along with the group. Even one dissenter decreases the incidence of conformity markedly—people are much more likely to diverge from a group when there is at least one other person to share that group's potential disapproval. People who follow the lead of an initial dissenter may even disagree with that person and be dissenting from the group for a totally different reason. However, knowing there is at least one other dissenting voice makes it easier for them to express their own opinions.

Situational factors like ambiguity and unanimity are not the sole determinants of conformity. Given the same situation, different individuals will conform to different degrees, so personal characteristics play a role as well. Persons who have a low status within a group or are unfamiliar with a particular situation are the ones most likely to conform. **Personality** traits, such as concern with being liked or desire to be right, also play a role. Cultural factors are important as well, as certain cultures are more likely than others to value group harmony over individual expression.

Further Reading

Cialdini, Robert B. *Influence: Science and Practice.* 3rd ed. New York: HarperCollins College Publishers, 1993.

Paulus, Paul B., ed. *Psychology of Group Influence.* 2nd ed. Hillsdale, NJ: L. Erlbaum, 1989.

Conscience

The moral dimension of human consciousness, the means by which humans modify instinctual drives to conform to laws and moral codes.

Sigmund Freud viewed the conscience as one of two components of the **superego**, the other being the **ego**-ideal. In this scheme, the conscience prevents people from doing things that are morally wrong, and the ego-ideal motivates people to do things that are considered morally right. This theory suggests that the conscience is developed by parents, who convey their beliefs to their children. They in turn internalize these moral codes by a process of identification with a parent.

Other psychologists have proposed different theories about the development of the conscience.

See also Moral Development.

Further Reading

Weissbud, Bernice. "How Kids Develop a Conscience." *Parents' Magazine* (December 1991): 156.

Consciousness

Awareness of external stimuli and of one's own mental activity.

Wilhelm Wundt's investigations of consciousness, begun in 1879, were central to the development of psychology as a field of study. Wundt's approach, called structuralism, sought to determine the structure of consciousness by recording the verbal descriptions provided by laboratory subjects to various stimuli, a method that became known as introspection. The next major approach to the study of consciousness was the functionalism of **William James,** who focused on how consciousness helps people adapt to their **environment.** Behaviorism, pioneered by **John B. Watson** in the early 1900s, shifted interest from conscious processes to observable behaviors, and the study of consciousness faded into the background for almost half a century, especially in the United States, until it was revived by the "cognitive revolution" that began in the 1950s and 1960s.

The existence of different levels of consciousness was at the heart of **Sigmund Freud**'s model of human mental functioning. In addition to the conscious level, consisting of thoughts and feelings of which one is aware, Freud proposed the existence of the **unconscious,** a repository for thoughts and feelings that are repressed because they are painful or unacceptable to the conscious mind for some other reason. He also formulated the concept of the preconscious, which functions as an intermediate or transitional level of mind between the unconscious and the conscious. A preconscious thought can quickly become conscious by receiving **attention,** and a conscious thought can slip into the preconscious when attention is withdrawn from it. In contrast, the repressed material contained in the unconscious can only be retrieved through some special technique, such as hypnosis or dream interpretation. (What Freud called the unconscious is today referred to by many psychologists as the subconscious.) Freud's contemporary, **Carl Jung,** posited the existence of a collective unconscious shared by all people which gathers together the experiences of

previous generations. The collective unconscious contains images and symbols, called **archetype**s, that Jung found are shared by people of diverse cultures and tend to emerge in dreams, myths, and other forms. In Jung's view, a thorough analysis of both the personal and collective unconscious was necessary to fully understand the individual **personality**.

People experience not only different levels, but also different states of consciousness, ranging from wakefulness (which may be either active or passive) to deep **sleep.** Although sleep suspends the voluntary exercise of both bodily functions and consciousness, it is a much more active state than was once thought. Tracking brain waves with the aid of electroencephalograms (EEGs), researchers have identified six stages of sleep (including a pre-sleep stage), each characterized by distinctive brain-wave frequencies. In **Rapid Eye Movement (REM)** sleep, which makes up 20% of sleep time, the same fast-frequency, low-amplitude beta waves that characterize waking states occur, and a person's physiological signs—heart rate, breathing, and blood pressure—also resemble those of a waking state. It is during REM sleep that dreams are experienced. Delta waves demarcate the deepest levels of sleep, when heart rate, respiration, temperature, and blood flow to the **brain** are reduced and growth hormone is secreted.

Certain waking states, which are accompanied by marked changes in mental processes, are considered states of altered consciousness. One of these is **hypnosis,** a highly responsive state induced by a hypnotist through the use of special techniques. While the term "hypnosis" comes from the Greek word for sleep (*hypnos*), hypnotized people are not really asleep. Their condition resembles sleep in that they are relaxed and out of touch with ordinary environmental demands, but their minds remain active and conscious. Other characteristics of hypnosis include lack of initiative, selective redistribution of attention, enhanced **ability** to fantasize, reduced reality testing, and increased suggestibility. Also, hypnosis is often followed by post-hypnotic amnesia, in which the person is unable to remember what happened during the hypnotic session. Hypnosis has proven useful in preventing or controlling various types of pain, including pain from dental work, childbirth, burns, arthritis, nerve damage, and migraine headaches.

In meditation, an altered state of consciousness is achieved by performing certain rituals and exercises. Typical characteristics of the meditative state include intensified **perception,** an altered sense of time, decreased distraction from external stimuli, and a sense that the experience is pleasurable and rewarding. While meditation is traditionally associated with Zen Buddhism, a secular form called Transcendental Meditation (TM) has been widely used in the United States for purposes of relaxation. It has been found that during this type of meditation, people consume less oxygen, eliminate less carbon dioxide, and breathe more slowly than when they are in an ordinary resting state.

Consciousness may be altered in a dramatic fashion by the use of psychoactive **drugs,** which affect the interaction of **neurotransmitter**s and receptors in the brain. They include illegal "street drugs," tranquilizers and other prescription medications, and such familiar substances as alcohol, tobacco, and coffee. The major categories of psychoactive drugs include depressants, which reduce activity of the **central nervous system**; sedatives, another type of depressant that includes barbiturates such as Seconal and Nembutal; anxiolytics (traditionally referred to as tranquilizers); narcotics—including heroin and its derivatives—which are addictive drugs that cause both drowsiness and euphoria, and are also pain-killers; psychostimulants, such as amphetamines and cocaine, which stimulate alertness, increase excitability, and elevate moods; and psychedelics or hallucinogens, such as marijuana and LSD. Psychedelics, which affect **moods,** thought, **memory,** and perception, are particularly known for their consciousness-altering properties. They can produce distortion of one's body image, loss of identity, dreamlike fantasies, and **hallucinations.** LSD (lysergic acid diethylamide), one of the most powerful psychedelic drugs, can cause hallucinations in which time is distorted, sounds produce visual sensations, and an out-of-body feeling is experienced.

Various states of consciousness are viewed differently by different cultures and even subcultures. In the United States, for example, hallucinations are devalued by mainstream culture as a bizarre sign of insanity, whereas the youth counterculture of the 1960s viewed drug-induced hallucinations as enlightening, "mind-expanding" experiences. In certain other societies, hallucinations are respected as an important therapeutic tool used by ritual healers.

Further Reading

Dennett, D.C. *Brainstorms.* Cambridge, MA: Bradford Books, 1980.

Freud, Sigmund. "The Unconscious." In *The Standard Edition of the Complete Psychological Works of Sigmund Freud.* London: Hogarth Press, 1962.

Contrast

The relative difference in intensity between two stimuli and their effect on each other.

Contrast, or contrast effect, is the effect a visual stimulus has on another. When one stimulus is present, it

Illustration of contrast effect. The center box is the same shade of gray in both the top and bottom drawings, but the different borders cause the centers to be perceived as different.

affects the other. As can be seen in the illustration, two gray boxes of equal intensity are surrounded by, in one case, a white field, and in the other, a black field. The perceived shade of gray is affected by the contrasting field.

Psychologists also study the contrast threshold, the point at which differences in two stimuli can be detected. These tests are used in the study of visual **perception** and the **ability** to perceive spatial relationships. Understanding contrast effect has practical applications. For example, black and yellow have the lowest contrast effect, which means the largest percentage of the population can clearly detect the difference between these two colors. Therefore, black and yellow are the colors used to mark school buses and on many traffic signs.

Control Group

In an experiment that focuses on the effects of a single condition or variable, the group that is exposed to all the conditions or variables except the one being studied.

Scientists often study how a particular condition or factor influences an outcome. In such an experiment, in which there are two groups of subjects, the group that is exposed to the condition or factor is called the experimental group. The other group, which provides a basis for comparison, is called the control group. For example, in a hypothetical study of the influence of the presence of loud music on the test performances of children, the control group would consist of the group of children not exposed to the loud music during the test. Their test scores would be compared with the experimental group, the group of children who were exposed to loud music during the test. In this type of **experimental design,** subjects would be randomly assigned to each group to ensure a reliable comparison.

Further Reading

Atkinson, Rita L.; Richard C. Atkinson; Edward E. Smith; and Ernest R. Hilgard. *Introduction to Psychology.* 9th ed. San Diego: Harcourt Brace Jovanovich, 1987.

Zimbardo, Philip G. *Psychology and Life.* 12th ed. Glenview, IL: Scott, Foresman, 1988.

Conversion Reaction

A psychological disorder characterized by physical symptoms for which no physiological cause can be found.

This condition was first described by **Sigmund Freud** as conversion hysteria because it involved the conversion of a repressed emotional problem to a physiological form. Today, conversion reaction is classified as a somatoform disorder in the American Psychiatric Association's *Diagnostic and Statistical Manual of Mental Disorders (DSM-IV).*

Conversion reaction is a very rare condition, accounting for about 2 percent of all psychiatric diagnoses, and usually first appears during **adolescence** or early adulthood, generally when an individual is under severe **stress.** Symptoms tend to be both specific and severe, and generally interferes with daily activities. A conversion disorder may serve as a way for a patient to avoid activities or situations associated with a source of emotional conflict or even shut down **conscious** awareness of the conflict itself. Another source of "secondary gain" is the attraction of **attention,** sympathy, and support that the patient may need but is unable to obtain in other ways.

Some of the most common symptoms of conversion disorder are paralysis, blindness or tunnel vision, seizures, loss of sensation, and disturbance of coordinated movements, such as walking. Other physical complaints include tremors, abdominal pain, and speech impairments such as aphonia, the inability to speak above a whisper. Sometimes a person will experience anesthesia in only one part of the body, such as "glove anesthesia," which affects the hand only up to the wrist, although such a problem could have no physiological origin since there is no cut-off point between the **nerve**s of the hand and arm. Symptoms may also involve the **endocrine glands** or **autonomic nervous system**s. If the symptoms of a conversion disorder are prolonged, they may produce physiological damage by interrupting the normal functioning of the body, and psychological damage by inducing excessive dependence on family members and other persons.

Further Reading

Freud, Sigmund. *The Standard Edition of the Complete Psychological Works of Sigmund Freud.* London: Hogarth Press, 1962.
——-. *Dora: An Analysis of a Case of Hysteria.* New York: Collier, 1963.

Correlation Method

A technique used to measure the likelihood of two behaviors relating to each other.

Psychologists are often interested in deciding whether two behaviors tend to occur together. One means of making this assessment involves using correlations. Sometimes two measurements are associated so that when the value of one increases, so does the other—a positive correlation. On the other hand, one value may increase systematically as the other decreases—a negative correlation.

For example, the number of correct answers on a student's test is generally positively related to the number of hours spent studying. Students who produce more correct answers have spent more hours studying; similarly, fewer correct answers occur with fewer hours spent studying.

One could also see whether the number of wrong answers on a test is associated with study time. This pattern is likely to produce a negative correlation: a greater number of wrong answers is associated with less study time. That is, the value of one variable increases (wrong answers) as the other decreases (hours spent studying).

Correlations allow an assessment of whether two variables are systematically related within a group of individuals. A single person may show behavior that differs from most of the rest of the group. For example, a given student might study for many hours and still not perform well on a test. This does not mean that study time and test grades are not related; it only means that exceptions exist for individuals, even if the rest of the group is predictable.

It is critical to remember that correlational approaches do not allow us to make statements about causation. Thus, greater study time may not necessarily cause higher grades. Students who are interested in a particular subject do better because of their interest; they also study more because they like the material. It may be their interest that is more important than the study time. One of the limitations of the correlational method is that although one variable (such as study time) may have a causal role on the other (such as test scores), one does not know that for certain because some other important factor (such as interest in the material) may be the most important element associated with both greater study time and higher test scores. When a third element is responsible for both variables (increase in study time and increase in grades), psychologists refer to this as the third variable problem.

The British scientist Sir **Francis Galton** developed the concept of the correlational method. The British statistician Karl Pearson (1857–1936) worked out the mathematical formulation. There are several different types of correlations; the most commonly used is called the Pearson Product-Moment Correlation.

See also Research Method; Scientific Method.

Counseling Psychology

An area of psychology which focuses on nurturing the development potential of relatively healthy individuals in all areas of their lives.

While the counseling psychologist may diagnose, assess, and treat **adjustment** difficulties, they often address problems which are more moderate than those encountered by the clinical psychologist. Clients of counseling psychologists are people who need help coping with the stresses of everyday life, and the focus is on strengthening their existing resources rather than overcoming disorders or deficits in particular areas. The counseling psychologist may use a number of tools in treating clients, including **psychotherapy,** workshops in such areas as assertiveness training or communications skills, and **psychological assessment**s. These tests are used to measure a person's aptitudes, interests, or **personality** characteristics and provide feedback which can facilitate the counseling process. Clients may be treated individually, in **group therapy,** or in family groups, depending on the nature of the problems and the specializa-

tion of the counselor. In contrast to a clinical psychotherapist, the counseling psychologist may intervene in the client's immediate **environment.** Also, unlike traditional psychotherapy, the relationship between counselor and client may extend to situations outside the office setting.

Counseling psychology has its roots in education and vocational guidance and has been closely linked with the use of mental testing, which is central to these fields. It has traditionally followed an educational rather than a medical model, considering those it helps as clients rather than patients. Its educational context is also evident in its emphasis on developmental models derived from the work of **Erik Erikson,** Robert Havighurst, Daniel Levinson, Roger Gould, and other theorists. Counseling psychologists work on helping clients remove obstacles to optimal development. A focus on adult development is helpful to many types of clients, such as women returning to the work force, or individuals undertaking second careers. Counseling psychology, paralleling a growing trend among health care providers, also advocates preventive as well remedial approaches to problems, seeking to identify "at risk" individuals and groups and intervene before a crisis occurs.

Of the psychotherapeutic models available to counseling psychology at its inception in the 1940s, Rogerian, or **client-centered therapy** has had the most influence. **Carl Rogers,** whose methods were more readily understood and adapted by counselors than those of **Sigmund Freud,** had a lasting influence on the techniques of vocational counseling and counseling psychology, which focus more on the process than on the outcome of the counseling relationship. Two other theoretical models that have been especially influential are decision-making theory and the social influence model. The former attempts to teach clients procedures and strategies for effective decision making, including such techniques as weighing the factors in a decision according to a numerical point system. Decision-making is related to counseling psychology's overall emphasis on problem solving.

Social influence theory, currently one of the prevailing theories in the field, involves the counselor's influence over the client based on how the client perceives him or her in terms of such factors as credibility and degree of expertise. Researchers have studied the behaviors that contribute to the counselor's social influence; the ways in which social influence can be maximized; and social influence in relation to such factors as race, gender, age, and social class. Over the years, the fields of counseling psychology and psychotherapy have begun to overlap as clinical psychologists have concentrated more on relatively healthy clients and counselors have grown to rely more heavily on psychotherapeutic techniques. There has also been a growing overlap between counseling and social work, as social workers have moved in the direction of therapeutic counseling themselves. Thus, there has been an overlap between these professions.

Most counselor training programs are offered by colleges of education rather than psychology departments. As the establishment of credentials has become more and more important (particularly with regard to payments by insurance companies), counseling psychology programs are offering (and requiring) an increased amount of training in basic psychology, which can include rigorous internship programs. Counseling psychology has its own division, Division 17, of the **American Psychological Association,** and its own professional publications, including *The Counseling Psychologist,* a quarterly, and the *Journal of Counseling Psychology,* which appears bimonthly.

Further Reading

Brammer, Lawrence M. *Therapeutic Psychology: Fundamentals of Counseling and Psychotherapy.* 5th ed. Englewood Cliffs, NJ: Prentice Hall, 1989.

Vernon, Ann, ed. *Counseling Children and Adolescents.* Denver, CO: Love, 1993.

Ronch, Judah L, William van Ornum, and Nicholas C. Stilwell, eds. *The Counseling Sourcebook: A Practical Reference on Contemporary Issues.* New York: Crossroad, 1994.

Creativity

The ability to juxtapose ideas in a new and unusual way in order to find solutions to problems, create new inventions, or produce works of art.

While it is generally associated with the arts, creativity can play a role in any human endeavor. Graham Wallas's 1962 study of well-known scientists and other innovators yielded a widely used breakdown of the creative process into four stages. The preparation stage consists of formulating a problem, studying previous work on it, and thinking intensely about it. In the incubation stage, there is no visible progress on the problem; it may be periodically "mulled over," but it is largely left dormant, allowing subconscious ideas about to emerge. At the illumination stage, an important insight about the problem is reached, often in a sudden, intuitive fashion. In the final, or verification, stage, the idea is tested and evaluated.

Creativity differs from the kinds of abilities measured by standard **intelligence** tests. Although creative people do tend to have average or above-average scores on **IQ tests**, beyond an IQ of about 120 there is little correlation between intelligence and creativity. J.P. Guilford first distinguished the thought processes of creative people from those of other people in terms of convergent and divergent thinking. Convergent thinking—the type required for traditional IQ tests—involves the application of logic and knowledge to narrow the number of possible solutions to a problem until one's thoughts "converge" on the most appropriate choice. In contrast, divergent thinking—the kind most closely associated with creativity and originality—involves being able to envision multiple ways to solve a problem. Guilford identified three aspects of divergent thinking: fluency entails the **ability** to come up with many different solutions to a problem in a short amount of time; flexibility is the capacity to consider many alternatives at the same time; and originality refers to the difference between a person's ideas and those of most other people.

Special tests, such as the Consequences Test, have been designed to assess creativity. Instead of being based on one correct answer for each question, as in conventional intelligence tests, the scoring on these tests is based on the number of different plausible responses generated for each question, or the extent to which a person's answers differ from those of most other test takers. Typical questions asked on such tests include "Imagine all of the things that might possibly happen if all national and local laws were suddenly abolished" and "Name as many uses as you can think of for a paper clip." While divergent thinking is important to the creative process, it is not the sole element necessary for creative achievement. Researchers have found little correlation between the scores of fifth and tenth graders on divergent thinking tests and their actual achievements in high school in such fields as art, drama, and science.

It appears that creative accomplishment requires both divergent and convergent thinking. Originality is not the only criterion of a successful solution to a problem: it must also be appropriate for its purpose, and convergent thinking allows one to evaluate ideas and discard them if they are inappropriate in the light of existing information. In addition, studies of people known for their creative accomplishments show that certain **personality** traits that may be impossible to measure on a test—such as **motivation,** initiative, tolerance for ambiguity, and independent judgment—are commonly associated with creativity. Other traits known to be shared by highly creative people include self-confidence, nonconformity, ambition, and perseverance. Albert Einstein (1879–1955) once remarked that for every hundred thoughts he had, one turned out to be correct.

In a 1986 study, a group of researchers identified three essential criteria for creative achievement: expertise in a specific field, which must be learned; creative skills, including divergent thinking; and the motivation to engage in creative activity for its own sake regardless of external reward. In this study, items created by people

Creativity, often associated with fine and performing arts, can be an important factor in all human endeavors, from problem-solving to interpersonal relations.

who were told that their work would be judged and possibly rewarded for creativity were found to be less creative than the results produced by those who were simply asked to work on a project with no prospect of external reward.

Creativity does not appear to be inherited. There is evidence that environmental influences play at least as great a role in the development of creativity as intelligence: the creative skills of identical twins reared apart vary more than their intellectual abilities. Studies have shown that reinforcing novel ideas in both children and adults leads to increased creativity. The originality of block arrangements produced by four-year-olds increased dramatically when novel designs were praised by adults; when this positive **reinforcement** was stopped, the children reverted to producing unimaginative patterns. Other studies have used similar techniques to boost creativity scores of fifth graders, improve the originality of stories written by sixth graders, and increase the ability of college students to produce novel word associations. One interesting finding in studies such as these is that positively reinforcing one kind of creative activity encourages original thinking in other areas as well. The play of children is closely related to the development of

creativity. The sensory stimulation that results from exposure to new objects and activities reinforces the exploratory impulse in both children and adults and results in an openness to new experiences and ideas that fosters creative thinking.

Further Reading
Briggs, John. *Fire in the Crucible: The Alchemy of Creative Genius.* New York: St. Martin's Press, 1988.
Guilford, J. P. *The Nature of Human Intelligence.* New York: McGraw-Hill, 1967.

Critical Period

A specified time span, also referred to as the optimal or sensitive period, during which certain events or experiences must occur in order for the development of an organism to proceed normally.

Although this term is used in a variety of contexts, the term most closely associated with **ethology**, the study of animal behavior in its natural **environment** from the perspective of evolutionary **adaptation**. The critical period plays an important role in the concept of **imprint-**

ing, first used by Konrad Lorenz in connection with the earliest process of social attachment in young animals. (However, the term imprinting is also applicable to any irreversible behavioral response acquired early in life and normally released by a specific triggering stimulus or situation.) In the most famous example of imprinting, Lorenz demonstrated that exposure to an appropriately maternal object during a critical period would activate the "following" instinct of newborn goslings: he successfully had a group of goslings follow him after he "impersonated" their absent mother.

Other examples of critical periods include the initial four months of life during which puppies must be exposed to humans in order to make good pets and the early months in which birds must be exposed to the characteristic song of their species in order to learn it. Critical periods vary in length: the period for identifying one's mother may last only a few hours, while the period for learning to identify a mate may take several months.

The specifically human phenomenon of **language** development also appears to be subject to a critical period. So-called "wild" or "feral" children deprived of human society for an extended period show that they have been unable to catch up on language due to lack of exposure early in life.

The term "critical period" is also used to describe physiological as well as behavioral phenomena. For example, the embryonic stage in humans is a critical period for certain types of growth (such as the appearance of the heart, eyes, ears, hands, and feet) which must occur for prenatal development to proceed normally.

Further Reading

Denny, M. Ray. *Comparative Psychology: Research in Animal Behavior.* New York: Dorset Press, 1970.

Lorenz, Konrad. *The Foundation of Ethology.* New York: Springer-Verlag, 1981.

Cross-Cultural Psychology

A subfield of psychology concerned with observing human behavior in contrasting cultures.

Studies in this discipline attempt to expand the compass of psychological research beyond the few highly industrialized nations on which it has traditionally focused. While definitions of what constitutes a culture vary widely, most experts concur that "culture" involves patterns of behavior, symbols, and values. The prominent anthropologist Clifford Geertz has described culture as ". . . a historically transmitted pattern of meanings embodied in symbols, a system of inherited conceptions expressed in symbolic forms by means of which men communicate, perpetuate, and develop their knowledge about and attitudes toward life."

While cross-cultural psychology and anthropology often overlap, both disciplines tend to focus on different aspects of a culture. For example, many issues of interest to psychologists are not addressed by anthropologists, who have their own concerns traditionally, including such topics as kinship, land distribution, and ritual. When anthropologists do concentrate on areas of psychology, they focus on activities whereby data can be collected through direct observation, such as the age of children at weaning or child rearing practices. However, there is no significant body of anthropological data on many of the more abstract questions commonly addressed by psychologists, such as cultural conceptions of **intelligence**.

Cross-cultural research can yield important information on many topics of interest to psychologists. In one of the best known studies, researchers found evidence that human perceptual processes develop differently depending on what types of shapes and angles people are exposed to daily in their environment. People living in countries such as the United States with many buildings containing 90-degree angles are susceptible to different optical illusions than those in rural African villages, where such buildings are not the norm. Cross-cultural studies have also discovered that the symptoms of most psychological disorders vary from one culture to another, and has led to a reconsideration of what constitutes normal human sexuality. For example, **homosexuality,** long considered pathological behavior in the United States, is approved of in other cultures and is even encouraged in some as a normal sexual outlet before marriage.

Collection of cross-cultural data can also shed new light on standard psychological theories. In the 1920s, the anthropologist Bronislaw Malinowski observed that young boys living in the Trobriand islands exhibited the type of hostility that **Sigmund Freud** had described in his formulation of the **Oedipus complex,** only it was directed not at their fathers but at a maternal uncle who was assigned the role of family disciplinarian. This observation posed a challenge to Freud's oedipal theory by raising the possibility that boys' tense relations with their fathers at a certain period in their lives may be a reaction to discipline rather than a manifestation of sexual jealousy. The questions raised by Malinowski's observation demonstrate a particularly valuable type of contribution that cross-cultural research can make to psychology. Psychological research often confounds, or merges, two variables in a situation in this case, the boy's anger toward his father and the father's sexual role in relation to the mother. A cross-cultural perspective can untangle such confounded variables when it finds them occurring separately in other cultures—e.g., the disciplinarian (the uncle), and the mother's lover (the father), as two separate persons.

Cross-cultural psychology may also be practiced within a given society by studying the contrasts between its dominant culture and subcultures. A subculture—defined as a group of people whose experiences differ from those of the majority culture—may be constituted in different ways. Often, it is an ethnic, racial, or religious group. Any group that develops its own customs, norms, and jargon may be considered a subculture, however, including such deviant groups as drug or gang subcultures. A prominent area of intersection between psychological inquiry and subcultures within the United States has been the issue of cultural bias in testing. Today, testing experts assert that there is no evidence for bias across race or social class in "standardized" intelligence and **achievement tests.** However, children whose primary language is not English should be tested in their primary language.

Further Reading

Barnouw, Victor. *Culture and Personality.* 4th ed. Homewood, IL: Dorsey Press, 1985.

Bock, Philip K. *Rethinking Psychological Anthropology: Continuity and Change in the Study of Human Action.* New York: W.H. Freeman, 1988.

Cross-Sectional Study

Research that collects data simultaneously from people of different ages, in contrast to a longitudinal study, which follows one group of subjects over a period of time.

A cross-sectional study is a research method where data are collected at the same time from people in different age categories. It contrasts with the method, known as longitudinal study, where the same group of subjects is studied over time. One weakness, or confounding variable, of the cross-sectional study is that its subjects, in addition to being different ages, are also born in different years, and their behavior may thus be influenced by differences in education, cultural influences, and medical treatment. In the longitudinal study, data can be obtained from subjects of different ages born within the same period of time. However, a confounding variable in longitudinal studies is the degree to which each person's environmental influences will vary from those of others over the period of time covered by the experiment.

Cults

Highly organized groups led by a dynamic leader who exercises strong control.

A cult is a structured group, most of whose members demonstrate unquestioned loyalty to a dynamic leader. The cult leader governs most, if not all, aspects of the lives of his or her followers, often insisting that they break all ties with the world outside of the cult. Such groups are usually thought of in terms of religion, although other types of cults can and do exist.

The proliferation of religious cults in the United States is considered by many experts as symptomatic of the general social discordance that has plagued postwar Western society. Cults offer the allure of an ordered world that is easily understood. Clear rules of behavior are enforced and nagging questions about meaning and purpose are dispelled by the leader, who defines members' lives in service to the cult's interest. It is probably most useful to examine the phenomenon of cults without dwelling on the sensationalistic practices of the flamboyant, the infamous, and the suicidal. When a psychologist examines a cult and its dynamics, what is actually observed is the mental condition of the member; in other words, what is it about the individual that allows them to willingly relinquish themselves to such rigid and dogmatic ways of thinking and living?

To help understand this process, it might be useful to consider that many social organizations other that what we traditionally think of as cults require strict adherence to a set of beliefs and, in turn, provide a sense of meaning and purpose to their followers. Behavior that is not normally considered as being cult-like can be seen as having some of the main characteristics of cults. The rigid social contract of the military, for instance, is considered by many psychologists as being cult-like. Other social organizations that have had a profound impact on the lives of its followers include self-help groups, such as Alcoholics Anonymous, where selflessness and devotion to the group are highly valued and rewarded. Certain types of political groups and terrorist organizations are still other examples of "cults" that defy the common definition of the term. Dr. Arthur Deikman, clinical professor of psychiatry at the University of California at San Francisco, is one of many psychologists who has observed cultic behavior in many areas of society other than in extremist religious groups. In the introduction to his 1990 book, *The Wrong Way Home: Uncovering the Patterns of Cult Behavior in American Society,* Deikman asserted that "behavior similar to that which takes place in extreme cults takes place in all of us," and suggested that "the longing for parents persists into adulthood and results in cult behavior that pervades normal society."

Because cultic behavior underlies more than extremist religious sects, many psychologists refer to these groups as charismatic groups. Marc Galanter, professor of psychiatry at New York University, defines the characteristics of charismatic groups in his study *Cults: Faith, Healing, and Coercion* (1989). According to Galanter, charismatic group members "1) have a shared belief system; 2) sustain a high level of social cohesiveness; 3) are strongly influenced by the group's behavioral norms, and 4) impute charismatic (or sometimes divine) power to the group or its leadership." Other psychologists have devised additional theories to explain the drawing power of charismatic groups, and some conclude that people who devote themselves to such groups have not yet achieved the developmental stage of individuation. Still other experts, drawing on the field of sociobiology, suggest that the need to be part of a group has biological, evolutionary roots traceable to that period in human history when to be banned from the dominant hunter-gatherer group meant almost certain death.

Whatever the origins of the psychological need to be a part of a defined group, the fact is most people do not fall under the sway of charismatic groups. Typically, such groups find recruits among young people. Usually, such a young person is approached by friendly, outgoing recruiters for the cult who express a deep interest in the person's life and offer empathy and understanding for the difficulties they may be experiencing. These difficulties may be in relation to a failed romance, an unhappy family life, or an existential crisis of the sort usually associated with late **adolescence** in which a young person has no idea how they fit in the world. The recruiters are often trained to provide a "friendly ear" to troubled young people, to validate their experiences as being common, and, finally, to suggest that other people (such as themselves) have found solace in their groups.

During the process of initiation, recruits may experience severe psychological disorders as they at once begin and resist immersion into an entirely new system. Abandoning old allegiances and belief systems can bring about intense guilt before the recruit completely immerses him or herself into the charismatic group. Some psychologists believe that such mental illnesses as **dissociative identity disorder**s, pathologic adjustment reactions, major depressive disorders, and others may be attributed to the agonizing process of joining a charismatic group. Once immersed in the cult, members will often cut all ties with their past lives, ending contact with their families and friends as they join a new social order that seems to give them meaning and purpose. This kind of behavior is obviously less true of charismatic groups such as the military and some types of self-help groups, but these symptoms can nonetheless appear in less extreme forms.

Interviews with former cult members have revealed that in extremist religious cults, there are often tremendous obstacles to leaving. These obstacles can come in the form of peer pressure, where loyal cult members will intervene in the case of a member who has doubts about the cult and longs for his or her old life, or the obstacles may be physical ones for those whose cult lives communally in an isolated area. Often, family members of persons in religious cults hire what are called "deprogrammers" to kidnap their loved ones and take them to some neutral place where they can be reasoned with sensibly without the interference of other cult members espousing the group's prevailing ideology.

Most psychologists would probably acknowledge that there exists a deep human need to belong to a group. Often, this need leads people to form what might be viewed as unhealthy allegiances to a person or group who, ultimately, does not truly have the person's interest at heart.

Further Reading

Deikman, Arthur J. *The Wrong Way Home: Uncovering Patterns of Cult Behavior in American Society.* Boston: Beacon Press, 1990.

Deutsch, A. "Tenacity of Attachment to a Cult Leader: A Psychiatric Perspective." *American Journal of Psychiatry* 137 (1980): 1569-73.

Galanter, Marc. *Cults: Faith, Healing and Coercion.* Oxford: Oxford University Press, 1989.

Hall, J.R. "The Apocalypse at Jonestown." In *In Gods We Trust: New Patterns of Religious Pluralism in America,* edited by T. Robbins and D. Anthony. New Brunswick, NJ: Transaction Books, 1981.

D

Charles Robert Darwin

Darwin, Charles Robert (1809–1882)

British naturalist whose theory of organic evolution through natural selection revolutionized science.

Charles Robert Darwin was born in Shrewsbury, England. His father was a successful provincial physician, and his grandfather, Erasmus Darwin (1731–1802), had been a distinguished intellectual figure. Young Darwin attended the Shrewsbury School, and his early failure to achieve academic distinction continued at Edinburgh University, where he studied medicine, and at Cambridge University, where he studied theology. While at Cambridge, however, Darwin enthusiastically pursued natural history as an avocation, drawing the attention of botanist John Stevens Henslow (1796–1861) and geologist Adam Sedgwick (1785–1873). In 1831, through his connection with Henslow, Darwin joined the expedition team aboard the survey ship H.M.S. *Beagle* headed for the coasts of South America, the Galápagos Islands, New Zealand, and Tasmania. There is some indication that Darwin went on the voyage in order to accompany Captain FitzRoy. FitzRoy, as captain, was not to socialize with the lower status crew members on the ship, and he was worried about maintaining his mental health during the long, solitary voyage. (FitzRoy later committed suicide.) During what turned out to be a five-year voyage, Darwin, a creationist, recorded his observations. Upon his return to England, Darwin developed his theory of evolution, one of the major intellectual achievements of the nineteenth century. However, because of his creationist perspective, some of the observations made during the voyage were not useful in the development of his evolutionary ideas. In 1858, when another scientist, Alfred Russell Wallace (1823–1913) shared his observations gathered in the Malay Archipelago, Darwin hastened to publish *The Origin of Species* to ensure his own work would receive recognition.

Darwin's theory of evolution postulates that all species on earth change over time, and that process is governed by the principles of natural selection. These principles hold that in the struggle for existence, some individuals, because of advantageous biological **adaptation,** are better able to occupy effectively a given ecological niche and therefore will produce more offspring than individuals who are less able. Realizing that his theory challenged biblically oriented views about the nature and origins of humans and animals, Darwin was extremely cautious and continued his research for another 18 years before publishing it in 1859 as *On the Origin of Species by Means of Natural Selection; or, the Preser-*

vation of Favoured Races in the Struggle for Life. Every copy of the book was sold on the first day of publication. Within a few years, scientists were convinced of the soundness of the theory, although popular debate about its ideological and theological implications has continued to the present.

Although **psychology** was one of the fields for which Darwin's theory had revolutionary implications, it was largely left to others—notably Darwin's cousin **Francis Galton**—to expand them publicly. However, toward the end of his career, Darwin published three books in which he explored how human mental qualities could be understood as the result of evolution. In *The Descent of Man* (1871), he supported the controversial position that human beings are descended from animal ancestors. In line with this idea, he argued that the mental activities of humans and animals are fundamentally similar. He identified the presence in animals of "human" qualities such as courage and devotion, and "human" **emotions,** including pride, **jealousy,** and shame. After examining these and other common mental functions, such as **memory,** attention, and dreaming, Darwin concluded that the mental difference between humans and the higher animals is one of degree rather than kind.

In *The Expression of the Emotions in Man and Animals* (1872), Darwin posited that human emotional expressions have evolved over time because of their link with reactions that have had adaptive or survival value. For example, an animal baring its teeth in rage is literally preparing to fight; thus its emotion gives it a physical advantage. Similarly, Darwin postulated that the "fight or flight" reaction, a heightened state of nervous **arousal,** was a mechanism that aided survival. He also put forth that human reactions which no longer have any clear survival value probably did in the past and that the similarity of emotional expression among all known human groups suggests a common descent from an earlier pre-human ancestor.

Darwin's final contribution to psychology was the publication in 1877 of *Biographical Sketch of an Infant,* based on a detailed log he had kept on the development of his eldest child, who was born in 1840. This milestone in the history of **child psychology** was probably the first publication of its type. One seminal idea expressed in this short work is that the individual's development parallels the development of the species to which it belongs. (Darwin had earlier made a similar observation about the development of the fetus before **birth.**)

Darwin's work had far-reaching influences on the theory and practice of psychology. Its emphasis on the individual's **adaptation** to the **environment** helped establish the "functional" view of the mind and of human behavior, influencing such thinkers as John Dewey and James Angell (1869–1949) in the United States, who together founded the functionalist movement at the University of Chicago. Darwin's conception of the continuity between humans and other species gave the study of animal behavior a new importance. **Sigmund Freud**'s younger colleague, George J. Romanes (1848–1894), to whom Darwin turned over his notes on animal behavior shortly before his death, established the field of **comparative psychology.** Paralleling the science of comparative anatomy, this field seeks to provide insights about human beings by studying the similarities and differences between human and animal psychological functioning. In addition, Darwin's principle of natural selection led to a greater interest in variation and individual differences among members of the same species.

Darwin's other books include *The Variations of Animals and Plants under Domestication* (1868), *Insectivorous Plants* (1875), and *The Power of Movement in Plants* (1880). He was awarded membership in the London Geological Society in 1836 and won election to the Royal Society in 1839.

Further Reading

Clark, Ronald W. *The Survival of Charles Darwin: A Biography of a Man and an Idea.* New York: Random House, 1984.
Darwin, Charles. *The Autobiography of Charles Darwin, 1809–1882.* Edited by Nora Barlow. New York: Norton, 1969.
De Beer, Gavin. *Charles Darwin: Evolution by Natural Selection.* London: Doubleday, 1963.
Gruber, Howard E. *Darwin on Man: A Psychological Study of Scientific Creativity.* London: Wildwood House, 1974.
Ridley, Mark. *The Darwin Reader.* New York: Norton, 1987.

Daydreaming

A temporary escape from daily reality by forming mental pictures, usually in spontaneous, brief episodes, of other experiences.

Daydreams are a form of **imagination.** In daydreams, the person forms a mental image of a past experience or of a situation that he or she has never actually experienced. Some psychologists use the acronym TUIT (Task-Unrelated Images and Thoughts) to describe episodes of daydreaming. A daydream may be triggered by a situation, a **memory,** or a sensory input (sight, taste, smell, sound, touch).

The daydreamer may use these mental pictures to escape from reality temporarily, to overcome a frustrating situation, or to satisfy hidden wishes. Almost all people daydream, although the frequency of daydreaming varies considerably from individual to individual. Psychologists estimate that one-third to one-half of a person's thoughts

Psychologists estimate that one-third to one-half of a person's thoughts while awake are daydreams.

natural component of the mental process for most individuals.

Similar to **dreams** experienced during **sleep**, daydreams occur in cycles set by biological cycles of temperature and **hormone** levels (psychologists estimate that the average person daydreams about every 90 minutes), and peak around the lunch hour (noon to 2 p.m.). Daydreaming first occurs for most people during childhood, sometime before age three, and these early daydreams set the pattern for adult daydreaming. Children who have positive, happy daydreams of success and achievement generally continue these types of mental images into adulthood; these daydreamers are most likely to benefit from the positive aspects of **mental imagery**. Daydreams become the impetus for problem-solving, creativity, or accomplishment. On the other hand, children whose daydreams are negative, scary, or visualize disasters are likely to experience **anxiety**, and this pattern will carry over into adulthood as well. A child's daydreams may take a visible or public form—the daydreamer talks about his mental images while he is experiencing them, and may even act out the scenario she or he is imagining. After age ten, however, the process of internalizing daydreaming begins.

It is not unusual for a daydream, or series of daydreams, to precede an episode of creative writing or invention. Athletes, musicians, and other performers use a form of daydreaming known as visualization. As the individual prepares for a competition or performance, he or she forms a mental picture of him- or herself executing and completing the task with the desired successful outcome.

Further Reading

Hogan, John. "Daydreaming: Experiments Reveal Links Between Memory and Sleep." *Scientific American* (October 1994): 32+.

Seligson, Susan V. "What Your Daydreams Really Mean." *Redbook* (July 1995): 51+.

Defense Mechanism

One of a number of techniques by which the ego diffuses anxiety and other unpleasant feelings, such as conflict, fear, and frustration.

The definition of defense mechanism was devised and evolved by **Sigmund Freud.** Defense mechanisms generally involve some distortion of reality, such as the **denial** of feelings, and people are usually not aware of using them. Originally viewed as signs of neurosis, defense mechanisms are now regarded as healthy, adaptive strategies for dealing with stressors when used appropri-

while awake are daydreams, although a single daydream rarely last more than a few minutes.

When the daydreamer begins to confuse the mental images with reality, the daydream is called an **hallucination.** Daydreaming is generally not harmful, unless the daydreaming episodes interfere with activities of daily living. When the daydreamer's daily routine is disrupted—a driver misses an exit on the freeway continuously, or a student does not hear the teacher assigning homework—he or she may want to consider whether the daydreams are a symptom of a psychological problem.

Although most psychologists view daydreams as generally healthy and natural, this was not always the case. In the 1960s, for example, textbooks used for training teachers provided strategies for combating daydreaming, using language similar to that used in describing drug use. **Sigmund Freud** felt that only unfulfilled individuals created fantasies, and that daydreaming and **fantasy** were early signs of mental illness. By the late 1980s, most psychologists considered daydreams a ately. They can spare individuals from potentially crippling feelings such as guilt or despair, giving them a chance to heal from painful experiences and find solutions to their problems. Defense mechanisms must still be viewed with caution, however, as they may also prevent effective problem solving if a person becomes habitually dependent on them.

A principal defense mechanism is **repression,** which consists of selectively forgetting disturbing material. A thought may either be prevented from entering consciousness or may be repressed even if it has already become conscious. Repressed material is stored in the **unconscious,** from which it may eventually be retrieved. Repression is a central concept in **psychoanalysis** as it allows for the formation of the unconscious. A related defense mechanism is suppression, in which stressful thoughts are avoided by not thinking about them, usually by replacing them with other thoughts. Unlike repression, in which the stressful thought is completely unavailable, in suppression the thought is available but is blocked by another thought. Suppression is sometimes practiced deliberately as a stress-reducing technique.

In denial, another major defense mechanism, a person denies the facts of an external reality that is too unpleasant to face. A person with a terminal illness, for example, may deny the fact that he or she is going to die. Denial can be healthy by giving people an initial "cushion" when facing very grim realities. When it cuts people off from reality in other situations, however, it can have harmful results, as in the situation of a person who fails to receive medical help for symptoms of a serious illness, or ignores warnings of inadequate job performance.

Projection consists of assigning to others characteristics or motivations that an individual would prefer not to recognize in themselves. By doing so, that person is able to blame others and avoid feeling guilt over their own undesirable tendencies. In displacement, another type of defense, an unacceptable impulse is redirected in one of two ways. In object displacement, a new object is substituted for the original one (for example, when a parent expresses anger at an employer by scolding his or her children). In drive displacement, the original feeling is transmuted into another one (such as sexual energy into **aggression** or vice versa), allowing the energy of the original impulse to be released but in a different form. Sublimation, a similar type of defense, also consists of diverting energy to a more appropriate or socially acceptable form than the one in which it first appeared. However, sublimation is generally associated specifically with the conversion of impulses to scientific, artistic, and other creative or intellectual activities.

Through intellectualization, another defense mechanism, a person will detach themselves from a painful or

anxiety-producing situation by dealing with it solely in intellectual, abstract terms and ignoring its emotional components. Rationalization, a related defense, consists of giving an intellectual reason or rationale for an emotionally motivated action in order to assign socially acceptable motives to one's behavior or to mask disappointment. In another defense mechanism, identification, a person takes on the characteristics of someone else. Identification can serve a number of purposes. Adopting the qualities of a beloved person lost through death, abandonment, or some other reason can ease the pain of loss. On the other hand, imitating someone perceived to be a threat can mitigate fear by letting an individual imagine that he or she has taken on the strength of the feared person. Identification can also be employed as a means of vicariously experiencing the gratification of a need that one is unable to fulfill by pretending to be someone who is able to pursue and satisfy the same need.

Reaction formation is characterized by dealing with unacceptable feelings through the adoption of diametrically opposite ones. Thus, a person with homosexual impulses may become heavily involved in heterosexual activity, or a parent may deal with hostile feelings toward a child by exhibiting exaggeratedly solicitous or generous behavior. Another defense mechanism, **regression,** consists of a person reverting to behavior characteristic of an earlier period of life in order to gain access to the sources of gratification experienced during that period.

Further Reading

Firestone, Robert. *Psychological Defenses in Everyday Life.* New York: Human Sciences Press, 1989.

Goleman, Daniel. *Vital Lies, Simple Truths: the Psychology of Self-deception.* New York : Simon and Schuster, 1985.

Delayed Response

A characteristic event of an experimental procedure in which the subject is not permitted to respond to a stimulus until some time after the stimulus has been removed.

A delayed response experiment might include placing a stimulus object inside one of several similar opaque containers while the subject is watching but is restrained, and then allowing the subject to search for the object after a certain period of delay. Delayed response experiments have been conducted in the psychological study of both animals and (usually very young) humans. Some psychologists believe that the ability to respond appropriately after a significant delay indicates the operation of some form of advanced mental functioning, and that investigations of delayed response are useful in the comparative psychological analysis of various species.

Delirium

A mental condition characterized by disorientation, confusion, uncontrolled imagination, reduced ability to focus or to maintain attention, and general inability to correctly comprehend immediate reality; often accompanied by illusions, delusions, and hallucinations.

Delirious behavior ranges from mildly inappropriate to maniacal, and is a symptom of a number of disorders. Delirium has been classified into several varieties, based primarily on causal factors. As an example, alcohol-withdrawal delirium, which is also called delirium tremens or D.T.s (because of the characteristic tremor), is an acute delirium related to physical deterioration and the abrupt lowering of blood alcohol levels upon cessation of alcohol intake after a period of abuse.

Delirium is believed to be caused by a chemical imbalance in the **brain,** which, in turn, may be caused by fever, drugs, head injury, disease, malnutrition, or other factors. The onset of delirium is usually fairly rapid, although the condition sometimes develops slowly, especially if a metabolic disorder is involved. Typically, delirium disappears soon after the underlying cause is successfully treated. Occasionally, however, recovery from delirium is limited by neurological or other damage.

Delusion

Beliefs that are in stark contrast to reality, often having to do with persecution or an exaggerated sense of importance or glory.

Delusions are generally experienced by people suffering from a severe psychotic disorder, usually **schizophrenia**, although delusional thinking can occur in other types of patients (as the result of drug or alcohol abuse, for instance). Typical delusional ideas are categorized into delusions of grandeur, in which a person imagines for him or herself some God-given purpose or, in some cases, believe they are in fact historical personalities of great importance. Another type of delusion are delusions of persecution, in which a patient will believe that some person or group is out to harm him. Still another set of delusions involve what are referred to as "command hallucinations," in which a person hears voices telling him or her to commit an act. These delusional thoughts can lead people to acts of self-mutilation or to violent criminal acts.

Many psychological disorders feature aspects of delusional thought. People suffering from **depression** often experience delusions such as beliefs that they are worthless, sinful, or too unlikable to engage productively in so-ciety. Other forms of delusional thinking occur in people with somatoform and **dissociative identity disorder**s. These include body dysmorphic disorder, **obsessive-compulsive disorder**, and multiple personality disorder.

John Junginger, a clinical scientist at Indiana University, studied 138 patients who exhibited delusional beliefs and developed a scale of "bizarreness." Junginger identified the 12 types of delusional beliefs (including those mentioned above) as well as several others, such as "insertion" and "control." After categorizing delusional thoughts as such, Junginger conducted another study, attempting to discern how well his categories could predict violent behavior. Describing the study in *Omni* magazine, Steve Nadis wrote that "Junginger suspects psychotics are more likely to act out their false beliefs if they have involved, highly 'systematized' delusions." That is, elaborate delusional beliefs correlate more highly with violent behavior than vague delusional beliefs; so that someone who believes that some unidentified person is out to hurt them is less likely to act violently than someone who believes that a specific neighbor has been sending him messages to kill himself through the walls.

While researchers such as Junginger have sought out methods to predict violence as a result of delusions, other psychologists have been attempting to explain the occurrence of delusional thoughts. One intriguing idea, proposed by G.A. Roberts in the *British Journal of Psychiatry* in 1991, is that delusions actually help psychotic and schizophrenic patients by providing them with a detailed sense of purpose for their lives. Roberts found that people currently exhibiting delusional behavior were less depressed than those who had been delusional but were recovering.

Further Reading
Nadis, Steve. "Dangerous Delusions: Making Sense of Senseless Behavior." *Omni* (December 1994): 32.

Starr, Cynthia. "A 'Secret Disorder' Yields to Serotonin Reuptake Inhibitors." *Drug Topics* (5 July 1993): 20.

Dementia

A gradual deterioration of mental functioning affecting all areas of cognition, including judgment, language, and memory.

Dementia generally occurs in the elderly, although it can appear at any age. Several substantial studies have been done to determine its prevalence, and in 1991 a major study was conducted which found that dementia occurred in just over 1 percent of the population aged 65 to 74; in approximately 4 percent in ages 75 to 84; and more than doubling to 10.14 percent in persons 85 and over. Other studies have concluded that many as 47 percent of

This elderly man, whose hobby is making whistles, shows no symptoms of dementia. Studies estimate that nearly half of all people over 85 exhibit some form of dementia.

people over 85 suffer from some form of dementia. Prevalence rates tend to be comparable between the sexes and across sociocultural barriers, such as education and class. It is also worth noting that, despite what is often commonly thought, dementia is not an inevitable consequence of **aging**.

Researchers have identified many types of dementia, including dementia resulting from **Alzheimer's disease,** vascular dementia, substance induced dementia, dementia due to multiple etiologies, dementia due to other general medical conditions, and dementia not otherwise specified. More than half of the persons diagnosed with dementia are classified as having dementia resulting from Alzheimer's disease. This type of dementia occurs in more than half of dementia cases in the United States. There is no definitive method in diagnosing this kind of dementia until after the patient's death and an autopsy can be performed on the **brain.** Alzheimer-related dementia is characterized by slow deterioration in the initial

stages, but the rate of cognitive loss speeds up as the disease progresses. Patients with this type of dementia can generally be expected to live eight years.

Vascular dementia is the second most common type of dementia and is caused by damage to the blood vessels that carry blood to the brain, usually by stroke. Because the area of the brain that is affected differs from person to person, the pattern of cognitive deterioration in this type of dementia is unpredictable. Other diseases that can cause dementia include human immunodeficiency virus (HIV), Parkinson's disease, Huntington's disease, Pick's disease, and Creutzfeldt-Jakob disease. The kind of dementia induced by these diseases is known as subcortical, meaning they affect mainly the interior structures of the brain, as opposed to cortical dementia (Alzheimer's and vascular) which affect the outer layers of the brain. Many of these subcortical diseases have been known for some time to result in dementia, but HIV-related dementia has only recently been described and diagnosed. Recent studies have indicated that between 29 to 87 percent of people with **AIDS** show significant signs of dementia.

Generally speaking, dementia has a gradual onset and can take different routes in different people. All sufferers, however, are eventually impaired in all areas of cognition. Initially, dementia can appear in **memory** loss, which may result in being able to vividly remember events from many years past while not being able to remember events of the very recent past. Other symptoms of dementia are agnosia, which is the technical term for not being able to recognize familiar objects, facial agnosia, the inability to recognize familiar faces, and visiospatial impairment, the inability to locate familiar places.

Along with cognitive deterioration, sufferers of dementia often experience related emotional disorders as they recognize their deterioration and experience **anxiety** about its continuation and worsening. Typical among reactions are **depression**, anxiety, **aggression**, and apathy. Psychologists are uncertain to what extent these symptoms are direct results of dementia or simply responses to its devastation. Dementia progressively deteriorates the brain and eventually sufferers are completely unable to care for themselves and, ultimately, the disease results in death.

Further Reading

Cooper, James W. Jr. "The Effects of Dementia." *American Druggist* (April 1993): 59.

Crystal, Howard. "Treating Severe Clinical Memory Disorders." *Newsweek* (3 May 1993): S6.

"Dementia: When You Suspect a Loved One's Problem." *Mayo Clinic Health Letter* (November 1995): 6

Dendrite

Nerve cell fibers that receive signals from other cells.

Dendrites are one of two types of short, threadlike fibers that extend from the cell body of a **nerve** cell, or neuron. The other type are called axons. Dendrites receive electrochemical signals, which are known as postsynaptic potentials, from the axons of other neurons, and the information contained in these signals is fired across a synaptic gap or cleft about 0.02 microns or about 8 millionths of an inch wide and transmitted toward the cell body, with the signals fading as they approach their destination. A single neuron can have many dendrites, each composed of numerous branches; together, they comprise the greater part of the neuron's receptive surface.

The number of axons and dendrites increases dramatically during infancy and childhood—possibly to facilitate the rapid development experienced during this period—and decrease in early **adolescence.** A child of six or seven has more dendrites than an adult.

See also Synapse.

Denial

A defense mechanism in which a person unconsciously ignores or reinterprets anything that feels threatening.

Denial is one of the **defense mechanisms** that may be employed by individuals in dealing with **stress** or risk. In denial, a person unconsciously ignores or reinterprets anything that induces high stress or threatens the individual's feeling of security. By paying attention to only certain parts of a situation or event, the person protects her or himself from other parts that are frightening or that would force the person to see a different reality than the one he or she wants to see. Denial is not the same as **repression**. In repression, a person completely buries an entire event, situation, or feeling in the **unconscious;** in denial, the event or situation is partly recalled and/or redefined in a nonthreatening way. For that reason, some prefer the terms *redefinition* or *reappraisal* for this defense mechanism, rather than denial.

Some examples of denial include: an alcohol abuser saying, "I'm not an alcoholic—I just like to have a drink now and then;" or the abuser's spouse saying, "He/She just drinks to relax." Denial is a basic part of any **addiction,** allowing addicts to continue their addictive behavior without seeing how destructive it is, either to themselves or to others. Many people also use denial when faced with a serious illness, refusing to recognize the true danger or to take the necessary steps to treat it.

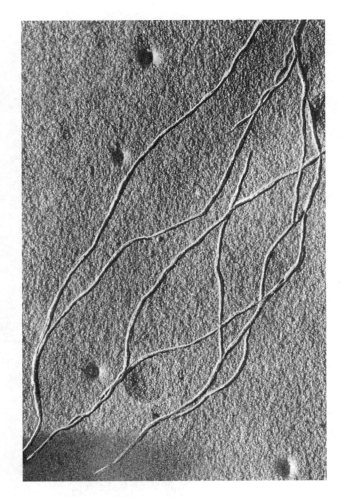

The long-chain molecules of DNA, photographed at magnification of 100,000 at the University of California at Berkeley. This photo, taken in 1954, was one of the first to document the 1953 discovery of the molecular structure of the fundamental element of heredity.

Studies have shown that people use denial spontaneously to protect themselves from threatening realities. Denial is very successful in reducing **fear** and **anxiety.** However, it can also get in the way of healing when it prevents a person from facing the truth.

Deoxyribonucleic Acid (DNA)

An organic substance occurring in chromosomes in the nuclei of cells, which encodes and carries genetic information, and is the fundamental element of heredity.

As the transmitter of inherited characteristics, deoxyribonucleic acid (DNA) replicates itself exactly and determines the structure of new organisms, which it does by governing the structure of their proteins. The Swiss researcher Friedrich Miescher first discovered DNA in 1869 when he extracted a substance (which he called nuclein) containing nitrogen and phosphorus from cell nuclei. The question of whether nucleic acids or proteins, or both, carried the information that make the genes of every organism unique was not answered, however, until the molecular structure of DNA was determined in 1953. This pioneering work was accomplished by an American biochemist, James D. Watson, and two British scientists, Francis Crick, a biochemist, and Maurice Wilkins, a biophysicist. The thousands of genes that make up each chromosome are composed of DNA, which consists of a five-carbon sugar (deoxyribose), phosphate, and four types of nitrogen-containing molecules (adenine, guanine, cytosine, and thymine). The sugar and phosphate combine to form the outer edges of a double helix, while the nitrogen-containing molecules appear in bonded pairs like rungs of a ladder connecting the outer edges. They are matched in an arrangement that always pairs adenine in one chain with thymine in the other, and guanine in one chain with cytosine in the other. A single DNA molecule may contain several thousand pairs.

The specific order and arrangement of these bonded pairs of molecules constitute the genetic code of the organism in which they exist by determining, through the production of **ribonucleic acid (RNA),** the type of protein produced by each gene, as it is these proteins that govern the structure and activities of all cells in an organism. Thus, DNA acts as coded message, providing a blueprint for the characteristics of all organisms, including human beings. When a cell divides to form new life, its DNA is "copied" by a separation of the two strands of the double helix, after which complementary strands are synthesized around each existing one. The end result is the formation of two new double helices, each identical to the original. All cells of a higher organism contain that organism's entire DNA pattern. However, only a small percentage of all the DNA messages are active in any cell at a given time, enabling different cells to "specialize."

Many viruses are also composed of DNA, which, in some cases, has a single-strand form rather than the two strands forming the edges of a double helix. Each particle of a virus contains only one DNA molecule, ranging in length from 5,000 to over 200,000 subunits. (The total length of DNA in a human cell is estimated at five billion subunits.) Radiation, thermal variations, or the presence of certain chemicals can cause changes, or "mistakes," in an organism's DNA pattern, resulting in a genetic mutation. In the course of evolution, such mutations provided the hereditary blueprints for the emergence of new species.

Since the 1970s, scientists have furthered their understanding of the molecular structure of genes through experiments with recombinant DNA. As its name suggests, this technique combines fragments of DNA from two different species, allowing an experimenter to purify, or clone, a gene from one species by inserting it into the DNA of another, which replicates it together with its own genetic material. The term "recombinant DNA" also refers to other laboratory techniques, such as splitting DNA with microbial enzymes called endonucleases, splicing fragments of DNA, and even synthesizing it chemically. Although controversial, gene cloning is an important scientific accomplishment which has enabled researchers to gain new understanding of the structure of genes through the ability to produce an unlimited number of gene copies gathered from a variety of organisms, including human ones.

See also Heredity.

Further Reading
Gribbin, John. *In Search of the Double Helix.* New York: McGraw-Hill, 1985.

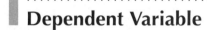

Dependent Variable

The variable measured in an experiment or study; what the experimenter measures.

When conducting research, a psychologist typically takes two or more similar groups of people or animals and exposes them to different treatments or situations. Then the researcher monitors a behavior of interest to see whether that behavior differs from one group to the next. This measurement is the dependent variable. A single experiment may involve more than one dependent variable.

When specifying the dependent variable, it must be clearly defined and measurable. In one experiment, researchers gathered a group of business executives who displayed evidence of Type A behavior (e.g., nonstop working, aggressiveness, and competitiveness). The researchers divided the executives into subgroups and either exposed them to a small amount of information regarding the health hazards of such behavior, provided them with support groups, or offered a course in **stress** management. The dependent variable was a score on a test that reflected Type A tendencies. Although **personality** is so complex that it cannot really be described by a single score, the test for Type A behavior provides a measurement that is objective and measurable. The executives who took the stress management course scored lower than those in the support groups; the highest test scores occurred in the group with the least exposure to information about stress management. The researchers concluded that the executives' test scores, the dependent variable, changed differently, depending on their group.

Further Reading

Levenkron, J. C.; J. D. Cohen; H. S. Mueller; and E. B. Fisher. "Modifying the Type A Coronary-Prone Behavior Pattern. *Journal of Consulting and Clinical Psychology* 51 (1983): 192-204.

Depression

Feelings of sadness, despair, and discouragement.

Depression may signify a **mood,** a symptom, or a syndrome. As a mood, it refers to temporary feelings of sadness, despair, and discouragement. As a symptom, it refers to these feelings when they persist and are associated with such problems as decreased pleasure, hopelessness, guilt, and disrupted sleeping and eating patterns. The entire syndrome is also referred to collectively as a depression or depressive disorder. At any given time between 10 and 20 percent of all people suffer some of the symptoms of depression. The **American Psychiatric Association** estimates that about one in five Americans experiences an episode of depression at least once in his or her lifetime.

Depression can generally be traced to a combination of physical, psychological, and environmental factors. Genetic inheritance makes some people more likely than others to suffer from depression. Over 60 percent of people who are treated for depression have family members who have been depressed at some time, and there is a 15 percent chance that immediate biological relatives of a depressed person will develop depression. Twin studies have also supported the existence of a genetic predisposition to depression, particularly bipolar depression. Researchers have found that depression is associated with changes in **brain** chemistry. The normal balance and functioning of two **neurotransmitters** in particular—serotonin and norepinephrine—appears to be disrupted in depressed persons, a finding that has led to the development of a variety of antidepressant **drugs.** Depression is also associated with an imbalance of cortisol, the main **hormone** secreted by the adrenal glands. Other physiological factors sometimes associated with depression include viral infections, low thyroid levels, and biological rhythms, including women's menstrual cycles—depression is a prominent symptom of **premenstrual syndrome (PMS).**

Life events, including developmental traumas, physical illness, problems in intimate relationships, and losses may trigger a depression. According to classic psychoanalytic theory, depression is the result of losing someone through death or abandonment and turning one's feelings of **anger** and resentment inward. For behaviorists, the link between such negative events as the death of a loved one, the end of a relationship, or the loss of a job is the removal of a source of reward. Cognitive theorists claim that depressed people develop destructive ways of thinking, which include blaming themselves when things go wrong, focusing on the negative side of events, and habitually jumping to excessively pessimistic conclusions.

Another psychological explanation of depression centers on the concept of **learned helplessness**, a phenomenon first observed in a laboratory setting when animals who had no control over their situations (such as being able to change them by pressing a lever) showed signs of depression. It has been found that lack of control over their own lives is also associated with depression in humans and may be especially relevant to depression in women, whose incidence of depression is twice that of men. Another factor that may be linked to depression in women is the tendency to dwell on negative events, a cognitive style that research has shown to be more common among women than among men, who are more likely to distract themselves from negative feelings by engaging in various forms of activity.

The *Diagnostic and Statistical Manual of Mental Disorders,* produced by the American Psychiatric Association, categorizes depression as an affective, or mood, disorder. Its criterion for clinical depression is the presence of at least five of the following symptoms almost every day for at least two weeks: depressed mood; loss of interest in activities; significant changes in appetite or weight; disturbed **sleep** patterns; agitated or slowed down movements; fatigue; feelings of worthlessness or inappropriate guilt; trouble concentrating; and preoccupation with death or **suicide.** In a major depressive episode, these symptoms can persist for six months or longer without treatment. Usually, major depression first occurs in one's late twenties. In severe cases, people may be almost completely incapacitated, losing the ability to work, socialize, and even care for themselves. The depressive episode may eventually lift completely, or some symptoms may persist for as long as two years. More than half the people who suffer from major depression experience more than one episode. A serious complication of major depression is the threat of suicide. Some 60 percent of people who commit suicide are depressed, and 15 percent of those diagnosed with depression eventually commit suicide.

In dysthymia, another type of depression, symptoms are less severe but more prolonged. The major symptom is a depressed mood that lasts at least two years, but at least some of the other symptoms of clinical depression are often present as well. **Bipolar disorder** (manic depression) is characterized by the alternation of depression and **mania,** an overly elated, energetic state. Characteristic symptoms of mania include an inappropriately cheerful mood; inflated optimism and self-esteem; the belief that one has extraordinary powers or abilities; excessive energy; racing thoughts; and irritability when confronted by obstacles or opposition. During manic episodes, people characteristically make unwise, irrational decisions and may even endanger their own lives. In bipolar disorder, manic episodes lasting days, weeks, or even months alternate with periods of depression. There may be a period of normalcy between the two or an immediate mood swing from one mode to the other.

Cyclothymic disorder, the bipolar equivalent of dysthymia, resembles bipolar disorder but consists of a less extreme pattern of mood swings. Another type of depression, seasonal affective disorder (SAD), follows an annual cycle triggered by seasonal variations in light and usually involves depression during the winter months; it is thought to be due to an excess of the sleep-inducing hormone melatonin. Sometimes depressions become severe enough to be classified as psychotic. These cases—which account for about 10 percent of all clinical depressions—are characterized by delusions or **hallucinations** and an especially high incidence of suicide.

Most people with clinical depression do not recognize that they have it and fail to seek treatment, blaming **stress** or physical ailments for their lack of well-being. Of those who do seek treatment either through **psychotherapy,** medication, or a combination of both, 80 percent improve, often within a matter of weeks. Psychotherapy alone is generally more effective for people with mild or moderate depression, while medication is advised for those whose depression is more severe or who have developed physical symptoms. Most persons receiving psychotherapy for their depression undergo short-term treatment lasting between 12 and 16 weeks. Treatment methods vary among different schools of therapy and individual therapists. **Cognitive behavior therapy** focuses on helping patients identify and change negative thought patterns; interpersonal and family therapies emphasize strategies for improving one's relationships with others; and behavioral therapy involves monitoring one's actions and modifying them through a system of incentives and rewards.

Two types of medication traditionally used to treat depression—tricyclic antidepressants and monoamine oxidase (MAO) inhibitors—increase the brain's supply of certain neurotransmitters, including norepinephrine and dopamine. Both medications are effective for many patients but can cause a variety of side effects, particularly MAO inhibitors. In recent years a new generation of antidepressants has been developed that affects levels of serotonin rather than norepinephrine. Fluoxitine (Prozac), the major drug in this group, has become the most widely used antidepressant in the United States. It is effective in 60 to 80 percent of those who take it and has fewer side effects than previous types of antidepressants.

Lithium is used to treat manic episodes in persons with bipolar disorder.

Whenever possible, persons suffering from depression should be urged to seek treatment through a private therapist, clinic, or hospital. There are special treatment centers for depression at medical centers throughout the country.

Further Reading

Hales, Dianne. *Depression.* New York: Chelsea House Publishers, 1989.

Jackson, Stanley W. *Melancholia and Depression: From Hippocratic Times to the Present.* New Haven: Yale University Press, 1986.

Papolos, Demitri, M.D., and Janice Papolos. *Overcoming Depression.* New York: Harper and Row, 1987.

Depth Perception

Ability to determine visually the distance between objects.

We can determine the relative distance of objects in two different ways. One uses cues involving only one eye; the second requires two eyes. When something is far from us, we rely on monocular cues, those that require the use of only one eye. For closer objects, we use both monocular cues and binocular cues, those that necessitate both eyes.

The ability to perceive depth seems to exist early in life. Research with infants has revealed that by two months of age, babies can perceive depth. Prior to that, they may be unable to do so in part because of weak eye muscles that do not let them use binocular depth cues.

Monocular Depth Cues. Psychologists have identified two different kinds of monocular cues. One comes into play when we use the muscles of the eye to change the shape of the eye's lens to focus on an object. We make use of the amount of muscular tension to give feedback about distance.

A second kind of monocular cue relates to external visual stimuli. These cues appear in the table below. Artists use these visual cues to make two dimensional paintings appear realistic. These cues may seem obvious to us now, but artistic renderings from earlier than about the sixteenth century often seem distorted because artists had not yet developed all the techniques to capture these visual cues.

Binocular Cues. Binocular cues require that we use both eyes. One cue makes use of the fact that when we look at a nearby object with both eyes, we bring our eyes together; the muscle tension associated with looking at close objects gives us information about their distance. The second binocular cue involves retinal disparity. This means that each eye (or, more specifically, the retina of each eye) has a slightly different perspective. The slight difference in appearance of an object in each eye when we gaze at it gives us further information about depth. Children's Viewmasters produce a three-dimensional image that has depth because of a slightly different picture that is delivered to each eye. In the natural world, because of the relatively small distance from one pupil to another (about 2.5 inches or 6.5 centimeters) binocular cues are effective only for objects that are within about 500 yards (455 m) of the viewer.

Animals that have eyes on front of the face, like primates, will be able to use binocular depth cues because the two eyes see almost, but not quite, the same scene; on the other hand, animals with eyes on the side of the head, like most birds, will be less able to use binocular cues because the visual fields of the two eyes do not overlap very much and each eye sees different scenes.

Descartes, René (1596–1650)

French philosopher and mathematician whose ideas included early and significant contributions to the field of psychology.

Descartes was born in France, near the small village of Le Haye. From the age of 10, he attended the most prestigious school in France, the Royal Collège of La Flèche, graduating at the age of 16. After spending some time sampling the amusements of Parisian society, followed by a period of solitary studies in philosophy and mathematics, Descartes briefly served as a soldier on the eve of the Thirty Years' War, joining first the Protestant and then the Catholic forces. Returning to the study of science and philosophy after the war, he spent several more years in Paris before moving to Holland at the age of 32. There Descartes wrote his most important works, *Discourse on Method* (1637), *Meditations on First Philosophy* (1642), and *Principles of Philosophy* (1644). Because his books aroused controversy among the Dutch Protestant clergy, Descartes, already wary after Galileo's condemnation by the Inquisition, published little for the remainder of his life, confining his thoughts largely to unpublished manuscripts and letters. His last published work was the *Passions of the Soul* (1649). Descartes remained in Holland for most of his life, although he moved frequently during his time there. In 1649, he left for Sweden at the invitation of Queen Christina and undertook to tutor her in philosophy. Only months after arriving in Sweden, Descartes died at the age of 53.

Descartes's philosophy is known for its glorification of human reason. He began with the premise that the only way to be sure of anything is to doubt everything ("I resolved to reject as false everything in which I could imagine the least doubt, in order to see if there afterwards remained anything that was entirely indubitable"). In so doing, Descartes arrived at the conclusion that the one thing he could be sure of was his own act of doubting—a mental process. From the certainty expressed in the famous statement, "I think, therefore I am," he built a philosophy that gave to the workings of the individual mind priority over both immediate sensory experience and re-

MONOCULAR CUE—HOW IT WORKS	
Aerial Perspective	Objects that are near seem crisper and clearer; far away objects appear fuzzier.
Height in Plane	Objects that are farther away appear higher in the visual scene.
Interposition	Objects that are nearer block objects that are farther away.
Linear Perspective	Lines that are parallel (e.g., railroad tracks) look like they come to a point in the distance. The farther the lines, the closer they are.
Motion Parallax	When you are moving and you fixate on a spot, objects closer to you than that spot appear to move in the direction opposite to your motion; objects farther than that spot appear to move in the same direction as you are moving.
Relative Size	If two objects are of the same size, the closer one is bigger.

René Descartes

ceived wisdom. Descartes postulated a radical mind-body dualism, claiming that the universe consisted of two utterly distinct substances: mind ("thinking substance" or *res cogitans)* and matter ("physical substance" or *res extensa*). Thus, he separated mental phenomena from the comprehensive mechanistic explanation he gave for the workings of matter and material things, including the human body, which he divided into ten physiological systems. These included such faculties as **memory** and **imagination,** along with the purely physiological functions of digestion, circulation, and respiration.

Descartes believed the primary site of interaction between mind and body to be the pineal gland (which he incorrectly thought to be unique to humans). He held that the will, an aspect of the mind, can move the pineal gland and cause the transmission of what he called animal spirits, which produce mechanical changes in the body; and, similarly, that changes in the body are transmitted to the pineal gland and can there affect the mind. His rationalistic ideas provided a basis for the Enlightenment and became the dominant system of philosophy until the work of David Hume (1711–1776) and Immanuel Kant (1724–1804). While many of Descartes's individual arguments have since been discredited, his overall view of the dualism between mind and body has been a powerful influ-ence on succeeding generations of philosophers and psychologists.

Further Reading

Popper, K., and J. Eccles. *The Self and Its Brain.* London, 1977.

Smith, Norman Kemp. *New Studies in the Philosophy of Descartes.* New York: Russell and Russell, 1963.

Vrooman, J. R. *Rene Descartes: A Biography.* New York: Putnam, 1970.

Desensitization

A behavior modification technique used to combat phobias and other irrational fears.

Developed by Joseph Wolpe in the 1950s, desensitization is a treatment method which weakens the learned association between **anxiety** and feared objects or situations by strengthening another response—in this case, relaxation—that is incompatible with anxiety. Relaxation responses are strengthened through progressive relaxation training, first developed by Edmund Jacobson in the 1930s. Clients first tighten and then relax 16 different muscle groups in various parts of the body, releasing the tension and focusing on the resulting feelings of relaxation. Once people learn how their muscles feel when they are truly relaxed, they develop the **ability** to reproduce this state voluntarily and in a variety of situations.

Next, the client outlines an "anxiety hierarchy," a list of situations or stimuli arranged in order from least to most anxiety-provoking. For a person who is afraid of flying, such a list might begin with seeing a picture of an airplane, eventually progress to driving to the airport, and end with taking an actual plane flight. With the aid of the therapist, the client then works through the list, either imagining or actually experiencing each situation while in a state of relaxation. When tolerance for each listed item is established, the client moves on to the next one. As clients face progressively more threatening situations, relaxation rather than **fear** becomes associated with the source of their anxiety, and they become gradually desensitized to it. While exposure through **mental imagery** does produce desensitization, actual real-life exposure to the feared stimulus whenever possible is more effective.

Further Reading

Craighead, W. Edward. *Behavior Modification: Principles, Issues, and Applications.* New York: Houghton Mifflin, 1976.

Skinner, B.F. *About Behaviorism.* New York: Knopf, 1974.

Wolpe, Joseph. *The Practice of Behavior Therapy.* Tarrytown, NY: Pergamon Press, 1990.

Determinism

A scientific perspective which specifies that events occur in completely predictable ways as a result of natural and physical laws.

Since ancient times, the origins of human behavior have been attributed to hidden or mystical forces. The Greek philosopher Democritus speculated, for example, that objects in our world consist of atoms; included among these "objects" was the soul, which was made of finer, smoother, and more spherical atoms than other physical objects. He rejected the concept of free will and claimed that all human behavior results from prior events. Some philosophers have advanced the argument that human behavior is deterministic, although most have resisted the idea that human beings merely react to external events and do not voluntarily select behaviors.

There is a clear dilemma in explaining human behavior through psychological principles. On the one hand, if psychology is a science of behavior, then there should be laws allowing the prediction of behavior, just as there are gravitational laws to predict the behavior of a falling object. On the other hand, objections have been raised by individuals who believe that humans control their own behaviors and possess free will. Part of the controversy relates to the concept of the mind and body as separate entities. In this view, the mind may not be subject to the same laws as the body. Wilhelm Wundt (1832–1920) attempted to make the distinction between determinism and indeterminism by suggesting that psychological processes could be creative and free, whereas the physiological processes in the **brain** were deterministic. This argument does not solve the problem for psychology, however, because psychologists consider mental processes appropriate for study within a scientific framework, thus subject to scientific laws.

Other psychologists like **William James,** who was interested in religion and believed in free will, recognized this conflict but was reluctant to abandon the concept that behaviors were not free. At one point, he suggested that mind and body operated in tandem, whereas on another occasion he concluded that they interacted. Clearly, James struggled with the issue and, like others, was unable to resolve it. The behaviorists were the most obvious proponents of determinism, dating back to **John B. Watson**, who claimed that **environment** was the single cause of behavior, and who made one of the most famous deterministic assertions ever: "Give me a dozen healthy infants . . . and my own specified world to bring them up in and I'll guarantee to take anyone at random and train him to become any type of specialist I might select—doctor, lawyer, artist, merchant, chief, and, yes, even beggar man and thief."

The psychologist with the greatest influence in this area, however, was **B. F. Skinner.** He adopted a stance called radical **behaviorism,** which disregarded free will and the internal causes of behavior. All behavior, Skinner maintained, was determined through **reinforcement** contingencies, that is, the pattern of reinforcements and **punishment**s in an individual's life. Although critics have claimed that Skinner's concept of determinism denied people of their humanity, he maintained that his approach could actually lead to more humane societies. For example, if people were not responsible for negative behaviors, they should not be punished, for they had no control over their behaviors. Instead, the environment that reinforced the unwanted behaviors should be changed so that desirable behaviors receive reinforcement and increase in frequency.

Sigmund Freud defined determinism in terms of the unconscious and contended that behavior is caused by internal, mental mechanisms. In some ways, Freud was more extreme than Skinner, who acknowledged that some behaviors are not predictable. The main difference between Freud and Skinner involved the origin of causation; Freud believed in underlying physiological processes while Skinner opted to focus on external causes. Thus, even though Freudians and Skinnerians differ on almost every conceivable dimension, they have at least one commonality in their reliance on determinism.

Those scientists who believe that behaviors are determined have recognized the difficulty in making explicit predictions. Thus, they have developed the concept of statistical determinism. This means that, even though behaviors are determined by fixed laws, predictions will never be perfect because so many different factors, most of them unknown, affect actions, which result in generally accurate predictions. The recently developed theory of chaos relates to making predictions about complex events such as behaviors. This theory suggests that in a cause-effect situation, small differences in initial conditions may lead to very different outcomes. This theory supports the notion that behaviors may not be completely predictable even though they may be dictated by fixed natural laws.

Further Reading

Doob, Leonard William. *Inevitability: Determinism, Fatalism, and Destiny.* New York: Greenwood Press, 1988.

Developmental Psychology

A field of psychology which examines how human behavior changes as a person matures through focusing on biological, emotional, physical, cognitive, and social changes that are age-related, sequential, and long-lasting.

Developmental psychologists study how characteristics and behaviors first appear and how and when they change. They study the relationships between different types of development, such as cognitive and social, as well as individual variations in development, both normal and deviant. Initially, developmental psychology focused on childhood but was subsequently expanded to cover changes that occur over the entire life span, from the intrauterine environment through childhood, **adolescence,** middle age, and **maturity.** Three processes that play a central role in development are growth, **maturation,** and learning. Growth refers to physical changes that are quantitative, such as increases in height or weight. Maturation involves anatomical, neurophysiological, and chemical transformations that change the way a person functions (such as a woman's passage into or out of childbearing age). Learning involves relatively long-term changes in behavior or performance acquired through observation, experience, or training.

One of the oldest questions in developmental psychology involves the **nature-nurture controversy,** which asks how and to what degree nature (inherited or genetic factors influencing development) contributes to a person's biological, emotional, cognitive, and social development, and to what degree it is the result of nurture (the influence of learning and experience in the **environment**). This issue has been debated for centuries by philosophers, who often argued strenuously for the predominance of one influence over the other (a famous example is the British philosopher John Locke's concept of the newborn human being as a blank slate, or *tabula rasa,* to be formed by experience). Pioneered by the American psychologist **Arnold Gesell,** the concept of maturation, which is central to developmental psychology, stresses the role of nature in human development. Gesell observed that the motor skills of children develop in a fixed order through a series of stages relatively unaffected by outside influences. The interplay of nature and nurture, rather than the importance of one over the other, however, has gained a greater emphasis in the work of more recent figures, notably the Swiss psychologist **Jean Piaget,** whose theory of cognitive development in children has been a model for much subsequent work in the field. Going beyond simplistic dichotomies, scientists have been able to gather substantial amounts of specific data on the effects of **heredity** and environment through family, twin, and adoption studies. Current concepts of maturation focus on models in which each stage of a developmental process is defined not only by innate characteristics but also by increased receptivity (or "readiness") toward certain environmental factors.

Developmental psychologists study the processes of growth, maturation, and learning that shape behavior over the entire life span

Another significant issue in the field of developmental psychology is the question of continuity versus stages, specifically, does an individual's development occur in a gradual and progressive (continuous) fashion, or in a distinct series of discrete stages? In his pioneering theory of cognitive development, Piaget delineated a sequence of developmental stages that occur in a fixed order with each dependent on the previous ones (sensorimotor, preoperational, concrete operational, and formal operational). Subsequent research has challenged some of his assumptions, finding in some cases that children are capable of advanced thinking at younger ages than those posited by Piaget. Observations such as these have led to the conclusion that cognitive development is more uneven and less systematic than previously thought, and that children's reasoning abilities in a specific situation may depend on variables—familiarity with certain objects, language comprehension, and prior experiences—that are not part of Piaget's system. One recent model advances the notion of cognitive development in "pockets" rather than globally uniform levels or stages. Another alternative that has been suggested is an information processing model focusing on gradual quantitative advances in memory and other learning abilities rather than qualitative progress through a series of stages.

In addition to Piaget, another major influence in the area of human development was **Erik Erikson,** whose eight stages of psychosocial development, encompassing the entire life span from infancy through old age, inspired an interest in the continuation of development past childhood. Erikson's work also popularized the concept of the adolescent "identity crisis" (a term he coined). Yet another type of development that has gained increased interest in recent years is **moral development,** which has been most extensively investigated by **Lawrence Kohlberg.** Presenting subjects with hypothetical moral dilemmas, Kohlberg found that moral reasoning in children develops through three distinct levels (consisting of two stages each) between the age of seven and adolescence. Like Piaget's theory, Kohlberg's stages do not necessarily occur at a given age but they do occur consistently in a given order. Also, not all individuals reach the final stage, at which following rules and obeying the social order is superseded by the imperative of the individual **conscience** to obey ethical principles that may transcend the law. The universality of some of Kohlberg's findings has been challenged in terms of applicability to non-Western cultures and women (Kohlberg's research focused on men). When Carol Gilligan questioned subjects about moral conflicts, the reactions of male and female respondents differed significantly, and Gilligan drew up her own model for women.

See also Cognitive Development Theory; Cognitive Psychology; Information-Processing Approach.

Further Reading

Anderson, Clifford. *The Stages of Life: A Groundbreaking Discovery: the Steps to Psychological Maturity.* New York: Atlantic Monthly Press, 1995.

Berger, Kathleen Stassen. *The Developing Person Through the Life Span.* 2nd ed. New York: Worth Publishers, 1988.

Cicchetti, Dante, and Donald J. Cohen, eds. *Developmental Psychopathology.* New York: J. Wiley, 1995.

Developmental Stages, Theories of

The various stages developmental psychologists theorize people go through as they develop from early life into childhood and beyond.

Developmental psychologists, by and large, study the way humans develop from an embryo into a full

STAGES OF DEVELOPMENT

Erik Erikson

"Trust versus mistrust" from birth to 18 months.

"Autonomy versus shame" from 1½ to 3 years

"Initiative versus guilt" from 3 to 6 years

"Industry versus inferiority" from 6 to 12 years

Jean Piaget

"Sensorimotor stage" from birth to 2 years

"Preoperational stage" from 2 to 7 years

"Concrete operational stage" from 7 to 12 years

"Formal operational stage" from 13 years to adult

Lawrence Kohlberg

"Preconventional stage," where moral decisions are based on how they *themselves* are effected

"Conventional stage," where moral judgments are based on the conventions of society, family, religion, or other social order. (Many people do not pass beyond this stage.)

"Post-conventional level," where moral judgments are based on personal beliefs.

grown adult, focusing mainly on the factors that contribute to **intelligence**, **personality**, morality, and lifestyle. Of special interest are the effects certain stimuli have on the development of humans. For instance, does genetics pre-program a person to be introverted, or is that personality trait the result of specific life events that caused him or her to retreat inward? Or, did intense study of music from an early age make someone a gifted musician, or is that something their genes had pre-programmed from the moment of conception?

Over the past hundred years or so, several prominent psychologists and psychiatrists have devised various theories seeking to quantify the developmental stages humans pass through, and in doing so, have sought to map out this difficult process. One of the more famous theories of developmental psychology was put forth by the psychological theorist **Erik Erikson** in 1963 in his important work *Childhood and Society.* In this work, Erikson suggests that psychosocial development, the changing ways we perceive ourselves individually and in relation to society, occurs in eight stages—only four of which deal with childhood. The first of Erikson's stages is "trust versus mistrust" and occurs from birth to 1½ years. The child formulates either a trusting or mistrusting relationship to the world around it, based on whether its immediate needs are met. These needs, at this young age, generally have to do with satisfaction of physical cravings (food, sleep, and comfort) and for feelings of **attachment**.

The second stage of development Erikson called "autonomy versus shame" and doubt—occurring between 1½ and 3 years of age. Here, young children learn to be independent and autonomous on the condition that they are adequately encouraged to explore their world and given the freedom to do so. On the other hand, children with overly restrictive or anxious parents who wield too great an influence over their children's behavior, stifling **creativity** and independent exploration of their environment, become shameful and self doubting.

Between the ages of three and six, children pass through the stage Erikson refers to as "initiative versus guilt." During this period of development, children seek to further explore their world by initiating new experiences. The guilt comes about when there are unexpected consequences involved in these initiations. The final stage of childhood development is called "industry versus inferiority," and it lasts from age six to 12. Here, children seek to become industrious in all areas of life, from school to interpersonal relations. Mastery of these skills, with adequate support at home and in school, brings about a sense of overall competence, whereas failure brings about a sense of inferiority.

Another prominent theorist in developmental psychology was **Jean Piaget**, who developed the four stages of cognitive development. He theorized that people pass from one stage to another not just as a matter of course, but only when they are confronted with the correct type of stimulation to initiate a change. Piaget believed that in the absence of the correct kinds of stimulation, children would never reach their full potential.

According to Piaget, from birth to two years of age, children are in the "sensorimotor" stage of cognitive development. During this stage, children first begin to develop motor skills. They also have little or no **ability** for what is called symbolic representation, that is, the ability to conceive of things existing outside of their immediate vicinity. Piaget called this ability object permanence. Piaget's next stage is called "preoperational" (from ages two to seven). In this stage, children begin to use language and other representational systems to conceive of, and even discuss, things or people who are not physically present. The chief marker of this stage is what Piaget called egocentric thought. That is, preoperational children can conceive of things that are not present, but they

can not conceive of others perceiving what *they* can not. The classic example of this kind of thinking is the young child who in order to hide simply covers his eyes, thinking that since he can no longer see, no one else can either.

Piaget's next stage is called "concrete operational" and covers the years 7 to 12. Here, children begin to develop clearer methods of thinking, and they start to overcome the egocentrism of the preoperational stage. They begin to better understand spatial relationships and matters of time, but they are largely bound by the concrete world and have trouble conceiving abstract thought. During the formal operational stage, from age 12 to adulthood, people develop the ability to think logically and systematically and to understand abstractions and the concepts of causality and choice. They see that different outcomes can proceed from different actions, and that they are free to choose between various actions depending on a desired outcome. According to Piaget, and to many who believe in his framework, not everyone reaches this stage of cognitive development. Some researchers assert that as few as 25 percent of the general population reaches the formal operational stage. Still others suggest that it is a culture-based phenomena and that in less technological societies, almost no one reaches the stage—mainly because such thinking is not valued or even necessary.

A final theory dealing with developmental psychology was devised by **Lawrence Kohlberg** and presented in his 1981 book *The Philosophy of Moral Development: Moral Stages and the Idea of Justice*. Kohlberg's stages deal with how children formulate moral reasoning at various stages of cognitive development. He called the earliest stage the "preconventional." Here, children base moral decisions on how they themselves are effected. Something is "right," in other words, if they are not likely to be punished for doing it. The next level is the "conventional" stage. During this stage, people base their moral judgments on the conventions of society (or of family or religion or some other social order). Something is "right" during this stage of development if it is something most people would agree is right. Many people do not pass beyond the conventional level of moral reasoning. If they do, they arrive at what Kohlberg calls the "post-conventional level," where moral judgments are based on personal beliefs. People in this stage of moral development will do what they consider is "right" even if it contradicts social norms.

See also Cognitive Development; Psychosexual Development.

Further Reading

Marse, Michele Black. "Is My Child Normal?" *Parents' Magazine* (September 1991): 68.

John Dewey

Dewey, John (1859–1952)

American philosopher, educator, and psychologist who made significant contributions to the establishment of the school of functional psychology.

John Dewey was born near Burlington, Vermont. After receiving his B.A. from the University of Vermont, he taught high school and studied philosophy independently before entering the graduate program in philosophy at Johns Hopkins University. After receiving his Ph.D. in 1884, Dewey served on the faculties of the University of Michigan, the University of Minnesota, the University of Chicago, and Columbia University. Dewey was a founder of the philosophical movement called pragmatism, and his writings on educational theory and practice were widely read and accepted. He held that the disciplines of philosophy, pedagogy, and **psychology** should be understood as closely interrelated. Dewey came to believe in an "instrumentalist" theory of knowledge, in which ideas are seen to exist primarily as instruments for the solution of problems encountered in the **environment.**

Dewey's work at the University of Chicago between 1894 and 1904—together with that of his colleague, Rowland Angell (1869–1949)—made that institution a world-renowned center of the functionalist movement in psychology. Dewey's functionalism was influenced by **Charles Darwin**'s theory of evolution, as well as by the ideas of **William James** and by Dewey's own instrumentalist philosophy. His 1896 paper, "The Reflex Arc Concept in Psychology," is generally considered the first major statement establishing the functionalist school. In this work, Dewey attacked the prevailing reductionist methods of such figures as Wilhelm Wundt (1832–1920) and Edward Titchener (1867–1927), who used stimulus-response analysis as the basis for psychological theories that reduced human experience to the simplest and most basic units possible. Dewey considered their approach flawed because it ignored both the continuity of human behavior and its significance in terms of **adaptation.** In contrast, **functionalism** sought to consider the total organism as it functioned in the environment—an active perceiver rather than a passive receiver of stimuli.

Dewey was also an educational reformer and a pioneer in the field of **educational psychology.** Paralleling his philosophical and psychological theories, his concept of instrumentalism in education stressed learning by doing, as opposed to authoritarian teaching methods and rote learning. Dewey's ideas have remained at the center of much educational philosophy in the United States. While at the University of Chicago, Dewey founded an experimental school to develop and study new educational methods, a project that won him both fame and controversy. He experimented with educational curricula and methods, successfully combining theory and practice, and also pioneered in advocating parental participation in the educational process. His first influential book on education, *The School and Society* (1899), was adapted from a series of lectures to parents of the pupils in his school at the University of Chicago. During his time at Columbia, he continued working on the applications of psychology to problems in education, and his work influenced educational ideas and practices throughout the world.

Dewey wrote the first American psychology textbook, titled *Psychology (1886)*, which was followed by William James's *The Principles of Psychology* four years later. Dewey served as president of the **American Psychological Association** from 1899 to 1900 and was the first president of the American Association of University Professors in 1915. In 1920 he helped organize the American Civil Liberties Union. In the following years, Dewey surveyed educational practices in several foreign countries, including Turkey, Mexico, and the Soviet Union. After his retirement in 1930, Dewey continued his writing and his advocacy of political and educational causes, including the advancement of adult education. Among Dewey's large body of writings are: *Applied Psy-*

CLASSIFICATION OF MENTAL DISORDERS

Disorders Usually First Diagnosed in Infancy, Childhood, or Adolescence

- Mental Retardation
- Learning Disorders
- Motor Skill Disorder
- Communication Disorders
- Pervasive Developmental Disorders
- Attention-Deficit and Disruptive Behavior Disorders
- Feeding and Eating Disorders of Infancy or Early Childhood
- Tic Disorders
- Elimination Disorders
- Other Disorders of Infancy, Childhood, or Adolescence

Delirium, Dementia, and Amnestic and Other Cognitive Disorders

- Delirium
- Dementia
- Amnestic Disorders
- Other Cognitive Disorders

Mental Disorders Due to a General Medical Condition Not Elsewhere Classified

Substance-Related Disorders

- Alcohol-Related Disorders
- Amphetamine Use Disorders
- Amphetamine-Induced Disorders
- Caffeine-Related Disorders
- Cannabis-Related Disorders
- Cocaine-Related Disorders
- Hallucinogen-Related Disorders
- Inhalant-Related Disorders
- Nicotine-Related Disorders
- Opioid-Related Disorders
- Phencyclidine-Related Disorders
- Sedative-, Hypnotic-, or Anxiolytic-Related Disorders
- Polysubstance-Related Disorder
- Other, or Unknown Substance-Related Disorders

Schizophrenia and Other Psychotic Disorders

Mood Disorders

- Depressive Disorders
- Bipolar Disorders

Anxiety Disorders

Somatoform Disorders

Factitious Disorders

Dissociative Disorders

Sexual and Gender Identity Disorders

- Sexual Dysfunctions
- Paraphilias
- Gender Identity Disorders

Eating Disorders

Sleep Disorders

- Primary Sleep Disorders
- Sleep Disorders Related to Another Mental Disorder

Impulse-Control Disorders Not Elsewhere Classified

Adjustment Disorders

Personality Disorders

Other Conditions

---

chology: An Introduction to the Principles and Practice of Education (1889), Interest as Related to Will (1896), Studies in Logical Theory (1903), How We Think (1910), Democracy and Education (1916), Experience and Nature (1925), Philosophy and Civilization (1931), Experience and Education (1938), and Freedom and Culture (1939).

See also Assessment, Psychological.

Further Reading

Boydston, Jo Ann. Guide to the Works of John Dewey. Edwardsville, IL: Southern Illinois University Press, 1972.

Hook, Sidney. John Dewey: An Intellectual Portrait. New York: John Day Co., 1939.

. . . .

Diagnostic and Statistical Manual of Mental Disorders (DSM)

An extensive reference work designed to facilitate the diagnosis and classification of mental disorders, produced by committees and work groups of the American Psychiatric Association. The fourth edition was published in 1994.

First published in 1917, the *Diagnostic and Statistical Manual of Mental Disorders* has added new categories. Beginning with the third edition, published in 1980, the *DSM* has recommended assessment of mental disorders according to five axes, or dimensions, that together establish an overall picture of a person's mental, emotional, and physical health, providing as complete a context as possible in which to make a proper diagnosis. The diagnostician evaluates the patient according to criteria for each axis to produce a comprehensive assessment of the patient's condition; the multiaxial system addresses the complex nature of more mental disorders.

Axis I lists 14 major clinical syndromes. These include disorders usually first diagnosed in childhood or **adolescence (hyperactivity, mental retardation, autism**); **dementia, amnesia,** and other cognitive disorders; substance-related disorders; **schizophrenia** and other conditions characterized by abnormalities in thinking, **perception,** and **emotion;** and sexual and gender identity disorders. Also listed in Axis I are **mood, anxiety,** somatoform, dissociative, eating, **sleep,** impulse control, and **adjustment** disorders, as well as factitious (false) disorders. Axis II is for assessment of **personality** disorders—lifelong, deeply ingrained patterns of behavior that are destructive to those who display them or to others. Some examples are narcissistic, dependent, avoidant, and antisocial personality types. This axis also includes developmental disorders in children. Axis III considers any organic medical problems that may be present. The fourth axis includes any environmental or psychosocial factors affecting a person's condition (such as the loss of a loved one, sexual abuse, **divorce,** career changes, poverty, or homelessness). In Axis V, the diagnostician assesses the person's level of functioning within the previous 12 months on a scale of 1 to 100.

One notable feature of *DSM-IV* is that it dispenses with two previously ubiquitous terms in the field of **psychology**—"neurosis" and "psychosis"—because they are now considered too vague. The term "neurosis" was generally used for a variety of conditions that involved some form of **anxiety,** whereas "psychosis" referred to conditions in which the patient had lost the ability to function normally in daily life and/or had lost touch with reality. Conditions that would formerly have been described as neurotic are now found in five Axis I classifications: mood disorders, anxiety disorders, somatoform disorders, **dissociative identity disorders,** and sexual disorders. Conditions formerly referred to as psychotic are now found in Axis I as well. Besides diagnostic criteria, the *DSM-IV* also provides information about mental and emotional disorders, covering areas such as probable cause, average age at onset, possible complications, amount of impairment, prevalence, gender ratio, predisposing factors, and family patterns.

DSM-IV contains the results of a comprehensive and systematic review of relevant published literature, including earlier editions of *DSM*. In cases where the evidence of a literature review was found to be insufficient

MULTIAXIAL CLASSIFICATION SYSTEM

Axis I – Clinical Disorders; Other Conditions That May Be a Focus of Clinical Attention

Axis II – Personality Disorders; Mental Retardation

Axis III – General Medical Conditions

Axis IV – Psychosocial and Environmental Problems

Axis V – Global Assessment of Functioning

to resolve a particular question, data sets were reanalyzed and issue-focused field trials were conducted. These literature reviews, data reanalyses, and field trials that form the basis of *DSM-IV* have been fully documented, condensed, and published separately as a reference record in a five volume set entitled *DSM-IV Sourcebook*. The *DSM-IV Sourcebook* also contains executive summaries of the rationales for the final decisions relative to inclusion in *DSM-IV*. The diagnostic, classificational, and statistical information presented in *DSM-IV* is widely used internationally by psychiatrists, other physicians, psychologists, nurses, social workers, and other health and mental health professionals in a variety of clinical, research, and educational settings.

Differential Psychology

The area of psychology concerned with measuring and comparing differences in individual and group behavior.

The earliest research in the field of differential psychology began in the late nineteenth century with **Francis Galton**'s investigation of the effects of **heredity** on individual **intelligence** and his pioneering work in intelligence testing, which was further advanced by **James McKeen Cattell** and **Alfred Binet.** It was Binet who developed the first standardized intelligence test. Growth in related areas such as genetics and **developmental psychology,** as well as advances in psychological testing, all broadened the scope of the field considerably. While individual differences are often conceived of, at least popularly, in terms of categories ("gifted," "slow learner"), they are actually measurable on a continuum which, for most traits, follows the normal probability or "bell" curve first derived from the study of heights of soldiers. The majority of subjects cluster near the center with a gradual decrease toward the extremes.

Some areas of research focused on today by psychologists working in differential psychology are the effect of heredity and **environment** on behavioral differences and differences in intelligence among individuals and groups. Observations about group differences can be misused and turn into stereotypes when **mean** characteristics are indiscriminately ascribed to all individuals in a group, and when differences between groups are viewed as unchangeable and solely hereditary.

Further Reading

Eysenck, Michael W. *Individual Differences: Normal and Abnormal.* Hillsdale, NJ: L. Erlbaum Associates, 1994.

Disability

Any physical, mental, sensory, or psychological impairment or deficiency resulting in the lack, loss, or substantial reduction of the ability to perform some normal function.

In the United States, the term disability is legally defined in the Rehabilitation Act (PL 93–112; 29 U.S.C. 794) Amendments of 1974 and the **Americans with Disabilities Act** (PL 101–336; 42 U.S.C. 12101) of 1990 as a physical or mental impairment that substantially limits one or more of the major life activities of an individual. Disabilities may be caused by congenital, traumatic, pathological, or other factors, and vary widely in severity. They may be temporary or permanent, correctable or irreversible. Physical disabilities include blindness, deafness, deformity, muscular and nervous disorders, paralysis, and loss of limbs. Paralysis is frequently caused by injuries to the spinal cord, with the extent of paralysis depending on the portion of the spine that is injured. Congenital disabilities include spina bifida, cystic fibrosis, and muscular dystrophy. Other causes of disabilities include cerebral hemorrhage, arthritis and other bone diseases, amputation, severe pulmonary or cardiac disease, nerve diseases, and the natural process of **aging.** Mental impairments are of two types: **mental illness** and **mental retardation.** Approximately 35 million people in the United States are disabled.

Professionals including physicians, physical and occupational therapists, social workers, and psychologists assist disabled persons in the rehabilitation process, helping them function at the highest possible physical, vocational, and social levels. Specialists in rehabilitation medicine, sometimes referred to as physiatrists, diagnose patients and plan individual treatment programs for the management of pain and disabilities resulting from musculoskeletal injuries. People with hearing or vision loss require special education, including instruction in lip reading, sign language, or Braille. Physical rehabilitation for individuals with musculoskeletal disabilities includes passive exercise of affected limbs and active exercise for parts of the body that are not affected. Occupational training, including counseling, helps persons whose disabilities make it necessary for them to find new jobs or careers. Rehabilitation also involves the services of speech pathologists, recreational therapists, home planning consultants, orthotists and prosthetists, driver educators, and dieticians.

Recent technological advances—especially those involving computer-aided devices—have aided immeasurably in mainstreaming the disabled into many areas of society. These include voice-recognition aids for the paralyzed; optical character-recognition devices for the blind; sip-and-puff air tubes that enable quadriplegics to type and control wheelchair movements with their mouths; and computerized electronic grids that translate eye movements into speech. In addition to access, mobility for the disabled has become an area of concern. The American Automobile Association (AAA) estimates that there are 500,000 licensed drivers in the United States with significant physical impairments and another 1.5 million with lesser disabilities. AAA auto clubs throughout the country are working to improve the mobility of disabled drivers and travelers through improved driver education for those with impairments and improved facilities for the handicapped traveler, including motorist rest areas on the highway.

Public attitudes toward the disabled have changed. Since the 1970s, advocates for the disabled have won passage of numerous laws on the federal, state, and local levels aimed at making education, employment, and public accommodation more accessible through the elimination of physical barriers to access, as well as affirmative action in the hiring and professional advancement of disabled people. Whereas many people with disabilities were formerly confined to their homes or to institutions, the current trend is geared toward reintegrating disabled persons into the community in ways that enable them the greatest possible amount of independence in both their living arrangements and their jobs. Wheelchair access at building entrances, curbs, and public restrooms has been greatly expanded and mandated by law. Braille signs are standard in public areas such as elevators.

Two major pieces of federal legislation have protected the rights of the disabled: a 1975 law guaranteeing disabled children a right to public education in the least restrictive setting possible and the 1990 Americans with Disabilities Act (ADA), which extends comprehensive civil rights protection in employment and access to public areas. Title I of the ADA, which prohibits discrimination by private employers on the basis of disability, is intended to ensure that the same performance standards and job requirements are applied to disabled persons as to persons who are not. In cases where functional limitations may interfere with job performance, employers are required to take any necessary steps to accommodate reasonably the needs of a disabled person, including adjustments to the work **environment** or to the way in which the job is customarily performed. The ADA also contains provisions ensuring nondiscrimination in state and local government services (Title II) and nondiscrimination in public accommodations and commercial facilities (Title III).

Further Reading
Davis, Lennard J. *Enforcing Normalcy: Disability, Deafness, and the Body.* New York: Verso, 1995.

Dissociation/Dissociative Disorders

The feeling of being detached from oneself, of being able to watch oneself as though from a distance; psychological disor-

CAUSES OF DISABILITIES IN CHILDREN UNDER AGE 17		
Condition	**Number (thousands)**	**Percent**
Learning disability	1435	29.5%
Speech problems	634	13.1%
Mental retardation	331	6.8%
Asthma	311	6.4%
Mental or emotional problem or disorder	305	6.3%
Blindness or vision problem	144	3.0%
Cerebral palsy	129	2.7%
Epilepsy or seizure disorder	128	2.6%
Impairment deformity of back, side, foot, or leg	121	2.5%
Deafness or serious trouble hearing	116	2.4%
Tonsilitis or repeated ear infections	80	1.6%
Hay fever or other respiratory allergies	76	1.6%
Missing legs, feet, toes, arms, hands, or fingers	70	1.4%
Autism	48	1.0%
Drug or alcohol problem or disorder	48	1.0%
Head or spinal cord injury	45	0.9%
Heart trouble	44	0.9%
Impairment deformity of finger, hand, or arm	27	0.6%
Cancer	26	0.5%
Diabetes	14	0.3%
Other	653	13.4%
Total	4858	100%

Source: Centers for Disease Control, U.S. Department of Health and Human Services.

ders having at their core long-term periods of such feelings when a specific cause may not be identified.

Dissociation, or the feeling of being detached from the reality of one's body, can be categorized into two types: depersonalization and derealization. Depersonalization is highlighted by a sense of not knowing who you are, or of questioning long-held beliefs about who you are. In derealization, persons perceive reality in a grossly distorted way. Psychologists have identified several types of disorders based on these feelings. These include depersonalization disorder, dissociative fugue, dissociative **amnesia,** dissociative trance disorder, and **dissociative identity disorder** (also known as multiple personality syndrome), among others.

Depersonalization disorder is a condition marked by a persistent feeling of not being real. The *DSM*-IV describes its symptoms as "persistent or recurrent experiences of feeling detached from, and as if one is an outside observer of, one's mental processes or body (e.g., feeling like one is in a dream)." While many people have experienced a similar feeling, persons actually suffering from this disorder are so overwhelmed by these feelings that they are unable to function normally in society. It is also critical to point out that in order to be diagnosed as having this disorder, these feelings cannot be caused by some specific **drug** or event. Depersonalization disorder, by itself, is a rare disorder, and, in fact, many of its symptoms are also symptomatic of other more common disorders, such as acute **stress** disorder and **panic** attacks.

Dissociative fugue is a strange phenomena in which persons will be stricken with a sudden **memory** loss that prompts them to flee their familiar surroundings. These flights are usually caused by some traumatic event. People suffering from this disorder will suddenly find themselves in a new surrounding, hundreds or even thousands of miles from their homes with no memories of the weeks, months, or even years that have elapsed since their flight. Incidence of dissociative fugue rarely appear until after **adolescence** and usually before the age of 50. Once a person has fallen into the behavior, however, it is more likely that it will recur.

Dissociative amnesia describes the condition of suddenly losing major chunks of memory. There are two types of this disorder: generalized amnesia, in which a person cannot remember anything about their lives, and localized amnesia, a common disorder in which a person forgets pieces of their identity but retains an overall understanding of who they are. Dissociative amnesia is generally caused by some traumatic event, such as a natural disaster, a violent crime, or war. In these instances, it is an adaptive mechanism that allows a person to continue his or her life without having to deal with an utterly horrific memory.

Dissociative trance disorder describes the trance-state that people experience in various kinds of religious ceremonies. Such people generally perform feats that would normally cause injury or severe **pain**—such as walking on hot coals—but because of their dissociated mental state, they are not harmed. This is a curious subcategory in that the condition is not considered a "disorder" in many cultures of the world. Western psychiatrists are divided as to whether this should really be considered a "disorder," since the word has negative implications. It has been proposed, however, that future editions of the *DSM* specify a diagnosis of trance and possession disorder as one of several dissociative disorders.

Further Reading

Goleman, Daniel. "Those Who Stay Calm in Disasters May Face Psychological Risk." *New York Times* (17 April 1994): 12.

Mukerjee, Madhursee. "Hidden Scars: Sexual and Other Abuse May Alter Brain Region." *Scientific American* (October 1995): 14.

Dissociative Identity Disorder

Also referred to as multiple personality disorder, a condition in which a person's identity dissociates, or fragments, creating additional, distinct identities that exist independently of each other within the same person.

Persons suffering from dissociative identity disorder (DID) adopt one or more distinct identities which co-exist within one individual. Each **personality** is distinct from the other in specific ways. For instance, tone of voice and mannerisms will be distinct, as well as posture, vocabulary, and everything else we normally think of as marking a personality. There are cases in which a person will have as many as 100 or more identities, while some people only exhibit the presence of one or two. In either case, the criteria for diagnosis are the same. This disorder was, until the publication of *DSM-IV,* referred to as multiple personality disorder. This name was abandoned for a variety of reasons, one having to do with psychiatric explicitness (it was thought that the name should reflect the dissociative aspect of the disorder).

The *DSM-IV* lists four criteria for diagnosing someone with dissociative identity disorder. The first being the presence of two or more distinct "identities or personality states." At least two personalities must take control of the person's identity regularly. The person must exhibit aspects of **amnesia**—that is, he or she forgets routine personal information. And, finally, the condition must not have been caused by "direct physiological effects," such as drug abuse or head trauma.

TWO FAMOUS CASES

The stories of two women with multiple personality disorder have been told both in books and films. A woman with 22 personalities was recounted in 1957 in a major motion picture starring Joanne Woodward and in a book by Corbett Thigpen, both titled *The Three Faces of Eve*. Twenty years later, in 1977, Caroline Sizemore, the 22nd personality to emerge in "Eve," described her experiences in a book titled *I'm Eve*. Although the woman known as "Eve" developed a total of 22 personalities, only three could exist at any one time—for a new one to emerge, an existing personality would "die."

The story of Sybil (a pseudonym) was published in 1973 by Flora Rheta Schreiber, who worked closely for a decade with Sybil and her New York psychiatrist Dr. Cornelia B. Wilbur. Sybil's sixteen distinct personalities emerged over a period of 40 years.

Both stories reveal fascinating insights—and raise though-provoking questions—about the unconscious mind, the interrelationship between remembering and forgetting, and the meaning of personality development. The separate and disctinct personalities manifested in these two cases feature unique physical traits and vocational interests. In their study of this disorder, scientists have been able to monitor unique patterns of brain wave activity for the unique multiple personalities.

Persons suffering from DID usually have a main personality that psychiatrists refer to as the "host." This is generally not the person's original personality, but is rather developed along the way. It is usually this personality that seeks psychiatric help. Psychiatrists refer to the other personalities as "alters" and the phase of transition between alters as the "switch." The number of alters in any given case can vary widely and can even vary across gender. That is, men can have female alters and women can have male alters. The physical changes that occur in a switch between alters is one of the most baffling aspects of dissociative identity disorder. People assume whole new physical postures and voices and vocabularies. One study conducted in 1986 found that in 37 percent of patients, alters even demonstrated different **handedness** from the host.

Statistically, sufferers of DID have an average of 15 identities. The disorder is far more common among fe-

males than males (as high as 9-to-1), and the usual age of onset is in early childhood, generally by the age of four. Once established, the disorder will last a lifetime if not treated. New identities can accumulate over time as the person faces new types of situations. For instance, as a sufferer confronts **sexuality** in **adolescence**, an identity may emerge that deals exclusively with this aspect of life. There are no reliable figures as to the prevalence of this disorder, although it has begun to be reported with increased frequency over the last several years. People with DID tend to have other severe disorders as well, such as **depression**, substance abuse, borderline **personality disorder** and eating disorders, among others.

In nearly every case of DID, horrific instances of physical or sexual **child abuse**—even torture—was present (one study of 100 DID patients found that 97 had suffered child abuse). It is believed that young children, faced with a routine of torture and neglect, create a fantasy world in order to escape the brutality. In this way, DID is similar to **post-traumatic stress disorder**, and recent thinking in psychiatry has suggested that the two disorders may be linked; some are even beginning to view DID as a severe subtype of post-traumatic stress disorder.

Treatment of dissociative identity disorder is a long and difficult process, and success (the complete integration of identity) is rare. A 1990 study found that of 20 patients studied, only five were successfully treated. Current treatment method involves having DID patients recall the memories of their childhoods. Because these childhood memories are often subconscious, treatment often includes **hypnosis** to help the patient remember. There is a danger here, however, as sometimes the recovered memories are so traumatic for the patient that they cause more harm.

There is considerable controversy about the nature, and even the existence, of dissociative identity disorder. One cause for the skepticism is the alarming increase in reports of the disorder over the last several decades. Eugene Levitt, a psychologist at the Indiana University School of Medicine, noted in an article published in *Insight on the News* (1993) that "In 1952 there was no listing for [DID] in the *DSM,* and there were only a handful of cases in the country. In 1980, the disorder [then known as multiple personality disorder] got its official listing in the *DSM,* and suddenly thousands of cases are springing up everywhere." Another area of contention is in the whole notion of suppressed memories, a crucial component in DID. Many experts dealing with memory say that it is nearly impossible for anyone to remember things that happened before the age three, the age when much of the abuse supposedly occurred to DID sufferers.

Regardless of the controversy, people diagnosed with this disorder are clearly suffering from some profound disorder. As Helen Friedman, a clinical psychologist in St. Louis told *Insight on the News,* "When you see it, it's just not fake."

Further Reading

Arbetter, Sandra. "Multiple Personality Disorder: Someone Else Lives Inside of Me." *Current Health* (2 November 1992): 17.

Mesic, Penelope. "Presence of Minds." *Chicago* (September 1992): 100.

Sileo, Chi Chi. "Multiple Personalities: The Experts Are Split." *Insight on the News* (25 October 1993): 18.

Sizemore, Chris Costner. *I'm Eve.* Garden City, NY: Doubleday, 1977.

Thigpen, Corbett H. *The Three Faces of Eve.* New York: Popular Library, 1957.

"When the Body Remembers." *Psychology Today* (April 1994): 9.

Videorecordings

Sybil [videorecording].

The Three Faces of Eve [videorecording]. Beverly Hills, CA: FoxVideo, 1993. Produced and directed from his screenplay by Nunnally Johnson. Originally released as motion picture in 1957.

Divorce

The legal dissolution of a marriage.

The divorce rate in the United States has been rising since the 1960s; currently half of all American couples who marry will divorce. Possible factors for the high incidence of divorce include the enactment of "no-fault" divorce laws that make it legally easier to get divorced; a decline in the number of couples who stay together for religious reasons; the increased financial independence of women; conflicts resulting from the growing number of dual-career marriages; and a greater social acceptance of divorce.

Divorce is generally preceded by a breakdown in communication between the partners. Other factors leading to divorce include alcoholism and drug abuse, domestic **violence,** extramarital affairs, and desertion. Divorce generally causes significant **stress** for all family members. After the death of one's spouse, it is considered the single greatest stressor on the Holmes and Rahe Social Readjustment Scale, which assigns point values to a variety of stress-producing life changes. Both partners must make financial adjustments—an area of much bitterness during divorce proceedings. Social relationships with friends and family often change, and the newly divorced person must face the challenges and insecurities of dating. Divorced parents have to adjust to raising children on their own or adapt to noncustodial parenthood. In

adults, divorce causes feelings of guilt over one's share of the responsibility for a failed marriage, **anger** toward one's spouse, and feelings of social, emotional, and financial insecurity. Also common to divorce are feelings of **anxiety**, incompetence, **depression**, and loneliness.

Children—who are involved in 70 percent of American divorces—may be even more severely affected than their parents, although this also depends on such factors as custody arrangements and parental **attitudes.** Divorce is often thought to be hardest on young children, who tend to blame themselves, fantasize that their parents will get back together, and worry about being abandoned. Sometimes the effects on younger children do not become apparent until they reach **adolescence**. Children who are teenagers at the time of the divorce are strongly affected as well. In one study, subjects who were in early adolescence when their parents divorced had troubled forming committed relationships ten years later. However, the effects of divorce must be weighed against the difficulty of continuing to live in a household characterized by conflict and estrangement. Researchers have found evidence that of the two alternatives, divorce can be the less emotionally damaging one. After an initial period of turmoil, stability generally returns to the lives of adults and children. Both may function more competently than they did before the divorce and show improved self-esteem. Most divorced people remarry within three years, but many second marriages have not been found to be successful.

Further Reading

Fisher, Helen E. *Anatomy of Love: The Natural History of Monogamy, Adultery, and Divorce.* New York: W. W. Norton, 1992.

DNA. See Deoxyribonucleic acid.

Double-blind. See Experimental design.

Down Syndrome

A hereditary mental disorder present at birth resulting from an abnormality in the number of chromosomes; also known Trisomy 21.

Down syndrome was named after John Langdon Haydon Down, a British physician and advocate of education for the mentally retarded, who first described it in 1866. In 1959, the French pediatrician Jerome Lejeune discovered that the disorder is caused by a chromosomal abnormality. Ninety-five percent of individuals with Down syndrome have Trisomy 21, an extra chromosome in the 21st pair (altogether, they have 47 chromosomes

Research has shown that children with Down syndrome benefit from early intervention—stimulation and close contact at an early age with family members and therapists.

instead of the normal 46); four percent have translocation, a chromosomal abnormality; and one percent have mosaicism. Down syndrome is characterized primarily by varying degrees of mental and motor retardation. Most people with the disorder are retarded. Individuals with Down syndrome have I.Q.s ranging from 20 to over 90, with the mean being 49. They are also prone to possible heart defects, poor vision and hearing, cataracts, and have a low resistance to respiratory infections. Until the discovery of antibiotics, most Down syndrome children died of pneumonia before reaching adulthood. People with Down syndrome are 20 times more likely than the general population to develop leukemia and a neurological condition similar to **Alzheimer's disease.**

Individuals with Down syndrome have a distinctive physical appearance characterized by almond-shaped eyes (on which the condition's former alternate name— mongolism—was based); a short, stocky build; a flat nose and large, protruding tongue (which makes normal speech difficult); a small skull flattened in the back; a short neck with extra skin; and small hands with short fingers. Other features include a fold of skin on the inner side of the eye; speckling at the edge of the iris; and a small amount of facial and body hair. Muscle tone is of-

ten poor, and newborns are prone to hypotonia, or "floppiness." It is often observed that people with Down syndrome tend to have docile temperaments; and are generally cheerful, cooperative, affectionate, and relaxed, although there are no scientific studies to confirm this. Their motor, speech, and sexual development is delayed, and their cognitive development may not peak until the age of 30 or 40. In infancy, speech development is delayed by about seven months.

Recent research has led to the conclusion that Down children are capable of expressing complex feelings, of developing richer personalities, and of mastering higher degrees of learning using adaptive strategies (such as computer-aided learning to teach reading and writing). One developmental program that began with Down children as young as 30 months old and stressed positive parent-child communication eventually enabled the children to read at a second-grade level. The theory is that early stimulation helps to develop connections in the brain that might otherwise not have developed.

Although most people with Down syndrome were institutionalized until the 1970s, those with only moderate retardation are capable of achieving some degree of self-sufficiency. Today, with changed social attitudes and expanded educational opportunities, many lead productive, fulfilling lives.

There are over 400,000 people in the United States with Down syndrome, which occurs in 1 out of about 600 births in people of every ethnic group and socioeconomic class. It is well-known that women over age 35 are at greater risk for bearing a child with Down syndrome. The incidence of the condition for mothers under 30 years old is one child in 1,500; for mothers over age 45, it is one in 65. However, it is less known that women under 35 actually bear 80 percent of Down infants, and recent studies suggest that the father's age may play a role as well. Prenatal detection of Down syndrome is possible through amniocentesis and chorionic villus sampling and is recommended for pregnant women over the age of 35.

See also Mental Retardation.

Further Information

National Down Syndrome Congress
    Address: 1800 Dempster Street
    Park Ridge, Illinois 60068-1146
    Telephone: 708-823-7550; (800) 232-NDSC
National Down Syndrome Society
    Address: 666 Broadway
    New York, New York 10012
    Telephone: 212-460-9330; (800) 221-4602

Draw-a-Person Test

A test used to measure nonverbal intelligence or to screen for emotional or behavior disorders.

Based on children's drawings of human figures, this test can be used with two different scoring systems for different purposes. One measures nonverbal **intelligence** while the other screens for emotional or **behavior**al **disorders**. During the testing session, which can be completed in 15 minutes, the child is asked to draw three figures—a man, a woman, and him- or herself. To evaluate intelligence, the test administrator uses the Draw-a-Person: QSS (Quantitative Scoring System). This system analyzes fourteen different aspects of the drawings, such as specific body parts and clothing, for various criteria, including presence or absence, detail, and proportion. In all, there are 64 scoring items for each drawing. A separate standard score is recorded for each drawing, and a total score for all three. The use of a nonverbal, nonthreatening task to evaluate intelligence is intended to eliminate possible sources of bias by reducing variables like primary language, verbal skills, communication disabilities, and sensitivity to working under pressure. However, test results can be influenced by previous drawing experience, a factor that may account for the tendency of middle-class children to score higher on this test than lower-class children, who often have fewer opportunities to draw. To assess the test-taker for emotional problems, the administrator uses the Draw-a-Person: SPED (Screening Procedure for Emotional Disturbance) to score the drawings. This system is composed of two types of criteria. For the first type, eight dimensions of each drawing are evaluated against norms for the child's age group. For the second type, 47 different items are considered for each drawing.

See also Intelligence Quotient, I.Q. Test.

Dreams

The sequence of imagery, thoughts, and emotions that pass through the mind during sleep.

Dreams defy the laws of physics, the principles of logic, and personal morality, and may reflect fears, frustrations, and personal desires. Often occurring in story-form with the dreamer as participant or observer, dreams usually involve several characters, motion, and may include sensations of **taste, smell, hearing,** or **pain.** The content of dreams clearly reflects daytime activities, even though these may be distorted to various degrees. While some people report dreaming only in black and white, others dream in color. "Lucid dreaming," in which the sleeper is actually aware of dreaming while the dream is taking place, is not uncommon. Research has indicated that everyone dreams during every night of normal **sleep.** Many people do not remember their dreams, however, and most people recall only the last dream they have prior to awakening. The memory shut-down theory suggests that memory may be one of the **brain**'s functions which rests during dreaming, hence we forget our dreams.

In order to understand how dreaming occurs, brain waves during sleep have been measured by an **electroencephalograph (EEG)**. Normally large and slow during sleep, these waves become smaller and faster during periods of sleep accompanied by rapid eye movements (called REM sleep), and it is during these period when dreams occur. During a normal eight-hour period of sleep, an average adult will dream three to five dreams lasting ten to thirty minutes each for a total of 100 minutes.

Dreams—which **Sigmund Freud** called "the royal road to the **unconscious**"—have provided psychologists and psychotherapists with abundant information about the structure, dynamics, and development of the human personality. Several theories attempt to explain why we dream. The oldest and most well-known is Freud's psychoanalytic theory, elucidated in *The Interpretation of Dreams* (1900), in which he suggested that dreams are disguised symbols of repressed desires and therefore offer us direct insight into the unconscious. According to Freud, the manifest content of dreams, such as daily events and memories, serve to disguise their latent content or unconscious wishes through a process he called dream-work, consisting of four operations. *Condensation* referred to the condensing of separate thoughts into a single image in order to fit the latent content into the brief framework of a dream. *Displacement* served to disguise the latent content by creating confusion between important and insignificant elements of the dream. *Symbolization* was a further effort to evade the "censor" of repressed desires by symbolizing certain objects with other objects, as in the case of phallic symbols. *Secondary revision* enables the dreamer to make the dream more coherent by additions that fill it in more intelligibly while he or she is recalling it.

Although **Carl Jung**'s system of analysis differed greatly from that of Freud, the Swiss psychologist agreed with Freud's basic view of dreams as compensating for repressed psychic elements. According to Jung's theory, significant dreams (those that involve the collective unconscious) are attempts to reveal an image, or **archetype,** that is not sufficiently "individuated" in the subject's personality. Another Swiss analyst, Medard Boss, offered yet another perspective on dreams as part of his system of "existential analysis." Under Boss's system, the significance of dreams lay close to their surface details rather than corresponding to an intricate symbolic pattern. Thus, for example, dreams set in a narrow, constricted room indicated that this was how the dreamer viewed his or her existence. Existential analysis was based on the feelings of the dreamer, the contents of the dream, and his or her response to them.

In contrast with the methods of these early dream analysts, modern researchers gather data from subjects in a sleep laboratory, a mode of investigation furthered in the 1950s. Calvin Hall, a pioneer in the content analysis of dreams, posits that dreams are meant to reveal rather than to conceal. Hall and his associates gathered dreams from a large and varied sampling of subjects and analyzed them for the following content categories: 1) human characters classified by sex, age, family members, friends and acquaintances, and strangers; 2) animals; 3) types of interactions among characters, such as aggressive or friendly; 4) positive and negative events; 5) success and failure; 6) indoor and outdoor settings; 7) objects; and 8) **emotion**s. Other investigators have devised their own systems of content analysis, such as the one outlined by David Foulkes in *A Grammar of Dreams*. The dreams of children have also been extensively assessed through laboratory testing and shown to be linked to their cognitive development. Content analysis has also yielded longitudinal information about individuals, including the observations that an adult's dreams remain strikingly similar over time and are strongly linked to the preoccupations of waking life, a phenomenon known as the continuity principle.

There have been recent attempts among scientists to discount the significance of dreams entirely. The activation-synthesis hypothesis created by J. Alan Hobson and Robert W. McCarley in 1977 holds that dreaming is a simple and unimportant by-product of random stimulation of brain cells activated during REM sleep. Another dream theory, the mental housecleaning hypothesis, suggests that we dream to rid our brains of useless, bizarre, or redundant information. A current synthesis of this theory sees dreaming as analogous to a computer's process of program inspection in which sleep is similar to "down" time and the dream becomes a moment of "online" time, a glimpse into a program being run at that moment.

See also Rapid Eye Movement (REM).

Further Reading

Andrews, Barbara. *Dreams and Waking Visions: A Journal.* New York: St. Martin's Press, 1989.

Guiley, Rosemary. *The Encyclopedia of Dreams: Symbols and Interpretations.* New York: Crossroad, 1993.

Drive Reduction Theory

A popular theory of the 1940s and 1950s that attributed behavior to the desire to reduce tension produced by primary (biological) or secondary (acquired) drives.

Many psychologists believed that all **motivation** depended upon the pleasure experienced when basic **needs** are met. A person who is hungry, for instance, eats in order to reduce the tension that hunger produces. All human behavior could be attributed to the pleasure gained when these drive-induced tensions were reduced.

Drive reduction theory lost favor over the years because it failed to explain human actions that produced, rather than reduced, tension. Many people enjoy riding roller coasters or skydiving, for instance, despite the fact that such activity may cause **fear** and **anxiety.** Similarly, drive theory could not adequately explain sexual behavior in humans or animals. For example, experiments showed that rats persisted in seeking sexual gratification even when their biological urges to mate were interrupted and thus tension was not reduced.

More modern motivational theory includes the principal of optimal arousal, that is, individuals act to maintain an appropriate—rather than a minimal—level of stimulation and **arousal.** Optimal levels vary from person to person, which explains why some people drive race cars and others prefer an evening at the symphony.

Further Reading

Atkinson, Rita L.; Richard C. Atkinson; Edward E. Smith; and Ernest R. Hilgard. *Introduction to Psychology.* 9th ed. San Diego: Harcourt Brace Jovanovich, 1987.

Zimbardo, Philip G. *Psychology and Life.* 12th ed. Glenview, IL: Scott, Foresman, 1988.

Drugs

Any chemical substance that alters normal biological processes.

Psychoactive drugs alter behavior, thought, or **emotion**s by changing biochemical reactions in the nervous system. They can be addictive (habit-forming), and they can be legal or illegal.

Drug abuse is the self-administration of drugs in ways that depart from medical or social norms, and it can lead to psychological or physical dependence. Physical dependence, or addiction, which can occur together with psychological dependence, is characterized by withdrawal symptoms and can involve increased tolerance for the drug. The causes of substance abuse are multiple: some people are high-risk for dependence due to genetic or physiological reasons; others become dependent on

Two popular stimulants that most people do not consider "drugs" are caffeine and nicotine.

drugs to cope with emotional or social problems, or physical **pain.**

Depressants reduce activity of the **central nervous system.** The most common depressive drug is alcohol, which calms, induces **sleep,** decreases inhibitions and fears, and slows reflexes. With continued use, the nervous system accommodates alcohol, requiring increasing amounts to achieve the alcoholic state, and produces withdrawal symptoms. Sedatives are another major category of depressants, notably barbiturates, such as Seconal and Nembutal. Overdoses can be fatal, and withdrawal symptoms are among the most severe for any drug. Anxiolytics (traditionally referred to as tranquilizers) are also sedatives and include the benzodiazepines (Librium, Valium) and meprobamate (Miltown). Many users of these drugs become both psychologically and physically dependent, and their withdrawal symptoms resemble those of barbiturate takers. Taken in combination with alcohol, anxiolytics can be fatal. Anxiolytics are still used in the clinical treatment of **anxiety** and are the most widely pre-

scribed and used legal drugs. Because they pose little danger of death from overdose, the benzodiazepines, have remained popular for the treatment of patients suffering from anxiety. A new member of this class of drug, Xanax, has also been widely used in the treatment of **panic** disorders and agoraphobia.

Narcotics, such as opiates which include heroin and its derivatives, are drugs with sedative properties; they are addictive and produce tolerance. They have a complex combination of effects, causing both drowsiness and euphoria, and are also pain-killers. Eaten, smoked, inhaled, or injected intravenously, heroin impairs the respiratory system, induces changes in the heart and blood vessels, constipation, and loss of appetite. It is derived from morphine, but is several times more powerful. An overdose of heroin can result in death.

Psychedelics, or hallucinogens, such as marijuana, are consciousness-altering drugs that affect **moods,** thought, **memory,** and **perception.** They can produce distortion of **body image,** loss of identity, and **hallucinations.** Usage can produce impaired performance on intellectual and psychomotor tasks, psychoses, and psychological dependence. LSD (lysergic acid diethylamide) is one of the most powerful psychedelic drugs. It can cause bizarre hallucinations, its effects are highly unpredictable, and some users suffer long-term side effects. While low doses of marijuana are considered relaxing and relieve anxiety with minimal health risks, long-term usage in larger amounts may cause major health hazards such as asthma and other respiratory disorders, suppression of the immune system, and heart problems.

Psychostimulants, such as amphetamines and cocaine, are drugs that in moderate or low doses increase mental and behavioral activity. They stimulate alertness, reduce fatigue, increase excitability, elevate moods, and depress appetites. Benzedrine, Dexedrine, Methedrine, (also called "uppers" or "speed"), raise the heart rate and blood pressure, constrict blood pressure, shrink mucous membranes (thus their use as decongestants), and reduce appetite. Many people abuse amphetamines in order to lose weight, remain productive and alert, or to "get high." The symptoms of severe amphetamine abuse can resemble those of paranoid **schizophrenia.** Cocaine and its derivative, "crack," are both highly addictive and take effect more rapidly than amphetamines. Overdoses, especially of crack, can be fatal, and small doses may induce cardiac arrest or stroke. Cocaine addiction is especially difficult to break.

Two popular stimulants that most people do not consider "drugs" are caffeine and nicotine. Caffeine is found in coffee, tea, chocolate, and many soft drinks. It decreases drowsiness and speeds up thought, but at high doses can produce anxiety and induce tremors. Caffeine is ad-

COCAINE

A crystalline alkaloid derived from the leaves of the South American coca plant, Erythroxylun coca.

Medically, cocaine can be used as a local anesthetic because it interrupts the conduction of nerve impulses, particularly in the mucous membranes of the eyes, nose, and throat. Illegally, cocaine is widely abused. As powdered cocaine hydrochloride, it is usually diluted with some other substance, such as aspirin, cornstarch lactose, or talc, and sucked into the nostrils or dissolved in water and injected intravenously. When cocaine is sniffed, it travels from the nasal tissue to the bloodstream and then to the brain, affecting the user within two or three minutes, and if injected, within 15 seconds. Its physiological effects include dilated pupils; elevated heart rate, blood pressure, and body temperature; rapid breathing; and an increased appetite. The drug may also augment norepinephrine and dopamine activity—an effect similar to that of amphetamines—and stimulate the cortex of the brain. Cocaine produces a quick but short "rush," characterized by temporary feelings of euphoria, self-confidence, well-being, and optimism, and hallucinations can also be present. The drug's pleasant effects peak in about 20 to 40 minutes and subside after about an hour, followed by a depression that induces a craving for the drug.

Cocaine can also be converted into a solid form by separating it from its hydrochloride base. This form, commonly known as "crack" cocaine, produces a high that is particularly fast and intense. It is extremely addictive, inducing constant cravings that can cost up to $500 a day to satisfy. Crack cocaine is usually smoked in a pipe or mixed with tobacco in a cigarette. As it has become cheaper to produce, its cost has dropped, and now crack cocaine cost less than one-fifth as much as regular cocaine.

Cocaine is a potent drug, and habituation and dependence may occur very quickly with its abuse. Cocaine users first become psychologically addicted to the drug, as the artificially-induced optimism and confidence they feel help them to cope with daily stresses. Soon, the cocaine user becomes physically addicted as well and often develops a secondary addiction to a depressant, such as alcohol or heroin, to help him or her "come down" from the drug's effects and to induce sleep. When taken internally in any form, cocaine has a highly toxic effect on the central nervous system. Frequent and/or long-term abuse of cocaine may cause overactivity, loss of appetite, nausea, heart problems, seizures, comas, strokes, and permanent brain damage. It can also precipitate delusional psychotic disorders.

Withdrawal from habitual cocaine abuse is characterized by severe physical and emotional discomfort and may last several weeks. Symptoms include muscle pains and spasms, and decreased energy levels and mental functioning. It is very difficult to withdraw from the drug without professional help. An overdose of cocaine stimulates the spinal cord, and may result in convulsions, depression of the entire nervous system, respiratory failure, and death. In the past 50 years, the incidence of cocaine use among Americans has risen dramatically (although there has been a slight decrease since the mid-1980s). A 1988 survey found that one in ten people had used the drug, with the number rising to one in four for adults between the ages of 18 and 25.

dictive; its withdrawal symptoms include headaches, fatigue, craving, and shakiness. They appear within 12 to 24 hours from the last intake, peak at around 48 hours, and continue for a week. Nicotine, the psychostimulant in tobacco, has a powerful effect on the **autonomic nervous system.** While some claim that nicotine addiction is more psychological than physical, it is associated with definite withdrawal symptoms, including cravings, restlessness, irritability, and weight gain. It can cause lung cancer, heart attack, respiratory disorders, and stroke. When used by pregnant women, it can harm their unborn children in a number of ways.

Certain classes of psychoactive drugs are used clinically to treat **depression, mania,** anxiety, and schizophrenia. Therapy for severe mental disorders was transformed in the 1950s with the discovery of neuroleptics (antipsychotics), which reduced psychotic symptoms, including **delusions,** paranoid suspicions, confusion, incoherence, and hallucinations. Phenothiazines, notably chlorpromazine, Thorazine, and Haldol, are the most commonly used antipsychotic drug.

Another drug, clozapine (Clozaril), has effects similar to those of phenothiazines but without the long-term side effect of movement disorders that afflicts at least 25 percent of phenothiazine users. However, about two percent of clozapine users are at risk for a different problem—agranulucytosis, a fatal blood disorder, and all patients who take the drug must be tested regularly for this side effect.

Antidepressants, a second class of therapeutic drugs, reduce symptoms of depression (depressed mood, fatigue, appetite loss, sleep disorders) in a majority of users. There are several types of antidepressants, including monoamine oxidase inhibitors (MAO-I), which can also relieve panic attacks; tricyclic antidepressants, which seem to be more effective for many patients; and a "second generation" of serotonin-related antidepressants. The best-known drug of this type, Prozac (fluoxetine), has become the most widely prescribed antidepressant in the United States due to its combination of effectiveness and lack of side effects. It also helps sufferers from **obsessive-compulsive disorder.** The drug lithium is used to relieve episodes of both mania and depression in patients with **bipolar disorder.**

See also Alcohol Dependence and Abuse.

Dyslexia

A developmental abnormality characterized by a severe impairment of the ability to learn to read.

In contrast to alexia, a condition in which an individual has lost the ability to read (usually due to **brain** injury or disease), dyslexia refers to an impairment or malfunction of that ability. Dyslexia occurs specifically in individuals whose inability to read is not attributed to low general cognitive **ability,** major neurological injury or deficit, or emotional disorder. The reading skills of a person with dyslexia are usually at a low level in relation to his or her IQ.

There is no complete consensus among psychologists, physicians, and educators about the nature and causes of dyslexia. However, it is now generally regarded as a combination of different reading deficiencies rather than a single impairment of the perceptual processes. The fact that reading disorders appear to be less frequent in cultures that use a pictorial rather than phonetic alphabet, such as Japanese, for example, suggest that a breakdown of visual-auditory perception is a contributing factor. It may also be the result of some form of inherent dysfunction involving the two hemispheres of the brain. Normally, the **right-brain hemisphere** is dominant when a child learns the shapes of letters, and the **left-brain hemisphere** takes command when the child learns to associate letters with speech sounds. It has been suggested that dyslexic children may either remain in the shape-learning

Korean-language advertisement for insurance that appeared in *The Korea Central Daily.* Dyslexia and other reading disorders appear to be less common in cultures that use a pictorial rather than phonetic alphabet.

stage, never fully develop the phonetic links, or they make the shift too soon, and are unable to fully absorb the letters' visual impact.

In general, dyslexia is manifested as a distinct lack of facility in creating or processing written language and is much more common in males than in females. Symptoms include persistent reversals of letters or words; bizarre spelling; disordered writing; difficulty in repeating or recalling long words or sequences of letters or digits; hesitant oral reading; leaving out or modifying words; failure to recognize words; and often a history of late speech development. Dyslexic children may have trouble recognizing words because by the time they identify one letter, the previous one has been forgotten. It also takes them longer than other children to name pictures, numbers, and colors.

Persons with dyslexia can benefit from special instructional methods. Treatment of developmental reading disorders has included corrective reading (special help by a teacher within the regular classroom setting), as well as remedial reading (provided by a specialist or tutor outside the regular classroom, often in small groups). Various remedial methods are used in treating dyslexia and other reading disorders. One method involves drills aimed at increasing automatic word recognition by repeated reading of short passages. Another method is having the teacher read with the student and then gradually decreasing his or her role until the student is reading alone. With the kinesthetic method, which is commonly used to treat severe reading disabilities, words are taught by a procedure involving multiple senses (visual, auditory, kinesthetic, tactual), referred to by the acronym VAKT. Exercises such as manually tracing a finger over sandpaper letters while pronouncing them provide an improved sensorimotor connection between visual perception and the reproduction of letters in speech or writing. Eventually, the tracing is eliminated, and the child concentrates on visual processing, looking at words while pronouncing them, attempting to visualize them with closed eyes and, finally, write them from **memory.**

When given sufficient remedial help to enable them to handle assignments, dyslexic individuals can complete high school and college. They generally need to devote considerably more time to their work than the average student, and those with a demonstrated reading disability are often allowed extra time on exams. Dyslexic students can benefit from making detailed organizational plans and schedules for the completion of schoolwork, and professional guidance by counselors and other administrative professionals can assist them in this and other facets of coping with academic work.

Further Reading

Miles, T.R. *Dyslexia.* Philadelphia: Open University Press, 1990.

E

Eating Disorders. See **Anorexia Nervosa; Bulimia Nervosa.**

Ebbinghaus, Hermann (1850–1909)

German psychologist whose work resulted in the development of scientifically reliable experimental methods for the quantitative measurement of rote learning and memory.

Born in Germany, Hermann Ebbinghaus received his formal education at the universities of Halle, Berlin, and Bonn, where he earned degrees in philosophy and history. After obtaining his philosophy degree in 1873, Ebbinghaus served in the Franco-Prussian War. For the next seven years following the war, he tutored and studied independently in Berlin, France, and England. In the late 1870s, Ebbinghaus became interested in the workings of human **memory**. In spite of Wilhelm Wundt's assertion in his newly published *Physiological Psychology* that memory could not be studied experimentally, Ebbinghaus decided to attempt such a study, applying to this new field the same sort of mathematical treatment that Gustav Fechner (1801–1887) had described in *Elements of Psychophysics* (1860) in connection with his study of sensation and **perception**.

Using himself as both sole experimenter and subject, Ebbinghaus embarked on an arduous process that involved repeatedly testing his memorization of nonsense words devised to eliminate variables caused by prior familiarity with the material being memorized. He created 2,300 one-syllable consonant-vowel-consonant combinations—such as *taz*, *bok*, and *lef*—to facilitate his study of learning independent of meaning. He divided syllables into a series of lists that he memorized under fixed conditions. Recording the average amount of time it took him to memorize these lists perfectly, he then varied the conditions to arrive at observations about the effects of such variables as speed, list length, and number of repetitions. He also studied the fac-

Hermann Ebbinghaus

tors involved in retention of the memorized material, comparing the initial memorization time with the time needed for a second memorization of the same material after a given period of time (such as 24 hours) and subsequent memorization attempts. These results showed the existence of a regular forgetting curve over time that approximated a mathematical function similar to that in Fechner's study. After a steep initial decline in learning time between the first and second memorization, the curve leveled off progressively with subsequent efforts.

Ebbinghaus also measured immediate memory, showing that a subject could generally remember between six and eight items after an initial look at one of his lists. In addition, he studied comparative learning rates for meaningful and meaningless material, concluding that meaningful items, such as words and sentences, could be learned much more efficiently than nonsense syllables. His experiments also yielded observations about the value of evenly spaced as opposed to massed memorization. A monumental amount of time and effort went into this ground-breaking research. For example, to determine the effects of number of repetitions on retention, Ebbinghaus tested himself on 420 lists of 16 syllables 340 times each, for a total of 14,280 trials. After careful accumulation and analysis of data, Ebbinghaus published the results of his research in the volume *On Memory* in 1885, while on the faculty of the University of Berlin. Although Wundt argued that results obtained by using nonsense syllables had limited applicability to the actual memorization of meaningful material, Ebbinghaus's work has been widely used as a model for research on human verbal learning, and *Über Gedachtnis (On Memory)* has remained one of the most cited and highly respected sourcebooks in the history of psychology.

In 1894, Ebbinghaus joined the faculty of the University of Breslau. While studying the mental capacities of children in 1897, he began developing a sentence completion test that is still widely used in the measurement of **intelligence.** This test, which he worked on until 1905, was probably the first successful test of **mental ability**. Ebbinghaus also served on the faculties of the Friedrich Wilhelm University and the University of Halle. He was a cofounder of the first German psychology journal, the *Journal of Psychology and Physiology of the Sense Organs,* in 1890, and also wrote two successful textbooks, *The Principles of Psychology* (1902) and *A Summary of Psychology* (1908), both of which went into several editions. His achievements represented a major advance for psychology as a distinct scientific discipline and many of his methods continue to be followed in verbal learning research.

See also Forgetting Curve; Intelligence Quotient, I.Q. test.

Educational Psychology

The study of the process of education, e.g., how people, especially children, learn and which teaching methods and materials are most successful.

Educational psychology departments in many universities provide training to educators, **school psychologist**s, and other educational professionals. Applied research in this field focuses on how to improve teaching, solve learning problems, and measure learning **ability**

The concerns of educational psychology include improving teaching, solving learning problems, and measuring learning ability and progress.

and progress. Other concerns of educational psychology include cognitive development, the dynamics of pupil behavior, and the psychological atmosphere of the classroom. Educational psychologists devise achievement tests, evaluate teaching methods, develop learning aids and curricula, and investigate how children of different ages learn. They often serve as researchers and educators at teacher training institutions, in university psychology departments, on the staffs of educational research organizations, and also work in government agencies, business, and the military. An educational psychologist might investigate areas as diverse as the causes of **dyslexia** and the measures that can be taken to help dyslexics improve their reading and learning skills; gender differences in mathematical ability; anxiety in education; the effect of **television** on study habits; the identification of **gifted children**; how teachers affect student behavior; and creative thinking in children of a specific grade level or age.

Educational psychology in the United States has its roots in the pioneering work of the 1890s by two of the country's foremost psychologists, **William James** and **John Dewey**. James—who is known for his 1899 volume, *Talks to Teachers on Psychology*—pioneered the concept of taking psychology out of the laboratory and applying it to problems in the real world. He advocated the study of educational problems in their natural **environment,** the classroom, and viewed classroom interactions and observations as a legitimate source of scientific data. John Dewey, the country's most famous advocate of active learning, founded an experimental school at the

University of Chicago to develop and study new educational methods. Dewey experimented with educational curricula and methods and advocated parental participation in the educational process. His philosophy of education stressed learning by doing, as opposed to authoritarian teaching methods and rote learning, and his ideas have had a strong impact on the theory and practice of education in the United States. Dewey's first influential book on education, *The School and Society* (1899), was adapted from a series of lectures to parents of the pupils in his school at the University of Chicago.

In the twentieth century, the theoretical and practical branches of educational psychology have developed separately from each other. The name most prominently associated with the scientific, experimental focus is that of **Edward L. Thorndike**, often called "the father of educational psychology." Applying the learning principles he had discovered in his animal research to humans, Thorndike became a pioneer in the application of psychological principles to such areas as the teaching of reading, language development, and mental testing. His *Introduction to the Theory of Mental and Social Measurements* (1904) gave users of **intelligence** tests access to statistical data about test results. Although Thorndike's emphases were on **conditioning** and scientific measurement, he was both directly and indirectly responsible for a number of curricular and methodological changes in education throughout the United States. Thorndike is especially well known as an opponent of the traditional Latin and Greek classical curriculum used in secondary schools, which he helped to discontinue by demonstrating that progress in one subject did not substantially influence progress in another—the major premise on which classical education had been based.

The work of Thorndike's contemporary, Charles Hubbard Judd (1873–1946), provided a marked contrast in its more pragmatic focus on transforming contemporary educational policies and practices. Judd served as director of the University of Chicago School of Education, where he disseminated his philosophy of education. His research interests were applied to the study of school subjects and teaching methods. Concerned with school organization as well, Judd recommended the establishment of both junior high schools and junior colleges and championed equal education opportunities for students of all backgrounds. His published books include *Psychology of High School Subjects* (1915), *Psychology of Secondary Education* (1927), and *Genetic Psychology for Teachers* (1939).

Other educational psychologists have focused their work on either measurement and learning theory or school and curriculum reform. The contributions of G. Stanley Hall (1844–1924) to the field of intelligence testing were especially significant and influential. He passed

on his view of intelligence as an inherited trait to two of his most famous students, **Arnold Gesell** and **Lewis Terman**. It was Terman who introduced the **Stanford-Binet Intelligence scales** in the United States in 1916, creating new norms based on American standardizing groups. Gesell also made important contributions to the study of human development, and by the 1930s, this subject had become a part of the standard educational psychology texts, and today it is a central area in the field. The learning process, a related area that is also traditionally studied, includes such issues as hierarchies of learning activities, the relationship of learning to motivation, and effective instructional methods.

The study of evaluation has remained a central part of the educational psychology and includes techniques for assessing learning, achievement, and behavior; analysis of individual differences; and methods of addressing learning problems. Another relevant area is that of **mental health** in the classroom (**personality** integration; adjustment problems; teacher-pupil interaction). In recent years, the trend has been toward a more "holistic" and humanistic approach that stresses the learner's affective needs in the context of cognitive processes. A growing area of emphasis for all education professionals is educating individuals with special needs. Current psychological theory and practice—as well as federal law—rejects the traditional exclusionary approach in dealing with disabled or emotionally troubled children and adolescents. Mainstreaming such students is now common practice, with the goal of expanding boundaries and reducing the barriers between exceptional or atypical students and mainstream students. Educational psychology must now concern itself with such issues as systems for classification of children and teenagers as mentally retarded or deviant; creation of alternative educational environments and intervention programs that promote the development of the special needs population and the requisite teaching strategies and skills; and the creation, where necessary, of individualized educational plans.

Division 15 of the **American Psychological Association (APA)** is devoted to educational psychology. Its members are mostly faculty members at universities, although some work in school settings. In 1982, nearly 14 percent of the members of the APA were members of this division and identified themselves as educational psychologists. Professional journals in educational psychology include *Journal of Educational Psychology, Educational Psychologist, Educational Researcher, Review of Educational Research,* and *American Educational Research Journal.*

Further Reading

Eysenck, Michael W. *Individual Differences: Normal and Abnormal.* Hillsdale, NJ: L. Erlbaum Associates, 1994.

Dembo, Myron H. *Applying Educational Psychology.* 5th ed. New York: Longman, 1994.

Farnham-Diggory, Sylvia. *Cognitive Processes in Education.* 2nd ed. New York: HarperCollins, 1992.

Effector

Peripheral tissue at the outer end of an efferent neural path (one leading away from the central nervous system).

An effector acts in special ways in response to a **nerve** impulse. In humans, effectors may either be muscles, which contract in response to neural stimuli, or glands, which produce secretions. The muscles are generally divided into two groupings: somatic effectors, which are the body's striated muscles (such as those found in the arm and back), and autonomic effectors, which are smooth muscles (such as the iris of the eye).

Both types of effectors are linked to the gray matter of the spinal cord, but each system originates in a different portion of it. The somatic effectors, which are responsible for powerful motor movements, are linked to the ventral horn cell, a large **neuron** in the ventral portion of the gray matter. The autonomic effectors receive impulses from the lateral part of the gray matter. The smooth muscles that are supplied by these effectors maintain the tone of blood vessels walls, thus helping to regulate blood pressure. Glandular secretions controlled by autonomic effectors include external secretions, such as sweat, and internal ones, such as the hormone epinephrine secreted by the adrenal medulla of the **brain**. Some nerve fibers that connect with autonomic effectors also pass through the ventral roots of the spinal nerves by way of a ganglion located outside the spinal cord and are then distributed to smooth muscles and glands.

Further Reading

ABC's of the Human Mind. Pleasantville, NY: Reader's Digest Association, 1990.

Ego

In psychoanalytic theory, the part of human personality that combines innate biological impulses (id) or drives with reality to produce appropriate behavior.

Sigmund Freud believed that human **personality** has three components: the **id**, the **ego** and the **superego**. In his scheme, the id urges immediate action on such basic needs as eating, drinking, and eliminating wastes without regard to consequences. The ego is that portion of the personality that imposes realistic limitations on such behavior. It decides whether id-motivated behavior is appropriate, given the prevailing social and environmental conditions.

While the id operates on the "**pleasure principle**," the ego uses the "reality principle" to determine whether to satisfy or delay fulfilling the id's demands. The ego considers the consequences of actions to modify the powerful drives of the id. A person's own concept of what is acceptable determines the ego's decisions. The ego also must "negotiate" with the superego (**conscience**) in the often bitter battle between the id's drives and a person's own sense of right and wrong. **Repression** and **anxiety** may result when the ego consistently overrides the id's extreme demands.

Further Reading

Atkinson, Rita L.; Richard C. Atkinson; Edward E. Smith; and Ernest R. Hilgard. *Introduction to Psychology.* 9th ed. San Diego: Harcourt Brace Jovanovich, 1987.

Zimbardo, Philip G. *Psychology and Life.* 12th ed. Glenview, IL: Scott, Foresman, 1988.

Electra complex. See **Oedipus complex.**

Electrical Stimulation of the Brain (ESB)

A procedure which involves the introduction of a weak electrical current into specific locations in the brain by using multiple microelectrodes to apply short pulses of electrical currents intended to mimic the natural flow of impulses through the neural pathways.

Electrical stimulation of the brain (ESB) is useful in a variety of situations, including neurosurgical operations and experimental research. In neurosurgery, this procedure may be used to assist physicians in determining which **brain** tissue should be removed. Because the patient must remain awake during the procedure, only a local anesthetic is administered. Focal **epilepsy** has been surgically treated by using electrical brain stimulation in conscious patients to determine the epileptic focus.

In experimental research, ESB does not control complex behavior patterns such as **depression**, but it can be employed quite successfully to control individual functions. Therefore, this procedure has proven useful in studying the relationships among various areas and structures of the brain and the activities they control. It has been found, for example, that stimulation of the visual cortex produces visual sensations, such as bursts of light or color (blind people have seen spots of light as a result of ESB). Similarly, stimulation of the auditory cortex results in aural sensation, while stimulating areas associated with motor control produces arm, leg, or other body movements. Stimulation of areas of the brain linked to association can induce memories of scenes or events.

In addition to research and experimental uses, electrical brain stimulation has been successfully used for some therapeutic purposes. Brain stem and cerebellar stimulation have aided in some movement disorders; peroneal nerve stimulation has been used to treat dropfoot in stroke victims; and transcutaneous nerve, dorsal-column, and deep-brain stimulation have proven useful in the relief of chronic severe **pain**.

Electrical brain stimulation has aided in mapping connections between different regions of the brain in animals, and has been used to induce many different types of behavior in animals, including eating, drinking, **aggression**, hoarding, and both sexual and maternal behavior. While hypothalamic stimulation is associated with such emotional responses as attack and defense, stimulation of the reticular formation in the brain stem can induce **sleep**. ESB has also confirmed the existence of a "reward center" in animals, whereby animals can be taught to stimulate their own brains mechanically by pressing a lever when such stimulation results in a pleasant sensation.

Electroconvulsive Therapy (ECT)

The application of a mild electric current to the brain to produce an epileptic-like seizure as a means of treating certain psychological disorders, primarily severe depression.

Electroconvulsive therapy, also known as ECT and electroshock therapy, was developed in the 1930s when various observations led physicians to conclude that epileptic seizures might prevent or relieve the symptoms of **schizophrenia**. After experiments with insulin and other potentially seizure-inducing drugs, Italian physicians pioneered the use of an electric current to create seizures in schizophrenic patients.

ECT was routinely used to treat **schizophrenia**, **depression**, and, in some cases, **mania**. It eventually became a source of controversy due to misuse and negative side effects. ECT was used indiscriminately and was often prescribed for treating disorders on which it had no real effect, such as **alcohol dependence**, and was used for punitive reasons. Patients typically experienced confusion and loss of **memory** after treatments, and even those whose condition improved eventually relapsed. Other side effects of ECT include speech defects, physical injury from the force of the convulsions, and cardiac arrest. Use of electroconvulsive therapy declined after 1960 with the introduction of antidepressant and antipsychotic **drugs**.

ECT is still used today but with less frequency and with modifications that have made the procedure safer and less unpleasant. Anesthetics and muscle relaxants are usually administered to prevent bone fractures or other injuries from muscle spasms. Patients receive approximately 4 to 10 treatments administered over a period of about two weeks. Confusion and memory loss are minimized by the common practice of applying the current only to the nondominant **brain** hemisphere, usually the **right-brain hemisphere**. Nevertheless, some memory loss still occurs; anterograde memory (the ability to learn new material) returns relatively rapidly following treatment, but retrograde memory (the ability to remember past events) is more strongly affected. There is a marked memory deficit one week after treatment which gradually improves over the next six or seven months. In many cases, however, subtle memory losses persist even beyond this point, and can be serious and debilitating for some patients.

About 100,000 people in the United States receive electroconvulsive therapy annually. ECT can only be administered with the informed consent of the patient and is used primarily for severely depressed patients who have not responded to antidepressant medications or whose suicidal impulses make it dangerous to wait until such medications can take effect. ECT is also administered to patients with **bipolar disorder**. Contrary to the theories of those who first pioneered its use, ECT is not an effective treatment for schizophrenia unless the patient is also suffering from depression. The rate of relapse after administration of ECT can be greatly diminished when it is accompanied by other forms of treatment.

Researchers are still not sure exactly how electroconvulsive therapy works, although it is known that the seizures rather than the electric current itself are the basis for the treatment's effects, and that seizures can affect the functioning of **neurotransmitters** in the brain, including norepinephrine and serotonin, which are associated with depression. They also increase the release of pituitary **hormones.** Because of its possible side effects, as well as the public's level of discomfort with both electrical shock and the idea of inducing seizures, ECT remains a controversial treatment method. In 1982, the city of Berkeley, California, passed a referendum making the administration of ECT a misdemeanor punishable by fines of up to $500 and six months in prison, but the law was later overturned.

Further Reading

Electroconvulsive Therapy: Theory and Practice. New York: Raven Press, 1979.

Electroencephalograph (EEG)

A device used to record the electrical activity of the brain.

Electroencephalography is used for a variety of research and diagnostic purposes. It is usually conducted using electrodes, metal discs attached to the scalp or to wires connected to the skull or even to the **brain** itself. The signals obtained through the electrodes must then be amplified in order to be interpreted. EEG patterns typically take the form of waves, which may be measured according to both their frequency and size (also referred to as amplitude). The electrical activity of animals' brains had been recorded as early as 1875, but it was not until 1929 that the first human EEG was reported by Austrian psychiatrist Anton Berger. Since then, it has been used to study the effects of **drugs** on the brain, as well as the **localization** of certain behavioral functions in specific areas of the brain. EEGs have also been widely used in **sleep** research. While the deeper stages of sleep are characterized by large, slow, irregular brain waves, and, in some cases, bursts of high-amplitude waves called "sleep spindles," REM (**rapid eye movement**) sleep, during which most vivid dreaming occurs, resembles the faster brain-wave pattern of the waking state.

As a diagnostic tool, EEGs have been used to diagnose **epilepsy,** strokes, infections, hemorrhages, inadequate blood supply to the brain, and certain tumors. They are especially useful because they can pinpoint the location of tumors and injuries to the brain. EEGs are also used to monitor patients in a coma and, during surgery, to indicate the effectiveness of anesthetics.

Further Reading
Cooper, R. *EEG Technology.* New York: Butterworth, 1980.

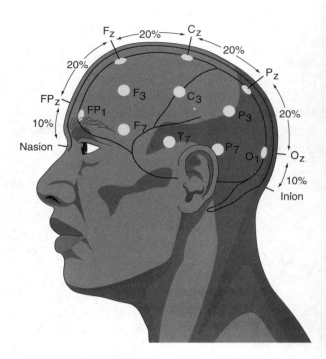

Placement of electrodes for an electroencephalograph.

Ellis, Albert (1913–)

American psychologist who originated rational-emotive therapy (RET), also known for his work as an author and counselor in the areas of marriage and sexuality.

Raised in the Bronx, New York, Albert Ellis was shy and physically frail when he was young. Although he had literary ambitions in his teens and twenties, he earned degrees in accounting and business. While in his twenties, he found that he had a gift for advising his friends on sexual matters and undertook an intensive independent study of human **sexuality**. Deciding to become a professional therapist, he earned a Ph.D. in **clinical psychology** at the Teachers College at Columbia University in 1947, followed by four years of psy-

choanalytic training with Charles R. Hulbeck at the Karen Horney Institute. By 1952, he had a full-time practice in Manhattan.

However, Ellis soon became dissatisfied with the limits of **psychoanalysis**. He found it slow and ineffective, and he was frustrated with the passive role it assigned to the therapist. In 1953 he began experimenting with different therapeutic techniques, and within two years he developed rational-emotive therapy (RET), which he then began to practice and advocate in writing. It was based on the idea that psychological problems are caused by self-defeating thoughts (such as "I must be loved or approved by everyone" and "If I don't find the perfect solution to this problem, a catastrophe will result"). Once such thoughts are changed, emotional and behavioral changes will follow. The therapist's task is to help the client recognize illogical and self-destructive ways of thinking and replace them with healthier, more positive ones. Ellis outlined an active role for the therapist: his own therapeutic style involved continually challenging the client's illogical and self-destructive ideas in a dynamic and provocative manner.

When Ellis first began promoting his new system of therapy, it was met with widespread professional opposition. However, the growing dissatisfaction with **behaviorism** created a climate that was more hospitable to a therapeutic method like RET that emphasized the role of **cognition** in changing behavior. Other psychologists, including Aaron Beck and social learning theorist Julian Rotter, developed their own cognitive-oriented therapies, and Ellis found himself the pioneer of a new school of therapy—the cognitive-behavioral approach. He has described himself as "the father of RET and the grandfather of cognitive-behavioral therapy." Ellis has also published numerous books on sexuality, including several popular best sellers (such as *Sex Without Guilt*) associated with the "sexual revolution" of the 1960s, and he was an innovator in the area of sex and marital therapy.

Further Reading

Bernard, M. E. *Staying Alive in an Irrational World: Albert Ellis and Rational-Emotive Therapy*. South Melbourne, Australia: Carlson/Macmillan, 1986.

Ellis, A., and W. Dryden. *The Essential Albert Ellis*. New York: Springer, 1990.

Emotion

A reaction, both psychological and physical, subjectively experienced as strong feelings, many of which prepare the body for immediate action.

In contrast to **moods**, which are generally longer-lasting, emotions are transitory, with relatively well-defined beginnings and endings. They also have valence, meaning that they are either positive or negative. Subjectively, emotions are experienced as passive phenomena. Even though it is possible to exert a measure of control over one's emotions, they are not initiated—they happen *to* people. Objectively, emotions involve internal physiological responses and expressive outward displays that are both learned and innate. Certain emotions themselves, considered to be primary emotions—joy, **anger**, sadness, **fear**, and love—are thought to be innate, while complex emotions—such as altruism, shame, guilt, and envy—seem to arise from social learning.

The first influential theory of emotion in modern times—the James-Lange theory—was formulated independently in the 1880s by both American psychologist and philosopher **William James** and Danish physiologist C.G. Lange (1834–1900). Both scientists arrived at the view that the physiological manifestations of emotion precede the subjective ones—rather than trembling because we are afraid, we are afraid because we tremble. Even though the **brain** responds to a threatening situation by activating peripheral responses, we do not consciously experience the emotion until these responses are activated. Thus, the **central nervous system** itself does not actually produce the emotion. Over the follow-

ing decades, this theory drew widespread response and criticism.

An alternative model of emotional experience was formulated in 1927 by Walter Cannon (1871–1945), who proposed that emotions do originate in the central nervous system. Cannon argued that nerve impulses first pass through the thalamus, from which subjective responses are routed through the cerebral cortex, directly creating the experience of fear at the same time that physiological responses are passing through the **hypothalamus**. The Cannon-Bard theory, whose name reflects later modifications by Phillip Bard, thus delineated the psychological and physiological components of emotion as simultaneous and argued that the experience of emotion comes directly from the central nervous system. Some more recent theorists have once again moved closer to the James-Lange model. The 1962 Schachter-Singer theory restores James's emphasis on the interpretation of physiological responses but adds another element—a cognitive evaluation of what caused the responses. This theory thus contradicts James's assertion that emotion is communicated solely on the basis of physical feedback, asserting that this feedback by itself is not clear enough to specify a particular emotion. Rather, the brain chooses one of many possible interpretations and "labels" the feedback pattern, and it is this labeling that results in the experiencing of a particular emotion.

Areas of the brain that play an important role in the production of emotions include the reticular formation, the limbic system, and the cerebral cortex. The reticular formation, within the brain stem, receives and filters sensory information before passing it on the limbic system and cortex. The limbic system includes the hypothalamus, which produces most of the peripheral responses to emotion through its control of the endocrine and **autonomic nervous systems**; the amygdala, which is associated with **fear** and aggressive behavior; the hippocampus; and parts of the **thalamus**. The frontal lobes of the cerebral cortex receive nerve impulses from the thalamus and play an active role in the experience and expression of emotions.

While the physiological changes associated with emotions are triggered by the brain, they are carried out by the endocrine and autonomic nervous systems. In response to fear or anger, for example, the brain signals the pituitary gland to release a **hormone** called ACTH, which in turn causes the adrenal glands to secrete cortisol, another hormone that triggers what is known as the fight-or-flight response, a combination of physical changes that prepare the body for action in dangerous situations. The heart beats faster, respiration is more rapid, the liver releases glucose into the bloodstream to supply added energy, fuels are mobilized from the body's stored fat, and the body generally goes into a state of high arous-

This mother smiles for the camera. Psychologists describe certain facial expressions of emotion, such as smiling, as innate and universal across cultures. Even blind persons smile, even though they have not seen others smiling, and therefore could not have learned to smile through imitation.

al. The pupils dilate, perspiration increases while secretion of saliva and mucous decreases, hairs on the body become erect, causing "goose pimples," and the digestive system slows down as blood is diverted to the brain and skeletal muscles. These changes are carried out with the aid of the sympathetic nervous system, one of two divisions of the autonomic nervous system. When the crisis is over, the parasympathetic nervous system, which conserves the body's energy and resources, returns things to their normal state.

Ways of expressing emotion may be either innate or culturally acquired. Certain facial expressions, such as smiling, have been found to be universal, even among blind persons, who have no means of imitating them. Other expressions vary across cultures. For example, the Chinese stick out their tongues to register surprise, in contrast to Americans and other Westerners, who raise their eyebrows and widen their eyes. In addition to the ways of communicating various emotions, people within a culture also learn certain unwritten codes governing emotional expression itself—what emotions can be openly expressed and under what circumstances. Cultural forces also influence how people

describe and categorize what they are feeling. An emotion that is commonly recognized in one society may be subsumed under another emotion in a different one. Some cultures, for example, do not distinguish between anger and sadness. Tahitians, who have no word for either sadness or guilt, have 46 words for various types of anger.

In daily life, emotional **arousal** may have beneficial or disruptive effects, depending on the situation and the intensity of the emotion. Moderate levels of arousal increase efficiency levels by making people more alert. However, intense emotions—either positive or negative—interfere with performance because central nervous system responses are channeled in too many directions at once. The effects of **arousal** on performance also depend on the difficulty of the task at hand; emotions interfere less with simple tasks than with more complicated ones.

Further Reading

Powell, Barbara. *The Complete Guide to Your Child's Emotional Health.* Danbury, CT: F. Watts, 1984.
Your Child's Emotional Health: Adolescence. New York: Macmillan, 1994.

Empathy

The capacity to vicariously experience and understand the thoughts and feelings of another person by putting oneself in that person's place.

While most forms of **psychotherapy** require some degree of empathy on the part of the counselor or therapist, the **client-centered therapy** pioneered by **Carl Rogers** places particular emphasis on this quality as part of the therapeutic experience. Instead of looking at the client from outside (external frame of reference), the client-centered therapist attempts to see things as they actually look to the client (internal frame of reference). Throughout each therapy session, the therapist demonstrates what Rogers termed "accurate empathetic understanding," showing sensitivity to the client's feelings through active listening that shows careful and perceptive attention to what the client is saying. The therapist employs standard behaviors common to all good listeners, making frequent eye contact with the client, nodding in agreement or understanding, and generally showing that he or she is listening attentively.

One unique way client-centered therapists demonstrate empathy with the client is through a special method called reflection, which consists of paraphrasing and/or summarizing what a client has just said. This technique lets therapists check the accuracy of their perceptions while showing clients that they are paying careful attention to and are interested in what is being said. Hearing their own thoughts and feelings repeated by another person can also help clients achieve new levels of insight and self-awareness. Clients generally respond to reflection by elaborating further on the thoughts they have just expressed. Empathy constitutes a major portion of the therapeutic work in client-centered therapy. By helping clients feel better about themselves, it gives them the self-confidence and energy to deal actively with their problems.

Further Reading

Rogers, Carl. *Client-Centered Therapy*. Boston: Houghton Mifflin, 1951.
———. *On Becoming a Person*. Boston: Houghton Mifflin, 1961.
———. *A Way of Being*. Boston: Houghton Mifflin, 1980.

Empiricism

Type of research that is based on direct observation.

Psychologists prefer to learn about behavior through direct observation or experience. This approach reflects what is called empiricism. Psychologists are well known for creating experiments, conducting interviews and using surveys, and carrying out case studies. The common feature of these approaches is that psychologists wait until observations are made before they draw any conclusions about the behaviors they are interested in.

Scientists often maintain that empiricism fosters healthy skepticism. By this they mean that they will not regard something as being true until they have made the observations themselves. Such an approach means that science can be self-correcting in the sense that when erroneous conclusions are drawn, others can test the original ideas to see if they are correct.

Empiricism is one of the hallmarks of any scientific endeavor. Other disciplines employ different approaches to gaining knowledge. For example, many philosophers use the *a priori* method rather than the empirical method. In the *a priori* method, one uses strictly rational, logical arguments to derive knowledge. Geometric proofs are an example of the use of the *a priori* method.

In everyday life, people accept ideas as being true or false based on authority or on intuition. In many cases, people hold beliefs because individuals who are experts have made pronouncements on some topic. For example, in religious matters, many people rely on the advice and guidance of their religious leaders in deciding on the correct way to lead their lives. Further, we often believe things because they seem intuitively obvious. Relying on authority and intuition may be very useful in some aspects of our lives, like those involving questions of morality.

Scientists prefer the empirical method in their work, however, because the topics of science lend themselves to observation and **measurement.** When something cannot be observed or measured, scientists are likely to conclude that it is outside the realm of science, even though it may be vitally important in some other realm.

Further Reading

Carruthers, Peter. *Human Knowledge and Human Nature: A New Introduction to an Ancient Debate*. Oxford, Eng.: Oxford University Press, 1992.
Grossmann, Reinhardt. *The Fourth Way: A Theory of Knowledge*. Bloomington: Indiana University Press, 1990.

Encounter Group

Group of individuals who engage in intensive and psychotherapeutic verbal and nonverbal interaction, with the general intention of increasing awareness of self and sensitivity to others, and improving interpersonal skills.

Encounter groups are formed, usually under the guidance and leadership of a **psychologist**s or therapist, to provide an **environment** for intensive interaction. In general, because the therapy takes place in a group setting, one of the goals of the encounter group is to improve the participants' interpersonal skills. A typical encounter group may consist of fewer that ten persons, one of whom is a trained specialist, or leader. The role of the leader is primarily to develop and maintain an atmosphere of psychological safety conducive to the free and honest expression of the ideas of group members. The leader remains, as much as possible, outside the actual discussion itself. Encounter group members are encouraged to fully examine and explore their reactions to, and feelings about, statements made, and issues raised, in the group. Proponents of the encounter group form of **psychotherapy** tend to believe that the behavior of an individual is shaped to a very large degree by responsive **adaptation** to the **attitudes** of other individuals, and that encounter groups enable individuals to discover and modify behavior that is perceived as inappropriate. The effectiveness of encounter groups is a matter of some dispute, and there is evidence which suggests that certain behavioral and attitudinal changes accomplished inside the group may not endure outside the group. Although early versions of encounter groups may have existed near the beginning of the 20th century, the encounter group technique as it is currently practiced is derived from sensitivity training procedures introduced shortly after World War II. Both the encounter group and sensitivity training techniques are now generally included in a wider array of techniques, some of which are controversial in the field of psychology, that were popularized beginning in the 1960s. These techniques are collectively referred to as the **human potential movement.**

Further Reading
Appelbaum, Stephen. *Out in Inner Space.* Garden City, NY: Anchor Press/Doubleday, 1970.

Endocrine Glands

Ductless glands which secrete chemical substances called hormones into the bloodstream which control the internal environment not only of each cell and organ, but of the entire body.

The endocrine glands: the pineal, pituitary, thyroid, parathyroids, thymus, adrenals, pancreas and gonads (ovaries or testes), comprise the endocrine system. The **hypothalamus,** the gland in the **brain** which serves as the command center, operates the endocrine system through the pituitary, a pea-sized gland located under it, which directs the work of all the other glands. The thyroid, a gland in the neck, regulates the body's metabolism. The parathyroids, which are attached to the thyroid, control the amount of calcium and phosphate in the

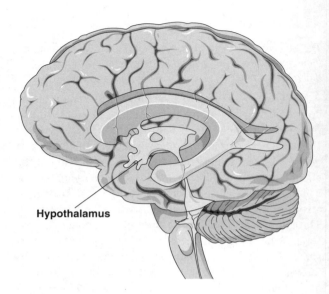

Hypothalamus

The hypothalamus is the command center for all the endocrine glands.

bloodstream. The adrenal glands, located near the kidneys, produce adrenaline which arouses the body to respond to **stress** and emergencies and other **hormones** active in carbohydrate metabolism. The pancreas secretes insulin which regulates the level of sugar in the bloodstream. The gonads regulate sexual development, ovulation, and growth of sex organs.

Further Reading
The Endocrine System: Miraculous Messengers. New York: Torstar Books, 1985.

Enuresis. See **Sleep Disorder.**

Environment

The combination of physical, social, and cultural conditions that influence an individual's development and behavior.

The relative importance of **heredity** and environment in shaping human lives—nature versus nurture—has long been a topic of debate taken up by thinkers as diverse as John Locke, **Charles Darwin**, and **Sigmund Freud,** and forms part of current policy debates in areas such as crime and education. Traditionally, this controversy pits those who believe that human nature and **intelligence** are biologically determined (eugenicists) against those who contend that, given a positive and enriching environment, most individuals have the potential for high levels of human development (euthenists). It is agreed that such human characteristics as sex,

The relative importance of heredity and environment in shaping personality has been a focus of debate among psychologists since the 1800s.

height, skin and hair color, and, to a certain extent, **temperament,** are genetically determined at conception. However, there is disagreement over the extent to which other aspects of human development—including behavior, **personality**, and intelligence—are influenced by such environmental factors as nutrition, emotional climate of the home, and quality of stimulation and parental feedback. In addition to the immediate family, many experts consider the social class and culture in which a child is raised as important environmental factors in determining his or her development.

Intelligence testing and race has resurfaced as a volatile topic in the nature/nurture debate, since African-Americans as a group score 10 to 15 points lower on standard **IQ test**s than whites. Some experts claim that this disparity demonstrates the differences in inherited ability among the two races, while others attribute the gap to environmental influences. In 1994, Richard Herrnstein and Charles Murray published *The Bell Curve,* in

which they asserted that low-income blacks have innately lower cognitive abilities than whites (based on the gap in IQ scores), a situation that cannot be significantly remedied through government social and educational programs. Many social scientists, however, consider environmental and genetic factors to be so closely intertwined as to make it impossible to clearly separate them. Thus, the contrasting positions of eugenicists and euthenists are actually at opposite ends of a continuum, with most observers of human behavior taking a middle position that emphasizes the interaction between biological predispositions and life experiences.

Social learning theorists refer to another layer of complexity in the relationship between environment and human behavior: the self-generated environment. This concept refers to the fact that a certain behavior or behaviors may produce environmental conditions that can affect future behavior. People who behave in an abrasive manner, for example, help create a hostile social environment, which in turn leads to further **hostility** on their part. Similarly, the behavior of friendly persons will tend to generate a supportive environment that reinforces and perpetuates their original behavior. Thus, a group of persons who find themselves in the same "potential environment" may experience different "actual environments" as a result of their contrasting behaviors.

Since the 1960s, environmental psychologists have studied the relationship between human behavior and the physical environment, including noise, pollution, and architectural design. Like ethologists, who study animal behavior in their natural habitat, environmental psychologists maintain a holistic view of human behavior that leads them to study it in its natural setting rather than in a laboratory, or at least to supplement laboratory experiments with field research. Environmental psychologists study such topics as the ways in which the architectural design of a psychiatric hospital affects its patients; the effects of aircraft noise on children at a school near an airport; and overcrowding in a college dormitory.

Environment psychology is basically an applied field geared toward solving specific problems rather than a theoretical area of study. Like social learning theory, it is heavily concerned with the reciprocal relationship between behavior and environment, including the ways in which people cope with their physical surroundings by altering them. One exception to this orientation is a position known as determinism, which has influenced much research into the effects of architecture on behavior. The determinist approach emphasizes the **adaptation** of people to their surroundings, and considers behavior largely as a function of those surroundings, with little reciprocity involved.

See also Eugenics; Jensen, Arthur.

Further Reading

Altman, Irwin. *The Environment and Social Behavior: Privacy, Personal Space, Territory, Crowding.* Monterey, CA: Brooks/Cole, 1975.

Gray, Jeffrey Alan. *The Psychology of Fear and Stress.* 2nd ed. New York: Cambridge University Press, 1988.

Environmental Deprivation. See **Environment.**

Epilepsy

A general term which describes a variety of symptoms caused by a pathological functioning of the brain.

The most notable of the symptoms of epilepsy is seizures or convulsions which are the manifestations of sudden periods of uncontrolled, involuntary electrical activity in the **brain.** Seizures may also be accompanied by violent muscular contractions and altered states of **consciousness.**

All epileptic seizures can be classified under two main headings: generalized seizures, which affect the whole brain, and partial seizures, which are localized in one part of the brain. Within these two categories are four types of epileptic seizures: tonic-clonic or grand mal; simple partial or Jacksonian; complex partial or psychomotor/temporal; and secondarily generalized seizures.

Tonic-clonic or grand mal seizures are the best known of generalized seizures, although not the most common type. They may involve violent muscular contractions or convulsions, the loss of consciousness as well as bladder and/or bowel control, frothing at the mouth, and a bluish tinge to the skin as oxygen intake decreases. Seizures may be preceded by an aura such as an odd **smell** or **taste,** a light, a sick feeling, or a feeling of warmth. They generally last for a minute or two and leave the person confused and/or drowsy.

An absence or petit mal seizure is also generalized but may last only a few seconds. The person is only briefly unconscious or may seem to daydream or stare blankly with a rhythmic twitching of the eyelid or facial muscles. This type of seizure may not be noticed by the person or by an observer.

A simple partial seizure, also called a Jacksonian seizure, is one in which the person remains conscious but cannot control their movements. Another form of it involves seeing strange, illusory people, hearing odd or uncommon sounds, and/or experiencing the feeling of "deja vu."

A complex partial seizure, also known as a psychomotor or temporal lobe seizure, produces a trance-like state in which the person moves as if in a daze but not out of conscious contact with others. During this time, the person may demonstrate behavior out of character with his/her normal **personality** and usually returns to awareness in a minute or two with some confusion or irritability but no memory of what happened. In a temporal lobe seizure, a person who is usually soft-spoken might suddenly become loud and aggressive or might laugh abruptly and uncontrollably without apparent cause.

A secondarily generalized seizure is one which is initially partial but which spreads in the brain to become generalized.

Approximately 1,500,000 people in the United States suffer from epilepsy, which generally appears first in childhood sometime between the ages of two and twenty. The cause of epilepsy is either idiopathic (no organic basis), which accounts for 75% of all cases, or symptomatic (identifiable organic brain pathology), which applies to only 25% of all cases. Factors which can trigger symptomatic cases of epilepsy include head injury, **mental retardation,** cerebral palsy, lead poisoning, severe infections such as meningitis, malaria, and measles, and poor nutrition. To the extent that any of these can be eliminated or treated, epilepsy is preventable. The condition is best controlled by anticonvulsant **drugs** whose dosage and type depend on the kind of seizure involved. It is estimated that seizures can be controlled in four out of five people and in some forms of epilepsy, especially absence seizures, many children tend to "grow out of it."

Research in the experimental treatment of epilepsy in 1961 led to one of the milestone discoveries in psychology when Joseph Bogen, a neurosurgeon, cut the corpus callosum of a patient with severe epilepsy in an attempt to reduce or eliminate his seizures. By severing that part of the brain connecting the two cerebral hemispheres and thus preventing transfer of information between the halves, researchers were able to establish a clear pattern of the different specialized functions of each hemisphere. Approximately one hundred of these operations have been performed since this date, yielding fascinating information on hemispheric specialization.

Further Reading

Burden, George. *Understanding Epilepsy.* 2nd ed. Brooklyn Heights, NY: Beekman, 1980.

Epilepsy: An Overview [videorecording]. Cleveland, OH: Cleveland Clinic Foundation, 1993.

Equilibrium Sense

One of two proprioceptive sensory systems that provide us with input about the positions of our own bodies.

The equilibrium sense, generally associated with balance, provides feedback about the positions and dizziness and nausea. Our sense of body position when we are at rest is provided by the vestibular sacs, which contain small crystals called otoliths (literally, "ear stones") that exert pressure on the hair cells. In their normal position, the otoliths inform our brains that we are standing or sitting upright. When the head is tilted, the position of the otoliths changes, and the signal sent to the brain changes accordingly. The neural connections of the vestibular system lead to the cerebellum, the eye muscles, and a part of the **autonomic nervous system** involved in digestion (which accounts for the link between dizziness and nausea).

Further Reading

Burke, Shirley R. *Human Anatomy and Physiology in Health and Disease.* New York: Delmar, 1992.

Martini, Frederic. *Fundamentals of Anatomy and Physiology.* Englewood Cliffs, NJ: Prentice-Hall, 1995.

Erikson, Erik (1902–1979)

German-born American psychoanalyst best known for his work with children and adolescents.

Erik Erikson was born in Frankfurt, Germany, to Danish parents. As a youth, he was a student and teacher of art. While teaching at a private school in Vienna, he became acquainted with **Anna Freud**, the daughter of **Sigmund Freud**. Erikson underwent **psychoanalysis,** and the experience made him decide to become an analyst himself. He was trained in psychoanalysis at the Vienna Psychoanalytic Institute and also studied the Montessori method of education, which focused on **child development.** Following Erikson's graduation from the Vienna Psychoanalytic Institute in 1933, the Nazis had just come to power in Germany, and he emigrated with his wife, first to Denmark and then to the United States, where he became the first child psychoanalyst in Boston. Erikson held positions at Massachusetts General Hospital, the Judge Baker Guidance Center, and at Harvard's Medical School and Psychological Clinic, establishing a solid reputation as an outstanding clinician. In 1936, Erikson accepted a position at Yale University, where he worked at the Institute of Human Relations and taught at the Medical School. After spending a year observing children on a Sioux reservation in South Dakota, he joined the faculty of the University of California at Berkeley, where he was affiliated with the Institute of Child Welfare, and opened a private practice as well. While in California, Erikson also studied children of the Yurok Native American tribe. After publishing the book for which he is best known, *Childhood and Society,* in 1950, he left Berkeley to join the staff of the Austen Riggs Center, a prominent psychiatric treatment facility in Stock-

This climber's equilibrium sense allows him to maintain balance while scaling this rocky facade.

movements of our heads and bodies in space. The other system—the **kinesthetic sense**—tells us about the orientation of different parts of our bodies in relation to each other. While the kinesthetic information needed by the **brain** comes from joints and muscle fibers throughout the body, the receptors for equilibrium are located in the semicircular canals and vestibular sacs of the inner ear. (The equilibrium sense is also called the vestibular sense, and the relevant parts of the inner ear are sometimes called the vestibular system or apparatus).

The semicircular canals are three pretzel-like curved tubes arranged at angles roughly perpendicular to each other, with the two vestibular sacs located at their base. Both the canals and sacs contain fluid and tiny hair cells, which act as receptors. When a person's head moves, the fluid disturbs the hair cells, which stimulate a branch of the auditory nerve, signaling the brain to make adjustments in the eyes and body. A movement at any given angle will have its primary effect on one of the three canals. Overstimulation from extreme movements will produce

Erik Erikson

bridge, Massachusetts, where he worked with emotionally troubled young people. In the 1960s, Erikson returned to Harvard as a professor of human development and remained at the university until his retirement in 1970.

Much of Erikson's work is concerned with the formation of individual **identity,** the creative operation of **consciousness** in a well-adjusted **personality,** and societal influences on child development. He differs from more traditional Freudians by assigning a significantly greater importance to development after the first few years of life, and by arguing that the **ego** plays a highly positive role in that development. Erikson is also noted for the illumination of his concept of the adolescent "identity crisis," a term which he coined. Erikson's theory of personality covers the entire human lifespan, which he divides into eight distinct stages, each with its own tasks and crisis. In **infancy,** the basic conflict is between trust and mistrust. A sense of trust is established according to the quality of the infant's relationship with its caregivers. Achievement of trust is considered especially important for development in the following stages. The crisis in early childhood, the next stage, is between the child's need for *autonomy* and the sense of doubt and shame brought on by learning to deal with rules and so-

cial demands for self-control, including physical control such as toilet training. Successfully negotiated, this stage leads to the emergence of independence and will power. Later in the preschool period comes the third stage, when the child begins to actively explore his or her **environment.** At this stage, there is a crisis over *initiative* and a possible sense of guilt about asserting control over his or her own activities. A sense of purpose, leading to the ability to pursue goals in spite of risks and possible failure, emerges with the resolution of this conflict. During the fourth stage, the early school years, the social context expands to include the school environment, where skills and mastery of tasks become a primary focus of **attention.** A conflict arises between *industry*, or the **ability** to work, and feelings of inferiority, and the former must triumph in order for the development of competence.

The goals of the first four stages—trust, autonomy, initiative, and industry—create the foundation for the successful negotiation of the fifth stage, in which the adolescent must form a stable identity and achieve a sense of self. While social issues such as "fitting in with the group" are important at this point, Erikson emphasizes the importance of achieving an individual identity based on self-knowledge and continuity of experience. Failure to resolve the conflicts of this stage results in identity or role confusion and affects the experiences of the three adult stages which follow. In young adulthood, the primary issue is *intimacy*, or the ability to love. In middle adulthood, it is *generativity*, or the ability to be productive, whether in work, parenting, or other activities, rather than stagnating. The key quality at this stage is the ability to care for others. Finally, at maturity, the challenge is to achieve a sense of *integrity* and wisdom with which to overcome despair over physical disintegration and death.

Erikson's mapping of the life cycle has had a profound impact on **developmental psychology,** especially in the area of adolescent behavior and in the shift to a life-span perspective among students of human development. He won both the Pulitzer Prize and the National Book Award for his writings, which include the psychobiographies *Young Man Luther* (1958) and *Gandhi's Truth* (1969). Erikson is also the author of *Insight and Responsibility* (1964) and *Identity, Youth, and Crisis* (1968).

See also Adolescence.

Further Reading

Coles, Robert. *Erik H. Erikson: The Growth of His Work.* Boston: Little, Brown & Co., 1970.

Ethnocentrism

An attitude of superiority about the ethnic group with which one is identified.

Ethnocentrism is a general belief that the ethnic group with which an individual is identified is superior to all other ethnic groups. Consequently, the individual persistently uses membership in the ethnic group as a primary criterion in the formation of relationships with others, and in evaluating or making judgments concerning other individuals. The term sociocentrism is sometimes used as a synonym of the term ethnocentrism, although sociocentrism is defined more narrowly. Sociocentrism involves the smaller social group rather than the larger ethnic group of the individual. Ethnic groups consist of individuals who are bound together, often closely, by a shared cultural structure and sense of ethnic identity. The central and defining feature of an ethnic group may be racial, religious, geopolitical, linguistic, traditional, tribal, or some combination of these or other characteristics. An ethnic group may be a majority or a minority of a population, and may be relatively dominant or powerless in a society. In varying degrees, ethnocentrism is an attribute of ethnic groups, past and present, throughout the world. The ethnocentric view that other ethnic groups and their members are inferior may be expressed in a number of ways: for example, through **prejudice,** paternalism, contempt, or hate crimes or other acts of **violence.**

Further Reading

Forbes, H. D. *Nationalism, Ethnocentrism, and Personality.* Chicago: University of Chicago Press, 1985.

Ethology

The study of animal behavior as observed in the natural environment and in the context of evolutionary adaptation.

The pioneering work of Konrad Lorenz and Niko Tinbergen in the 1930s established a theoretical foundation for ethology, which has had an effect on such wide-ranging disciplines as genetics, anthropology, and political science in addition to **psychology.** Ethologists believe that an animal must be studied on its own terms rather than primarily in relation to human beings, with a focus on its normal behavior and **environment.** They study animal behavior from the dual perspective of both "proximate explanations" (which concern the individual lifetime of an animal) and "ultimate explanations" (which concern an animal's phylogenetic past). Proximate explanations answer questions about how a specific behavior occurs; ultimate explanations answer questions about why a behavior occurs.

Much of the field work performed by ethologists is based on the notion that an animal's behavior is generally adapted to its environment in much the same way as its physical characteristics. From the ethologist's point of view, a laboratory environment constrains animal behavior too much to provide a true understanding of its full range of functions and activities. However, the field work of ethologists consists of more than mere passive observation of animals in their natural habitats. In order to make observations about the behavior of an animal in its environment, ethologists often modify that environment. In a now-classic experiment, Lorenz managed to substitute himself for a mother goose, whose goslings then proceeded to follow him in single file wherever he went. In another well-known experiment, Tinbergen conducted a study of ground-nesting black-headed gulls to explain why a mother gull removes all traces of eggshell from its nest after a chick hatches. He hypothesized that the eggshell might be removed to prevent injuries, disease, or the attention of predatory birds. By placing pieces of shell in exposed locations away from the gulls' nests, Tinbergen found that the white interior of the shells were visible from the air and did indeed attract predators.

The ethologist's method of studying an animal begins with the creation of an ethogram, an objective description of its behavior patterns, including hunting, eating, sleeping, fighting, and nest-building. Four types of questions are raised about each activity: the cause of the behavior, development (within the lifetime of the individual animal), evolution (within the lifetime of the species), and adaptive function (how it helps the animal's species survive). Then, the researcher may turn to existing data on related species in various habitats and/or conduct independent research with reference to the animal's natural environment. Experiments may be conducted within the environment itself, or by investigating the effects of removing the animal from that environment. Laboratory studies may also be done, but these will usually be in relation to some aspect of the animal's own habitat.

Early theories of ethology focused on instinctive behaviors called fixed action patterns (FAPs), unlearned actions activated by "innate releasing mechanisms" that were thought to occur in response to specific stimuli. For example, submissive behavior could be regarded as a stimulus triggering an end to **aggression** on the part of a dominant animal. More recently, the focus of ethological theory has shifted to include an increasing awareness of behaviors that cannot be attributed to innate genetic processes, and learning has come to play a greater role in explanations of animal behavior. One example is the changing attitude toward the key concept of **imprinting,** first used by Lorenz to describe a nonreversible behavioral response acquired early in life, normally released by a specific triggering stimulus or situation. The differences between imprinting and ordinary learning include the fact that imprinting can take place only during a limited "critical period," what is imprinted cannot be forgotten, and imprinting does not occur in response to a reward. Imprinting was initially regarded as totally innate, but subsequent research has found that **conditioning** plays a role in this process.

Initially, ethology encompassed broad areas of behavioral study. More recently it has emphasized detailed study of particular behaviors. An emerging subfield, molecular ethology, focuses on how behaviors are affected by a single gene. Additional subdisciplines derived from classical ethology include sociobiology, which also involves gene study, and behavioral ecology, which relates behavior to the ecological conditions in which it occurs.

See also Adaptation; Comparative Psychology; Genetic Psychology.

Further Reading

Moynihan, Martin. *The New World Primates: Adaptive Radiation and the Evolution of Social Behavior, Languages, and Intelligence.* Princeton, NJ: Princeton University Press, 1976.

Eugenics

The systematic attempt to increase desirable genetic traits and to decrease undesirable genetic traits in a population.

As **Charles Darwin**'s ideas on evolutionary theory gained acceptance in the late 1800s, the public's faith in science as a source for social remedies increased in popularity, and scientists have looked for ways to "improve" humanity. British scientist **Francis Galton** introduced the ideas that led to a scientific approach to eugenics, including the concept of "positive eugenics" in which he encouraged the healthiest and most intelligent to marry one another and procreate. Although Galton's theories did not gain widespread acceptance in England, in the United States his ideas were interpreted in programs of "negative eugenics," designed to keep certain people from bearing children. Negative eugenics included such extreme measures as castration and sterilization as well as the institutionalization of people considered "defective" or "undesirable."

Racial, social, and moral issues were key factors in the American eugenics movement. Its victims included individuals diagnosed with **mental retardation,** psychiatric symptoms, **epilepsy,** or **deafness,** and people considered to be of low moral stature—unwed mothers, thieves, and prostitutes, for such behaviors were thought to be genetically based. A number of states enacted mis-

cegenation laws that prohibited marriage between people of different races because it was believed that mixing the genes of different races would allow undesirable traits to proliferate in the dominant population. In an attempt to keep the "unfit" from procreating, legislators passed compulsory sterilization laws. Indiana was the first state to pass such legislation in 1907; by 1932, thirty states had similar laws. Prior to these statutes, however, compulsory sterilization had been an accepted practice in parts of the Midwest, and by the end of the eugenics movement, approximately 20,000 people had been sterilized.

In one particularly noteworthy case, the state of Virginia had ordered that Carrie Buck, an allegedly retarded women, be sterilized against her will. Later, Buck sued the state in a case that ultimately went to the Supreme Court. With a single dissenting vote, the Court upheld the existing sterilization laws, with Chief Justice Oliver Wendell Holmes handing down the opinion that it would be better to sterilize a feebleminded woman than to allow her to bear children who would ultimately become thieves and murderers. Recent investigations have revealed that Carrie Buck was completely normal intellectually, as was a daughter—conceived before the sterilization in a case of rape—who, before her death at the age of eight, performed quite satisfactorily in school. The daughter, Vivian Dobbs, had been diagnosed as retarded at six months of age during a cursory examination by a social worker.

In some cases, **mental retardation** was diagnosed on the basis of **intelligence** test scores. One prominent psychologist, Henry H. Goddard (1866–1957) actively campaigned to keep mentally retarded individuals from having children, and segregated students living at the New Jersey Vineland Training School for Feeble-Minded Girls and Boys by sex so that they could not procreate. Goddard also worked to keep "defective" immigrants from entering the United States. In one instance, he used **Alfred Binet**'s intelligence test to assess 35 Jews, 22 Hungarians, 50 Italians, and 45 Russians at Ellis Island in New York as they entered the country, and concluded that on average, over 80 percent of the immigrants scored so low as to be reflective of mental retardation. In this case, low test scores are not surprising given that the immigrants were tested in a language foreign to them (English), were probably intimidated by the testing situation, and were unfamiliar with American culture. Subsequent immigration laws included provisions relating to the of intelligence quotients of potential immigrants.

Many of the tenets of the American eugenics movement were initially promulgated by the American Breeder's Association. While reputable scientific research did not support many of the ideas of the eugenicists, they did attempt to invoke science as the foundation for their ideas. The "research" employed was often regarded as low quality by the top scientists of the day, and its "findings" were considered flawed. In fact, Goddard's discredited research involving the famous lineage of the **Kallikak family** is now regarded as an example of poorly conceived and biased science.

American eugenics laws were widely supported up until World War II, when evidence of atrocities committed at Nazi death camps were publicized. The eugenics movement can be seen as more a socially than a scientifically based enterprise; only when the malignant implications of eugenics became clear did the American public withdraw its support.

See also Heredity; Jukes family; Nature-Nurture Controversy.

Further Reading

Bajema, Carl Jay, ed. *Eugenics: Then and Now.* Stroudsburg, PA: Dowden, Hutchinson & Ross, 1976.

Darwin, Leonard. *What Is Eugenics?* London: Watts, 1928.

East, Edward Murray. *Mankind at the Crossroads.* New York: C. Scribner's Sons, 1923.

Goddard, Henry Herbert. *The Kallikak Family: A Study in the Heredity of Feeble-Mindedness.* New York: Macmillan, 1927.

Packard, Vance Oakley. *The People Shapers.* Boston: Little, Brown, 1977.

Experimental Design

Careful and detailed plan of an experiment.

In simple psychological experiments, one characteristic—the **independent variable**—is manipulated by the experimenter to enable the study of its effects on another characteristic—the **dependent variable**. In many experiments, the independent variable is a characteristic that can either be present or absent. In these cases, one group of subjects represent the experiment group, where the independent variable characteristic exists. The other group of subjects represent the **control group,** where the independent variable is absent.

The validity of psychological research relies on sound procedures in which the experimental manipulation of an independent variable can be seen as the sole reason for the differences in behavior in two groups. Research has shown, however, that an experimenter can unknowingly affect the outcome of a study by influencing the behavior of the research participants.

When the goal of an experiment is more complicated, the experimenter must design a test that will test the effects of more than one variable. These are called multivariate experiments, and their design requires sophisticated understanding of statistics and careful planning of the variable manipulations.

When the actual experiment is conducted, subjects are selected according to specifications of the independent and dependent variables. People who participate as research subjects often want to be helpful as possible and can be very sensitive to the subtle cues on the part of the experimenter. As a result, the person may use a small smile or a frown by the experimenter as a cue for future behavior. The subject may be as unaware of this condition, known as experimenter bias, as the experimenter.

Experimenter bias is not limited to research with people. Studies have shown that animals (e.g., laboratory rats) may act differently depending on the expectations of the experimenter. For example, when experimenters expected rats to learn a maze-running task quickly, the rats tended to do so; on the other hand, animals expected not to learn quickly showed slower learning. This difference in learning resulted even when the animals were actually very similar; the experimenter's expectations seemed to play a causal role in producing the differences.

Some of the studies that have examined experimenter bias have been criticized because those studies may have had methodological flaws. Nonetheless, most researchers agree that they need to control for the experimenter bias. Some strategies for reducing such bias include automation of research procedures. In this way, an experimenter cannot provide cues to the participant because the procedure is mechanical. Computer-directed experiments can be very useful in reducing this bias.

Another means of eliminating experimenter bias if to create a double blind procedure in which neither the subject nor the experimenter knows which condition the subject is in. In this way, the experimenter is not able to influence the subject to act in a particular way because the researcher does not know what to expect from that subject.

The results of experiments can also be influenced by characteristics of an experimenter, such as sex, race, euthanasic or other personal factors. As such, a subject might act in an unnatural way not because of any behavior on the part of the experimenter, but because of the subject's own biases.

Further Reading

Christensen, Larry B. *Experimental Methodology.* 5th ed. Boston: Allyn and Bacon, 1991.

Elmes, David G. *Research Methods in Psychology.* 4th ed. St. Paul: West Publishing Company, 1992.

Martin, David W. *Doing Psychology Experiments.* 2nd ed. Monterey, CA: Brooks/Cole, 1985.

Experimental Psychology

The scientific investigation of basic behavioral processes including sensation, emotion, and motivation, as well as such cognitive processes as perception, memory, learning, problem-solving, and language.

Experimental psychologists work to understand the underlying causes of **behavior** by studying humans and animals. Animals are studied within and outside laboratory settings for a variety of reasons. A researcher may wish to learn more about a particular species, to study how different species are interrelated, to investigate the evolutionary significance of certain behaviors, or to learn more about human behavior.

Experimental psychology flourished in the second half of the nineteenth century with the work of such figures as G. T. Fechner (1801–1887), whose *Elements of Psychology* (1860) is considered the first study in the field, and Wilhelm Wundt (1832–1920), who established the first psychological laboratory in 1879. Others, including **Hermann Ebbinghaus** and E.B. Titchener (1867–1927), used laboratory methods to investigate such areas as sensation, **memory, reaction time,** and rudimentary levels of learning. While controlled laboratory studies continue to make major contributions to the field of psychology, experimental methods have also been used in such diverse areas as **child development**, clinical diagnosis, and social problems. Thus, the concept of experimentation can no longer be limited to the laboratory, and "experimental psychology" is now defined by method and by the kinds of processes being investigated, rather than its setting.

An experiment in any setting tests a hypothesis, a tentative explanation for an observed phenomenon or a prediction about the outcome of a specific event based on theoretical assumptions. All experiments consist of an **independent variable,** which is manipulated by the researcher, and a **dependent variable,** whose outcome will be linked to the independent variable. For example, in an experiment to test the **sleep**-inducing properties of the **hormone** melatonin, the administration of the hormone would be the independent variable, and the resulting amount of sleep would be the dependent variable.

In simplest terms, the effects of the independent variable are determined by comparing two groups which are as similar to each other as possible, with the exception that only one group has been exposed to the independent variable being tested. That group is called the experimental group; the other group, which provides a baseline for measurement, is called the **control group.**

Although ideally the experimental and control groups will be as similar as possible, in practice, most psychological research is complicated by a variety of factors. For example, some random variables—differences in both the subjects themselves and in the testing conditions—are unavoidable and have the potential to disrupt the experiment. In addition, many experiments include more than one group of subjects, and establishing a true control group is not possible. One method of offsetting these problems is to randomly assign subjects to each group, thus distributing the effect of uncontrollable variables as evenly as possible.

The subjects' **attitudes** toward the experimental situation is another condition that may influence the results. This phenomenon is best demonstrated by what is referred to as the **placebo effect.** Subjects in experiments that test medical and psychological treatments often show improvement solely because they believe the treatment has been administered. Thus, the administration of a placebo (a supposed treatment that in fact contains no active ingredient) to a control group can disclose to the experimenter whether improvement in the subjects' conditions has been caused by the treatment itself or only by the subjects' belief that their condition will improve. Interference may come from an additional variable, experimenter bias, the unintentional effect of the experimenter's attitudes, behavior, or personal interests on the results of an experiment. The experimenter may, for example, read instructions to two groups of research subjects differently, or unintentionally allow one group slightly more or less time to complete an experiment. A particularly powerful type of experimenter bias is the **self-fulfilling prophecy,** whereas the researcher's expectations influence the results. In a well-known example, when laboratory assistants working with two groups of randomly selected rats were told that one group was brighter than the other, they treated the rats in such a way that the supposedly "brighter" group learned to negotiate a maze faster than the other group. Subtle differences in the assistants' handling of the "brighter" group had produced the results they were conditioned to expect.

In experiments utilizing a placebo, experimenter bias may be prevented by a double blind design, in which not only the subjects but also the persons administering the experiment are unaware of which is the control group and what results are expected. In general, experimenters can minimize bias by making a vigilant attempt to recognize it when it appears, as well as resisting the temptation to intentionally influence the outcome of any experiment. The results of experiments are generally presented in a report or article that follows a standard format of introduction, method, results, and conclusion.

Experimental research can also be conducted through quasi-experiments, studies which lack the control of a true experiment because one or more of its requirements cannot be met, such as the deliberate use of an independent variable or the random assignment of subjects to different groups. Studies of the effects of **drugs** on pregnant women, for instance, are based on data about women who have already been pregnant and either taken or not taken drugs. Thus, the researcher has no control over the assignment of subjects or the choices with which they are presented, but he or she can still measure differences between the two populations and obtain significant findings. These findings gain validity when they are based on data obtained from large numbers of subjects and when their results can be replicated a number of times. Such studies provide a basis for investigations that would otherwise be impossible.

See also Experimental Design; Research Methods.

Further Reading

D'Amato, M. R. *Experimental Psychology: Methodology, Psychophysics, and Learning.* New York: McGraw-Hill, 1970

Kantowitz, Barry H. *Experimental Psychology: Understanding Psychological Research.* 5th ed. St. Paul: West Publishing Company, 1994.

Experimenter Bias. See **Experimental design.**

Extinction

The elimination of a conditioned response by withholding reinforcement.

In **classical/respondent conditioning**, the learned response disappears when the association between conditioned and unconditioned stimuli is eliminated. For example, when a **conditioned stimulus** (a light) is presented with an unconditioned stimulus (meat), a dog may be trained to salivate in response to the conditioned stimulus. If the unconditioned stimulus does not appear at least some of the time, however, its association with the conditioned stimulus will be lost, and extinction of the dog's learned or conditioned response will occur. As a result, the dog will stop salivating in response to the light.

In **operant conditioning**, the experimental subject acquires a conditioned response by learning that its actions will bring about specific consequences, either positive or negative. When the link between this operant response and its consequences is not reinforced, extinction of the response occurs. Thus, a rat that has learned that pressing a lever in its cage will produce a food pellet will gradually stop pressing the lever if the food pellets fail to appear.

Just as behavioral therapies use **reinforcement** to foster desirable behaviors, they may achieve the extinction of undesirable ones by removing various forms of reinforcement. For example, rowdy or otherwise inappropriate behavior by children is often "rewarded" by attention from both adults and peers. Sending a child to "time out" short circuits this process and can eliminate the undesirable behavior by removing the reward. Although it works slowly, extinction is a popular technique for modifying behavior in children.

Further Reading

Craighead, W. Edward. *Behavior Modification: Principles, Issues, and Applications.* Boston: Houghton Mifflin, 1976.

Skinner, B.F. *About Behaviorism.* New York: Knopf, 1974.

Extroversion. See **Introversion/Extroversion.**

Family Size

The size of a family has a significant effect on the interrelationships among its members and can play a major role in the formation of a child's personality.

Family size is a significant factor in child development, but must be considered as only one part of a larger picture, however. Other factors, such as the parents' personality traits, and the gender and spacing of the children, contribute significantly to the formation of a child's personality. Children of large families have a greater opportunity to learn cooperation at an early age than children of smaller families as they must learn to get along with siblings. They also take on more responsibility, both for themselves and often for younger brothers and sisters. In addition, children in large families must cope with the emotional crises of sibling rivalry, from which they may learn important lessons that will aid them later in life. This factor, however, may also be a disadvantage; either the older child who was "dethroned" from a privileged position or the younger child who is in the eldest child's shadow may suffer feelings of inferiority. Children in large families tend to adopt specific roles in order to attain a measure of uniqueness and thus gain parental **attention**.

Children in small families receive a greater amount of individual attention and tend to be comfortable around adults at an early age. They may also be overprotected, however, which can result in dependence, lack of initiative, and **fear** of risk, and the increased parental attention may also take the form of excessive scrutiny and pressure to live up to other people's expectations. Researchers have found that only children are often loners and have the lowest need for **affiliation**. They tend to have high IQs and are successful academically. However, only children have also been found to have more psychological problems than children from larger families.

Family Therapy

Treatment of two or more individuals within the same family system in order to change unhealthy patterns of interaction.

Many times when an individual seeks psychological help, the therapist focuses on the individual's problem. In family therapy, the problems of the identified patient (a troubled teen, for example) are considered symptomatic of dysfunctional relationships within the family as a whole. The therapist addresses these relationships rather than the apparent problems of any one individual, seeking to understand the role played by each member in maintaining the family system. Family therapy grew out of the traditional emphasis of psychodynamic theories on the effect of early family relationships on an individual's psychological make-up. Another motivating factor in the focus on family systems was the observation that the improvement made by hospitalized mental patients was often reversed when they returned to their family settings.

There are a variety of approaches to family therapy. The object relations approach emphasizes **unconscious** processes, including the projection of unacceptable **personality** traits onto another family member, and the parents' relationship with their own parents. This approach focuses more than other methods on family history and less on symptoms, resulting in a lengthier therapeutic process. Ivan Boszormenyi-Nagy, a well-known adherent of this orientation, would only agree to treat families when members of three generations could participate in therapy sessions. The Bowen Theory, like the object relations approach, deals with intergenerational issues and projective processes. Based on the observations of Murray Bowen, this method attempts to help individuals come "unstuck" from the family system so that they can establish real identities instead of the "pseudo" identities dictated by their enmeshment in family dynamics. Central to this approach is the concept of triangulation, in which two persons (generally a couple) deal with the tension between them by using a third person as a buffer.

Eight adult siblings pause during a family wedding celebration to pose with their mother, spouses, and children for a group photo. Psychologists have observed that children in large families tend to adopt specific roles to gain a measure of uniqueness.

Bowen Theory is basically a cognitive approach, with thoughts emphasized over emotions.

Structural family therapy focuses on present family structure rather than on the past. This approach, designed by founder Salvador Minuchin, concentrates on changing interactions that reinforce existing behavior, such as the formation of alliances among some family members against others. Minuchin theorized that the family actually needs a troubled member in the family in order for the system to continue functioning in its accustomed way: if that person becomes healthier, others are threatened with the disruption of their existing system. The structural approach also views faulty communication as a key element in perpetuating destructive patterns of interaction among family members.

Several other family therapy approaches are primarily concerned with communication, including those centered at the Mental Research Institute in Palo Alto, California, and at the Ackerman Institute in New York. The work at both of these centers is strongly influenced by the communication theories of Gregory Bateson, particularly his concept of the double bind. (Bateson used the term "double bind" to describe the situation where communication and behavior conflict. For example, an adult uses a warm, comforting voice to communicate with a child while administering **punishment**. This can result in a child exhibiting strange or inappropriate behavior when reacting to a warm, comforting tone of voice from others.) Virginia Satir's work combines the teaching of family communication skills with a phenomenological approach that emphasizes the promotion of self-esteem. There are also behavioral approaches to family therapy that involve creating behavioral "contracts" by family members, as well as the establishment of rules and **reinforcement** procedures.

Further Reading

Minuchin, Salvador. *Family Therapy Techniques.* Cambridge, MA: Harvard University Press, 1981.

Satir, Virginia. *Conjoint Family Therapy.* Palo Alto, CA: Science and Behavior Books, 1983.

Fantasy

A set of mental images that generally have no basis in reality.

A fantasy is inspired by **imagination** characterized by mental images that do not necessarily have any relationship to reality. In **psychoanalysis,** fantasy is regarded as an **defense mechanism**. For example, after being reprimanded by a supervisor, a worker may fantasize about taking over the company and firing the supervisor. Similarly, a child may fantasize about running away from home in retaliation against her parents for punishing her.

Vivid fantasies are often a part of childhood, diminishing as a child grows older. In the majority of individuals, fantasy is not a cause for concern; as long as the fantasizer is aware that the fantasy is not real, the formation of these mental images may be considered normal. When the line between fantasy and reality becomes blurred, however, it is possible that some form of mental illness is present. When the individual regards his fantasy as reality, it has become an **hallucination.** In such situations, the hallucination may be a symptom of **schizophrenia,** and professional evaluation by a psychologist or psychiatrist is required.

Further Reading

Klinger, Eric. *Daydreaming: Using Waking Fantasy and Imagery for Self-Knowledge and Creativity.* Los Angeles, CA: J. P. Tarcher, 1990.

"What Your Fantasies Reveal About You." *American Health* (April 1995): 68+.

▌ Fear

An intense emotional state caused by specific external stimuli and associated with avoidance, self defense, and escape.

Fear is one of the primary **emotion**s, together with joy, **anger**, and grief. Fear generally refers to feelings elicited by tangible, realistic dangers, as opposed to **anxiety,** which often arises out of proportion to the actual threat or danger involved. Fear may be provoked by exposure to traumatic situations, observations of other people exhibiting fear, or the receipt of frightening information. Repeated or prolonged exposure to fear can lead to disorders such as combat fatigue, which is characterized by long-term anxiety and other emotional disturbances.

Fear is accompanied by a series of physiological changes produced by the **autonomic nervous system** and adrenal glands, including increased heart rate, rapid breathing, tenseness or trembling of muscles, increased sweating, and dryness of the mouth. Blood is diverted from other parts of the body to the areas where energy is most needed, either to run from danger or to forcibly protect oneself, a reaction known as the "fight or flight" response. This sudden diversion of excess blood from the cerebral cortex of the **brain** may also cause fainting,

which in animals may actually serve an adaptive function to protect them from predators. In the 1880s, **William James** concluded that the physiological changes associated with fear actually constitute the emotion itself (e.g., "we are afraid because we tremble"), a view that has been challenged by cognitive psychologists since the 1950s.

Fears first appear in human infants at about seven months of age. Young children generally have more fears than older persons and their fears are experienced more intensely. Within families, studies have shown that middle children as a group experience fewer fears than older or younger siblings. Researchers have disagreed about the extent to which fear is innate or learned, with behaviorists arguing that it is largely learned. Animals have been conditioned to fear previously neutral stimuli through various methods including association, the exposure to paired neutral and fear-producing stimuli to the point where the neutral stimuli become associated with fear, even when presented alone. Certain innate fears such as fear of loud noises, **pain,** and injury appear to be universal. Species-specific innate fears have also been documented, including a fear of hawk-like shapes in certain animals and a fear of snakes in humans and other primates.

When a person confronts real dangers, fear can be an important means of self-preservation. However, many people are plagued by chronic and unrealistic fears, including **phobias** and obsessions, that cause much unnecessary distress and can severely reduce their ability to function normally in society. While it is possible to reduce pathological fears through drug treatment, the results are temporary and drugs do not address the root cause of the problem. Mental health professionals offer various types of psychological treatment that either attempt to deal with the underlying cause of the fear through a psychodynamic approach or address the fear directly through behavioral therapy. Behavioral techniques include **desensitization** (gradually increasing exposure to the feared object), flooding (sudden, intensive exposure to the feared object or stimulus), and **modeling** (observing another person being exposed to the feared object without being harmed).

Further Reading

Bemis, Judith. *Embracing the Fear: Learning to Manage Anxiety and Panic Attacks.* St. Paul, MN: Hazelden, 1994.

Forgione, Albert G. *Fear: Learning to Cope.* New York: Van Nostrand Reinhold, 1977.

Nardo, Don. *Anxiety and Phobias.* New York: Chelsea House, 1991.

Feral Children

Lost or abandoned human children raised in extreme social isolation, either surviving in the wild through their own efforts or "adopted" by animals.

The study of children reared in complete or nearly complete isolation from human contact can provide important information to psychologists studying various aspects of **socialization.** After their return to human society, feral children often continue to be seriously retarded, raising the question of whether or not such children manifested abnormalities before their removal from society. Interest in wild or feral children dates back to Carl Linnaeus's 1758 classification of *loco ferus*—"feral" or "wolf" men, characterized as four-footed, non-speaking, and hairy.

The most famous case of a human being surviving in total isolation for an extended period of time is that of Victor, the "wild boy of Aveyron," discovered in 1799. Lost or abandoned in childhood, he had apparently survived on his own in the wild up to the age of approximately 11. **Philippe Pinel,** the renowned director of the asylum at Bicêtre, France, declared Victor an incurable idiot, but Jean-Marc-Gaspard Itard, a physician and teacher of the deaf, undertook to educate him. Although he remained almost totally unable to speak, Victor showed great improvements in socialization and cognitive **ability** in the course of several years spent working with Itard. In 1807, Itard published *Rapports sur le sauvage de l'Aveyron (Reports on the Wild Boy of Aveyron),* a classic work on human educability, detailing his work with Victor between the years 1801–05.

Unlike Victor, the young man named Kaspar Hauser who appeared in Nuremberg, Germany, in 1828 had apparently been locked up in isolation for an extended period, but without being totally deprived of human care. A 17-year-old with the mentality of a child of three, Hauser was reeducated over the next five years, regaining many of the faculties that had been stunted by extreme social and **sensory deprivation,** to the point where he could communicate verbally although his speech was substandard. After an earlier assassination attempt, Hauser was murdered in 1833, presumably by someone who sought to prevent his origins from becoming known.

Despite the persistence and popularity of stories about children reared by animals throughout history, well-documented cases of such children are very rare, and in most of these cases the documentation begins with the discovery of the child, so that virtually nothing is known about the time actually spent in the company of animals. In the best-known modern case of zoanthropy (humans living among animals), however, researchers did have some opportunities to observe the behavior of

NELL

A contemporary depiction of feral humans is the 1994 feature film *Nell,* which is based on the true story of a young woman introduced to society after living for years in near-isolation inside her mother's house. In *Nell,* actress Jodie Foster starred in the title role. The character is a backwoods woman who, having grown up away from people, has developed her own language. Foster used a variety of strategies to understand how to interpret the character, described as a feral or wild child.

two children—the so-called Wolf Children of Midnapore—while they were in the company of wolves, actually removing them from the embrace of a pair of wolf cubs in order to take them back to society. Kamala and Amala, two young girls, were observed living with wolves in India in 1920, when Kamala was approximately eight years of age, and Amala about one and a half. Not only did they exhibit the physical behavior of wolves—running on all fours, eating raw meat, and staying active at night—they displayed physiological **adaptation**s to their feral life, including modifications of the jaw resulting from chewing on bones. Taken to an orphanage run by J.A.L. Singh, the girls were cared for and exposed to human society. Amala, the younger one, died within two years, but Kamala achieved a modicum of socialization over the nine remaining years she lived.

The study of feral children has engaged some of the central philosophical and scientific controversies about human nature, including the nature/nurture debate as well as questions about which human activities require social instruction, whether or not there is a critical period for **language acquisition**, and to what extent can education compensate for delayed development and limited **intelligence.** Itard's pioneering work with the "wild boy of Aveyron" has had a profound impact on both education of the disabled and early childhood education. In 1909, the renowned Italian educator and physician Maria Montessori (1870–1952) wrote that she considered her own achievements a "summing up" of previous progress, giving Itard a prominent place among those whose work she saw herself as continuing.

See also Nature/Nurture Controversy.

Further Reading

Candland, Douglas Keith. *Feral Children and Clever Animals: Reflections on Human Nature.* New York: Oxford University Press, 1993.

Singh, Joseph. *Wolf Children and Feral Man.* Hamden, CT: Archon Books, 1966.

Ruben vase (left) and borderless square.

Figure-Ground Perception

The ability to differentiate visually between an object and its background.

A person's **ability** to separate an object from its surrounding visual field is referred to as figure-ground perception. The object that a person focuses on is called the figure; everything else is referred to as background, or simply ground.

Psychologists have created different kinds of stimuli in order to study how people separate figure from ground. In some cases, these stimuli involve simple ambiguous figures like the famous face-vase figure that can be interpreted as two faces looking at one another or a goblet, depending on what aspect a person focuses on. In other situations, complex stimuli can be used to demonstrate figure-ground relationships. For example, the 3-D Magic Eye pictures involve relaxing the muscles of the eyes to see a three-dimensional figure-ground picture. Until a viewer positions the eyes appropriately, the stimulus is invisible; when the eye muscles are appropriately relaxed, the three-dimensional figure emerges.

The interpretations that people derive from these stimuli are real, even though the objects are ambiguous or are nonexistent. A good example of this involves illusory or subjective contours. In the illustration, people will see an entire square, complete with borders (contours), even though the borders do not really exist.

Psychologists have also demonstrated figure-ground principles with auditory stimuli. For example, some people have claimed that there are satanic or otherwise harmful lyrics embedded backwards in some rock music. In most cases, when people first listen to the music backwards, they hear absolutely nothing that resembles speech. When somebody tells them to listen for particular words or phrases, however, people report hearing satanic words. As with illusory contours, the words are not really there until someone's **attention** is focused appropriately on a particular set of sounds.

Further Reading

Coren, S., and L.M. Ward. *Sensation and Perception.* 3rd ed. San Diego: Harcourt Brace Jovanovich, 1989.

Fixation

An intense psychological association with a past event or series of events that triggers certain feelings or behaviors in a person when confronted with similar events or series of events.

Sigmund Freud theorized that the developmental stages of **infancy** and early childhood chart our lives in ways that are difficult to change. He believed that most adult neuroses could be attributed to a fixation developed during one of these stages of early life. Freud was especially concerned about how these stages were related to sexual development in later life, and in this he was, and continues to be, quite controversial. In his time, it was considered by many to be outlandish that an infant sucking on her mother's breast was experiencing sexual gratification, yet Freud classified it as such and composed a theory of **psychosexual development**.

Freud's theory of psychosexual development suggests that children pass through several stages in their earliest years. These stages are the oral stage, the anal stage, the phallic stage, the latency stage, and genital stage. During each stage, children learn to gratify themselves (Freud would say sexually) via distinct patterns of behavior. During the oral stage, for instance, children learn that the highest level of physical gratification occurs through oral stimulation. (They feed by sucking, they routinely place objects in their mouths, etc.) It was Freud's view that during any one of these stages a person could become fixated—that is, they could be so gratified or, on the other hand, so unfulfilled, that they are marked for life by this fixation. Someone who has a fixation at the oral stage of development, for instance, might suck his or her thumb, eat or drink excessively, chew pencils, or smoke cigarettes. Adults fixated during this period of development are also thought to be inclined toward clinging, dependent relationships. Those fixated during the anal phase of psychosexual development are typically thought of as being overly controlling and obsessed with neatness or cleanliness.

Freud also considered **regression** closely linked to fixation. In his famous *Introductory Lectures on Psycho-Analysis,* he spoke of human development as a journey into new territory, much like an early migration of primitive peoples into new territory. He states that as people migrated into new, unexplored territory, certain members of the party might stop along the way at a place that offered them the prospect of a good life. These stopping points would be analogous to the fixations people develop in early life, attaching themselves to a period of safety and security before the entire journey of life is fully accomplished.

Further Reading

Freud, Sigmund. *Introductory Lectures on Psycho-Analysis.* New York: W.W. Norton & Co., 1966.

Forensic Psychology

The application of psychology to lawmaking, law enforcement, the examination of witnesses, and the treatment of the criminal; also known as legal psychology.

Forensic psychologists often work within the judicial system in such diverse areas as determining an inmate's readiness for parole; evaluation of rehabilitation programs; criminal competency; tort liability and damages; eyewitness testimony and evidence; jury selection; and police training. Forensic psychology may also be employed in other areas of jurisprudence, including patent and trademark disputes, divorce and custody cases, product liability, and taxation.

Forensic psychologists advise their clients in several ways, including diagnostic appraisals, which may be used to determine the competency of the client to stand trial, and contributing to defense strategy. They are also called upon to render clinically-based opinions on a wide variety of issues arising from their diagnoses, such as the best interests of a child in a custody case, or the readiness of a prisoner for parole. Finally, forensic psychologists advise on the prognosis and treatment of the individuals under evaluation. In most cases, they obtain a "forensic history," which includes hospital records, police reports, witness statements, and provide relevant research. Besides submitting reports on their findings, they are sometimes required to testify in court.

In a typical criminal case, the forensic psychologist may be hired by a defense attorney to evaluate the defendant. (A case will commonly entail the services of a psychologist, for example, if an insanity defense is being considered.) The psychologist is briefed on the circumstances of the crime and examines records detailing the defendant's previous criminal record and any history of mental or emotional problems and treatment. In pretrial preparations, the psychologist may administer **personality** and **intelligence** tests to the defendant. Afterwards, the psychologist reports the evaluation findings to the attorney and may be asked to testify at pretrial hearings, the trial itself, or the sentencing.

The most common type of civil case in which a psychologist may be consulted are lawsuits to recover damages for injuries resulting from car accidents. The first task is to become familiarized with the case, which includes an examination of the client's medical records relating to the accident, as well as his or her previous medical history and any records that indicate the client's level of functioning at work or in other settings prior to the accident. The psychologist must then evaluate the plaintiff's emotional or cognitive problems, being careful to distinguish those problems caused by the accident from any preexisting ones.

Forensic psychologists are regularly consulted in child custody cases. In many situations it is the court itself that hires a psychologist to evaluate both parents, children, and other relevant family members. These evaluations may involve visits to the home of each parent, which provide additional information on the relationship between parent and child and on a child's possible future **environment.** Such interviews, by their relatively informal nature, serve to facilitate communication with the child.

In addition to providing expert consultation on a contractual basis, forensic psychologists are also employed by community mental health centers, police departments, and prisons. They may train police officers to handle diverse situations like domestic abuse, **suicide** threats, and hostage crises, and how to control crowds. Those who work in prisons provide clinical services to inmates. In addition to the applied work performed by forensic psychologists in these and other settings, some members of the field specialize solely in research, investigating areas such as eyewitness and expert testimony, jury selection, and the jury decision process.

Regardless of specialty, forensic psychologists must be familiar with relevant case law, respect issues of confidentiality, and continually keep apprised of new research in the field. Joint Ph.D.-J.D. programs have been in existence since the early 1970s. It is also possible to earn a Ph.D. in psychology with a specialization in forensic or correctional psychology, and the curricula of graduate programs in psychology include a growing number of law-related courses.

Organizations for forensic psychologists include the American Association for Correctional Psychology and the American Psychology-Law Society. Forensic Psychology has had its own division in the **American Psychological Association** since 1980 (Division 4). The American Board of Forensic Psychology has provided referrals to qualified professionals in the field since its establishment in 1978 as well as promoting the discipline of forensic psychology to the general public. The Board certifies practitioners who have amassed at least 1,000 hours of experience within a five-year period. Applicants must also submit a work sample and undergo a three-hour examination administered by their peers.

Further Information

American Association for Correctional Psychology

(Formerly: American Association of Correctional Psychologists)
  Address: West Virginia University
  College of Graduate Studies Institute
  Morgantown, West Virginia 25112
  Telephone: (304) 766-1929

American Psychology-Law Society
  Address: University of Massachusetts Medical Center
  Department of Psychology
  55 Lake Avenue N.
  Worcester, Massachusetts 01655
  Telephone: (508) 856-3625

Further Reading

Cooke, Gerald, ed. *The Role of the Forensic Psychologist.* Springfield, IL: Thomas, 1980.

Criminal Justice and Behavior. Volume 1-, March 1974- .

Law and Human Behavior. Volume 1- , 1977- .

Lipsitt, Paul D. and Dennis Sales. *New Directions in Psycho-legal Research.* New York: Van Nostrand Reinhold, 1980.

Schwitzgebel, Robert L., and R. Kirkland Schwitzgebel. *Law and Psychological Practice.* New York: Wiley, 1980.

Forgetting Curve

The general, predictable pattern of the process of forgetting learned information.

Psychologists have been interested in the processes of learning and forgetting since the early days of the discipline. The researcher who pioneered this field, **Hermann Ebbinghaus** (1850–1909), invented the nonsense syllable in order to be able to assess "pure" learning, that is, learning free of meaning, and the rate at which we forget. He served as his own subject and learned an incredible number of lists of nonsense syllables. He used material with little or no meaning because he was aware that learning new information is influenced by what we already know. He decided to create learning situations that were free of prior knowledge.

The way that we forget is highly predictable, following what psychologists call the forgetting curve. When we acquire knowledge, much of our forgetting occurs right away. Ebbinghaus discovered that a significant amount of information was forgotten within twenty minutes of learning; over half of the nonsense material he learned was forgotten within an hour. Although he forgot within a day almost two thirds of the material he learned, retention of the material did not decline much beyond that period. In other words, if information is retained for a day, the knowledge was there to stay.

Ebbinghaus's forgetting curve is actually much more dramatic that a forgetting curve would be for meaningful material. When the learner is able to connect new information with old information, he still might forget what was learned, but the amount and speed of forgetting is likely to be less that Ebbinghaus experienced.

See also Ebbinghaus, Hermann

Free Association

One of the basic techniques of classic psychoanalysis in which the patient says everything that comes to mind without editing or censoring.

The use of free association was pioneered by **Sigmund Freud**, the founder of **psychoanalysis**, after he became dissatisfied with the **hypnosis**-based "cathartic" treatment of hysterical symptoms practiced by his colleague Josef Breuer (1842–1925), through which patients were able to recall traumatic experiences while under hypnosis and express the original **emotions** that had been repressed and forgotten. Freud found the limitations of hypnosis unsatisfactory and began the task of finding another similarly cathartic treatment method. By the late 1890s, he had worked out the essential components of his system of psychoanalysis, including the use of free association as a method of exploring the **unconscious**, identifying repressed memories and the reasons for their **repression**, and enabling patients to know themselves more fully. The patient, relaxed on a couch in his office, was directed to engage in a free association of ideas that could yield useful insights and to reveal frankly whatever came to mind. Freud, seated behind the patient, would listen to and interpret these associations.

For free association to be effective, it is important for the patient to share his or her thoughts freely without regard to whether they are logical, consistent, or socially appropriate. Even thoughts that seem trivial, bizarre, or embarrassing should be reported without hesitation. Initially, free association can be difficult, because people are accustomed to editing their thoughts, presenting them in a logical, linear fashion, and leaving out potentially embarrassing material. However, the technique becomes more comfortable with practice and with encouragement by the therapist. The more closely the patient can replicate his or her stream of **consciousness**, the more likely it is that defenses will be lowered and repressed material brought to light. Besides the content of the thoughts themselves, the connections between them may also offer important information to the therapist.

Further Reading

Freud, Sigmund. *An Outline of Psychoanalysis.* New York: W.W. Norton, 1989.

Free-Recall Learning

The presentation of material to the learner with the subsequent task of recalling as much as possible about the material without any cues.

A typical experiment involving the use of words as stimuli may include unrelated or related words, single or multiple presentations of the words, and single or multiple tests involving **memory.** In a free-recall test, the learner organizes the information by memory, and the process of recall often reveals the mental processes that the learner uses. For example, words positioned at the beginning and the end of a list are most likely to be remembered, a phenomenon called the serial position effect. Further, any unusual stimuli have a greater chance of being recalled, a phenomenon called the von Restorff effect.

Learners tend to organize related material in ways that enhance recall. One process, clustering, involves placing words that are associated with one another in one "location" in memory. The advantage of clustering is that recall is easier because the person can search one mental "location" and find several stimuli. The disadvantage of this strategy is that people may erroneously think that certain stimuli occurred because they are associated with the clustered items. Such falsely remembered words are referred to as intrusions.

As a rule, an individual can remember an average of about seven stimuli in a typical free recall task. This generally translates into a total of five to nine items. Psychologists refer to the "magic number seven, plus or minus two," as the amount that people can remember without engaging in rehearsal or other memory-enhancing tactics. Researchers have discovered that people can recall about seven items, but the "items" are not limited to words. If given a list of book titles, for example, a learner might be able to recall about seven titles, even though each title consists of multiple words. The critical element is the number of meaningful units, not simply the number of words. If the learners have to recall the stimuli in the same order in which they were presented, the results are less successful than if the learners can retrieve the stimuli in their own preferred order.

Frequency (Audition)

Technical definition of the range of sounds audible to humans.

Humans can detect sound waves with frequencies that vary from approximately 20 to 20,000 Hz. Probably of greatest interest to psychologists are the frequencies around 500-2,000 Hz, the range in which sounds important to speech typically occur. Humans are most responsive to sounds between 1,000 and 5,000 Hz, and are not likely to hear very low or very high frequencies unless they are fairly intense. For example, the average person is approximately 100 times more sensitive to a sound at 3,000 Hz than to one at 100 Hz. People can best differentiate between two similar pitches when they are between 1,000 and 5,000 Hz.

The relationship between frequency and pitch is predictable but not always simple. That is, as frequency increases, pitch becomes higher. At the same time, if the frequency is doubled, the resulting sound does not have a pitch twice as high. In fact, if one listens to a sound at a given frequency, then a second sound at twice the frequency, the pitch would have increased by one octave in pitch. Each doubling of frequencies involves a one-octave change, for example, the Middle C note on a piano has a frequency of 261.2; the C note one octave higher is

522.4, a change of 261.2 Hz. The next C note on the piano has a frequency of 1046.4 Hz, or a change of 523.2 Hz.

When an individual hears a complex sound consisting of many different wavelengths, such as a human voice, music, and most sounds in nature, the ear separates the sound into its different frequencies. This separation begins in the inner ear, specifically the basilar membrane within the cochlea. The basilar membrane is a strip of tissue that is wide at one end and narrow at the other. When the ear responds to a low frequency sound, the entire length of the basilar membrane vibrates; for a high frequency sound, the movement of the membrane is more restricted to locations nearer the narrow end. Thus, a person can hear the different frequencies (and their associated pitches) as separate sounds.

The ability to hear declines with age, although the loss is greatest for high frequency sounds. At age 70, for example, sensitivity to sounds at 1,000 Hz is maintained, whereas sensitivity to sounds at 8,000 Hz is markedly diminished. As many as 75 percent of people over 70 years of age have experienced some deterioration in their **hearing**.

Frequency Distribution

Systematic representation of data, arranged so that the observed frequency of occurrence of data falling within certain ranges, classes, or categories is shown.

When data is presented in a frequency distribution, the objective is to show the number of times a particular value or range of values occurs. Common forms of presentation of frequency distribution include the frequency polygon, the bar graph, and the frequency curve, which associate a number (the frequency) with each range, class, or category of data. A grouped frequency distribution is a kind of frequency distribution in which groups of ranges, classes, or categories are presented. Grouped frequency distributions are generally used when the number of different ranges, classes, or categories is large. A cumulative frequency distribution is a representation in which each successive division includes all of the items in previous divisions (so that, for example, the last division includes all of the data in the entire distribution). A probability distribution is similar to a frequency distribution, except that in a probability distribution the observed probability of occurrence is associated with each range, class, or category. The sum of the probabilities in a probability distribution is one, while the sum of the frequencies in a frequency distribution is the total number of data items.

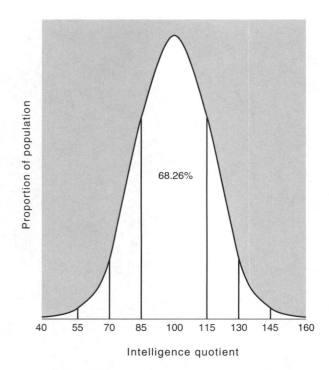

A normal distribution curve, popularly called the bell curve, with half the scores on each side of the midpoint. This sample curve illustrates the distribution of IQs in a hypothetical population.

Further Reading

Berman, Simeon M. *Mathematical Statistics: An Introduction Based on the Normal Distribution.* Scranton, PA: Intext Educational Publishers, 1971.

Peavy, J. Virgil. *Descriptive Statistics: Measures of Central Tendency and Dispersion.* Atlanta, GA: U.S. Dept. of Health and Human Services/Public Health Service, Centers for Disease Control, 1981.

Freud, Anna (1895–1982)

Austrian psychoanalyst and pioneer in the field of child psychoanalysis; daughter of psychoanalyst Sigmund Freud.

A seminal figure in the field of child **psychoanalysis** and development, Anna Freud was born in Vienna, Austria, the youngest child of **Sigmund Freud.** She was educated at private schools in Vienna, and at age 19 began two years of study to become a teacher. As the youngest of six children, she became her father's lifelong traveling companion and student. When Freud was 23 years old, she underwent psychoanalysis, with her father as analyst. Despite the fact that psychoanalysis at that time—and until around the mid-1920s—was less formal than it has become, it was nonetheless unusual for a child to become the patient, or analysand, of a parent.

Anna Freud

Anna Freud's own interest was in children and their development. Influenced by her father's psychoanalytic theories, she believed that children experience a series of stages of normal psychological development. She also felt strongly that, in order to work with children, psychoanalysts need a thorough understanding of these stages, knowledge she believed was best acquired through direct observation of children. With Dorothy Burlingham, Freud founded a nursery school for poor children in Vienna, becoming an international leader in treating children's mental illnesses. Freud turned her attention to the study of the **ego**, especially in adolescence, publishing *The Ego and the Mechanisms of Defense* (1936) in honor of her father's 80th birthday.

After the Nazis took control in Austria in 1938, the Freuds emigrated to London, England, where Sigmund Freud died a year later. In 1947, Freud and Burlingham established the Hampstead Child Therapy Course and Clinic in London, which provided training opportunities for individuals interested in the psychological and emotional development of children. From the 1950s until her death, psychoanalysts, child psychologists, and teachers worldwide sought opportunities to hear Freud lecture, and to benefit from the insights she developed from a lifetime of working with children. Freud's other writings include *The Psychoanalytical Treatment of Children*

(1946), *Normality and Pathology in Childhood* (1965), and the seven-volume *Writings of Anna Freud* (1973).

Further Reading

Coles, Robert. *Anna Freud: The Dream of Psychoanalysis.* Reading, MA: Addison-Wesley Publishing Company, Inc., 1992.

Freud, Sigmund (1856–1939)

Austrian neurologist and the founder of psychoanalysis.

Sigmund Freud was born in Moravia. When he was three years old, his family moved to Vienna, the city where he was to live until the last year of his life. At the age of 17, Freud entered the University of Vienna's medical school, where he pursued a variety of research interests. Although primarily interested in physiological research, Freud was forced to enter into clinical practice due to the difficulty of obtaining a university appointment—aggravated, in his case, by anti-Semitic **attitudes** and policies. After additional independent research and clinical work at the General Hospital of Vienna, Freud entered private practice, specializing in the treatment of patients with neurological and hysterical disorders.

During this period, Freud learned about his colleague Josef Breuer's "cathartic" treatment of hysterical symptoms, which disappeared when a patient recalled traumatic experiences while under **hypnosis** and was able to express original emotions that had been repressed and forgotten. Pursuing this idea further, Freud spent several months in France studying Jean-Martin Charcot's method of treating hysteria by hypnosis. Upon his return to Vienna, Freud began the task of finding a similar method of treatment that did not require hypnosis, whose limitations he found unsatisfactory. In addition to learning by observing the symptoms and experiences of his patients, Freud also engaged in a rigorous self-analysis based on his own **dreams.** In 1895, he and Breuer published *Studies on Hysteria*, a landmark text in the history of **psychoanalysis,** and in 1900 Freud's own groundbreaking work, *The Interpretation of Dreams*, appeared.

By this time, Freud had worked out the essential components of his system of psychoanalysis, including the use of **free association** and **catharsis** as a method of exploring the **unconscious,** identifying repressed memories and the reasons for their **repression,** and enabling patients to know themselves more fully. The patient, relaxed on a couch in his office, was directed to engage in a free association of ideas that could yield useful insights, and was asked to reveal frankly whatever came to mind. Through both his work with patients and his own self-analysis, Freud came to believe that mental disorders

Sigmund Freud

which have no apparent physiological cause are symbolic reactions to psychological shocks, usually of a sexual nature, and that the memories associated with these shocks, although they have been repressed into the unconscious, indirectly affect the content not only of dreams but of conscious activity.

Freud published *The Psychopathology of Everyday Life* in 1904 and three more works the following year, including *Three Essays on the Theory of Sexuality*, which set forth his ideas about the development of the human sex instinct, or **libido**, including his theory of childhood **sexuality** and the **Oedipus complex.** While recognition from the scientific community and the general public was slow in coming, by the early 1900s Freud had attracted a circle of followers, including **Carl Jung, Alfred Adler,** and Otto Rank (1884–1939), who held weekly discussion meetings at his home and later became known as the Vienna Psychological Society. Although Jung and Adler were eventually to break with Freud, forming their own theories and schools of analysis, their early support helped establish psychoanalysis as a movement of international importance. In 1909, Freud was invited to speak at Clark University in Worcester, Massachusetts, by its president, the distinguished psychologist G. Stanley Hall (1844–1924), and was awarded an honorary doctorate. After World War I, Freud gained increasing fame as psy-choanalysis became fashionable in intellectual circles and was popularized by the media.

Freud contended that the human **personality** is governed by forces called "instincts" or "drives." Later, he came to believe in the existence of a death instinct, or death wish (Thanatos), directed either outward as **aggression** or inward as self-destructive behavior (noted mainly as repetition compulsions). He constructed a comprehensive theory on the structure of the psyche, which he viewed as divided into three parts. The **id,** corresponding to the unconscious, is concerned with the satisfaction of primitive desires and with self-preservation. It operates according to the pleasure principle and outside the realm of social rules or moral dictates. The **ego,** associated with reason, controls the forces of the id to bring it into line with the reality principle and make socialization possible, and channels the forces of the id into acceptable activities. The critical, moral **superego—or con-science**—developed in early childhood, monitors and censors the ego, turning external values into internalized, self-imposed rules with which to inhibit the id. Freud viewed individual behavior as the result of the interaction among these three components of the psyche.

At the core of Freud's psychological structure is the repression of unfulfilled instinctual demands. An unconscious process, repression is accomplished through a series of **defense mechanisms.** Those most commonly named by Freud include **denial** (failure to perceive the source of **anxiety**); rationalization (justification of an action by an acceptable motive); displacement (directing repressed feelings toward an acceptable substitute); projection (attributing one's own unacceptable impulse to others); and sublimation (transforming an unacceptable instinctual demand into a socially acceptable activity).

Freud continued modifying his theories in the 1920s and changed a number of his fundamental views, including his theories of **motivation** and anxiety. In 1923, he developed cancer of the jaw (he had been a heavy cigar smoker throughout his life) and underwent numerous operations for this disease over the next 16 years. Life in Vienna became increasingly precarious for Freud with the rise of Nazism in the 1930s, and he emigrated to London in 1938, only to die of his illness the following year. Many of the concepts and theories Freud introduced—such as the role of the unconscious, the effect of childhood experiences on adult behavior, and the operation of defense mechanisms—continue to be a source of both controversy and inspiration. His books include *Totem and Taboo* (1913), *General Introduction to Psychoanalysis* (1916), *The Ego and the Id* (1923), and *Civilization and Its Discontents* (1930).

See also Consciousness; Memory.

Further Reading

Fromm, Erich. *Sigmund Freud's Mission.* New York: Grove Press, 1959.

Gay, Peter. *Freud: A Life for Our Time.* New York: Norton, 1988.

Fromm, Erich (1900–1980)

German-born American psychoanalyst, social philosopher, and scholar whose writings have attracted the interest of a large general audience.

Erich Fromm was born in Frankfurt, Germany, and studied sociology and psychology at the universities of Frankfurt and Heidelberg, where he received his Ph.D. in 1922. Fromm was trained in **psychoanalysis** at the University of Munich and at the Psychoanalytic Institute of Berlin. In 1925, he began his practice and was associated with the influential Institute for Social Research in Frankfurt. Although Fromm began his professional career as a disciple of **Sigmund Freud,** he soon began to differ with the Freudian emphasis on **unconscious** drives and neglect of the effects of social and economic forces on **personality.** The theories he developed integrate **psychology** with cultural analysis and Marxist historical materialism. Fromm argued that each socioeconomic class fosters a particular **character,** governed by ideas that justify and maintain it and that the ultimate purpose of social character is to orient the individual toward those tasks that will assure the perpetuation of the socioeconomic system.

Fromm consistently advocated the primacy of personal relationships and devotion to the common good over subservience to a mechanistic superstate in his work. He believed that humanity had a dual relationship with nature, which they belong to but also transcend. According to Fromm, the unique character of human existence gives rise to five basic **needs.** First, human beings, having lost their original oneness with nature, need relatedness in order to overcome their essential isolation. They also need to transcend their own nature, as well as the passivity and randomness of existence, which can be accomplished either positively—by loving and creating—or negatively, through hatred and destruction. The individual also requires a sense of rootedness, or belonging, in order to gain a feeling of security, and needs a sense of **identity** as well. The remaining need is for orientation, or a means of facing one's existential situation by finding meaning and value in existence. Orientation can be achieved either through **assimilation** (relating to things) or **socialization** (relating to people).

Fromm identified several character orientations found in Western society. The *receptive character* can only take and not give; the *hoarding character*, threatened by the outside world, can not share; the *exploitative character* satisfies desires through force and deviousness; and the *marketing character*—created by the impersonal nature of modern society—sees itself as a cog in a machine, or as a commodity to be bought or sold. Contrasting with these negative orientations is the *productive character*, capable of loving and realizing its full potential, and devoted to the common good of humanity. Fromm later described two additional character types: the *necrophilous character*, attracted to death, and the *biophilous character*, drawn to life.

Fromm emigrated to the United States in 1934, following the rise of Nazism in Germany. In America, Fromm became increasingly controversial in orthodox Freudian circles. He served on the faculties of, and lectured at, several universities in the United States, including Columbia University and Yale University, and in Mexico. In 1941, Fromm wrote *Escape from Freedom,* an analysis of totalitarianism that would become a classic in political philosophy and intellectual history as well as in **psychology.** According to Fromm, the "escape" from freedom experienced upon reaching adulthood and gaining independence from one's parents leads to a profound sense of loneliness and isolation, which the individual attempts to escape by establishing some type of bond with society. In Fromm's view, totalitarianism offered the individual a refuge from individual isolation through social **conformity** and submission to authority. Among his other important books in the areas of psychology, ethics, religion, and history are *Man for Himself* (1947), *Psychoanalysis and Religion* (1950), *The Forgotten Language* (1951), *The Sane Society* (1955), *The Art of Loving* (1956), *Beyond the Chains of Illusion* (1962), *The Heart of Man* (1964), *You Shall Be As Gods* (1966), *The Revolution of Hope* (1968), *Social Character in a Mexican Village* (1970), *The Anatomy of Human Destructiveness* (1973), and *To Have or To Be* (1976).

Fromm's work has had a deep and lasting influence on Western thought. One central thesis that appears in much of his writing is that **alienation** is the most serious and fundamental problem of Western civilization. In his view, Western culture must be transformed—through the application of psychoanalytic principles to social issues—into societies that recognize the primacy of human beings as responsible, sovereign individuals and that are conducive to the attainment of individual freedom, which he sees as the ultimate goal of humanity's existence.

Further Reading

Funk, Rainer. *Erich Fromm: The Courage to be Human.* New York: Human Sciences Press, 1989.

Functional Disorder

A psychological disorder for which no organic cause can be found.

Disorders traditionally classified as neuroses (including a variety of **anxiety** and **mood** disorders as well as psychosomatic illnesses) are generally regarded as functional disorders. While conditions classified as psychotic are usually believed to have biological origins, neurotic conditions are generally believed to be caused by developmental, psychosocial, or **personality** factors. Psychotic disorders not associated with damage to **brain** tissue from a head injury, infection, or similar causes are also considered functional disorders.

Many mental health professionals are uncomfortable with the term "functional disorder" for a variety of reasons. First, its meaning is often distorted. While the term is essentially a designation of what a disorder is *not* (i.e., organic), it tends to be interpreted as making positive statements about what the disorder *is* (i.e., induced by environmental or psychosocial factors) when, in fact, such causes may not have been scientifically proven. In addition, "functional" as a classification continually becomes outdated as new discoveries are made about the origins of certain disorders. **Schizophrenia,** for example, would be considered an *organic* disorder if a biochemical cause for the disease—which some researchers believe exists—could be verified. By comparison, the current system of classifying disorders in the ***Diagnostic and Statistical Manual of Mental Disorders***, which is organized by the mental faculty or area of behavior that is impaired, is much less likely to become outdated due to new research. A further objection to the term functional disorder is that it implies an artificial separation of the mind and body, as a number of disorders have both organic and functional components.

Functional Fixedness

A limitation in perception.

In solving problems, humans try to focus on the best strategy to reach the goal. Sometimes problems are more difficult to solve than they need to be because the available solutions are not clear or obvious. That is, humans form mental sets, ways of viewing the potential solutions, that actually hinder progress.

When people develop functional fixedness, they recognize tools only for their obvious function. For example, an object is regarded as having only one fixed function. The problem-solver cannot alter his or her mental set to see that the tool may have multiple uses.

A common theatrical situation involves a group of people who want to enter a locked room when they have no key. A solution often arises when somebody thinks to insert a credit card between the door and the door jamb, releasing the lock. In real life, if one needs to get into a locked room, a useful implement might be present that would help solve your problem. Unfortunately, the person may not recognize that it will help because he or she is a victim of functional fixedness.

In many cases, people are quite adept at avoiding functional fixedness, as when using a nail clipper as a screwdriver or the heel of a shoe as a nutcracker.

Functionalism

A psychological approach, popular in the early part of the twentieth century, that focused on how consciousness functions to help human beings adapt to their environment.

The goal of the first **psychologist**s was to determine the structure of **consciousness** just as chemists had found the structure of chemicals. Thus, the school of psychology associated with this approach earned the name structuralism. This perspective began in Germany in the laboratory of Wilhelm Wundt (1832–1920).

Before long, however, psychologists suggested that psychology should not concern itself with the structure of consciousness because, they argued, consciousness was always changing so it had no basic structure. Instead, they suggested that psychology should focus on the function or purpose of consciousness and how it leads to adaptive behavior. This approach to psychology was consistent with **Charles Darwin**'s theory of evolution, which exerted a significant impact on the character of psychology. The school of functionalism developed and flourished in the United States, which quickly surpassed Germany as the primary location of scientific psychology.

In 1892, George Trumbull Ladd (1842–1921), one of the early presidents of the **American Psychological Association**, had declared that objective psychology should not replace the subjective psychology of the structuralists. By 1900, however, most psychologists agreed with a later president, Joseph Jastrow, that psychology was the science of mental content, not of structure. At that point, structuralism still had some adherents, but it was fast becoming a minor part of psychology.

The early functionalists included the pre-eminent psychologist and philosopher **William James**. James promoted the idea that the mind and consciousness itself would not exist if it did not serve some practical, adaptive purpose. It had evolved because it presented advantages. Along with this idea, James maintained that psychology should be practical and should be developed to make a difference in people's lives.

One of the difficulties that concerned the functionalists was how to reconcile the objective, scientific nature of psychology with its focus on consciousness, which by its nature is not directly observable. Although psychologists like William James accepted the reality of consciousness and the role of the will in people's lives, even he was unable to resolve the issue of scientific acceptance of consciousness and will within functionalism.

Other functionalists, like **John Dewey**, developed ideas that moved ever farther from the realm that structuralism had created. Dewey, for example, used James's ideas as the basis for his writings, but asserted that consciousness and the will were not relevant concepts for scientific psychology. Instead, the behavior is the critical issue and should be considered in the context in which it occurs. For example, a stimulus might be important in one circumstance, but irrelevant in another. A person's response to that stimulus depends on the value of that stimulus in the current situation. Thus, practical and adaptive responses characterize behavior, not some unseen force like consciousness.

This dilemma of how to deal with a phenomenon as subjective as consciousness within the context of an objective psychology ultimately led to the abandonment of functionalism in favor of **behaviorism**, which rejected everything dealing with consciousness. By 1912, very few psychologists regarded psychology as the study of mental content—the focus was on behavior instead. As it turned out, the school of functionalism provided a temporary framework for the replacement of structuralism, but was itself supplanted by the school of behaviorism.

Interestingly, functionalism drew criticism from both the structuralists and from the behaviorists. The structuralists accused the functionalists of failing to define the concepts that were important to functionalism. Further, the structuralists declared that the functionalists were simply not studying psychology at all; psychology to a structuralist involved mental content and nothing else. Finally, the functionalists drew criticism for applying psychology; the structuralists opposed applications in the name of psychology.

On the other hand, behaviorists were uncomfortable with the functionalists' acceptance of consciousness and sought to make psychology the study of behavior. Eventually, the behavioral approach gained ascendance and reigned for the next half century.

Functionalism was important in the development of psychology because it broadened the scope of psychological research and application. Because of the wider perspective, psychologists accepted the validity of research with animals, with children, and with people having psychiatric disabilities. Further, functionalists introduced a wide variety of research techniques that were beyond the boundaries of structural psychology, like physiological measures, mental tests, and questionnaires. The functionalist legacy endures in psychology today.

Some historians have suggested that functional psychology was consistent with the progressivism that characterized American psychology at the end of the nineteenth century: more people were moving to and living in urban areas, science seemed to hold all the answers for creating a Utopian society, educational reform was underway, and many societal changes faced America. It is not surprising that psychologists began to consider the role that psychology could play in developing a better society.

Further Reading

Biro, J.I., and Robert W. Shahan, eds. *Mind, Brain, and Function: Essays in the Philosophy of Mind.* Norman: University of Oklahoma Press, 1982.

Leahey, T. H. *A History of Modern Psychology.* 2nd ed. Englewood Cliffs, NJ: Prentice-Hall, 1994.

Putnam, Hilary. *Representation and Reality.* Cambridge, MA: MIT Press, 1988.

Schultz, D. P., and S. E. Schultz *A History of Modern Psychology.* 6th ed. Fort Worth, TX: Harcourt Brace College Publishers, 1996.

G

Galton, Sir Francis (1822–1911)

English scientist, explorer, and principal figure in the early history of eugenics.

Born in Birmingham, England, Francis Galton was descended from founders of the Quaker religion. He learned to read before the age of three and became competent in Latin and mathematics by age five. Nevertheless, Galton's formal education was unsuccessful. A rebellious student, he left school at the age of 16 to receive medical training at hospitals in Birmingham and London. Entering Cambridge University two years later, Galton failed to attain the high academic ranking he sought, and this precipitated a mental breakdown, although he did eventually earn his degree.

After several years of living on an inheritance from his father who died in 1845, Galton led a two-year expedition to the interior of southwest Africa, winning a gold medal from the Royal Geographical Society for a highly detailed map he produced from data obtained on this trip. He also became a fellow of both the Royal Geographical Society and the Royal Society. During the next ten years, Galton was preoccupied with geographical and meteorological studies. Among his other achievements, Galton created the world's first weather maps.

The 1859 publication of *On the Origin of Species* by Galton's cousin, **Charles Darwin,** turned Galton's attention to the subject of **heredity.** Theorizing that the operating principles of Darwin's theory of evolution provided the potential for the positive biological transformation of humankind, Galton began to study the inheritance of intellectual characteristics among human beings. Based on quantitative studies of prominent individuals and their family trees, he concluded that intellectual ability is inherited in much the same way as physical traits, and he later published his findings in *Hereditary Genius* (1869).

Sir Francis Galton

Galton's belief in the hereditary nature of **intelligence** led him to the idea that society should encourage superior individuals to procreate, while those with lesser mental abilities should be discouraged from doing so, a concept for which he coined the term "**eugenics**," denoting the scientific attempt to genetically improve the human species through selective parenthood. It is interesting to note that Galton's approach to eugenics was to encourage the "best specimens" to procreate. This differed from the American approach referred to as "negative eugenics," where the "worst specimens" were prevented from procreating.

Galton carried out further research to distinguish between the effects of heredity and those of **environment.** He polled members of the Royal Society about their lives, using a new research tool of his own devising that was to have a long life as an information-gathering device: the questionnaire. Eventually, Galton modified his original theories to recognize the effects of education and other environmental factors on **mental ability,** although he continued to regard heredity as the preeminent influence.

Galton made significant contributions in many areas. His strong interest in individual psychological differences led him to pioneer intelligence testing, inventing the word-association test. He also was the first known investigator to study twins who had been separated from each other as a means of offering insight into the **nature-nurture controversy.** In his late sixties, Galton discovered the analytical device known as the "regression line" for studying the correlations between sets of data. In 1909, he was knighted in recognition of his manifold accomplishments in such diverse fields as geography, meteorology, biology, statistics, **psychology,** and even criminology (he had developed a system for classifying fingerprints). While many of Galton's specific conclusions and research methods turned out to have been flawed, his work provided a foundation for the study of individual differences by both **psychologists** and educators. Among Galton's many publications are *Tropical South Africa* (1853), *The Art of Travel* (1855), *Hereditary Genius* (1869), *English Men of Science: Their Nature and Nurture* (1874), *Inquiries into Human Faculty and Its Development* (1883), and *Memories of My Life* (1908).

Further Reading

Forrest, D.W. *Francis Galton: The Life and Work of a Victorian Genius.* London: Elek, 1974.

Pearson, Karl. *The Life, Letters and Labours of Francis Galton.* Cambridge, England: Cambridge University Press, 1914-30.

Gender Bias

Differences in the treatment of males and females.

Gender bias, and its corollary, gender equity, describe the comparison of opportunities and treatment available to males with those available to females. Today, gender bias is observed and discussed in societies and cultures worldwide. Parents and teachers of young people are especially concerned with unequal treatment of boys and girls, particularly the effect these differences have on **child development**. Economic development professionals have observed that, from subsistence to advanced economies, women are assigned different workloads, have different responsibilities for child and family welfare, and receive different rewards for performance.

In the United States, the Education Amendments of 1972 were passed by the U.S. Congress. These included Title IX, introduced by Representative Edith Green of Oregon, requiring educational institutions that receive federal funds to provide equal opportunities in all activities for girls and boys. Title IX applies to all schools, public and private, that receive money from the federal government, from kindergarten through higher education.

However, in 1992 a study published by the American Association of University Women (AAUW) revealed that enforcement of this law has been lax nationwide. The AAUW's report, "How Schools Shortchange Girls," which compiled results from hundreds of research studies and articles on gender bias at every educational level, concluded that schools continue to perpetuate subtle discrimination against girls, stereotyping them as studious and well-behaved, while more aggressive students, usually the boys, may receive more attention from the teacher. Additionally, a 1989 study of books used in high school literature classes found that 90 percent of the most frequently assigned books were written by males; a year later, an evaluation of school textbooks specifically written to comply with gender-equity guidelines in California revealed lingering bias toward males in both language usage and in accounts of historical milestones.

Female students are affected by gender bias in many subtle but significant ways. Girls have lower expectations for their success in math and science; are more likely to attribute academic success to luck rather than to **ability**, and are more likely to equate academic failure to lack of ability (boys are more likely to attribute failure to lack of effort). Boys are more likely that girls to challenge the teacher when they do not agree with an answer. Generally, girls earn higher grades than boys, but boys outperform girls on **standardized tests**. Boys with higher **SAT** scores are more likely than girls with equal or better grades to be awarded academic scholarships.

The ramifications of gender bias are not limited to the educational arena. Researchers have shown that in most cultures the lack of decision-making power among females regarding sexual and economic matters contributes to population growth and confines women to subservient roles to men—usually their fathers, and later, their husbands. Although women make up 45 percent of the workforce in the United States, 60 percent of professional women are in traditionally female occupations such as nursing and teaching.

Gender stereotypes defining appropriate activities and behavior for men and women are prevalent in every culture, even though they may differ slightly from culture to culture. Awareness of the existence of these biases will help to overcome their negative effects.

Further Reading

Childs, Ruth Axman. *Gender Bias and Fairness.* Washington, DC: ERIC Clearinghouse on Texts, Measurement, and Evaluation, 1990.

Gay, Kathleen. *Rights and Respect: What You Need to Know About Gender Bias.* Brookfield, CT: Millbrook Press, 1995.

Walker, Michael. "Gender Bias: Is Your Daughter's School Prepping Her for Failure?" *Better Homes and Gardens* (April 1993): 40+.

Gender Identity Disorder

A condition, sometimes called transsexualism, in which an individual develops a gender identity inconsistent with their anatomical and genetic sex.

Researchers have suggested that both early **socialization** and prenatal **hormones** may play an important role in the development of transsexuality. It is estimated that about 1 in 20,000 males and 1 in 50,000 females are transsexuals. Gender identity disorder generally begin to manifest between the ages of two and four, in which a child displays a preference for the clothing and typical activities of the opposite sex and also prefer playmates of the opposite sex. Young boys like to play house (assuming a female role), draw pictures of girls, and play with dolls. Girls with gender identity disorder prefer short hairstyles and boys' clothing, have negative feelings about maturing physically as they approach **adolescence,** and show little interest in typically female pastimes, preferring the traditionally rougher male modes of play, including contact sports. Cross-gender behavior carries a greater social stigma for boys than girls; girls with gender identity disorder experience less overall social rejection, at least until adolescence. Approximately five times more boys than girls are referred to therapists for the disorder.

Most children outgrow gender identity disorder with time and the influence of their parents and peers. Adolescents with gender identity disorder are prone to low self-esteem, social isolation, and distress, and are especially vulnerable to **depression** and **suicide.** Preoccupied with cross-gender wishes, they fail to develop both romantic relationships with the opposite sex and peer relationships with members of their own sex, and their relationships with their parents may suffer as well. Approximately 75 percent of boys with gender identity disorder display a homosexual or bisexual orientation by late adolescence or early adulthood, although without a continuation of the disorder. Most of the remaining 25 percent become

heterosexual, also without a continuation of the disorder, and those individuals in whom gender identity disorder persists into adulthood may develop either a homosexual or heterosexual orientation.

The major symptom of gender identity disorder in adults is the desire to live as a member of the opposite sex by adopting its social role, behavior, and physical appearance. Some transsexuals become obsessed with activities that reduce gender-related stress, including cross-dressing (dressing as a member of the opposite sex), which may be practiced either privately or in public. (*Transvestism* is a condition in which individuals cross-dress primarily for sexual **arousal.**) Both male and female transsexuals may elect to alter their primary and secondary sexual characteristics by undergoing surgery to make their genitals as much like those of the opposite sex as possible. Sex-change surgery was pioneered in Europe in the early 1930s and had gained international notoriety after the procedure was performed on a former American soldier named George (Christine) Jorgenson in Denmark in 1952.

Public awareness of transsexualism has increased through the publicity surrounding such prominent figures as British travel writer Jan Morris (who wrote about her experiences in her book *Conundrum*) and American tennis star Renee Richards. As of the mid-1970s, it was estimated that more than 2,500 Americans had undergone sex-change operations, and in Europe 1 in 30,000 males and 1 in 100,000 females sought sex-change surgery. The operation itself is accompanied by hormone treatments that aid in acquiring the secondary sex characteristics of the desired sex. While a number of individuals have gone on to lead happy, productive lives following sex-change operations, others fail to make the transition and continue to suffer from gender identity disorder.

See also Heterosexuality; Homosexuality; Sex Identity; Sexuality.

Further Reading

Morrison, James. *DSM-IV Made Easy: The Clinician's Guide to Diagnosis.* New York: The Guilford Press, 1995

General Adaptation Syndrome

A profound physiological reaction of an organism to severe stress, consisting of three stages.

The first stage of the general adaptation syndrome is alarm reaction, and includes the shock phase and the countershock phase. In the shock phase, there are significant changes in several organic systems. For example,

General Adaptation Syndrome

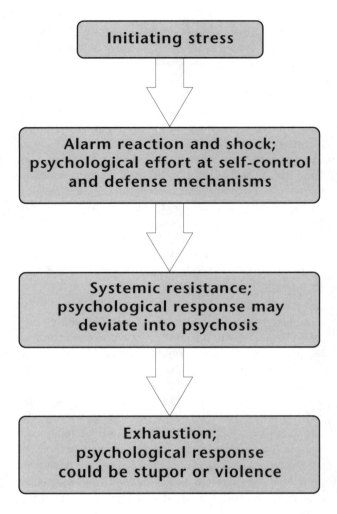

Initiating stress

Alarm reaction and shock; psychological effort at self-control and defense mechanisms

Systemic resistance; psychological response may deviate into psychosis

Exhaustion; psychological response could be stupor or violence

body temperature and blood pressure are lowered, and muscle tone is decreased. In the countershock phase, there is a defensive response to these changes, including an increased production of adrenocortical **hormones.** The second is resistance, during which the affected systems recover toward their normal levels of functioning. The third stage is exhaustion, and is reached if the defenses of the organism are unable to withstand the **stress.** In the exhaustion stage, the shock phase of the alarm reaction is essentially repeated, resulting in death.

Further Reading

Selye, Hans. *The Stress of Life.* New York: McGraw-Hill, 1978.

Genetic Psychology. See **Developmental Psychology.**

Genital Stage. See **Psychosexual Development.**

Gesell, Arnold (1880–1961)

American psychologist and pediatrician whose principal area of study was the mental and physical development of normal individuals from birth through adolescence.

Arnold Gesell was born in Alma, Wisconsin, and received his bachelor's degree from the University of Wisconsin. In 1906, he earned his Ph.D. from Clark University, where he was motivated to specialize in **child development** by studying with the prominent American psychologist G. Stanley Hall (1844–1924). Gesell received his M.D. from Yale University in 1915. After briefly holding a position at the Los Angeles State Normal School, he was appointed an assistant professor of at Yale University, where he established the Clinic of Child Development and served as its director from 1911 to 1948. He was later a consultant with the Gesell Institute of Child Development. Gesell's early work involved the study of **mental retardation** in children, but he soon became convinced that an understanding of normal development is necessary for the understanding of abnormal development.

Gesell was among the first to implement a quantitative study of human development from **birth** through **adolescence,** focusing his research on the extensive study of a small number of children. He began with pre-school children and later extended his work to ages 5 to 10 and 10 to 16. From his findings, Gesell concluded that mental and physical development in infants, children, and adolescents are comparable and parallel orderly processes. In his clinic, he trained researchers to collect data and produced reports that had a widespread influence on both parents and educators. The results of his research were utilized in creating the Gesell Development Schedules, which can be used with children between four weeks and six years of age. The test measures responses to standardized materials and situations both qualitatively and quantitatively. Areas emphasized include motor and language development, adaptive behavior, and personal-social behavior. The results of the test are expressed first as developmental age (DA), which is then converted into developmental quotient (DQ), representing "the portion of normal development that is present at any age." A separate developmental quotient may be obtained for each of the functions on which the scale is built.

In the 1940s and 1950s, Gesell was widely regarded as the nation's foremost authority on child rearing and development, and developmental quotients based on his development schedules were widely used as an assessment of children's **intelligence.** He wrote several best-

Arnold Gesell

selling books, including *Infant and Child in the Culture of Today* (1943) and *The Child from Five to Ten* (1946), both co-authored with Frances L. Ilg. Gesell argued, in widely read publications, that the best way to raise children requires reasonable guidance, rather than permissiveness or rigidity. His influence was also felt through the many child psychologists and pediatricians he helped educate. Eventually, the preeminence of Gesell's ideas gave way to theories that stressed the importance of environmental rather than internal elements in child development, as the ideas of **Jerome S. Bruner** and **Jean Piaget** gained prominence. Gesell was criticized for basing his work too rigidly on observation of a small number of research subjects who were all children of white, middle-class parents in a single New England city. He was also faulted for allowing too little leeway for individual and cultural differences in growth patterns.

Although the developmental quotient is no longer accepted as a valid measure of intellectual ability, Gesell remains an important pioneer in child development, and is recognized for his advances in the methodology of observing and measuring behavior. He also inaugurated the use of photography and observation through one-way mirrors as research tools. Gesell was also a prolific author, whose other books include *An Atlas of Infant Be-*

havior (1934) and *Youth: The Years from Ten to Sixteen* (1956).

See also Infancy.

Further Reading

Ames, Louise Bates. *Arnold Gesell: Themes of His Work.* New York: Human Sciences Press, 1989.

Gestalt Principles of Organization

Principles of perceptual organization proposed by the early 20th-century German psychologists of the Gestalt school.

The psychologists in Germany who proposed the Gestalt principles of organization developed theories and research focusing on the effects of holistic patterns or configurations (the rough meaning of the German term *Gestalt*) on **perception**. Much of their work emphasized the concept that the whole affects the way in which parts are perceived: "the whole is more than the sum of its parts."

The Gestalt principles of organization involve observations about the ways in which we group together various stimuli to arrive at perceptions of patterns and shapes. For example, at the most basic level the principle of proximity leads us to group together objects that are close to each other spatially. We also have a powerful tendency to group together mentally items that are similar to each other in terms of their appearance, texture, or other properties. Other qualities that govern our perceptions are continuity and closure: if part of an object (or person) is blocked from view, we assume that it is a continuous whole and automatically "fill in" the missing part or parts.

The attribute of simplicity also affects perception. People will interpret something they see in a manner that provides the simplest possible explanation. For example, if all other things are equal and one has a choice of perceiving a drawing as either two- or three-dimensional, it will be perceived as two-dimensional. However, if its features make it more complex to interpret in two dimensions than in three, one will automatically perceive it as three-dimensional. A final influence on perception, called "common fate," has to do with movement. Visual stimuli (such as a flock of birds or a marching band) that are moving in the same direction and at the same speed are perceived as belonging together.

Further Reading

Köhler, Wolfgang. *The Task of Gestalt Psychology.* Princeton, NJ: Princeton University Press, 1972.

Members of this drill team, moving in unison in one direction, are perceived by observers as belonging together. Gestaltists labelled this the "common fate" influence on perception.

Gestalt Psychology

The school of psychology that emphasizes the study of experience and behavior as wholes rather than independently functioning, disparate parts.

The Gestaltists were at odds with the popular school of psychology of the day, known as structuralism, whose proponents believed that the mind consists of units or elements and could be understood by mapping and studying them in combination. The Gestalt psychologists believed that mental experience was dependent not on a simple combination of elements but on the organization and patterning of experience and of one's perceptions. Thus, they held that behavior must be studied in all its complexity rather than separated into discrete components, and that **perception,** learning, and other cognitive functions should be seen as structured wholes.

The Gestalt school of psychology was founded in the early twentieth century by the German psychologist Max Wertheimer and his younger colleagues, Kurt Koffka and **Wolfgang Köhler.** The association between the three men began in 1910 with early studies of perception that ultimately led to the wide-ranging Gestalt view of the whole as more than the sum of its parts. Investigating the phenomenon of "apparent perception"—on which motion pictures are based—they discovered that when two lights were flashed in succession under specific conditions, an illusion of continuous motion was produced. The subject perceived a single light which appeared to move from the position of the first light to the position of the second light. This and other experiments led the Gestaltists to conclude that the mind imposes its own patterns of organization on the stimuli it receives rather than merely recording them, and that the significance of the mental "wholes" thus formed transcends that of their component parts. In a series of lectures in 1913, Wertheimer outlined a new psychological approach based on the belief that mental operations consist mainly of these organic "wholes" rather than the chains of associated sensations and impressions emphasized by Wilhelm Wundt (1832–1920) and other psychological researchers of the day.

In the same year Köhler began six years of experimental animal research on the Canary Islands during which he made many discoveries that applied Gestalt theories to animal learning and perception. One of his most famous experiments was with chickens which he trained to peck grains from either the lighter or darker of two sheets of paper. The chickens trained to prefer the light color were presented with a choice between that color and a new sheet that was still lighter, a majority switched to the new sheet. Similarly, chickens trained to prefer the darker color, when presented with a parallel choice, chose a new, darker color. These results, Köhler maintained, proved that what the chickens had learned was an association with a *relationship*, rather than with a specific color. This finding, which contradicted contemporary behaviorist theories, became known as the Gestalt *law of transposition*, because the test subjects had transposed their original experience to a new set of circumstances.

Although its founders conceived of Gestalt theory as a way to understand **motivation,** learning, and other cognitive processes, much early Gestalt research was concentrated in the area of perception. In the dozen years following the first studies in apparent motion, additional rules of perception were discovered. Among the most well-known are laws involving *proximity* (objects that are closer together are more likely to be seen as belonging together); *similarity* (similar elements are perceived as belonging together); *continuity* (sensations that seem to create a continuous form are perceived as belonging together); *closure* (the tendency that makes people mentally fill in missing areas to create a whole); *texture* (the tendency to group together items with a similar texture); *simplicity* (grouping items together in the simplest way possible); and *common fate* (grouping together sets of objects moving in the same direction at the same speed).

Another well-known Gestalt concept illustrating the significance of the whole involves the interdependence of figure and ground. The Gestaltists introduced the idea that perception occurs in "fields" consisting of a figure (which receives most of the viewer's **attention**) and a ground (the background). Neither figure nor ground can exist without the contrast they provide for each other: thus, they form an inseparable whole that can only be understood as part of a dynamic process greater than the sum of its individual parts. (The phenomenon of figure and ground is most often illustrated by the Rubin vase, which can be perceived as either two dark profiles on a white background, or a white vase on a dark background.) Köhler's work with primates during this period yielded important findings—transferable to humans—on learning and **problem solving** that contributed further to the body of Gestalt theory. His experiments emphasized "insight learning," through which the test subject finds a solution to a problem by suddenly "seeing it whole" rather than through random trial and error attempts, or reward-driven **conditioning.** Hence, Köhler offered a basis for viewing learning as the result of higher-level thinking involving the creative reorganization of data to produce new ways of envisioning a problem.

In 1921, Köhler was appointed to the most prestigious position in German psychology—directorship of the Psychological Institute at the University of Berlin. Under his leadership, it became a center for Gestalt studies, which remained a major force in German psychology until the mid-1930s, when Nazi pressure led to Köhler's resignation and emigration to the United States. Articles and books published in English by Kurt Koffka had also popularized Gestalt psychology in the United States beginning in 1922, and both Koffka and Köhler received invitations to lecture in America throughout the 1920s. By the early 1930s, however, the Gestalt school had become subordinated to the reigning enthusiasm for **behaviorism,** a movement antithetical to its principles.

While the Gestaltists were at odds with many popular psychological views of their time, including those held in introspective psychology, they did maintain the value of an unstructured form of introspection known as "phenomenology." Phenomenological investigation explored questions regarding personal perception of motion, size, and color and provided additional feedback regarding perception and its importance in psychological experiences. This information influenced later perception-centered theories involving problem solving, **memory,** and learning.

See also Gestalt Principles of Organization.

Further Reading

Köhler, Wolfgang. *The Task of Gestalt Psychology.* Princeton, NJ: Princeton University Press, 1972.

McConville, Mark. *Adolescence: Psychotherapy and the Emergent Self.* San Francisco, CA: Jossey-Bass Publishers, 1995.

Gifted Children

Children whose IQ scores range 135 or higher, or children who perform in the top 3 to 5 percent of all students.

The most extensive study of gifted students, initiated by **Lewis Terman,** found high **intelligence quotient,** or IQ, to be a valid predictor of future success. Terman and his colleagues tracked the lifetime development and progress of over 1,500 children with IQs over 135 for 60 years beginning in 1922 and evaluated them in terms of academic and professional achievement, income levels, physical and **mental health,** and other variables. Terman's study discredited two popular myths about giftedness. One was that high IQs are associated with genius: the vast majority of the persons studied had not matured into creative geniuses. The other myth was that exceptionally bright children were socially maladjusted "bookworms" and loners. By and large, the subjects of

More research is needed on strategies for identifying and teaching gifted children, a subject of debate among educators since the 1950s.

as opposed to the "convergent" thinking of less creative people, who approached problems in a more logical, narrow manner. The fact that convergent rather than divergent thinking is generally tested in IQ tests—which ask for one correct answer to a problem, for example—may provide a key to the lack of correlation between giftedness as defined by IQ and creative achievement.

School systems throughout the country have special classes for gifted children, and some accommodate them through such programs as early admissions, accelerated learning, advanced and/or independent study, and mentoring programs. However, recent research suggests that children in gifted programs do not score higher on **achievement tests** than those in regular classes. In addition to questioning their academic value, some educators and psychologists have voiced concern about the ways in which segregating gifted students may affect their social skills. Areas for further research on giftedness include strategies for identifying and teaching gifted children; developmental differences between gifted and average children; and development throughout the life span of gifted and talented individuals.

Further Reading

Berger, Gilda. *The Gifted and Talented.* F. Watts, 1980.
Howe, Michael J. *The Origins of Exceptional Abilities.* Cambridge, MA: B. Blackwell, 1990.
Tuttle, Frederick B. *Characteristics and Identification of Gifted and Talented Students.* Washington, DC: National Education Association, 1988.

Group Therapy

The simultaneous treatment of several clients who meet regularly under the guidance of a therapist to obtain relief from particular symptoms or to pursue personal change.

Group therapy has numerous advantages over individual therapy. The therapist's knowledge about the clients offers an added dimension through the opportunity of observing them interact with each other. Clients are helped by listening to others discuss their problems (including problems more severe than theirs) and by realizing that they are not alone. They also gain hope by watching the progress of other members and experience the satisfaction of being helpful to others. Groups give the individual client the chance to model positive behavior they observe in others. Besides learning from each other, the trust and cohesiveness developed within the group can bolster each member's self-confidence and interpersonal skills. Group therapy gives clients an opportunity to test these new skills in a safe **environment.** In addition, the group experience may be therapeutic by offering the clients a chance to reenact or revise the way in

Terman's study led successful lives, both professionally and socially. Over 85 percent accelerated beyond their designated grade level in school. All but 11 finished high school, and two-thirds graduated from college. An unusually high percentage earned professional and other postgraduate degrees. As adults their salaries were above the national average, and they also enjoyed exceptionally good physical and **mental health**.

Many have advocated a broader definition of giftedness, one that goes beyond IQ scores alone and recognizes qualities such as **creativity**, curiosity, drive, and self-direction. J.P. Guilford, a prominent researcher in the area of creativity, began advocating a more inclusive definition of giftedness in the 1950s, the period during which he introduced the term "divergent thinking" to characterize the thought processes of creative individuals—those most likely to make original contributions to society. He found that their thinking was distinguished by a tendency to envision multiple solutions to problems, which they relate to their primary families. Finally, group therapy is cost-effective, reducing the use of the therapist's total time.

The average group has six to twelve clients who meet at least once a week. All matters discussed by the group remain confidential. The therapist's functions include facilitating member participation and interaction, focusing conversation, mediating **conflicts** among members, offering emotional support when needed, facilitating the establishment of group rules, and ensuring that the rules are followed.

Nevertheless, there are also some possible disadvantages to group therapy. Some clients may be less comfortable speaking openly in a group setting than in individual therapy, and some group feedback may actually be harmful to members. In addition, the process of group interaction itself may become a focal point of discussion, consuming a disproportionate amount of time compared with that spent on the actual problems from which its members are seeking relief. There are many different types of therapy groups, and a wide variety of approaches are used in them. Some groups are organized around a specific problem (such as **alcohol dependence**) or a type of client (such as single parents), or with the goal of acquiring a particular skill (such as assertiveness training). Groups can be open or closed to accepting new members after the initial session, and their meetings may be either time-limited or open-ended sessions.

Group therapy first came into widespread practice following World War II and employs numerous methods of **psychotherapy,** including psychodynamic, behavioral, and phenomenological. In Fritz Perls' application of his Gestalt approach to group work, the therapist tends to work with one group member at a time. Other approaches, such as J.L. Moreno's psychodrama **(role playing)** method, stresses the interaction among group members. Psychodrama calls for the group to act out scenes relevant to the situation of a particular member under the therapist's guidance. Influenced by Moreno's approach, new action-based methods were introduced in the 1960s, including **encounter groups, sensitivity training,** marathon groups, and transactional analysis, whose foremost spokesperson was Eric Berne. Marathon groups, which can last for extended periods of time, are geared toward wearing down the members' defenses to allow for more intense interaction. In addition to the adaptation of individual psychotherapeutic methods for groups, the popularity of group therapy has also grown out of the development of methods initially intended for groups, including Kurt Lewin's work with T-groups at the National Training Laboratories in Bethel, Maine, during the 1940s and similar work by researchers at the Tavistock Institute in London.

Group therapy is practiced in a variety of settings, including both inpatient and outpatient facilities, and is used to treat **anxiety, mood,** and **personality** disorders as well as psychoses. Since the 1980s, techniques borrowed from group therapy have been widely used by a profusion of self-help groups consisting of people who share a specific problem or situation ranging from single parenthood and overeating to drug **addiction, child abuse,** and cancer. The primary difference of these groups from traditional group therapy sessions is the absence of facilitation by a mental health professional.

Further Reading

Friedman, William H. *Practical Group Therapy: A Guide for Clinicians.* San Francisco: Jossey-Bass, 1989.

Helmering, Doris Wild. *Group Therapy—Who Needs It?* Millbrae, CA: Celestial Arts, 1976.

Hallucinations

Compelling perceptual experiences which may be visual, tactile, olfactory, or auditory, but which lack a physical stimulus.

Although hallucinations are false perceptions, they carry the force of reality and are a definitive sign of **mental illness.** Hallucinations may be caused by organic deterioration or **functional disorders**, and can occur in **normal** people while asleep or awake, or as a result of sensory deprivation. Generally not positive experiences, hallucinations are often described as frightening and distressing. A person under a hallucinatory state may be either alert and intelligent or incoherent, depending on the type and degree of the disturbance.

One psychological condition commonly characterized by hallucinations is **schizophrenia.** In schizophrenia, the hallucinations are usually auditory, involving one or more voices. The voices may issue commands, comment on or seem to narrate the person's actions, or sound like an overheard conversation, and can be analyzed for greater insight into the patient's emotional state. Auditory hallucinations can also occur in severe **depression** and **mania;** seriously depressed persons may hear voices making derogatory remarks about them or threatening them with bodily harm. Visual hallucinations, on the other hand, are more likely to characterize organic neurological disturbances, such as **epilepsy,** and may occur prior to an epileptic seizure. Hallucinations involving the senses of **smell** and **touch** are less frequent than visual or auditory ones; however, tactile hallucinations have proven useful in the study and diagnosis of schizophrenia. Together with fearfulness and agitation, hallucinations are also a component of **delirium** tremens, which can afflict persons suffering from **alcohol dependence.**

Hallucinations can also be induced by ingesting **drugs** that alter the chemistry of the **brain.** (The technical name used for drug-induced hallucinations is hallucinosis.) The most widely known hallucinogens, or mind-altering drugs, are LSD, psilocybin, peyote, and mescaline, which act on the brain to produce perceptual, sensory, and cognitive experiences that are not occurring in reality. Effects vary from user to user and also individually from one experience to the next. Hallucinations produced by LSD are usually visual in nature. On an LSD "trip," for example, hallucinations can last eight to ten hours while those produced by mescaline average six to eight hours. Two illegal drugs manufactured to produce psychoactive effects, PCP (phencyclidine) and MDMA (Ecstasy), are not true hallucinogens, but both produce hallucinations of **body image** as well as psychoses. A person may also experience hallucinations while attempting to withdraw from a drug, such as "pink elephants" and other visual hallucinations from alcohol withdrawal. Withdrawal symptoms from cocaine are associated with the hallucinatory tactile sensation of something crawling under one's skin, often termed "the cocaine bug."

Other causes of hallucinations are **hypnosis,** lack of **sleep, stress,** illness, and fatigue, which can produce a rare and unique hallucination known as "the doppelganger." A person who has this experience sees his or her mirror image facing him or her three or four feet away, appearing as a transparent projection on a glassy surface. The hypnagogic hallucinations that occur in the zone between sleep and waking are both visual and auditory, and are strikingly detailed to those who can remember them. Sensory deprivation in subjects of laboratory experiments over a period of time has also been shown to produce hallucinations, as has electrical stimulation of the brain. Experiences called pseudohallucinations involve the **perception** of vivid images without the sense that they are actually located in external space—the perceiver recognizes that they are not real. Associated with isolation and emotional distress, they include such examples as shipwrecked sailors visualizing rescue boats or travelers stranded in the desert visualizing an oasis. Pseudohallucinations do not have the same psychiatric significance as true hallucinations.

People suffering from hallucinations may try to conceal them from others because of their negative connotations, and may receive more drastic forms of treatment or inadequate prognoses because of them. In contrast to mainstream cultural opinion, however, users of hallucinogens in the United States view hallucinations as positive and potentially enlightening, and in other cultures they are regarded for their healing faculties. In the Moche culture of coastal Peru, for example, traditional healers may ingest mescaline as part of a healing ritual in the belief that the hallucinations produced by it offer insight into the patient's condition and thus aid in the healing process.

Further Reading

Andrews, Barbara. *Dreams and Waking Visions: A Journal.* New York: St. Martin's Press, 1989.

Guiley, Rosemary. *The Encyclopedia of Dreams: Symbols and Interpretations.* New York: Crossroad, 1993.

Halo Effect

A type of bias where one characteristic of a person or one factor in a situation affects the evaluation of the person's other traits.

Halo effect is a phenomenon that occurs when one is influenced by a person's strengths, weaknesses, physical appearance, behavior, or any other single factor. The halo effect is most often apparent in situations where one person is responsible for evaluating or assessing another in some way. Examples of such situations include assessment of applicants for jobs, scholarships, or awards; designating job or committee assignments based on perceived capabilities or past performance; and in evaluating academic, job, or athletic performance. The halo effect can undermine an individual's effort to be objective in making judgments because all people respond to others in a variety of ways, making true objectivity nearly impossible. However, the halo effect causes one characteristic or quality of an individual to override all others.

To counteract the halo effect, decision makers can break the evaluation process into specific steps, evaluating only one characteristic at a time, but human judgments can never be free of complex influences.

Handedness

The tendency to use either the right or left hand more frequently.

Research in hemispheric specialization of the **brain** has revealed that each cerebral hemisphere tends to be associated predominantly with movement in the opposite side of the body. Thus, the right side of the brain is the dominant hemisphere for left-handed people and the left hemisphere controls movements of the right-handed peo-

This young artist holds the paintbrush naturally in her right hand.

ple. However, research has also yielded evidence of bilateral specialization with skills learned with either hand. Experiments have shown that when a task is learned by the right hand, information is stored not only by the hemisphere receiving sensory information from that hand (left), but also by the opposite hemisphere. The information crosses over via the corpus callosum, the bundle of **nerve** fibers connecting the left and right hemispheres, and leaves some **memory** trace in the opposite hemisphere, thus transferring the learning bilaterally. For this reason, left-handed people can write, play tennis, throw darts, etc. with the right hand although with much less skill.

See also Left Brain Hemisphere; Left Handedness; Right Brain Hemisphere; Right Handedness.

Further Reading

Coren, Stanley. *The Left-Hander Syndrome: The Causes and Consequences of Left-Handedness.* New York: Vintage Books, 1993.

Health Psychology

A subfield of psychology devoted to health maintenance, including research on the relationship between mental and physical health, guidance in improving individual health through lifestyle changes, and analysis and improvement of the health care system.

Health psychology is a diverse area with a variety of emphases. Medical psychology focuses on the clinical treatment of patients with physical illnesses, offering practical advice people can use in order to improve their health. While there is special emphasis on **psychosomatic disorders**—those that have traditionally been most closely related to psychological factors—the current trend is toward a holistic perspective that considers all physical health inseparable from a patient's emotional state. As part of this trend, psychologists and pediatricians have joined forces in the growing area of pediatric psychology, collaborating to meet the health and developmental needs of children and their families. Another focal point is rehabilitation psychology, which teams mental health professionals with health care providers who care for patients with physical disabilities and chronic conditions, often in institutional settings.

Another province of health psychology is the study of "health behavior"—how people take care of or neglect their health, either in a preventative context or when they are ill. This area includes such concerns as drug abuse, utilization of health care resources, and adjustment to chronic illness. Health psychology also addresses the health care system itself, including analysis of the outreach, diagnostic, and prescription processes, provider-patient interaction, and the training of health care personnel.

See also Applied Psychology.

Hearing

The ability to perceive sound.

The ear, the receptive organ for hearing, has three major parts: the outer, middle and inner ear. The pinna or outer ear—the part of the ear attached to the head, funnels sound waves through the outer ear. The sound waves pass down the auditory canal to the middle ear, where they strike the tympanic membrane, or eardrum, causing it to vibrate. These vibrations are picked up by three

DECIBEL RATINGS AND HAZARDOUS LEVEL OF NOISE	
Decibel level	**Example of sounds**
30	Soft whisper
35	Noise may prevent the listener from falling asleep
40	Quiet office noise level
50	Quiet conversation
60	Average television, sewing machine, lively conversation
70	Busy traffic, noisy restaurant
80	Heavy city traffic, factory noise, alarm clock
90	Cocktail party, lawn mower
100	Pneumatic drill
120	Sandblasting, thunder
140	Jet airplane
180	Rocket launching pad
Above 110 decibels, hearing may become painful Above 120 decibels is considered deafening Above 135, hearing will become extremely painful and hearing loss may result if exposure is prolonged Above 180, hearing loss is almost certain with any exposure.	

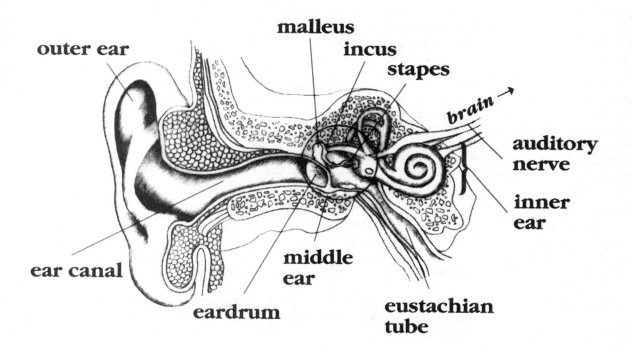

outer ear

malleus
incus
stapes

brain →

auditory
nerve

inner
ear

ear canal

middle
ear

eardrum

eustachian
tube

The human ear. Sound is captured by the outer ear (pinna), travels into the ear (auditory) canal to the middle ear, where it causes the eardrum (tympanic membrane) to vibrate. These vibrations are transferred to the malleus (hammer), incus (anvil), and stapes (stirrup).

small bones (ossicles) in the middle ear named for their shapes: the malleus (hammer), incus (anvil), and stapes (stirrup). The stirrup is attached to a thin membrane called the oval window, which is much smaller than the eardrum and consequently receives more pressure.

As the oval window vibrates from the increased pressure, the fluid in the coiled, tubular cochlea (inner ear) begins to vibrate the membrane of the cochlea (basilar membrane) which, in turn, bends fine, hairlike cells on its surface. These auditory receptors generate miniature electrical forces which trigger nerve impulses that then travel via the auditory **nerve,** first to the thalamus and then to the primary auditory cortex in the temporal lobe of the **brain.** Here, transformed into auditory but meaningless sensations, the impulses are relayed to association areas of the brain which convert them into meaningful sounds by examining the activity patterns of the **neurons,** or nerve cells, to determine sound frequencies. Although the ear changes sound waves into neural impulses, it is the brain that actually "hears," or perceives the sound as meaningful.

The auditory system contains about 25,000 cochlear neurons that can process a wide range of sounds. The sounds we hear are determined by two characteristics of sound waves: their amplitude (the difference in air pressure between the peak and baseline of a wave) and their **frequency** (the number of waves that pass by a given point every second). Loudness of sound is influenced by a complex relationship between the wavelength and amplitude of the wave; the greater the amplitude, the faster the neurons fire impulses to the brain, and the louder the sound that is heard. Loudness of sound is usually expressed in decibels (dB). A whisper is about 30 dB, normal conversation is about 60 dB, and a subway train is about 90 dB. Sounds above 120 dB are generally painful to the human ear. The loudest rock band on record was measured at 160 dB.

Pitch (how high or low a tone sounds) is a function of frequency. Sounds with high frequencies are heard as having a high pitch; those with low frequencies are heard as low-pitched. The normal frequency range of human hearing is 20 to 20,000 Hz. Frequencies of some commonly heard sounds include the human voice (120 to approximately 1,100 Hz), middle C on the piano (256 Hz), and the highest note on the piano (4,100 Hz). Differences in frequency are discerned, or coded, by the human ear in two ways, frequency matching and place. The lowest sound frequencies are coded by frequency matching,. duplicating the frequency with the firing rate of auditory nerve fibers. Frequencies in the low to moderate range

DEAFNESS

Deafness, the inability to hear, can result from a conductive loss, nerve deafness, or damage to the auditory areas of the brain. In a conductive loss, sound waves are unable to reach the inner ear due to disease or obstruction of the auditory conductive system (the external auditory canal; the eardrum, or tympanic membrane; or structures and spaces in the middle ear). Conductive deafness may be caused by middle ear infections, otosclerosis (a bony growth developing where the stapes, a stirrup-shaped bone, connects to the oval window), tumors, a perforated tympanic membrane (eardrum), and blockage of the Eustachian tube. Nerve, or sensorineural deafness, refers to two different but related types of impairment, both affecting the inner ear. Sensory hearing loss involves damage, degeneration, or developmental failure of the hair cells in the cochlea's organ of Corti, which help transform vibrations into nerve impulses. Neural loss involves the auditory nerve or other parts of the cochlea. Sensorineural hearing loss occurs as a result of disease, birth defects, aging, or exposure to loud sounds.

While many types of hearing loss occur suddenly, auditory loss from aging occurs progressively and is also known as presbycusis. It may begin as early as the thirties and affects both ears equally. Another type of gradual hearing loss is that caused by exposure to loud noise over an extended period of time, which mostly affects hearing in the range of 4,000 Hz. With additional damage, however, it may extend to the speech range, impairing speech discrimination in especially noisy situations.

Damage to the auditory areas of the brain through severe head injury, tumors, or strokes can also prevent either the perception or the interpretation of sound. Certain drugs, especially antibiotics of the mycin group, can cause reduced hearing or total deafness. Mixed hearing loss—usually associated with chronic otis media or otosclerosis—has elements of both conductive and sensorineural deafness. Other conditions associated with deafness are ischemia (tissue anemia) of the cochlea due to blocked blood vessels; rupture of the oval or round window of the middle ear; Ménière's disease; syphilis; and mumps. Prenatal and birth-related causes of deafness include viral infections (including maternal rubella); ototoxic drugs taken during pregnancy; jaundice; and low birth weight. Heredity plays a role in hearing impairment. Otosclerosis is an example of a type of hearing loss that can be inherited. Approximately 2 million Americans are profoundly deaf, and an additional 21 million are hard of hearing.

Either congenital or prelingual deafness (before the acquisition of speech) affects between 1 and 2 out of 1,000 children. A person's degree of hearing loss can be shown in decibels on an audiogram and is generally assigned to one of five classifications: mild (up to 40 decibels); moderate (41-65); severe (66-80); very severe (81-100); and profound (101 or greater).

Children who are prelingually hearing impaired have more complex psychological, educational, and social problems than those who lose their hearing once they learn to speak. In the late 1990s, research indicates that deaf children are most successful in learning to communicate in a total language development program when they learn sign language first instead of being forced to learn speech. The prelingually hearing impaired can learn to speak intelligibly and develop other communication and linguistic skills. While they show a significant delay in acquiring verbal skills, these children attain normative levels when it comes to nonverbal or practical abilities.

Hearing aids work by amplifying sounds to increase an individual's residual hearing, but they do not correct hearing problems. Sound may be distorted and the quality may be unpleasant. Although conventional hearing aids are ineffective in nerve deafness, scientists are currently developing an artificial cochlea.

There are a number of different educational services available to hearing impaired persons in the United States. Children with hearing loss may attend special classes, or small tutorial groups in regular schools, or be mainstreamed into regular classes. In addition, there are several colleges that specifically serve hearing impaired students. Psychological studies of the hearing impaired have departed from their former emphasis on similarities and differences between the hearing and hearing impaired populations in order to concentrate more exclusively on the hearing impaired and their needs.

Since the 1950s, geneticists have studied the ways in which physical traits are passed on from parent to child. In the 1990s, quantitative or biometrical geneticists have expanded the research to include the ways in which such traits as intelligence, behavior, and personality are inherited.

are coded both by frequency matching and by the place on the basilar membrane where the sound wave peaks. High frequencies are coded solely by the placement of the wave peak

Loss of hearing can result from conductive or sensorineural deafness or damage to auditory areas of the brain. In conductive hearing loss, the sound waves are unable to reach the inner ear due to disease or obstruction of the auditory conductive system (the external auditory canal; the eardrum, or tympanic membrane; or structures and spaces in the middle ear). Sensorineural hearing loss refers to two different but related types of impairment, both affecting the inner ear. Sensory hearing loss involves damage, degeneration, or developmental failure of the hair cells in the cochlea's organ of Corti, while neural loss involves the auditory nerve or other parts of the cochlea. Sensorineural hearing loss occurs as a result of disease, birth defects, **aging,** or continual exposure to loud sounds. Damage to the auditory areas of the brain through severe head injury, tumors, or strokes can also prevent either the perception or the interpretation of sound.

Further Reading

Davis, Lennard J. *Enforcing Normalcy: Disability, Deafness, and the Body.* New York: Verso, 1995.

Heredity

The process by which the genetic code of parents is passed on to their children.

There are certain traits that parents pass on to their children, including eye color, hair color, height, and other physical characteristics. The coding for these traits are contained inside **DNA** molecules that are present within all human cells. Since the discovery of DNA by James Watson (1928–) in the 1950s, the science of genetics has focused on the study of DNA and the ways in which physical traits are passed on from generation to generation. Within genetics, a special branch of DNA science—called quantitative, or biometrical, genetics—has emerged, which studies the heritability of such traits as **intelligence**, behavior, and **personality**. This branch focuses on the effects of polygenes in the creation of certain phenotypes. Polygenes, as the name implies, refer to the interaction of several genes; and phenotypes are certain variable characteristics of behavior or personality. Quantitative geneticists, therefore, study the effects of groups of genes on the development of personality and other abstract variables. They rarely, it should be noted, are able to pinpoint a behavior's genesis to a specific gene. Specific genes have been found to cause a small number of diseases, however, such as Huntington's disease and other degenerative disorders.

In studying personality traits and intelligence, the latest research in quantitative genetics suggests that the heritability rate for many characteristics hovers around 50 percent. In 1988 a study of twins reared apart revealed the heritability of 11 common character traits. The findings, published in the *Journal of Personality and Social Psychology,* reported that social potency is 61% influenced by genes; traditionalism, 60%; **stress** reaction, 55%; absorption (having a vivid imagination), 55%; **alienation**, 55%; well-being, 54%; harm avoidance (avoiding dangerous activities), 51%; **aggression**, 48%; achievement, 46%; control, 43%; and social closeness, 33 percent.

Other recent studies have compiled lists of traits most influenced by **heredity.** Physical characteristics that are most genetically determined include height, weight, tone of voice, tooth decay, athletic **ability,** and age of death, among others. Intellectual capabilities include **memory**, IQ scores, age of **language acquisition,** reading disabilities, and **mental retardation**. Emotional characteristics found to be most influenced by heredity were **shyness**, extroversion, neuroses, **schizophrenia, anxiety,** and **alcohol dependence.** It is important to note that these are tendencies and not absolutes. Many children of alcoholics, for instance, do not become alcoholics themselves. Many social and cultural factors intervene as humans develop, and the child of an alcoholic, who may be genetically vulnerable to acquiring the disease, may avoid drinking from witnessing the devastation caused by the disease. (For a fuller discussion of the role of **environment,** see **Nature-Nurture Controversy.**)

Recent work has shown that genes can both be influenced by the environment and can even influence the environments in which we find ourselves. A 1990 study found that animals raised in environments requiring significant motor activity actually developed new structures in the **brain** that were significantly different from the brain structures of animals raised in environments lacking motor stimuli. Observations from such experiments have revealed that complex environments actually "turn on" sets of genes that control other genes, whose job it is to build new cerebral structures. Therefore, living in an environment that provides challenges can genetically alter a person's make-up. Additionally, a genetic predisposition to **introversion** can cause people to isolate themselves, thus changing their environment and, in the process, altering their development of social skills. This, then, contributes further to their genetic predisposition to introversion.

There also appears to be universal, inherited behavior patterns in humans. Common behaviors across diverse cultures include the patterns of protest among infants and small children at being separated from their mothers. A study conducted in 1976 found that separation protests emerge, peak, and then disappear in nearly identical ways across five widely diverse cultures. Other studies have found universal facial expressions for common emotions, even among pre-literate hunter-gatherer cultures that have had no exposure to media. It used to be thought that the human smile was learned through observation and **imitation**, but a 1975 study found that children who had been blind from birth began smiling at the same age as sighted children. Many of these behaviors are thought to be instinctual. Aside from the infant/developmental behaviors already mentioned, other inherited behavior patterns in humans include sex, aggression, **fear**, and curiosity/exploration.

Further Reading

Beal, Eileen. "Charting the Future? Researching Heredity Quotient in African American Families." *American Visions* (October-November 1994): 44.

Berkowitz, Ari. "Our Genes, Ourselves?" *BioScience* (January 1996): 42.

Metzler, Kristan. "The Apple Doesn't Fall Far in Families Linked to Crime." *Insight on the News* (29 August 1994): 17.

Tellegen, A. "Personality Similarity in Twins Reared Apart and Together." *Journal of Personality and Social Psychology* 54 (1988): 1031.

Heterosexuality

Sexual attraction to members of the opposite sex.

The sex drive, or sexual desire, is an unlearned, powerful drive that humans share with other animal species. Heterosexuals experience sexual desire in relation to members of the opposite sex. This contrasts with homosexuals, where the object of sexual desire is a member of one's own sex. Most researchers believe that children begin to notice physical differences between males and females by about age two. As children grow, they learn about sex roles and sex differences by observing their parents and other adults, including teachers, child care providers, and from play experiences and the **attitudes** and behavior of peers. Gender identity becomes firmly established, that is, the young boy understands that he is a boy, and thinks of himself as a boy.

A heterosexual couple walks on the beach.

Sex researcher Alfred Kinsey (1894–1956), who founded the Institute for Sex Research at Indiana University in 1942, believed that sexual orientation in humans is complex, ranging from exclusively homosexual to exclusively heterosexual, with most people's sexual desires falling somewhere between the two. In fact, some individuals practice bisexuality, that is, they engage in sexual relations with both members of their own sex and members of the opposite sex. Kinsey's controversial study, popularly known as the "Kinsey Report" was published in 1948 under the title *Sexual Behavior in the Human Male*. His theory caused heated public discussion, since sexual behavior was considered a taboo subject for public discussion and study. In fact, until the late 1960s, any sexual behavior outside of exclusively heterosexual was considered either a **mental illness** or perversion. Although **homosexuality** continues to be prohibited by law in many locales, it is no longer listed as a mental disorder by the **American Psychiatric Association.**

Although much research into underlying causes of sexual orientation has been done, little conclusion evidence has emerged about why one individual is heterosexual and another homosexual. Researchers have studied biological and genetic determinants, **hormone** levels, and environmental factors. It seems from evidence available in the mid-1990s that environmental and biological factors combine in the complex process of human development to establish sexual orientation.

See also Gender Identity Disorder; Sex Identity; Sexuality.

Further Reading

Fisher, Seymour. *Sexual Images of the Self: the Psychology of Erotic Sensations and Illusions.* Hillsdale, NJ: L. Erlbaum Associates, 1989.

Levand, Rhonda. *Sexual Evolution.* Berkeley, CA: Celestial Arts, 1991.

Heuristics

A methodical procedure for discovering solutions to problems.

The principal feature of heuristics is the formulation of a hypothetical solution to a problem at the beginning of an investigation of the problem. This working hypothesis serves to direct the course of the investigation, and is modified and refined as relevant facts are discovered and analyzed. During the course of the investigation, the heuristic method reduces the range, and increases the plausibility, of possible solutions of the problem. Unlike an algorithm, however, which is a methodical procedure that necessarily produces the solution of a problem, heuristics does not necessarily lead to the solution of a problem. Heuristics has been fundamental in the acquisition of scientific knowledge, and, in fact, is an essential component of many forms of complex human behavior.

Histrionic Personality Disorder

A maladaptive or inflexible pattern of behavior characterized by emotional instability, excitability, over-reactivity and self-dramatization.

Individuals with histrionic personality disorder tend to seek attention by exaggerating events, even if insignificant, and are immature, self-centered and often vain. They react emotionally to the slightest provocation. Histrionic personality disorder is classified by psychologists with the group of personality disorders characterized by overly dramatic, emotional, impulsive or erratic reactions. People with histrionic personality disorder seek stimulation and novelty and easily become bored with routine situations and relationships. Their low tolerance for inactivity leads to hedonistic or impulsive actions. They tend to be preoccupied with their appearance and attractiveness, and their demeanor is often charming and seductive, even if this behavior is inappropriate. These individuals pursue a fast-paced social and romantic lifestyle, although their relationships usually are shallow and fleeting. They also tend to be dependent on others.

The use of the term "histrionic" by professional in psychology is relatively recent and replaces the term "hysterical," which has been dropped due to its negative and sexist associations. Women are more likely than men to be diagnosed with histrionic personality disorder, although this may at least partly reflect gender and cultural biases that cause this pattern of behavior to be less easily recognized in men. Individuals with histrionic personality disorder can benefit from psychodynamic therapy or **group therapy**. The latter can help by enabling these individuals to learn how they relate to others and try out new ways of relating. The goals for individuals who undergo therapy should include gaining more control over emotional reactions and understanding how their overly dramatic behavior undermines their relationships or careers. Medication is ineffective in treating histrionic personality disorder, although it might be prescribed for accompanying symptoms, such as **anxiety** or **depression**.

Further Reading

Morrison, James. *DSM-IV Made Easy: The Clinician's Guide to Diagnosis.* New York: The Guilford Press, 1995.

Holtzman Inkblot Test

A projective test used for the assessment of personality characteristics

The Holtzman Inkblot Test was developed in an attempt to minimize certain statistical difficulties that arise in the analysis of Rorschach results. In the Holtzman Inkblot Test, the subject responds to each of a series of 45 ambiguous inkblots. These responses are scored to describe and to classify the **personality** of the subject. The main difference between the Holtzman Inkblot Test and the Rorschach Inkblot Test is that in the Holtzman Inkblot Test the subject is permitted to make only one response per inkblot. The empirical validity of the Holtzman Inkblot Test, and other projective techniques, is disputed by some authorities.

See also Rorschach Technique.

Further Reading

Holtzman, Wayne. *Inkblot Perception and Personality.* Austin: University of Texas Press, 1961.

Homosexuality

Sexual thoughts, feelings, fantasies, and overt sexual acts involving a member of one's own sex. The term may refer to any incidence of homosexual behavior, a long-term pattern of attraction to partners of one's own sex, or a psychological identity (currently termed gay or lesbian in the United States) implying membership in a minority group.

Because of the continuing stigmatization of homosexuals, it is impossible to gauge accurately the number of homosexuals in the United States. Alfred Kinsey's studies in the 1940s and 1950s indicated that 10 percent of males admitted to engaging regularly in homosexual behavior for at least three years between the ages of 16 and 55. For women, the figure was between 2 and 6 percent. In surveys conducted in the 1970s and 1980s, approximately 5 to 7 percent of American males reported engaging in some type of homosexual behavior in adulthood.

Sexual orientation appears differently among different individuals. Some people may realize they are gay after having multiple homosexual experiences, while others may form a gay **identity** before ever engaging in sex. In addition, some persons experience attraction to others of the same sex without developing a homosexual identity. Both biological and **environmental** explanations have been advanced for homosexuality. Studies of identical **twins** offer some support for a hereditary component, and it is also thought by some researchers that a mother's **hormone** levels during pregnancy may affect the sexual orientation of her child later in life. The environmental emphasis focuses on such factors as early family dynamics, the **modeling** of behaviors observed in the parent of the opposite sex, and social learning throughout the life span. **Psychoanalysis** in particular stresses the development of childhood **sexuality**, including fixations of the **libido.** Homosexuality is also studied as a cultural phenomenon whose origins and significance vary from one society to another, a view that conflicts with attempts to determine a biological—and hence universal—basis for homosexual behavior. Researchers generally agree that homosexuality is too complex a phenomenon to have a single cause or explanation.

Condemned by the teachings of Judeo-Christianity since the Middle Ages and perhaps even earlier, homosexuality was further stigmatized in the following centuries, first legally and later by medicine and psychiatry, which declared it a pathology. While this view was supported by some early figures in the history of psychology, such as Richard von Kraft-Ebing (who called homosexuality a degenerative disease), others, including **Sigmund Freud** and Havelock Ellis, adopted a more tolerant view. Ellis regarded homosexuality as a normal behavioral variant, like **left-handedness.** Nevertheless, the mental health professions in the United States continued to treat homosexuality as a form of psychopathology throughout of the twentieth century. As recently as the 1970s, the American sex therapists **William Masters** and Virginia Johnson were "converting" gays to **heterosexuality,** although critics have asserted that those patients with whom they were successful were actually bisexual.

The **American Psychiatric Association (APA)** listed homosexuality as a disorder in its ***Diagnostic and Statistical Manual of Mental Disorders (DSM)*** until 1980, when it was replaced by "ego-dystonic homosexuality," confined to situations in which an individual's homosexual orientation was a source of distress or interfered with his or her ability to function normally. By 1986, the *DSM* contained no diagnosis that referred specifically to homosexuality. Rather than attempting to alter their sexual orientation, psychologists today are concerned with helping homosexuals acknowledge and accept it, disclose it to others, "come out," develop fulfilling intimate relationships, and cope with anti-gay **attitudes** and behaviors. They are assisted in overcoming internalized homophobia (fear of, aversion to, or prejudice against homosexuals) based on stereotypes about gays and lesbians. Current scientific studies have replaced the former emphasis on pathology, focusing instead on the effects of anti-gay discrimination, **stereotyping,** and the diversity of the homosexual population itself.

While the gay rights movement has been highly visible since the 1970s and has made significant progress in fighting anti-homosexual attitudes, laws, and behavior, homophobia remains widespread in the United States. Almost half the states still have sodomy laws which make homosexual acts between consenting adults illegal. It has been found that homophobic attitudes are most likely to be held by individuals who are older, less educated, male, rural, and living in the South or the Midwest. The appearance of **AIDS** (acquired immunodeficiency syndrome) in the 1980s and its disproportionate occurences in homosexual men contributed to a new wave of intolerance against gays. Reports of "gay-bashing"—violence against gays and lesbians—have increased, and homosexual groups have organized to protect their communities and lobby for punitive legislation to deal with hate crimes. The 1990 Hate Crime Statistics Act, which mandates the collection of data on such crimes, was the first federal legislation to explicitly protect gays and lesbians.

Psychotherapeutic services geared toward homosexuals have grown in scope and importance since the advent of AIDS. Guidance and solace from mental health professionals have played a major role in helping the gay community deal with the epidemic and cope with the magnitude of its losses. Assistance has been provided in a variety of settings, individually and in groups, to those living with the disease, as well as their partners and families.

See also Gender Identity Disorder; Heterosexuality; Sex Identity; Sexuality.

Further Reading
Fisher, Seymour. *Sexual Images of the Self: The Psychology of Erotic Sensations and Illusions.* Hillsdale, NJ: L. Erlbaum Associates, 1989.

Levand, Rhonda. *Sexual Evolution.* Berkeley, CA: Celestial Arts, 1991.

Hormone

In humans and many other animals and plants, any of a large number of organic chemical substances that regulate certain bodily functions.

Hormones strongly influence human physiology, behavior, and mental processes. Secreted through the blood in precisely controlled quantities, they regulate functions ranging from physical growth to **stress** responses. The major hormone-producing glands include the thyroid, which controls the body's metabolic rate; the pancreas, which controls insulin and glucose levels; the adrenal cortex, which regulates carbohydrate and salt metabolism; the adrenal medulla, which prepares the body for action by releasing adrenalin; and the testes and ovaries, which regulate male and female sexual behavior and the functioning of the reproductive organs.

The pituitary gland, which secretes hormones that regulate the functions of the other endocrine glands, is controlled by a portion of the **brain** called the **hypothalamus.** Thus it is the brain that has ultimate control over the endocrine system and the production of hormones. In addition to carrying messages, the hormones also provide feedback to the brain and pituitary gland, guiding them in adjusting the amount of each hormone released to keep it within the correct range. Each hormone acts only on specific target organs, producing effects that are coordinated throughout the body.

Any action of the endocrine system thus involves four main elements: the brain, the pituitary gland, the endocrine organ, and the target organs. For example, in response to stress, the brain signals the pituitary gland to release a hormone called ACTH, which in turn causes the adrenal glands to secrete cortisol, another hormone that triggers what is known as the fight-or-flight response, a combination of physical changes that prepare the body for action in dangerous situations. The heart beats faster, respiration is more rapid, the liver releases glucose into the bloodstream to supply added energy, fuels are mobilized from the body's stored fat, and the body generally goes into a state of high arousal.

Other important hormones include estrogen and testosterone, which regulate the female and male reproductive systems; vasopressin, which controls the kidneys and blood pressure; thyroxine, which governs metabolism and physical development; and insulin, which regulates the body's utilization of glucose.

Horney, Karen (1885–1952)

German-born American psychoanalyst who was among the leading theorists of psychoanalysis in the United States, and co-founder of the American Institute of Psychoanalysis.

Karen Horney was born in Hamburg, Germany, and educated at the University of Berlin and the University of Freiberg. She emigrated to the United States in 1932, after having taught for two years at the Berlin Institute of Psychoanalysis. From 1932–34, she was assistant director of the Chicago Institute for Psychoanalysis; she then left for New York City. In 1935, she was elected to the New York Psychoanalytic Society. Horney believed that **personality** is significantly affected by the **unconscious** mind, but she also theorized that both interpersonal relationships and societal factors were key factors contributing to mental development. She became increasingly outspoken in her disagreements with the theories developed by **Sigmund Freud** on the nature of neuroses and personality. Where Freud advanced a biological basis for neuroses, Horney believed that the **environment** of childhood played a key role in personality development. She felt strongly that negative experiences in early childhood could trigger **anxiety** in adulthood. In 1936, Horney published her first book, *The Neurotic Personality of Our Time,* a highly readable work. This was followed in 1939 by *New Ways in Psychoanalysis,* and *Self Analysis* in 1942.

In 1942, Horney cofounded the American Institute for Psychoanalysis. She is best known for broadening the perspective of psychoanalysis to consider childhood, environment, and interpersonal relationship. In 1955, three years after her death, the Karen Horney Clinic was established in New York City in her honor. The Clinic provides psychoanalysis and training for analysts.

Further Reading
Rolka, Gail Meyer. *100 Women Who Shaped World History.* San Francisco: Bluewood Books, 1994.
Sayers, Janet. *Mothers of Psychoanalysis.* New York: W.W. Norton, 1991.

Hostility

A persistent feeling of anger or resentment combined with a strong desire to express it or retaliate.

Hostility is a strong impulse inspired by feelings of **anger** or resentment. Though hostile impulses are normal, and everyone has them from time to time (for example, when frustrated, offended, or deprived of something), a hostile person feels those impulses regularly. She or he is always ready to take offense or feel frustrated in some way. This is often described as "having a chip on one's shoulder." Hostility can play a part in **anxiety** attacks, **depression**, compulsions, and **paranoia**. On a larger scale, hostility leads to violent crime, invasions, wars, and other acts of **aggression**.

Further Reading
Lerner, Harriet Goldhor. *The Dance of Anger: A Woman's Guide to Changing the Patterns of Intimate Relationships.* New York: Perennial Library, Harper & Row, 1989.
Williams, Redford, M.D., and Virginia Williams, Ph.D. *Anger Kills: Seventeen Strategies for Controlling the Hostility that Can Harm Your Health.* New York: HarperPerennial, 1993.

Howes, Ethel Dench Puffer. See **Puffer, Ethel Dench.**

Human Potential Movement

A movement that focused on helping normal persons achieve their full potential through an eclectic combination of therapeutic methods and disciplines. The movement's values include tolerance, a basic optimism about human nature, the necessity of honest interpersonal communication, the importance of living life to the fullest in the "here and now," and a spirit of experimentation and openness to new experiences.

William James, an early proponent of human potential and altered states of **consciousness,** is considered a forerunner of the human potential movement. However, modern interest in human potential can be traced most directly to the humanistic psychological approach of such figures as **Carl Rogers** and **Abraham Maslow** in the 1950s. Humanistic psychology was sometimes referred to as the Third Force because it presented an alternative to the prevailing psychoanalytic and behaviorist meth-

Hostility at its most intense may lead, on an interpersonal level, to violent crime or acts of aggression. On an international level, hostility may be the impetus for military invasions and even war.

ods. Rejecting the view of behavior as determined by childhood events or conditioned responses to external stimuli, humanistic practitioners emphasized the individual's power to grow and change in the present and embraced the goal of self-fulfillment through the removal of obstacles.

Maslow, together with Rogers, Rollo May, and Charlotte Buhler, founded the American Association of Humanistic Psychology. Subscribing to a positive, optimistic view of human nature, he popularized the concept of **self-actualization**, based on his study of exceptionally successful, rather than exceptionally troubled, people. Selecting a group of "self-actualized" figures from history, including Abraham Lincoln (1809–1865), Albert Einstein (1879–1955), and Eleanor Roosevelt (1884–1962), Maslow constructed a list of their characteristics, some of which later became trademark values of the human potential movement (acceptance of themselves and others, spontaneity, identification with humanity, democratic values, creativity). In Maslow's widely popularized hierarchy of **motivation**, the basic human **need**s were arranged at the bottom of a pyramid, with self-actualization at the highest level. Another of Maslow's ideas was the concept of the "peak experience," a transcendent moment of self-actualization characterized by feelings of joy, wholeness, and fulfillment.

The philosophy of Carl Rogers's **client-centered therapy** (which had been developed by 1940 but peaked in popularity in the 1950s) resembled Maslow's ideas in its view of human impulses as basically positive and in its respect for the inner resources and innate potential of each client. Another strong influence on the development of the human potential movement was the **sensitivity training** inaugurated by Gestalt psychologist Kurt Lewin (1890–1947) in his T-groups at the National Training Laboratories in the late 1940s and 1950s. Under the influence of such figures as Maslow and Rogers, sensitivity training—which had initially been used to train professionals in business, industry, and other fields—evolved into the **encounter groups** of the 1960s and 1970s. Encounter groups used the basic T-group techniques but shifted their emphasis toward personal growth, stressing such factors as self-expression and intense emotional experience.

At the center of the human potential movement was the growth center, for which the model was the Esalen Institute at Big Sur in California. Independent of any university or other institution, Esalen offered workshops by psychologists and authors on many topics of interest to humanists. Its founder, Michael Murphy, envisioned it as a place where humanistic psychology could be integrated with Eastern philosophies. In the mid-1960s its roster of presenters included philosopher Alan Watts (1915–1973), historian Arnold Toynbee (1889–1975), theologian Paul Tillich (1886–1965), and chemist Linus Pauling (1901–1994). Maslow became affiliated with Esalen in 1966. By the early 1970s there were an estimated 150 to 200 growth centers modeled after Esalen throughout the United States.

California's status as the hub of the human potential movement was further enhanced when Carl Rogers moved to La Jolla in 1964, writing and lecturing at the Western Behavioral Science Institute and later at the Center for Studies of the Person. Central tenets of his therapeutic approach were expanded into areas such as philosophy and educational reform that transcended the boundaries of psychology, and the phrases "person-centered approach" and "a way of being" began to replace "client-centered approach." Rogers also became a leader in the encounter group movement, adapting the principles of client-centered therapy to a group model. These included the belief that individuals can solve their own problems and reach their full potential in a supportive, permissive environment. Rogers's model called for the group leader to act as a non-authoritarian facilitator, creating a non-threatening atmosphere conducive to open and honest sharing among group members.

Besides encounter groups and a variety of non-traditional therapies (including Gestalt therapy, psychodrama, transactional analysis, primal scream therapy, and Morita therapy), the human potential movement also embraced a number of disciplines and practices (both Eastern and Western) involving healing, self-improvement, and self-awareness, including Zen Buddhism, astrology, art, dance, and various systems of body movement and manipulation. While the flashier and most eccentric aspects of the human potential movement have largely been relegated to fads of the 1960s and 1970s, such as primal scream therapy and EST (Erhard Seminars Training), it endures in other forms. The American Society of Humanistic Psychologists is still an active, well-organized group. Journals in the field include the *Journal of Humanistic Psychology, Journal of Creative Behavior, Journal of Transpersonal Psychology,* and others. Beyond this, the legacy of the human potential movement can be seen in the continuing popularity of self-improvement workshops and books and even in the recent proliferation of 12-step groups, as well as in the many ways its values and principles continue to influence the professional work of therapists with a variety of orientations.

Further Reading

Maslow, Abraham. *Toward a Psychology of Being.* Princeton: Van Nostrand, 1962.
Rogers, Carl. *On Becoming a Person.* Boston: Houghton Mifflin, 1961.
Severin, F., ed. *Humanistic Viewpoints in Psychology.* New York: McGraw-Hill, 1965.

Humor

The mental faculty of discovering, expressing, or appreciating the ludicrous or absurdly incongruous.

Sigmund Freud considered humor an outlet for discharging pent up psychic energy and diminishing the importance of potentially damaging events. Since the 1970s, research on humor has shifted from a Freudian focus to an emphasis on its cognitive dimensions, including investigations involving information-processing theory. Humor has been found to depend on the disparity between expectations and **perceptions,** generally termed "incongruity." Not all incongruity, however, is humorous; for humor to be evoked, the incongruous must somehow be meaningful or appropriate, and must be at least partially resolved. Research has shown the importance of humor both in social interaction and human development. Developmental psychologists consider humor a form of **play** characterized by the manipulation of images, symbols, and ideas. Based on this definition, humor can first be detected in infants at about 18 months of age with the acquisition of the **ability** to manipulate symbols. Some researchers believe that humor can be considered present in infants as young as four months old if the criterion used is the ability to perceive incongruities in a playful light and resolve them in some manner. Most research thus far has focused on responsiveness to humor rather than on its instigation, production, or behavioral consequences.

Humor serves a number of social functions. It can serve as a coping strategy, to cement allegiances, or to test the status of relationships. One of the main signs of a healthy **ego** is the ability to laugh at one's own foibles and mistakes. Humor can be used to lend social acceptability to forbidden feelings or **attitudes,** a phenomenon at least as old as the Renaissance fool or Court Jester who was given license to voice unpleasant truths and mock those in positions of authority. Research has also led to the view that humor is a way of countering **anxiety** by reasserting mastery over a situation. Feelings of helplessness have been found to characterize both anxiety and **depression.** (One of the signs of depression is the inability to appreciate or use humor.) Humor gives people an opportunity to stand outside the dire aspects of a situation, however briefly, and assert a measure of control through the ability to laugh at their predicament. This dynamic, which drives the phenomenon known as "gallows humor," is expressed in the following witticism about two contrasting cities: "In Berlin, the situation is serious but not hopeless; in Vienna, the situation is hopeless but not serious."

Further Reading

Dix, Albert S. *Humor: the Bright Side of Pain.* New York, NY: Carlton Press, 1989.

Green, Lila. *Making Sense of Humor: How to Add Joy to Your Life.* Glen Rock, NJ: Knowledge, Ideas, and Trends, 1994.

Hyperactivity

Childhood behavior or syndrome of behaviors characterized by excessive non-goal-directed motor behavior, short attention span, impulsiveness, and excitability.

The term "hyperactivity" is somewhat ambiguous, as it refers to a symptom characterizing a variety of medical and behavioral disorders. However, it is also used to describe a common syndrome—first described in medical journals over a century ago—associated with perceptual and learning difficulties in individuals of normal **intelligence.** In describing this syndrome, the term hyperactivity is inaccurately used interchangeably with **attention deficit disorder** and also referred to as **attention-deficit hyperactivity disorder,** or ADHD. At times, hyperactivity may also be used synonymously with the terms hyperkinesis, **minimal brain dysfunction,** and learning disability.

Hyperactivity is one of the most common childhood **behavior disorders.** Thought to affect up to 10 percent of the population, it is more common in boys than in girls (the ratio may be as high as 10 to 1). While the scope of this condition often does not become apparent until a child reaches school age, it usually appears very early (often in **infancy**), and some researchers have claimed that it can even be detected through fetal monitoring during the late stages of pregnancy. The disorder has been shown to persist beyond **adolescence,** as manifested in such symptoms as **attention** difficulties and impulsiveness. It has also been associated with later emotional and educational problems and antisocial behavior.

While the exact origin of hyperactivity has not been determined, it has been linked to **heredity,** maternal consumption of alcohol and cigarettes during pregnancy, poisoning by lead and other toxic substances, allergic reactions, and environmental factors including early emotional deprivation and maternal **depression.** Hyperactivity has also been associated with metabolic and endocrine disorders, such as hyperthyroidism; senso-

ry disorders, including blindness and deafness; maturational lag; and impairments of the **central nervous system,** such as acute encephalitis. It may also accompany **mood** and **anxiety** disorders (such as depression and **phobias**), **personality** disorders, and psychoses. Some researchers have linked the condition to diet, recommending diets free of artificial coloring and sugar. Hyperactivity has also been associated with physiological **brain** abnormalities including minor brain stem damage (minimal brain dysfunction), which affects attention span and motor activity but not intelligence. Assessment of hyperactivity differs among cultures: behavior that one society labels hyperactive may be considered **normal** in another. In one study, for example, Chinese and Indonesian participants exhibited a greater degree of hyperactivity than did their American and Japanese counterparts. Behavior termed hyperactive in the United States is classified as a **conduct disorder** in Great Britain.

Hyperactive children consistently exhibit a high level of activity even when it is inappropriate, are unable to inhibit this activity on command, and often seem capable of responding to a situation at only one particular speed. They even move excessively in their **sleep.** Hyperactive children are often blamed and punished for not controlling themselves when, in fact, they are unable to do so even if they want to. The sedentary activities demanded in school make it especially difficult for them to cooperate in that setting, and the usual methods of controlling behavior, such as reward and **punishment,** is unsuccessful. Hyperactivity may be diagnosed through neurological, psychological, or educational evaluation. In clinical research, it can be diagnosed and studied through **electroencephalographic (EEG)** tests that measure **arousal** of the **central nervous system.** In applied settings, it is often diagnosed using **rating scales**—completed by teachers or parents—that measure such traits and behaviors as restlessness; excitability and impulsiveness; undertaking projects and leaving them unfinished; fidgeting; inattention; crying; mood changes; and outbursts of temper.

A variety of therapies are available to treat hyperactivity, of which medications such as stimulants, tranquilizers, and antidepressants has been the most successful. Paradoxically, stimulants have been the most effective. These drugs include methylphenidate (Ritalin), dextroamphetamine (Dexedrine), and pemoline (Cylert). Up to 80 percent of hyperactive children to whom stimulants were administered have shown a reduction in symptoms, including aggressiveness, purposeless behavior, and impulsivity, and improvements in **attention span** and social **adaptation.** Stimulants, however, have both short- and long-term side effects, including insomnia, decreased appetite, weight loss, abdominal pain, and headaches. Adverse emotional effects have also been observed in some hyperactive children, although these can usually be controlled by changing the dosage of the medication. While long-term use of stimulants has been found to retard the physical growth rate of children, they catch up through a growth spurt when the medication is discontinued and reach normal height by adolescence.

Psychological treatment is of limited use in dealing with hyperactivity since the condition is not generally psychological in origin. Formerly, hyperactivity was thought to involve an impairment in the thinking process that prevented a child from remaining focused on a single concept or project. Alternatively, it was regarded by some as a means of "acting out" to get parental attention. However, cognitive and behavioral approaches to treatment have had only limited success in affecting hyperactivity. While these therapies may result in temporary improvement, in most cases children will later revert to their previous behavior patterns. Counseling, guidance, therapy, and educational intervention can be effective, however, in dealing with secondary problems resulting from hyperactivity, such as low self-esteem or strained relationships with family members, and they are often used to complement a pharmacological treatment regimen. **Psychotherapy** can also help family members to better understand and cope with hyperactive children.

Most hyperactive children grow up to lead normal adult lives, although approximately one-third of them may exhibit antisocial behavior. While they are no more likely than the general population to develop severe psychiatric disorders, some may benefit from long-term psychological help, possibly including medication. Adults whose childhood hyperactivity was never diagnosed and treated may remain restless, moody, easily distracted, and have difficulty concentrating.

See also Attention Deficit Disorder; Attention Deficit Hyperactivity Disorder.

Further Reading

Diagnostic and Statistical Manual of Mental Disorders. 3rd & 4th eds. 1994. Washington, D.C.: American Psychiatric Association.

Graham, Janis. "Pay Attention!" *Parenting* (September 1995): 118-24.

Hans, James. *The Mysteries of Attention.* Albany: SUNY Press, 1993.

Williams, Laurie C. "Understanding ADHD." *Essence* (July 1995): 102-04.

Hyperkinetic Children. See **Attention Deficit Hyperactivity Disorder (ADHD); Hyperactivity.**

Hypnosis

A temporary narrowing of conscious awareness.

Hypnosis, or hypnotism, has been practiced since ancient times, but it remains difficult to define accurately and completely. Although the word hypnosis comes from the Greek word *hypnos,* for **sleep,** hypnosis is actually an intense state of concentration.

MYTHS ABOUT HYPNOSIS	
Myth	**Scientific response**
Hypnosis places the subject in someone else's control.	Magicians and other entertainers use the illusion of power to control their subjects' behavior. In reality, people who act silly or respond to instructions to do foolish things do so because they want to. The hypnotist creates a setting where the subject will follow suggestions—but the subject must be willing to cooperate.
A subject can become "stuck" in a trance.	Subjects can come out of a hypnotic state any time they wish. The subject has control of the process of hypnosis, with the hypnotist simply guiding him or her.
The hypnotists can plant a suggestion in the subjects mind—even for something to be done in the future.	It is impossible for anyone to be implanted with suggestions to do anything against his or her will.
Hypnosis may be used to improve accuracy of the subject's memory.	Memories recovered under hypnosis are no more reliable than others.

MESMERISM

Franz Anton Mesmer, an Austrian physician practicing in the late 1700s, believed that the stars emitted a subtle magnetic fluid that flowed over humans and other beings on earth. He called this force "animal magnetism," and conducted extensive scientific experiments to prove its existence. After his work was denounced by other scientists in Vienna, Mesmer emigrated to Paris, where he established a flourishing medical practice.

Mesmer's technique focused on the passage of magnetic fluids between the physician and patient—in what later would be known as hypnosis. Patients were treated in groups, and would typically tremble when touched by Mesmer's iron wand. While Mesmer received little support from his colleagues and often used theatrics to dramatize his results, his work is believed to have instigated the scientific investigation of hypnotism.

In 1784, Mesmer was the subject of an investigation by a consortium of government officials and scientists (whose panel included the American scientist and ambassador to France, Benjamin Franklin, French chemist Antoine Lavoisier, and Joseph Gullotin, the inventor of the guillotine). While their report concluded that there was insufficient evidence to prove the existence of animal magnetism or magnetic fluid, they did concede that one person could influence another at will through stimulation of the imagination. Despite the lack of support from the scientific community, mesmerism flourished in Europe and the United States. An American mesmerist, Elisha Perkins, sold George Washington a set of metal pieces that were purported to have magnetic qualities that, when applied to the body, could cure pain.

In the 1840s and 1850s, two Englishmen contributed to the development of hypnosis as a phenomenon for scientific investigation. Medical writer John Braid became the first to describe mesmerism as a trance state, and was the first to suggest that hypnosis was a psychological phenomenon. James Esdaile, an English physician practicing in India, used hypnotism to anesthetize over 250 patients on whom he performed surgery.

In the late 1800s, the French scientist Jean Martin Charcot performed experiments using hypnosis. Among his students were Sigmund Freud, the founder of psychoanalysis, and French psychologist Alfred Binet. As a result of his study with Charcot, Freud's early work studying the unconscious mind was done on hypnotized patients.

There are three degrees of hypnosis. Under light hypnosis, the subject becomes sleepy and follows simple directions; under deep hypnosis, the person experiences dulling of sensory **perception**, similar to that of anesthesia. Under deep hypnosis, the subject can move about, open his or her eyes, and can even undergo medical procedures with no additional anesthetic. Magicians and illusionists use deep hypnosis to make a subject behave in unusual ways, such as to suspend the subject's body between two chairs in a posture that is completely stiff. The magician suggests that the subject's body become stiff and rigid, and the result is muscle tension powerful enough to support the body completely. Many researchers contend that the key factor in hypnosis is the subject's willingness to cooperate with the hypnotist, combined with the subject's belief that hypnosis works. People who are easily hypnotized are described as "suggestible"; in fact, if the subject expects to be successfully hypnotized, it is much more likely that he or she will.

Hypnotic induction is the process by which hypnosis is accomplished. In most situations, the induction is performed by an individual on a willing subject. Classical hypnotic induction involves a series of steps. First, sensory input to the subject is restricted, and the subject is instructed to stop moving. Second, the subject's focus of **attention** is narrowed. This may be accomplished by asking him or her to focus on a specific point of light or a spot on the wall. Finally, the hypnotist begins a pattern of monotonous repetition. The hypnotist may repeatedly tell the subject to relax, to breathe slowly and deeply, and to focus attention on a fixed point. It is estimated that about 70 percent of all people can be hypnotized at some level. Within that group, an estimated 30 percent are in the low range, 60 percent in the middle, and 10 percent are highly hypnotizable using the classical approach to hypnotic induction. The claim that a person could be hypnotized against his or her will is controversial in the scientific community. Many scientists feel that an unwilling subject would be difficult to hypnotize, and most scientists raise ethical questions about any attempts to do so.

While in an hypnotic trance, some subjects are able to recall forgotten experiences. This can be useful in treating **amnesia** or milder forms of **memory** loss. Interestingly, many subjects do not recall anything that happened while they were in the hypnotic trance; the hypnotist may direct the person to perform some act or engage in a specific behavior after the trance state has ended. This is termed *post-hypnotic trance* or *post-hypnotic suggestion,* and it is successful in only a small percentage of people who are able to be hypnotized. The post-hypnotic suggestion only works for behaviors that the subject is willing and able to perform; an unscrupulous hypnotist could not enlist an unwilling subject in criminal activity, for example, by post-hypnotic suggestion. Ending the trance is usually accomplished by a preset signal given by the hypnotist. On occasion, the subject may wake from the trance without the signal being given. It is unusual for a hypnotist to have difficulty ending the induced trance. Some people are able to hypnotize themselves in a process called autohypnosis.

Medical applications of hypnotic suggestion are in dentistry, where dentists use hypnosis to complete dental work on a relaxed patient without the need for anesthesia; in medical emergencies when victims under a state of shock are more responsive to hypnotic induction; and in childbirth. In cases of traumatic injury, hypnotic induction not only helps control pain but may limit the damage of the injury. A patient in an hypnotic trance can remain immobile for extended periods of time, avoiding aggravation of the injury prior to treatment.

Some psychotherapists employ hypnotic induction as a method in helping patients reduce **stress,** break self-destructive habits (such as smoking and overeating), gain access to memories, and make positive behavioral changes. Psychiatrists and psychologists may also use hypnosis to learn more about the human mind, and to help patients understand their own emotional and **personality** development. This application of hypnosis is termed *hypnotherapy.* In law enforcement, victims of and witnesses to crimes are sometimes hypnotized to help them remember important clues.

Patients who are responsive to being hypnotized must, first of all, be willing participants in the hypnosis process. One psychiatrist, Dr. Herbert Spiegel, developed the Hypnotic Induction Profile (HIP) to determine whether an individual is a good prospect for hypnosis. When the subject rolls his or her eyes back into the head, Dr. Spiegel suggests that person is likely to be successfully hypnotized if a great deal of white is visible on the eyeball. Other qualities included in Dr. Spiegel's profile include a trusting personality, preference for emotional rather than rational thinking, high empathy for others, and an intense capacity for concentration. Other researchers have studied the hypnotic situation and theorize that creating a setting where the subject is more likely to believe that hypnosis will work is a key to suc-

cessful hypnosis. These scientists contend that the situation, combined with the subject's motivation, has greater influence that any personality trait or physical characteristic.

There is no specific course of training, certification examination, or other credential qualifying a person to use hypnosis. The **American Psychiatric Association**, the **American Psychological Association**, and the American Dental Association have all endorsed the technique. Doctors throughout the United States now use hypnosis to overcome the pain of chronic headaches, backaches, childbirth, cancer, severe burns, dental **phobias**, and more. Some surgeons use hypnosis in the operating room, not only to reduce the amount of anesthesia patients need, but also to lessen **anxiety** and postoperative swelling and bleeding.

Further Information

American Society of Clinical Hypnosis
>**Address:** 2200 East Devon Avenue, Suite 291
>Des Plaines, Illinois 60018
>**Telephone:** (847) 297-3317

Society for Clinical and Experimental Hypnosis
>**Address:** 3905 Vincennes Road, Suite 304
>Indianapolis, Indiana 46268
>**Telephone:** (800) 214-1738

Further Reading

Edmonston, William E. *The Induction of Hypnosis.* New York: Wiley, 1986.

Inglis, Brian. *Trance: A Natural History of Altered States of Mind.* London: Grafton, 1989.

Kirby, Vivian. *Hypnotism: Hocus Pocus or Science?* New York: J. Messner, 1985.

Manfred, Erica. "The New Uses of Hypnosis." *Cosmopolitan* (February 1996): 104+.

Starker, Steven. *Fantastic Thought: All About Dreams, Daydreams, Hallucinations, and Hypnosis.* New York: Prentice-Hall, 1982.

Hypochondria

A mental disorder characterized by an excessive and habitual preoccupation with personal health and a tendency to interpret insignificant or imaginary conditions as evidence of serious disease; also called hypochondriasis.

Typically, hypochondriacs not only falsely believe that they have a serious disease (often, but not exclusively, of the heart or another internal organ), they persist in this belief even after being assured that they do not have the disease by a physician (or, usually, by many physicians). Hypochondriacs seem to have an increased sensitivity to internal sensations. It is also thought that serious childhood illness or experience with disease in a family member or friend may be associated with hypochondria, and that psychological **stress** in early adulthood related to disease or death may precipitate or worsen this condition.

Further Reading

Baur, Susan. *Hypochondria.* Berkeley: University of California Press, 1988.

Hypothalamus

A section of the forebrain, connected to other parts of the forebrain and midbrain, that is involved in many complex behaviors.

The hypothalamus, which together with the **thalamus** makes up the section of the forebrain called the diencephalon, is involved in such aspects of behavior as **motivation, emotion,** eating, drinking, and **sexuality.** Lying under the thalamus, the hypothalamus weighs only a fraction of an ounce and is a little larger than the tip of the thumb. It is connected to the **autonomic nervous system,** and controls the entire endocrine system using the pituitary gland to direct the work of all the other **endocrine glands.** If a particular section of the hypothalamus is destroyed, an overwhelming urge to eat results; damage to another section of a male's hypothalamus can reduce the sex drive. Yet another part of the hypothalamus, the suprachiasmatic nuclei (SCN), is the site of a person's "internal clock" that regulates biological rhythms according to a cycle of roughly 24 hours. From the SCN, signals reach areas of the hindbrain that regulate **sleep** and wakefulness. With **neurons** firing on a 24- or 25-hour cycle, it determines the periods of greatest alertness—whether one is "morning person" or a "night person." Pathways from the SCN to the eyes connect its circadian rhythms to external cycles of light and dark.

Different roles have been identified for various sections of the hypothalamus in interpreting and acting on hunger signals. The ventromedial nucleus, whose neurons detect blood levels of glucose, signals when it is time to stop eating. Rats in whom this part of the hypothalamus has been destroyed will eat extremely large quantities of food, enough to triple their body weight. Similarly, the lateral hypothalamus signals when it is time to begin eating. Yet another area, the paraventricular nucleus, appears to motivate the desire for particular types of foods, depending on which **neurotransmitters** are acting on it at a particular time.

See also Brain.

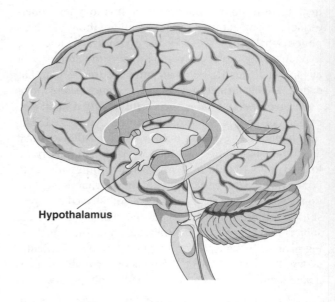

Hypothalamus

The hypothalamus is slightly larger than the tip of an adult human's thumb, and plays a role in many behaviors, such as motivation, eating and drinking, and sexuality.

Hypothesis Testing

The method psychologists employ to prove or disprove the validity of their hypotheses.

When psychologists engage in research, they generate specific questions called hypotheses. Research hypotheses are informed speculations about the likely results of a project. In a typical research design, researchers might want to know whether people in two groups differ in their behavior. For example, psychologists have asked whether the amount that we can remember increases if we can find a way to organize related information. The hypothesis here might be that the organization of related information increases the amount that a person can remember in a learning task.

The researcher knows that such a strategy might have no effect, however. Learning may not change or it may actually worsen. In research, psychologists set up their projects to find out which of two conclusions is more likely, the research hypothesis (i.e., whether organizing related information helps **memory**) or its complement (i.e., whether organizing related information does not help memory). The possibility that organizing related information will make no difference is called the Null Hypothesis, because it speculates that there may be no change in learning. (The word "null" means "nothing" or "none.") The other possibility, that organizing related information helps to learn, is called the Research Hypothesis or the Alternate Hypothesis. To see which hypothesis

HYPOTHESIS TESTING		
	You conclude that the two groups differ so you reject the Null Hypothesis.	You conclude that the two groups do not differ so you fail to reject the Null Hypothesis.
Two groups really do differ	You correctly rejected the Null Hypothesis. You made a good decision.	You made a Type II error. You should have said there is a difference, but you made a mistake and said there wasn't.
Two groups really do not differ	You made a Type I error. You said that the groups are different, but you made a mistake.	You correctly failed to reject the Null Hypothesis. You said that the groups are not different, and you were right.

is true, people will be randomly assigned to one of two groups that differ in the way they are told to learn. Then the memory of the people in the two groups is compared.

As a rule, psychologists attempt to rule out the Null Hypothesis and to accept the Research Hypothesis because their research typically tries to focus on changes from one situation to the next, not failure to change. In hypothesis testing, psychologists are aware that they may make erroneous conclusions. For example, they might reject the Null Hypothesis and conclude that performance of people in two groups is different, that is, that one group remembers more than the other because they organize the information differently. In reality, one group might have gotten lucky and if the study were performed a second time, the result might be different. In hypothesis testing, this mistaken conclusion is called a Type I error.

Sometimes researchers erroneously conclude that the difference in the way the two groups learn is not important. That is, they fail to reject the Null Hypothesis when they should. This kind of error is called a Type II error. The table below indicates the relationship among errors and correct decisions.

Unfortunately, when researchers conduct a single experiment, they may be making an error without realizing it. This is why other researchers may try to replicate the research of others in order to spot any errors that previous researchers may have made.

See also Scientific Method.

Id

In psychoanalytic theory, the most primitive, unconscious element of human personality.

Sigmund Freud believed that human **personality** consisted of three components: the id, the **ego,** and the **superego**. The id is the part of the personality that includes such basic biological impulses or drives as eating, drinking, eliminating wastes, avoiding **pain**, attaining sexual pleasure, and **aggression**. The id operates on the "pleasure principle," seeking to satisfy these basic urges immediately with no regard to consequences. Only when tempered through interaction with the ego (reality) and superego (**conscience**) does the id conform to what is considered socially acceptable behavior.

According to Freud, **anxiety** is caused by the conflict between the id's powerful impulses and the modifying forces of the ego and superego. The more id-driven impulses are stifled through physical reality or societal norms, the greater the level of anxiety. People express their anxiety in various ways, including nervousness, displaced aggression, and serious anxiety disorders. Healthy personalities are those that have learned to balance the id, ego and superego forces.

Further Reading

Atkinson, Rita L.; Richard C. Atkinson; Edward E. Smith; and Ernest R. Hilgard. *Introduction to Psychology.* 9th ed. San Diego: Harcourt Brace Jovanovich, 1987.

Zimbardo, Philip G. *Psychology and Life.* 12th ed. Glenview, IL: Scott, Foresman, 1988.

Identity

A person's mental representation of who he or she is.

Components of identity include a sense of personal continuity and of uniqueness from other people. In addition to carving out a personal identity based on the **need**

This young man has chosen to wear a punk hairstyle, thus affiliating with a rebellious segment of society. Identity formation begins in childhood, but becomes a driving force in adolescence, according to Erik Erikson. Many adolescents experiment with alternative identities.

for uniqueness, people also acquire a social identity based on their membership in various groups—familial, ethnic, occupational, and others. These group identities, in addition to satisfying the need for **affiliation**, help people define themselves in the eyes of both others and themselves.

Identity formation has been most extensively described by **Erik Erikson** in his theory of **developmental stages**, which extends from birth through adulthood. According to Erikson, identity formation, while beginning in childhood, gains prominence during **adolescence**. Faced with physical growth, sexual maturation, and impending career choices, adolescents must accomplish the task of integrating their prior experiences and characteristics into a stable identity. Erikson coined the phrase identity crisis to describe the temporary instability and confusion adolescents experience as they struggle with alternatives and choices. To cope with the uncertainties of this stage, adolescents may overidentify with heroes and mentors, fall in love, and bond together in cliques, excluding others on the basis of real or imagined differences.

According to Erikson, successful resolution of this crisis depends on one's progress through previous developmental stages, centering on fundamental issues of trust, autonomy, and initiative. By the age of 21, about half of all adolescents are thought to have resolved their identity crises and are ready to move on to the adult challenges of love and work. Others, however, are unable to achieve an integrated adult identity, either because they have failed to resolve the identity crisis or because they have experienced no crisis. J. E. Marcia identified four common ways in which adolescents deal with the challenge of identity formation. Those who experience, confront, and resolve the identity crisis are referred to as "identity-achieved." Others, termed "identity-foreclosed," make commitments (often conventional ones, identical or similar to those of their parents) without questioning them or investigating alternatives. Those who are "identity-diffused" shrink from making defining choices about their futures and remain arrested, unable to make whole-hearted commitments to careers, values, or another person. In contrast, those in the "moratorium" group, while unable to make such commitments, are struggling to do so and experience an ongoing though unresolved crisis as they try to "find themselves."

Although the phrase "identity crisis" was initially popularized in connection with adolescence, it is not limited to this time frame: Erikson himself initially formulated the concept in connection with World War II veterans. A variety of changes that affect one's work, status, or interpersonal relationships can bring on a crisis that forces one to redefine oneself in terms of values, priorities, and chosen activities or lifestyle. In *Passages*, Gail Sheehy proposed that there are actually "predictable crises of adult life" that generally challenge people's conceptions of themselves and result either in personal growth or stagnation.

See also Self-Concept.

Further Reading
Erikson, Erik H. *Childhood and Society*. New York: W. W. Norton, 1950.
Josselson, Ruthellen. *Finding Herself: Pathways to Identity Development in Women*. San Francisco: Jossey-Bass, 1987.
Sheehy, Gail. *Passages: Predictable Crises of Adult Life*. New York: E.P. Dutton, 1976.

Imagination

A complex cognitive process of forming a mental scene that includes elements which are not, at the moment, being perceived by the senses.

Imagination involves the synthetic combining of aspects of memories or experiences into a mental construction that differs from past or present perceived reality, and may anticipate future reality. Generally regarded as one of the "higher mental functions," it is not thought to be present in animals. Imagination may be fantastic, fanciful, wishful, or problem-solving, and may differ from reality to a slight or great extent. Imagination is generally considered to be a foundation of artistic expression, and, within limits, to be a healthy, creative, higher mental function.

Observers as diverse as Plato and Samuel Taylor Coleridge have noted two contrasting types of imagination. One is largely imitative and concerned with mentally reconstructing past events or images. Among the imitative types of imagination is eidetic imagery, which consists of rich and vividly recalled images and is especially characteristic of children up to the age of six. Afterimages, such as the green image that appears after looking at the color red, are a type of imitative image and are produced by sense receptors. A synesthetic image is produced by the conjunction of two senses such as occurs when hearing a certain piece of music elicits a visual image with which it is associated in the mind of the listener. Hypnagogic images are unusually clear images produced in the state between **sleep** and waking. **Hallucinations** are vivid, detailed images produced in the absence of external stimuli and generally confused with real images. **Dreams** are images occurring in a sleeping state that are usually not confused with reality once the sleeper awakes.

In contrast to imitative images, creative imagination is associated with thought and involves the restructuring, rather than merely the retention, of sensory impressions. It was this faculty that Coleridge called "imagination" as opposed to "fancy," his name for imitative imagining. One common form of creative imagination is **daydreaming.** At one time, daydreaming and fantasies were regarded as compensatory activities that had the function of "letting off steam," but recent research has cast doubt on that theory. Creative imagination is the basis for achievements in the realms of both art and science, and students of behavior have analyzed the creative process in hopes of being able to encourage greater creativity through various types of training. New discoveries about the specialized functions of the right- and **left-brain hemispheres** have revealed that the **right-brain hemisphere** is the center for much of the mental functioning commonly regarded as creative: it is the side associated with intuitive leaps of insight and the ability to synthesize existing elements into new wholes. These findings have been applied by educators seeking to enhance individual creativity in areas including writing and drawing.

After falling into neglect as an area of inquiry during the period when **behaviorism** was preeminent, mental imagery has become a significant topic of study for cognitive psychologists. Researchers have found that imagery plays a significant role in **emotion, motivation,** sexual behavior, and many aspects of **cognition,** including learning, **language acquisition, memory,** problem-solving, and **perception. Mental imagery** has also been found to be a useful technique in clinical work. In addition to Gestalt therapy, which has traditionally involved the use of images, a number of image-based therapies have emerged in the United States and elsewhere. Mental images have also been used as a diagnostic tool to reveal feelings and **attitudes** not accessible through verbalization.

Further Reading

Bronowski, Jacob. *The Origins of Knowledge and Imagination.* New Haven, CT: Yale University Press, 1978.

Imitation

The act of mimicking or copying; also called modeling or social learning.

Unlike behaviorist models of learning through various forms of conditioning, imitation occurs naturally without outside stimulus or reward. In a child's early years, an enormous amount of learning is done through imitation of parents, peers, and **modeling** based on other stimuli, such as **television**. Imitative learning occurs in primates, both human and nonhuman, but has not conclusively been proved to exist in other species.

The foremost researcher in the area of imitative learning is **Alfred Bandura**, whose work has focused on how modeling—especially the modeling of aggressive behavior—affects the thoughts, feelings, and behavior of children. Bandura's research revealed that imitation may

result in the acquisition of new responses as well as the facilitation or inhibition of existing ones. While modeling will occur in situations where neither the observer nor the model is rewarded for performing a particular action, Bandura found that **punishment** and reward can have an effect on the modeling situation. A child will more readily imitate a model who is being rewarded for an act than one who is being punished. Thus, the child can learn without actually being rewarded or punished himself—a concept known as vicarious learning. Similarly, Bandura has shown that when a model is exposed to stimuli intended to have a conditioning effect, a person who simply observes this process, even without participating in it directly, will tend to become conditioned by the stimuli as well.

Further Reading

Meinhold, Patricia. *Child Psychology: Development and Behavior Analysis.* Dubuque, IA: Kendall/Hunt Publishing Co., 1993.

Owens, Karen. *The World of the Child.* New York: Holt, Rinehart, and Winston, 1987.

Papalia, Diane E. *A Child's World: Infancy through Adolescence.* 5th ed. New York: McGraw-Hill, 1990.

Imprinting

A type of learning characteristic of fowls that occurs only during a critical period of development soon after birth.

Imprinting is the process that prompts ducklings to form an attachment to their mothers—or whatever other moving object that appears—within the first two days of life. Ethologists, scientists who study the behavior of animals in their natural **environment**, noted the process of imprinting as they observed newly hatched ducklings. They discovered that if a duckling were introduced to another moving object, alive or not, during a critical period after birth, the duckling would follow that object as if it were the mother. Humans and even wooden decoys successfully served as maternal substitutes after as little as ten minutes of imprinting. It has been discovered that once the process takes place, the ducklings will follow the substitute, even through adverse circumstances, in preference to a live duck. Imprinting does not take place anytime after the first two days of life because by that time, it is believed, ducklings develop a **fear** of strange objects. There is little evidence that imprinting occurs in humans or most other animals. It has been noted to some extent in dogs, sheep, and guinea pigs. The discovery and study of imprinting have prompted continued examination of the relative roles of **instinct** and acquired behavior in the process of learning.

Further Reading

Bower, Gordon H., and Ernest R. Hilgard. *Theories of Learning.* Englewood Cliffs, NJ: Prentice-Hall, 1981.

Incest

Prohibited sexual relations between members of a close kinship group, such as between parents and children or between brothers and sisters. The term is often expanded to include not only actual intercourse but other sexual acts as well.

While the incest taboo is nearly universal and exists in nearly all societies, notions of kinship vary greatly from culture to culture. Thus, some cultures would consider sexual relations between first cousins incest, while others would not. The same premise holds true for intercourse between a stepfather and stepdaughter. The very rare exceptions to incest, such as those found in ancient Egyptian and Incan societies, usually involve mandatory incestuous unions within royal families, which may have been motivated by economic or theocratic considerations.

In classical psychoanalytic theory, the **psychosexual development** of children between the ages of three and five is characterized by incestuous desires toward the parent of the opposite sex. **Sigmund Freud** called these desires in males the **Oedipus complex,** referring to the inadvertent incest between the title character and his mother in the classical Greek tragedy, *Oedipus Rex.* Freud asserted that young boys form a sexual attachment to their mothers, accompanied by resentment and **hostility** toward their fathers, whom they regard as rivals for their mother's **attention.** The fear of retaliation by the father, which takes the form of castration **anxiety,** leads the boy to renounce his forbidden desires and begin to identify with his father, thus assuming his proper gender identity together with a **superego** composed of his father's moral values. Freud posited roughly the same condition, in reverse, for girls, which he called the Electra complex. While largely recognizing the widespread existence of incestuous desires (which many claim is indirectly demonstrated by the very universality of the incest taboo), contemporary psychologists differ widely with respect to the developmental and other importance they attribute to these desires.

Among the various types of incest, sexual relations between brother and sister and between father and daughter are thought to occur more frequently than mother-son incest, which is believed to be rare. The phenomenon of covert incest has been noted between mother and son, however, in which the mother acts toward her son in a sexual manner without actually seducing him. Usually, other members of the family are aware of the incestuous relationship, and it will govern the psychodynamics of the entire family structure. According to contemporary reports by incest survivors, most child sexual abuse is committed by male relatives. Fathers who abuse their daughters tend to have a history of psychological problems and emotional deprivation, and will often implement an incestuous relationship with more than one daughter. In many cases, the mother is aware of the abuse and either feels powerless to stop it or colludes with the father for reasons of her own.

Contrary to popular assumptions and stereotypes, incest occurs at all levels of society, is likely to happen in middle and upper-class families as in poor families, and takes place in families that appear outwardly happy, respectable, and well adjusted. Adults who have been incest victims in childhood are prone to **depression,** sexual dysfunction, and abusive behavior. Incest involving an adult victim is extremely rare. Although there has been increasing public awareness of this problem in recent years, it is believed that most cases of incest remain unreported due to the stigma involved and the powerlessness of dependent children ensnared in incestuous relationships. Over the years, many (more or less speculative) theories have been advanced regarding the origin, nature, structure, function, and interpretation of the incest taboo, but none has been generally accepted as completely definitive. One practical function of the taboo is that the prohibition of incest decreases the incidence of birth defects and recessive genetic disorders.

Further Reading

Maisch, Herbert. *Incest.* New York: Stein and Day, 1972.

Independent Variable

The variable the experimenter manipulates.

In experimental research, psychologists create two or more groups that are as similar as possible except for a single change that the psychologist makes from one group to the next. That single element that varies across groups is called the independent variable. In more complex research, the experimenter may include more than one independent variable.

In one experiment dealing with eyewitness testimony and jury decisions, researchers exposed the eyewitnesses to staged crimes and then had them "testify" what they observed. One group of participants saw the staged crime under good lighting conditions; a second group had a less favorable viewing condition, and the third group had only a poor view of the scene. The independent variable was the viewing condition which had three levels, or different variations: good, moderate, and poor visibility.

The researchers investigated whether the "jurors" accepted the testimony as believable and the degree of confidence of the eyewitnesses in their own testimony. The degree to which the jurors accepted the testimony and the stated degree of confidence by the witnesses themselves were **dependent variables**. The results revealed that the jurors were more likely to believe witnesses who had seen the crime in the best lighting.

The researchers concluded that the independent variable (e.g., the amount of light available for viewing the crime) had affected one dependent variable (e.g., the jurors' acceptance of the testimony). At the same time, the independent variable did not affect the confidence of the eyewitnesses concerning their own testimony.

Further Reading

Lindsay, R. C.; G. L. Wells; and C. M. Rumple. "Can People Detect Eyewitness Identification Accuracy Within and Across Situations?" *Journal of Applied Psychology* 67 (1981): 79-89.

Industrial Psychology

The subfield of applied psychology in which practical problems in the workplace are addressed through the application of psychological principles.

Some industrial psychologists, also called personnel or organizational psychologists, may be employed by companies to administer tests which measure employee aptitudes or skills in hiring and placement programs. Others work for consulting firms which offer their services to companies on a contractual basis to solve specific problems. The projects which they work on may include facilitating interpersonal relationships within a company by training management personnel in human relations skills, analyzing and recommending changes in employee training programs, or conducting research to determine what influences consumers to purchase particular products. A distinguishing characteristic of industrial psychology is that the focus of research and other work is to solve specific practical problems.

See also Applied Psychology; Vocational Aptitude Tests.

Infancy

Very early childhood, generally referring to the period up to age two. During this important formative period, children begin to

A grandmother interacts with her infant granddaughter. Infants need stimulus from their environment, and are especially responsive to facial expressions.

develop habits and behavior patterns, and acquire many basic skills, including speech.

Compared to the young of other mammals, human infants are precocious in some ways—notably sensory development—and relatively helpless in others, such as physical strength and mobility. At **birth,** the average American infant weighs approximately 7.5 pounds (3.37 kg), although a baby born 28 weeks after conception may weigh as little as two pounds (0.9 kg). The average length of an American newborn is about 21 inches (53 cm).

Infants are born with several **reflexes** that are activated by particular stimuli, such as the grasping reflex when a finger is placed in the palm of a baby's hand. Other reflexes include rooting (turning the mouth toward the breast or bottle) and sucking. Many early reflexes—such as reaching and performing a step-like motion—disappear, only to reappear later. While the most important senses in human adults are vision and hearing, infants acquire much of their information about the world through touch. At birth, a baby's eyes and the pathways between the eyes and the **brain** are not fully developed; the eyesight of a newborn is estimated at 20–600 (an object viewed from 20 feet [609 cm] away appears as a distance of 600 feet [182 m] by an adult with 20-20 vision). The senses of newborns are particularly well adapted for bonding with their caregivers. Infants can see large objects close up and are especially interested in faces, and their **hearing** is most acute in the range of human speech.

In the first year, the shape and proportion of an infant's body are better suited to crawling on all fours than to walking erect. During the first three months of life, infants also lack the lower body strength and muscular control to support their weight standing upright. The urge to stand and walk upright is very strong, however, and babies work hard to accomplish this task. By seven to eight months, infants can usually stand holding on to a playpen or other object; at 10 or 11 months they can walk with assistance, and by 13 months they can usually take a few steps unaided.

As infants are developing physically, they are also developing cognitively in their **ability** to perform such mental processes as thinking, knowing, and remembering. The theory of childhood cognitive development developed by the Swiss psychology **Jean Piaget** describes four stages of increasingly complex and abstract thought that occur between birth and **adolescence,** each qualitatively different from but dependent upon the stages before it. The first, or sensorimotor, stage, (birth to approximately two years), is a time of nonverbal, experimental basic learning when infants gradually gain mastery of their own bodies and external objects. By sucking, shaking, banging, hitting, and other physical acts, children at this age learn about the properties of objects and how to manipulate them. The main goal at this stage is to achieve what Piaget termed "object constancy," or permanence: the sense that objects exist even when they are not visible and that they are independent of the infant's own actions. This sense forms the basis for the **perception** of a stable universe. The sensorimotor stage is followed by the preoperational stage (ages two to six), which involves the association of objects with words.

Infants are born with different **temperaments**. There are "easy babies," who are cheerful and seldom fuss; difficult babies, who are often irritable; and timid babies, who are wary when approaching new situations. Most people believe that temperament is inborn, although there is little hard evidence to prove it. Temperament's interaction with a variety of environmental factors, including parental expectations, determines the course of an individual's development. The most im-

portant aspect of an infant's **socialization** is forming secure **attachments**, primarily to parents or other principal caregivers. Attachment problems may have a negative effect on a child's normal development. Initially, infants will respond positively to all contact with adults, even though they recognize familiar faces and prefer their mother or other primary caregiver. By the age of three months, babies will begin to smile in response to outside stimuli, maintain eye contact, and vocalize, as distinguished from crying. Eventually, they will advance to what Piaget called the "secondary level" of concentration, at which they are aware of social changes in addition to objects and events. During this period, infants enjoy social contact and will fuss when left alone. They are able to distinguish their parents from other people, will smile and vocalize at familiar people, and will cry when those individuals are absent. At the age of six or seven months, when infants develop of conception of object permanence, an especially strong bond begins to form with the primary caregiver, usually the mother. This is accompanied by separation **anxiety** (distress at being separated from the primary caregiver) and stranger anxiety (shyness or **fear** in the presence of strangers). Such behaviors are an integral part of normal cognitive development and displays a healthy attachment to the primary caregiver.

During the second year of life, the infant's focus of socialization extends beyond the primary caregiver to the family unit as a whole and includes gaining some control over emotions and accepting discipline. In **Erik Erikson**'s eight-stage theory of **personality,** the most important task in the first 18 months of an infant's life is establishing a basic sense of trust in the world, accomplished initially by the attachment formed with the primary caregivers. Sometime after his or her first birthday, an infant begins developing a tremendous **need** for autonomy, inevitably accompanied by a sense of doubt and shame brought on by learning to follow rules and social demands for self-control, including physical control (such as toilet training). The conflict between autonomy and doubt occupies much of a child's second year and continues into the third. Successfully negotiated, this stage leads to the emergence of independence and will power, and a sense of self-awareness—which appears to depend upon a combination of cognitive development, socialization, and linguistic skills—slowly develops during the second year of life.

Further Reading

Owens, Karen. *The World of the Child.* New York: Holt, Rinehart, and Winston, 1987.

Papalia, Diane E. *A Child's World: Infancy through Adolescence.* 5th ed. New York: McGraw-Hill, 1990.

Inferiority Complex

A psychological condition that exists when a person's feelings of inadequacy are so intense that daily living is impaired.

The term "inferiority complex" was coined in the 1920s by French psychologist **Alfred Adler**, a one-time follower of **Sigmund Freud** who became disenchanted with Freud's emphasis on the influence of **unconscious** factors as motivators in human behavior. While Adler subscribed to the notion that underlying motivations play a part in directing **personality**, he introduced the notion of "ego psychology" in an effort to give equal importance to the role of conscious factors in determining behavior. According to Adler, all humans experience feelings of inferiority as children and spend the rest of their lives trying to compensate for those feelings. As people replace the dependence of childhood with the independence of adulthood, the feelings of inferiority persist in varying intensity in different people. For some people, the sense of inferiority serves as a positive motivating factor, as they strive to improve themselves in an effort to neutralize the negative feelings of inferiority. Some, however, become dominated—and, as a result, crippled—by an overwhelming sense of inadequacy. These people, whose thoughts are so overtaken by these feelings that they cannot function normally, are said to have an inferiority complex. The opposite of inferiority complex, a superiority complex, can also result from the inevitable early feelings of inferiority, Adler believed. This results when a person overcompensates and places too much emphasis on striving for perfection.

Further Reading

Clark, John, ed. *The Mind: Into the Inner World*. New York: Torstar Books, 1986.

Hergenhahn, B.R. *An Introduction to Theories of Personality*. Englewood Cliffs, NJ: Prentice-Hall, 1980.

Zimbardo, Philip G. *Psychology and Life*. Glenview, IL: Scott, Foresman, 1988.

Information-Processing Approach

A leading orientation in experimental psychology that focuses on how people select, process, and internalize information and how they use it to make decisions and guide their behavior.

The information-processing approach is associated with the development of high-speed computers in the 1950s. Researchers—most notably Herbert Simon and his colleagues—demonstrated that computers could be used to simulate human **intelligence**. This development led to the realization that computer-oriented information-processing models could provide new insight into how the human mind receives, stores, retrieves, and uses information. The information-processing approach was one of several developments that ended the decades-long dominance of **behaviorism** in American psychology. Rather than on conditioned, externally observable behavior, it focused on innate mental capacities. By enabling experimental psychologists to test theories about complex mental processes through computer simulation, information-processing models helped reestablish internal thought processes as a legitimate area of scientific inquiry.

The information-processing approach to human **cognition** encompasses several basic stages. Information received from external or internal stimuli is inputted through the senses and transformed by a variety of mental operations (including representation by symbols). It receives attention through the perceptual processes and is stored in either short-term or long-term **memory**, where it interacts with previously stored information to generate a response, or output. These stages may take place in a number of different arrangements. The simplest is the serial model, in which the stages occur in succession like a chain reaction, with the output of each stage becoming the input of the succeeding one. However, stages can also occur simultaneously, a phenomenon known as parallel processing. Serial and parallel processing can also be combined in what are known as hybrid models. Another important characteristic of information-processing models is resource allocation—the way in which energy is distributed in the system. This refers to the fact that the efficiency of each stage in the process may depend on whether certain other stages are operating at the same time.

One of the many areas investigated through the use of information-processing models is human error. Errors that occur during the early stages of processing, such as misunderstandings, are called mistakes, as distinguished from slips, which occur during the selection or execution of responses. The increased understanding of error provided by information-processing models has been useful in eliminating a variety of technical and industrial problems by isolating and addressing their causes. Those problems classified as mistakes often involve the size of an information load and the way it is handled, while slips are commonly remedied by redesigning instruments and equipment so they can be used more efficiently.

Another area that has been investigated using an information-processing approach is reaction time—the amount of time needed to respond to a stimulus in a particular situation. Reaction time is an important feature in the design of automobiles and many other products. Factors influencing reaction time include complexity of the decision required before action can be taken; stimulus-response compatibility (the physical convenience of the reaction); expectancy (it takes longer to respond to an unexpected stimulus); and the relative importance of speed and accuracy in the required response.

Further Reading

Johnson-Laird, Philip N. *The Computer and the Mind: An Introduction to Cognitive Science.* Cambridge, MA: Harvard University Press, 1988.

Lindsay, Peter H. *Human Information Processing: An Introduction to Psychology.* San Diego: Academic Press, 1977.

Newell, A., and H. A. Simon. *Human Problem Solving.* Englewood Cliffs, NJ: Prentice-Hall, 1972.

Insomnia. See **Sleep Disorders.**

Instinct

The inborn tendency of every member of a certain species to behave in the same way given the same situation or set of stimuli.

Behavior is considered instinctive only if it occurs in the same form in all members of a species. Instincts must be unlearned and characteristic of a specific species. Animals provide the best examples of instinctive behavior. Birds naturally build nests without being taught and feed and protect their young in the exact same ways. Other animals, such as squirrels or dogs, behave in manners characteristic of only squirrels or dogs. Ethologists, scientists who study animals in their natural **environments**, devote much of their efforts to the observation of instinctive behavior.

Throughout history, theorists have speculated on the role of instinct in determining human behavior. While it has been widely accepted that animal behavior is governed largely by innate, **unconscious** tendencies, the presence and power of instincts in humans have been a source of controversy. Early Christian theorists believed that only animals were guided by instincts, asserting that the absence of instinct-governed behavior and the presence of a moral code provided the major distinction between humans and animals. Instinct assumed a more prominent place in behavior theory in later years. In the late 1800s, **William James** proposed that human behavior is determined largely by instinct, and that people have even more instinctual urges than less complex animals. James believed that certain biological instincts are shared with animals, while human social instincts like sympathy, love, and modesty also provide powerful behavioral forces.

Sigmund Freud considered instincts to be basic building blocks of human behavior and play a central role in his drive theory, which postulates that human behavior is motivated by the desire to reduce the tension caused by unfulfilled instinctive urges or drives. For instance, people eat when they are hungry because unsatiated hunger causes tension, which is reduced by eating. For Freud, the life instinct (Eros) and its components motivate people to stay alive and reproduce. The death instinct (Thanatos) represents the negative forces of nature. Another theorist, William McDougall, described instincts simply as "inherited dispositions."

The debate continues today over the role of instinct in human behavior, as the balance between learned behavior and innate urges remains a subject ripe for continued research and discussion. It is useful to note a nonscientific use of the term instinct. In casual conversation, a person may use instinct to mean "natural" or "automatic—in describing a baseball player's instinct for batting, for example. This use of the term would not meet the scientist's criteria for instinct.

See also Drive Reduction Theory.

Further Reading

Atkinson, Rita L.; Richard C. Atkinson; Edward E. Smith; and Ernest R. Hilgard. *Introduction to Psychology.* 9th ed. San Diego: Harcourt Brace Jovanovich, 1987.

Zimbardo, Philip G. *Psychology and Life.* 12th ed. Glenview, IL: Scott, Foresman, 1988.

Instrumental Behavior

Behavior exhibited by persons in response to certain stimuli.

Instrumental behavior is a concept that grew out of the **behavior therapy** movement, originating in the 1950s with the work of H.J. Eysenck. Behavior therapy asserts that neuroses are not the symptoms of underlying disorders (as **Sigmund Freud** theorized), but are in fact disorders in and of themselves. Further, these disorders are learned responses to traumatic experiences in much the same way that animals can be demonstrated to learn a response to instrumental, or operant, **conditioning**.

In the classic behaviorist experiments of **Ivan Pavlov** and **B.F. Skinner**, it was shown that animals could be trained to respond in a learned way to external stimuli. Humans also respond in a similar manner. If, for instance, a child has a difficult, painful relationship with his older brother, who is athletic and popular, he may develop a **fear** or hatred of all popular, athletic males that will stay with him throughout life—even after the original stimuli for the reaction (his older brother) is absent. This behavior is referred to as instrumental behavior.

In treating a patient to eliminate instrumental behaviors, behavioral therapists rely on several fairly well-tested techniques. Perhaps the most popular is counterconditioning, a process in which a therapist links the stimuli to a different instrumental behavior, or conditioned response. Other methods include flooding and **modeling**. In flooding, a therapist will attempt to expose a patient to an overload of the **anxiety**-producing stimuli in order to lessen its effect. In modeling, the patient is exposed to someone who has successfully dealt with a similar anxiety-producing stimuli.

Intelligence

An abstract concept whose definition is continually evolving and often dependent upon current social values as much as scientific ideas. Modern definitions encompass diverse aspects of thought and reasoning and are concerned with how a person uses information they possess, not merely the knowledge they have acquired.

The concept of intelligence has been surrounded by controversy since it was first proposed as a psychological construct. Part of the problem stems from the fact that nobody has been able to develop an adequate definition of what intelligence really means. In everyday life, we have a general understanding that some people are "smart," but when we try to define "smart" precisely, we often have difficulty because a person can be gifted in one area and average or below in another. Because of this problem, some psychologists have developed theories that include multiple components of intelligence.

Early views of intelligence. One of the first commonly accepted notions of intelligence was that it involved a single, core psychological trait. That is, a person's intelligence could be seen as having a single main component; this level of intelligence could be represented by the letter g. Psychologists recognized that other, specific mental strengths also existed, but the intelligence tests generally concentrated on measuring g. The foremost early proponent of this idea was the British psychologist and statistician Charles Spearman (1863–1945).

In the 1940s, however, a different view of intelligence emerged. The new development involved the concept that intelligence was multifaceted. The American psychologist L. L. Thurstone (1887–1955) rejected Spearman's emphasis on g and instead suggested that intelligence consisted of more specific abilities. He identified seven primary intellectual abilities: word fluency, verbal comprehension, spatial **ability**, perceptual speed, numerical ability, inductive reasoning, and **memory**.

Taking Thurstone's concept even further, J. P. Guilford developed the theory that intelligence consisted of as many as five different operations or processes (evaluation, convergent production, divergent production, mem-

ory, and **cognition**), five different types of content (visual, auditory, symbolic, semantic, and behavioral), and six different products (units, classes, relations, systems, transformations, and implications). Each of these different components was seen as independent; the result was a theory of intelligence that consisted of 150 different elements.

Although the idea of many different components of intelligence has grown in favor among psychologists and laypersons, the approach to intelligence testing remains more closely tied to the ideas of Charles Spearman. Tests of intelligence also tend to mirror the values of our culture, which are linked to academic skills like verbal and mathematical ability, although more performance-oriented tests also exist.

Current views of intelligence. In the past few decades, psychologists have expanded the notion of what constitutes intelligence. The newer definitions of intelligence encompass more diverse aspects of thought and reasoning. For example, psychologist Robert Sternberg developed a triarchic theory of intelligence that states that behaviors must be viewed within the context of a particular culture (i.e., in some cultures, a given behavior might be highly regarded whereas in another, the same behavior is given low regard); that a person's experiences affect the expression of intelligence; and that certain cognitive processes control all intelligent behavior. When all of these aspects of intelligence are viewed together, the importance of how people use their intelligence becomes more important than the question of "how much" intelligence a person has. Sternberg has suggested that current intelligence tests focus too much on what a person has already learned rather than on how well a person acquires new skills or knowledge. Another multifaceted approach to intelligence is Howard Gardner's proposal that people have seven intelligences: logical-mathematical, linguistic, musical, spatial, bodily-kinesthetic, interpersonal, and intrapersonal.

One feature that characterizes the newly developing concept of intelligence is that it has taken on broader meaning than the initial views of a single underlying trait (e.g., Spearman's g). Sternberg and Gardner's emergent ideas suggest that any simple attempt at defining intelligence will be inadequate because of the wide variety of skills, abilities, and potential that people manifest.

Societal implications of the views of intelligence. The initial foray into systematic mental testing began with the French psychologists **Alfred Binet** and Thèodore Simon (1873–1961). The French government charged them in 1904 with the task of creating a means to identify children whose learning was subnormal so that they could receive special education. The 1908 version of Binet and Simon's test formed the basis of the influential

Stanford-Binet test that was translated into English and adapted for use in the United States by American psychologist **Lewis Terman**. In this application, the concept of the **intelligence quotient** (IQ) emerged as it is now used.

With the adoption of widespread testing using the Stanford-Binet and two versions created for the Army in World War I, the concept of the intelligence test departed from Binet and Simon's initial view. Intelligence became associated with a fixed, innate, hereditary value. That is, one's intelligence, as revealed by **IQ tests**, was locked at a certain level because of what was seen as its hereditary basis. Although a number of well-known and respected psychologists objected to this characterization of intelligence, it gained popularity, especially among the public.

At this time, people placed great faith in the role of science in improving society; intelligence tests were seen as a specific application of science that could be used beneficially. Unfortunately, because of the nature of the tests and because of many people's willingness to accept test results uncritically, people of racial minorities and certain ethnic groups were deemed to be genetically inferior with regard to intelligence compared to the majority.

Some scholars have claimed that immigration laws that restricted entry into the United States of "inferior" groups were based on the results of early intelligence testing. This claim seems to have some merit, although many psychologists objected to the conclusions that resulted from mass intelligence testing. In large part, the immigration laws seemed to reflect the attitudes of Americans in general regarding certain groups of people.

Some of the same controversies that surfaced in the early years of intelligence testing have recurred repeatedly throughout this century. They include the question of the relative effects of **environment** versus **heredity**, the degree to which intelligence can change, the extent of cultural bias in tests, and even whether intelligence tests provide any useful information at all.

Part of the difficulty also involves how intelligence is defined. Some early psychologists thought that measuring the speed of sensory processes and reaction times might indicate an individual's intelligence. This approach provided no useful results. Subsequently, tests reflecting white American culture and its values provided the benchmark for assessing intelligence. Although such tests indicate the degree of academic success that an individual is likely to experience, many have questioned the link to the abstract notion of intelligence, which extends beyond academic areas. The current approach to intelligence involves how people use the information they possess, not merely the knowledge they have acquired. Intelligence is not a concrete and objective entity, though psychologists have looked for different ways to assess it.

The particular definition of intelligence that has currency at any given time reflects the social values of the time as much as the scientific ideas.

Further Reading

Gould, S.J. *The Mismeasure of Man.* New York: W.W. Norton, 1981.
Hothersall, D. *History of Psychology.* 2nd ed. New York: McGraw-Hill, 1990.

Intelligence Quotient, IQ Test

An index of intelligence based on standardized test scores.

Psychologists have been interested in the concept of **intelligence** since **Alfred Binet** and Thèodore Simon (1873–1961) were commissioned by the Minister of Public Education in Paris to develop a test to differentiate students who would profit from a normal education from those who would not.

Binet and Simon based their test on judgment, decision making, and critical thinking. Their test succeeded where earlier attempts at assessing intelligence by **Sir Francis Galton** and by **James McKeen Cattell** failed; those earlier attempts involved simple tests of sensation and perception rather than more abstract thought. Current intelligence tests follow Binet and Simon's lead in that most tests are highly linked to academic performance and the kinds of tasks associated with school work.

Some critics of standardized intelligence tests have questioned the adequacy of these tests on the grounds of cultural bias. They claim that IQ tests discriminate against members of minority groups because the tests reflect the vocabulary, cultural references, and values of the mainstream, or dominant, culture. The average IQ scores of African Americans and Hispanic Americans are 12–15 points lower than those of European Americans, although Asian Americans average 4–6 points higher than those of European Americans.

In the late 1960s educational psychologist **Arthur Jensen** drew fire for claiming that the difference in average performance between whites and blacks on intelligence tests is the result of innate differences rather than contrasts in parental upbringing, formal schooling, or other environmental factors. More recently, a new round of controversy was ignited with the 1994 publication of *The Bell Curve* by Richard Herrnstein and Charles Murray, which emphasizes the fact that despite the affirmative action programs of the past 20 years, black Americans as a group still score 10–15 points lower on standard IQ tests than whites.

Additional criticisms have involved the prospect that intelligence consists of components other than those related to academic work. Psychologist Howard Gardner is one of the foremost proponents of the idea that people possess multiple intelligences. His model includes such components as linguistic, logical-mathematical, spatial, musical, bodily-kinesthetic, interpersonal, and intrapersonal elements. Psychologist Robert Sternberg has proposed a three-element theory of intelligence called Triarchic Theory of Intelligence that integrates analytic, creative, and practical abilities. Traditional tests of intelligence, according to Sternberg and Gardner, fail to account for the complexity of human intelligence.

How intelligence scores have been computed

Binet advanced the practice of intelligence testing and suggested that children's intelligence be based on their **mental age**; that is, the mental age should be compared to an "average" child of a given age.

German psychologist Wilhelm Stern developed the intelligence quotient, or IQ, so that the relative intelligence of children of different ages might be assessed. Stern established the practice of finding the IQ of a child by dividing mental age by chronological age and multiplying by 100. This technique creates the pattern in which the average score is 100. Although the means of computing IQ scores differs today, psychologists have continued the practice of using 100 as the average IQ score. In current scoring, the test administrator computes the number of correct responses on the test and compares them to norms. Depending on whether the score is above or below the typical score for that age group, the IQ score will be either above or below 100.

Major contemporary intelligence tests

Binet and Simon's test was developed for use in English by the American psychologist **Lewis Terman** at Stanford University; thus, the **Stanford-Binet Intelligence Scales** was born. It has gone through a number of revisions since its creation and is still widely used.

Other tests of intelligence have also been developed. Psychologist David Wechsler has created tests for children at the preschool level, for older children, and for adults. These tests are named the *Wechsler Preschool and Primary Scale of Intelligence (WPSSI)*, the *Wechsler Intelligence Scale for Children (WISC-III)*, and the *Wechsler Adult Intelligence Scale—Revised (WAIS-R)*.

Assessing the effectiveness of intelligence tests

In order to understand the potential utility of intelligence tests, one must understand two critical concepts: reliability and validity. Reliability refers to the tendency of tests to produce stable scores. If a test produces different scores when people take it on separate occasions, one should question whether the test is measuring anything useful. Modern intelligence tests show reasonable reliability over the short term, but over a period of years, people's IQ scores tend to fluctuate.

The second concept, validity, refers to how useful the test is in providing information about the concept being investigated. In this case, do IQ scores reveal anything useful about those who take them? In general, validity is harder to assess than reliability because it is difficult to determine exactly what intelligence really means.

With respect to IQ scores, research has revealed that they are adequate predictors of academic success and that IQ scores predict later career success to a certain extent. Nonetheless, psychologists have identified several potential variables that influence the validity of IQ results. These factors include the motivation of those taking the test and environmental factors that might lead test takers to be more or less familiar with the content of the test.

Historic uses of intelligence tests

IQ testing gained widespread use during World War I. Psychologists tested nearly one and three-quarter million army inductees. The mental age of almost half, they concluded, was under thirteen. This meant that nearly half of the adult population of the United States, by their reckoning, was mentally deficient. They attributed the problem to the low intelligence of recent immigrants, mostly from southern and eastern Europe. Further, they claimed that the intelligence tests reflected the genetic inferiority of some groups of people. At the time, the results of the testing were taken to suggest a serious problem in the United States, that it was becoming a nation at risk.

In reality, most contemporary psychologists have concluded that testing conditions were quite problematic, that the research was generally not sound, and that the results of the massive wartime testing revealed nothing of importance. Some of the original researchers also changed their minds about the conclusions they initially drew.

Although controversy still surrounds the use of intelligence tests and whether intelligence is primarily determined through **environment** or genetics, most psychologists recognize that no single factor is the sole determinant of something as complex as intelligence.

Further Reading
Bridge, R. Gary. *The Determinants of Educational Outcomes: The Impact of Families, Peers, Teachers, and Schools.* Ballinger Publishing Co., 1979.

Eysenck, H. J. *The IQ Argument: Race, Intelligence, and Education.* Peru, IL: Library Press, 1971.

Herrnstein, Richard J., and Charles Murray. *The Bell Curve: Intelligence and Class Structure in American Life.* New York: Free Press, 1994.

Wise, Paula Sachs. *The Use of Assessment Techniques by Applied Psychologists.* Belmont, CA: Wadsworth Publishing Co., 1989.

Interest Inventory

A test that determines a person's preferences for specific fields or activities.

An interest inventory is a testing instrument designed for the purpose of measuring and evaluating the level of an individual's interest in, or preference for, a variety of activities; also known as interest test. Testing methods include direct observation of behavior, ability tests, and self-reporting inventories of interest in educational, social, recreational, and vocational activities. The activities usually represented in interest inventories are variously related to occupational areas, and these instruments and their results are often used in vocational guidance.

The first widely used interest inventory was the Strong Vocational Interest Blank, developed in 1927 by E.K. Strong. The original test was designed for men only; a version for women was developed in 1933. In 1974 the Strong test was merged into the Strong-Campbell Interest Inventory, which was further revised in 1981. The test contains 325 activities, subjects, etc. Takers of this test are asked whether they like, dislike, or are indifferent to 325 items representing a wide variety of school subjects, occupations, activities, and types of people. They are also asked to choose their favorite among pairs of activities and indicate which of 14 selected characteristics apply to them. The Strong-Campbell test is scored according to 162 separate occupational scales as well as 23 scales that group together various types of occupations ("basic interest scales"). Examinees are also scored on six "general occupational themes" derived from J.L. Holland's interest classification scheme (realistic, investigative, artistic, social, enterprising, and conventional).

The other most commonly administered interest inventory is the Kuder Preference Record, originally developed in 1939. The Kuder Preference Record contains 168 items, each of which lists three broad choices concerning occupational interests, from which the individual selects the one that is most preferred. The test is scored on 10 interest scales consisting of items having a high degree of correlation with each other. A typical score profile will have high and low scores on one or more of the scales and average scores on the rest.

Other interest inventories include the Guilford-Zimmerman Interest Inventory, the G-S-Z Interest Survey, the California Occupational Preference Survey, the Jackson Vocational Interest Survey, and the Ohio Vocational Interest Survey. There are also inventories designed especially for children, for the disabled, and for those interested in the skilled trades.

Interest inventories are widely used in vocational counseling, both with adolescents and adults. Since these tests measure only interest and not ability, their value as predictors of occupational success, while significant, is limited. They are especially useful in helping high school and college students become familiar with career options and aware of their vocational interests. Interest inventories are also used in employee selection and classification.

Internal-External Control (I-E)

A personality variable first described by social learning theorist Julian B. Rotter.

Julian B. Rotter, a social learning theorist, developed a system of categorizing **personality** in the 1960s. People categorized as *internals* view themselves as able to control events, while *externals* view the events in their lives as chiefly determined by factors outside their control. The internal orientation is regarded as the healthier one and has been shown to characterize individuals with above-average resistance to **stress**. A personality test developed by Rotter, the *Internal-External Locus of Control Scale,* or *I-E,* measures the beliefs individuals hold about their ability to influence the outcomes of situations in their lives. Scores on this test have been correlated with a variety of differences in how people behave. In a work situation, for example, externals function more effectively when their pace is controlled by a machine, while internals are more comfortable setting their own pace. Internals are less likely than externals to develop stress-related illnesses, and they have fewer accidents. However, they are generally more health-conscious and more likely than externals to seek medical treatment when they do become ill. They are more likely to take risks, attempt to influence the opinions and behavior of others, and resist the attempts of others to influence them. They are also more likely to participate in social activism.

Further Reading

Rotter, Julian B. *The Development and Applications of a Social Learning Theory of Personality.* New York: Praeger, 1982.

Interpersonal Attraction

A favorable attitude toward, or a fondness for, another person.

Both personal characteristics and **environment** play a role in interpersonal attraction. A major determinant of attraction is propinquity, or physical proximity. People who come into contact regularly and have no prior negative feelings about each other generally become attracted to each other as their degree of mutual familiarity and comfort level increases. The situation in which people first meet also determines how they will feel about each other. One is more likely to feel friendly toward a person first encountered in pleasant, comfortable circumstances.

People are generally drawn to each other when they perceive similarities with each other. The more **attitudes** and opinions two people share, the greater the probability that they will like each other. It has also been shown that disagreement on important issues decreases attraction. One of the most important shared attitudes is that liking and disliking the same people creates an especially strong bond between two individuals. The connection between interpersonal attraction and similar attitudes is complex because once two people become friends, they begin to influence each other's attitudes.

Personality type is another determinant of interpersonal attraction. In areas involving control, such as dominance, **competition,** and self-confidence, people tend to pair up with their opposites. Thus, for example, the complementary pairing of a dominant person with a submissive one. People gravitate to others who are like themselves in terms of characteristics related to **affiliation**, including sociability, friendliness, and warmth. Another important factor in interpersonal attraction, especially during the initial encounter, is that of physical appearance, even among members of the same sex. Each culture has fairly standard ideas about physical appearance that serve as powerful determinants in how we perceive **character.** Kindness, sensitivity, **intelligence,** modesty, and sociability are among those characteristics that are often attributed to physically attractive individuals in research studies. In one study, attractive job applicants (both male and female) were given markedly preferential treatment by prospective employers compared with equally qualified candidates who were less attractive. There is also evidence that physical appearance has a greater role in the attraction of males to females than vice versa. Behavior, as well as appearance, influences interpersonal attraction. No matter what the circumstances are, behavior is often seen as reflecting a person's general traits (such as kindness or **aggression**) rather than as a response to a specific situation.

The type of interpersonal attraction that has particular interest to most people is attraction to the opposite

One view on interpersonal attraction holds that people select potential mates whose status, physical attractiveness, and personal qualities are roughly equivalent to their own.

sex. To a certain extent, romantic attraction is influenced by evolutionary considerations: the survival of the species. Some experts claim that when people select potential mates, they look for someone whose status, physical attractiveness, and personal qualities are roughly equivalent to their own. According to another theory, a person will choose a partner who will enhance his or her own self-image or persona. Researchers generally acknowledge a specific set of courting or flirting behaviors, employed by both sexes to attract each other. Initially, both men and women use varied repertoires of body language to signal interest and/or availability. Men may stretch, exaggerate ordinary motions (such as stirring a drink), or engage in preening motions, such as smoothing the hair or adjusting neckties, and younger men often affect a swagger. Women draw attention to themselves by tossing or playing with their hair, tilting their heads, raising their eyebrows, giggling, or blushing. The first connection is generally made through eye contact, often an intent gaze which is then lowered or averted. If the eye contact is positively received, a smile often follows and a conversation is initiated.

Conversations initiated by romantic attraction are generally light and often include laughter. If the attraction progresses, the next step is casual touching in innocuous areas such as the shoulder, wrist, or forearm. The final step in the initial romantic attraction is known as mirroring or body synchrony, which is a matching of nonverbal body language. With bodies aligned and facing each other, the couple begins to move in tandem, leaning toward each other, crossing their legs, or tilting their heads. By these actions, the couple mutually transmit the messages that they like and are like each other. This mirroring activity is not confined to romantic relationships. Infants begin to mirror adult behavior shortly after birth, and the technique is consciously practiced by therapists, salespeople, and others whose work depends on establishing a sense of closeness with others. Generally, the adoption of each other's postures may be seen in virtually any grouping of individuals who feel comfortable with and are close to each other.

Further Reading

Berscheid, Ellen. *Interpersonal Attraction*. 2nd ed. Reading, MA: Addison-Wesley, 1978.

Bull, Ray. *The Social Psychology of Facial Appearance*. New York: Springer-Verlag, 1988.

Introversion/Extroversion

In trait theories of personality, the scale that represents a person's tendency to direct their attention inward (introversion) or outward toward the external environment (extroversion).

Most of the varying theories of **personality** that base their hypotheses on the study of **traits**, or characteristics, include some measure of introversion and extroversion. Generally, people described as introverted share some or all of these characteristics: shyness, quietness, nonsocial, withdrawn, passive, cautious. Extroverted people are thought to be sociable, outgoing, impulsive, energetic, active, and confident. Some theorists believe each person can be labeled as either an introvert or an extrovert. Others believe most people share some of the characteristics of each. Critics have claimed that any such efforts to label people as either introvert or extrovert have little value because they are too simplistic and ignore the complexities inherent in human personality.

Carl Jung proposed as early as 1913 that introversion and extroversion describe the two basic orientations of human nature. A person was either inwardly oriented—taken with ideas and the imagination and most comfortable alone—or directed toward the outside world, comfortably seeking contact with other people and striving for new experiences. An outgoing, confident manner went hand-in-hand with this outward orientation. A model proposed by British psychologist Hans Eysenck designates introversion/extroversion as one of the two main dimensions of personality. According to Eysenck's model, introversion/extroversion was represented on one axis and stability/instability on another. After answering a set of psychological questions, subjects were then rated according to each scale depending upon their responses. Equal measures of introversion and instability (or neuroticism), as rated by the responses, equaled an anxious, withdrawn personality. An extroverted, instable combination was judged to be an attention-seeking personality. Those who were extroverted and stable were thought to be outgoing and capable; the combination of introversion and stability represented a meticulous, responsible personality.

Eysenck also conducted tests that have revealed other possible dimensions to the introversion/extroversion scheme. He discovered that introverts generally have lower pain thresholds than those labeled as extroverts. They also tend to learn faster under certain conditions. Extroverts, he found, perform most tasks better when they are externally aroused. Eysenck and others have also found that the **neurotransmitter** dopamine is present in higher concentrations in extroverts than introverts. It is not known whether the higher level of the chemical causes the tendency to be extroverted, or if it inherently is present at higher levels in extroverts.

Further Reading

Clark, John, ed. *The Mind: Into the Inner World*. New York: Torstar Books, 1986.

Hergenhahn, B.R. *An Introduction to Theories of Personality*. Englewood Cliffs, NJ: Prentice-Hall, 1980.

Zimbardo, Philip G. *Psychology and Life*. Glenview, IL: Scott, Foresman, 1988.

J

James, William (1842–1910)

American philosopher and psychologist who was the principal figure in the establishment and development of functionalism.

William James was born in New York City to a wealthy, educated family that included the future novelist, Henry James, his younger brother. The family traveled extensively in Europe and America in James's youth. James studied chemistry, physiology, and medicine at Harvard College, but was unable to settle on a career, his indecision intensified by physical ailments and **depression.** In 1872, at the invitation of Harvard's president, Charles Eliot, James began teaching physiology at Harvard and achieved a reputation as a committed and inspiring instructor. Throughout the 1870s, his interest in **psychology**—initially sparked by an article by the German physiologist Wilhelm Wundt (1832–1920)—grew. In 1875, James taught the first psychology course offered at an American university and in the same year received funding for the first psychological laboratory in the United States.

James began writing *The Principles of Psychology* in 1878 and published it in 1890. It had been intended as a textbook, but the original version, over 1,000 pages in length, was unsuitable for this purpose (James wrote an abridged version shortly afterwards). Nevertheless, the original text became a seminal work in the field, lauded for James's influential ideas and accessible writing style. James believed that psychology should be seen as closely linked to physiology and other biological sciences. He was among the earliest to argue that mental activity should be understood as dynamic functional processes rather than discrete structural states. The overall name generally associated with this outlook is **functionalism,** and it contrasts with the structural division of **consciousness** into separate elements that was the practice among early German psychologists, including Wundt, whose ideas James eventually came to reject. Influenced by **Charles Darwin**'s theories of evolution in *On the Origin of Species*, the functionalist view held that the true goal

William James

of psychology was the study of how consciousness functions to aid human beings in adapting to their **environment.**

Probably the most well-known individual topic treated in *Principles of Psychology* is the concept of thought as an unbroken but constantly changing stream, which added the phrase "stream of consciousness" to the English language. Following in the footsteps of the Greek philosopher Heraclitus, James argues that the exact same sensation or idea can never occur twice, and that all experiences are molded by the ones that precede them. He also emphasized the continuous quality of consciousness, even when interrupted by such phenomena as seizures or **sleep,** the thoughts that precede and follow an interruption seem unbroken. In contrast, scientific attempts to "break up" or "freeze" consciousness in order to study its disparate elements, such as those of Wundt or Edward Titchener (1867–1927), seemed misguided to James. Also treated prominently in *Principles of Psychology* is the importance and power of habits, as a force either to resist or cultivate, depending on the circumstances.

An especially influential part of James's book is the chapter on **emotion,** which expresses a principle that became known as the James–Lange Theory because the Danish physiologist Carl Lange published similar views at about the same time as James. The theory states that physical responses to stimuli precede emotional ones. In other words, James posited that emotions actually result from rather than cause physical changes. Based on this conclusion, James argued that a person's emotional state could be improved by changing his or her physical activities or **attitudes.**

Related to this observation about emotion were James's theories of the human will, which were also central to *Principles of Psychology* and contained the germ of his later philosophy of pragmatism. His emphasis on the will had its roots in his personal life: while in his twenties, an essay on free will by the French philosopher Charles-Bernard Renouvier (1815–1903) had inspired him to overcome his emotional problems. James rejected the idea of human beings responding passively to outside influences without power over their circumstances. Having himself triumphed by a strenuous exertion of the will, he recommended this course for others as well, defining an act of will as one characterized by focusing one's attention strongly on the object to be attained.

James served as president of the **American Psychological Association** in 1894 and 1904. He applied some of his psychological theories to his other studies, including education and religion. In 1909, the year before his death, James traveled to Clark University to meet **Sigmund Freud,** the founder of **psychoanalysis,** during the latter's only visit to the United States. In addition to *Principles of Psychology* and his other books, James had a great impact on psychology in America through his teaching. The work of his student G. Stanley Hall (1844–1924) provided a link between James's psychological theories and the functionalist school of psychology that flourished during the 1920s. James's other books include *The Will to Believe and Other Essays* (1897), *The Varieties of Religious Experience* (1902), *Pragmatism* (1907), *A Pluralistic Universe* (1909), *The*

Meaning of Truth (1909), and *Essays in Radical Empiricism* (1912).

Toward the end of his career, James concentrated his work in the area of philosophy and maintained few ties to the field of psychology.

Further Reading
Perry, Ralph B. *The Thought and Character of William James.* Cambridge, MA: Harvard University Press, 1948.

Jealousy

An envious emotional attitude primarily directed by an individual toward someone perceived as a rival for the affections of a loved one or for something one desires, such as a job, promotion, or award.

Jealousy is a combination of emotional reactions, including **fear, anger,** and **anxiety.** Studies have shown that men and women tend to feel jealous for different reasons; for instance, physical attractiveness in a perceived rival is more likely to incite jealousy in a woman than in a man. Everyone occasionally experience normal jealousy; caring about anyone or anything means that one will become uncomfortable and anxious at the prospect of losing the desired person or object to another. An unhealthy degree of apathy would be required for an individual never to experience jealousy.

The opposite extreme is pathological jealousy, also called morbid jealousy, which differs significantly from normal jealousy in its degree of intensity. Stronger and more long-lasting than normal jealousy, it is generally characterized by serious feelings of insecurity and inadequacy, as well as suspiciousness or **paranoia.** Whereas healthy individuals recover from jealousy fairly rapidly, either by realizing that it is unfounded or through some other coping mechanism, pathologically jealous people become obsessed by their fears and constantly look for signs that their suspicions are true, to the point where they may find it difficult to function normally. Excessive jealousy is unhealthy and destructive in all relationships. By making people behave in ways that will alienate others, jealousy becomes a **self-fulfilling prophecy,** depriving its victims of the affection or success they are so anxious to protect. Individuals suffering from morbid jealousy are prone to severe anxiety, **depression,** difficulty in controlling anger, and may engage in self-destructive behavior or elicit suicidal tendencies.

Further Reading
White, Gregory. *Jealousy.* New York: Guilford Press, 1989.

Jensen, Arthur R. (1923–)

American educational psychologist whose work has concentrated in the areastudy of human intelligence.

Arthur Jensen was born in San Diego, California, and attended the University of California at Berkeley, San Diego State College, and Columbia University. He completed a clinical internship at the University of Maryland's Psychiatric Institute in 1956, after which he won a two-year postdoctoral research fellowship with the Institute of Psychiatry at the University of London, where he worked with Hans J. Eysenck, a prominent psychologist known for his evolutionary approach to human behavior. Eysenck's work in **personality** theory, measurement, and **intelligence**—areas that were to become Jensen's specialty—challenged humanistic, psychodynamic approaches that stressed the importance of social factors in human behavior. In 1958, Jensen joined the faculty at the University of California at Berkeley, serving as a professor of educational psychology, and also served as a research psychologist at the Institute of Human Learning. After early work in the area of verbal learning, Jensen turned to the study of individual differences in human learning and intelligence.

Jensen claimed, on the basis of his research, that general cognitive **ability** is essentially an inherited trait, determined predominantly by genetic factors rather than by environmental conditions. He also contended that while associative learning, or memorizing ability, is equally distributed among the races, conceptual learning, or synthesizing ability, occurs with significantly greater frequency in whites than in blacks. He suggested that from the data, one might conclude that on average, white Americans are more intelligent than African-Americans. Jensen suggested that the difference in average performance between whites and blacks on intelligence tests might be the result of innate differences rather than contrasts in parental upbringing, formal schooling, or other environmental factors. Jensen further surmised from the data that federal educational programs such as Head Start could only raise the IQs of disadvantage children by only a few points and are therefore not worthy of funding. The relative influence of **heredity** and **environment** on intelligence tests had been an area of debate since their inception in the 1920s, and the prevailing view of Jensen's contemporaries was that environmental factors in the home and school play the decisive role.

In 1969, Jensen published his views in a long article entitled "How Much Can We Boost IQ and Scholastic Achievement?" in the *Harvard Education Review,* which rekindled the age-old debate of the relative importance of genetics in determining intellectual ability. Jensen's work was often misquoted by the media and was popularly denounced on college campuses. The belief in a genetic basis for individual and racial differences in intelligence and scholastic performance came to be known as "jensenism." Although Jensen's work in human intelligence has received a mixed reception from professionals in the field, his prolific publications have engaged the serious attention of many researchers and educators in the years since. Jensen's books include *Genetics and Education* (1973), *Educability and Group Differences* (1973), *Bias in Mental Testing* (1979), and *Straight Talk about Mental Tests (1980).*

See also Nature-Nurture Controversy.

Further Reading

Jensen, Arthur. "How Much Can We Boost IQ and Scholastic Achievement?" *Harvard Education Review* 39 (Winter/Summer 1969): 1-123; 449-83.

Jukes Family

Pseudonym for the family involved in a psychological study of antisocial behavior.

One of the goals of 19th-century American scientists was to determine why some people engaged in undesirable or antisocial behavior. A family from Ulster County in upstate New York provided a great deal of material for speculation about the origins of such behavior. The family was referred to as the Jukes family (the actual family name was kept anonymous).

One of the initial researchers of the Jukes family was Elisha Harris (1824–1884), a New York City physician. He identified a family that, for six generations, had included large numbers of paupers, criminals, and vagrants. He traced the family to a woman he referred to as "Margaret, mother of criminals." Margaret and her two sisters produced 600 descendants over an 85-year period, many of whom lived on the fringes of society. For example, in one generation that produced 14 children, nine served a total of 50 years in state prison, and the other five were frequently jailed for petty crimes or spent time in poorhouses.

After Harris's discovery, Richard Dugale (1841–1883) studied the family history intensively. He concluded that the repeated appearance of undesirable behaviors could be traced to environmental rather than hereditary factors. Dugale advocated for decent housing and education for people from damaging **environment**s.

After Dugale's death, some of his contemporaries reinterpreted his research in light of hereditarian influences. Instead of advancing the idea that environment influenced the behavior of the Jukes, the notion that antisocial behavior was passed from one generation to the next like any other biological trait was favored. Proponents of this idea included the widely respected physician and author Oliver Wendell Holmes (1809–1894). Holmes's son later became a United States Supreme Court Justice and issued a famous ruling that allowed legal, involuntary sterilization of people deemed to be genetically "unfit."

Later research has revealed that the original settlers in Ulster County, like the Jukes, included people who could not adapt to the urban life in 19th-century New York City and moved north, living an itinerant life of trapping and hunting. (The name "Jukes" came from the slang term "to juke," which described the behavior of chickens who did not deposit their eggs in nests, but rather laid them in any convenient spot.) When the area became more densely populated, such individuals lost most of their hunting and trapping land and their way of life. They were looked down upon by later settlers, who preferred to live in houses within a community. The earlier inhabitants, including the Jukes, were forced to live a marginal existence, which foreshadowed their troubles with society.

See also Eugenics; Kallikak Family; Nature-Nurture Controversy.

Carl Jung

Jung, Carl (1875–1961)

Swiss psychiatrist and founder of analytic psychology.

Carl Jung was born in Switzerland, the son of a Swiss Reform pastor. Having decided to become a **psychiatrist,** he enrolled in medical school at the University of Basel, from which he received his degree in 1900. Serving as an assistant at the University of Zurich Psychiatric Clinic, Jung worked under psychiatrist Eugen Bleuler (1857–1939), a psychiatrist renowned for his work on **schizophrenia.** Jung also traveled to France to study with the well-known psychiatrist Pierre Janet (1859–1947) as well. In 1905, he was appointed to a faculty position in **psychiatry** at the University of Zurich and became a senior physician at its clinic. Eventually, a growing private practice forced him to resign his university position. Jung's early published studies on schizophrenia established his reputation, and he also won recognition for developing a word association test.

Jung had read **Sigmund Freud**'s *The Interpretation of Dreams* shortly after its publication in 1900 and entered into a correspondence with its author. The two men met in 1907 and began a close association that was to last for over six years. In 1909, they both traveled to the United States to participate in the 20th-anniversary commemoration at Clark University in Worcester, Massachusetts at the invitation of American psychologist, G. Stanley

Hall (1844–1924). Jung became part of a weekly discussion group that met at Freud's house and included, among others, **Alfred Adler** and Otto Rank (1884–1939). This group evolved into the Vienna Psychoanalytic Society, and Jung became its first president in 1911. Jung had begun to develop concepts about **psychoanalysis** and the nature of the **unconscious** that differed from those of Freud, however, especially Freud's insistence on the sexual basis of neurosis. After the publication of Jung's *Psychology of the Unconscious* in 1912, the disagreement between the two men grew, and their relationship ended in 1914. At this period, Jung underwent a period of personal turmoil and, like Freud at a similar juncture in his own life, undertook a thorough self-analysis based on his **dreams.** Jung also explored myths and symbols, an interest he was to investigate further in the 1920s with trips to Africa and the southwestern United States to study the myths and religions of non-Western cultures.

Jung developed his own system of psychoanalysis, which he called analytical psychology, that reflected his interest in symbolism, mythology, and spirituality. A major premise of analytical psychology is that the individual **personality,** or psyche, functions on three levels. The *ego* operates at the conscious level, while the *personal* *unconscious* includes experiences that have been repressed, forgotten, or kept from **consciousness** in some other way. It is also the site of complexes—groups of feelings, thoughts, and memories, usually organized around a significant person (such as a parent) or object (such as money). At the deepest and most powerful level, Jung posited the existence of a racial or *collective unconscious,* which gathers together the experiences of previous generations and even animal ancestors, preserving traces of humanity's evolutionary development over time. The collective unconscious is a repository of shared images and symbols, called *archetypes*, that emerge in dreams, myths, and other forms. These include such common themes as **birth,** rebirth, death, the hero, the earth mother, and the demon. Certain archetypes form separate systems within the personality, including the *persona,* or public image; the *anima* and *animus,* or gender characteristics; the *shadow,* or animal instincts; and the *self,* which strives for unity and wholeness. In Jung's view, a thorough analysis of both the personal and collective unconscious is necessary to fully understand the individual personality.

Perhaps Jung's best-known contribution is his theory that individuals can be categorized according to general attitudinal type as either introverted (inward-looking) or extroverted (outward-looking). The psychic wholeness, or individuation, for which human beings strive depends on reconciling these tendencies as well as the four functional aspects of the mind that are split into opposing pairs: sensing versus intuiting as ways of knowing, and thinking versus feeling as ways of evaluating. If any of these personality characteristics is overly dominant in the conscious mind, its opposite will be exaggerated in the unconscious. These pairs of functions have been widely adapted in vocational and other types of testing.

From 1932 to 1942, Jung was a professor at the Federal Polytechnical University of Zurich. Although his health forced him to resign, he continued writing about analytical psychology for the rest of his life and promoting the attainment of psychic wholeness through personal transformation and self-discovery. Jung's work has been influential in disciplines other than psychology, and his own writing includes works on religion, the arts, literature, and occult topics including alchemy, astrology, yoga, fortune telling, and flying saucers. Jung's autobiography, *Memories, Dreams, Reflections,* was published in 1961, the year of his death. Institutes of analytical psychology have been established throughout the world, although its international center remains the C.J. Jung Institute in Zurich, founded in 1948. Jung was a prolific writer; his collected works fill 19 volumes, but many of his writings were not published in English until after 1965. Shortly before his death, Jung completed work on *Man and His Symbols,* which has served as a popular introduction to his ideas on symbols and dreams.

See also Archetype; Character; Introversion-extroversion.

Further Reading

Fordham, Frieda. *An Introduction to Jung's Psychology.* New York: Penguin Books, 1966.

Just Noticeable Difference

Scientific calculation of the average detectable difference between two measurable qualities, such as weight, brightness of light, loudness of sound.

When we try to compare two different objects to see if they are the same or different on some dimension (e.g.,

JUST NOTICEABLE DIFFERENCE (JND)	
Type of Stimulus	**Percentage Change Needed**
Electric shock	1.3
Heaviness	2.0
Line length	2.9
Vibration frequency	4.0 (approximate)
Loudness	4.8
Salt concentration	2.0
Brightness	7.9

weight), the difference between the two that is barely big enough to be noticed is called the just noticeable difference (JND). Just noticeable differences have been studied for many dimensions (e.g., brightness of lights, loudness of sounds, weight, line length, and others).

The human sensory system does not respond identically to the same stimuli on different occasions. As a result, if an individual attempted to identify whether two objects were of the same or different weight he or she might detect a difference on one occasion but will fail to notice it on another occasion. Psychologists calculate the just noticeable difference as an average detectable difference across a large number of trials. The JND does not stay the same when the magnitude of the stimuli change. In assessing heaviness, for example, the difference between two stimuli of 10 and 11 grams could be detected, but we would not be able to detect the difference between 100 and 101 grams. As the magnitude of the stimuli grow, we need a larger actual difference for detection. The percentage of change remains constant in general. To detect the difference in heaviness, one stimulus would have to be approximately 2 percent heavier than the other; otherwise, we will not be able to spot the difference.

The corresponding table presents the percentage difference necessary for a JND on several dimensions. These values will differ from one person to the next, and from one occasion to the next. However, they do represent generally accurate values. Psychologists refer to these values as Weber fractions, named after Ernst Weber (1795–1878), a German physiologist whose pioneering research on sensation had a great impact on psychological studies.

Further Reading

Nietzel, Michael T. *Introduction to Clinical Psychology.* 3rd ed. Englewood Cliffs, NJ: Prentice Hall, 1991.

Juvenile Delinquency

Chronic antisocial behavior by persons 18 years of age or younger that is beyond parental control and is often subjected to legal and punitive action.

According to the Federal Bureau of Investigation (FBI) and the Centers for Disease Control (CDC), the arrest rate of American juveniles (persons 18 years of age or younger) committing violent crimes increased from 137 percent in 1965 to 430 percent in 1990. While teenagers are the population most likely to commit crimes, their delinquency is related to the overall incidence of crime in society: teen crime increases as adult crime does. The majority of violent teenage crime is committed by males. While the same delinquency rates are attribut-

ed to both whites and nonwhites, nonwhites have a higher arrest rate.

In spite of the emotional turbulence associated with **adolescence**, most teenagers find legal, nonviolent ways to express feelings of **anger** and frustration and to establish self-esteem. Nonetheless, some teenagers turn to criminal activity for these purposes and as a reaction to peer pressure. A number of factors have been linked to the rise in teen crime, including family **violence**. Parents who physically or verbally abuse each other or their children are much more likely to raise children who will commit crimes. In a study conducted in 1989, for example, 80 out of 95 incarcerated juvenile delinquents had witnessed or been victims of severe family violence. A similar incidence of abuse was found in a study of teenage murderers.

The growing poverty rate in the U.S., particularly among children, has also been attributed to juvenile delinquency. In the late 1980s, the National Education Association predicted that 40 percent of secondary school students will live below the poverty line. The anger and frustration of low-income youths excluded from the "good life" depicted in the mass media, coupled with the lack of visible opportunities to carve out productive paths for themselves, leads many to crime, much of it drug-related. A dramatic link has been found between drug use and criminal activity: people who abuse illegal drugs, such as cocaine and heroin, have been found to commit six times as many crimes as non-drug users.

For many poor inner-city youths, juvenile delinquency begins with participation in the drug trade. Children as young as 9 or 10 are paid as much as $100 a day to serve as lookouts while drug deals are taking place. Next, they become runners and may eventually graduate to being dealers. The introduction of crack cocaine, one of the most powerfully addictive drugs in existence, in the mid-1980s, has contributed to drug-related delinquency. The neglected children of crack-addicted parents are especially likely to be pulled into the drug culture themselves.

The wealth gained from the drug trade has further escalated levels of juvenile delinquency by fueling the rise of violent street gangs. Many gangs are highly organized operations with formal hierarchies and strict codes of dress and behavior. With millions of dollars in drug money behind them, they are expanding from major urban areas to smaller communities. Teens, both poor and middle-class, join gangs for status, respect, and a feeling of belonging denied them in other areas of their lives. Some are pressured into joining to avoid harassment from gang members. Once in a gang, teens are much more likely to be involved in violent acts.

The juvenile justice system has been criticized as outdated and ineffective in dealing with the volume and nature of today's teen crime. A teenager must be either 16 or 18 years of age (depending on the state) to be tried as an adult in criminal court, regardless of the crime committed. Child offenders under the age of 13 are considered juvenile delinquents and can only be tried in family court, no matter what type of crime they have committed. Unless the offender has already committed two serious crimes, the maximum punishment is 18 months in a youth facility. Teenagers between the ages of 13 and 16 are classified as "juvenile offenders." They are rarely photographed or fingerprinted, even in cases involving rape or murder, and usually receive lenient sentences. Most are confined for period of less than four months.

Of approximately 2 million juveniles arrested each year, an estimated 50 percent are released immediately. Those whose cases are tried in court are often given suspended sentences or put on probation. Of those who are sentenced to prison, most return to criminal activity upon their release, and many fear that these young offenders come out of prisons even more violent. In addition, the unmanageable caseloads of probation officers in many cities makes it impossible to keep track of juveniles adequately. Thus, those teens who turn to crime face little in the way of a deterrent, a situation that has caused many authorities to place a large share of the blame for teen crime on the failure of the juvenile justice system.

Alternative community-based programs for all but the most violent teens have had some success in reducing juvenile crime. These include group homes which offer counseling and education; wilderness programs such as Outward Bound; crisis counseling programs that provide emergency aid to teenagers and their families; and placement in a foster home, when a stable home environment is lacking.

Further Reading

Binder, Arnold. *Juvenile Delinquency: Historical, Cultural, Legal Perspectives.* New York: Macmillan, 1988.

Grinney, Ellen Heath. *Delinquency and Criminal Behavior.* New York: Chelsea House Publishers, 1992.

Trojanowicz, Robert C. *Juvenile Delinquency: Concepts and Control.* New York: Prentice Hall, 1983.

Kallikak Family

Pseudonym for a family involved in a psychological study of the hereditary aspects of intelligence.

The history of **intelligence** testing in the United States has been troublesome from the beginning. Although psychologists attempted to conduct legitimate research and apply psychological knowledge to the study of intelligence, some of the early work was quite unscientific and led to dubious results.

One case involved the descendants of an anonymous man referred to as Martin Kallikak. This man produced two different lines of descent, one with a supposedly "feebleminded" bar maid with whom he had had sexual relations and one with his wife, reputed to be an honest Quaker woman. The offsprings from the two women generated two lineages that could not have been more different. The pseudonym "Kallikak" was taken from two Greek words: *kallos,* meaning beauty (referring to the descendants of the Quaker woman) and *kakos,* meaning bad (referring to the descendants of the bar maid).

The psychologist Henry Goddard (1866–1957) investigated these two groups over a two-year period. According to psychology historian David Hothersall, Goddard discovered that the inferior branch of Martin Kallikak's family included "46 normal people, 143 who were definitely feebleminded, 36 illegitimate births, 33 sexually immoral people, 3 epileptics, and 24 alcoholics. These people were horse thieves, paupers, convicts, prostitutes, criminals, and keepers of houses of ill repute. On the other hand, Quaker side of the family included only 3 somewhat mentally "degenerate people, 2 alcoholics, 1 sexually loose person, and no illegitimate births or epileptics."

These patterns of behavior were believed to be the results of **heredity**, rather than **environment**, even though the two environments were radically different. Goddard also believed that intelligence was determined by heredity, just like the inclination toward prostitution, theft, and poverty.

Goddard was also a supporter of the **eugenics** movement in the United States. One of the solutions that he proposed for controlling the creation of the "defective classes" was sterilization, which he advocated as being as simple as having a tooth extracted. Later in his career, Goddard retracted some of his earlier conclusions and maintained that, although intelligence had a hereditary basis, morons (at that time a technical term) might beget other morons, but they could be educated and made useful to society.

See also Jukes Family; Nature-Nurture Controversy.

Further Reading

Goddard, Henry Herbert. *The Kallikak Family: A Study in the Heredity of Feeble-Mindedness.* New York: Macmillan, 1927.

Gould, S. J. *The Mismeasure of Man.* New York: W. W. Norton, 1981.

Kinesthetic Sense

The ability to know accurately the positions and movements of one's skeletal joints.

Kinesthesis refers to sensory input that occurs within the body. Postural and movement information are communicated via sensory systems by tension and compression of muscles in the body. Even when the body remains stationary, the kinesthetic sense can monitor its position. Humans possess three specialized types of **neurons** responsive to **touch** and stretching that help keep track of body movement and position. The first class, called Pacinian corpuscles, lies in the deep subcutaneous fatty tissue and responds to pressure. The second class of neurons surrounds the internal organs, and the third class is associated with muscles, tendons, and joints. These neurons work in concert with one another and with cortical neurons as the body moves.

The ability to assess the weight of an object is another function of kinesthesia. When an individual picks up an object, the tension in his/her muscles generates signals that are used to adjust posture. This sense does not operate in isolation from other senses. For example, the size-weight illusion results in a mismatch between how heavy an object looks and how heavy the muscles "think" it should be. In general, larger objects are judged as being heavier than smaller objects of the same weight.

The kinesthetic sense does not mediate equilibrium, or sense of balance. Balance involves different sensory pathways and originates in large part within the inner ear.

Further Reading

Bartenieff, Irmgard. *Body Movement: Coping with the Environment.* New York: Gordon and Breach Science Publishers, 1980.

Moving Parts (videorecording). Princeton, NJ: Films for the Humanities, 1985.

Kleptomania

One of the impulse control disorders, characterized by an overwhelming impulse to steal.

Persons with this disorder, popularly referred to as kleptomaniacs, experience a recurring urge to steal that they are unable to resist. They do not steal for the value of the item, for its use, or because they cannot afford the purchase. The individual knows that it is wrong to steal. Stolen items are often thrown or given away, secretly returned to the store from which they were taken, or hidden.

Persons with this disorder describe a feeling of tension prior to committing the theft, and a feeling of relief or pleasure while stealing the item.

Kleptomania is a rare disorder. It can begin at any age, and is reported to be more common among females. Kleptomania is different from deliberate theft or shoplifting, which is much more common; it is estimated that less than 5 percent of individuals who shoplift exhibit symptoms of kleptomania. Shoplifting often involves two or more individuals working together; among adolescents, peers sometimes challenge or dare each other to commit an act of shoplifting. Individuals with kleptomania are not influenced by peers, nor are they motivated by a **need** for the item stolen. This disorder may persist despite arrests for shoplifting; the individual is apparently not deterred by the consequences of stealing, but may feel guilty afterwards.

Further Reading

Morrison, James. *DSM-IV Made Easy: The Clinician's Guide to Diagnosis.* New York: The Guilford Press, 1995.

Kohlberg, Lawrence (1927–1987)

American psychologist whose work has been centered in the area of the development of moral reasoning.

Lawrence Kohlberg was born in Bronxville, New York, and received his B.A. (1948) and Ph.D. (1958) from the University of Chicago. He served as an assistant professor at Yale University from 1959 to 1961 and was a fellow of the Center of Advanced Study of Behavioral Science in 1962. Kohlberg began teaching at the University of Chicago in 1963, where he remained until his 1967 appointment to the faculty of Harvard University, where he has served as professor of education and **social psychology.** Kohlberg is best known for his work in the development of moral reasoning in children and adolescents. Seeking to expand on **Jean Piaget**'s work in cognitive development and to determine whether there are universal stages in **moral development** as well, Kohlberg conducted a long-term study in which he recorded the responses of boys aged seven through **adolescence** to hypothetical dilemmas requiring a moral choice. (The most famous sample question is whether the husband of a critically ill woman is justified in stealing a drug that could save her life if the pharmacist is charging much more than he can afford to pay.) Based on the results of his study, Kohlberg concluded that children and adults progress through six stages in the development of moral reasoning. He also concluded that moral development is directly related to cognitive development, with older children able to base their responses on increasingly broad and abstract ethical standards.

In evaluating his research, Kohlberg was primarily interested not in the children's responses themselves, but in the reasoning behind them. Based on their thought processes, he discerned a gradual evolution from self-interest to principled behavior and developed a chronological scheme of moral development consisting of three levels, each made up of two separate stages. Each stage involves increasingly complex thought patterns, and as children arrive at a given stage they tend to consider the bases for previous judgments as invalid. Children from the ages of seven through ten act on the *preconventional* level, at which they defer to adults and obey rules based on the immediate consequences of their actions. The behavior of children at this level is essentially premoral. At Stage 1, they obey rules in order to avoid **punishment,** while at Stage 2 their behavior is mostly motivated by the desire to obtain rewards. Starting at around age ten, children enter the *conventional* level, where their behavior is guided by the opinions of other people and the desire to conform. At Stage 3, the emphasis is on being a "good boy" or "good girl" in order to win approval and avoid disapproval, while at Stage 4 the concept of doing one's duty and upholding the social order becomes predominant. At this stage, respecting and obeying authority (of parents, teachers, God) is an end in itself, without reference to higher principles. By the age of 13, most moral questions are resolved on the conventional level.

During adolescence, children move beyond this level and become capable of *postconventional* morality, which requires the **ability** to formulate abstract moral principles, which are then obeyed to avoid self-condemnation rather than the censure of others. At Stage 5, adolescents are guided by a "social contract" orientation toward the welfare of the community, the rights of others, and existing laws. At Stage 6, their actions are guided by ethical standards that transcend the actual laws of their society and are based on such abstract concepts as freedom, dignity, and justice. However, Kohlberg's scheme does not imply that all adolescents negotiate the passage to postconventional morality. Progress through the different stages depends upon the type of thinking that a child or adolescent is capable of at a given point, and also on the negotiation of previous stages. Kohlberg points out that many people never pass beyond the conventional level, and that the most clearly principled response at Stage 6 was expressed by fewer than 10 percent of adolescents over the age of 16. (In relation to the dilemma of the stolen drug, such a response would clearly articulate the existence of a moral law that transcends society's laws about stealing, and the sanctity of human life over financial gain.)

Kohlberg's system is closely related to Piaget's theories, both in its emphasis on cognitive development and in its designation of a chronological series of stages, each dependent on the preceding ones. It also has important implications for the **nature-nurture controversy,** as it stresses the role of innate rather than environmental factors in moral development. According to Kohlberg, progress from one level or stage to the next involves an internal cognitive reorganization that is more complex than a mere acquisition of precepts from peers, parents, and other authorities. Kohlberg's most famous book is *The Philosophy of Moral Development: Moral Stages and the Idea of Justice,* the first volume in a series entitled *Essays on Moral Development.* The second volume, The *Psychology of Moral Development,* was published in 1984.

See also Cognitive Development Theory.

Further Reading

Alper, Joseph. "The Roots of Morality," *Science 85,* (March 1985): 70.

Kohlberg, Lawrence. *Child Psychology and Childhood Education: A Cognitive-Developmental View.* New York: Longman, 1987.

Wolfgang Köhler

Power, F. Clark. *Lawrence Kohlberg's Approach to Moral Education.* New York: Columbia University Press, 1989.

Köhler, Wolfgang (1887–1967)

German psychologist and principal figure in the development of Gestalt psychology.

Wolfgang Köhler was born in Revel, Estonia, and grew up in Wolfenbüttel, Germany. He studied at the universities of Bonn and Tübingen, and at the Friedrich Wilhelm University of Berlin, where he received his Ph.D. in 1909, writing a dissertation on psychoacoustics under the direction of Carl Stumpf (1848–1936). In 1910, Köhler began a long professional association with Max Wertheimer (1880–1943) when he and Kurt Koffka (1886–1941), both assistants to Friedrich Schumann at the University of Frankfurt, served as research subjects for an experiment of Wertheimer's involving **perception** of moving pictures. Within the next ten years, the three men were to found the Gestalt movement in psychology. In reaction to the prevailing behavioristic methods of Wilhelm Wundt (1832–1920) and others, the Gestalt psychologists held that behavior must be studied in all its complexity rather than separated into discrete components. Köhler's early work convinced him that perception, learning, and other cognitive functions should be seen as structured wholes.

Unlike Koffka and Wertheimer, Köhler concentrated on animal research. Beginning in 1913, he spent more than six years as director of the anthropoid research facility of the Prussian Academy of Sciences on the island of Tenerife, where he made many discoveries applying Gestalt theories to animal learning and perception. His observations and conclusions from this period contributed to a radical revision of **learning theory**. One of his most famous experiments centered on chickens which he trained to peck grains from either the lighter or darker of two sheets of paper. When the chickens who had been trained to prefer the light color were presented with a choice between that color and a new sheet that was still lighter, a majority switched to the new sheet. Similarly, chickens trained to prefer the darker color, when presented with a parallel choice, chose a new, darker color. These results, Köhler maintained, showed that what the chickens had learned was an **association** with a *relationship*, rather than with a specific color. This finding, which flew in the face of behaviorist theories deemphasizing the importance of relationships, became known as the Gestalt *law of transposition*, because the test subjects had transposed their original experience to a new set of circumstances.

Köhler also conducted a series of experiments in which chimpanzees were confronted with the problem of obtaining bananas that were hung just out of reach by using "tools"—bamboo poles and stacked boxes. The chimpanzees varied in their ability to arrive at the correct combination of actions needed to solve the problem. Often, a test subject would suddenly find a solution at a seemingly random point. This research led Köhler to the concept of learning by a sudden leap of the imagination, or "insight," in which a relationship that had not been seen before was suddenly perceived, a formulation in conflict with the trial-and-error theory of learning resulting from **Edward Thorndike**'s puzzle box experiments. Based on this work, Köhler published *The Mentality of Apes* in 1917, demonstrating that Gestalt theory could be applied to animal behavior.

Köhler returned to Germany after World War I, and in 1921 was appointed to the most prestigious position in German psychology, director of the Psychological Institute at the University of Berlin. For the next 14 years he made the Institute a center for Gestalt studies and was a noted spokesman for the movement. In 1935, however, Köhler resigned due to conflicts with the Nazis, and emigrated to the United States, where he served on the faculties of Swarthmore and Dartmouth Colleges. In 1959, he was appointed president of the **American Psychological Association.** There has been some speculation that he was a spy during World War I, a thesis explored by his biographer, Ronald Ley. Köhler's books include *Gestalt Psychology* (1929), *The Place of Value in a World of Facts* (1938), and *Dynamics in Psychology* (1940).

See also Behaviorism; Cognitive Development Theory; Gestalt Psychology.

Further Reading

Ley, Ronald. *A Whisper of Espionage.* Garden City Park, NY: Avery Publishing Group, 1990.

Petermann, Bruno. *The Gestalt Theory and the Problem of Configuration.* London: K. Paul, 1932.

Ladd-Franklin, Christine (1847–1930)

American psychologist, logician, and an internationally recognized authority on the theory of color vision.

Born in Windsor, Connecticut, Christine Ladd-Franklin spent her early childhood in New York City. Her father was a prominent merchant and her mother was a feminist. Following her mother's death when Ladd-Franklin was 13, she moved to Portsmouth, New Hampshire, to live with her paternal grandmother. Ladd-Franklin attended the Wesleyan Academy in Wilbraham, Massachusetts for two years, taking classes with boys preparing to enter Harvard University, and was the valedictorian of her graduating class in 1865. After graduating from Vassar College in 1869 with a primary interest in mathematics and science, she taught in secondary schools in Pennsylvania, New York, and Massachusetts for more than a decade and also published numerous articles on mathematics during this period. In 1878, she applied for admission to Johns Hopkins University for advanced study in mathematics. Because of her extraordinary intellectual ability, Ladd-Franklin was awarded the stipend of a fellow, although not the actual title because women were not permitted to pursue graduate study at the time. Despite completing requirements for the doctorate in 1882, she was denied the degree until 1926.

At the completion of her fellowship in 1882, Ladd-Franklin married Fabian Franklin, a mathematics professor at Johns Hopkins University, and gave birth to two children, one of whom died in infancy. Atypical for married women of the time, and without a formal academic affiliation, she continued to publish scholarly papers, several of which appeared in the *American Journal of Mathematics*. After hearing Charles S. Peirce (1839–1914) lecture at Johns Hopkins, Ladd-Franklin became interested in symbolic logic and wrote a paper, "The Algebra of Logic," that was published in 1883 in a book of essays by Peirce and his students. In her paper, praised as

Christine Ladd-Franklin

a landmark achievement by Harvard philosopher Josiah Royce (1815–1916), Ladd-Franklin reduced all syllogisms to a single formula, in which the three parts form an "inconsistent triad."

Ladd-Franklin's mathematical interests ultimately led her to make important contributions to the field of **psychology.** In 1886, she became interested in the geometrical relationship between binocular vision and points in space and published a paper on this topic in the first volume of the *American Journal of Psychology* the following year. During the 1891-92 academic year, Ladd-Franklin took advantage of her husband's sabbatical leave from Johns Hopkins and travelled to Europe to conduct research in **color vision** in the laboratories of Georg Müller (1850–1934) in Göttingen, and Hermann von Helmholtz (1821–1894) in Berlin, where she also attended lectures by Arthur König. In contrast to the prevailing three-color and opponent-color explanations of color vision, Ladd-Franklin developed an evolutionary theory that posited three stages in the development of color vision. Presenting her work at the International Congress of Psychology in London in 1892, she argued that black-white vision was the most primitive stage, since it occurs under the greatest variety of conditions, including under very low illumination and at the extreme edges of the visual field. The color white, she theorized, later became differentiated into blue and yellow, with yellow ultimately differentiated into red-green vision. Ladd-Franklin's theory was well-received and remained influential for some years, and its emphasis on evolution is still valid today.

After returning to the United States, Ladd-Franklin taught, lectured, and pursued research. She continued publishing and presented papers at meetings of both the American Philosophical Association and the **American Psychological Association,** as well as at international congresses. She lectured in philosophy and logic at Johns Hopkins between 1904 and 1909, and served as an associate editor in those fields for Baldwin's *Dictionary of Philosophy and Psychology*. Moving to New York City with her husband in 1910 when he became an associate editor of the *New York Evening Post*, Ladd-Franklin began lecturing at Columbia University. She published an influential paper on the visual phenomenon known as "blue arcs" in 1926, when she was in her late seventies, and in 1929, a year before her death, a collection of her papers on vision was published under the title *Colour and Colour Theories*. In her writings and active correspondence with colleagues, Ladd-Franklin challenged the mores of the day, championing the cause of women in matters of equal rights, access to education and the professions, and the right to vote.

Further Reading

Scarborough, Elizabeth, and Laurel Furumoto. *Untold Lives: The First Generation of American Women Psychologists.* New York: Columbia University Press, 1987, pp. 109–129.

Language Acquisition

The process by which children acquire their first language in early childhood.

Human infants are acutely attuned to the human voice and prefer it above all other sounds. In fact, they prefer the higher pitch ranges characteristic of female voices. They are also attentive to the human face, particularly the eyes, which they stare at even more if that person is talking. These preferences are present at **birth**, and some research indicates that babies even listen to their mother's voice during the last few months of pregnancy. Babies who were read to by their mothers while in the womb showed the **ability** to pick out her voice from among other female voices.

At the beginning of **infancy**, vegetative noises and crying predominate. Observers note that by the age of four months, the baby's repertoire has expanded in more interesting ways. By this point, babies are smiling at care givers and in doing so they engage in a cooing noise that is irresistible to most parents. When the baby is being fed or changed, she will frequently lock gazes with her care giver and coo in a pleasant way, often making noises that sound like "hi," and gurgles. It is common for the care giver to respond by echoing these noises, thereby creating an elaborate interchange that can last many minutes. This may not happen universally, however, as not all cultures take the baby's vocalization so seriously. The nature of the sounds made at this stage is not fully speech-like, though there are open mouths noises such as vowels and an occasional "closure" akin to a consonant, but without the full properties that normally make a syllable out of the two. At some point between four and six months, the infant begins producing more speech-like syllables, with a full resonant vowel and an appropriate "closure" of the stream of sound, approaching a true consonant. This stage is called "canonical babbling."

At about six to eight months, the range of vocalizations grows dramatically, and babies can spend hours practicing the sounds they can make with their mouths. Not all of these are human phonemes, and not all of them are found in the language around them. Research has shown that Japanese and American infants sound alike at this stage, and even congenitally deaf infants babble, though less frequently. These facts suggest that the infant is "exercising" her speech organs, but is not being guided very much, if at all, by what she had heard.

An infant's first words make their appearance any time between 9 and 15 months of age, depending on the child's precocity and the parent's enthusiasm in noticing. That is, the baby begins making sounds that occur fairly reliably in some situations and are at least a vague approximation to an adult sounding word. After several months of slow growth, however, there is an explosion of new words, often called the "word spurt." This usually coincides with an interest in what things are called, e.g., the child asking some variant of "what's that?" Vocabulary climbs precipitously from then on—an estimated nine new words a day from ages 2 to 18. These develop-

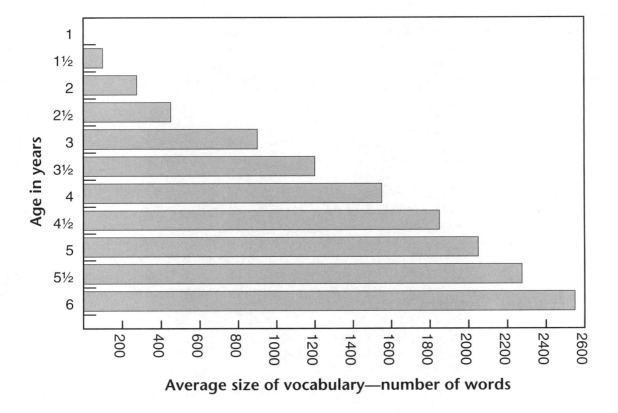

Average vocabulary growth of children from ages 1 to 7.

ments are noted in all cultures that have been studied to date. The child often names foods, pets, animals, family members, toys, vehicles, and clothing that the child can manipulate manually. Children vary in that some develop an early vocabulary almost exclusively of "thing" words and actions, whereas others develop a social language: words for social routines, expressions of love, and greetings. Researchers differ as to whether these are seen as different styles inherent in the child or whether their social **environment** encourages them in different ways. Researchers agree that the child learns most effectively from social and interactive routines with an accomplished talker (who may be an older child), and not, at least at the start, from passive observations of adults talking, or from radio or TV programs. Experiments and observations show that children pick up words at this stage most rapidly when the care giver uses them to name or comment on what the child is already focused on. Young children also frequently name objects at an intermediate level of abstraction known as the *basic object* level. That is, they will use the word "dog" rather than the more specific "collie," or the more general "animal." This coincides with the naming practices of most parents, and seems to be the level of greatest utility for the two-year old.

Most toddlers produce their first two-word sentence at 18 to 24 months, usually once they have acquired between 50 and 500 words. Before their first sentence, they often achieve the effect of complex expressions by stringing together their simple words—Book, Mine, Read—but then their first sentence puts these words under a single intonational envelope, with no pause. Their first sentences are not profound, but they represent a major advance in the expression of meaning. For children learning English, their first sentences are *telegraphic*, that is, content words predominate, primarily the nouns and verbs necessary in the situation. Words that have grammatical functions, but do not themselves make reference, such as articles, prepositions, and auxiliary verbs, do not occur very often.

The child's vocabulary grows enormously between the ages of two and five, and vocabulary size is frequently used by researchers as an index of the child's development. In addition to learning many new nouns and verbs, the child must organize vocabulary, for example, into hierarchies: that Rover is also a dog, a corgi, an animal, a living thing, and so on. The child also learns about opposites and relatedness—all necessary forms of connection among words in the "inner lexicon." The child also becomes better able to learn words from linguistic context alone, rapidly homing in on the meaning after only a few scattered exposures. This is a surprisingly effective process, though hardly fail-safe: after being told that screens were to stop flies from bringing germs into the house, one child concluded that germs were "things flies play with."

Researchers have been acutely aware that the child's language learning does not take place in a vacuum or a laboratory—it is enmeshed in the social relationships and circumstances of the child. The child uses language for communication with peers, siblings, parents, and increasingly, relative strangers. All of these individuals make special demands on the child in terms of their different status, knowledge, requirements of politeness, clarity or formality, to which the child must adjust and adapt, and the preschool child is only beginning this process of language socialization. Even four-year-olds adjust their style, pitch, and sentence length when talking to younger children or infants rather than peers or older people, and in other cultures they master formal devices that acknowledge the status or group membership of different people. It is recognized, however, that the three-year-old child is rather poor at predicting what others know or think, and therefore will be rather egocentric in expressing him or herself. Especially when communicating across a barrier or over a telephone, a child of this age might be unable to supply the right kind of information to a listener. However, other researchers show that children become increasingly adept at "repairing" their own communicative breakdowns as they get older.

Skill in producing a coherent narrative is one of the culminating achievements of language acquisition, but it is acquired late and varies widely according to opportunity for practice and experience with stories. In part, this is because creating a narrative is a cultural event: different cultures have different rules for how stories are structured, which much be learned. Initially, children tend to focus just on the actions, with little **attention** to the motives, or reasons, or consequences of those actions, and little overarching structure that might explain the events. Young children also fail to use the linguistic devices that maintain cohesion among referents, so they may switch from talking about one character to another and call them all "he," to the bewilderment of the listener. Reading and writing in the grade school years depends on this ability and nurture it further, and one of the best predictors of reading readiness is how much children were read to in the first few years. As children begin to read and write, there are further gains in their vocabulary (and new ways to acquire it) and new syntactic forms emerge that are relatively rare in speaking but play important roles in the text, such as stage-setting and maintaining cohesion. Mastery of these devices requires a sensitivity to the reader's needs, and it is a lifelong developmental process.

Further Reading

Berko-Gleason, J. *The Development of Language*. New York: Macmillan, 1993.

Goodluck, H. *Language Acquisition: A Linguistic Introduction.* Cambridge, MA: Blackwell Publishers, 1991.

Law of Effect

A principle associated with learning and behavior which states that behaviors that lead to satisfying outcomes are more likely to be repeated than behaviors that lead to unwanted outcomes.

Psychologists have been interested in the factors that are important in behavior change and control since psychology emerged as a discipline. One of the first principles associated with learning and behavior was the Law of Effect, which states that behaviors that lead to satisfying outcomes are likely to be repeated, whereas behaviors that lead to undesired outcomes are less likely to recur.

This principle, which most learning theorists accept as valid, was developed by **Edward Lee Thorndike**, who provided the basis for the field of **operant conditioning**. Prior to Thorndike, many psychologists interested in animal behavior attributed learning to reasoning on the animal's part. Thorndike instead theorized that animals learn by trial and error. When something works to the animal's satisfaction, the animal draws a connection or association between the behavior and positive outcome. This association forms the basis for later behavior. When the animal makes an error, on the other hand, no association is formed between the behavior that led to the error and a positive outcome, so the ineffective behavior is less likely to recur.

Initially, Thorndike drew parallels between positive outcomes, which would be termed **reinforcement**s by the behaviorists, and negative outcomes, which would be referred to as **punishment**s. Later, however, he asserted that punishment was ineffective in removing the connection between the behavior and the result. Instead, he suggested that, following a punishment, behavior was likely to be less predictable.

Thorndike also developed his Law of Exercise, which states that responses that occur in a given situation become more strongly associated with that situation. He suggested that these two laws could account for all behavior. As such, psychologists had no need to refer to abstract thought in defining the way that behavior is learned. Everything is associated with the effects of reward and punishment, according to Thorndike.

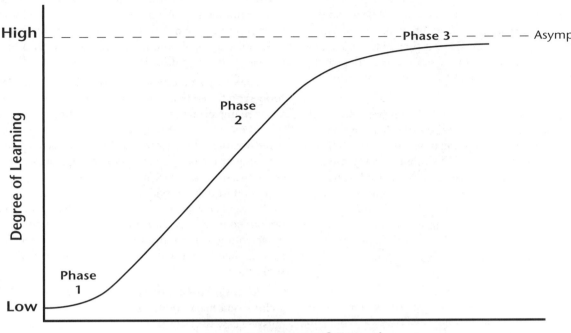

High ⎯ ⎯ ⎯ ⎯ ⎯ ⎯ ⎯ ⎯ ⎯ ⎯ ⎯ ⎯ ⎯ ⎯ ⎯ ⎯ ⎯ –Phase 3– ⎯ ⎯ ⎯ ⎯ Asymptote

Phase
2

Degree of Learning

Phase
1

Low

Amount of Practice

The learning curve illustrates the process of learning new information or acquiring a new skill. The asymptote represent the maximal level of performance, after which no further improvement is possible.

Further Reading

Clifford, G. J. *Edward L. Thorndike: The Sane Positivist.* Middletown, PA: Wesleyan University Press, 1984.
Mackintosh, N. J. *Conditioning and Associative Learning.* New York: Oxford University Press, 1983.

Learned Helplessness

A condition of extreme, pathological helplessness in an individual that arises after exposure to a series of unavoidable or inescapable negative experiences, considered to be learned behavior.

It has been argued that based on their experiences of actual powerlessness to positively affect their circumstances, individuals who display learned helplessness form a belief that such powerlessness is a constant and necessary component of their lives. The persistence of this belief, even in the presence of obvious evidence that it is false, is characteristic of this condition.

Further Reading

Peterson, Christopher. *Learned Helplessness.* New York: Oxford University Press, 1993.

Learning. See **Learning Theory**.

Learning Curve

The timeline of learning.

When a person is introduced to new information or a new skill, it may take several learning sessions to acquire that knowledge or skill. Psychologists refer to this acquisition process as the learning curve. In general, this term refers to the time it takes an individual to develop knowledge or a new skill.

Behavioral psychologists have noted that the degree, or strength, of learning reflects three factors. First, the degree of learning is associated with the number of **reinforcement**s received during the acquisition of the behavior. In animal research, these reinforcements may be food pellets; in human research, the reinforcement may simply be knowledge about the number of correct and incorrect answers. In general, as the reinforcement increases, so does the performance level.

Second, there is a maximal level of performance associated with any behavior. This maximum is called the asymptote. Once this asymptote is reached, no further improvement in performance is possible.

Third, the greatest increase in the acquisition of the behavior will occur in the initial phases of learning. As the performance of the behavior approaches the asymptote, there is increasingly less room for further improvement.

Psychologists often use graphs to depict learning curves. The amount of practice at a task appears on the horizontal axis; the strength or accuracy of a response is recorded on the vertical axis. For a single individual, the tendency is to improve over time or practice, although an improvement may be temporarily followed by a decline in performance.

When a large number of individuals are tested and their average performance plotted, the learning curve gives the appearance of a gradual, smooth improvement over time. In the hypothetical learning curve in the accompanying graph, phase one reflects a period of familiarization with the task in which little learning takes place. In the second phase, there is a great deal of learning over a short period of time. In the final phase, the degree of learning is approaching asymptote, that is, the maximum. Any further change in performance will be minimal.

Further Reading

Teplitz, Charles J. *The Learning Curve Deskbook: A Reference Guide to Theory, Calculations, and Applications.* New York: Quorum Books, 1991.

Learning Disability

An umbrella term describing learning problems that are not attributed to low intelligence, inadequate education, physical disability, or emotional disturbance.

Learning disabilities generally include difficulties in communicating or reading, but can encompass many different combinations of symptoms involving behavioral, social, or motor problems. Some types of learning disabilities are thought to affect between two and five percent of the literate population worldwide. They occur with equal frequency in persons of varying **intelligence** and socioeconomic levels but are four times more common in males than in females.

Persons with learning disabilities may have trouble with either receptive language (comprehending written and spoken words) or expressive language (speaking and writing). Specific problems include failure to comprehend either abstract or concrete terms, difficulty connecting words within a sentence or sentences within a paragraph, and trouble recognizing groups of words. Short-term **memory** problems are also common, as are letter or word reversal, and difficulties with categorization and problem-solving. In addition to these cognitive difficulties, learning disabilities can affect people, especially children, socially and emotionally. Lack of success at academic tasks that pose no comparable problem for their peers threaten children's self-esteem and social **ad-**

justment and can lead to social withdrawal, psychosomatic symptoms, or disruptive classroom behavior. This issue is further complicated by the fact that the disruptive behavior may be due to hyperactivity, which often accompanies learning disorders.

The most common learning disability is **dyslexia**, formerly referred to as "word blindness," which involves a severe impairment of reading and writing ability. Dyslexics commonly reverse letters and words, exhibit disordered writing with chaotic spelling, and have difficulty repeating or recalling long words or sequences of letters or numbers. It also takes them longer than other people to process information: one of the major characteristics of dyslexics in an academic setting is that they require extra time to complete assignments and exams. **Aphasia**, another common learning disability, affects speech and hearing, interfering with the ability to understand words spoken at normal speeds.

Attention deficit hyperactivity disorder (ADHD), a childhood behavioral syndrome characterized by impulsiveness, excitability, and non-goal-directed motor behavior, is also considered a learning disability, since it is associated with perceptual and learning difficulties in individuals of normal intelligence. ADHD involves attention problems that interfere with learning, including an inability to concentrate, difficulty in finishing tasks, and a tendency to be easily distracted. Students with ADHD have trouble organizing and carrying out assignments and, like persons with dyslexia, they often benefit by being given extra time in which to complete written work. While ADHD is considered a childhood disorder, its characteristic **attention** difficulties have been shown to persist beyond **adolescence**.

Public Law 94–142, the 1977 act guaranteeing equal educational opportunities to handicapped persons, included learning disabilities in its definition of "handicapped," thus requiring the provision of services to the learning disabled by all states and localities. Children exhibiting signs of learning disabilities are identified as early as possible so that remediation can begin, as well as accommodation by such means as substituting oral for written work when needed, as appropriate. Learning disabled students are offered special college and career counseling, and both public and private colleges and universities commonly offer special services, such as tutors and note takers, to students with documented learning disabilities.

Further Reading

Cruickshank, William M. *Learning Disabilities: The Struggle from Adolescence Toward Adulthood.* Syracuse, NY: Syracuse University Press, 1980.

Dockrell, Julie. *Children's Learning Difficulties: A Cognitive Approach.* Cambridge, MA: Blackwell, 1993.

Farnham-Diggory, Sylvia. *The Learning-Disabled Child.* Cambridge, MA: Harvard University Press, 1992.

Learning Theory

Theory about how people learn and modify pre-existing thoughts and behavior.

Psychologists have suggested a variety of theories to explain the process of learning. During the first half of the 20th century, American psychologists approached the concept of learning primarily in terms of behaviorist principles that focused on the automatic formation of associations between stimuli and responses. One form of associative learning—**classical conditioning**—is based on the pairing of two stimuli. Through an association with an unconditioned stimulus (such as meat offered to a dog), a **conditioned stimulus** (such as a bell) eventually elicits a **conditioned response** (salivation), even when the unconditioned stimulus is absent. Principles of classical conditioning include the **extinction** of the response if the conditioned and unconditioned stimuli cease to be paired, and the generalization of the response to stimuli that are similar but not identical to the original ones. In **operant conditioning**, a response is learned because it leads to a particular consequence (**reinforcement**), and it is strengthened each time it is reinforced. Positive reinforcement strengthens a response if it is presented afterwards, while negative reinforcement strengthens it by being withheld. Once a response has been learned, it may be sustained by partial reinforcement, which is provided only after selective responses.

In contrast to theories of classical and operant conditioning, which describe learning in terms of observable behavior, intervening variable theories introduce such elements as **memory**, **motivation**, and **cognition**. Edward Tolman demonstrated in the 1920s that learning can involve knowledge without observable performance. The performance of rats who negotiated the same maze on consecutive days with no reward improved drastically after the introduction of a goal box with food, leading to the conclusion that they had developed "cognitive maps" of the maze earlier, even in the absence of a reward, although this "latent learning" had not been reflected in their observable behavior. Even earlier, **Wolfgang Köhler**, a founder of the Gestalt school of psychology, had argued for the place of cognition in learning. Based on experiments conducted on the island of Tenerife during World War I, Köhler concluded that insight played a role in problem-solving by chimpanzees. Rather than simply stumbling on solutions through trial and error, the animals he observed seemed to demonstrate a holistic un-

By watching his father use a camera, this two-year old can imitate the behavior with a toy through the process Albert Bandura termed modeling.

derstanding of problems, such as getting hold of fruit that was placed out of reach, by arriving at solutions in a sudden moment of revelation or insight.

The **drive-reduction theory** of Clark L. Hull and Kenneth W. Spence, which became influential in the 1930s, introduced motivation as an intervening variable in the form of homeostasis, the tendency to maintain equilibrium by adjusting physiological responses. An imbalance creates **need**s, which in turn create drives. Actions can be seen as attempts to reduce these drives by meeting the associated needs. According to drive-reduction theory, the association of stimulus and response in classical and operant conditioning only results in learning if accompanied by drive reduction.

In recent decades, cognitive theories such as those of social learning theorist **Albert Bandura** have been influential. Bandura is particularly known for his work on observational learning, also referred to as **modeling** or **imitation**. It is common knowledge that children learn by watching their parents, other adults, and their peers. According to Bandura, the extent to which children and adults learn behaviors through imitation is influenced not only by the observed activity itself but also by its consequences. Behavior that is rewarded is more readily imitated than behavior that is punished. Bandura coined the term "vicarious conditioning" for learning based on the observed consequences of others' actions, listing the following requirements for this type of learning: **attention** to the behavior; retention of what is seen; **ability** to reproduce the behavior; and motivation. Cognitive approaches such as Bandura's have led to an enhanced understanding of how **conditioning** works, while conditioning principles have helped researchers better understand certain facets of cognition.

Computers play an important role in current research on learning, both in the areas of computer-assisted learning and in the attempt to further understand the neurological processes involved in learning through the development of computer-based neural networks that can simulate various forms of learning.

Further Reading

Bower, G. H., and E. Hilgard. *Theories of Learning.* 5th ed. Englewood Cliffs, NJ: Prentice-Hall, 1981.

Grippin, Pauline. *Learning Theory and Learning Outcomes: The Connection.* Lanham, MD: University Press of America, 1984.

Norman, D.A. *Learning and Memory.* San Francisco: Freeman, 1982.

Learning-to-Learn

The phenomenon of greater improvement in speed of learning as one's experience with learning increases.

When people try to learn a new behavior, the first attempts are often not very successful. After a time, however, they seem to get the idea of the behavior and the pace of learning increases. This phenomenon of greater improvement in speed of learning is called learning-to-learn (LTL). There are two general reasons for the existence of LTL. First, negative transfer diminishes. When people have learned to do something, they have often developed schemas or learning sets, that is, ways to approach those tasks. When a new behavior is required, old approaches that may be irrelevant or that may get in the way must be discarded. Learning becomes easier when irrelevant or distracting behaviors disappear. Second, there may be positive transfer of previous knowledge that might be usefully applied to the situation.

Learning-to-learn is most obvious in tasks that are somewhat complicated or varied. LTL occurs when the learner realizes how the various components of an overall behavior fit together. When learners must deal with a lot of information, they can develop the required higher order principles that allow them to develop a general perspective on the behavior. As a result, subsequent learning fits together because it fits in more naturally with the person's overall perspective. When the behavior to be learned is simple, no such perspective is needed, so LTL is less relevant.

Left-Brain Hemisphere

The hemisphere of the brain that specializes in spoken and written language, logic, number skills, and scientific concepts.

The left-brain hemisphere neurologically controls the right side of the body and is connected to the **right-brain hemisphere** by an extensive bundle of over a million **nerve** fibers called the corpus callosum. Scientific study of the **brain** hemispheres dates back to the 1800s. In the 1860s, French physician Paul Broca (1824–1880) observed speech dysfunction in patients with lesions on the left frontal lobes of their brains. Initially, the discovery of specialized functioning of the right and left sides of the brain led to the assumption that all higher reasoning **ability** resided in the left-brain hemisphere, which was thus regarded as dominant overall. The right-brain hemisphere was thought to possess only lower-level capabilities and was considered subordinate to the left-brain hemisphere.

Interest in the functions of the brain hemispheres was revived in the 1960s, with Roger Sperry's studies of patients who had the corpus callosum severed to control epileptic seizures. It was discovered that each hemisphere of the brain specialized in performing certain types of functions, a phenomenon now known as *lateralization*. While the left-brain hemisphere performs functions involving logic and language more efficiently, the right-brain hemisphere is more adept in the areas of music, art, and spatial relations. Each hemisphere processes information differently; the left-brain hemisphere is thought to function in a logical and sequential way; the right appears to synthesize material simultaneously. These differences can also be investigated in normal patients (in whom the hemispheres are connected) by temporarily disabling a single brain hemisphere with sodium amytal, a fast-acting barbiturate, and by other means.

Lateralization varies considerably among individuals. Two factors known to affect it are **handedness** and gender. In one experiment, almost all right-handed persons were unable to speak when their left-brain hemispheres were disabled. In contrast, the incidence decreased to 20 to 40 percent among left-handed people, indicating that only this percentage had their speech centers located in the left-brain hemisphere. Other left-handed subjects appear to use both hemispheres for speech. In general, each gender is known to excel at certain lateralized functions: women are more adept in language-based skills, perceptual fluency tasks (such as identifying matching terms rapidly), and arithmetic calculations. Men are generally more proficient in envisioning and manipulating objects in space. It has also been found that brain function in males is more lateralized than in females. Men who have had one brain hemisphere disabled are more debilitated than similarly affected women. In particular, men display more language difficulties than women when the left hemisphere is damaged. However, it is also known that the sexes are more dependent on different areas of each hemisphere, so the assessment of function after damage also depends on where the damage is localized. In addition, conclusions about lateralization and gender are complicated by the fact that those functions at which members of a particular gender appear to be more adept are often those they are likely to have done more of (such as men manipulating tools), raising the question of **environment**al as opposed to biological factors.

When the left-brain hemisphere is damaged, the result is often severe **aphasia**—difficulty using or understanding spoken or written language. Damage localized in the left temporal cortex can cause Wernicke's aphasia, which disturbs the ability to comprehend language. A different condition, called Broca's aphasia, results from damage to the left frontal cortex and interferes with a person's ability to produce language. Persons affected with this disorder experience halting speech, and they often have difficulty recalling even the most familiar words.

Additional methods for studying brain hemispheres include autopsies of cadavers that reveal the location of brain lesions, observation of dysfunction in living patients with known brain lesions, and electrical stimulation of various areas of the brain. **Biofeedback** instruments have also contributed to the body of knowledge about brain hemispheres; when wired to a research subject, they show a higher electrical discharge from whichever hemisphere is active at a given point in time, while recording alpha rhythms from an inactive hemisphere. Researchers have also made use of the discovery that the eyes will typically move away from the more active hemisphere and toward the side of the body controlled by that hemisphere.

See also Cerebellum; Cerebral Cortex.

Left-Handedness

The tendency to use the left hand more frequently than the right hand.

Because control of movement in the human body is specialized, the cerebral hemisphere of the **brain** which is opposite from that side of the body, movement in left-handed people is controlled by the **right-brain hemisphere.** Research has shown that most people who use their left hands to write, hammer a nail, and throw a ball still have their language centers on the left side of the brain. In a 1981 study conducted by Springer and Deutsch, 95 percent of right-handers had speech localized on the left side of the brain and 70 percent of left-handers showed the same pattern. However, for 15 percent of left-handers, the right hemisphere controls speech. The remaining 15 percent of left-handers have bilateral (both hemispheres) control of speech processes. This research suggests that even though the right hemisphere is dominant in control of movement on the left side of the body (i.e., **handedness**), other types of motor skills are often localized in the same brain areas as for right-handers.

It is interesting to note that the expression of handedness differs widely across cultures. For example, it is speculated that ancient cultures, for hygiene purposes, kept the right hand clean for eating and used the left hand for dirtier tasks. Thus, it may be that more people appear to be right handed because of cultural constraints.

See also Right-Handedness.

Further Reading
Coren, Stanley. *The Left-Hander Syndrome: The Causes and Consequences of Left-Handedness.* New York: Vintage Books, 1993.

Libido

In Freudian psychology, a term designating psychic or sexual energy.

The term libido, which **Sigmund Freud** used as early as 1894 and as late as the 1930s, underwent changes as he expanded, developed, and revised his theories of **sexuality**, **personality** development, and **motivation**. In Freud's early works, it is associated specifically with sexuality. Libido is central to the theory of **psychosexual development** outlined in *Three Essays on the Theory of Sexuality* (1905). It is the energy that is repeatedly redirected to different erogenous zones throughout the stages of pregenital sexuality (oral, anal, phallic) that take place between **birth** and the age of about five years. After the latency period, the libido reemerges in its mature manifestation at the genital stage that begins in **adolescence**. During all these permutations, the libido also shifts from being primarily autoerotic and narcissistic to being directed at a love object.

When Freud reformulated his theory of motivation around 1920, he defined libido more broadly in terms of opposed life and death instincts (Eros and Thanatos). Libido in this context is the source of the life instincts that motivate not only sexuality and other basic drives but also more complex human activities such as the creation of art.

Further Reading

Freud, Sigmund. *New Introductory Lectures on Psychoanalysis*. New York: W. W. Norton, 1933.

Hall, Calvin S. *A Primer of Freudian Psychology*. New York: Harper and Row, 1982.

Localization (Brain Function)

Refers to the concept that different areas of the brain control different aspects of behavior.

Theories of localization first gained scientific credence in the 1860s with Paul Broca's discovery that damage to a specific part of the **brain**—the left frontal lobe—was associated with speech impairment. Other discoveries followed: in 1874, Carl Wernicke identified the part of the brain responsible for receptive speech (the upper rear part of the left temporal lobe, known as Wernicke's area), and in 1870 Gustav Fritsch and J. L. Hitzig found that stimulating different parts of the **cerebral cortex** produced movement in different areas of the body. By the beginning of the twentieth century, detailed maps were available showing the functions of the different areas of the brain.

Not all researchers have agreed with theories of localization, however. An influential conflicting view is the equipotential theory, which asserts that all areas of the brain are equally active in overall mental functioning. According to this theory, the effects of damage to the brain are determined by the extent rather than the location of the damage. Early exponents of this view—including Goldstein and Lashley—believed that basic motor and sensory functions are localized, but that higher mental functions are not. There is still controversy between adherents of the localization and equipotential theories of brain function. Some experts advocate a combination of the two theories, while others search for new alternatives, such as that proposed by J. Hughlings Jackson in 1973. Jackson claimed that the most basic skills were localized but that most complex mental functions combined these so extensively that the whole brain was actually involved in most types of behavior.

Further Reading

Corballis, Michael C. *The Lopsided Ape: Evolution of the Generative Mind*. New York: Oxford University Press, 1991.

Edwards, Betty. *Drawing on the Right Side of the Brain*. Los Angeles: J. P. Tarcher, 1979.

Hampden-Turner, Charles. *Maps of the Mind*. New York: Collier Books, 1981.

Localization (Sensory)

The ability of animals and humans to determine the origin of a sensory input.

One of the highly developed abilities that humans and other animals possess is the **ability** to determine where a sensory input originates.

The capacity to localize a sound, for example, depends on two general mechanisms. The first is relevant for low **frequency** (i.e., low pitch) sounds and involves the fact that sound coming from a given source arrives at our ears at slightly different times. The second mechanisms applies to high frequency (i.e., high pitch) sounds; if such a sound comes from one side, one ear hears it more loudly than the other and we can detect location based on differences in the loudness of the sound at each ear.

Low frequency sounds that come from the noise-making source will enter the nearer ear first; these sound waves will bend around our head and arrive at the far ear a short time later. If the sound is almost directly in front of us, the sound arrives at one ear an extremely short time ahead of its arrival at the other ear. Humans can detect differences of perhaps 10 millionths of a second in arrival time. If the sound comes from the side, the difference in time of arrival at the two ears is longer. In either case, our **brain** executes quick computations to inform us about the location of the sound. Other animals, like nocturnal owls, have shown greater sensitivity to differences in time of arrival.

The second mechanism involves intensity differences in sound waves traveling to the ears. High frequency sound waves do not bend around the head like low frequency waves. Instead, high frequency sound waves tend to reflect off the surface of the head. As a consequence, a sound coming from one side of the head will show greater intensity in one ear; that is, it will be slightly louder in one ear. The brain uses this intensity difference to tell us where a sound originates.

In general, we locate sounds below about 1500 Hz (i.e., 1500 cycles per second) by analyzing differences in time of arrival at each ear; above 1500 Hz, we use intensity differences. Sounds that are right around 1500 Hz are hardest to localize. Further, we are likely to confuse sounds that are directly in front of us, above us, and behind us because their positions are such that we cannot use time of arrival and intensity differences.

Finally, sometimes we ignore the cues for sound localization if logic tells us that the sound should be coming from another direction. For example, when we listen to somebody on a stage, we may hear the sounds they produce from a loudspeaker that is above us. Nonetheless, we localize the sound as coming from the person on the stage because it seems more logical. Psychologists refer to this phenomenon as "visual capture."

Further Reading

Corballis, Michael C. *The Lopsided Ape: Evolution of the Generative Mind.* New York: Oxford University Press, 1991.
Hampden-Turner, Charles. *Maps of the Mind.* New York: Collier Books, 1981

Longitudinal Study

A research method used to study changes in individual or group behavior over an extended period of time by repeatedly measuring the same subjects.

Longitudinal research is one of two major methods used in **developmental psychology.** The other is cross-sectional research, in which members of different age groups are studied at the same point in time. In longitudinal research, results are recorded for the same *cohort,* or group of subjects, throughout the course of the study.

An example of a longitudinal study might be an examination of the effects of premature **birth** on a child's **memory** development by selecting a group of premature infants and a group of normal term infants and testing each group repeatedly at different points across a span of time. An advantage of the longitudinal study is that it allows the researcher to focus on the same subjects as they mature; it also records developmental patterns and determines how specific characteristics can affect later development, thus tracing continuity or stability in those subjects across time. A disadvantage of the longitudinal study is that researchers must wait for their subjects to age in order to obtain the results, and during this time some may drop out of the study for a variety of reasons. Another disadvantage is that some of the changes observed in members of the cohort group may actually be due to the effects of the assessment itself.

See also Cross-sectional Study Methods; Research Methods.

Mania

A description of the condition opposite depression in manic-depressive psychosis, or bipolar disorder. It is characterized by a mood of elation without apparent reason.

Most episodes of mania—elation without reasonable cause or justification—are followed in short order by **depression**; together they represent the opposites described as **bipolar disorder**. Manic episodes are characterized by intense feelings of energy and enthusiasm, uncharacteristic self-confidence, continuous talking, and little need for **sleep**. People experiencing a manic period tend to make grandiose plans and maintain inflated beliefs about their own personal abilities. While manic people appear to be joyful and celebratory, their mood corresponds little to conditions they are experiencing in reality. Expressions of **hostility** and irritability also are common during manic episodes.

Further Reading

Duke, Patty. *Call Me Anna.* New York: Bantam, 1987.

Jamison, Kay. *Touched with Fire: Manic-Depressive Illness and the Artistic Temperament.* New York: Free Press, 1993

Manic-Depressive Psychosis. See **Bipolar Disorder.**

Marijuana

The common name of a small number of varieties of Cannabis sativa, *or Indian hemp plant, which contain tetrahydrocannabinol (THC), a psychoactive drug.*

Cannabis, in the form of marijuana, hashish (a dried resinous material that seeps from cannabis leaves and is more potent than marijuana), or other cannabinoids, is probably the most often used illegal substance in the world. In the United States, marijuana use became widespread among young people in the 1960s. By 1979, 68 percent of young adults between the ages of 18 and 25 had experimented with it at least once, and it was reported that as of the same year the total number of people in the U.S. who had tried the drug was 50 million. In the late 1980s, it was estimated that about 50 to 60 percent of people between the ages of 21 and 29 had tried marijuana at least once.

Marijuana and hashish are usually smoked, but may also be ingested orally, and are sometimes added to food or beverages. The psychoactive substance of cannabis is tetrahydrocannabinol, or THC, especially delta-9-tetrahydrocannabinol. Delta-9-THC can be synthesized, is known to affect the **central nervous system,** and has been legally used to treat side-effects of **chemotherapy** and weight loss in persons affected with **AIDS.** Other legal therapeutic uses of marijuana include the treatment of glaucoma and **epilepsy.**

The effects of cannabis use vary from individual to individual, depending on the physical and psychological condition of the user, the amount of THC consumed, and many other factors. Technically, marijuana is classified as a hallucinogen, but its effects are usually much milder than those of other **drugs** in this category, such as LSD, mescaline, and psilocybin. When it is inhaled through a marijuana cigarette, THC reaches its highest concentration in the blood within a half hour, and is absorbed by the **brain** and other organs, and can affect **consciousness** for several hours. THC can remain stored in body fat for several weeks. Marijuana users commonly experience feelings of euphoria, self-confidence, reduced inhibition, relaxation, and a floating sensation. Feelings of giddiness and mild feelings of **paranoia** are also common. Physiological effects include increases in pulse and heart rates, reddened eyes, dryness of the mouth, and an increased appetite. The initial euphoric feelings after ingesting marijuana are generally followed by sleepiness. Although marijuana has been known to produce psychological dependence, there is little tendency to become physically dependent on it, and withdrawal from the drug does not pose medical problems. Recently, receptors for THC have been discovered in the brain, together with a naturally-occurring substance—anandamide—that binds the chemical to its receptors and may be a **neurotransmitter.**

Documented negative effects of marijuana use include impairment in **perception,** sensory motor coordination, short-term **memory,** and **panic** attacks, and is also linked to impairment of the immune system, lowered testosterone levels in males, and chromosome damage. If taken by pregnant women, marijuana affects the developing fetus. Long-term marijuana smokers display similar respiratory dysfunctions as tobacco smokers In research on rats, THC has been found to destroy cells in the hippocampus, a part of the brain that is important in the formation of new memories. Psychologically, chronic use of marijuana has been associated with a loss of ambition known as amotivational syndrome. Authorities differ with respect to the physical and psychological risks of short-term and long-term use/abuse of cannabis. Current penalties for the illegal possession of marijuana, hashish, or other form of cannabis can be extremely severe.

See also Drugs.

Further Reading
Grinspoon, Lester. *Marijuana Reconsidered.* Oakland, CA: Quick American Archives, 1994.

Marriage Counseling

A clinical specialty of family and marital therapy.

There are many different approaches to marriage counseling, which may be used alone or combined with other methods by the therapist. Among the oldest is the psychodynamic approach, which attributes problems within a marriage to the unresolved conflicts and **need**s of each spouse. Each client's personal history and underlying motivations are central to this mode of therapy. Therapists using this approach apply the principles of psychoanalysis in their treatment; they may either treat both marriage partners individually, or treat one spouse in collaboration with another therapist who treats the other.

Marriage counseling that follows a systems approach stresses the interaction between partners as the origin of marital difficulties, rather than their actions or **personality**. Behavior and communication patterns are analyzed as well as the interlocking roles portrayed by the couple or members of the family. Family members may be conditioned to consistently play "the strong one" or "the weak one," or such other roles as "scapegoat," "caretaker," or "clown." Although initially it may seem that only one member of a family system is troubled, on closer inspection his or her difficulties are often found to be symptomatic of an unhealthy pattern in which all the members play an active part. Systems theory is actually an umbrella term for a range of therapies, and systems-oriented counseling may take a variety of forms, including both short- and long-term therapy.

A popular individual treatment approach also used in marriage counseling is Rogerian or **client-centered therapy**, also referred to as humanistic therapy. Here, the emphasis is on communication and the open sharing of feelings. Through specially formulated exercises, couples work on improving their speaking and listening skills and enhancing their capacity for emotional honesty. Another widely employed mode of marriage counseling is based on a behavioral approach, in which marital problems are treated as dysfunctional behaviors that can be observed and modified. Couples are made aware of destructive behavior patterns, often by systematically recording their behavior until certain patterns emerge. The therapist then coaches them in various modifying strategies with the goal of achieving positive, mutually reinforcing interactions. Behavior-oriented therapy also focuses on improving a couple's problem-solving and **conflict-resolution** skills.

Marriage counselors may conduct therapy sessions with both spouses, treating one as the primary client and the other one only occasionally, while another therapist treats the other spouse. An increasing number of therapists counsel couples in pairs, with married therapists sometimes working together as a team. Theoretically, the relationship between the co-therapists is supposed to serve as a model for their clients. Marriage counseling in groups, which is becoming increasingly common, offers clients some of the same advantages that group therapy offers individuals. Sex counseling, which had previously been part of marital therapy, emerged as an independent field following the pioneering work of **William Masters** and Virginia Johnson in the 1950s and 1960s. Couples seeking treatment for sexual dysfunction have the option of working with a sex therapist.

Marriage counseling is usually practiced by licensed individuals with specialized training in psychology, psychiatry, and counseling, or by persons without such training, including members of the clergy. The first marriage counseling centers were established in the 1930s, and the American Association of Marriage and Family Therapy (formally the American Association of Marriage Counselors) was founded in 1942.

Further Reading
Brammer, Lawrence M. *Therapeutic Psychology: Fundamentals of Counseling and Psychotherapy.* 5th ed. Englewood Cliffs, NJ: Prentice Hall, 1989.

Ronch, Judah L, William van Ornum, and Nicholas C. Stilwell, eds. *The Counseling Sourcebook: A Practical Reference on Contemporary Issues.* New York: Crossroad, 1994.

Maslow, Abraham (1908–1970)

American psychologist.

A central figure in humanistic psychology and in the **human potential movement**, Abraham Maslow is known especially for his theory of **motivation**. He was born and raised in Brooklyn, New York, and received his Ph.D. in psychology from the University of Wisconsin in 1934. Maslow then began medical studies, which he discontinued within a year, after which he was offered a postdoctoral research fellowship to work with **Edward Thorndike** at Columbia University. After moving to New York, Maslow met many prominent European psychologists and social scientists who had fled Nazi Germany. Several of these emigrés became his mentors, including psychoanalysts **Alfred Adler**, **Erich Fromm**, and **Karen Horney** and Gestalt psychologists Max Wertheimer (1880–1943) and Kurt Koffka (1886–1941). In 1937 Maslow began teaching at the newly opened Brooklyn College. At the urging of anthropologist Ruth Benedict (1887–1948), whom Maslow had met at Columbia, he spent the summer of 1938 doing field work on a Blackfoot Indian reservation in Alberta, Canada, with financial support from the Social Science Research Council. In 1951 Maslow became the head of the psychology department at Brandeis University, where he remained until a year before his death in 1970.

During the 1940s, Maslow began to work out his theory of human motivation, which was eventually published in *Motivation and Human Personality* in 1954. Rejecting the determinism of both the psychoanalytic and behaviorist approaches, Maslow took an optimistic approach to human behavior that emphasized developing one's full potential. Instead of basing his psychological model on people with mental and emotional problems, he used as his point of reference a collection of exceptionally dynamic and successful historical and contemporary figures whom he considered "self-actualizers," including Thomas Jefferson (1743–1826), Abraham Lincoln (1809–1865), Jane Addams (1860–1935), Albert Einstein (1879–1955), and Eleanor Roosevelt (1884–1962). In addition to drawing up a list of the common traits of self-actualized individuals, Maslow placed **self-actualization** at the peak of his hierarchy of human motivations, the concept for which he is best known today.

This hierarchy is generally portrayed as a pyramid with five levels, ranging from the most basic **need**s at the

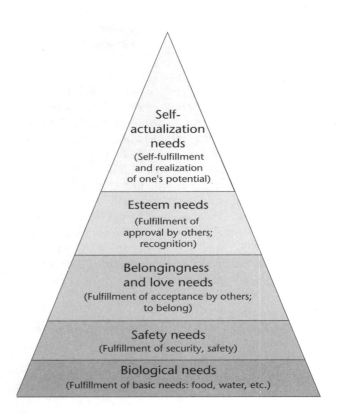

Maslow's hierarchy of needs.

bottom to the most complex and sophisticated at the top. From bottom to top, the levels are biological needs (food, water, shelter); safety; belongingness and love; the need to be esteemed by others; and self-actualization, the need to realize one's full potential. According to Maslow, the needs at each level must be met before one can move on to the next level. With so many other issues to concern them, the vast majority of people never grapple with self-actualization; Maslow considered fewer than one percent of the population to be self-actualized individuals. However, he believed that all human beings still possessed an innate (if unmet) need to reach this state.

During the 1950s and 1960s, Maslow became associated with the movement known as humanistic psychology, which he also referred to as the Third Force because it offered an alternative to the prevailing schools of **psychoanalysis** and **behaviorism** in both theory and therapeutic practice. Like Maslow, colleagues such as **Carl Rogers** and Rollo May rejected the idea that human behavior was determined by childhood events or **conditioning** and stressed instead the individual's power to grow and change in the present. They believed that the goal of **psychotherapy** was to remove the obstacles that prevented their clients from self-actualizing.

As humanistic psychology gave birth to the human potential movement of the 1960s, Maslow became one of its central figures, lecturing at the Esalen Institute at Big Sur, California, which offered workshops by psychologists, social scientists, philosophers, and other intellectual figures. During these years, he also popularized the concept of the peak experience, an unusual moment of extreme joy, serenity, beauty, or wonder that he believed was closely related to self-actualization. In 1967 and 1968, Maslow served as president of the **American Psychological Association**. In 1969, he moved to Menlo Park, California, where he died of a heart attack a year later. In his lifetime Maslow published over 100 articles in magazines and professional journals. His other books include *Toward a Psychology of Being* (1962), *Religions, Values, and Peak Experiences* (1964), *Eupsychian Management* (1965), *The Psychology of Science* (1966), and a posthumous collection of papers entitled *The Farther Reaches of Human Nature* (1971).

Further Reading
Hoffman, Edward. *The Right to be Human: A Biography of Abraham Maslow.* Los Angeles: Tarcher, 1988.

Maslow's Hierarchy of Needs. See Maslow, Abraham.

Masochism. See Paraphilia.

Masters, William (1915–)

American physician and researcher who, in collaboration with Virginia Johnson, pioneered in the physiological study of human sexual function.

William Masters was born in Cleveland, Ohio, grew up in Kansas City, and did his undergraduate work at Hamilton College. He received his M.D. degree in 1943 from the University of Rochester School of Medicine, where he assisted in the laboratory research of George Washington Corner, who was studying and comparing the reproductive systems of animals and humans. Masters's interest in the study of **sexuality** was reinforced when he learned of the research done by Alfred Kinsey (1894–1956) at the University of Indiana, where he had interviewed men and women about their sexual experiences. Masters completed his internship and residency at St. Louis Hospital and Barnes Hospital, choosing obstetrics and gynecology as a speciality. He also did an internship in pathology at the Washington University School of Medicine.

In 1947, Masters was appointed to the faculty of Washington University, where he conducted research in areas including **hormone**-replacement therapy for postmenopausal women. In 1954, he began researching the physiology of sex by collecting data about sexual stimulation in a laboratory situation. His work, which took place at Washington University, was supported by a grant from the United States Institute of Health. By 1956, Virginia Johnson, a sociology student, was assisting Masters interview and screen research volunteers. Over an 11-year period, Masters studied 382 women and 312 men ranging in age from 18 to 89, recording their sexual responses using electrocardiographs and **electroencephalographs.**

Masters established the Reproductive Biology Research Foundation in 1964. Two years later, Masters and Johnson published the results of their long-term laboratory investigation of the physiology of human sexual activity in *Human Sexual Response*. This book is generally considered to be the first major scientific analysis of the subject, and was produced to provide physicians and **psychologists** with factual information useful in the treatment of sexual dysfunction. Despite the book's promotion solely as a serious research work, it won wide popular acclaim, and its authors were soon in demand as speakers and lecturers.

Since 1959, Masters and Johnson had been applying their studies to counseling sexually dysfunctional couples, working together as a team so that each member of a couple would have a therapist of the same sex to relate to. Having found sexual functioning susceptible to **conditioning,** much like other human and animal behaviors, they used learning strategies based on the theories of **Ivan Pavlov, B. F. Skinner,** Wolpe, and others. Following the principles of **operant conditioning** and **desensitization,** they helped their patients "unlearn" blocks involving **arousal** and/or orgasm. Masters and Johnson were married in 1971 and became co-directors of the Masters and Johnson Institute in 1973. In their 1979 work, *Homosexuality in Perspective*, Masters and Johnson detailed the results of studies based on the responses of homosexuals and lesbians, whose sexual preferences they claimed to be able to change.

Masters retired from private practice in gynecology in 1981, although he and his wife continued to operate the Masters and Johnson Institute, which moved to a new location that year. In 1988, they co-authored the book *Crisis: Heterosexual Behavior in the Age of AIDS* with Robert Kolodny, attracting criticism within the medical community—including that of then Attorney General C. Everett Koop—for their prediction that the **AIDS** epidemic would spread to the heterosexual population. Masters and Johnson were divorced in 1992, ending their work together at the Institute. Their other books include *Human Sexual Inadequacy* (1970), *The Pleasure Bond* (1974), *Human Sexuality* (1988), and *Heterosexuality* (1994).

Further Reading

Robinson, Paul. *The Modernization of Sex.* New York: Harper & Row, 1976.

Masturbation. See **Autoeroticism**.

Mead, Margaret (1901–1978)

American anthropologist whose work emphasized the relationship between culture and personality formation.

Margaret Mead was born in Philadelphia to a family of educators. In her youth, her main influences were her mother and maternal grandmother, both of whom had raised families and also pursued careers. Mead's formal education before entering college was sporadic, and she was mainly educated at home by her grandmother. An unhappy year at DePauw University turned Mead against coeducation, and she subsequently transferred to Barnard College. She first concentrated in English and **psychology** but became interested in anthropology under the influence of Columbia University anthropologists Franz Boas (1858–1942) and Ruth Benedict (1887–1948). Boas was urgently organizing ethnographic investigations of primitive cultures throughout the world before eventual contact with modern society, and he convinced Mead that she could make a contribution to this burgeoning field. After receiving her M.A. in psychology in 1924, she conducted her first field work in American Samoa, where she observed adolescent girls to determine if the turmoil associated with **adolescence** in the West is universal. Living with her research subjects in a Samoan village, Mead was the first American to use the participant-observer method developed by British anthropologist Bronislaw Malinowski (1884–1942). Upon her return to the United States, she received her Ph.D. in anthropology in 1929 and published *Coming of Age in Samoa* (1928), in which she presented a portrait of Samoan culture as free from the *sturm und drang* of the teen years in Western societies because preparation for adulthood is a continuous process that begins early in life rather than a series of stages, which create a more stressful transition process.

Mead did extensive field work throughout the 1920s and 1930s. After her initial trip, she was always joined by a collaborator. These included her second husband, New Zealand psychologist Reo Fortune, and her third husband, the British anthropologist Gregory Bateson, whom she married in 1935. Mead and Bateson conducted two years of intensive field work together in Bali, pursuing their different research interests. They pioneered the use of film as a resource for anthropological research, shooting some 22,000 feet of film as well as thousands of still photographs. Besides the Balinese, groups studied by Mead included the Manus people of the Admiralty Islands, and the Arapesh, Mundugumor, Tchambuli, and Iatmul of New Guinea. A tireless investigator, she made many repeat visits to her research sites; over a 47-year period, she observed the Manus people seven times. Having studied seven different Pacific cultures as well as the Omaha tribe of North America, Mead became convinced of the importance of culture as a determinant of **personality,** following in the footsteps of **Alfred Adler** in the field of psychology and Ruth Benedict in anthropology. Mead detailed her theories of **character** formation and culture in *Sex and Temperament in Three Primitive Societies* (1935) and expanded further on the role of culture in gender formation in her 1949 work, *Male and Female: A Study of the Sexes in a Changing World.* (Although Mead's stature as an anthropologist is unquestioned, there has been some speculation that her subjects may have systematically lied to her during her investigations.) In contrast to **Sigmund Freud**'s dictum, "anatomy is destiny," Mead found gender roles to be culturally determined rather than innate, noting that behavior regarded as masculine in one culture could be considered feminine in another.

Mead's professional skills were enlisted by the United States government during World War II to analyze the cultural characteristics of its wartime adversaries, the Germans and Japanese, and facilitate relations with its allies, especially the British. From 1926 to 1964, Mead was associated with the American Museum of Natural History in New York City as a curator of ethnology, eventually attaining the status of curator emeritus. She became an adjunct professor at Columbia in 1954 and also held a number of visiting professorships elsewhere. Mead was also the chairperson of the Social Sciences division of Fordham University beginning in 1968. She served as president of the World Federation of Mental Health (1956–57), the American Anthropological Association (1960), and the American Association for the Advancement of Science (1975). Beginning in the 1960s, Mead's influence expanded to include a wider audience, as she agreed to write a monthly column for *Redbook* magazine, in which she discussed topics she had concentrated on for much of her career—child-rearing practices and the family. In turn, she used her readers' letters to learn more about the concerns of American women. Mead was posthumously awarded the Presidential Medal of Freedom. Her other books include *Growing Up in New Guinea* (1930), *Balinese Character* (with Gregory Bateson, 1942), *Soviet Attitudes Toward Authority* (1951), *Childhood in Contemporary Societies* (1955), *Anthropology: A Human Science* (1964), *Blackberry Winter* (1972), an autobiographical account of her early life, and *Letters from the Field, 1925–1975* (1977).

See also Child Development; Conditioning; Sexuality.

Further Reading

Bateson, Mary Catherine. *With a Daughter's Eye: A Memoir of Margaret Mead and Gregory Bateson.* New York: William Morrow, 1984.

Foerstel, Lenora, and Angela Gilliam, eds. *Confronting the Margaret Mead Legacy: Scholarship, Empire, and the South Pacific.* Philadelphia: Temple University Press, 1992.

Holmes, Lowell D. *Quest for the Real Samoa: The Mead/Freeman Controversy and Beyond.* South Hadley, MA: Bergin & Garvey, 1987.

Rice, Edward. *Margaret Mead: A Portrait.* New York: Harper & Row, 1979.

Mean

The sum of the values of the points in a data set divided by the number of points.

In statistics, the mean refers to the value that results when all the scores in a data set are added together and the total is divided by the number of scores in the data set. In the example, the mean for a set of fifteen data points is calculated. The mean balances the scores on either side of it. Also called the arithmetic mean or average, the mean is one of the measures of central tendency; the others being the **median** and the **mode.**

EXAMPLE

Heights in centimeters of fifteen children are:

124, 137, 129, 144, 136, 157, 129, 130, 130, 131, 125, 128, 133, 133, 129

Sum equal 1995; divide by 15 to get the mean of **133**.

Further Reading

Peavy, J. Virgil. *Descriptive Statistics: Measures of Central Tendency and Dispersion.* Atlanta, GA: U.S. Dept. of Health and Human Services/Public Health Service, Centers for Disease Control, 1981.

Measurement

The assessment of a trait or feature against a standard scale.

Psychologists rely heavily on measurements for very different purposes, ranging from clinical diagnoses based on test scores to the effects of an **independent variable** on a **dependent variable** in an experiment. Several different issues arise when considering measurement. One consideration is whether the measurement shows reliability and validity. Reliability refers to consistency: if the results of a test or measurement are reliable, a person should receive a similar score if tested on different occasions. Validity refers to whether the measurement will be useful for the purposes for which it is intended.

The **Scholastic Assessment Test (SAT)** is reasonably reliable, for example, because many students obtain nearly the same score if they take the test more than once. If the test score is valid, it should be useful for predicting how well a student will perform in college. Research suggests that the SAT is a sufficient but not perfect predictor of how well students will perform in their first year in college; thus, it shows some validity. However, a test can be reliable without being valid. If a person wanted to make a prediction about an individual's **personality** based on an SAT score, they would not succeed very well because the SAT is not a valid test for that purpose, even though it would still be reliable.

Another dimension of measurement involves what is called the scale of measurement. There are four different scales of measurement: nominal, ordinal, interval, and ratio. Nominal scales involve simple categorization but does not make use of the notion of comparisons like larger, bigger, and better. Ordinal scales involve ranking different elements in some dimension. Interval scales are used to assess by how much two measurements differ, and ratio scales can determine the difference between measurements and by how much. One advantage of more complex scales of measurement is that they can be applied to more sophisticated research. More complex scales also lend themselves to more useful statistical tests that give researchers more confidence in the results of their work.

Median

The middle value in a group of measurements.

In statistics, the median represents the middle value in a group of measurements. It is a commonly used indicator of what measurement is typical or **normal** for a group. The median is joined by the mean and the mode to create a grouping called measures of central tendency. Although the **mean** is used more frequently than the median, the median is still an important measure of central tendency because it is not affected by the presence or a score that is extremely high or extremely low relative to the other numbers in the group.

See also Mode.

EXAMPLE:

125–128–129–129–129–130–130–131–133

The median is **129**.

Further Reading

Peavy, J. Virgil. *Descriptive Statistics: Measures of Central Tendency and Dispersion*. Atlanta, GA: U.S. Dept. of Health and Human Services/Public Health Service, Centers for Disease Control, 1981.

Medical Psychology. See **Health Psychology.**

Melancholia

Melancholia is both an outdated term for depression itself and, currently, a clinically defined characteristic of major depression listed in the Diagnostic and Statistical Manual of Mental Disorders.

The term "melancholia" is derived from the Greek words *melas*, meaning black, and *chole*, meaning bile, and is a vestige of the ancient belief that a person's health and **temperament** are determined by the relative proportions of the four cardinal humors, or body fluids, which are blood, phlegm, choler (yellow bile), and melancholy (black bile). The central feature of melancholic **depression** is persistent and unremitting sadness. Persons suffering from this disorder are unable to enjoy normally pleasurable experiences, even brief ones, and they exhibit a greatly reduced sensitivity to pleasurable stimuli.

Melancholic depression is characterized by other features as well. The quality of the depressed **mood** is unique, differing from the sadness that an emotionally healthy person would feel even in response to a very painful event, such as the death of a loved one. The depression tends to be worse in the morning and associated with early morning awakening (at least two hours before the normal waking time). There is often a marked change in the affected person's physical movements, which can become either agitated or slowed down. Many persons suffering from melancholic depression show significant weight loss, with or without anorexic behavior. A final feature is the presence of intense and inappropriate guilt feelings.

A person is officially classified as suffering from depression with melancholic features when the persistent feelings of unhappiness are accompanied by at least three of the other symptoms listed above. Individuals with melancholic depression generally respond to antidepressant medications or **electroconvulsive therapy.** Depression with melancholic features occurs equally in both men and women but more often in older persons and more frequently in hospital inpatients than outpatients. Organic conditions associated with melancholic depression include hyperadrenocorticism, reduced **rapid eye movement (REM)** latency, and dexamethasone nonsuppression.

Further Reading

Ostow, Mortimer. *The Psychology of Melancholy*. New York: Harper & Row, 1970.

Memory

The ability to store and later recall previously learned facts and experiences.

The **brain**'s capacity to remember remains one of the least understood areas of science. What is understood is that memory is a process that occurs constantly and in various stages. There are three stages in the memory process: encoding, storage, and retrieval. Conditions present during each of these stages affect the quality of the memory, and breakdowns at any of these points can cause memory failure.

The first stage, encoding, is the reception by the brain of some physical input that is changed into a form that the memory accepts. When a person is introduced to someone new, for example, that person's name becomes a part of memory. Before information can be encoded, it first must be recognized and noted by the recipient. During the second stage, storage, learned facts or experiences are retained in either short-term or long-term memory. In the third, or retrieval, stage, memory allows the previously learned facts or experiences to be recalled. Each of these stages play an important role in both short-term and long-term memory, although it is believed they work differently depending on which memory is used.

As the term implies, short-term memory is used for items that need to be recalled over short periods of time, sometimes as little as seconds. It is believed that short-term memories are encoded either visually or acoustically. Visual encoding is primary for recalling faces, places, and other visual experiences, while acoustic encoding is most important for verbal material. After looking up a number in a telephone book, for example, most people repeat the number to themselves several times before dialing the number. Rather than visualizing the written form of the numbers, the sound of the words becomes the means for recall. Experiments have demonstrated the importance of acoustic coding in the **ability** to recall lists of words or letters as well. When subjects were asked to re-

Stages of Memory

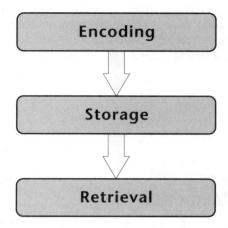

```
Encoding
   ↓
Storage
   ↓
Retrieval
```

call a sequence of letters, those who made errors replaced the correct letter with a similarly sounding letter, for example "D" instead of "T."

Adequate operation of short-term memory is crucial when performing such everyday activities as reading or conversing. However, the capacity of short-term memory is quite limited. Studies have shown consistently that there is room in short-term memory for an average of seven items, plus or minus two (known as magic number seven). In experiments in which subjects are asked to recall a series of unrelated numbers or words, for example, some are able to recall nine and others only five, but most will recall seven words. As the list of things to be remembered increases, new items can displace previous items in the current list. Memory uses a process called "chunking" to increase the capacity of short-term memory. While most people still can use only seven "slots" of memory, facts or information can be grouped in meaningful ways to form a chunk of memory. These chunks of related items then act as one item within short-term memory.

Long-term memory contains information that has been stored for longer periods of time, ranging from a few minutes to a lifetime. When translating information for long-term memory, the brain uses meaning as a primary method for encoding. When attempting to recall a list of unrelated words, for instance, subjects often try to link the words in a sentence. The more the meaning of the information is elaborated, the more it will be recalled. Voices, odors, and tastes also are stored in long-term memory, which indicates that other means of encoding besides meaning, are also used. Items are regularly transferred back and forth from short-term to long-term memory. For example, rehearsing facts can transfer short-term memory into long-term. The chunking process in long-

term memory can increase the capacity of short-term memory when various chunks of information are called upon to be used.

The breakdown in the retrieval of information from either memory can be the result of various factors, including interference, decay, or storage problems. In addition, researchers believe it is unlikely that all experiences or facts are stored in memory and thus are available for retrieval. Emotional factors, including anxiety, also contribute to memory failure in certain situations. Test anxiety, for example, may cause a student to forget factual information despite how well it has been learned. **Amnesia**, a partial or total loss of memory, may be caused by stroke, injury to the brain, surgery, **alcohol dependence,** encephalitis, and **electroconvulsive therapy** (ECT).

Many methods can be used to improve memory. Long-term memory may be improved using mnemonic, or memory-aiding, systems. One, the "method of loci" system, encourages an association between various images and unrelated words. The "key word" method of learning a foreign language links the pronunciation of a new word with a picture that corresponds to the sound of the word. Context is another powerful memory aid that recognizes that people recall more easily facts or events more easily if they are placed in the same **environment** in which they learned them. For example, a person is more likely to recall specific memories from high school if they go to the school and retrace their paths.

Imposing a meaningful organization on an unrelated group of facts or words also improves memory. The EGBDF notes that represent the lines on a musical staff often are recalled using the sentence, "Every good boy does fine." The sentence has nothing to do with music; rather, it places a meaning on letters that, at first glance, seem random. Another notable mnemonic system, the PQRST method, is helpful in assisting students learn textbook material. The letters correspond to the five steps of the method: preview, question, read, self-recitation and test.

See also Mnemonic Strategies; Serial Learning; Serial Position Function.

Further Reading

Atkinson, Rita L.; Richard C. Atkinson; Edward E. Smith; and Ernest R. Hilgard. *Introduction to Psychology.* 9th ed. San Diego: Harcourt Brace Jovanovich, 1987.

Bolles, Edmund Blair. *Remembering and Forgetting: Inquiries Into the Nature of Memory.* New York: Walker and Co., 1988.

Zimbardo, Philip G. *Psychology and Life.* 12th ed. Glenview, IL: Scott, Foresman, 1988.

Memory Improvement. See **Memory** and **Mnemonic Strategies**.

Mental Ability. See **Intelligence**.

Mental Age

A scale used to correlate intelligence to the typical changes that occur as a child matures.

French psychologist and educator **Alfred Binet** theorized that a child who appears to have limited mental abilities is able to perform on a level characteristic of younger children; conversely, a child who appears to be gifted is able to perform on the level of older children. In 1905 Binet, in collaboration with Thèophile Simon, developed a scale on which mental age could be compared to the chronological age. Thus, a bright child's mental age is higher than his or her chronological age.

In 1916, **Lewis Terman**, a psychologist at Stanford University, devised an intelligence test based on Binet's work (referred to today as the **Stanford-Binet Intelligence Scale**) and was administered to assess American school children. Terman maintained the concept of mental age in devising his formula for calculating the intelligence quotient (IQ). The formula is IQ = mental age/ chronological age multiplied by 100. Thus if the child's mental age equals her chronological age, her IQ will equal 100.

Mental Health

Personal well-being, characterized by self-acceptance and feelings of emotional security.

After decades of concentrating on **mental illness** and emotional disorders, many psychologists during the 1950s turned their focus toward the promotion of mental health. Attempts to prevent mental illness joined the emphasis on treatment methods, and promotion of "self-help" in many cases replaced the dependence on professionals and drug therapies. American psychologist Gordon Allport (1897–1967) viewed the difference between an emotionally healthy person and a neurotic one as the difference in outlook between the past and the future. Healthy people motivate themselves toward the future; unhealthy ones dwell on events in the past that have caused their current condition. Allport also considered these qualities characteristic of mentally healthy individuals: capacity for self-extension; capacity for warm human interactions; demonstrated emotional security and self-acceptance; realistic perceptions of one's own talents and abilities; sense of humor, and a unifying philosophy of life such as religion.

Most psychologists point to qualities such as initiative, a forward-looking attitude, capacity for warm human interactions, and a sense of humor as signs of mental health.

In the United States, the Community Mental Health Centers Act of 1963 attempted to localize and individualize the promotion of personal well-being. Community mental health centers were established for outpatient treatment, emergency service, and short-term hospitalizations. Professional therapists and paraprofessionals consulted with schools, courts, and other local agencies to devise and maintain prevention programs, particularly for young people. Halfway houses enabled formerly ill patients to make an easier transition back to everyday life. Youth centers provided an available source of counseling for jobs and personal problems. Hot lines became staffed 24 hours a day in attempts to prevent **suicide** and **child abuse**.

Aided in large part by these community mental health centers, mental health professionals have strived to reduce the severity of existing disorders through the use of traditional therapies, the duration of disorders that do occur, and the incidence of new mental illness cases.

In addition, attempts have been to decrease the stigma attached to mental illness by making mental health services more commonly available. Self-help strategies have also played an important role in the mental health arena. People with particular anxieties are encouraged to reduce them through training. For example, people afraid to speak in public are encouraged to take classes to help them cope with their **anxiety** and overcome it so that it does not interfere with their personal or professional lives. The proliferation of self-help support groups are also outgrowths of the efforts to personalize, rather than institutionalize, mental health care. People who participate in such groups not only learn to cope with the **stresses** that erode their well-being, they also receive the social support thought to be equally important in building strong mental health.

Further Reading

Hergenhahn, B.R. *An Introduction to Theories of Personality.* Englewood Cliffs, NJ: Prentice-Hall, 1980.

Zimbardo, Philip G. *Psychology and Life.* Glenview, IL: Scott, Foresman, 1988.

Mental Hospitals

Institutions for the mentally ill, formerly called asylums, and now called psychiatric institutions.

Beginning in the Middle Ages, mental hospitals were basically prisons. By the end of the eighteenth century, the term asylum was used, and some reforms were being implemented when the notion was introduced that psychological disturbances, like physical ailments, could be viewed as diseases requiring treatment rather than crimes calling for imprisonment. By the late 1800s, reactions against conditions in mental hospitals led to a reform movement in the care and treatment of people with mental disorders. The Mental Health Act of 1946 and the Community Mental Health Centers Act of 1963 allotted federal funds for the establishment of community treatment centers, which provide a variety of services—including short-term and partial hospitalization—in an effort toward the deinstitutionalization of mental patients. As of the late 1990s, institutions for the treatment of mental disorders are called psychiatric institutions. These institutions—along with mental health centers and halfway houses—form a system for treatment of mental disorders at all levels of severity.

See also Psychiatric Institution.

Further Reading

Wyer, Robert S., Jr., ed. *Knowledge and Memory: The Real Story.* Hillsdale, NJ: Lawrence Erlbaum, 1995.

Hartmann, Ernest. *Boundaries in the Mind: A New Psychology of Personality Difference.* New York: Basic Books, 1991.

Mental Illness. See **Psychological Disorder.**

Mental Imagery

A picture created by the imagination with no visual stimulus required.

Mental images are created by the **brain** from memories, **imagination**, or a combination of both. In the 1990s, scientists were gaining knowledge of how the brain forms these visual pictures without input from the eyes. According to researchers at Harvard University, the brain may generate these mental pictures in the area of the brain responsible for vision. Stephen Kosslyn, a psychologist, used positron emission tomography (PET) technology to examine the flow of blood in the brains of twelve men. The men were asked to close their eyes and imagine total darkness. Subsequently, they were asked to imagine a series of different items. The tests seem to indicate that the primary visual cortex, the area of the brain that interprets vision, was activated when creating the imagined images.

See also Daydreams; Dreams; Fantasy.

Further Reading

Bower, Bruce. "Brain Scans Set Sights on Mind's Eye." *Science News* (December 2, 1995): 372.

Mental Retardation

A condition characterized by abnormally low general cognitive development and intellectual functioning.

The American Association on Mental Retardation (formerly the American Association of Mental Deficiency) defines mental retardation as "significantly subaverage general intellectual functioning existing concurrently with deficits in adaptive behavior, and manifested during the developmental period." This definition means that a mentally retarded individual has an unusually low **intelligence quotient**, or IQ, and also shows deficiency in the skills needed for daily living ("adaptive behavior"). In addition, the last part of the definition means that people who develop intellectual and behavioral deficits in adulthood (from an event such as a stroke or other trauma) are not considered mentally retarded.

Mental retardation is divided into four classification levels—mild, moderate, severe, and profound—depending on IQ as measured by such standardized intelligence tests as the **Stanford–Binet Intelligence Scale** and the **Wechsler Intelligence Scales.** Mild mental retardation is the condition of individuals whose measured IQ is in the range of 50-69. A large majority of the mentally retarded fall into this category. These individuals usually display no overt signs of retardation, show fairly effective social behavior, and are capable of learning elementary school material and some skills. As adults, they can often hold down a semiskilled job, but need some assistance with financial and social matters. They are generally at the intellectual level of a fourth or fifth grade child. Three important ways in which the mildly retarded differ from **normal** individuals are: 1) performing certain mental tasks more slowly, such as accessing information from long-term **memory**; 2) knowing fewer facts about the world; and 3) low levels of competence at certain mental strategies important to problem solving and learning.

Moderate mental retardation is the condition of individuals whose measured IQ is in the range of 35-49. As adults, these individuals have a **mental age** of between six and eight years, and their retardation is readily apparent upon even casual contact. They must be taught self-care and other practical skills. Although moderately retarded people usually develop some communication capability, they remain functionally illiterate. These individuals mostly remain dependent on their families, but can be taught to perform some types of labor, usually of an unskilled and repetitive nature.

Severe mental retardation is the condition of individuals whose measured IQ is in the range of 20-34. These individuals, most of whom have neurological damage, have a mental age between roughly four and six years. Although they can learn to talk and can be taught to care for personal needs, severely retarded people usually develop poor or no social skills, and cannot benefit from academic or vocational training. Such individuals need constant care and supervision.

Profound mental retardation is the condition of individuals whose measured IQ is below 20. These individuals have a mental age below three years and eight months, and many are nonambulatory and/or physically handicapped. They develop minimal sensorimotor functioning and require highly structured **environment**s and constant custodial care. The use of **behavior modification** techniques has increased the number of profoundly retarded individuals who are able to feed themselves and look after their own hygienic needs.

More than half of the cases of mental retardation have no known organic cause, and those that do are usually in the severe or profound ranges. Of those cases that have a known biological origin, the majority involve such genetic disorders as **Down syndrome,** Turner's syndrome, and phenylketonuria (PKU). Other biological causes include rubella (German measles), contracted by the mother during pregnancy; **birth trauma** that deprive an infant of oxygen; infections such as meningitis or encephalitis; head injuries; asphyxiation; and prenatal exposure to toxins. There is speculation that mild mental retardation may be the result of a genetic predisposition combined with cultural deprivation, including such environmental factors such as infant neglect, poor stimulation, or lack of learning experiences. This phenomenon is called *familial retardation,* because those affected by it are more likely to have one or more relatives who are also retarded than persons whose retardation is of a genetic basis.

Although there is no cure for mental retardation, retarded individuals can learn to be productive and self-sufficient, and the quality of life can be enhanced even for the severely and profoundly retarded. Much of the current debate over education of the mentally retarded revolves around mainstreaming—teaching children with disabilities, including mental disabilities, in the same classroom as ordinary students.

See also Learning Disability.

Further Information

American Association of Mental Retardation (AAMR)
> **Address:** 444 North Capitol St. NW, Suite 846, Washington, DC 20001
> **Telephone:** 202-387-1968

Further Reading

Zigler, Edward. *Understanding Mental Retardation.* Cambridge, Eng.: Cambridge University Press, 1986.

Metapsychology

Umbrella term used to describe the attempt to establish general principles to explain all psychological phenomena.

Metapsychology describes the effort to construct or to postulate a systematic and comprehensive set of general principles encompassing all of psychology, specifically including elements that are theoretical in addition to elements that are considered to have been empirically demonstrated; also known as nomothetic psychology. In classical Freudian psychoanalytical theory, the term metapsychology is used in reference to the analysis of the dynamic (instinctive), topological (association with **id**, **ego**, or **superego**), and economic (allocation of psychic energy) aspects of mental processes. The term metapsychology is sometimes used as a synonym of the term parapsychology. Parapsychology is a field of study that involves the investigation of paranormal phenomena, such as extrasensory perception, precognition, telepathy, clairvoyance, and telekinesis, that are (presumably) not explainable in terms of scientifically established principles or natural laws.

Meyer, Adolf (1866–1950)

Swiss-born American psychiatrist who developed the concept of psychobiology.

Adolph Meyer was born in Niederweningen, Switzerland, and received an extensive medical education in neurology in Zurich, obtaining his M.D. in 1892. He emigrated to the United States in the same year. Beginning in 1893, Meyer worked for several hospitals, including a state hospital in Kankakee, Illinois, as a pathologist, and the New York State Hospital Service Pathological Institute, where he was involved with the training of **psychiatrists.** Meyer later joined the faculty of Cornell Medical College in New York City, where he served as professor of **psychiatry.** In 1909 G. Stanley Hall (1844–1924), a prominent psychologist and former student of **William James,** invited Meyer to Clark College in Worcester, Massachusetts, on the occasion of the college's twentieth anniversary, where he met with **Sigmund Freud** and **Carl Jung.** In following year Meyer was appointed professor of psychiatry at Johns Hopkins University and director of its Henry Phipps Psychiatric Clinic, which became an internationally renowned training center for psychiatrists.

Meyer became so influential in his adopted country that he was known as "the dean of American psychiatry," and his work has had a wide influence on psychiatric theory and practice. In Meyer's view, the diagnosis and treatment of a mental disorder must include a thorough understanding of the patient as a whole person. This approach, which would today be termed "holistic," involved studying the patient from various perspectives—medical, biographical, educational, and even artistic. It was this goal that led him to introduce the use of the individual case history, bringing together in one place information about a patient's physical condition, past history, family life, work situation, and other facts that could be relevant to treatment. Meyer also pioneered in promoting visits to the patient's family in order for the psychiatrist to understand the **environment** in which the patient lived, and to which he or she would return when treatment was completed.

Meyer believed that the constituent elements of human existence are actively interrelated, from the lowest biochemical level to the highest cognitive level. Arguing that psychological factors may be as important as neuropathology in causing mental illness, Meyer advocated integrating the studies of human psychology and biology into a single system that he called psychobiology. The goal of psychobiological therapy was the successful integration of different aspects of the patient's **personality.** Steps involved in this **psychotherapy** included analyzing the psychological, sociological, and biological factors relevant to the patient's illness; working with the patient on a conscious level, staying close to the original complaint; and utilizing a combination of treatment methods satisfactory to both psychiatrist and patient.

Through therapy that addressed both short-term and long-term problems, Meyer's goal was to help the patient adjust as well as possible to life and change. Part of the therapy process consisted of aiding the patient in modifying unhealthy adjustments to his or her situation through guidance, suggestion, and reeducation, which Meyer called "habit training." His emphasis on habits extended to include **schizophrenia,** which he viewed as caused by harmful habits acquired over a long period of time, in combination with biological factors, including **heredity.** Neurosis, Meyer believed, differed from psychosis in that only a part of the personality was involved. He viewed neurotic patients as suffering from unrealistic expectations and the inability to accept themselves as they were.

Meyer, together with **Clifford Beers,** was also a founder of the mental hygiene movement (and the one who suggested its name). The goal of this movement was to educate the public about mental illness and achieve more humane treatment of institutionalized patients. Meyer contributed significantly to the medical literature on psychiatry. His papers were collected and published in *Collected Papers* (1950–1952).

Middle Years

While there is no exact consensus as to the age range of this period of life, it generally refers to the ages between approximately 40 and 60, with the lower limit sometimes placed as low as age 35 and the upper one as high as 65 years of age.

In **Erik Erikson's** influential scheme of human development, middle age is the period in which an individual is presented with the developmental task of choosing between ego stagnation (self-interest) and generativity, the capacity to care for others and make a positive contribution to society by being productive in work, parenting, or other activities. **Carl Jung** characterized the middle years as a time for self-realization and the exploration of spiritual and social values once the practical tasks of finding an occupation and establishing a family have been accomplished.

For many people, middle age is a stable period in which they are settled in a long-term love relationship, have committed themselves to a career, and have established a family and a permanent home. The middle years can also be a time of exploration and radical change, sometimes fueled by the much-publicized "midlife crisis." For some individuals, failure to achieve goals set earlier in life or reassessment of those goals may produce discontent or even despair, resulting in major lifestyle changes, both professional and personal. It is important to note that personal and professional growth at midlife may also be indicative of an individual's socioeconomic status: the poor generally have less flexibility and fewer opportunities to make sweeping changes in their lives at this stage.

The ability to realize one's full potential in middle age is also closely related to developmental experiences earlier in life. Unresolved issues of childhood and **adolescence** are often felt keenly during this period, and the greatest number of **psychotherapy** clients are thought to be of middle aged. In addition, coping with aging parents and their eventual deaths compels middle-aged individuals to acknowledge their own mortality, resulting in a restructuring of priorities. Professionally, people may change careers, return to school, or enter into business for themselves, voluntarily decreasing their earning potential or accepting a lower measure of financial security in order to pursue their dreams while they still have a chance. Some women who have stayed home to raise children often reenter the job market at midlife, a challenge that can involve major personal reassessments and lifestyle changes.

Women in midlife are confronted with the approaching end of their childbearing years and begin experiencing symptoms of menopause. Men commonly become concerned about their levels of sexual prowess and activity in middle age. Affluent, well-educated men are especially prone to engaging in extramarital affairs at this time, often with younger women. Both sexes also face the disengagement of their children, first through the detachment of adolescence, and then when the children finally leave the family home.

Further Reading

Anderson, Clifford. *The Stages of Life: A Groundbreaking Discovery: the Steps to Psychological Maturity.* New York: Atlantic Monthly Press, 1995.

Berger, Kathleen Stassen. *The Developing Person Through the Life Span.* 2nd ed. New York: Worth Publishers, 1988.

Inglehart, Marita Rosc. *Reactions to Critical Life Events: A Social Psychological Analysis.* New York: Praeger, 1991.

Zimbardo, Philip G. *The Psychology of Attitude Change and Social Influence.* Philadelphia: Temple University Press, 1991.

Milgram's Obedience Experiment

A controversial experiment on conformity and obedience conducted in the early 1960s.

Stanley Milgram (1933–1984), an American experimental psychologist at Yale University, conducted a series of experiments on **conformity** and obedience to authority. In these experiments, Milgram recruited subjects—ordinary citizens—through newspaper advertisements offering four dollars for one hour's participation in a "study of **memory**." When the subject arrived at the experimental laboratory, he or she was assigned the role of "teacher," and asked to read a series of word pairs to another subject, or learner. The teacher-subject then would test the learner's **ability** to recall the pairs by reading back the first word in each pair. Whenever the learner made a mistake, the teacher-subject was instructed to administer **punishment** in the form of electric shock. This instruction, by an authority figure or employer to administer **pain** to a human being, is at the heart of the controversy.

The teacher-subject watched as the learner was strapped into a chair and an electrode was attached to the learner's wrist. The teacher was encouraged by the experimenters to continue to administer the shocks. Milgram found that the 65 percent of the teacher-subjects would continue to do what they were told, even though the learners could be heard pleading and screaming, and concluded that most people will follow the instructions of an authority figure as long as they considered the authority as legitimate. Many psychologists and others questioned the ethics of conducting such experiments, where participants were encouraged, in the name of scientific experimentation, to inflict pain on others. Another aspect of the controversy surrounding Milgram's work focused on the implications of his findings for the future of societies and their authority figures.

Further Reading

Milgram, Stanley. "Behavior Study of Obedience." *Journal of Abnormal Psychology,* 1963.

_____. "Some Conditions of Obedience and Disobedience to Authority," *Human Relations,* 1965.

_____. "Issues in the Study of Authority: A Reply to Baumrind," *American Psychologist,* 1964.

Minimal Brain Dysfunction

A term often used either in connection (or interchangeably) with hyperactivity and/or attention deficit disorder.

Minimal brain dysfunction was formally defined in 1966 by Samuel Clements as a combination of average or above average **intelligence** with certain mild to severe learning or behavioral disabilities characterizing deviant functioning of the **central nervous system.** It can involve impairments in visual or auditory **perception**, conceptualization, language, and **memory,** and difficulty controlling **attention,** impulses, and motor function. Minimal brain dysfunction is thought to be associated with minor damage to the brain stem, the part of the **brain** that controls **arousal.** A likely cause of this type of damage is oxygen deprivation during childbirth. While such damage does not affect intelligence, it does have an effect on motor activity and **attention span.** Minimal brain disorder usually does not become apparent until a child reaches school age.

Minimal brain dysfunction has also been linked to **heredity**; poor nutrition; exposure to toxic substances; and illness *in utero.* Other symptoms that may be associated with the disorder include poor or inaccurate **body image,** immaturity, difficulties with coordination, both hypoactivity and **hyperactivity,** difficulty with writing or calculating, speech and communication problems, and cognitive difficulties. Secondary problems can include social, affective, and **personality** disturbances.

Mnemonic Strategies

Any technique used for the purpose of either assisting in the memorizing of specific material or improving the function of memory in general.

The basic coding procedure common to most mnemonic strategies is to mentally associate, in some manner, items of new or unfamiliar information with various interconnected parts of a familiar, known whole. Mnemonic devices range from the very simple to the remarkably complex. An example of a very simple mnemonic device is the use of the acronymic word HOMES to remember the names of the Great Lakes (Huron, Ontario, Michigan, Erie, and Superior). An example of a remarkably complex mnemonic device is the ancient Greek and Roman system of topical mnemonics, in which a large imaginary house, or even a town full of large imaginary houses, is intricately subdivided into thousands of quadrates, or **memory** places, each of which is available to be associated with an item of material to be remembered. The difficulties encountered in the application of mnemonic strategies appear to increase as the amount of information to be mastered increases, and involve issues such as ambiguity, confusion, and complexity.

MNEMONIC DEVICE FOR THE FIVE GREAT LAKES

This mnemonic device can help the learner remember the names of the five U.S. great lakes.

H - Huron

O - Ontario

M - Michigan

E - Erie

S - Superior

There are several commonly employed mnemonic devices. For example, the *method of loci* is a system where objects to be remembered are imagined to be arranged in geographical locations, or locations in a building, the map or layout of which is well-known. The learner uses this map or layout to remember unordered items, such as a shopping list, by placing the grocery items on the map, and recalling them later in a well-known order. In this way, no items will be forgotten or missed.

Further Reading

Higbee, Kenneth. *Your Memory: How It Works and How to Improve It.* New York: Paragon House, 1993.

Maguire, Jack. *Your Guide to a Better Memory.* New York: Berkley Books, 1995.

Sandstrom, Robert. *The Ultimate Memory Book: Remember Anything Quickly and Easily.* Granada Hills, CA: Stepping Stone Books, 1990.

Mode

One of the measures of central tendency in statistics.

In **statistics,** the mode is a descriptive number that indicates the most frequently occurring score or scores in a group of numbers. Along with the **mean** and the **median**, the mode constitutes the grouping of descriptive statistics known as measures of central tendency. Although the mode is the easiest of the measures of central tendency to determine, it is the least used because it gives only a crude estimate of typical scores.

See also Median; Mean.

EXAMPLE

124–125–128–129–129–**130–130–130–130–**
131–133–133–133

The mode is **130**.

Further Reading

Peavy, J. Virgil. *Descriptive Statistics: Measures of Central Tendency and Dispersion.* Atlanta, GA: U.S. Dept. of Health and Human Services/Public Health Service, Centers for Disease Control, 1981.

Modeling

The process of learning by watching others; a therapeutic technique used to effect behavioral change.

The use of modeling in **psychotherapy** was influenced by the research of social learning theorist **Albert Bandura**, who studied observational learning in children, particularly in relation to **aggression**. Bandura pioneered the concept of vicarious **conditioning**, by which one learns not only from the observed **behavior** of others but also from whether that behavior is rewarded or punished. Bandura also concluded that certain conditions determine whether or not people learn from observed behavior. They must pay **attention** and retain what they have observed, and they must be capable of and motivated to reproduce the behavior. The effects of observed behavior are also stronger if the model has characteristics similar to those of the observer or is particularly attractive or powerful (the principle behind celebrity endorsements).

Modeling is also used as a therapeutic technique for changing one's behavior and has been especially effective in the treatment of **phobia**s. As with systematic **desensitization**, an individual is exposed to the feared object or situation in progressively **anxiety**-provoking forms. However, this series of confrontations, instead of being imagined or experienced directly, is first modeled by another person. In symbolic modeling, the person receiving treatment has also had relaxation training, and his or her task is to watch the series of modeled situations (live or on film) while remaining relaxed. As soon as a situation or action provokes anxiety, it is discontinued and the observer returns to a state of relaxation. In another effective technique, "live modeling with participation," the observer actively imitates the behavior of a live model in a series of confrontations with a feared object or situation. For example, persons being treated to overcome fear of snakes—watching and imitating a model—gradually progress from touching a snake with a gloved hand to retrieving a loose snake bare-handed and letting it crawl on their bodies.

In individual therapy sessions, the therapist may model anxiety-producing behaviors while the client, remaining relaxed, first watches and then imitates them. In therapy involving social skills and assertiveness training, this technique may take the form of behavioral rehearsal, in which the therapist models and then helps the client practice new, more socially adaptive behaviors.

See also Imitation.

Further Reading

Bandura, Albert. *Principles of Behavior Modification.* New York: Holt, Rinehart, and Winston, 1969.
Contemporary Behavior Therapy: Conceptual and Empirical Foundations. Guilford Press, 1982.

Mood

Loosely defined and subjectively experienced general emotional condition.

A mood, while relatively pervasive, is typically neither highly intense nor sustained over an extended period of time. Examples of mood include happiness, sadness, contemplativeness, and irritability. The definitions of phrases to describe moods—such as good mood and bad mood—are imprecise. In addition, the range of what is regarded as a **normal** or appropriate mood varies considerably from individual to individual and from culture to culture.

See also Affect; Emotion.

Further reading

Kuiken, Don, ed. *Mood and Memory.* Newbury Park, CA: Sage Publications, 1991.

Moral Development

Development of the ability to differentiate between right and wrong.

The roots of moral behavior in human beings have been explained differently by theorists with varying psychological orientations. The psychoanalytic viewpoint approaches moral behavior in terms of guilt. Psychoanalyst **Sigmund Freud** related the beginnings of the **conscience** to the formation of the **superego** during the Oedipal stage that occurs between the ages of 3 and 5. Guilty over forbidden feelings toward the parent of the opposite sex, a child internalizes the values and prohibitions of the same-

A contemplative moment. Moods—which range from sadness to happiness, from optimism to discouragement—are rarely intense or sustained over a long period of time.

sex parent, and these form the basis for the superego. Further guilt results if the rules of the superego are subsequently violated. Behaviorists and social learning theorists believe that moral behavior is learned: behaviorists focus on the conditioned fear of **punishment** for transgression, while social learning theorists emphasize the importance of **imitation** and **reinforcement**.

The best known work on moral development was developed by cognitive theorist **Lawrence Kohlberg**. Kohlberg was influenced by **Jean Piaget**'s 1932 work *The Moral Judgment of the Child,* which sought to draw distinctions between moral judgments that are governed by social constraints and those that arise internally. Based on a long-term study that assessed the ways in which children and adolescents respond to moral dilemmas, Kohlberg evolved a six-stage framework based on the principle that moral development is based on how children think about moral choices and how they justify their decisions. Kohlberg found that older children were able to base their responses on increasingly broad and abstract ethical standards. Based on their thought processes, he discerned a gradual evolution from self-interest to principled behavior and designed a chronological scheme of moral development consisting of three levels, each made up of two separate stages. Progress through the different stages depends upon the type of **thinking** that a child or adolescent is capable of at a given point, and also on the negotiation of previous stages. Each stage involves increasingly complex thought patterns, and as children arrive at a given stage they tend to consider the bases for previous judgments as invalid.

The most famous sample question in Kohlberg's study is whether the husband of a critically ill woman is justified in stealing a drug that could save her life if the pharmacist is charging more than he can afford to pay. Children at the preconventional level (ages 7 through about 10) give responses such as "If you steal the drug, you'll be sent to jail" or "If you let your wife die, you'll get into trouble." Their moral judgment is based on deferring to adults and obeying rules based on the immediate consequences of their actions. The behavior of children at this level is essentially premoral. At the beginning of the preconventional level (Stage 1), the emphasis is on avoiding punishment; in Stage 2 it shifts to obtaining rewards.

Kohlberg's second level is the conventional level, which begins around the age of 10. During this period, the behavior of children is guided by the opinions of other people and the desire to conform. In the first stage of the conventional level (Stage 3) the emphasis is on being a "good boy" or "good girl" in order to win approval and avoid disapproval, while at Stage 4 the concepts of doing one's duty and upholding the social order become paramount. Typical responses to the drug-stealing question at the conventional level might be "The man should steal the drug because his family will approve" or "He should not steal the drug because stealing is illegal." At this stage, respecting and obeying authority (of parents, teachers, God) is an end in itself, without reference to higher principles.

While the final level outlined by Kohlberg—that of postconventional morality—may be attained by adolescents, there are adults whose moral reasoning never reaches this stage, which involves going beyond self-interest and conventional morality to formulate one's own moral principles, which are then obeyed to avoid self-condemnation rather than the censure of others. At Stage 5 one is primarily concerned with the welfare of the community, the rights of others, and existing law, while actions at Stage 6 are guided by ethical standards that transcend the law and are based on abstract concepts such as freedom, dignity, and justice. In relation to the dilemma of the stolen drug, these standards would exact a response based on the existence of a moral law that transcends society's laws about stealing, and the sanctity of human life over financial gain. However, Kohlberg has pointed out that the most clearly principled responses at Stage 6 were expressed by fewer than 10 percent of adolescents over the age of 16.

Kohlberg's theory has been criticized as applying only to constitutional democracies and North American males. Additional studies have found that his stages tend to apply to behavior in other cultures as well, although the first four stages are more universal than the last two. An important critique of Kohlberg's work is found in the 1982 book *In a Different Voice* by his colleague Carol Gilligan. Gilligan criticizes the fact that all of Kohlberg's original research was done on boys and men and claims that his theory defines morality in largely male terms. She describes the contrasting responses of an eleven-year-old boy and girl to the "stolen drug" dilemma. The boy (entering Kohlberg's postconventional stage) unequivocally supports stealing the drug because human life is more valuable than money. The girl, by comparison, expresses the hope that a better solution can be reached if the husband and druggist "talk it out" and expresses concern over what will happen to the relationship between the man and his wife if he goes to jail for stealing the drug.

Based on findings from her own research, Gilligan outlines a female "ethic of care" that places more value on preserving relationships and fulfilling responsibilities than on implementing an abstract concept of justice, noting that Kohlberg assigns behavior based on the needs and approval of others to a considerably lower stage (Stage 3) than behavior based on abstract principles (Stage 6). She also suggests that moral reasoning in North American women is based more on concern for specific individuals than on impersonal ideas of fairness. Gilligan's ideas, which prompted Kohlberg to make some revisions in his earlier work, have been highly influential in recent academic and political debates about gender.

Further Reading

Coles, Robert. *The Moral Life of Children.* Boston: Houghton Mifflin, 1987.

Gilligan, Carol. *In a Different Voice: Psychological Theory and Women's Development.* Cambridge, MA: Harvard University Press, 1982.

Kohlberg, Lawrence. *The Psychology of Moral Development: The Nature and Validity of Moral Stages.* New York: Harper and Row, 1984.

Motivation

The drive that produces goal-directed behavior.

The study of motivation is concerned with the influences that govern the initiation, direction, intensity, and

Motivation to ride a horse may be considered stimulus-seeking, based on a person's internal need for cognitive, physical, and emotional stimulation.

persistence of behavior. Three categories of motives have been recognized by many researchers: primary or biological (hunger and the regulation of food intake); stimulus-seeking (internal needs for cognitive, physical, and emotional stimulation, or intrinsic and extrinsic rewards); and learned (motives acquired through reward and **punishment,** or by observation of others).

Instinct theories, which were popular early in the twentieth century, take a biological approach to motivation. Ethologists study instinctual animal behavior to find patterns that are unlearned, uniform in expression, and universal in a species. Similarly, instinct theory in humans emphasizes the inborn, automatic, involuntary, and unlearned processes which control and direct human behavior. Scientific development of the instinct theory consisted largely of drawing up lists of instincts. In 1908, William McDougall (1871–1938) postulated 18 human instincts; within 20 years, the list of instincts had grown to 10,000. Although instinct theory has since been abandoned, its evolutionary perspective has been adopted by sociobiologists considering a wide range of human behavior, from **aggression** to **interpersonal attraction**, from the standpoint of natural selection and the survival of humans as a species.

Drive-reduction theory, which is biologically-oriented but also encompasses learning, centers on the concept of *homeostasis,* or equilibrium. According to this theory, humans are constantly striving to maintain homeostasis by adjusting themselves to change. Any imbalance creates a **need** and a resulting drive—a state of **arousal** that prompts action to restore the sense of balance and thereby reduce the drive. The drive called thirst, for example, prompts us to drink, after which the thirst is reduced. In drive-reduction theory, motivation is seen not just as a result of biological instincts, but rather as a combination of learning and biology. The *primary drives,* such as hunger and thirst, are basic physiological needs that are unlearned. However, there is also a system of learned drives known as *secondary drives* that are not biological (such as the desire for money) but that prompt action in much the same way as the primary drives.

Another biologically-oriented theory of motivation is arousal theory, which posits that each person is driven to achieve his or her optimum level of arousal, acting in ways that will increase this level when it is too low and decrease it when it is too high. Peak performance of tasks is usually associated with moderate levels of arousal. Researchers have found that difficult tasks (at which people might "freeze" from nervousness) are best accomplished at moderate arousal levels, while easier ones can be successfully completed at higher levels.

Psychologically-oriented theories of motivation emphasize external **environment**al factors and the role of thoughts and expectations in motivation. Incentive theory argues that motivation results from environmental stimuli in the form of positive and negative incentives, and the value these incentives hold at a given time. Food, for example, would be a stronger incentive when a person is hungry. Cognitive theories emphasize the importance of mental processes in goal-directed behavior. Many theorists have agreed, for example, that people are more strongly motivated when they project a positive outcome to their actions. Achievement-oriented individuals learn at an early age to strive for excellence, maintain optimis-

tic expectations, and to not be readily discouraged by failure. Conversely, individuals who consistently **fear** failure have been found to set goals that are too high or too low and become easily discouraged by obstacles. The concept of **learned helplessness** centers on how behavior is affected by the degree of control that is possible in a given situation.

American psychologist **Abraham Maslow** developed a five-level hierarchy of needs, or motives, that influence human behavior. The "lower" physiological and biological urges at the bottom of the hierarchy must be at least partially satisfied before people will be motivated by those urges closer to the top. The levels in Maslow's system are as follows: 1) *biological* (food, water, oxygen, sleep); 2) *safety*; 3) *belongingness and love* (participating in affectionate sexual and non-sexual relationships, belonging to social groups); 4) *esteem* (being respected as an individual); and 5) **self-actualization** (becoming all that one is capable of being).

In addition to individual motivations themselves, conflicts between different motivations exert a strong influence on human behavior. Four basic types of conflict have been identified: 1) *approach-approach* conflicts, in which a person must choose between two desirable activities that cannot both be pursued; 2) *avoidance-avoidance* conflicts, in which neither choice in a situation is considered acceptable and one must choose the lesser of two evils; 3) *approach-avoidance* conflicts, where one event or activity has both positive and negative features; and 4) *multiple approach-avoidance* conflicts involving two or more alternatives, all of which have both positive and negative features.

See also Cognitive Development Theory; Environment; Ethology.

Further Reading

Hoffman, Edward. *The Right to be Human: A Biography of Abraham Maslow.* Los Angeles: Tarcher, 1988.

Multiple Personality. See **Dissociation Identity Disorder**.

Myelin Sheath. See **Nervous System**.

Narcissism

A personality disorder characterized by excessive love for and preoccupation with one's self.

Clinically, narcissism is considered a **personality disorder** and is listed in the *Diagnostic and Statistical Manual of Mental Disorders (DSM IV)*. Individuals with this disorder display an exaggerated sense of their own importance and abilities, brag about their accomplishments, and downplay the achievements of others. They believe themselves to be uniquely gifted and commonly engage in fantasies of fabulous success, power, or fame. Arrogant and egotistical, narcissistics are often snobs, defining themselves by their **ability** to associate with (or purchase the services of) the "best" people, and display a sense of entitlement, expecting (and taking for granted) special treatment and concessions from others. Paradoxically, individuals with narcissistic personality disorder are generally very insecure and have low self-esteem. They require the continual **attention** and admiration of others and find it difficult to cope with adversity or criticism, which may result in either rage and counterattack or social withdrawal. Because narcissistics cannot handle failure, they will take great lengths to avoid risks and situations in which defeat is a possibility. Another common characteristic of narcissistic individuals is envy and the expectation that others are envious as well. The self-aggrandizement and self-absorption of narcissistic individuals is accompanied by a pronounced lack of interest in and empathy for others. They expect people to be devoted to them but have no impulse to reciprocate, being unable to identify with the feelings of others or anticipate their needs. Narcissistics are exploiters; their relationships are often based on what other people can do for them.

The first psychologist to address narcissism was Havelock Ellis (1859–1939) in a paper on **autoeroticism** published in 1898. **Sigmund Freud** claimed that sexual perversion is linked to the narcissistic substitution of the self for one's mother as the primacy love object in **infancy.** In 1933, psychoanalyst Wilhelm Reich (1897–1957)

described the "phallic-narcissistic" personality type in terms that foreshadow the present-day definition: self-assured, arrogant, and disdainful. The social-learning-oriented criteria for narcissistic personality disorder drawn up by Theodore Milton in 1969 were included in the third edition of the *Diagnostic and Statistical Manual of Mental Disorders* (and are very similar to those found in the current edition of *DSM)*: 1) inflated self-image; 2) exploitative; 3) cognitive expansiveness; 4) insouciant temperament; 5) deficient social conscience.

Secondary features of narcissism include feelings of shame or humiliation, **depression,** and **mania.** Narcissistic personality disorder has also been linked to **anorexia nervosa,** substance-related disorders (especially cocaine abuse), and other personality disorders. The incidence of the disorder in the American population is estimated at under 1 percent, and approximately 50 and 75 percent of those diagnosed are male.

Further Reading

Morrison, James. *DSM-IV Made Easy: The Clinician's Guide to Diagnosis*. New York: The Guilford Press, 1995.

National Association of School Psychologists

Organization of school psychologists and related professionals, with members in the United States and 25 other countries.

The National Association of School Psychologists (NASP) has over 18,000 members from the United States and abroad. Founded in 1969, NASP is dedicated to serving the **mental health** and educational needs of school age children and adolescents. Members are school psychologists or professional in related fields. The association encourages professional development and provides publications, meetings, workshops, and seminars for its members, and maintains a resource library and a placement service for school psychologists. In addition, NASP plays an activist role on behalf of school-age children, is-suing position statements and resolutions to its member-ship, the general public, and government officials at all levels on such issues as **violence** in media and toys; leg-islative priorities; advocacy for appropriate educational services for all children; **corporal punishment;** and **rac-ism, prejudice,** and discrimination.

NASP operates a national certification program for school psychologists. In addition, NASP is approved by the **American Psychological Association** and the Na-tional Board of Certified Counselors to provide continu-ing education for psychologists and National Certified Counselors. This allows participants in NASP's conven-tion workshops and regional workshops to apply these sessions to their state's requirements for renewal of pro-fessional licenses.

Further Information
National Association of School Psychologists
> **Address:** 4340 East-West Highway, Suite 402
> Bethesda, MD 20814-4411
> Telephone: 301/657-0270

National Institute of Mential Health

A component of the U.S. Department of Health and Human Ser-vices, with a mission to increase knowledge and understanding in all aspects of mental health, and to develop effective strate-gies to promote mental health and to prevent or treat mental ill-ness.

The National Institute of Mental Health conducts and supports research in a very broad array of areas of mental health and illness. The Institute also collects and analyzes a vast amount of scientific data, widely distrib-utes those data and analyses, and provides technical as-sistance to numerous federal, state, local, and private agencies and organizations. The National Institute of Mental Health consists of nine principal divisions and of-fices, and oversees the administration of a hospital.

Nature/Nurture Controversy

Colloquial term for the two views of human development, one emphasizing heredity and the other environment.

The nature/nurture controversy is an age-old dispute among behavioral psychologists, philosophers, theolo-gians, and theorists of **consciousness** as to the source of the creation of human **personality**: Does it develop pri-marily from biology (nature), or from the **environment**s

The nature/nurture debate continues: which is the more powerful influence on personality development—the genetic factors inher-ited from the parents, or the conditions of the environment in which the child is raised?

in which we are raised (nurture)? People have been pon-dering the role of nature and environment since the time of Hippocrates (c. 460–c. 377 B.C.). He, for instance, linked human behavior to four bodily fluids, or humors: yellow bile, blood, black bile, and phlegm. Hippocrates classified personalities into four types related to these four humors: choleric (yellow bile), or hot-tempered; sanguine (blood), or confident; melancholic (black bile), or moody; and phlegmatic, or slow to take action.

Unlike Hippocrates, the philosopher John Locke (1632–1704), whose ideas were a precursor to **behavior-ism**, believed that behaviors were externally determined. Similarly, the philosopher Jean-Jacques Rousseau (1712–1778) theorized that people were born essentially good, and that positive aspects of the environmental con-tribute to the development of behavior. Locke believed that people were born essentially blank, like a black-board, and who they "became" was entirely the result of their experiences.

The first scientist of the modern era to seriously con-sider the genetic and environmental effects in personality development was Sir **Francis Galton,** a wealthy British scientist. He dabbled in the arts and sciences but became primarily interested in what we today call genetics after his cousin, **Charles Darwin,** published *The Origin of the Species* in 1859. He was fascinated by the idea of genetic pre-programming and sought to uncover the ways in which humans are predestined. Many of his experiments were eccentric and ill-conceived, but his contributions to the field are still considered vital. His studies, curiously, led to the development of the science of fingerprinting and to the concept of the word association test. He also coined the term **"eugenics"** and believed that science would one day be able to direct, with absolute precision, the development patterns of human evolution. Taking the other position in this early debate was **John Watson**, the eminent behaviorist who once made the outlandish claim—which he later modified—that he could turn babies into any kind of specialist he wanted.

Over the years, much research has been done in the nature/nurture controversy, and today nearly everyone agrees that both nature and nurture play crucial roles in human development. This outlook has come to be known as interactionism and is the dominant system of belief among biologists, psychologists, and philosophers nearly everywhere.

Much of the research in the late 20th century has focused on **twins** who were separated at birth. In studying such pairs, psychologists can be relatively certain that any behavior the twins share has a genetic component, and those behaviors that are different have environmental causes. There are many famous cases of twins separated at birth being reunited later in life to find that they have many things in common. One of the most striking studies of twins, reported in a 1995 *New Yorker* article, was conducted by Thomas Bouchard, a professor of psychology at the University of Minnesota and founder of the Center for Twin and Adoptive Research. The twins, Daphne Goodship and Barbara Herbert, had been separated at birth and sent to economically different areas of London. Wright writes, "When they finally met, at King's Cross Station in May of 1979, each was wearing a beige dress and a brown velvet jacket. . . . Both had the eccentric habit of pushing up their noses, which they called 'squidging.' Both had fallen down the stairs at the age of fifteen and had weak ankles as a result. At sixteen, each had met at a local dance the man she was going to marry. The twins suffered miscarriages with their first children, then proceeded to have two boys followed by a girl. And both laughed more than anyone they knew. . . . Neither had ever voted, except once, when she was employed as a polling clerk."

Twin researchers, buoyed by stunning accounts like this, have been boldly asserting that nature determines who we are to a far greater degree than nurture. But twin research has its critics. One commonly pointed out flaw in twin research is that twins often mythologize, i.e.,

imagine or manufacture stories about, their shared characteristics. Also in dispute is how "different" the environments really are. Because adoption agencies screen applicants, families generally have certain shared socio-economic characteristics. In addition, little research has been conducted on "disconfirming evidence," that is, to ask the question, "Are there twins who show no remarkable similarities?" The nature/nurture controversy is far from settled.

See also Jukes Family and Kallikak Family.

Further Reading
Bouchard, Thomas. "Genes, Personality, and Environment." *Science* (17 June 1994): 1700.

Cohen, Jack, and Ian Stewart. "Our Genes Aren't Us." *Discover* (April 1994).

Cowley, Geoffrey. "It's Time to Rethink Nature and Nurture." *Newsweek* (27 March 1995): 52-53.

Gallagher, Winifred. "How We Become What We Are." *Atlantic Monthly* (September 1994): 39-55.

Wright, Lawrence. "Double Mystery." *New Yorker* (7 August 1995): 45-62.

Necrophilia. See **Paraphilia**.

Need

A physiological or psychological requirement for the well-being of an organism.

The term need describes those physiological or psychological elements that are necessary for an organism to thrive. Deprivation of an essential need, such as food or water, triggers energy that takes the form of a basic drive to obtain the unfulfilled need. However, needs do not always lead to the actions appropriate to meeting them. In some cases, conflicts between competing needs prevents such action. In other cases, values may take precedence over needs (for example, hunger strikes by political activists).

Abraham Maslow outlined a hierarchy of needs that influence human behavior. Maslow's system takes the form of a pyramid in which the most basic needs at the bottom must be at least partly satisfied before the higher ones can be. At the base of the pyramid are primary biological needs, including food, water, oxygen, activity, and **sleep.** At the next level is the need for safety, followed by belongingness, or the need to be part of social groups and participate in relationships, both sexual and nonsexual. The highest needs outlined by Maslow are the need to be esteemed by others and, at the top of the pyramid, the need for **self-actualization,** or realizing one's greatest potential. This includes developing one's interests and participating as fully as possible in relationships with others and in the life of the community. According to Maslow, individuals achieve full self-actualization only rarely. While other research has supported the idea that basic needs generally take precedence over more sophisticated ones, Maslow's system has been challenged for being overly simplistic and rigid.

Neocortex

The exterior covering of the cerebral hemispheres of the brain.

The neocortex, the exterior covering of the cerebral hemispheres of the **brain,** is approximately 2 millimeters thick and consists of six thin layers of cells. The cortex is convoluted, furrowed, and, if stretched out, would measure 1.5 square feet. In terms of function, the cortex is divided into four lobes distinguished by the lateral and central fissures: the frontal lobe; parietal lobe (which controls sense of **touch** and body position); temporal lobe (which controls speech, **hearing** and **vision**); and occipital lobe, which also controls vision.

See also Left-Brain Hemisphere; Right-Brain Hemisphere.

Further Reading

Hoffman, Edward. *The Right to be Human: A Biography of Abraham Maslow.* Los Angeles: Tarcher, 1988.

Nerve

The common name for neuron, the basic fiber, or bundles of fibers, that transmit information to and from the muscles, glands, organs, spinal cord, and brain.

Nerves form the network of connections that receive signals, known as sensory input, from the **environment** and within the body and transmit the body's responses, or instructions for action, to the muscles, organs, and glands. The **central nervous system**, comprised of the **brain** and spinal cord, sends information throughout the body over the network of nerves known collectively as the peripheral nervous system. The nerves of the peripheral nervous system are in pairs, with one usually leading to the left side and the other to the right side of the body. There are 12 nerve pairs, called cranial nerves, that connect directly to the brain and control such functions as **vision** and **hearing**. Thirty-one nerve pairs are connected directly to the spinal cord, branching out to the rest of the body.

The peripheral nervous system may be further subdivided into the **autonomic nervous system**, which regulates involuntary functions such as breathing, digestion, beating of the heart, and the somatic nervous system, which controls voluntary functions, such as walking, picking up a pencil, and reading this page. The cells of the central nervous system do not have the ability to regenerate, and are not replaced directly if they are damaged.

See also Neuron.

Nervous System

An electrochemical conducting network that transmits messages from the brain through the nerves to locations throughout the body.

The nervous system is responsible for the perception of external and internal conditions and the body's response to them. It has two major divisions: the central and peripheral nervous systems. The **central nervous system** (CNS), consisting of the **brain** and the spinal cord, is that part of the nervous system that is encased in bone; the brain is located in the cranial cavity of the skull, and the spinal cord in the spinal column, or backbone. Both are protected by cerebrospinal fluid and a series of three membranes called meninges. The CNS receives information from the skin and muscles and sends out motor commands as well.

The brain functions as the center of instinctive, emotional, and cognitive processes. It is composed of three primary divisions, the forebrain, midbrain, and hindbrain, and divided into the left and right hemispheres. The first division, the forebrain, is the largest and most complicated of the brain structures and is responsible for most types of complex mental activity and behavior. The forebrain consists of two main divisions: the diencephalon and the cerebrum. The **thalamus** and **hypothalamus** make up the diencephalon. The parts of the cerebrum—the larger part of the forebrain—include the corpus callosum, striatum, septum, hippocampus, and amygdala, all covered by the **cerebral cortex.**

The midbrain, or mesencephalon, is the small area near the lower middle of the brain. Portions of the midbrain have been shown to control smooth and reflexive movements and it is important in the regulation of **attention, sleep,** and **arousal.** The hindbrain (rhombencephalon), which is basically a continuation of the spinal cord, is the part of the brain that receives incoming messages first. Lying beneath the cerebral hemispheres, it consists of three structures: the **cerebellum,** the medulla, and the pons, which control such vital functions of the **autonomic nervous system** as breathing, blood pressure, and heart rate.

The spinal cord is a long bundle of neural tissue continuous with the brain that occupies the interior canal

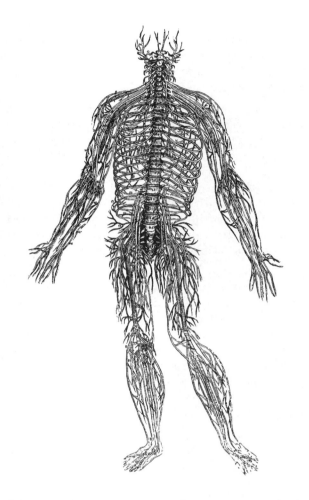

The peripheral nervous system carries out sensory and motor functions.

of the spinal column and functions as the primary communication link between the brain and the body. It is the origin of 31 bilateral pairs of spinal **nerves** which radiate outward from the central nervous system through openings between adjacent vertebrae. The spinal cord receives signals from the peripheral senses and relays them to the brain.

The peripheral nervous system (PNS) includes all parts of the nervous system not covered by bone and carries out sensory and motor functions. It is composed of 12 pairs of cranial and 31 pairs of spinal nerves which lead to the left and right sides of the body. The PNS is divided into two subsystems: the somatic and autonomic nervous systems. The somatic nervous system senses and acts upon the external world. Its sensory **neurons** transmit signals from receptor cells located in sense organs, such as the skin and eye, to the CNS. Motor neurons carry outgoing messages from the CNS to neuromuscular cells (**effectors**) found in muscles, joints, glands, and organs, which facilitate action. The skeletal muscles, which

are responsible for bodily movement, are controlled by the somatic nervous system.

The autonomic nervous system (ANS) relays messages between the CNS and the heart, lungs, and other glands and organs. These messages increase or decrease their activity in accordance with demands placed on the body. The ANS affects activities that are basically outside of conscious control, such as respiration and digestion. The autonomic nervous system is further subdivided into two branches. The sympathetic system speeds up muscles and mobilizes the body for action. This is the system responsible for the reaction to danger known as the "fight or flight" response. In contrast, the parasympathetic system, which slows down muscles, regulates bodily functions to conserve energy. For example, it is this system that slows heart rate and blood flow after a large meal is eaten to conserve energy for digestion. Disorders of the autonomic nervous system involve reactions such as fainting, uncontrollable sweating, and sexual dysfunction.

The nervous system is composed of two types of cells: **neuron**s, which transmit information through electrochemical impulses, and glial cells, which hold the neurons together and help them communicate with each other. There are three kinds of neurons. *Receptor* neurons register stimulation from the **environment** (such as cells in the eye responding to light or skin cells responding to pressure). When they are stimulated, they send signals to the brain, which are then converted into various types of information. *Motor,* or effector neurons transmit messages from the brain and spinal cord that provide for muscular contraction, which results in movement. Finally, *interneurons* transmit signals between different parts of the nervous system. Most neurons are composed of five parts: the *cell body*, which contains the nucleus; ***dendrites***, short fibers that usually receive signals from other neurons; the *axon*, a long fiber leading away from the cell body that transmits signals to other neurons, muscles, or glands; the *myelin sheath,* a fatty substance that insulates the axon; and *synapses,* minute gaps through which signals are transmitted between neurons. The many axon and dendrite fibers radiating from neurons permit each one to be in contact with many thousands of other neurons.

Communication at the synapses between neurons relies on chemicals called **neurotransmitters.** More than 50 different neurotransmitters have been identified, and more are constantly being discovered. Recently, it was found that the gases nitric oxide and carbon monoxide are neurotransmitters. Different transmitters predominate in different parts of the nervous system, and a particular neurotransmitter may perform different functions in different locations. Researchers have proposed that almost all drugs work through interaction with neurotransmitters. Important neurotransmitters include acetylcholine

(ACh), which is used by motor neurons in the spinal cord; the catecholamines (including norepinephrine and dopamine), which are important in the **arousal** of the sympathetic nervous system; serotonin, which affects body temperature, sensory perception, and the onset of **sleep;** and a group of transmitters called endorphins, which are involved in the relief of **pain.**

Among the major functions of the central nervous system is that of the *reflex arc,* which provides immediate, involuntary reaction to potentially harmful stimulireactions commonly referred to as *reflexes* (such as drawing one's hand back from a hot stove). The reflex arc is a circuit of neurons by which signals travel from a sensory receptor to a motor neuron, rapidly turning sensory input into action. The complexity of the nervous system makes it a challenge to study—millions of neurons may lie beneath a single square centimeter of brain surface, each synapsing with as many as 600 other neurons, and many different parts of the brain may be involved in a single task.

Further Reading

The Mind and Beyond. Alexandria, VA: Time-Life Books, 1991.

Neuron

Technical term for nerve cell.

Neurons are the basic working unit of the **nervous system,** sending, receiving, and storing signals through a unique blend of electricity and chemistry. The human brain has more than 100 billion neurons.

Neurons that receive information and transmit it to the spinal cord or brain are classified as *afferent* or *sensory;* those that carry information from the brain or spinal cord to the muscles or glands are classified as *efferent* or *motor.* The third type of neuron connects the vast network of neurons and may be referred to as *interneuron, association neuron, internuncial neuron, connector neuron,* and *adjustor neuron.*

Although neurons come in many sizes and shapes, they all have certain features in common. Each neuron has a *cell body* where the components necessary to keep the neuron alive are centered. Additionally, each neuron has two types of fiber. The *axon* is a large tentacle and is often quite long. (For example, the axons connecting the toes with the spinal cord are more than a meter in length.) The function of the axon is to conduct nerve impulses to other neurons or to muscles and glands. The signals transmitted by the axon are received by other neurons through the second type of fiber, the **dendrites**. The dendrites are usually relatively short and have many branch-

es to receive stimulation from other neurons. In many cases, the axon (but not the cell body or the dendrites) has a white, fatty covering called the *myelin sheath.* This covering is believed to increase the speed with which nerve impulses are sent down the axon.

An unstimulated neuron has a negative electrical charge. The introduction of a stimulus makes the charge a little less negative until a critical point—the threshold—is reached. Then the membrane surrounding the neuron changes, opening channels briefly to allowing positively charged sodium *ions* to enter the cell. Thus, the inside of the neuron becomes positive in charge for a millisecond (thousandth of a second) or so. This brief change in electrical charge is the nerve impulse, or spike, after which the neuron is restored to its original resting charge.

This weak electrical impulse travels down the axon to the **synapse.** The synapse or *synaptic gap* forms the connection between neurons, and is actually a place where the neurons almost touch, but are separated by a gap no wider than a few billionths of an inch. At the synapses, information is passed from one neuron to another by chemicals known as **neurotransmitter**s. The neurotransmitter then combines with specialized receptor molecules of the receiving cell.

Neurotransmitters either excite the receiving cell (that is, increase its tendency to fire nerve impulses) or inhibit it (decrease its tendency to fire impulses), and often both actions are required to accomplish the desired response. For example, the neurons controlling the muscles that pull your arm down (the triceps) must be inhibited when you are trying to reach up to your nose (biceps excited); if they are not, you will have difficulty bending your arm.

Physiological psychologists are interested in the involvement of the nervous system in behavior and experience. The chemistry and operation of the nervous system is a key component in the complex human puzzle. A number of chemical substances act as neurotransmitters at synapses in the nervous system and at the junction between nerves and muscles. These include acetylcholine, dopamine, epinephrine (adrenalin), and neuropeptides (enkephalins, endorphins, etc.). A decrease in acetylocholine has been noted in **Alzheimer's disease** which causes deterioration of the thought processes; shortage of dopamine has been linked to **Parkinson's disease,** whereas elevated dopamine has been observed in **schizophrenics**.

Drugs that affect behavior and experience—the *psychoactive drugs*—generally work on the nervous system by influencing the flow of information across synapses. For instance, they may interfere with one or several of the stages in synaptic transmission, or they may have ac-

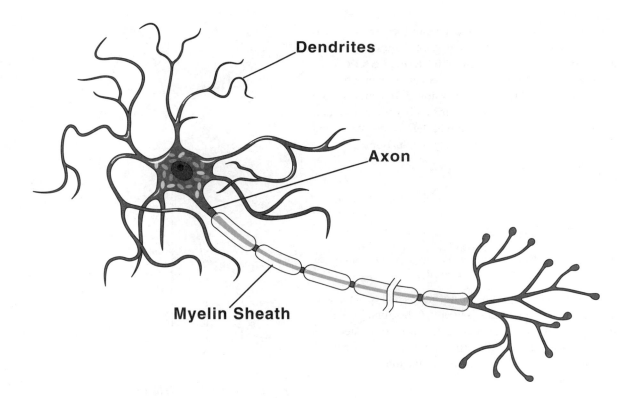

Dendrites

Axon

Myelin Sheath

A motor neuron

tions like the natural neurotransmitters and excite or inhibit receiving cells. This is also true of the drugs which are used in the treatment of certain **psychological disorders**.

Neurotic Disorders. See **Anxiety.**

Neurotransmitter

Chemical substances or molecules which aid in message transmission between neurons.

Communication at the **synapses** between **neurons** relies on chemicals called neurotransmitters. Secreted from a part of one neuron (the axon) into the synaptic gap between two others, neurotransmitters diffuse across this space and combine with specific proteins on the surface of the receiving cell, triggering an electrochemical response in the target cell. Afterward, neurotransmitters are either destroyed or reabsorbed back into the neuron for storage and reuse. The release of neurotransmitters by a neuron has three main functions: 1) exciting a second neuron, thus causing it to depolarize; 2) inhibiting a second neuron, which prevents it from depolarizing; and 3) stimulating a muscle fiber to contract.

More than 50 different neurotransmitters have been identified, and more are constantly being discovered. Researchers have proposed that almost all drugs work through interaction with neurotransmitters. Important neurotransmitters include acetylcholine (ACh), which is used by motor neurons in the spinal cord; the catecholamines (including norepinephrine and dopamine), which are important in the **arousal** of the sympathetic nervous system; serotonin, which affects body temperature, sensory **perception,** and the onset of **sleep;** and a group of transmitters called endorphins, which are involved in the relief of **pain.** In recent years, it has been recognized that biochemical imbalances in the **brain** play an important role in **mental illness.** Low levels of norepinephrine characterize some varieties of **depression,** for example, and an imbalance of dopamine is considered a factor in **schizophrenia.**

Norm

A measure of central tendency in statistics, describing a value's frequency.

In testing, norms are figures describing the frequency with which particular scores appear. They provide information about whether a score is above or below average and about what percentage of the persons tested received that score. Norms may apply to tests of mental ability or achievement, such as **IQ tests** or **SATs**. They are also used in **personality** assessment to measure variables such as **anxiety**, **introversion-extroversion**, and **paranoia**. The term "norm" may also refer to social norms, unwritten social rules that define acceptable and unacceptable behavior in a variety of situations.

See also Mean; Median; Mode.

Normal

Represents the characteristics that are typical for—that is, exhibited by—most members of a particular group.

For statistical purposes, normal means whatever is average for a given group of people ("the **norm**"). Therefore, the term normal does include those group members who deviate significantly from the measures of central tendency (the **mean**, the **median**, or the **mode**) of a given distribution.

The term normal is fundamentally statistical and quantitative. In testing and measuring, for example, normal can be defined as a central cluster of scores in relation to a larger grouping. In **intelligence** testing normal is also defined by the average, or mean, which is established as an IQ score of around 100.

However, in many contexts normal is a subjective term that is very difficult to define. In the absence of fixed standards, normal and abnormal are often defined in terms of each other. However, rather than a simple pairing of opposites, they are generally thought of as points on a continuum of social adjustment, with normal people possessing certain positive traits to a greater degree, while abnormal people are characterized by deficiencies in these traits. Some of the traits that help define psychological normalcy are efficient **perception** of reality; self-knowledge; self-control; **ability** to form affectionate relationships; self-esteem; and productivity. The notion of defining normalcy in terms of social adjustment has its detractors, who argue that such a definition places too much emphasis on **conformity** and too little on such traits as individuality and **creativity.**

Further Reading

Martin, David W. *Doing Psychology Experiments.* 2nd ed. Monterey, CA: Brooks/Cole, 1985.

Berman, Simeon M. *Mathematical Statistics: An Introduction Based on the Normal Distribution.* Scranton, PA: Intext Educational Publishers, 1971.

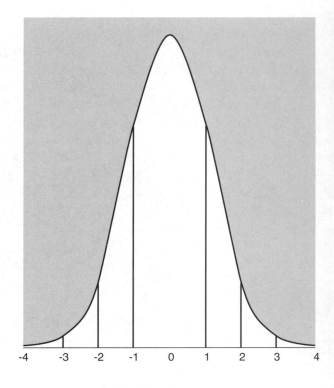

An example of the bell-shaped curve of a normal distribution.

Normal Distribution

The common pattern of numbers in which the majority of the measurements tend to cluster near the mean of distribution.

Psychological research involves measurement of behavior. This measurement results in numbers that differ from one another individually but that are predictable as a group. One of the common patterns of numbers involves most of the measurements being clustered together near the mean of the distribution, with fewer cases occurring as they deviate farther from the **mean**. When a frequency distribution is drawn in pictorial form, the resulting pattern produces the bell-shaped curve that scientists call a normal distribution.

When measurements produce a normal distribution, certain things are predictable. First, the mean, **median**, and **mode** are all equal. Second, a scientist can predict how far from the mean most scores are likely to fall. Thus, it is possible to determine which scores are more likely to occur and the proportion of score likely to be above or below any given score.

Many behavioral measurements result in normal distributions. For example, scores on **intelligence** tests are likely to be normally distributed. The mean is about 100 and a typical person is likely to score within about 15 points of the mean, that is, between 85 and 115. If the psychologist knows the mean and the typical deviation from the mean (called the standard deviation), the researcher can determine what proportion of scores is likely to fall in any given range. For instance, in the range between one standard deviation below the mean (about 85 for **IQ** scores) and one deviation above the mean (about 115 for IQ scores), one expects to find the scores of about two thirds of all test takers. Further, only about two and a half percent of test takers will score higher than two standard deviations above the mean (about 130).

Although psychologists rely on the fact that many measurements are normally distributed, there are certain cases where scores are unlikely to be normally distributed. Whenever scores cannot be higher than some upper value or smaller than some lower value, a non-normal distribution may occur. For example, salaries are not normally distributed because there is a lower value (i.e., nobody can make less than zero dollars), but there is no upper value. Consequently, there will be some high salaries that will not be balanced by corresponding, lower salaries. It is important to know whether scores are normally distributed because it makes a difference in the kind of statistical tests that are appropriate for analyzing and interpreting the numbers.

Further Reading

Berman, Simeon M. *Mathematical Statistics: An Introduction Based on the Normal Distribution.* Scranton, PA: Intext Educational Publishers, 1971.

Martin, David W. *Doing Psychology Experiments.* 2nd ed. Monterey, CA: Brooks/Cole, 1985.

Obesity

A condition of having an excessive accumulation of fat in the body, resulting in a body weight that is at least 20 percent above normal when measured against standard tables of optimal weight ranges according to age, sex, height, and body type.

Individuals who are 20 percent overweight are considered *slightly* obese. Those who are 40 percent above standard weight are *moderately* obese, while those 50 percent above it are *morbidly* obese. Persons who exceed desired weight levels by 100 pounds (45 kg) or more are *hyperobese*. Obesity is a serious health problem in the United States. Studies suggests that between 10 and 20 percent of Americans are slightly to moderately obese. Obesity places stress on the body's organs, and is associated with joint problems, high blood pressure, indigestion, dizzy spells, rashes, menstrual disorders, and premature **aging.** Generally, when compared to persons of normal weight, obese individuals suffer more severely from many diseases, including degenerative diseases of the heart and arteries, and a shorter life expectancy. Obesity can also cause complications during childbirth and surgery.

Obesity may be familial, as the body weight of children appears to be linked to that of their parents. Children of obese parents have been found to be 13 times more likely than other children to be obese, suggesting a genetic predisposition to body fat accumulation. Recent animal research suggests the existence of a "fat gene," and the tendency toward a body type with an unusually high number of fat cells—termed *endomorphic*—appears to be inherited. However, the generational transmission of obesity may be as cultural as it is genetic, as early feeding patterns may produce unhealthy eating habits.

Some cases of obesity have a purely physiological cause, such as glandular malfunction or a disorder of the **hypothalamus.** Individuals with a low production of the **hormone** thyroxin tend to metabolize food slowly, which results in excess unburned calories. When more calories are consumed than the body can metabolize, excess calories are stored in the body as fat, or adipose tissue. Some persons with hypoglycemia have a specific metabolic problem with carbohydrates that can also lead to the storage of unburned calories as fat.

In the great majority of cases, however, obesity is caused by overeating. Overeating itself often combines

OBESITY IN ADOLESCENTS YOUTHS (AGES 6 TO 17) IN THE UNITED STATES	
Prevalence of overweight	Doubled since 1965
Number who are overweight	4.7 million
Percent who are overweight	11 percent
Related disorders	Elevated blood cholesterol; high blood pressure; increased adult mortality
Social consequences	Excluded from peer groups, discriminated against by adults, experience psychological stress, poor body image and low self-esteem.

Source: Centers for Disease Control, U.S. department of Health and Human Services.

physical and psychological components. People may eat compulsively to overcome **fear** or social maladjustment, express defiance, or avoid intimate relationships. However, researchers have also suggested physical correlates for overeating, including deficits in the **neurotransmitter** serotonin that increase cravings for carbohydrates, and possibly a higher "set point" for body weight that makes obese persons feel hungry more often than thinner people. This raised set point could result from both genetics and early nutritional habits. Lack of exercise and sedentary living also contribute to obesity.

The most effective treatment of obesity includes both the reduction of surplus body fat and the elimination of causative factors, and is best accomplished under medical supervision. An appropriate weight loss plan includes exercise (which burns calories without slowing metabolism), reduced food intake, **behavior modification** to change food-related **attitudes** and behavior, and **psychotherapy** if there are underlying psychological causes for overeating. Other possible treatment measures include hormone therapy, appetite-suppressant **drugs,** and surgical intervention to alter satiety signals by reducing the size of the stomach and intestines.

Behavior modification has been especially successful and widely used in the treatment of obesity. Treatment techniques include stimulus control (removing environmental cues that play a role in inappropriate eating), eating management (slowing the pace of eating to allow satiation to catch up with it), contingency management (applying a system of positive **reinforcement** and **punishments**), and self-monitoring of daily dietary intake and factors associated with it. Despite all of the available treatments, the difficulty of reversing obesity in adults makes preventative treatment an important factor during childhood. Today, an increasing percentage of children in the United States are overweight. Recent studies have shown that metabolic rates of children are lower when they watch **television** than when they are at rest. Unhealthy eating patterns and behaviors associated with obesity can be addressed by programs in nutrition, exercise, and **stress** management involving both children and families.

Obsessive-Compulsive Disorder (OCD)

A condition characterized by persistent, unwanted thoughts (obsessions) and repetitive, uncontrollable ritualistic behaviors (compulsions).

Obsessive-compulsive disorder (OCD), which is classified as an **anxiety** disorder in the **American Psychiatric Association**'s *Diagnostic and Statistical Manual of Mental Disorders,* affects males and females equally. About 2.5 percent of the American population will suffer from OCD in the course of their lives. Symptoms usually begin in **adolescence** or early adulthood.

The symptoms of obsessive-compulsive disorder mask basic conflicts and anxieties that persons affected by them are unwilling or unable to face. Often, the individual have repressed unacceptable impulses that would endanger their self-esteem or their relationships with others, and the obsessive-compulsive symptoms are a way of alleviating the anxiety induced by this **repression**. It has been suggested that persons suffering from OCD did not receive adequate parenting and developed obsessive-compulsive symptoms as a means of compensating for the lack of safety and security experienced in childhood. Compulsive rituals also give people a sense of order and control over events. The obsessions, or unwanted thoughts, commonly include **fear** of contamination (often through routine actions such as shaking hands or touching doorknobs), doubts about whether one has done something correctly, a **need** to arrange things in a particular order, aggressive or otherwise frightening impulses (such as recurrent thoughts of hurting one's children), and unwanted sexual thoughts. Because such obsessions are characteristically unrelated or out of proportion to real-life situations, one principal way of relieving the resulting anxiety is to engage in compulsive, ritualistic behaviors. Thus, the fear of contamination commonly leads to such actions as excessive handwashing or showering, and doubts about having performed a task result in compulsive checking to see if doors are locked or other activities have been performed. Other compulsive behaviors include repeatedly arranging things in a certain order and mental activities such as counting or repeating certain words. Adults with obsessive-compulsive disorder generally recognize that their thoughts and/or behaviors are unreasonable, although the degree of awareness varies from one individual to another, and for a single individual in different situations.

OCD can severely disrupt the lives of those who suffer from it. The rituals they undergo to reduce their anxiety tend to multiply until people have little time or energy for anything else. Many feel compelled to take lengthy baths or showers several times a day and to change their clothes or underwear frequently as well. Compulsive arranging or ordering of household items such as clothes or books may take hours. In persons who fear contamination, ordinary activities like cooking turn into complicated, time-consuming procedures that incorporate numerous rituals, such as washing already clean pots several times in scalding water before using them. In addition to interfering with work, school, and other activities, obsessive-compulsive disorder also tends to disrupt social functioning, as its sufferers withdraw from friends and family because of their preoccupation with obsessive thoughts, or in order to avoid having their compulsive rituals interrupted.

The prognosis for persons with obsessive-compulsive disorder varies. With treatment, many achieve partial or even complete recovery. If onset occurred at a young age such aspects of normal adolescent development as the formation of peer relationships and psychosexual maturation may have been disrupted. In addition, people with OCD sometimes suffer from other disorders as well, such as anxiety or **depression**. The presence of supportive friends and family affects the outlook for improvement, as it is easier for someone who can look to others for emotional support to abandon reliance on obsessive-compulsive behaviors.

Psychotherapy, often in combination with antidepressant medication, is generally the best course of treatment for obsessive-compulsive disorder. Therapy that involves other family members is often helpful, both in order to obtain insight into the nature of the anxiety troubling the OCD sufferer and also as a means of encouraging environmental changes that will aid in his or her recovery. Fluoxetine (Prozac) and other serotonin-related drugs, including clomipramine (Anafranil), have been effective in treating OCD.

Further Reading

Levenkron, Steven. *Obsessive-Compulsive Disorders: Treating and Understanding Crippling Habits.* New York: Warner Books, 1991.

Melville, Joy. *Phobias and Obsessions.* Coward, McCann, and Geoghegan, 1977.

Oedipus Complex

The theory that children are torn between feelings of love for one parent while feeling a sense of competition with the other; first put forth by Sigmund Freud as one possible cause of neuroses in later life.

Sigmund Freud first suggested the existence of what he would later call the Oedipus complex in *The Interpretation of Dreams* (1900). In this work, he describes a subconscious feelings in children of intense competition and even hatred toward the parent of the same sex, and feelings of romantic love toward the parent of the opposite sex. He felt that if these conflicting feelings were not successfully resolved, they would contribute to neuroses in later life. The name "Oedipus" refers to *Oedipus Rex,* the classic Greek play by Sophocles, which tells the story of Oedipus, who is abandoned at birth by his parents, King Lauis and Queen Jocasta. He later comes back and, as foretold by prophecy, kills his father and marries

his mother before finding out his true identity. Freud saw in the play an archetypal dynamic being played out, and so coopted the character's name for his description.

In traditional Freudian psychoanalytical theory, the term Electra complex was used when these unconscious wishes were attributed to a young girl and centered around sexual involvement with her father and jealous rivalry with her mother. Like Oedipus, Electra is a figure in Greek mythology who participated in the killing of her parent (in Electra's case, her mother). Contemporary psychology no longer distinguishes this complex by gender, and the Electra complex is included in the definition of the Oedipus complex.

Modern interpretations of Freudian theories are often critical, and his Oedipus theory has been no exception. Many current psychologists think of it as too simplistic, and the authors of the *Oxford Companion to the Mind* (1987) state, "Freud's formula . . . gives a one-sided and too simple an account of the complex interactions of the family." It would be fair to say that this is the current view of Freud's Oedipal notions. Yet, looking to Freud's *Introductory Lectures on Psychoanalysis* (1920), Freud writes, "I do not wish to assert that the Oedipus complex exhausts the relation of children to their parents: it can easily be far more complicated. The Oedipus complex can, moreover, be developed to a greater or lesser strength, it can even be reversed; but it is a regular and very important factor in a child's mental life."

Further Reading

Montrelay, Michele. "Why Did You Tell Me I Love Mommy and That's Why I'm Frightened When I Love You." *American Imago* (Summer 1994): 213.

Sophocles. *Oedipus Rex.* Cambridge, England: Cambridge University Press, 1982.

Tabin, Johanna. *On the Way to Self.* New York: Columbia University Press, 1985.

Operant Conditioning

Use of reward and punishment to modify behavior.

Psychologists distinguish two types of conditioning, operant and classical. Operant conditioning involves the use of **reinforcement** and **punishment** to change behavior. In general, psychologists agree that reinforcement is a more effective means of changing behavior than punishment because reinforcement lets a person know what behavior will be rewarded, while punishment often fails to provide information about appropriate behavior.

The noted psychologist **B.F. Skinner** popularized many of the ideas and procedures used in operant conditioning, although **Edward L. Thorndike** developed the

	POSITIVE	NEGATIVE
REINFORCEMENT		
The frequency of a behavior is increased because of the behavior of the subject.	When a person receives reinforcement after engaging in some behavior, the person is likely to repeat that behavior.	When a person experiences a negative state and does something to eliminate the undesired state, the person is likely to repeat that behavior.
PUNISHMENT		
The frequency of a behavior is decreased because of the behavior of the subject.	When a person engages in a behavior and something negative is applied as a result, that behavior is less likely to be repeated.	When a person engages in a behavior and something positive is taken away, that behavior is less likely to be repeated.

first principles of operant conditioning around the turn of the century.

The basic process of operant conditioning involves gradually changing an organism's behavior so that the behavior evolves in the direction of the final, desired action. This process is called shaping a behavior through successive approximations. At each point in the shaping process, the subject must perform an action successively closer to the desired behavior in order to be rewarded. For example, in training a rat to press a lever, the researcher would first reinforce any movement made by the animal toward the lever, and reward the rat each time it moved closer to the lever.

Behaviors can also be eliminated with operant conditioning techniques. One way is through the process of **extinction** in which an animal receives no reinforcement for behaviors that were previously reinforced. The speed of extinction depends on many factors, including the nature of the reinforcement the animal has received. For example, if an animal learned a behavior by being reinforced every time it performed some action, extinction would occur much more quickly than if the animal received reinforcement only some of the time during **shaping**.

Another means of eliminating behavior is through punishment. If the animal displays an undesired behavior, it receives some punishment; ultimately, that behavior will diminish in frequency.

Some of the terminology in operant conditioning can be confusing. For example, although the meaning of the term positive reinforcement is clear (i.e., a reward), the meaning of the term negative reinforcement is more difficult. Contrary to common usage, the term negative reinforcement does not mean punishment. The accompanying table describes conditions of reinforcement and punishment and their effects on behavior.

Although much of the research on operant conditioning has been done with animals, the principles of conditioning can often be used with people as well.

See also Classical/Respondent Conditioning.

Further Reading

Mackintosh, N. J. *Conditioning and Associative Learning.* New York: Oxford University Press, 1983.

Organic Disorder

Disorder caused by a known pathological condition.

In general, any disorder that is caused by a known pathological condition of an organic structure may be categorized as an organic disorder, or more specifically, as an organic mental disorder, or a psychological disorder. An example is **delirium,** a disorder that is caused by a known physical dysfunction of the **brain.** Most psychologists and psychiatrists now believe that virtually all serious, or psychotic, mental disorders will eventually be proven to have an organic cause. Consequently, many psychologists and psychiatrists prefer not to use the term organic mental disorder because the term implies that those disorders which have not yet been shown to have an organic cause do not have an organic cause, and that functional disorders (a term that has often been contrasted with the term organic disorders) have no organic causal component.

Organizational Psychology. See **Industrial Psychology.**

Origin of Species. See **Darwin, Charles.**

Otis, Arthur (1886–1964)

American psychologist whose most enduring work was done in the field of group intelligence testing.

Arthur Otis was born in Denver, Colorado, and educated at Stanford University. He served on the faculty of Stanford University, and held various consulting and research positions at several U.S. government agencies. He was also an editor of tests in mathematics for an educational publishing company. Otis introduced and developed the Otis Group Intelligence Scale, which is considered to be the earliest scientifically reliable instrument for the **intelligence** testing of subjects in groups. First published in 1918, the Otis Group Intelligence Scale consisted of verbal and nonverbal items and became very widely used, especially in schools. The test was substantially revised by Roger Lennon, and continues to be used. Otis' books include: *Statistical Method in Educational Measurement* (1925), *Modern School Arithmetic* (1929), and *Primary Arithmetic Through Experience* (1939).

See also Intelligence Quotient, I.Q. Test.

Overachiever

A person, usually a student, whose academic achievement is disproportionate to his or her performance on standardized intelligence tests.

The terms "overachiever" and "underachiever," both of which refer to gaps between academic performance and **IQ** test scores, are generally not used by either educators or psychologists. Sometimes the term is used in informal communication to describe a person intent on gathering tangible or recognized symbols of accomplishment, such as educational degrees, awards, and honorary positions.

Pain

Physical suffering resulting from some sort of injury or disease, experienced through the central nervous system.

Pain is a complex phenomenon that scientists are still struggling to understand. Its purpose is to alert the body of damage or danger to its system, yet scientists do not fully understand the level and intensity of pain sometimes experienced by people. Long-lasting, severe pain does not serve the same purpose as acute pain, which triggers an immediate physical response. Pain that persists without diminishing over long periods of time is known as chronic pain. It is estimated that almost one-third of all Americans suffer from some form of chronic pain. Of these, 70 million have back pain, 36 million have arthritis, 20 million suffer from migraine headaches, and at least 800,000 Americans suffer severe pain associated with the growth of cancerous tumors. An additional kind of pain is psychological pain. Recent research has shown that the chemicals produced by **anxiety** are similar to those that are released in response to physical injury.

Pain signals travel through the body along billions of special nerve cells reserved specifically for transmitting pain messages. These cells are known as nociceptors. The chemical **neurotransmitter**s carrying the message include prostaglandins, bradykinin—the most painful substance known to humans—and a chemical known as P, which stands for pain. Prostaglandins are manufactured from fatty acids in nearly every tissue in the body. Analgesic pain relievers, such as aspirin and ibuprofen, work by inhibiting prostaglandin production.

After an injury, cells near the trauma site release these chemicals into the **central nervous system**. In the spinal cord, they are carried by the dorsal horn, and it is at this point that the body pulls away from the source of the pain. When the signal reaches the **brain**, it is first processed by the **thalamus** and then passed to the **cerebral cortex**. Here, the brain fully processes the informa-tion, locates its source in the body, and begins sending signals to relieve the pain.

As they travel, the pain messages are sorted according to severity. Recent research has discovered that the body has two distinct pathways for transmitting pain messages. The epicritic system is used to transmit messages of sudden, intense pain, such as that caused by cuts or burns. The **neurons** that transmit such messages are called A fibers, and they are built to transmit messages quickly. The protopathic system is used to transmit less severe messages of pain, such as the kind one might experience from overstrenuous exercise. The C fibers of the protopathic system do not send messages as quickly as A fibers.

In 1965, Ronald Melzack and Patrick Wall, leading pain researchers at the Massachusetts Institute of Technology, proposed what has come to be known as the gate theory of pain. This theory holds that the **nervous system** has the capacity to process only limited amounts of information at a time. For example, if the body is overwhelmed by multiple messages, the nervous system will "shut down" certain messages. This would explain why rubbing an injury often lessens its pain. The rubbing, in essence, competes with the injury for space in the nervous system.

One application of the gate theory is the use of small bursts of electricity to help manage pain. Experiments were first conducted on animals, whose brains were stimulated electronically at certain points, shutting down their capacity to feel pain. The animals were then operated on using no anesthetic. This method has been adapted for humans as well and has led to the development of a pain relief method known as transcutaneous electrical nerve stimulation, or TENS. In this technique, pain sufferers are jolted with tiny bits of electricity at strategic points. As predicted by the gate theory, the nerve endings at the point of the shock are overwhelmed and divert some of the space in the central nervous system to processing it, thereby relieving the original pain.

Chronic pain, on the other hand, presents its own set of problems. Treating chronic pain is difficult because by its very nature, such pain damages the central nervous system, making it weaker and more susceptible to pain. This residue of pain is called pain **memory.** Problems also arise when nerve cells are damaged by chemotherapy, diabetes, shingles, and other diseases. And in the case of arthritis and other inflammatory diseases, the body's threshold for pain is lowered, thus causing increased pain from "less" stimuli.

Treatments for pain vary widely. For mild pain, the most common form of treatment is aspirin, a medication discovered in the 19th century and derived from salicin, a chemical found in the bark of the willow tree. Today, there are several aspirin-like drugs on the market for the relief of minor, inflammatory pain, including ibuprofen and acetaminophen. For more severe pain, opiates—derived from the opium poppy, a common flowering plant—are often used. Opiates work by attaching themselves, on the molecular level, to nerve cells normally used to transmit pain messages. (The place on the nerve cells where the opiates reside are called opiate receptors). Opiates work very well in relieving pain, but are quite dangerous and can become addictive.

In the 1970s, scientists began looking for natural opiate-like substances, and found that the body does indeed produce its own painkillers, which has come to be called opioids. The two most common opioids are endorphins and enkephalins. These chemicals attach themselves to the opiate receptors in nerve cells just as opiates do. It has been found that the body can be stimulated to release these chemicals by TENS and by acupuncture, a Chinese method of placing tiny needles at specific points in the body to relieve pain. Other methods for treating pain include **hypnotism**, massage, and **biofeedback**.

Further Reading

Arnold, Caroline. *Pain: What Is It? How Do We Deal With It?* New York: William Morrow and Company, 1986.

Atkinson, Jim. "Nerve Center." *Texas Monthly* (June 1994): 54.

Bower, Bruce. "Brain Changes Linked to Phantom-Limb Pain." *Science News* (10 June 1995).

Chase, Marilyn. "When Treating Pain, All Roads Lead to the Brain." *Wall Street Journal* (17 October 1994): B1.

Strobel, Gabrielle. "Pain Message Travels via Diffuse Signal." *Science News* (27 November 1993).

"Tips for Coping with Chronic Agony." *USA Today Magazine* (October 1993): 3.

Paired-Associate Learning

Strategy used by psychologists to study learning.

Paired-associate (PA) learning was invented by **Mary Whiton Calkins** in 1894 and involves the pairing of two items (usually words)—a stimulus and a response.

For example, words such as *calendar* (stimulus) and *shoe* (response) may be paired, and when the learner is prompted with the stimulus, he responds with the appropriate word (*shoe*).

The study of PA learning has been important for a number of reasons. Psychologists view it as representative of the kind of learning that people engage in every day. For example, when learning a new word, a person must pair the word itself with the concept it represents. This is the essence of PA learning. Another reason is that it allows researchers to study the associations between stimuli and responses. Although this stimulus-response approach has lost some of its importance in contemporary psychology, researchers—especially behaviorists—have been interested in how stimulus-response links are formed and broken.

Psychological research has revealed that when people learn paired associates, they engage in two separate mental processes. The first is the learning of the response; the second is the formation of a bond between the two words. This second process seems to produce a one-way association in many circumstances. That is, a learner is much more likely to remember the response word if given the stimulus; people have a harder time remembering the stimulus if presented with the response word.

This pattern holds true when the response has never been used as a stimulus. On the other hand, if a particular word (e.g., *cloud*) has been used both as a stimulus and as a response (e.g., *cloud-pen* and *bag-cloud*), the learner gets accustomed to using the word in two ways. In later testing, the subject is likely to remember the word pair correctly when presented with either word. Based on research such as this, psychologists have concluded that learners remember the word pair as a unit, not as a stimulus that simply leads to a response.

Further Reading

Deese, J., and S.H. Hulse. *The Psychology of Learning*. 3rd ed. New York: McGrawHill, 1967.

Panic

An acute feeling of intense fear, accentuated by increased heart rate, shortness of breath, sweating, and mild convulsions.

Feelings of **fear** and panic are common to all species, and humans are certainly no exception. Psychologically speaking, however, panic can be an obtrusive, life-altering phenomena for many people who suffer panic attacks. Such attacks occur commonly in people suffering from various **phobia**s. People suffering from agoraphobia, for instance, can expect to suffer panic attacks when out in public. While panic attacks are generally short-lived, their recurrence and the severity of the physical symptoms that accompany them can lead people to fear them so intensely that they develop a more severe condition known as **anxiety disorder**.

Panic attacks usually originate as realistic responses to fearful or **stress**ful experiences, usually in childhood. In more mature persons, however, memories of fearful events are put in perspective, and people generally do not feel the same fear they felt as a child when confronting a similar situation as an adult. Often, however, certain people will be susceptible to a variety of subconscious triggers. For instance, a person may experience intense fear every time he or she goes to the mall, not because of the mall, per se, but perhaps because they once had a very fearful experience, like being lost from a parent, in a mall. Panic attacks can also be caused by internal reactions. For example, increased heart rate can remind a person of an early panic experience and every time his or her heart rate increases, the person experiences another panic attack.

Psychiatrists have documented the physical manifestations of panic, and are fairly certain that there is a genetic component to panic attacks. Neurologically, recent psychiatric research has identified a **brain** circuit called the flight/fight system, or FFS. This neurologic area, when stimulated in animals, produces features of tremendous fear and panic. Research in this area is still very new, and with each finding there are controversies and conflicting views. Brain imaging technology should help psychiatrists better understand the neurology of panic attacks, but they are still largely a mystery.

Further Reading

Chase, Marilyn. "Psychiatry Finds Answers to Mystery of Panic Attacks." *Wall Street Journal* (12 June 1995): B1.

Segal, Mariah. "Panic Disorder: The Heart That Goes Thump in the Night—and Day." *FDA Consumer* (April 1992): 22.

Seymour, Lesley Jane. "Fear of Almost Everything." *Mademoiselle* (September 1993): 252.

"What Triggers Panic Attacks?" *USA Today Magazine* (October 1992): 2.

Paranoia

A pervasive feeling of distrust of others.

Paranoia is an ever-present feeling of suspicion that others cannot be trusted. Such feelings are not based on fact or reality; insecurity and low self-esteem often exaggerate these emotions. Typically, paranoia is not seen in children, but in most cases it begins to develop in late **adolescence** and early adulthood. Most people experience feelings of paranoia, usually in response to a threatening situation or in connection with feelings of insecurity

based on real circumstances. These feelings are related to the mild **anxiety** people experience at some points during their lives.

The fourth edition of ***Diagnostic and Statistical Manual of Mental Disorders (DSM-IV)*** includes diagnostic criteria for the more serious condition, paranoid personality disorder. According to the *DSM-IV*, individuals afflicted with this disorder assume, with little concrete evidence to support the assumption, that others plan to exploit, harm, or deceive him or her; and continually analyzes the motivations of friends, family, and others to confirm his or her doubts about their trustworthiness; expects friends and family to abandon him or her in times of trouble or **stress**; avoids revealing personal information because of **fear** that it will be used against him or her; interprets remarks and actions as having hidden, demeaning, and threatening connotations; and is unwilling to forgive an insult. The behavior of an individual with paranoid personality disorder may compel others to react with **anger** or **hostility**. This tends to reinforce the individual's suspiciousness and feelings that friends and associates are "against" him or her.

In the 1990s, the term "everyday paranoia (EP)" came into usage among psychologists to describe the intense **anxiety** that was becoming prevalent in society. Everyday paranoia is sparked by fear of losing one's job, feelings of inadequacy when confronting a new interpersonal or romantic relationship, or insecurity in a marriage or other long-term relationship. Low self-esteem and feelings of insecurity contribute to a person's susceptibility to feelings of everyday paranoia. Stressful situations—economic insecurity, divorce, a move, a job change—can also reinforce a person's paranoia. Almost everyone experiences feelings of suspicion or insecurity—and in fact, paranoia can be a mechanism for coping with misfortune or personal problems. Rather than view the situation as "bad luck" or personal failure or incompetence, paranoia places the responsibility for the problem on some "enemy."

The term paranoia is used erroneously at times to define special life circumstances. Members of minority groups and new immigrants may exhibit guarded behavior due to unfamiliarity with their new **environment** and lack of knowledge of language and cultural norms. This display of suspicion of authority figures and lack of trust in outsiders is based on a real lack of understanding of the person's surroundings, and does not represent an abnormal reaction. In addition, the term "political paranoia" is used to describe **attitudes** shared by members of groups on the fringes of society who suspect that government agencies are conspiring to control the lives of citizens by imposing new values, or suspect that other dominant groups are persecuting them. The growth of paramilitary organizations in the United States in recent years appears to be indicative of such feelings of political paranoia among a small percentage of citizens.

Further Reading

Diagnostic and Statistical Manual of Mental Disorders. 4th ed. Washington, DC: American Psychiatric Association, 1994.

Goodwin, Jan. "Paranoia." *Cosmopolitan* (August 1994):184+.

Kelly, Michael. "The Road to Paranoia." *The New Yorker* (June 19, 1995): 60+.

Paranoid Personality. See **Personality Disorder.**

Paraphilia

Sexual feelings or behaviors that may involve sexual partners that are not human, not consenting, or that involve suffering by one or both partners.

To diagnose an individual with a paraphilia, the psychologist or other diagnostician must confirm recurrent, intense, sexually arousing feelings, fantasies, or behaviors over a period of at least six months. According to the *Diagnostic and Statistical Manual of Mental Disorders (DSM-IV),* it is not uncommon for an individual to have more than one paraphilia.

Bestiality

Bestiality is a term that describes sexual feelings or behaviors involving animals. Termed zoophilia by the fourth edition of *Diagnostic and Statistical Manual of Mental Disorders (DSM-IV),* this is a relatively uncommon disorder. The disorder does not specify an animal or category of animals; the person with zoophilia may focus sexual feelings on domesticated animals, such as dogs, or farm animals, such as sheep or goats.

Exhibitionism

Exhibitionism is the exposure of genitals to a non-consenting stranger. In some cases, the individual may also engage in **autoeroticism** while exposing himself. Generally, no additional contact with the observer is sought; the individual is stimulated sexually by gaining the attention of and startling the observer.

Masochism (Sexual)

Masochism is a term applied to a specific sexual disorder but which also has a broader usage. The sexual disorder involves pleasure and excitement produced by **pain,** either inflicted by others or by oneself. It usually begins in childhood or **adolescence** and is chronic. Masochism is the only paraphilia in which any noticeable number of women participate—about 5 percent of masochists are female. The term comes from the name of a nineteenth century Austrian writer, Leopold von Sacher-Masoch, whose novels often included characters who were obsessed with the combination of sex and pain.

In the broader sense, masochism refers to any experience of receiving pleasure or satisfaction from suffering pain. The psychoanalytic view is that masochism is **aggression** turned inward, onto the self, when a person feels too guilty or afraid to express it outwardly.

Pedophilia

Pedophilia involves sexual activity with a child, generally under age 13. The *Diagnostic and Statistical Manual of Mental Disorders* describes a criterion that the individual with pedophilia be over 16 years of age and be at least five years older than the child. Individuals with this disorder may be attracted to either males or females or both, although incidents of pedophilic activity are almost twice as likely to be repeated by those individuals attracted to males. Individuals with this disorder develop procedures and strategies for gaining access to and trust of children.

Sadomasochism

Sadomasochism applies to deviant sexual behavior in which an individual achieves gratification either by experiencing pain (masochism) or inflicting it on another (sadism).

In psychoanalytic theory, sadism is related to the **fear** of castration, while the behaviorist explanation of sadomasochism is that its constituent feelings are physiologically similar to sexual **arousal.** Separate but parallel descriptions are given for sexual sadism and sexual masochism in the *Diagnostic and Statistical Manual of Mental Disorders (DSM-IV).* The clinical diagnostic criteria for both are recurrence of the behavior over a period of at least six months, and significant distress or impairment of the ability to function as a result of the behavior or associated urges or fantasies. Either type of behavior may be limited to fantasies (sometimes while one is engaged in outwardly nondeviant sex) or acted out with a consenting partner, a non-consenting partner, or in the case of masochism, alone. Sadomasochism occurs in both males and females, and in both heterosexual and homosexual relationships.

Sadistic activities, which may express dominance or inflict pain and /or humiliation on the other person, include restraint, blindfolding, whipping, burning, **rape,** stabbing, strangulation, and even death. Masochists may seek to be the object of some of these acts as well as other types of humiliation, including forced cross-dressing. A particularly dangerous and fatal masochistic practice is hypoxyphilia, which consists of deliberately cutting off one's oxygen supply through mechanical or chemical means. Both sadistic and masochistic fantasies usually begin in childhood, and the disorders usually manifest in early adulthood. When associated with antisocial personality disorder, it may result in serious injury to others or death.

Voyeurism

Voyeurism is a paraphilia in which a person finds sexual excitement in watching unsuspecting people who are nude, undressing, or having sex. Voyeurs are almost always male, and the victims are usually strangers. A voyeur may fantasize about having sex with the victim but almost never actually pursues this. The voyeur may return to watch the same stranger repeatedly, but there is rarely physical contact.

Voyeurs are popularly known as "peeping Toms," based on the eleventh-century legend of Lady Godiva. According to the story, Tom was a tailor who "peeped" at Lady Godiva as she rode naked through the streets of Coventry, England, in a sacrificial act to get her husband to lower taxes. Tom was struck with blindness for not looking away like everyone else did.

Further Reading

Baumeister, Roy F. *Escaping the Self: Alcoholism, Spirituality, Masochism, and Other Flights from the Burden of Selfhood.* New York: Basic Books, 1991.

Caplan, Paula J. *The Myth of Women's Masochism.* Toronto: University of Toronto Press, 1993.

Carnes, Patrick. *Out of the Shadows: Understanding Sexual Addiction.* 2nd ed. Center City, MN: Hazelden Educational Materials, 1992.

Parapsychology

Meaning "beside psychology," term used to describe the study of paranormal, or psi, phenomena, the most significant being extra-sensory perception (ESP) and psychokinesis (PK).

The study of paranormal activities and phenomena has been riddled with controversy since its conception. It is claimed that some people, utilizing senses beyond the ordinary, exhibit powers that cannot be explained by traditional science. Skeptics of the paranormal point to the fact that in over a century since the first serious studies of the paranormal began, usually dated to the opening of the Society for Psychical Research in London in 1882, no replicable demonstration of any such powers has ever been conducted. Yet many people continue to believe in the existence of the paranormal.

The most studied and debated paranormal phenomena are ESP and psychokinesis. ESP is an acronym for extra-sensory perception and encompasses clairvoyance, the **ability** to perceive something without the use of the senses, and telepathy, the ability to communicate with another person without the use of the senses. (Parapsychologists currently refer to telepathy as "anomalous processes of information or energy transfer.")

Clairvoyance was the first paranormal phenomena to be seriously considered by scientists, probably because devising tests to prove or disprove its existence was easy. In the late 1920s, many such tests were devised by J.B. Rhine, a psychology professor who had left Harvard University to help found the Parapsychology Laboratory at Duke University. Rhine's tests often produced positive results for clairvoyance, and at the time his work was seriously regarded. In recent decades, however, much of Rhine's work has been discredited as being biased, careless, and, in some cases, utterly fraudulent.

Recent studies have proven more reputable but far from conclusive. One such study revealed statistically significant telepathic abilities among 100 men and 140 women tested in Scotland over six years in the mid-1980s. In the tests, "senders" focused on images or video clips and attempted to send those impressions to a "receiver" in a sensory-isolated room. The researchers reported that one in three sessions led to a "hit," meaning that the receiver reported visualizing images similar to those being sent. A hit is expected to occur by chance in one in four instances. On the other hand, the Central Intelligence Agency of the United States discounted the existence of ESP after conducting its own experiments in "remote viewing." The agency concluded that there were not enough evidence for its existence.

Psychokinesis (PK) is the ability to manipulate physical objects with the mind. Probably the most infamous purveyor of psychokinetic powers was the Israeli psychic and entertainer Uri Geller, who became an international celebrity by bending spoons, supposedly with his mind. During his career, he would never demonstrate his spoon bending ability in a controlled **environment**, and he was on several occasions shown to be faking. Another form of PK is known as spontaneous PK, in which a physical action occurs in response to psychological trauma. There are personal accounts, for instance, of clocks and watches stopping at the moment of a loved one's death. J.B. Rhine was one of the first to conduct experiments in PK, primarily with the use of dice. He tested a subject's ability to influence the outcome of a toss and found that many people demonstrated a slight ability, beyond chance, of "controlling" the dice.

There are other phenomena studies by parapsychologists, including hauntings, UFOs, near-death and after-death experiences, out-of-body experiences, psychic healing, and many others. All of these share the curious nature of ESP and PK in that, anecdotally speaking, occurrences are widespread, believed by members of many cultures, and discussed throughout history. Yet none have been scientifically demonstrated or reproduced. Despite the lack of proof, many people firmly believe in the paranormal, as evidenced by personal testimony, the popularity of television shows such as *The X-Files*, and by the huge profits generated by psychic phone lines and other occult enterprises. One of the reasons the scientific community is skeptical about paranormal phenomena is that there is no apparent basis in physical laws for such phenomena. In every other scientific discipline, it is possible to speculate reasonably that events occur as they do because they follow a recognized natural law, such as gravity or conservation of energy. Parapsychologists have failed to develop adequate theoretical reasons for the existence of the phenomena they purport to demonstrate. Nevertheless, it seems that most people are open to the possibility of the paranormal despite the lack of evidence.

Further Reading

Blackmore, Susan. "Psi in Psychology." *Skeptical Inquirer* (Summer 1994): 351.

Bower, B. "CIA Studies Fan Debate Over Psi Abilities." *Science News* (9 December 1995): 390.

————. "Scientists Peer into the Mind's Psi." *Science News* (29 January 1994): 68.

Irwin, H.J. *An Introduction to Parapsychology.* Jefferson, NC: McFarland & Co., 1989.

Jaroff, Leon. "Weird Science: Catering to Viewers' Growing Appetite for Paranormal . . ." *Time* (15 May 1995): 75.

Yam, Philip. "A Skeptically Inquiring Mind." *Scientific American* (July 1995): 34.

Parkinson's Disease

A relatively common degenerative disorder of the central nervous system.

Parkinson's disease is a degenerative disorder of the **central nervous system** named for James Parkinson (1755–1824), the physician who first described it in 1817. This disorder is also called paralysis agitans, shaking palsy, or parkinsonism.

Typically, the symptoms of Parkinson's disease begin to appear in late middle life, and the course of the disease is slowly progressive over 20 years or more. In its advanced stages, Parkinson's disease is characterized by poorly articulated speech, difficulty in chewing and swallowing, loss of motor coordination, a general tendency toward exhaustion, and especially by stooped posture, positioning the arms in front of the body when walking, caution and slowness of movement, rigidity of facial expression, and tremor of the hands. Mental ability and the senses are not directly affected by this disease. Parkinson's disease is believed to be caused by a deficiency of dopamine in the basal ganglia of the **brain.**

Further Reading

McGoon, Dwight. *The Parkinson's Handbook.* New York: Norton, 1990.

Passive-Aggressive Personality

A pattern of behavior formerly classified as a personality disorder.

Formerly listed among the **personality disorders** in the **American Psychiatric Association's** *Diagnostic and Statistical Manual of Mental Disorders,* the passive-aggressive personality type has been described by a number of psychologists and psychiatrists, including **Karen Horney,** Karl Menninger, and Wilhelm Reich (1897–1957). Its main distinguishing feature is indirect resistance to the demands or expectations of others through stubbornness, forgetfulness, inefficiency, procrastination, and other covert means. Rather than refusing outright to perform a task, the passive-aggressive person will do it badly or procrastinate until the deadline for its completion has passed. Passive-aggressive people, at one time called "ill-tempered depressives," are also generally moody, discontented, and critical of others, and they tend to see themselves as victims, feeling that they are singled out for bad luck and ill treatment by others. In their interpersonal relationships, they are unable to find a healthy balance between dependence and assertiveness.

Passive **aggression** also refers more generally to a type of behavior not limited to a certain personality type and characterized by the covert expression of aggressive feelings one is unable or unwilling to express directly. Passive aggression may be expressed in a variety of ways, including tardiness for an event or job about which one has negative feelings or poor performance of a task one resents.

Further Reading

Cicchetti, Dante, and Donald J. Cohen (eds.) *Developmental Psychopathology.* New York: J. Wiley, 1995.

Eysenck, Michael W. *Individual Differences: Normal and Abnormal.* Hillsdale, NJ: L. Erlbaum Associates, 1994.

Ivan Pavlov

Pavlov, Ivan (1849–1936)

Russian physiologist and Nobel Laureate best known for his development of the concept of the conditioned reflex, or conditioned response.

Ivan Pavlov was born into an impoverished family in the rural village of Ryazan, Russia. He won a government scholarship to the University of St. Petersburg and studied medicine at the Imperial Medical Academy, receiving his degree in 1883. In 1890, Pavlov was appointed to a professorship at the St. Petersburg Military Academy and a few years later joined the faculty of the University of St. Petersburg. He organized the Institute of Experimental Medicine in 1895, which was to be his research laboratory for the next 40 years.

In the 1890s, Pavlov investigated the workings of the digestive system—focusing on digestive secretions—using special surgically created openings in the digestive tracts of dogs, a project strongly influenced by the work of an earlier physiologist, Ivan Sechenov (1829–1905). As a result of this research, Pavlov was awarded the Nobel Prize for Physiology and Medicine in 1904. During his investigations in this area, Pavlov observed that normal, healthy dogs would salivate upon seeing their keeper, apparently in anticipation of being fed. This led him,

through a systematic series of experiments, to formulate the principles of the **conditioned response**, which he believed could be applied to humans as well as to animals. According to Pavlov's system, an *unconditioned stimulus*, such as offering food to a dog, produced a response, or *unconditioned reflex*, that required no training (salivation). In contrast, a normally neutral act, such as ringing a bell, became a **conditioned stimulus** when associated with the offering of food and eventually would produce salivation also, but as a *conditioned reflex*. According to Pavlov, the conditioned reflex was a physiological phenomenon caused by the creation of new reflexive pathways created in the cortex of the **brain** by the conditioning process. In further studies of the cortex, Pavlov posited the presence of two important processes that accompany conditioning: *excitation*, which leads to the acquisition of conditioned responses, and *inhibition*, which suppresses them. He eventually came to believe that cortical inhibition was an important factor in the **sleep** process.

Pavlov continued working with conditioned reflexes throughout the early decades of the twentieth century, generating several addition principles through further experimentation. The principle of *timing* dictated that the neutral stimulus must precede the unconditioned reflex in order to become a conditioned stimulus. (In other words, a buzzer would have to go off before food was offered to a dog in order for the dog to associate the food and buzzer with each other). The concept of **extinction** referred to the fact that a conditioned response could be "unlearned" if the neutral stimulus (buzzer) was repeatedly used without **reinforcement** (food). *Generalization* was the name given to the observation that a stimulus similar to the conditioned stimulus would still produce a response as the dog generalized from its original experience to a similar one, but the response would be less pronounced in proportion to the difference between the stimuli. Finally, testing the limits of the dogs' ability to differentiate among stimuli led, unexpectedly, to *experimental neuroses*, similar to mental breakdowns in humans, when the subjects were forced to confront conflicting or ambiguous stimuli for any length of time. Observing the ways in which neurotic symptoms differed among test subjects led Pavlov between 1916 and 1936 to formulate a theory of four different types of **temperament** linked to physiological differences based on differences in excitatory and inhibitory activity. Attempting to extend the implications of this theory to human psychopathology, Pavlov helped establish the Soviet Union's continuing tradition of organically-based psychiatric treatment.

Pavlov, who died of pneumonia in 1936, tried to apply his ideas to psychiatry, and was influential enough to be considered one of the founders of Russian psychiatry, and he remains a dominant figure in Russian psychology.

Although he never considered himself a psychologist, Pavlov's ultimate belief in **conditioning** as the fundamental unit of learning in humans and animals provided one of the cornerstones of the behaviorist school of psychology in the United States. It is ironic that, although Pavlov was a staunch critic of communism, in the late 1920s Joseph Stalin (1879–1953) chose Pavlov's work as the basis for a new Soviet psychology. Pavlov's books include *Lectures on the Work of the Principal Digestive Glands* (1897), *Lectures on Conditioned Reflexes* (1928), and *Conditioned Reflexes and Psychiatry* (1941).

See also Behaviorism.

Further Reading

Babkin, Boris P. *Pavlov: A Biography.* Chicago: University of Chicago Press, 1949.

Pavlovian Conditioning. See **Classical / Respondent Conditioning.**

Pedophilia. See **Paraphilia.**

Perception

The area of psychology associated with the functioning of sensory systems and how information from the external world is interpreted.

Psychologists have identified two general ways in which humans perceive their **environment**. One involves what is called "top-down" processing. In this mode, what is perceived depends on such factors as expectations and knowledge. That is, sensory events are interpreted based on a combination of what occurs in the external world and on existing thoughts, experience, and expectations. When a perception is based on what is expected, it is called a perceptual set, a predisposition to experience an event in a particular way. One example of such a predisposition involves hearing potentially disturbing words or phrases when rock music is played backwards. Although most people will not detect such words or phrases when they first listen to the backward sounds (when they do not have a perceptual set), these same people will hear them quite clearly if they are then told what to listen for. Psychologists regard this process as involving a perceptual set because perception of the distressing message does not occur until the individual is primed to hear it.

Motivation can also influence the way an event is perceived. At sporting events, the same episode can be interpreted in exactly opposite ways by fans of two different teams. In this instance, people are interpreting the episode with what they regard as an open mind, but their

subjectivity colors their perceptions. The alternate approach is "bottom-up" processing that relies less on what is already known or expected and more on the nature of the external stimulus. If there are no preconceived notions of what to expect, cues present in the stimulus are used to a greater extent. One part of this process is called feature analysis, which involves taking the elementary cues in a situation and attempting to put them together to create a meaningful stimulus. When children listen to an initially unfamiliar set of sounds, like the "Pledge of Allegiance," they often hear words and phrases that adults (who use top-down processing) do not hear. Thus, the phrase "one nation indivisible," may be heard by a child as "one naked individual." The child has heard the correct number of syllables, some key sounds, and the rhythm of the phrase, but too many features are unclear, resulting in an inaccurate perception. In general, many psychologists have concluded that perceptual abilities rely both on external stimuli and on expectation and knowledge.

Much of the research in perception has involved vision for two general reasons. First, psychologists recognize that these this sense dominates much of human perception and, second, it is easier to study than audition (**hearing**) or the minor senses like **taste, smell, touch,** and balance. Other perceptual research has investigated the way people pay **attention** to the world around them and learn to ignore information that is irrelevant to their needs at any given moment.

Within the realm of vision, several areas have especially captured the attention of psychologists: **depth perception,** form perception, perceptual constancy, and perceptual organization. When a visual scene contains information that includes conflicting information about depth, form, and organization, the result is a visual illusion, commonly referred to as an optical illusion. Such illusions can occur when there is too little information available to generate an accurate interpretation of the stimulus; when experience leads to the formulation of a specific interpretation; or when the sensory systems process information in a consistent, but inaccurate, fashion. Illusions are completely normal, unlike **delusions** that may reflect abnormal psychological processes.

Another aspect of perception that psychologists have studied intensively is attention. Often, people can selectively attend to different aspects of their world and tune others out. In a loud, crowded room, for example, a person can understand a single speaker by turning his or her attention to the location of the speaker and concentrating on the **frequency** (pitch) of the speaker's voice; the individual can also use the meaning of the conversation to help in concentration and to ignore irrelevant speech. In some cases, however, we seem incapable of ignoring information. One common example is the "cocktail party phenomenon." If something is holding our attention but an individual within earshot speaks our name, our attention is quickly diverted to that individual. When we perceive a stimulus that is important to us (like our name), our attention switches. One famous example that involves an inability to ignore information is the Stroop effect. If words are printed in colored ink, it is normally an easy task to name the color of the ink. If the words are color names, however, (e.g., "RED") that appear in a different ink color (e.g., the word "RED" in green ink), we have difficulty naming the ink color because we tend to read the word instead of paying attention to the ink color. This process seems entirely automatic in proficient readers.

Research on the perceptual capabilities of young children is more difficult because of insufficient communication skills. At **birth**, infants can see objects clearly only when those objects are about eight inches (20 cm) from the eye, but distance vision improves within the first month. Infants also exhibit depth perception and appear to have some **color vision**. Similarly, infants can detect speech sounds shortly after birth and can locate the origin of sounds in the environment, as is smell and taste. Within a few days following birth, breast-fed babies can differentiate their own mother's milk from that of another mother, and also prefer odors that adults like and respond more negatively to the types of odors adults do not like.

Further Reading

Chapman, Elwood N. *Attitude: Your Most Priceless Possession.* 2nd ed. Los Altos, CA: Crisp Publications, 1990.

Eiser, J. Richard. *Social Psychology: Attitudes, Cognition, and Social Behaviour.* New York: Cambridge University Press, 1986.

Personality

The unique pattern of psychological and behavioral characteristics by which each person can be distinguished from other people.

Personality is fundamental to the study of psychology. The major systems evolved by psychiatrists and psychologists since **Sigmund Freud** to explain human mental and behavioral processes can be considered theories of personality. These theories generally provide ways of describing personal characteristics and behavior, establish an overall framework for organizing a wide range of information, and address such issues as individual differences, personality development from **birth** through adulthood, and the causes, nature, and treatment of psychological disorders.

At the heart of the field of psychology is the study of personality. Psychologists examine personality development from birth through adulthood, and the causes, nature, and treatment of psychological disorders.

Type Theory of Personality

Perhaps the earliest known theory of personality is that of the Greek physician Hippocrates (c. 400 B.C.), who characterized human behavior in terms of four **temperaments**, each associated with a different bodily fluid, or "humor." The sanguine, or optimistic, type was associated with blood; the phlegmatic type (slow and lethargic) with phlegm; the melancholic type (sad, depressed) with black bile; and the choleric (angry) type with yellow bile. Individual personality was determined by the amount of each of the four humors. Hippocrates' system remained influential in Western Europe throughout the medieval and Renaissance periods. Abundant references to the four humors can be found in the plays of Shakespeare, and the terms with which Hippocrates labeled the four personality types are still in common use today. The theory of temperaments is among a variety of systems that deal with human personality by dividing it into types. A widely popularized (but scientifically dubious) modern typology of personality was developed in the 1940s by William Sheldon, an American psychologist. Sheldon classified personality into three categories based on body types: the endomorph (heavy and easy-going), mesomorph (muscular and aggressive), and ectomorph (thin and intellectual or artistic).

Trait Theory of Personality

A major weakness of Sheldon's morphological classification system and other type theories in general is the element of oversimplification inherent in placing individuals into a single category, which ignores the fact that every personality represents a unique combination of qualities. Systems that address personality as a combination of qualities or dimensions are called trait theories. Well-known trait theorist Gordon Allport (1897–1967) extensively investigated the ways in which traits combine to form normal personalities, cataloguing over 18,000 separate traits over a period of 30 years. He proposed that each person has about seven central traits that dominate his or her behavior. Allport's attempt to make trait analysis more manageable and useful by simplifying it was expanded by subsequent researchers, who found ways to group traits into clusters through a process known as factor analysis. Raymond B. Cattell reduced Allport's extensive list to 16 fundamental groups of interrelated characteristics, and Hans Eysenck claimed that personality could be described based on three fundamental factors: psychoticism (such antisocial traits as cruelty and rejection of social customs), **introversion-extroversion**, and emotionality-stability (also called neuroticism). Eysenck also formulated a quadrant based on intersecting emotional-stable and introverted-extroverted axes.

Psychodynamic Theory of Personality

Twentieth-century views on personality have been heavily influenced by the psychodynamic approach of Sigmund Freud. Freud proposed a three-part personality structure consisting of the **id** (concerned with the gratification of basic instincts), the **ego** (which mediates between the demands of the id and the constraints of society), and the **superego** (through which parental and social values are internalized). In contrast to type or trait theories of personality, the dynamic model proposed by Freud involved an ongoing element of conflict, and it was these conflicts that Freud saw as the primary determinant of personality. His psychoanalytic method was designed to help patients resolve their conflicts by exploring **unconscious** thoughts, motivations, and conflicts through the use of **free association** and other techniques. Another distinctive feature of Freudian **psychoanalysis** is its emphasis on the importance of childhood experiences in personality formation. Other psychodynamic models were later developed by colleagues and followers of Freud, including **Carl Jung**, **Alfred Adler**, and Otto Rank (1884–1939), as well as other neo-Freudians such as **Erich Fromm**, **Karen Horney**, Harry Stack Sullivan (1892–1949), and **Erik Erikson**.

Phenomenological Theory of Personality

Another major view of personality developed during the twentieth century is the phenomenological approach, which emphasizes people's self-**perception**s and their drive for **self-actualization** as determinants of personality. This optimistic orientation holds that people are innately inclined toward goodness, love, and creativity and that the primary natural **motivation** is the drive to fulfill one's potential. **Carl Rogers**, the figure whose name is most closely associated with phenomenological theories of personality, viewed authentic experience of one's self as the basic component of growth and well-being. This experience together with one's self-concept can become distorted when other people make the positive regard we need dependent on conditions that require the suppression of our true feelings. The **client-centered therapy** developed by Rogers relies on the therapist's continuous demonstration of **empathy** and unconditional positive regard to give clients the self-confidence to express and act on their true feelings and beliefs. Another prominent exponent of the phenomenological approach was **Abraham Maslow**, who placed self-actualization at the top of his hierarchy of human needs. Maslow focused on the need to replace a deficiency orientation, which consists of focusing on what one does not have, with a growth orientation based on satisfaction with one's **identity** and capabilities.

Behavioral Theory of Personality

The behaviorist approach views personality as a pattern of learned behaviors acquired through either classical (Pavlovian) or operant (Skinnerian) **conditioning** and shaped by **reinforcement** in the form of rewards or **punishment**. A relatively recent extension of **behaviorism**, the cognitive-behavioral approach emphasizes the role **cognition** plays in the learning process. Cognitive and social learning theorists focus not only on the outward behaviors people demonstrate but also on their expectations and their thoughts about others, themselves, and their own behavior. For example, one variable in the general theory of personality developed by social learning theorist Julian B. Rotter is internal-external orientation. "Internals" think of themselves as controlling events, while "externals" view events as largely outside their control. Like phenomenological theorists, those who take a social learning approach also emphasize people's perceptions of themselves and their abilities (a concept called "self-efficacy" by **Albert Bandura**). Another characteristic that sets the cognitive-behavioral approach apart from traditional forms of behaviorism is its focus on learning that takes place in social situations through observation and reinforcement, which contrasts with the dependence of classical and **operant conditioning** models on laboratory research.

Aside from theories about personality structure and dynamics, a major area of investigation in the study of personality is how it develops in the course of a person's lifetime. The Freudian approach includes an extensive description of **psychosexual development** from birth up to adulthood. Erik Erikson outlined eight stages of development spanning the entire human lifetime, from birth to death. In contrast, various other approaches, such as those of Jung, Adler, and Rogers, have rejected the notion of separate developmental stages.

An area of increasing interest is the study of how personality varies across cultures. In order to know whether observations about personality structure and formation reflect universal truths or merely cultural influences, it is necessary to study and compare personality characteristics in different societies. For example, significant differences have been found between personality development in the individualistic cultures of the West and in collectivist societies such as Japan, where children are taught from a young age that fitting in with the group takes precedence over the recognition of individual achievement. Cross-cultural differences may also be observed within a given society by studying the contrasts between its dominant culture and its subcultures (usually ethnic, racial, or religious groups).

Further Reading

Allport, Gordon W. *Personality and Social Encounter: Selected Essays.* Boston: Beacon Press, 1960.
Eysenck, Hans. *The Structure of Human Personality.* London: Methuen, 1970.
Mischel, Walter. *Introduction to Personality.* 4th ed. New York: Holt, Rinehart, and Winston, 1986.

Personality Disorders

Long-standing, deeply ingrained patterns of socially maladaptive behavior that are detrimental to those who display them or to others.

Personality disorders constitute a separate diagnostic category (Axis II) in the American Psychiatric Association's *Diagnostic and Statistical Manual of Mental Disorders (DSM-IV).* Unlike the major mental disorders (Axis I), which are characterized by periods of illness and remission, personality disorders are generally ongoing. Often, they first appear in childhood or **adolescence** and persist throughout a person's lifetime. Aside from their persistence, the other major characteristic of personality disorders is inflexibility. Persons affected by these disorders have rigid personality traits and coping styles that they are unable to adapt to changing situations and that impair their social and/or occupational functioning. A further difference between personality disorders and the major clinical syndromes listed in Axis I of *DSM-IV* is that people with personality disorders generally do not perceive that there is anything wrong with their behavior and are not motivated to change it. Although the *DSM-IV* lists specific descriptions of ten personality disorders, these conditions are often difficult to diagnose. Some characteristics of the various disorders overlap. In other cases, the complexity of human behavior makes it difficult to pinpoint a clear dividing line between pathology and normality in the **assessment** of personality. There also has been relatively little research done on some of the personality disorders listed in *DSM-IV*.

The most effectively-diagnosed personality disorder is the antisocial personality. The outstanding traits of this disturbance are an inability to feel love, **empathy**, or loyalty towards other people and a lack of guilt or remorse for one's actions. Due to the lack of **conscience** that characterizes it, the condition that is currently known as antisocial personality disorder was labeled moral insanity in the nineteenth century. More recent names associated with this personality type are psychopath and sociopath. Unable to base their actions on anything except their own immediate desires, persons with this disorder demonstrate a pattern of impulsive, irresponsible, thoughtless, and sometimes criminal behavior. They are often intelligent, articulate individuals with an ability to charm and manipulate others; at their most dangerous, they can become violent criminals who are particularly dangerous to society because of their ability to gain the trust of others combined with their lack of **conscience** or remorse.

There are both biological and psychosocial theories of the origin of antisocial personality disorder. Two of the major components of the antisocial personality—the constant need for thrills and excitement and the lack of **anxiety** about **punishment**—may be at least partially explained by research suggesting that antisocial individuals experience chronic underarousal of the central and autonomic nervous systems. In one experiment, anticipation of an electric shock produced a dramatically lower increase of tension in teenagers diagnosed with antisocial personality disorder than in other individuals. In terms of environmental influences, connections have been suggested between the antisocial personality and various patterns of familial interaction, including parental rejection or inconsistency and the retraction of punishment when repentance is claimed.

Some personality disorders resemble chronic but milder versions of the mental disorders listed in Axis I of *DSM-IV*. In schizotypal personality disorder, for example, the schizophrenic's **hallucination**s or voices are moderated to the less extreme symptom of an "illusion" that others are present when they are not. Speech patterns, while not incoherent like those of **schizophrenia**, tend to be vague and digressive. Similarly, avoidant personality disorder has characteristics that resemble those of social **phobia**, including hypersensitivity to possible rejection and the resulting social withdrawal in spite of a strong need for love and acceptance. The paranoid and schizoid personality disorders are usually manifested primarily in odd or eccentric behavior. The former is characterized mainly by suspiciousness of others, extreme vigilance against anticipated misdeeds, and insistence on personal autonomy. The latter involves emotional coldness and passivity, indifference to the feelings of others, and trouble forming close relationships.

Several personality disorders, including antisocial personality, are associated with extreme and erratic behavior. The most dramatic is the histrionic personality type, which is characterized by persistent **attention**-getting behavior that includes exaggerated emotional displays (such as tantrums) and overreaction to trivial problems and events. Manipulative **suicide** attempts may also occur. Narcissistic personality disorder consists primarily of an inflated sense of self-importance coupled with a lack of empathy for others. Individuals with this disorder display an exaggerated sense of their own importance and abilities and tend to fantasize about them. Such persons also have a sense of entitlement, expecting (and taking for granted) special treatment and concessions from others. Paradoxically, individuals with narcissistic personality disorder are generally very insecure and suffer from low self-esteem. Another personality disorder that is characterized by erratic behavior is the borderline personality. Individuals with this disorder are extremely unstable and inconsistent in their feelings about themselves and others and tend toward impulsive and unpredictable behavior.

Several personality disorders are manifested primarily by anxiety and **fear**fulness. In addition to the avoidant personality, these include the dependent, compulsive, and **passive-aggressive personality disorder**s. Persons with dependent personality disorder are extremely passive and tend to subordinate their own **need**s to those of others. Due to their lack of self-confidence, they avoid asserting themselves and allow others to take responsibility for their lives. Compulsive personality disorder is characterized by behavioral rigidity, excessive emotional restraint, and overly conscientious compliance with rules. Persons with this disorder are overly cautious and indecisive and tend to procrastinate and to become overly upset by deviations from rules and routines. Passive-aggressive personality disorder involves covert **aggression** expressed by a refusal to meet the expectations of others in such areas as adequate job performance, which may be sabotaged through procrastination, forgetfulness, and inefficiency. This disorder is also characterized by irritability, volatility, and a tendency to blame others for one's problems.

Further Reading

Beck, Aaron. *Cognitive Therapy of Personality Disorders.* Guilford Press, 1990.

Millon, T. *Disorders of Personality.* New York: Wiley, 1981.

Personality Inventory

A method of personality assessment based on a questionnaire asking a person to report feelings or reactions in certain situations.

Personality inventories, also called objective tests, are standardized and can be administered to a number of people at the same time. A psychologist need not be present when the test is given, and the answers can usually be scored by a computer. Scores are obtained by comparison with **norms** for each category on the test. A personality inventory may measure one factor, such as **anxiety** level, or it may measure a number of different personality traits at the same time, such as the Sixteen Personality Factor Questionnaire (16 PF).

The personality inventory used most often for diagnosing psychological disorders is the Minnesota Multiphasic Personality Inventory, generally referred to as the MMPI. It consists of 550 statements that the test taker has to mark as "true," "false," or "cannot say." Answers are scored according to how they correspond with those given by persons with various psychological disorders, including **depression**, hysteria, **paranoia**, psychopathic deviancy, and **schizophrenia**. The MMPI was originally developed (and is still used) for the diagnosis of these and other serious psychological problems. However enough responses have been collected from people with less severe problems to allow for reliable scoring of responses from these persons as well. Many people with no severe disorder are now given the MMPI as an assessment tool when they begin **psychotherapy**, with scoring geared toward personality attributes rather than clinical disorders.

The California Psychological Inventory (CPI), based on less extreme measures of personality than the MMPI, assesses traits, including dominance, responsibility, self-acceptance, and **socialization**. In addition, some parts of the test specifically measure traits relevant to academic achievement. Another inventory designed to measure a spectrum of personality variables in normal populations is the Personality Research Form (PRF), whose measurement scales include affiliation, autonomy, change, endurance, and exhibition. The Neuroticism Extroversion Openness Personality Inventory, Revised (NEO-PI-R) also measures common dimensions of personality such as sensitivity and extroversion, but it differs from other tests in its inclusion of both "private" and "public" versions. The questions in the private version are answered like those in other personality inventories, but the public version consists of having another person acquainted with the test taker answer questions about him or her. Significant discrepancies between the two versions can be an important source of information for those interpreting the test.

Further Reading

Cronbach, L.J. *Essentials of Psychological Testing.* New York: Harper and Row, 1970.

Sundberg, N. *The Assessment of Persons.* Englewood Cliffs, NJ: Prentice-Hall, 1977.

Phallic Stage. See **Psychosexual Development.**

Philosophical Psychology

The area of study where psychology and philosophy intersect, focusing on metaphysical and speculative problems in the study of mental processes.

One of the central questions in philosophical psychology has been the relationship between the mind and body, a perennial area of inquiry throughout the history of philosophy. Other topics considered in this discipline include **memory, perception,** and **consciousness;** the nature of the self; the existence of free will; the relationship between thought and **emotion;** and so-called irrational phenomena, such as self-deception.

The study of the mind and mental processes was traditionally the province of philosophers, but philosophy and psychology began to diverge with the advent of **experimental psychology** as practiced by such figures as Gustav Fechner (1801–1887) and Wilhelm Wundt (1832–1920) in the nineteenth century. In the twentieth century, the separation of the two disciplines became standard in American universities, resulting in the establishment of professional associations and journals devoted to psychology and its practitioners. This schism was further entrenched with the rise of **behaviorism,** which advocated behavior as the sole focus of psychology and rejected introspective inquiry and the study of consciousness. In 1925, the prominent American behaviorist **John Watson** predicted the demise of philosophy as a field of inquiry altogether.

In the 1950s, however, psychologists and philosophers increasingly found themselves once again on common ground. The "cognitive revolution" shifted the focus of psychology back to mental processes and such topics as **language acquisition** and mental representation. In turn, philosophy has demonstrated a growing interest in the empirical side of psychology; philosophers have studied the clinical foundations of **psychoanalysis** as well as topics such as **behavior modification.** Representative journals in philosophical psychology include *Philosophy of Science, Mind, British Journal of Psychology,* and *The Philosophical Review.*

Further Reading

Russell, Bertrand. *The Analysis of Mind.* New York: Macmillan, 1921.

Strawson, Peter. *Individuals: An Essay in Descriptive Metaphysics.* Garden City, NY: Doubleday, 1959.

Phobia

An excessive, unrealistic fear of a specific object, situation, or activity that causes a person to avoid that object, situation, or activity.

Unlike generalized anxiety, phobias involve specific, identifiable but usually irrational **fear**s. Phobias are common occurrences among a large segment of the population. People with phobias recognize that their fears are irrational, yet avoid the source to spare themselves of the resulting **anxiety.** Phobias are classified as disorders only when they interfere substantially with a person's daily life.

Psychologists have identified three categories of phobic disorders. The first, simple phobia, is defined in ***Diagnostic and Statistical Manual of Mental Disorders*** as a persistent, irrational fear of, and compelling desire to avoid, an object or a situation other than being alone, or in public places away from home (agoraphobia) or of humiliation or embarrassment in certain social situations (social phobia). Simple phobia causes considerable distress when confronted because the person realizes that the fear is excessive and irrational. Such phobias are not indicative of other mental disorders. Almost any object or situation can be the cause of a simple phobia. Common phobias include fear of snakes (ophidiophobia), enclosed places (claustrophobia), and spiders (arachnophobia). Fear of heights, doctors and dentists, loud noises, storms, and the sight of blood also are experienced by large numbers of people. Animal phobias, the

The person who has a fear of heights may experience anxiety during a visit to an amusement park. Most individuals with simple phobias do not seek treatment; they simply avoid the situation.

most common type of simple phobia, usually develop in early childhood. Most people do not seek treatment for simple phobias; they simply avoid the object or situation.

The second category of phobic disorders are social phobias. People with social phobias avoid social situations because they are afraid of embarrassing themselves. Fear of public speaking, fear of using public toilets, and fear of eating in public are common social phobias. Most social phobias develop over a period of time, beginning in **adolescence** or the early 20s, and rarely over the age of 30.

Agoraphobia, the third category of phobic disorders, is the most disabling and the most difficult to treat. Agoraphobia can be defined as the fear of being alone, or the fear of being in public places in unfamiliar settings. Some agoraphobics fear open spaces, like large bodies of water or open fields without fences. Most agoraphobics fear more than one situation, which contributes to the disabling nature of the disorder. The list of fears is long and extensive: public transportation, bridges, tunnels, crowd-

ed theaters, or simply being home alone. Agoraphobia rarely begins before age 18 or after 35. Sometimes it appears to be precipitated by major illness or **stress**.

Like other anxiety disorders, phobias can be treated with drugs, behavior therapy or both. Drug therapy usually includes minor tranquilizers like Librium or Valium, taken before a situation in which a phobia is likely to be introduced. Behavior therapy attempts to reduce a patient's anxiety through exposure to the phobia. For example, patients are guided step-by-step from imaginary confrontation of the phobia (visualizing a snake, for example) to actually experiencing it (holding a real snake). Gradual **desensitization** is most successful in treating simple phobias.

Further Reading

Atkinson, Rita L.; Richard C. Atkinson; Edward E. Smith; and Ernest R. Hilgard. *Introduction to Psychology.* 9th ed. San Diego: Harcourt Brace Jovanovich, 1987.

Goodwin, Donald W. *Anxiety.* New York: Oxford University Press, 1986.

Zimbardo, Philip G. *Psychology and Life.* 12th ed. Glenview, IL: Scott, Foresman, 1988.

Phrenology

An approach, primarily of historical interest, to describing the thinking process based on the belief that different mental capacities are controlled by specific locations in the brain.

Although people recognize the **brain** as the center of mental processes, this contemporary view has not always been accepted. Philosophers and scientists have proposed different ideas throughout history about the process of thinking that have since been rejected as inaccurate. One such rejected approach was phrenology. Phrenologists believed that our different mental capacities were controlled by specific locations in the brain. Although scientists today recognize the general validity of this belief, the problem was that the phrenologists developed ideas that did not really describe the way the brain functions.

German scientist Franz Joseph Gall (1758–1828), a recognized expert on anatomy, proposed the initial ideas on phrenology. He proposed that some areas of the brain were highly developed in certain individuals, which lead to specific behaviors. For instance, he claimed that pickpockets were acquisitive (i.e., possessed the desire to own things) because of excess development of an area on the side of the head. One of Gall's contemporaries, Johann Spurzheim (1776–1832) identified 35 different mental faculties and suggested the location in the brain that related to each one. Each trait was claimed to lead to a certain behavior; the inclination toward that behavior could be detected by assessing the bumps on a person's

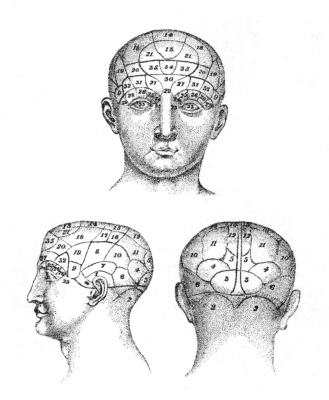

Spurzheim's Phrenological Chart of the Human Head.

AFFECTIVE FACULTIES.—I. *Propensities:* *, alimentiveness; 1, destructiveness; 2, amativeness; 3, philoprogenitiveness; 4, adhesiveness; 5, inhabitiveness; 6, combativeness; 7, secretiveness; 8, acquisitiveness; 9, constructiveness. II. *Sentiments:* 10, cautiousness; 11, approbativeness; 12, self-esteem; 13, benevolence; 14, reverence; 15, firmness; 16, consientiousness; 17, hope; 18, marvelousness; 19, ideality; 20, mirthfulness; 21, initation. INTELLECTUAL FACULTIES.—I. *Perceptive:* 22, individuality; 23, configuration; 24, size; 25, weight and resistance; 26, coloring; 27, locality; 28, order; 29, calculation; 30, eventuality; 31, time; 32, tone; 33, language. II. *Reflective:* 34, comparison; 35, causality.

skull. Scientists now recognize that the shape of the skull does not relate to the shape of the brain.

From the start, phrenology was controversial. For instance, the Roman Catholic church pressured the Austrian government to prevent Gall from lecturing in an area that the Church regarded as materialistic and atheistic. This tactic apparently served to increase the interest in phrenology. Although Gall developed his ideas with a serious scientific perspective, Spurzheim was more of an entrepreneur. He coined the term phrenology (which Gall never accepted), popularized it, and brought it to the United States. Spurzheim's goal was to reform education, religion, and penology using principles of phrenology. He died shortly after arriving in America, however. Spurzheim's work was continued by the British phrenolo-

gist George Combe (1788–1858), whose book on phrenology, *Constitution of Man,* was quite popular. According to psychology historian David Hothersall, Combe was highly respected by scientists in the United States. He was elected to the National Academy of Sciences. Interestingly, at one point he was asked to justify slavery on the grounds that people of African descent had "inferior" skulls. Combe refused, noting that educated slaves were the intellectual equals of white people. Similarly, Combe rejected the second-class status of women, asserting that they were not intellectually or emotionally inferior to men.

Two enterprising brothers, Orson and Lorenzo Fowler, marketed phrenology as a means by which people could improve themselves. Unlike Gall, who believed that **heredity** dictated one's strengths and weaknesses, the Fowlers preached the **environment**al message that people could improve themselves by practice and could overcome weaknesses by virtue of their will. They wrote extensively for popular audiences and published a journal of phrenology that existed from the 1840s to 1911. They also set up a clinic in New York where clients could be tested; they toured the United States, giving advice wherever they went; and they emphasized the practical vision of phrenology, minimizing the scientific aspects of their field.

Meanwhile, scientists and philosophers quickly dismissed phrenological ideas. Leading biologists and physicians of the day showed that the specific locations deemed important by the phrenologists were not associated with specific mental processes. Similarly, careful research in the area revealed that phrenologists were susceptible to biased observations in cases in which the research supported phrenological claims. During the 19th century, at the height of phrenology's popularity among the general public, scientists regarded the field with disdain and characterized it as a discipline dressed up to look like science. Nonetheless, phrenology exerted a positive influence on the fields of physiology and, later, biology, and sparked research on the relationship between the brain and behavior.

Further Reading

Cooter, Roger. *The Cultural Meaning of Popular Science.* Cambridge, Eng.: Cambridge University Press, 1984.

Hothersall, David. *History of Psychology.* 2nd ed. New York: McGraw-Hill, 1990.

Physiological Psychology

The area of experimental psychology concerned specifically with how biology shapes behavior and mental processes.

The area of experimental known as physiological psychology has evolved in the 1990s. Increasingly, the field is being referred to as behavioral neuroscience, replacing physiological psychology and biological psychology. Nonetheless, the goals of psychologists in this field remain the same: to utilize basic research to explain behavior in physiological terms, working on the assumption that for every behavioral event there is a corresponding physical event or series of events.

The physiological psychologist (or behavioral neuroscientist) is also concerned with the functioning of the adrenal glands and with the physical processes involved in sensation. Although physiological psychology is concerned with physical organisms, it is distinguished from such life sciences as physiology and biology by its focus on behavior. Researchers may investigate questions such as how the **brain** controls physical movements or regulates eating; the role of sex **hormones** in violent behavior; the effects of **drugs** on **memory** and **personality;** the physiological basis for **sleep** and **dream**ing; and the areas of the brain devoted to language functions. Physiological psychology overlaps with the field of neurobiology, which is the study of the **nervous system** and its functions. A related field is psychopharmacology, the study of drugs and behavior.

Another subfield of physiological psychology, psychophysiology, deals with the measurement of physiological responses as they relate to behavior. Practical applications include lie detector tests; clinical tests of vision and hearing; tests of brain activity in individuals with **mental retardation** and neurological and behavioral disorders; and **biofeedback** training.

Further Reading

Asimov, Isaac. *The Human Brain: Its Capacities and Functions.* New York: Penguin, 1994.

Guiley, Rosemary. *The Encyclopedia of Dreams: Symbols and Interpretations.* New York: Crossroad, 1993.

Mind and Brain: Readings from Scientific American Magazine. New York: W.H. Freeman, 1993.

Piaget, Jean (1896–1980)

Swiss psychologist whose work was concentrated in the study of the development of intellectual processes in children.

Piaget was born in Neuchatel, Switzerland, the son of a history professor. Turning to nature studies at an early age as an escape from an emotionally turbulent family life, he published a paper on birds by the age of 10. Between the ages of 15 and 19, Piaget published 21 papers on mollusks in international journals and was offered a curatorship by a museum director who was unaware that he was still in high school. Piaget received his Ph.D. in natural history from the University of Neuchatel at the

Jean Piaget

age of 22. He next became interested in **psychology** and studied briefly with **Carl Jung** in Zurich, where he also worked in two laboratories. Traveling to Paris, he worked with Theodore Simon, a pioneer in psychological testing and a colleague of **Alfred Binet**'s, at the Sorbonne. When Simon put Piaget in charge of standardizing a set of children's **intelligence** tests developed by Cyril Burt (1883–1971) in England, he inadvertently led the young Swiss scientist to his life's work.

Although Piaget's task was to calculate the number of right and wrong answers given by each child, he immediately became interested in the reasoning behind "wrong" answers. Respecting the children's subjective point of view, he questioned his subjects closely and discovered significant differences between their underlying thought processes and those of adults, as well as differences in the thought processes of children belonging to different age groups. Where the developers of previous intelligence tests had been interested in *quantitative,* "psychometric" measures of reasoning **ability**, Piaget embarked on the project of studying the ways in which intelligence develops *qualitatively* with age, labeling his new field of study "genetic epistemology." By learning how children view the world, Piaget realized, he could make important discoveries about the nature of human knowledge itself. Two central concepts of genetic epistemology are *functional invariants* and *structures.* Functional invariants are inborn, universal mental processes that are independent of age; the main ones identified by Piaget are accommodation, **assimilation,** and organization. In contrast, structures are cognitive processes that change with age.

The study of cognitive development occupied Piaget for the rest of his life. In 1921, he became the director of research at the Jean-Jacques Rousseau Institute in Geneva, and later served as a professor of philosophy at the University of Neuchatel. Piaget was also a faculty member at the Sorbonne and the University of Geneva. From 1952 on, Piaget directed the newly formed Center for Genetic Epistemology at the University of Geneva, where he remained until his death in 1980.

Piaget's tireless research at all of his posts—as well as observation conducted at home on his own three children—eventually yielded a complete portrait of mental development from **infancy** to **adolescence.** Piaget's influential theory of cognitive development in children describes four stages of increasingly complex and abstract thought, each qualitatively different from but dependent on the ones preceding it. The first, or sensorimotor, stage (**birth** to approximately 2 years old) is a time of nonverbal, experimental basic learning when infants gradually gain mastery of their own bodies and external objects. By sucking, shaking, banging, hitting, and other physical acts, children at this age learn about the properties of objects and how to manipulate them. The main goal at this stage is to achieve what Piaget terms "object constancy," or permanence, which is the sense that objects have a continuing existence outside our immediate sensory experience. This sense, which forms the basis for the **perception** of a stable universe, is repeatedly tested and developed through "peekaboo" games in which objects are made to repeatedly disappear and reappear.

Once children begin to recognize objects as constant and begin to name them, they are ready to enter the preoperational stage (ages 2 to 6 years), which involves the association of objects with words. Children at this stage still do not have the ability to think about objects using key concepts such as causality, time, volume, reversability, and perspective. They also lack an understanding of "conservation of quantity"—the fact that substances retain the same volume even when shifted into containers of different sizes and shapes. Also, the child's focus at this stage (as at the previous one) is egocentric, denoting an inability to consider things from someone else's perspective. Other qualities characterizing this stage are centration (**attention** to only one feature of a situation) and irreversability (inability to reverse direction of thought).

The third, or concrete operations, stage (6 to 11 years of age) is a period during which categorizing activities and the earliest logical operations occur. At this stage, children understand the conservation of quantity, can perform such operations as counting and classifying, and have an increased understanding of relationships. Concrete operational children also lose their egocentric focus, becoming aware that events have causes outside themselves. The fourth, or formal operations, stage (ages 12 and higher) is characterized by the gradual emergence of a mature ability to reason. Children become capable of dealing with abstract relationships like probability and ratio. At this stage, scientific reasoning becomes possible, involving the formulation and testing of hypotheses and predictions. A network of ideas emerges, with everything related to everything else, and abstract concepts and moral values become as important as concrete objects.

Piaget's hundreds of studies in genetic epistemology have been central to the development of **child psychology** in the twentieth century. His ideas revolutionized the study of this field in France and Switzerland in the 1920s and gained currency in the United States beginning in the late 1950s, as **child psychologists** became dissatisfied with traditional theories about learning. Piaget is cited in psychological literature more often than any other figure, with the exception of **Sigmund Freud.** Although he had no formal academic training in psychology, Piaget has received honorary degrees from prestigious institutions and was honored by the **American Psychological Association** for his distinguished contributions to psychology. Even the growing trend toward revision and modification of his work in "neo-" "post-" and "anti-" Piagetian papers is further evidence of his influence. Piaget's theories have, naturally, been of great interest to educators as well as psychologists. In addition to using the stages of cognitive development as guidelines for teaching methods and curricula, some educators have focused on the possibility of accelerating student development and learning.

Piaget's many works include *The Language and Thought of the Child* (1926), *The Construction of Reality in the Child* (1954), *The Origin of Intelligence in Children* (1954), *The Early Growth of Logic in the Child* (1964), and *The Development of Thought* (1977).

See also Cognitive Development Theory; Developmental Psychology.

Further Reading

Boden, M. A. *Piaget.* New York: Viking Press, 1980.

Evans, Richard I. *Jean Piaget: The Man and His Ideas.* New York: Dutton, 1973.

Flavell, John. *The Developmental Psychology of Jean Piaget.* New York: Van Nostrand, 1963.

Statue of Philippe Pinel outside the Salpêtrière hospital in Paris, France.

Ginsburg, Herbert, and Sylvia Opper. *Piaget's Theory of Intellectual Development.* Englewood Cliffs, NJ: Prentice-Hall, 1988.

Piaget, Jean, and Barbel Inhelder. *The Growth of Logical Thinking from Childhood to Adolescence.* New York: Basic Books, 1958.

Pinel, Philippe (1745–1826)

French physician and one of the founders of psychiatry.

Philippe Pinel was born near Toulouse, France, the son of a surgeon. After first studying literature and theology, he pursued medical studies at the University of Toulouse, receiving his M.D. in 1773. In 1778, Pinel moved to Paris, where he worked as a publisher, translator of scientific writings, and teacher of mathematics. He also wrote and published articles, a number of them about mental disorders, a topic in which he had become interested due to the illness of a friend. In 1792, Pinel was appointed chief physician and director of the Bicêtre asylum, where he was able to put into practice his ideas on treatment of the mentally ill, who were commonly kept chained in dungeons at the time. Pinel petitioned to the Revolutionary Committee for permission to remove the chains from some of the patients as an experiment, and to allow them to exercise in the open air. When these steps proved to be effective, he was able to change the conditions at the hospital and discontinue the customary methods of treatment, which included bloodletting, purging, and physical abuse.

Rejecting the prevailing popular notion that mental illness was caused by demonic possession, Pinel was among the first to believe that mental disorders could be caused by psychological or social **stress,** congenital conditions, or physiological injury. He strongly argued for the humane treatment of mental patients, including a friendly interaction between doctor and patient, and for the maintenance and preservation of detailed case histories for the purpose of treatment and research. In 1795, Pinel was appointed chief physician at Salpêtrière, where he effected reforms similar to those at Bicétre. Pinel remained at Salpêtrière for the remainder of his career. His student, Jean Esquirol, succeeded him and expanded his reform efforts throughout France. The success of Pinel's methods also influenced practices in other countries, including England.

In 1795, Pinel was appointed to the faculty of the newly opened medical school in Paris, where he was professor of medical pathology for the next 20 years. He was elected to the Academy of Science in 1804 and the Academy of Medicine in 1820. Besides his work in hospitals, Pinel also treated patients privately as a consulting physician. Although he is regarded today as a pioneering figure in **psychiatry,** during his lifetime Pinel was known chiefly for his contributions to internal medicine, especially his authoritative classification of diseases in the textbook *Nosographie philosophique* (1798), in which he divided diseases into five classes—fevers, phlegmasias, hemorrhages, neuroses, and diseases caused by organic lesions. Pinel's extensive contributions to medical research also include data on the development, prognosis, and frequency of occurrence of various illnesses, and experiments measuring the effectiveness of medicines. Pinel established an inoculation clinic at Salpêtrière in 1799, and the first vaccination in Paris was given there in April of the following year.

In addition to transforming psychiatric facilities from prisons into hospitals, Pinel did much to establish psychiatry formally as a separate branch of medicine, publishing numerous articles on the topic which were collected in "Recherches et observations sur le traitement moral des aliénés" (1799) and his book *Traîte medico-philosophique de l'aliénation mentale* (*Medical-Philosophical Treatise on Mental Alienation or Mania*, 1801), which is considered a classic of psychiatry. Pinel's practice of interacting individually with his patients in a humane and understanding manner represented the first known attempt at **psychotherapy.** He also emphasized the importance of physical hygiene and exercise, and pioneered in recommending productive work for mental patients. In addition, Pinel concerned himself with the proper administration of psychiatric facilities, including the training of their personnel.

Placebo Effect

In research, a scientifically significant response that cannot be explained by physiological variables and is assumed to be psychological in origin.

Placebos are substances with no known pharmacological value that are given to members of a **control group** in an experiment. In studies determining the effectiveness of a particular **drug,** for example, the experimental group is given the drug being studied and the control group is given a placebo, which is made to look exactly like the actual drug. Neither group, nor the researchers, knows which received the drug and which the placebo. If the members of each group show similar responses, the placebo effect has been produced. For reasons not completely understood, the patients given the placebo have experienced the effects of the drug without actually taking it. In such cases, the drug itself is considered ineffective.

The placebo effect has been noted since ancient times, when animal parts or other naturally occurring substances were given as treatment for various human diseases and ailments. Throughout medical history, patients have recovered from illnesses after healers employed substances or methods that scientifically should have no effect. It is believed that patients' expectations that their condition will improve plays a major role in producing the placebo effect.

The use of placebos in **psychotherapy** is controversial, with some critics contending that it links therapists with "quack" treatments rather than legitimate, scientifically measurable methods. However, most researchers agree that the placebo effect, while not completely understood, plays a major and beneficial role in both physiological and psychological treatment.

Further Reading

Atkinson, Rita L.; Richard C. Atkinson; Edward E. Smith; and Ernest R. Hilgard. *Introduction to Psychology.* 9th ed. San Diego: Harcourt Brace Jovanovich, 1987.
Zimbardo, Philip G. *Psychology and Life.* 12th ed. Glenview, IL: Scott, Foresman, 1988.

Play

Activity that is not required, but is enjoyed.

While the term "play" may refer to an extremely varied range of activities, certain broad, defining characteristics have been noted. Perhaps the most basic one is that play is something that is not required. Although the enjoyment derived from it may be needed emotionally, no single play activity itself is necessary for survival. Thus play is referred to as "autotelic"—it is engaged in for its own sake, with the reward inherent in the activity itself. Nevertheless, in spite of its detachment from survival and financial gain, play is engaged in wholeheartedly. During the time allotted to play, it commands a person's entire attention.

Play takes place in a realm divorced from ordinary reality and governed by its own rules, which may be more complex and absolute than those of many "serious" activities. It is also bound in terms of both time and space. The period during which one engages in play has time limits: it begins, proceeds, and inevitably ends when one returns to "real life." Play is also set apart in space— a person generally goes somewhere special (even if it is

Child engaged in classic play activity, building a sandcastle.

only the "play room" or the "playground") to engage in play. The relationship between play and tension has also been noted. While tension is not absent from play itself, the ultimate result is the reduction of tension and conflict. Based on this feature, play has often been viewed as a "safety valve" for the harmless discharge of tensions and conflicts.

In children, play is a necessary vehicle for normal physical, social, and cognitive development. The well known early 20th-century American psychologist G. Stanley Hall (1844–1924) viewed the evolution of children's play as recapitulating the evolution of the human species. Individually, play develops in stages that correspond to a child's social and cognitive development. Initially, a child's play is solitary in nature. Next comes parallel play, where children are in each others' company but playing independently. Socially, the final stage is cooperative play, which consists of organized activities characterized by social roles.

Jean Piaget formulated a series of developmental stages of play that corresponded to the successive stages in his influential theory of cognitive development in children. The sensorimotor stage (**birth** to approximately two years old), when children are focused on gaining mastery of their own bodies and external objects, is characterized by "practice play" consisting of repeated patterns of movement or sound, such as sucking, shaking, banging, babbling, and, eventually, "peekaboo" games in which objects are made to repeatedly disappear and reappear. As children learn more about the properties of objects and learn how to manipulate them, they begin to monitor the effects of play on their **environment,** and their relationship with that environment becomes increasingly systematic.

The preoperational stage (ages 2-7 years) is marked by the ability to master symbolic functions, including the association of objects with words, and the transition from an egocentric focus to an awareness that events have causes outside themselves. At this stage, children begin to engage in make-believe games marked by the use of objects for purposes other than their intended function. Between the ages of 4 and 7, when their **thinking** is still dominated by intuition rather than logic, children first become interested in games characterized by rules, structure, and social interaction. As they move through the concrete operational stage (ages 7–11), during which categorizing activities and the earliest logical operations occur, the types of rules governing their play and the reasons for following them change. At first, rules are centered on the sensorimotor aspects of play and largely provide structure and repetition. Gradually, they become more focused on the social aspects of play and are connected with acceptance by the group. By the fourth, or formal operations stage (ages 12 and higher), with the gradual emergence of a mature ability to reason, competitive games and games with codes of rules begin to predominate.

While other psychologists have proposed schemes that vary from this one theory, there is general agreement on its broad outlines. Some additional categorizations of children's play that have been proposed include diversive play, composed of aimless activities that serve as a diversion when a child is bored; mimetic play, which is repetitious, structured, and symbolic; and cathartic play, which is therapeutic in nature.

Further Reading

Dolinar, Kathleen J. *Learning Through Play: Curriculum and Activities for the Inclusive Classroom.* Albany, NY: Delmar, 1994.

Moyles, Janet R. *The Excellence of Play.* Philadelphia: Open University Press, 1994.

Hughes, Fergus P. *Children, Play, and Development.* Boston: Allyn and Bacon, 1991.

Pleasure Principle

The theoretical principle that humans make decisions to seek pleasure and minimize pain.

Among other principles, Freudian psychology states that there is a basic human tendency to seek pleasure and avoid **pain**. It arises from the desire for unrestrained expression of both the life instinct (Eros) associated with **sexuality** and the death instinct (Thanatos) associated with **aggression** and destructiveness. Freud described the pleasure principle in terms of the **need** to discharge or reduce tensions—experienced as pain or discomfort—created internally or by external stimuli. The **id**, which operates on the pleasure principle, is the instrument for discharging these tensions. However, it is held in check by the **ego**, operating on the opposed reality principle, which mediates between the primitive desires of the id and the constraints of the external world.

The promptings of the pleasure principle, which are often compared to the demands of a child, seek immediate gratification and are ungoverned by social or moral rules. The reality principle opposes many of these promptings, denying them altogether or postponing gratification either until a socially appropriate time (waiting until a meal to eat) or so that greater pleasure may be achieved in the long run (studying for a degree or training for a sport).

Further Reading

Freud, Sigmund. *New Introductory Lectures on Psychoanalysis.* New York: W. W. Norton, 1933.

Hall, Calvin S. *A Primer of Freudian Psychology.* New York: Harper and Row, 1982.

Pornography

Any printed or pictorial material containing representations of sexually obscene behavior, intended to sexually arouse its audience.

There is an obvious and necessary imprecision in this definition of the term pornography, in the sense that what is considered to be sexually obscene behavior, and, for that matter, what might sexually arouse an audience, vary quite widely from time to time, from place to place, and from individual to individual. Nearly all modern societies have laws that prohibit the possession or distribution of at least some forms of pornography, although the statutory suppression and criminalization of sexually obscene material is a relatively recent phenomenon, and is significantly predated by the legal censorship of material that was judged to be sacrilegious or antireligious (religiously obscene) or seditious or treasonous (politically obscene). Generally, laws against pornography have been based on the controversial assumption that exposure to pornography morally corrupts individuals and is a cause of sexual crimes. In the United States, legislation concerning pornography dates from the middle of the 19th century. Since that time, the admittedly elusive legal definition of what constitutes pornography and can be regulated by law has evolved into material that portrays sexual conduct in a patently offensive way and appeals to prurient interest in sex, as judged by an average person applying contemporary community standards, and which, on the whole, does not have serious literary, artistic, political, or scientific value. When necessary, the judgment of whether or not material is pornographic is usually made by a jury. Many authorities have concluded that, because of the constantly shifting moral connotations of the concept of sexual obscenity, it is not possible to completely and objectively define the term pornography, and that, in the final analysis, pornography is in the eye of the beholder.

Further Reading

Hunter, Ian. *On Pornography.* New York: St. Martin's Press, 1993.

Post-Traumatic Stress Disorder (PTSD)

A psychological disorder that develops in response to an extremely traumatic event that threatens a person's safety or life.

Although the term post-traumatic stress disorder is relatively new, the symptoms of PTSD can be recognized in many guises throughout history, from the reactions to the great fire of London that Samuel Pepys (1633–1703) described in the 1600s to the shell shock of soldiers in World War I. Some psychologists suspect that the "hysterical" women treated by Josef Breuer (1842–1925) and **Sigmund Freud** at the turn of the twentieth century may have been suffering from symptoms of PTSD as a result of childhood sexual abuse or battering by their husbands.

Post-traumatic stress disorder has been classified as an **anxiety** disorder in the **American Psychiatric Association**'s *Diagnostic and Statistical Manual of Mental Disorders* since 1980. People suffering from PTSD repeatedly re-experience the traumatic event vividly in their thoughts, **perceptions**, images, or **dreams**. They may be aware that they are recollecting a previous experience, or they may have **hallucinations, delusions,** or dissociative flashbacks that make them feel as though the trauma is actually recurring in the present. Children may engage in repetitive **play** that expresses some aspect of the trauma. A related symptom is the consistent avoidance of people, objects, situations, and other stimuli connected with the event. PTSD sufferers usually experience heightened **arousal** in the form of agitation, irritability, insomnia, difficulty concentrating, or being easily startled. In contrast, they often "shut down" emotionally and become incapable of expressing certain feelings, especially those associated with affection and intimacy. Children who have been traumatized may stop talking altogether or refuse to discuss the traumatic event that affected them. They may also experience physical symptoms such as headaches or stomach aches.

Events that may lead to post-traumatic stress disorder include natural disasters (earthquakes, floods, hurricanes) or serious accidents such as automobile or plane crashes. However, PTSD is most likely to be caused by traumas in which death and injury are inflicted by other human beings: war, torture, **rape**, terrorism, and other types of personal assault that violate one's sense of self-esteem and personal integrity. (PTSD also tends to be more severe and long-lasting when it results from traumas of this nature.) In addition to the direct experience of traumatic events, PTSD can also be caused by witnessing such events or by learning of serious harm to a family member or a close friend. Specific populations in which PTSD has been studied include Vietnam veterans and Holocaust survivors.

Among the disorders listed in the *Diagnostic and Statistical Manual,* the diagnosis for PTSD is unique in its focus on external events rather than internal predispositions or **personality** features. Studies have found that such factors as race, sex, socioeconomic status, and even previous psychiatric history have little to do with the incidence of PTSD. Whether a person develops PTSD is much more closely related to the severity and duration of the traumatic event experienced than to any preexisting characteristics or situations. Physiologically, post-traumatic stress disorder is thought to be related to changes in **brain** chemistry and levels of **stress**-related **hormones.** When a person is subjected to excessive stress levels on a prolonged basis, the adrenal glands—which fuel the "fight-or-flight" reaction by producing adrenaline—may be permanently damaged. One possible result is over-functioning during subsequent stress, causing hyper-arousal symptoms such as insomnia, jumpiness, and irritability. The brain's **neurotransmitters**, which play a role in transmitting **nerve** impulses from one cell to another, may be depleted by severe stress, leading to **mood** swings, outbursts of temper, and **depression.**

Post-traumatic stress disorder can affect persons of any age and is thought to occur in as many as 30 percent of disaster victims. In men, it is most commonly caused by war; in women, by rape. Symptoms usually begin within one to three months of the trauma, although in some cases they are delayed by months or even years. If left undiagnosed and untreated, PTSD can last for de-cades. However, over half of all affected persons who receive treatment recover completely within three months. Short-term **psychotherapy** (12 to 20 sessions) has been the single most effective treatment for PTSD. It may be accompanied by medication for specific purposes, but medication alone or for extended periods is not recommended as a course of treatment. Sleeping pills may help survivors cope in the immediate aftermath of a trauma, anti-anxiety medications may temporarily ease emotional distress, and antidepressants may reduce nightmares, flashbacks, and **panic** attacks.

The primary goal of psychotherapy is to have the person confront and work through the traumatic experience. **Hypnosis** may be especially valuable in retrieving thoughts and memories that have been blocked. One technique used by therapists is to focus on measures that PTSD sufferers took to save or otherwise assert themselves in the face of traumatic events, thus helping to allay the feelings of powerlessness and loss of control that play a large part in the disorder. Behavioral techniques such as relaxation training and systematic **desensitization** to "triggering" stimuli have also proven helpful. Support groups consisting of other persons who have experienced the same or similar traumas have facilitated the healing process for many persons with PTSD.

See also Combat Neurosis.

Further Information

The International Society for Traumatic Stress Studies
Address: 435 North Michigan Ave., Suite 1717, Chicago, IL 60611
Telephone: 312-644-0828.

Further Reading

Matsakis, Aphrodite. *I Can't Get Over It: A Handbook for Trauma Survivors.* Oakland, CA: New Harbinger Publications, 1992.
McCann, Lisa. *Psychological Trauma and the Adult Survivor: Theory, Therapy, and Transformation.* New York: Brunner/Mazel, 1990.
Porterfield, Kay Marie. *Straight Talk about Post-Traumatic Stress Disorder: Coping with the Aftermath of Trauma.* New York: Facts on File, 1996.

Power

One's capacity to act or to influence the behavior of others.

Power may be defined in both personal and interpersonal terms. In the first sense, it refers to one's physical, intellectual, or moral capacity to act. In the second, it denotes the **ability** to influence the behavior of others. Philosophers have often described power as an integral facet of human existence. Psychologist Harry Stack Sullivan

ROLLO MAY'S INTRAPSYCHIC POWER LEVELS

Survival and sustenance: to exist

Self-affirmation: recognition and self-esteem

Self-assertion: affirmation of one's existence

Aggression: active pursuit of power and territory

Violence: separate from reason

(1892–1949) has claimed that power is a more crucial **motivation** than hunger or thirst.

Rollo May has written about power in terms of individual human potential, referring to the roots of the word "power" in the Latin word *posse,* which means "to be able." May distinguishes among five levels of intrapsychic power. The most basic level, the power to be, is literally the power to exist, which is threatened if one is denied the basic conditions of human sustenance. The second level, self-affirmation, goes beyond mere survival and involves recognition and esteem by others, while the third, self-assertion, refers to the more strenuous affirmation of one's existence that is required in the face of opposition. The next level of power, **aggression,** develops when one's access to other forms of self-assertion is blocked. In contrast to self-assertion, which May views as essentially defensive, aggression involves the active pursuit of power or territory. The endpoint in May's continuum of power is **violence,** which, unlike the other levels, is divorced from reason and verbal persuasion.

Power in its other sense—that of power over others—is a fundamental feature of all relationships, whether each party has a certain degree of power over the other (which is usually the case) or all the power resides with one party. Power may be based on force, acknowledged expertise, the possession of specific information that people want, the ability to reward others, or legitimization (the **perception** that one has the right to exercise it).

Other bases for power include identification with those who wield it and reciprocity (indebtedness to the wielder of power for providing a prior benefit of some sort). May has described various types of interpersonal power, ranging from harmful to beneficial: exploitative (characterized solely by brute force); manipulative (various types of power over another person); competitive (power *against* another); nurturing (power *for* another person); and integrative (power *with* another person).

Further Reading

May, Rollo. *Power and Innocence: A Search for the Sources of Violence.* New York: W. W. Norton, 1972.

Tillich, Paul. *Love, Power, and Justice: Ontological Analyses and Ethical Applications.* New York: Oxford University Press, 1960.

Preconscious

In psychoanalytic theory, knowledge, images, emotions, and other mental phenomena that are not present in immediate consciousness but are quickly accessible and can be brought into consciousness easily without the use of special techniques.

Sigmund Freud theorized that the human mind was divided into three parts: the conscious, preconscious, and **unconscious.** This schema first appeared in his earliest model of mental functioning, published in his classic work, *The Interpretation of Dreams* (1900). Freud believed that the preconscious functions as an intermediate or transitional level of the mind—between the unconscious and the conscious—through which repressed material passes.

Freud described this arrangement spatially, depicting the unconscious as a large room crowded with thoughts and the conscious area as a smaller reception room, with a doorkeeper between the two rooms selectively admitting thoughts from the unconscious to the consciousness. Those thoughts that are restricted to the unconscious area remain repressed, meaning that they are totally invisible to the conscious self, and can be recovered only by **hypnosis, free association,** or some other technique. Not all thoughts allowed into the "reception area" necessarily become conscious, however. Rather, they become *available* for **consciousness,** with one or another becoming conscious at a given time when **attention** is drawn to it in some way. Thus, the smaller room might more properly be thought of as a preconscious area, in which are gathered all of the thoughts that are not deliberately repressed. Because of their relative closeness to each other, Freud actually grouped the conscious and preconscious systems together in contrast to the unconscious, emphasizing that thoughts in the conscious and preconscious categories do not differ in any essential way and can be distinguished only functionally. A preconscious thought can quickly become conscious by receiving attention, and a conscious thought can slip into the preconscious when attention is withdrawn from it.

Further Reading

Firestone, Robert. *Psychological Defenses in Everyday Life.* New York: Human Sciences Press, 1989.

Goleman, Daniel. *Vital Lies, Simple Truths: the Psychology of Self-Deception.* New York: Simon and Schuster, 1985.

Prejudice

A positive or negative attitude toward an individual based on his or her membership in a religious, racial, ethnic, political, or other group.

Prejudice has cognitive, affective, and behavioral components. Based on *beliefs*, it can affect one's *emotions* and *behavior*, sometimes leading to discrimination. Prejudiced beliefs primarily take the form of **stereotype**s, overall impressions based on the assumption that all members of a group possess similar attributes.

Various theories have been proposed to explain the causes and dynamics of prejudice. In the 1940s, a University of California study on anti-Semitism and other forms of prejudice created a profile of a particular personality type—the **authoritarian personality**—believed to be associated with prejudice. Persons fitting this profile are typically raised by strict, emotionally distant parents who exact rigid adherence to rules and commands. Obedience is ensured through both verbal and physical **punishment**, and independent thought and action are discouraged. As adults, people fitting this personality type define their world in terms of a social hierarchy, deferring to persons of higher status and acting with **hostility** and contempt toward those they regard as inferior. They often discriminate against or overtly persecute those whom they perceive to be of lower status. It has also been suggested that they may also be projecting their own weaknesses and **fea**rs onto the groups they denigrate. Other traits associated with this personality type include strict obedience to rules and authority, **conformity**, admiration of powerful figures, and inability to tolerate ambiguity. The California study also found that those who are prejudiced against one group are likely to be prejudiced against other groups as well.

Investigators have also studied prejudice as a pattern of learned **attitudes** and behaviors. People are not born prejudiced: many prejudices are formed against groups with which a person has never had any contact. They acquire prejudiced views by observing and listening to others, particularly one's parents and other elders. Cultural influences such as movies and **television** may also create or perpetuate stereotypes. The ways in which women, ethnic groups, and racial minorities are represented in the media and by the entertainment industry have been the target of much discussion and criticism. Cognitive theories have proposed that stereotypes are unavoidable because they help people categorize and make sense of a complex and diverse society.

It is a popular belief that prejudices can be overcome by direct contact between people of different backgrounds. However, social psychologists have noted that contact alone cannot eliminate stereotypes and prejudice—in fact, some types of contact can even reinforce prejudiced beliefs. For change to occur, contact between different groups must meet certain conditions: 1) members of the groups should be of equal status. 2) The interaction should move beyond the confines of ritualized interactions (such as those between employer and employee or customer and salesperson) and into personal acquaintance.

Exposure to persons who dispel or contradict stereotypes about a particular group can also help a prejudiced person to rethink his views. For example, the growing willingness of gays to be open about their sexual orientation has helped dispel the stereotype that all gay men are effeminate. Another important element in overcoming prejudice is the social support of one's community. During the civil rights struggles of the 1950s and 1960s, the lack of community support for desegregation and school busing further increased prejudiced feelings and behavior among some individuals. Finally, cooperative effort is an effective way of reducing prejudice. Working together toward a common goal can bring different groups of people together.

See also Racism.

Further Reading

Adorno, Theodor, et al. *The Authoritarian Personality.* New York: Harper and Row, 1950.

Allport, Gordon. *The Nature of Prejudice.* Reading, MA: Addison-Wesley Publishing Co., 1954.

Terkel, Studs. *Race: How Blacks and Whites Think and Feel About the American Obsession.* New York: New Press, 1992.

Premenstrual Syndrome (PMS)

Symptoms that occur several days before the onset, and sometimes during the first day of, menstruation.

Premenstrual syndrome (PMS) exhibits both physiological and psychological symptoms. The primary physiological symptoms are water retention and bloating, slightly enlarged and tender breasts, and food cravings. Psychological symptoms include irritability and **depression.** The full range of symptoms that have been attributed to PMS is extremely broad: as many as 150 have been identified. Because the symptoms are so varied from one woman to another (and even within the same woman at different times) it has been very difficult to arrive at a clinical definition of PMS. In addition, researchers disagree over whether PMS consists solely of symptoms that disappear completely at the onset of menstruation or of the premenstrual intensification of symptoms or conditions that are present, although to a lesser degree, during the rest of the month. Most women with premenstrual syndrome typically suffer from more than one symptom during each menstrual cycle.

Although there is no conclusive evidence that PMS is caused by **hormone** imbalances, some women have been successfully treated by hormonal therapy, which consists of oral contraceptives and monthly injections of progesterone. Recent research has linked premenstrual syndrome to an inadequate number of progesterone receptors or to the failure of those receptors to function properly, suggesting that PMS may be a disorder of progesterone response rather than progesterone deficiency. Other studies have posited a link between PMS and **brain** opioid (opiate-like) activity, based on alleged similarities between the symptoms of PMS and those of heroin withdrawal. Regular aerobic exercise, which helps stabilize opioid levels in the brain, has been shown to decrease PMS.

The physiological effects of PMS can be reduced through natural means, including **stress** management, dietary changes, acupressure massage, yoga, regular exercise, and adequate rest. Nutritional supplements, such as vitamins A, E, and B-6 have been shown to aid in the treatment of PMS, as have calcium and magnesium. Some physicians prescribe diuretics to treat water retention or tranquilizers for the treatment of irritability and **mood** swings. Recent research has suggested that drugs which increase the brain's serotonin levels, such Prozac, may also be helpful in treating PMS.

Although PMS has received much attention from the medical establishment, some women's health experts believe that its severity and significance have been exaggerated, and claim that only a small percentage of women have premenstrual symptoms so disabling that it interferes with work or other aspects of their lives. They also contend that the increased awareness of PMS contributes to a cultural bias that disproportionately attributes a woman's fluctuations in mood to her menstrual cycle, when the moods of both males and females will fluctuate within the course of a month for many reasons—both physiological and **environment**al—that have nothing to do with menstruation. In a recent investigation into the link between a woman's psychological characteristics and premenstrual syndrome, it was noted that whether or not women report PMS has less to do with the number and severity of their actual symptoms than with their general outlook on life, including levels of self-esteem and the ability to express feelings and manage stress.

Further Reading

Dalton, Katharina. *PMS: the Essential Guide to Treatment Options.* London, Eng.: Thorsons, 1994.

PMS: It's Not in Your Head. [videorecording] Omaha, NB: Envision Communications, 1993.

Programmed Learning

A method of self-instruction that enlists machines or specially prepared books to teach information.

Originally introduced in the mid-1950s by behaviorist **B.F. Skinner**, programmed instruction is a system whereby the learner uses specially prepared books or equipment to learn without a teacher. It was intended to free teachers from burdensome drills and repetitive problem-solving inherent in teaching basic academic subjects like spelling, arithmetic, and reading. Skinner based his ideas on the principle of **operant conditioning**, which theorized that learning takes place when a reinforcing stimulus is presented to reward a correct response. In early programmed instruction, students punched answers to simple math problems into a type of keyboard. If the answer was correct, the machine would advance to another problem. Incorrect answers would not advance. Skinner believed such learning could, in fact, be superior to traditional teacher-based instruction because children were rewarded immediately and individually for correct answers rather than waiting for a teacher to correct written answers or respond verbally. Programmed instruction quickly became popular and spawned much educational research and commercial enterprise in the production of programmed instructional materials. It is considered the antecedent of modern computer-assisted learning.

Two types of programmed learning can be compared. Linear programming involves a simple step-by-step procedure. There is a single set of materials and students work from one problem to the next until the end of the program. Branching programming is more complex. Students choose from multiple-choice answers and then are prompted to proceed to another page of the book depending on their answer. If a correct answer is given, students move on to another page with more information to learn and more questions to answer. An incorrect answer leads to comments on why the answer is incorrect and a direction to return to the original question to make another selection.

Just as the programming developed more complexity over the years, so did the teaching machines themselves. Early, simple machines were little more than electronic workbooks. Later machines allowed students to be instructed on more complex material that required more than one-word or one-number responses. In some, students could write their responses and move ahead by comparing their answers to acceptable answers. Programmed-learning books differ from traditional workbooks because they actually teach new information through this step-by-step stimulus-response method rather than simply offering practice material for already-learned skills.

Research has shown that programmed learning often is as successful, and sometimes more successful, than traditional teacher-based learning because it recognizes the different abilities and needs of individual children. Students who have mastered the material can move ahead more quickly, while those who need more practice are repeatedly exposed to the problems. Programmed learning also allows teachers more time to concentrate on more complex tasks. One criticism of programmed learning centers on the lack of student-teacher interaction. It has been shown that some students thrive more fully with the human motivation inherent in more traditional learning situations.

Further Reading

Bower, Gordon H., and Ernest R. Hilgard. *Theories of Learning.* Englewood Cliffs, NJ: Prentice-Hall, 1981.

Projective Techniques

Unstructured tests used for personality assessment that rely on the subject's interpretation of ambiguous stimuli.

Projective techniques involve asking subjects to interpret or fill in visual stimuli, complete sentences, or report what associations particular words bring to mind. Because of the leeway provided by the tests, subjects project their own personalities onto the stimulus, often revealing personal conflicts, **motivations**, coping styles, and other characteristics.

The best known projective test is the **Rorschach** test, created in the 1920s by Swiss psychologist Hermann Rorschach (1884–1922). It consists of a series of 10 cards, each containing a complicated inkblot. Some are in black and white, some in color. Subjects are asked to describe what they see in each card. Test scores are based on several parameters: 1) what part of the blot a person focuses on; 2) what particular details determine the response; 3) the content of the responses (what objects, persons, or situations they involve); and 4) the frequency with which a particular response has been given by previous test takers. A number of different scoring methods have been devised for the Rorschach test, some aimed at providing greater objectivity and validity for this highly impressionistic form of assessment. However, many psychologists still interpret the test freely according to their subjective impressions. Some also take into account the subject's demeanor while taking the test (cooperative, anxious, defensive, etc.).

Another widely used projective test is the Thematic Apperception Test (TAT) introduced at Harvard University in 1935 by Henry Murray. Test takers look at a series of up to 20 pictures of people in a variety of recognizable settings and construct a story about what is happening in each one. They are asked to describe not only what is happening at the moment shown in the picture but also what events led up to the present situation and what the characters are thinking and feeling. They are encouraged to interpret the pictures as freely and imaginatively as they want and to be completely open and honest in their responses. As with the Rorschach test, the psychologist often interprets the test results subjectively, focusing on any recurring themes in responses to the different pictures. However, scoring methods have also been developed that focus on specific aspects of the subjects' responses, including **aggression**, expression of **need**s, and **perception**s of reality.

Still another type of projective technique is the sentence completion test. Many tests of this type have been developed, some of which investigate particular **personality** features. Others are designed specifically for children or adolescents. Subjects are asked to complete sentences with such open-ended beginnings as "I wish . . ." or "My mother . . ." Although the same sentence beginnings are shown to different test takers, there are no norms for comparing their answers to those of previous subjects. Still other types of projective tests have been developed, including some that ask the subject to create drawings or complete a story.

Compared to the more objective questionnaire-type personality **assessment**s, projective tests are difficult to score, and questions are often raised about their degree of reliability and validity. In most cases, not enough research has been done on such tests to determine scientifically how effective they actually are in assessing personality. Results of the Thematic Apperception Test obtained by different scorers have proven relatively reliable when specific features (such as aggression) are measured. However, the reliability of the Rorschach test, which has also been researched, has generally proven unsatisfactory because test results are dependent on the psychologist's judgment. Different interpretations of the same set of responses may vary significantly. Although newer scoring systems—including one that allows for computer scoring—may yield greater reliability, free interpretation of the test is valuable to clinicians.

In addition to their weaknesses in terms of reliability and validation, projective tests also require more time and skill to administer than more objective testing methods. However, they continue to be employed because of their usefulness in helping psychologists obtain a comprehensive picture of an individual's personality. The results are most useful when combined with information obtained from personal observation, other test scores, and familiarity with a client's previous history. In addition, projective tests make it especially difficult for subjects to skew their answers in a particular direction as they sometimes attempt to do with other types of assessment.

See also Rorschach Technique

Further Reading

Cronbach, L.J. *Essentials of Psychological Testing.* New York: Harper and Row, 1970.

Sundberg, N. *The Assessment of Persons.* Englewood Cliffs, NJ: Prentice-Hall, 1977.

Psychiatric Institution

Institutions for the persons with mental disorders, formerly called asylums or mental hospitals.

Introduced during the Middle Ages, mental hospitals were basically prisons designed to control people who exhibited disturbed behavior and separate them from the general population. Patients were kept, often chained, in darkened cells, where they suffered from neglect and were commonly subjected to physical abuse. This type of treatment also reflected the popular belief that the mentally ill were demonically possessed and that by inflicting **pain** on them one was combating Satanic forces.

The first major advance toward more humane forms of institutionalization began with the reforms implemented by **Philippe Pinel** in 1792, when he was appointed chief physician and director of the Bicêtre asylum in Paris. As an experiment, Pinel was allowed to remove the chains from some of his patients and allow them to exercise in the open air. When these steps proved to be effective, Pinel was able to institute other changes at the hospital and discontinue such customary methods of treatment as bloodletting and purging. Moved to clean, sunny rooms and treated compassionately, many patients who were diagnosed as hopelessly insane had improved to the point where they were able to return to their families. Pinel was among the first to posit that mental disorders could be attributed to psychological or social **stress**, congenital conditions, or physiological injury. In addition to advocating the humane treatment of mental patients and the maintenance and preservation of detailed case histories for the purposes of treatment and research, Pinel also emphasized the importance of physical hygiene and exercise and pioneered in recommending productive work for mental patients.

Pinel's student, Jean Esquirol, expanded his reform efforts throughout France. The success of Pinel's methods also influenced practices in other countries. In the United States, **Benjamin Rush**, who in 1787 took charge of treating mental patients at the Pennsylvania Hospital, established the medical model of mental illness, a perspective from which psychological disturbances, like physical ailments, are viewed as diseases requiring treatment rather than crimes calling for imprisonment. While Rush was not an innovator in terms of treatment methods like his contemporary Pinel, his work eventually earned him the title "father of American psychiatry."

Despite such enlightened attitudes toward the mentally ill, conditions in most American psychiatric institutions had deteriorated during the nineteenth century. The U. S. Congress turned over financial responsibility for care of the mentally ill to the states, including the funding of treatment facilities. The loss of federal funds contributed to the decrease in doctor-to-patient ratios, the prevalence of unqualified personnel, and increased overcrowding. Reactions against such conditions in psychiatric institutions included the state hospital movement led by Dorothea Dix in the 1840s and the mental hygiene movement begun by **Clifford Beers** at the beginning of the twentieth century. Beers, who was institutionalized in 1900 following a **suicide** attempt, found the treatment of mental patients inhumane and ineffective, which he documented in *A Mind That Found Itself* (1908), a popular autobiographical study of his confinement and recovery. In the following year, Beers organized the National Committee for Mental Hygiene, which lobbied for improved treatment of mental patients.

While conditions in psychiatric institutions have improved in recent decades, the quality of patient care still varies, ranging from comfortable, pleasant facilities that provide individual and group **psychotherapy**, occupational therapy, and recreational activities to primarily custodial institutions offering little treatment besides medication. Due to greater funding, private hospitals are generally superior to public institutions. In contrast to the previous acceptance of long-term institutionalization as the norm, involuntary commitment to psychiatric institutions is avoided if at all possible. Commitment to a psychiatric institution is now considered as a last resort if other options—such as mental health clinics and halfway houses—have failed.

During the twentieth century, the federal government has assumed increased responsibility for the care of the mentally ill, funding programs for training and research through the Mental Health Act of 1946 and establishing the Joint Commission on Mental Illness and Health in 1955. The Community Mental Health Centers Act of 1963 allotted federal funds for the establishment of community treatment centers, which provide a variety of services including short-term and partial hospitalization in an effort toward the deinstitutionalization of mental patients.

Further Reading

Hartmann, Ernest. *Boundaries in the Mind: A New Psychology of Personality Difference.* New York: Basic Books, 1991.

Wyer, Robert S., Jr., ed. *Knowledge and Memory: The Real Story.* Hillsdale, NJ: Lawrence Erlbaum, 1995.

Psychiatry/Psychiatrist

A physician who specializes in the diagnosis and treatment of mental disorders.

Psychiatrists treat patients privately and in hospital settings through a combination of **psychotherapy** and medication. There are about 41,000 practicing psychiatrists in the United States. Their training consists of four years of medical school, followed by one year of internship and at least three years of psychiatric residency. Psychiatrists may receive certification from the American Board of Psychiatry and Neurology (ABPN), which requires two years of clinical experience beyond residency and the successful completion of a written and an oral test. Unlike a medical license, board certification is not legally required in order to practice psychiatry.

Psychiatrists may practice general psychiatry or choose a specialty, such as child psychiatry, geriatric psychiatry, treatment of substance abuse, forensic (legal) psychiatry, emergency psychiatry, **mental retardation**, community psychiatry, or public health. Some focus their research and clinical work primarily on psychoactive medication, in which case they are referred to as psychopharmacologists. Psychiatrists may be called upon to address numerous social issues, including **juvenile delinquency**, family and marital dysfunction, legal competency in criminal and financial matters, and treatment of mental and emotional problems among prison inmates and in the military.

Psychiatrists treat the biological, psychological, and social components of mental illness simultaneously. They can investigate whether symptoms of mental disorders have physical causes, such as a **hormone** imbalance or an adverse reaction to medication, or whether psychological symptoms are contributing to physical conditions, such as cardiovascular problems and high blood pressure. Because they are licensed physicians, psychiatrists, unlike psychologists and psychiatric social workers, can prescribe medication; they are also able to admit patients to the hospital. Other mental health professionals who cannot prescribe medication themselves often establish a professional relationship with a psychiatrist.

Psychiatrists may work in private offices, private psychiatric hospitals, community hospitals, state and federal hospitals, or community mental centers. Often, they combine work in several settings. As of 1988, 15 percent of psychiatrists belonged to group practices. In addition to their clinical work, psychiatrists often engage in related professional activities, including teaching, research, and administration. The **American Psychiatric Association**, the oldest medical specialty organization in the United States, supports the profession by offering continuing education and research opportunities, keeping members informed about new research and public policy issues, helping to educate the public about **mental health** issues, and serving as an advocate for people affected by mental illness.

Traditional psychiatry has been challenged in a variety of ways since the end of World War II. The most widespread and significant change has been the removal of the **psychiatric hospital** from its central role in the practice of psychiatry. This development resulted from a number of factors: the financial inability of state governments to remedy the deteriorating condition of many institutions; the discovery of new, more effective drugs enabling patients to medicate themselves at home; social activists' charges of abuse and neglect in state mental facilities; and activism by former mental patients protesting involuntary institutionalization and treatment. In addition, a growing movement, led by Karl Menninger, sought to replace state mental hospitals with community mental health centers. The Community Mental Health Centers Act of 1963 allotted federal funds for the establishment of community treatment centers, which provide a variety of services, including short-term and partial hospitalization. The establishment of these centers has contributed to the growing trend toward the deinstitutionalization of mental patients.

In the 1960s and 1970s radical critics within the profession, such as Thomas Szasz and R. D. Laing, challenged basic assumptions about psychiatric treatment and about the medical model of mental illness itself. Sociologists, including Erving Goffman and Thomas Scheff, produced critiques of mental institutions as a form of social control, and the anti-psychiatry ideas of French philosopher Michel Foucault gained currency among American intellectuals. Psychiatry also came under fire from the feminist movement, which saw it as a vehicle for controlling women. Feminist authors Kate Millett and Shulamith Firestone have portrayed **psychoanalysis** as instrumental in suppressing the original feminist movement of the late 19th and early 20th centuries by labeling women's legitimate dissatisfaction and agitation as hysteria and providing an intellectual theory that aided in legitimizing society's continuing subordination of women. Published in 1972, Phyllis Chesler's *Women and Madness* was a landmark in feminist criticism.

Advances in neuroscience, endocrinology, and immunology have had a major effect on the way psychiatry is practiced today. The study of **neurotransmitters**—chemicals in the **brain** that are related to **anxiety, depression**, and other disorders—have been significant both in the development of new medications and in the way psychiatrists think about **mood**, **personality**, and behavior. Currently, a major (and highly publicized) issue in psychiatry is the use of Prozac and other specialized serotonin reuptake inhibitors (SSRIs), a new class of antidepressants that has fewer side effects than drugs previously used to treat depression. These drugs have become controversial because of their potential use for "cosmetic psychopharmacology," the transformation of mood and personality in persons with no diagnosable mental disorder. Both psychiatrists and others in the medical and mental health professions must confront the issue of using psychoactive drugs as "mood brighteners" to make clinically healthy individuals more energetic, assertive, and resilient.

Another contemporary development with wide-ranging implications for psychiatry is the growth of health maintenance organizations (HMOs) and managed care programs, whose cost-containment policies have already had a significant effect on the way psychiatry is practiced. Expensive long-term psychotherapy is discouraged by such organizations, and medication is generally favored over therapy. Recently, concern has been expressed over the practice of promoting cheaper medications over more expensive ones, even when those that cost more offer greater benefits.

Further Reading

Coles, Robert. *The Mind's Fate: A Psychiatrist Looks at His Profession.* Boston: Little, Brown and Co., 1995.

Kramer, Peter D. *Listening to Prozac: A Psychiatrist Explores Antidepressant Drugs and the Remaking of the Self.* New York: Viking, 1993.

Laing, R. D. *Wisdom, Madness, and Folly: The Making of a Psychiatrist.* New York: McGraw-Hill, 1985.

Psychoanalysis

A theory of personality and associated method of psychotherapy developed by Sigmund Freud.

As a theory, psychoanalysis has exercised enormous influence on 20th-century ideas about human behavior and mental processes, not only among psychologists but in fields as diverse as art, literature, education, medicine, and the social sciences. As the first form of **psychotherapy**, its methods have affected all subsequent therapy systems, even those that depart drastically from **Sigmund Freud**'s own practices and beliefs.

The psychoanalytic method grew out of Freud's early work with nervous patients in Vienna. Impressed by the "talking cure" of his colleague, Josef Breuer (1842–1925), who was able to relieve hysterical symptoms by helping patients remember and confront traumatic memories, Freud evolved a similar system that, unlike Breu-

er's, did not use **hypnosis** to retrieve repressed thoughts and feelings. Instead, Freud relied on associations that surfaced when his patients spoke freely to him in a relaxed state (**free association**) and on the interpretation of their **dreams** to reveal material that had been relegated to the **unconscious**. Working with this material involved overcoming resistance by patients when they felt their control over sensitive areas threatened. A central feature of psychoanalysis is **transference**, the process by which patients transfer to the therapist their feelings toward and reactions to some other important figure or figures in their lives. Transference reveals to both the therapist and patient important beliefs and attitudes held by the patient as well as characteristic patterns of relating to others.

Psychoanalysis works on several different levels. Reliving and expressing strong reactions to emotional experiences in the safety of the therapy session has a cathartic effect (also called abreaction) that can be a source of relief and healing. Psychoanalysis also operates on the principle that the insight gained by understanding the reasons for one's **motivations** and behavior has therapeutic value. Finally, working through conflicts over an extended period of time strengthens one's ability to confront them without undue **anxiety**. Initially psychoanalysis was an extremely intensive and lengthy process. Patients met with their therapists for 50-minute sessions several times a week, often for years. Currently, psychoanalytically oriented therapists commonly see their patients once a week and agree on a limited term of therapy in which to address certain issues and attain specific goals.

Based on his clinical observations as well as a thorough self-analysis, Freud evolved a comprehensive theory of **personality** that focused on the conflicts all persons face in satisfying their basic drives—such as hunger, sex, and **aggression**—in the face of social constraints. At the heart of this theory is a three-part personality structure consisting of the **id**, which seeks immediate gratification of one's **instincts**, the **superego**, which internalizes society's values and prohibitions, and the **ego**, which mediates between the id and the superego. The ego operates on the conscious level, organizing one's actions to achieve goals as satisfactorily as possible within the limits laid down by the superego. The activities of the id and, to a certain extent, the superego are **unconscious**. Thoughts and feelings are relegated to the unconscious when their taboo or otherwise frightening nature would cause more anxiety than a person is able to handle. According to Freud, the source of much human anxiety is unconscious material that comes too close to **consciousness**. The ego's ways of dealing with anxiety include a variety of **defense mechanisms**, such as **denial**, **repression**, projection, sublimation, rationalization, and **regression**.

One of the best known and most controversial aspects of Freud's psychoanalytic theory is the central role of **sexuality** in psychic conflict, behavior, and personality formation. Proposing that sexuality is a basic drive from **birth**, Freud created an outline of childhood **psychosexual development** divided into chronological stages, with each stage (except latency) focused on a different erogenous zone (oral, anal, and phallic). Included in this sequence is the Oedipal crisis, a major developmental turning point that results in the formation of the superego and the assumption of one's gender identification. In contrast to the sexual, or life-preserving, instincts that Freud associated with the term "**libido**," he eventually came to believe in the existence of Thanatos, a death instinct or death wish, directed either outward in aggression or inward in self-destructive behavior and expressed primarily in repetitive behavior.

By the early 1900s Freud had attracted a circle of followers—including **Carl Jung**, **Alfred Adler**, and Otto Rank (1884–1939)—which eventually became known as the Vienna Psychological Society. Although their early support helped establish psychoanalysis as a movement of international importance, several of Freud's colleagues later broke away to formulate their own psychoanalytic systems. Alfred Adler's individual psychology emphasized the importance of social rather than sexual urges in determining personality, while Jung pioneered the concept of the collective unconscious whose psychic content is passed down between generations and contains universal **archetype**s that can be found in the myths and belief systems of many different cultures throughout history.

A later generation of "neo-Freudians," following Adler's example, emphasized the importance of social needs (such as security and acceptance) in personality formation. These included **Erich Fromm**, **Karen Horney**, and Harry Stack Sullivan (1892–1949). Sullivan in particular saw personality primarily as the pattern of a person's interactions with others. Another important figure, **Erik Erikson**, charted human development in terms of psychosocial stages, many of whose goals (trust, autonomy, intimacy, generativity) had an interpersonal component. Ego psychologists, including Freud's daughter, **Anna Freud,** give the ego a more important role than that assigned by classical psychoanalysis, assigning to it language, **perception,** learning, and other important functions. New psychodynamic theories (the term for psychoanalysis and other theories based on identifying and resolving unconscious conflicts) have continued to be developed, including the object relations theories of Melanie Klein (1882–1960), Otto Kernberg, and Heinz Kohut, which give primary importance to an infant's **attachment** to its mother or other primary caregiver.

In recent years, Freud's theories have come under attack from a variety of directions. Feminists have criticized his emphasis on male psychosexual development and on the role played by male anatomy in forming the attitudes of both sexes. With growing awareness of the extent of childhood sexual abuse, Freud's dismissal of his patients' memories of abuse as hysterical has been questioned. Attention has also been drawn to the restriction of his clinical observations to a relatively small group of upper-class female patients, casting doubt on the applicability of his theories to other populations and cultures. Despite the criticism of Freud and the declining popularity of psychoanalytic therapy, psychoanalysis remains an influential intellectual force.

Further Reading

Hall, Calvin S. *A Primer of Freudian Psychology.* New York: Harper and Row, 1982.

Menninger, K., and P.S. Holzman. *Theory of Psychoanalytic Technique.* New York: Basic Books, 1973.

Mitchell, Juliet. *Psychoanalysis* and *Feminism.* New York; Vintage Books, 1975.

Psychoanalytic Theory. See **Psychoanalysis**.

Psychodrama. See **Role Playing**.

Psychological Abstracts

Monthly journal published by the American Psychological Association.

Founded in 1927, *Psychological Abstracts* contains nonevaluative summary abstracts of literature in the field of psychology and related disciplines, which are grouped into 22 major classification categories. It includes summaries of technical reports as well as journal articles and books. Each edition is collected into a cumulative volume every six months, with an index listing both the volume's contents and the national and international journals in which the abstracted literature appear. These journals are cited within the volume by codes listed in each monthly issue. A table of contents near the beginning of each issue guides readers to broad general areas that they may wish to investigate, while the subject indexes in the cumulative volumes refers them to articles on a particular topic.

In addition to research articles, *Psychological Abstracts* features theoretical discussions and reviews of other investigations, and also contains an author index for readers who would like to follow up their research by studying additional articles or books by a given author.

PsycLIT®, the CD-ROM version of *Psychological Abstracts,* became available in 1993, and is used by many academic and large public libraries. *PsycLIT®,* a two-CD set which is updated quarterly, includes over 670,000 records. *PsycLIT®* indexes and abstracts articles dating from 1973 from 1,300 professional journals. The database also indexes and abstracts books and book chapters dating from 1987.

Further Information

EBSCO Publishing
    Address: 10 Estes Street, Ispwich, MA 01938
    Telephone: 800-653-2726

Psychological Disorder

A condition characterized by patterns of thought, emotion, or behavior that are maladaptive, disruptive, or uncomfortable either for the person affected or for others.

While psychological disorders are generally signaled by some form of abnormal behavior or thought process, abnormality can be difficult to define, especially since it varies from culture to culture. Psychologists have several standard approaches to defining abnormality for diagnostic purposes. One is the statistical approach, which evaluates behavior by determining how closely it conforms to or deviates from that of the majority of people. Behavior may also be evaluated by whether it conforms to social rules and cultural norms, an approach that avoids condemning nonconformists as abnormal for behavior that, while unusual, may not violate social standards and may even be valued in their culture. Yet another way to gauge the normality of behavior is by whether it is adaptive or maladaptive—and to what extent it interferes with the conduct of everyday life. In some situations, psychologists may also evaluate normality solely on the basis of whether or not a person is made unhappy or uncomfortable by his or her own behavior.

The official standard for the classification of psychological disorders is the American Psychiatric Association's *Diagnostic and Statistical Manual of Mental Disorders,* whose most recent edition is also referred to as *DSM-IV.* Its five dimensions, or axes for evaluating behavior and thought patterns, provide a thorough context in which to assess an individual's psychological profile. Axis I lists major mental disorders that may affect a patient. Axis II is for assessing of **personality disorders**—lifelong, deeply ingrained patterns of behavior that are destructive to those who display them or to others. Axis III deals with any organic medical problems that may be present. The fourth axis includes any **environment**al or psychosocial factors affecting a person's condition (such as the loss of a loved one, sexual abuse, divorce, career changes, poverty, or homelessness). In Axis V, the diagnostician assesses the person's level of functioning within the previous 12 months on a scale of one to 100.

Conditions that would formerly have been described as neurotic are now found in five Axis I classifications: **anxiety** disorders, somatoform disorders, dissociative disorders, mood disorders, and sexual disorders. **Anxiety disorders**—conditions involving longstanding, intense, or disruptive anxiety—are the most common of psychological disorders among Americans. These include **phobia**s (a strong fear of a specific object or situation); generalized anxiety (a diffuse, free-floating anxiety); **panic** disorder (an acute anxiety attack often accompanied by agoraphobia, or fear of being separated from a safe place); and **obsessive-compulsive disorder** (a repetitive, uncontrollable behavior triggered by persistent, unwanted thoughts).

Somatoform disorders are characterized by psychological problems that take a physical, or somatic, form. A person suffering from a somatoform disorder will show persistent physical symptoms for which no physiological cause can be found. Included among these disorders are hypochondriasis (a strong, unjustified fear of contracting a serious disease); **pain** disorder (severe pain with no apparent physical cause); and somatization disorder (complaints about a variety of physical problems). Another somatoform condition, conversion disorder (formerly called conversion hysteria), is characterized by apparent blindness, deafness, paralysis, or insensitivity to pain with no physiological cause. Conversion disorders, which are most prevalent in **adolescence** or early adulthood, are usually accompanied by some form of severe **stress** and often appear to elicit surprisingly little concern in the patient. **Dissociative disorders** involve the fragmentation, or **dissociation,** of personality components that are usually integrated, such as **memory, consciousness,** or even **identity** itself. These disorders include **amnesia**, **dissociative identity disorder,** and dissociative fugue (in which amnesia is accompanied by assumption of a new identity in a new location).

Mood disorders (also called affective disorders), are characterized by extremes of mood, abnormal mood fluctuations, or inconsistency between mood and the surrounding events or **environment.** The two leading mood disorders are **depression** and **bipolar disorder.** Major depressive disorder is characterized by feelings and behaviors that many people experience at times—sadness, guilt, fatigue, loss of appetite—but it is distinguished by their persistence and severity. Major depression may be accompanied by feelings of inadequacy and worthlessness, weight loss or gain, **sleep** disturbances, difficulty concentrating and making decisions, and, in the most severe cases, **delusion**s and suicidal impulses. Depression is a major problem in the United States; one-third of all psychiatric outpatients suffer from depression. The percentage of Americans who will experience at least one major depressive episode during their lives has been estimated at between eight and 12 percent for men and between 20 and 26 percent for women. Bipolar disorder (also known as manic depression) is characterized by the alternation of depression with **mania,** an abnormally active and elated emotional state in which a person becomes overly optimistic, energetic, and convinced of his or her own powers and abilities. Manic episodes can result in impulsive and unwise decisions, and may even pose physical dangers.

The *DSM-IV* list of mental disorders also includes psychotic disorders, which are severe conditions characterized by abnormalities in **thinking,** false beliefs, and other symptoms indicating a highly distorted **perception** of reality and severe interference with the capacity to function normally. Probably the best known of these disorders is **schizophrenia,** which seriously disrupts communication and other normal functions, including profound disturbances in thinking, **emotion,** perception, and behavior. About one percent of Americans suffer from schizophrenia. Other mental disorders listed in *DSM-IV* include eating and **sleep disorders;** impulse control and **adjustment** disorders; substance-related disorders; cognitive disorders, such as **delirium,** and **dementia;** and disorders usually diagnosed in **infancy,** childhood, or **adolescence**, such as **hyperactivity, mental retardation,** and **autism.** Personality disorders, which are listed in Axis II of *DSM-IV,* include narcissistic, dependent, avoidant, and antisocial personality types. This axis also includes developmental disorders in children.

Psychological Testing. See **Assessment, Psychological**.

Psychology/Psychologist

The science which studies behavior and mental processes.

As psychology has grown and changed throughout its history, it has been defined in numerous ways. As early as 400 B.C., the ancient Greeks philosophized about the relationship of **personality** characteristics to physiological traits. Since then, philosophers have proposed theories to explain human behavior. In the late 1800s the emergence of scientific method gave the study of psychology a new focus. In 1879, the first psychological laboratory was opened in Leipzig, Germany, by Wilhelm Wundt (1832–1920), and soon afterwards the first experimental studies of **memory** were published. Wundt was instrumental in establishing psychology as the study of conscious experience, which he viewed as made up of elemental sensations. In addition to the type of psychology practiced by Wundt—which became known as structuralism—other early schools of psychology were **functionalism,** which led to the development of **behaviorism,** and **Gestalt psychology.** The **American Psychological Association** was founded in 1892 with the goals of encouraging research, enhancing professional competence, and disseminating knowledge about the field.

With the ascendance of the Viennese psychologist **Sigmund Freud** and his method of **psychoanalysis** early in the twentieth century, emphasis shifted from conscious experience to **unconscious** processes investigated by means of **free association** and other techniques. According to Freud, behavior and mental processes were the result of mostly unconscious struggles within each person between the drive to satisfy basic **instinct**s, such as sex or **aggression,** and the limits imposed by society. At the same time that Freud's views were gaining popularity in Europe, an American psychology professor, **John B. Watson,** was pioneering the behavioral approach, which focuses on observing and measuring external behaviors rather than the internal workings of the mind. **B.F. Skinner,** who spent decades studying the effects of reward and **punishment** on behavior, helped maintain the predominance of **behaviorism** in the United States through the 1950s and 1960s. Since the 1970s, many psychologists have been influenced by the cognitive approach, which is concerned with the relationship of mental processes to behavior. **Cognitive psychology** focuses on how people take in, perceive, and store information, and how they process and act on that information.

Additional psychological perspectives include the neurobiological approach, focusing on relating behavior to internal processes within the **brain** and **nervous system,** and the phenomenological approach, which is most concerned with the individual's subjective experience of the world rather than the application of psychological theory to behavior. While all these approaches differ in their explanations of individual behavior, each contributes an important perspective to the psychological image of the total human being. Most psychologists apply the principles of various approaches in studying and understanding human nature.

Along with several approaches to psychology there are also numerous subfields in which these approaches may be applied. Most subfields can be categorized under one of two major areas of psychology referred to as basic and **applied psychology.** Individual psychologists may specialize in one of the subfields in either of these areas. The subfields are often overlapping areas of interest rather than isolated domains. Basic psychology encompasses the subfields concerned with the advancement of psychological theory and research. **Experimental psychology** employs laboratory experiments to study basic behavioral processes shared by different species, including sensation, **perception,** learning, **memory,** communication, and **motivation. Physiological psychology** is concerned with the ways in which biology shapes behavior and mental processes, and **developmental psychology** is concerned with behavioral development over the entire life span. Other subfields include **social psychology,** quantitative psychology, and the psychology of personality.

Applied psychology is the area of psychology concerned with applying psychological research and theory to problems posed by everyday life. It includes **clinical psychology,** the largest single field in psychology. Clinical psychologists—accounting for 40 percent of all psychologists—are involved in **psychotherapy** and psychological testing. Like clinical psychologists, counseling psychologists apply psychological principles to diagnose and treat individual emotional and behavioral problems. Other subfields of applied psychology include **school psychology,** which involves the evaluation and placement of students; **educational psychology,** which investigates the psychological aspects of the learning process; and **industrial psychology** and organizational psychology, which study the relationship between people and their jobs. Community psychologists investigate **environment**al factors that contribute to mental and emotional disorders; health psychologists deal with the psychological aspects of physical illness, investigating the connections between the mind and a person's physical condition; and consumer psychologists study the preferences and buying habits of consumers as well as their reactions to certain advertising.

In response to society's changing needs, new fields of psychology are constantly emerging. One new type of specialization, called environmental psychology, focuses on the relationship between people and their physical surroundings. Its areas of inquiry include such issues as the effects of overcrowding and noise on urban dwellers and the effects of building design. Another relatively new specialty is **forensic psychology,** involving the application of psychology to law enforcement and the judicial system. Forensic psychologists may help create personality profiles of criminals, formulate principles for jury selection, or study the problems involved in eyewitness testimony. Yet another emerging area is program evaluation, whose practitioners evaluate the effectiveness and cost efficiency of government programs.

Depending on the nature of their work, psychologists may practice in a variety of settings, including colleges and universities, hospitals and community mental health centers, schools, and businesses. A growing number of psychologists work in private practice and may

CONCEPTS IN PSYCHOPHYSICS

Absolute threshold: as the stimulus strengthens from undetectable, the point at which the person first detects it.

Signal detection theory: theory pertaining to the interaction of the sensory capabilities and decision-making factors in detecting a stimulus.

Difference thresholds: at what point can one differentiate between two stimuli. This point is termed just-noticeable difference.

Scaling: using rating scales to assign relative values (for example, rating on a scale of one to ten) to sensory experiences.

also specialize in multiple subfields. Most psychologists earn a Ph.D. degree in the field, which requires completion of a four- to six-year program offered by a university psychology department. The course of study includes a broad overview of the field, as well as specialization in a particular subfield, and completion of a dissertation and an internship. Students who intend to practice only applied psychology rather than conduct research have the option of obtaining a Psy.D. degree, which does not entail writing a dissertation.

See also Behavior Therapy; Cognitive Development Theory; Counseling Psychology; Developmental Psychology; Experimental Psychology; Health Psychology; Research Methods.

Psychophysics

The subfield of psychology that deals with the transformation from the physical to the psychological through detection, identification, discrimination, and scaling.

Psychophysics originated with the research of Gustav Fechner (1801–1887), who first studied the relationship between incoming physical stimuli and the responses to them. Psychophysicists have generally used two approaches in studying our sensitivity to stimuli around us: measuring the **absolute threshold** or discovering the difference threshold. In studying the absolute threshold using the method of constant stimuli, an experimenter will, for example, produce an extremely faint tone which the listener cannot hear, then gradually increase the intensity until the person can just hear it; on the next trial, the experimenter will play a sound that is clearly heard, then reduce its intensity until the listener can no longer hear it. Thresholds can also be ascertained through the method of constant stimuli. In this approach, stimuli of varying intensity are randomly presented. Although an observer's measured threshold will change depending on methodology, this technique gives an estimate of an individual's sensitivity.

A different psychophysical approach combines the concept of sensory abilities with the decisions and strategies that an observer uses to maximize performance in a difficult task. Rather than try to identify a single point for the threshold, psychophysicists who employ the **signal detection theory** have developed ways to measure an observer's sensitivity to stimuli in ways that go beyond the simple concept of the threshold. Some psychophysical research involves the identification of stimuli. There may be no question as to whether we can detect a stimulus, but sometimes we cannot identify it. For example, people can often detect odors but cannot identify them. Research in this area has centered on determining how much information is needed to allow a person to identify a stimulus. Identification constitutes a relatively small part of psychophysical research, although such research has important practical applications. For example, in the development of useful telephones, researchers had to assess how much "noise" or unwanted sound could accompany speech in a phone conversation so that a listener could understand what was said—that is, identify the spoken words accurately.

A third area of psychophysics involves discrimination of different stimuli, or difference thresholds. No two physical stimuli are absolutely identical, although they may seem to be. The question of interest here is how large must the difference be between two stimuli in order for us to detect it. The amount by which two stimuli must differ in order for us to detect the difference is referred to as the JND, or **just noticeable difference.** Research has indicated that for stimuli of low intensity, we can detect a difference that is small, as the intensity increases, we need a larger difference. Sometimes psychophysicists use reaction time as a measure of how different two stimuli are from one another. When two stimuli are very similar, it takes a longer time to decide if they are different, whereas large differences lead to fast reaction times.

The final area of interest to psychophysicists is scaling, the activity of deciding how large or small something is or how much of it is present. Any sensory experience can be scaled. For instance, if the attractiveness of a painting is rated on a scale of one to ten, it is being scaled. If the painting is rated nine, it is considered more attractive than a painting rated eight. This simple example gives the concept underlying scaling, but psychologists have developed more complicated techniques and sophisticated mathematical approaches to scaling.

Psychosexual Development

Psychoanalytical theory of development based on sexual impulses.

Austrian psychotherapist **Sigmund Freud** described **personality** development during childhood in terms of stages based on shifts in the primary location of sexual impulses. During each stage libidinal pleasure is derived from a particular area of the body—called an erogenous zone—and the activities centered in that area. If the problems and conflicts of a particular stage are not adequately resolved, the child—and, later, the adult—may remain fixated at that stage. A **fixation** consists of a conscious or **unconscious** preoccupation with an area of the body (such as the mouth in a compulsive eater), as well as certain personality **traits**. Freud believed that some degree of fixation is present in everyone and that it is an important determinant of personality.

During the three pregenital stages that occur in a child's first five years, **sexuality** is narcissistic: it is directed toward the child's own body as a source of pleasure rather than outward. In the oral stage, which occupies approximately the first year of life, pleasurable impulses are concentrated in the area of the mouth and lips, the infant's source of nourishment. The child derives pleasure from sucking, mouthing, swallowing, and, later, biting and chewing food. The mouth is also used for exploring. The primary emotional issues at this stage of life are nurturance and dependency. A person who develops an oral fixation—for example, by being weaned too early or too late—is likely to focus on forms of oral gratification such as smoking, drinking, or compulsive eating. Personality traits may include excessive dependency and desire for the approval of others or a drive to acquire possessions that recalls the infant's drive to incorporate food.

The next stage—the anal stage—takes place during the infant's second year. At this point, voluntary control of elimination becomes physically possible and is inculcated through toilet training. This is a child's first major experience with discipline and outside authority and requires the subordination of natural **instinct**s to social demands. Experiences at this stage play a role in determining a person's degree of initiative and **attitude** toward authority. A child who is harshly disciplined in the course of toilet training may later rebel against authority or become overly fastidious, controlled, or stingy. Conversely, a child who is rewarded and praised for attempts to control elimination is more likely to develop a willingness to "let go" that is associated with generosity and creativity.

Between the ages of two and three years, the focus of a child's attention and pleasure shifts from the anal to the genital area, initiating what Freud termed the phallic stage. During this period, important changes take place in the child's attitude toward his or her parents. Sexual longings are experienced toward the parent of the opposite sex, accompanied by feelings of rivalry and **hostility** for the same-sex parent. Freud called this situation the **Oedipus complex** for its similarity to the plot of the Greek tragedy *Oedipus Rex,* in which the central character unknowingly kills his father and marries his mother. While the broad outlines of the Oedipal stage are similar for both sexes, it takes a somewhat different course in male and female children. A boy fears that his father will punish him for his feelings toward his mother by removing the locus of these feelings, the penis. This **fear**, which Freud called castration **anxiety**, causes the boy to abandon his incestuous attachment to his mother and begin to identify with his father, imitating him and adopting his values, a process that results in the formation of the boy's **superego**. To describe the experience undergone by girls in the Oedipal stage, Freud used the term "Electra complex," which was derived from the name of a figure in Greek mythology who was strongly attached to her father, Agamemnon, and participated in avenging his death at the hands of her mother, Clytemnestra. Paralleling the castration anxiety felt by boys, girls, according to Freud, experience penis envy. The girl blames her mother for depriving her of a penis and desires her father because he possesses one. Ultimately, the girl, like the boy, represses her incestuous desires and comes to identify with the same-sex parent, the mother, through the development of a superego.

As the phallic stage ends, its conflicts are resolved or repressed, and it is followed by the latency period, during which sexual impulses are dormant. The latency period separates pregenital sexuality from the genital stage, which begins with **adolescence** and lasts through adulthood. In the genital stage, **narcissism** is replaced by focusing sexual energy on a partner of the opposite sex, ultimately resulting in sexual union and extending to feelings such as friendship, altruism, and love.

Further Reading

Freud, Sigmund. *New Introductory Lectures on Psychoanalysis,* Chapter Five. New York: W. W. Norton and Co., 1933.

Hall, Calvin S. *A Primer of Freudian Psychology.* New York: Harper and Row, 1982.

Psychosis. See **Psychotic Disorder.**

Psychosomatic Disorders

Physical illnesses that are believed to be psychologically based; also referred to as psychophysiological disorders.

The **American Psychiatric Association**'s *Diagnostic and Statistical Manual of Mental Disorders (DSM-*

IV) classifies psychosomatic illnesses under "Psychological Factors Affecting Physical Conditions." Physicians have been aware that people's mental and emotional states influence their physical well-being since the time of Hippocrates. In the twentieth century, the discoveries of psychologists have shed new light on how the mind and body interact to produce health or illness. **Sigmund Freud** introduced the idea that **unconscious** thoughts can be converted into physical symptoms (**conversion reaction**). The formal study of psychosomatic illnesses began in Europe in the 1920s, and by 1939, the journal *Psychosomatic Medicine* had been founded in the United States. Eventually, sophisticated laboratory experiments replaced clinical observation as the primary method of studying psychosomatic illness. Researchers in the field of psychophysiology measured such responses as blood pressure, heart rate, and skin temperature to determine the physiological effects of human behavior. Animal research have also contributed to the growing body of knowledge about psychosomatic disorders. Three theories have been particularly popular in explaining why certain persons develop psychosomatic disorders and what determines the forms these illnesses take. One theory contends that psychological **stress** affects bodily organs that are constitutionally weak or weakened by stress. Another links specific types of illness with particular types of stress. Still another theory suggests that physiological predispositions combined with psychological stress to produce psychosomatic illness.

The parts of the body most commonly affected by psychosomatic disorders are the gastrointestinal and respiratory systems. Gastrointestinal disorders include gastric and duodenal ulcers, ulcerative colitis, and irritable bowel syndrome. (**Anorexia nervosa** and **bulimia** are sometimes considered psychosomatic disorders, but they also appear under the category of "**anxiety disorder—eating disorders**" in *DSM-IV.*) Respiratory problems caused or worsened by psychological factors include asthma and hyperventilation syndrome. Cardiovascular complaints include coronary artery disease, hypertension, tachycardia (speeded-up and irregular heart rhythm), and migraine headaches. Psychosomatic disorders also affect the skin (eczema, allergies, and neurodermatitis) and genitourinary system (menstrual disorders and sexual dysfunction).

Probably the most well-known psychosomatic connection is that of stress and coronary heart disease. The term "Type A" has been used for over twenty years to describe the aggressive, competitive, impatient, controlling type of person whom researchers have found to be more prone to heart disease than people who are more easygoing and mild-mannered and less hostile and concerned with time. In 1981, a panel appointed by the National Heart, Lung, and Blood Institute found that Type A behavior poses a greater risk of coronary heart disease and myocardial infarction (heart attack) than do cigarette smoking, age, hypertension, or a high serum cholesterol count.

Emotional stress can also affect the immune system, raising the risk to the body from such foreign invaders as bacteria, viruses, and cancer cells. People under stress are more likely to develop infectious diseases, including those stemming from the reactivation of latent herpes viruses. It is known that several of the body's reactions to stress, including the release of cortisol, adrenaline, and other **hormones**, suppress the activity of the immune system. A special field, psychoneuroimmunology, studies how the interaction of psychological and physiological reactions affects the functioning of the immune system.

People suffering from psychosomatic disorders have been helped by treatment of either their physical symptoms, the underlying psychological causes, or both. If the disorder is in an advanced stage (such as in severe asthma attacks, perforated ulcers, or debilitating colitis) symptomatic treatment must be undertaken initially as an emergency measure before the emotional component can be addressed. Psychological approaches range from classic **psychoanalysis**, which addresses a person's early traumas and conflicts, to **behavior therapy** that focuses on changing learned behaviors that create or increase anxiety. Medications such as tranquilizers or antidepressants may be effective in relieving symptoms of psychosomatic disorders. **Hypnosis** has successfully been used to treat hyperventilation, ulcers, migraine headaches, and other complaints. Today, psychologists commonly treat psychosomatic ailments with the aid of such relaxation techniques as progressive relaxation, autogenic training, transcendental meditation, and yoga. **Biofeedback** has been used in treating a number of different clinical problems, including tachycardia, hypertension, and both tension and migraine headaches.

Further Reading
Mind, Body, Medicine: How to Use Your Mind for Better Health. Consumer Reports Books, 1993.

Psychosurgery

Highly controversial medical procedures where areas of the brain are destroyed or disabled through surgery as treatment for mental illness.

Psychosurgery involves severing or otherwise disabling areas of the **brain** to treat a **personality disorder**, **behavior disorder** or other **mental illness**. The most common form of psychosurgery is the lobotomy, where the nerves connecting the frontal lobes of the brain and the **thalamus** or **hypothalamus** are severed. Performed first in the late 1930s, by the 1940s lobotomies were recommended for patients diagnosed with **schizophrenia**, severe **obsessive-compulsive disorder**, severe depression, and uncontrollable aggressive behavior. Other psychosurgeries also involve severing nerve connections to the hypothalamus, since it plays a key role in controlling **emotion**s. Psychosurgery has been recommended less frequently as more effective **drugs** for treatment of psychological disorders have been developed.

Further Reading
Rodgers, Joann Ellison. *Psychosurgery: Damaging the Brain to Save the Mind.* New York: HarperCollins Publishers, 1992.
Valenstein, Elliott S. *The Psychosurgery Debate: Scientific, Legal, and Ethical Perspectives.* San Francisco: W. H. Freeman, 1980.

Psychotherapy

The treatment of psychological disorders and problems of adjustment through the use of psychological techniques rather than through physical or biological means.

Numerous methods of intervention are encompassed by the term psychotherapy, all of which are aimed at aiding individuals in changing their behaviors, thoughts, and **emotion**s in ways which help them to overcome psychological problems. Psychotherapy is practiced by a variety of professionals, including the psychoanalyst, who practices Freudian **psychoanalysis**, the **psychiatrist**, the clinical psychologist, the counseling psychologist, the psychiatric social worker and, in the psychiatric hospital, by the psychiatric nurse. Some practitioners, such as the psychoanalyst, believe that change is contingent on a client's understanding of his unconscious conflicts. Others, like the cognitive behavior therapist, believe that individuals can learn new skills that will aid in their recovery without analyzing the factors that have led to their problems.

Regardless of these variations in methods, there are a number of features that most forms of psychotherapy share. There is interaction between a therapist and client (or group of clients in **group therapy**) in which a relationship of mutual warmth and trust is developed. The therapy is based on a theory that either helps explain the source of the client's problems or offers a way of alleviating them (or does both). The theory prescribes certain procedures for the therapist to follow in helping the client. Often, the client is encouraged to express inner thoughts and feelings openly and the therapist generally provides reassurance and support. The therapist also attempts to provide clients with insight and new skills to help them find more workable solutions to their problems. People may receive therapy as inpatients in a hospital or other institution, or as outpatients residing in the community. Some persons seek therapy as a means of personal growth even though they may not be confronting major problems in their lives at the time.

Psychoanalysis was the first formalized method of psychotherapy. Developed by **Sigmund Freud** in the late nineteenth century, it is based on the assumption that human behavior and mental processes are based on **unconscious** conflicts between instinctual desires and the restrictions imposed by society, and it focuses on bringing these conflicts to the surface where they can be understood and treated. Significant aspects of the psychoanalytic method that have influenced other forms of therapy include individualized analysis and treatment of clients; investigation of the relationship between a person's past history and current problems; the focus on thoughts and emotions; and emphasis on the client-therapist relationship. Although it is not as predominant as it once was, classical psychoanalysis as developed by Freud is still practiced, as well as a number of variations that may retain the broad emphasis on uncovering unconscious **motivation** and breaking down defenses that alter the methods of treatment. Collectively, such therapies (including psychoanalysis) are known as *psychodynamic therapy.*

Those seeking psychotherapy today have many other options as well. *Phenomenological therapy* (also called humanistic therapy). It de-emphasizes the doctor-patient aspect of psychotherapy and regards treatment as an encounter between equals that should occur in a close, supportive, non-judgmental atmosphere. Therapy is viewed as a growth experience, with the patient free to chart his or her own future rather than being enslaved by the past. Two well-known forms of phenomenological therapy are the **client-centered therapy** pioneered by **Carl Rogers** (also known as nondirective therapy) and Gestalt therapy, developed by Fritz Perls. Client-centered therapy is based on **empathy** and an unconditional positive regard toward the client by the therapist, who listens without interrupting or evaluating what the client says. Derived from but not identical with **Gestalt psychology,** which emphasizes the organization of perception and experience into meaningful patterns, or wholes, Gestalt therapy is based on the principle that each person's reality depends on how he or she perceives and organizes experience. Often working in groups, clients are encouraged to actively confront their own feelings in the present (the "here and now"), as well as their evasions of them, sometimes using techniques such as **role-playing** exercises.

In contrast to the psychodynamic and phenomenological approaches, behavior-oriented therapies are geared toward helping clients to identify their problems as learned behaviors that can be modified without looking for unconscious motivations or hidden meanings. Behavioral approaches derive from the work of researchers such as **John Watson**, **Ivan Pavlov**, and **B.F. Skinner** on **operant conditioning** in animals. By the 1950s and 1960s, operant conditioning was being studied as a way of altering maladaptive behavior in humans, and by 1970 behavior therapy was a popular alternative to previous approaches. The various types of behavior therapy rely on a good client-therapist relationship; careful observation and monitoring of the behaviors (or thought processes) to be changed; and of a teacher-like role for the therapist, who assigns the client "homework" and helps him or her develop plans for dealing with specific problems. **Behavior therapy** that relies on classical conditioning principles is known as **behavior modification** and makes use of such techniques as systematic **desensitization, modeling,** positive **reinforcement, extinction** (weakening of undesirable behaviors), aversive conditioning, and **punishment.** Behavior therapy may be used to alter not only overt behavior but also the thought patterns that drive it. This type of treatment is known as **cognitive behavior therapy.** One well-known type of cognitive-behavior therapy is rational-emotive therapy (RET), developed by Albert Ellis, which attempts to help people rid themselves of self-defeating or problem-causing thoughts, such as "I fail at whatever I try," or "I must be perfect to be a worthwhile person." Clients learn to replace such thoughts with alternative thoughts that are positive and calming—a process called cognitive restructuring. Another cognitively-oriented therapy is *cognitive therapy*, created by Aaron Beck. It is often used with persons suffering from **depression** or **anxiety** disorders. It is based on challenging negative styles of **thinking** and reducing the tendency of depressed people to blame all negative events on their own perceived incompetence by helping them develop more optimistic ways of thinking.

See also Human Potential Movement.

Further Reading

Ammerman, Robert T., and Michel Hersen, eds. *Handbook of Behavior Therapy with Children and Adults: A Developmental and Longitudinal Perspective.* New York: Allyn and Bacon, 1993.

Craighead, Linda W. *Cognitive and Behavioral Interventions: An Empirical Approach to Mental Health Problems.* Boston: Allyn and Bacon, 1994.

Kanfer, Frederick H., and Arnold P. Goldstein, eds. *Helping People Change: A Textbook of Methods.* 4th ed. New York: Pergamon Press, 1991.

O'Leary, K. Daniel, and G. Terence Wilson. *Behavior Therapy: Application and Outcome.* Englewood Cliffs, NJ: Prentice-Hall, 1975.

Stern, Richard. *The Practice of Behavioural and Cognitive Psychotherapy.* New York: Cambridge University Press, 1991.

Psychotic Disorders

A diagnostic term formerly used in a general way to designate the most severe psychological disorders; now used in a much narrower sense in connection with specific symptoms and conditions.

Formerly, all psychological disorders were considered either psychotic or neurotic. Psychotic disorders were those that rendered patients unable to function normally in their daily lives and left them "out of touch with reality." They were associated with impaired **memory**, language, and speech and an inability to think rationally. Neurotic disorders, by comparison, were characterized chiefly by **anxiety**; any impairment of functioning was primarily social. Psychotic conditions were attributed to physiological causes, neurotic conditions to psychosocial ones. Other distinguishing features associated primarily with psychotic disorders were hospitalization and treatment by biological methods—medication and **electroconvulsive therapy**. With the development of new types of psychoactive **drugs** in the 1950s and 1960s, medication became a common form of therapy for anxiety, **depression**, and other problems categorized as neurotic.

"Psychotic" and "neurotic" are no longer employed as major categories in the **American Psychiatric Association**'s *Diagnostic and Statistical Manual of Mental Disorders (DSM-IV)*. Instead, disorders that formerly belonged to either one category or the other appear side by side in Axis I of the manual under the heading "Clinical Syndromes." The term "psychotic" still appears in *DSM-IV,* most prominently in the categorization "Schizophrenia and Other Psychotic Disorders." The disorders in this section have as their defining feature symptoms considered psychotic, which in this context can refer to **delusion**s, **hallucination**s, and other positive symptoms of **schizophrenia**, such as confused speech and catatonia.

In other parts of *DSM-IV,* "psychotic" is also used to describe aspects of a disorder even when they are not its defining feature, as in "Major Depressive Disorder with Psychotic Features."

Further Reading

Hales, Dianne, and Robert E. Hales, M.D. *Caring for the Mind: The Comprehensive Guide to Mental Health.* New York: Bantam Books, 1995.

Puberty

The period of physiological development during which sexual maturity is reached.

The physical changes of puberty are initiated and controlled in the **brain** by the **hypothalamus** and the anterior pituitary gland. While these changes usually begin at about age ten for girls and twelve for boys, the timing may vary. In some teenagers, the changes happen slowly and may take as many as five to six years. For others, puberty is completed in as short a time as one year. Patterns of physical maturation may be influenced by genetic factors as well as **environment**al factors, including emotional problems. Despite the differences in the onset and speed of the changes, they generally occur in the same order in both sexes. For girls, the sequence is as follows: an initial growth spurt, breast development, appearance of straight, then kinky pubic hair, a period of maximum annual growth, menarche (onset of menstruation), and appearance of auxiliary hair. Development occurs in boys in the following order: initial growth spurt, enlargement of the testes, appearance of straight pubic hair, early deepening of the voice, first ejaculation, the appearance of kinky pubic hair, maximum growth spurt, facial hair,

ADOLSCENTS WHO HAVE BECOME SEXUALLY ACTIVE*						
Sexually active by age	All (Number)	All (Percent)	Boys (Number)	Boys (Percent)	Girls (Number)	Girls (Percent)
13	749	8.6%	389	14.7%	350	2.7%
14	509	17.7%	263	24.6%	246	10.8%
15	320	31.2%	166	35.0%	154	27.3%
16	169	54.9%	82	63.1%	87	47.1%
17	78	68.6%	38	72.1%	40	65.8%

*This table reports data on the number and percent of adolescents who have become sexually active by a certain age. Data was gathered by the National Longitudinal Survey of Youth, 1988–92.

auxiliary hair, late voice change, and development of beard and chest hair.

Adolescent emotional responses to puberty vary, depending on the individual pattern of physical change experienced and on gender. Boys feel good about themselves if they mature early and often lack self-confidence if they mature late. Girls, however, may feel embarrassed by early physical maturity, which may lead to increased distance from their parents and peers and, possibly, early sexual activity. Teenagers are more concerned about secondary characteristics such as breast development or voice change because these features can be perceived by others. Besides concern with breast size and height, girls commonly become preoccupied with menstruation, which represents an important rite of passage in femininity.

Adolescent boys are concerned with their height, muscle development, shoulder breadth, and other traditional features of masculinity. Teenagers also become preoccupied with other physical characteristics that have no direct connection with sexual maturity. One is acne, which first appears during **adolescence**, when secretions from the sebaceous glands increase. Because it is so visible, acne can strongly affect self-confidence, depending on its severity. Another physical preoccupation is weight gain. Girls are especially vulnerable to eating disorders, notably **anorexia nervosa** and **bulimia.** The peak times of onset of anorexia are ages 12 to 13 and age 17. The American Anorexia/Bulimia Association (AABA) estimates that one percent of American teenage girls become anorexic.

In addition to changes in physical appearance, the emergence of teenage **sexuality** has important effects on behavior. Statistics indicate that a growing number of American teens are sexually active, resulting in over one million teen pregnancies each year. Teenage girls are more prone to encounter difficult pregnancies and deliveries, and have higher rates of toxemia and anemia than older women. Adolescent pregnancies and motherhood can be severely disruptive to a teenager's psychological development; the number of teenage mothers who attempt **suicide** is seven times greater than that of teenage girls without children. Teen mothers are less likely to marry or become self-supporting than are women who become mothers later in life, and fewer than 50 percent graduate from high school. Another major consequence of teenage sexuality is the exposure to **AIDS** and other sexually-transmitted diseases. In 1993, AIDS was the nation's fourth leading cause of death of women between the ages of 15 and 44. Increases in the number of women carrying the HIV virus through heterosexual sex has been greatest among 20 to 29-year-olds, most of whom were probably infected as teenagers, and high-risk sexual behavior among heterosexual teens, particularly African-American and Hispanic males, continues. Much of the AIDS prevention effort in the United States has been directed toward promoting safer sex practices, including abstinence (especially among young people) and the use of latex condoms, which greatly reduce the chance of infection.

Further Reading

Erikson, Erik. *Identity, Youth, and Crisis.* New York: W. W. Norton, 1968.

Stress, Risk, and Resilience in Children and Adolescence. New York: Cambridge University Press, 1994.

Puffer, Ethel Dench (1872–1950)

American educator and psychologist.

Ethel Dench Puffer was born in Framingham, Massachusetts, the eldest of four daughters. Her family was of native New England stock and highly educated by the standard of the era. After graduating from Smith College in 1891 at the age of 19 and teaching high school for one year in New Hampshire, Puffer returned to Smith as an instructor of mathematics, where she taught for the next three years while developing a keen interest in **psychology.** In 1895, Puffer traveled to Germany to study aesthetics under Hugo Münsterberg (1863–1916), then a professor of psychology at the University of Freiberg. On the strength of her research, she was awarded a fellowship for graduate study by the Association of Collegiate Alumnae. Enrolling in Radcliffe College in 1897 and working again under Münsterberg at Harvard University, she earned a certificate stating she had completed work equivalent to that of a doctoral candidate for the Harvard Ph.D. Because of the restrictions against granting the Harvard degree to women, however, Puffer was forced to make a special appeal to Radcliffe to grant her the doctoral degree. In 1902, she was one of the first four women to be offered the Radcliffe Ph.D.

Restricted from many research opportunities because of her gender, Puffer returned to teaching psychology at Radcliffe, Wellesley, and Simmons Colleges, and published a book, *The Psychology of Beauty,* in 1905, based on her research in aesthetics. In 1908, her marriage to Benjamin Howes further impacted her career due to cultural norms of the period which did not permit married women to work outside of the home. She continued to write scholarly articles through her forties while raising two children. Puffer's published reflections of the role of women and the conflict between marriage and career in the *Atlantic Monthly* in 1922 brought attention to one of the basic dilemmas confronting educated women of that time.

Further Reading

Scarborough, Elizabeth and Laurel Furumoto. *Untold Lives: The First Generation of American Women Psychologists.* New York: Columbia University Press, 1987, pp. 70-90.

Punishment

In learning theory, a stimulus that is likely to eliminate an unwanted behavior or reduce the frequency of that behavior.

Punishments can be applied in two different ways. A pleasant situation can be terminated or a negative situation can be created when an unwanted or undesirable behavior occurs. More specifically, if an animal or person does something inappropriate, the punisher can either apply something hurtful or take something that is pleasant away. In either case, the animal or person is less likely to repeat the behavior. Punishment is often confused with negative **reinforcement**, in part because of the word "negative." One way to distinguish between the terms is to remember that, by definition, punishment is designed to eliminate a behavior, whereas reinforcement is designed to make a behavior more likely to occur. **B. F. Skinner** suggested that punishment did not change behavior as effectively as reinforcement. Although punishment may reduce unwanted behavior, it can lead to unwanted consequences that are more negative than the original, undesired behavior. An individual can learn to avoid punishment without changing behavior, such as refraining from the behavior when the punisher is present, but engaging in the behavior when the punisher is absent. Further, the person being punished may learn that aggressive behavior is appropriate and may later mimic the punisher's actions. In addition, punishment may lead to physical or psychological harm. For instance, extreme physical punishment may cause bodily injury as well as creating **stress** and **anxiety,** or may lower an individual's self-esteem.

Although reinforcement is more effective in changing behavior, psychologists have identified ways to maximize the effectiveness of punishment in changing behavior. A critical element is to ensure that the person being punished knows not only what behavior is being punished, but is also given information about what alternate behaviors are appropriate. Further, positive reinforcement should be coupled with punishment when possible, and the punishment should involve the withholding of something positive rather than the application of physical or emotional **pain**. Any type of punishment should be as mild as possible while still being effective in stopping the unwanted behavior, as stronger punishment may be less effective than weaker punishment. The pun-

PUNISHMENT	
Positive punishment	**Negative punishment**
When the subject—a person or animal—engages in a behavior and something negative is applied as a result, the behavior is less likely to be repeated.	When the subject—a person or animal—engages in a behavior and something positive is taken away, that behavior is less likely to be repeated.

isher should also make certain that the punishment is swift and impossible to escape.

The relationship between punishment and its effects is complex. For example, research has revealed that when people who are depressed, they tend to overestimate the amount of punishment they encounter while simultaneously underestimating the amount of reinforcement. Thus, punishment may affect a depressed person differently than a person not suffering from **depression**. The effects of punishment include cognitive and emotional factors as well as the nature of the punishment itself.

Further Reading

Mackintosh, N. J. *Conditioning and Associative Learning.* New York: Oxford University Press, 1983.

Pyromania

An impulse to start fires.

Pyromania is a rare condition and little is known about its origins. Nearly all pyromaniacs are male, and the behavior often begins in childhood. An individual suffering from pyromania may set a fire in order to experience a particular tension and release that is often sexual in nature. Pyromaniacs are obsessed with fire and everything associated with it, such as firefighters, firefighting equipment, and scenes of fire disasters. They may set off false alarms just to be near fire engines and see firefighters at work. Some pyromaniacs may even become volunteer firefighters in order to carry out their obsession.

Not all arsonists are pyromaniacs. Fires are set for political or financial reasons, to cover up another crime, or to express **anger** or take revenge. **Hallucinations** or **delusions** may lead others to start a fire.

Further Reading

Morrison, James. *DSM-IV Made Easy: The Clinician's Guide to Diagnosis.* New York: The Guilford Press, 1995.

R

Racism

The belief that members of one (or more) races are inferior to members of other races.

Racism is most commonly used to describe the belief that members of one's own race are superior physically, mentally, culturally, and morally to members of other races. Racist beliefs provide the foundation for extending special rights, privileges, and opportunities to the race that is believed to be superior, and to withholding rights, privileges, and opportunities from the races believed to be inferior. No scientific evidence supports racist claims, although racism exists in all countries and cultures. The definition of racism has evolved to describe **prejudice** against a group of people based on the belief that human groups are unequal genetically, and that members of some racial groups are thus inferior. Sociologists distinguish between *individual racism,* a term describing **attitudes** and beliefs of individuals, and *institutional racism,* which denotes governmental and organizational policies that restrict minority groups or demean them by the application of **stereotypes**. While such policies are being corrected to eliminate institutional racism, individual racism nonetheless persists.

Scientists have acknowledged individual differences among ethnic and racial groups, citing the importance of **environment** in shaping performance and measurable **ability**. When test results appear to indicate differences in ability and performance that follow racial lines, the effect of environment must be considered in interpreting the results. In addition, tests and other instruments for evaluating ability may be biased to favor knowledge and experiences of one racial or ethnic group over others. Thus, test scores must be analyzed with great caution with regard to patterns of performance and their relationship to race.

By studying genetic patterns in humans, scientists have demonstrated that genetic differences between races are not very significant. As humans migrate from continent to continent and ethnic groups intermingle, racial categories will have less meaning, but prejudice is not likely to disappear.

See also Ethnocentrism; Eugenics.

Further Reading
Balibar, Etienne. "Racism and Anti-Racism." *UNESCO Courier* (March 1996): 14+.

Dawes, Kwame. "Clothed Against Naked Racism." *World Press Review* (April 1996): 32+.

Jacquard, Albert. "An Unscientific Notion." *UNESCO Courier* (March 1996): 22+.

Wieviorka, Michel. "The Seeds of Hate: Racism and Nationalism After World War II." *UNESCO Courier* (March 1996): 104+.

Rape

Sexual intercourse forced on a person without the person's consent.

Rape is essentially an act of **power** and dominance. Although an estimated 15 to 40 percent of American women are victims of rape or attempted rape, men are raped as well. Women are more likely to be raped by someone they know; between 50 and 70 percent of all rapes occur within the context of a romantic relationship, and more than half the time the assault takes place in the victim's home. Rape is one of the most underreported crimes in the United States, due to the victim's fear of embarrassment, humiliation, or retaliation by the rapist. Estimates of the percentage of rapes reported to authorities range from 10 to 50 percent. Because of the difficulty of obtaining a conviction, about two percent of all rapists are convicted, and most serve approximately half of their original sentence.

A survey conducted in 1987 found that 57 percent of women who have been raped develop **post-traumatic stress disorder.** These women may lose their appetite, become easily startled, and suffer from headaches, **sleep disorders,** or fatigue. Many women have difficulty

INSTITUTIONAL RACISM

Institutional racism is defined as governmental and organizational policies that restrict minority groups or demean them. An example from U.S. history is the internment of Japanese Americans from 1942–45. Following the Japanese attack on Pearl Harbor, the U.S. became involved in World War II, and the U.S. military ordered persons of Japanese descent—the majority of them U.S. citizens—to be forcibly removed from their homes and imprisoned in internment camps. Norman Y. Mineta, representative to the U.S. Congress from California, was among those interned. An excerpt from a speech given on February 15, 1992 on the 50th anniversary of this institutional act of racism, follows:

Fifty years ago...our life as a community was forever transformed by an attack not of our making. The Government of the United States—our government—decided that American of Japanese ancestry were a categorical threat to the United States. No matter that these threats were unproven, or that we were American citizens or permanent resident aliens. All were tarred with the same indiscriminate brush of racial hatred and fear. One by one, Japanese American communities along the West Coast disappeared: removed into stark, barren camps scattered throughout some of the most inhospitable regions of the United States. . . . None of us can predict who might next fall target to hysteria, racism, and weak political leadership. But I do believe that we can ensure that such a tragedy as our internment never befalls anyone every again here in the United States.

Congressman Norman Y. Mineta

maintaining a **normal** life following a rape, and may repress the experience for an extended period before they are able to talk about it. Over the past 20 years feminist organizations have fought successfully to change public attitudes toward rape as well as treatment of rape victims. Efforts have been made to increase the sensitivity of police and hospital personnel to rape victims through special training programs. Today, women police officers routinely investigate rape cases. Rape crisis centers in local communities throughout the nation counsel rape victims and perform other services, such as instruction on rape prevention, providing hotline services and legal advice, and supplying hospital emergency room advocates to offer emotional support to victims and assure that they are treated fairly by physicians and the police.

Despite these and other advances in combating rape, it remains a difficult crime to prosecute. Traditionally, rape victims have been questioned about their sexual histories, although most states now place restrictions on the admissibility and usage of such information at trial. In some states, evidence by witnesses or proof of bodily injury to the victim are still required; in other states, a struggle between the woman and her attacker must be proven. Most states require physical evidence of recent sexual intercourse in which the victim most undergo a medical examination within 24 hours of the assault.

In recent years, increased attention has been focused on "date" or "acquaintance" rape, a widespread phenomena that is particularly insidious because women who are victimized in this way are more likely to blame themselves and are less likely to seek help or prosecute their attackers. A 1987 study of acquaintance rape at 32 college campuses sponsored by *Ms.* magazine found that one in four women surveyed were victims of rape or at-

RAPE: DOES THE VICTIM KNOW THE OFFENDER?	
Offender was a stranger	68,140
Rate per 1,000 persons for cases involveing strangers	0.3
Offender was a nonstranger*	72,790
Rate per 1,000 persons for cases involveing nonstrangers	0.4

*A "nonstranger" offender is someone who is either related to, well-known to, or casually acquainted with the victim.
Source: *Statistics on Crime & Punishment,* p. 32.

tempted rape, that most rape victims knew their attackers, and over half the assaults were date rapes. Only 27 percent of the women identified themselves as rape victims, and five percent reported the rapes to police. Of the acquaintance rape victims in the *Ms.* magazine survey, 38 percent were between 14 and 17 years old. Rape can be particularly devastating for adolescents; the damage it inflicts on the victim's sense of personal integrity interferes with the fragile personal **identity** and sense of self-esteem that are being forged during this period. It also upsets the adolescent's need to assert some control over her **environment**. Young rape victims, who are often sexually inactive at the time of the attack, may have their ideas and feelings about sex distorted by the experience. Often, they have daily encounters with their attacker or his friends at school or social events, adding to their sense of shame and humiliation. Most are unlikely to report the rape to parents or other adults, fearing they will be blamed or that their parents may press charges against their own wishes.

Further Reading
Brownmiller, Susan. *Against Our Will: Men, Women, and Rape.* Bantam, 1986.
Guernsey, JoAnn B. *The Facts about Rape.* Crestwood, 1990.
Parrot, Andrea. *Coping with Date Rape and Acquaintance Rape.* Rosen Publishers, 1988.

Rapid Eye Movement (REM)

The stage of sleep most closely associated with dreaming.

First described in 1953 by Nathaniel Kleitman and Eugene Aserinsky, rapid eye movement (REM) **sleep** is also called active sleep because the EEG (**electroencephalogram**) patterns in this stage are similar to the patterns during the awake stage. The four stages of slow-wave, or non-REM, sleep are accompanied by deep breathing, a relatively slow heartbeat, and lowered blood pressure. In contrast, levels of physiological **arousal** during REM sleep resemble those of the waking state. In some ways, however, people are more deeply asleep dur-

ing the REM stage than at other times: the major muscle groups go limp in a sort of paralysis, and people are hardest to waken during REM sleep. The contradictions between the active, "awake" features of REM sleep and its soundness have caused some people to refer to REM sleep as "paradoxical sleep." At **birth** about 50 percent of all sleep is REM sleep, but by the age of 10 this figure drops to 25 percent.

In the course of a night, periods of REM sleep occur every 90 to 100 minutes, becoming longer as the night progresses, in contrast to the deeper stage four sleep, most of which occurs early in the night. About 80 percent of the time, people awakened from REM sleep will say they have been dreaming, while those awakened during other sleep stages rarely report **dreams**. Experiments have shown that people repeatedly awakened during the REM stage for several nights will compensate by spending twice as much time in REM sleep the first night they are left alone, an observation that has led to much speculation about the role of this type of sleep.

Some researchers have hypothesized that REM sleep strengthens neural connections in the **brain**, a theory supported by the fact that infants and children, whose brains are still developing, require larger amounts of REM sleep than adults. It has also been suggested that REM sleep may be linked to a specific **neurotransmitter,** norepinephrine, which helps maintain alertness when people are awake. In addition, REM sleep has been investigated in connection with learning and **memory** in studies that showed decreased retention of learned skills in persons who were deprived of REM sleep. However, a contrasting (and controversial) theory maintains that the REM stage is a way for the body to "empty" the brain so that its neural networks do not become overloaded.

Further Reading
Hartmann, Ernest. *The Functions of Sleep.* New Haven, CT: Yale University Press, 1973.
Hobson, J. Allan. *Sleep.* New York: Scientific American Library, 1989.
———. *The Dreaming Brain.* New York: Basic Books, 1988.

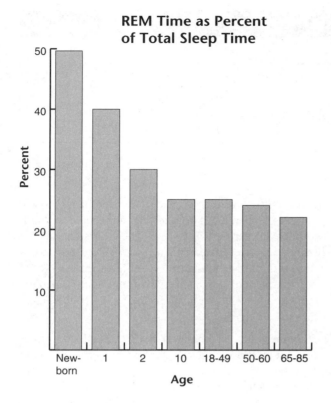

REM Time as Percent of Total Sleep Time

REM sleep decreases from about 50 percent of a newborn baby's sleep to about 25 percent by age 10.

Rating Scale

Any instrument designed to assist in the measurement of subjective evaluations of, or reactions to, a person, object, event, statement, or other item of interest.

Several varieties of rating scales have been developed. One common form of rating scale presents the rater with a spectrum of potential responses that includes antithetical elements at each end of a range of intermediate possibilities, on which the rater is expected to indicate the position that most accurately represents the rater's response to the subject in question. Another form of rating scale presents the rater with a list of characteristics or attributes from which the rater is expected to select those which the rater believes apply to the subject in question. Rating scale instruments are used in psychological research primarily to assess qualities for which no objective measurement techniques have been developed.

Further Reading

Bech, Per. *Rating Scales for Psychopathology, Health Status, and Quality of Life.* New York: Springer-Verlag, 1993.

Reaction Formation

A term coined by Sigmund Freud to describe behavior that masks the individual's true, but possibly unacknowledged, feelings.

When a person possesses a **character** trait, **attitude**, or **emotion** that he does not like, he may conceal it with behavior that outwardly expresses the opposite of his true feelings. For example, a worker with an unreasonable boss may always act pleasant and eager to please, even in situations when **anger** would be appropriate and justified. A new mother, resentful of the constraints her baby places on her mobility, may react by becoming overly protective of the child. It is difficult to confirm the presence of the underlying motive, especially when the individual's true feelings are unacknowledged.

See also Denial.

Reaction Time

Generally, in psychological measurement, the interval of time between the presentation of a stimulus to a subject and the beginning of the subject's response to that stimulus.

Several categories of reaction time, such as simple reaction time, have been established and studied in **experimental psychology.** In a simple reaction time experiment, the subject is presented with one simple stimulus, such as a light, and instructed to perform one simple response, such as pressing a button. In a discrimination reaction time experiment, the subject is presented with one of two or more different stimuli, such as a red light and a green light, and instructed to perform a response to only one of the stimuli, such as pressing a button when the red light is presented but not when the green light is presented. In a choice reaction time experiment, the subject is presented with one of two or more different stimuli, such as a red light and a green light, and instructed to perform different responses depending upon which stimulus is presented, such as pressing a red button when the red light is presented and pressing a green button when the green light is presented. There are other types, and many variations of reaction time experiments.

Readiness Test

A test designed to assess the developmental condition of an individual to determine whether or not, or to what extent, the individual could gain from some particular experience.

Readiness tests are commonly used in educational situations, and often include the **measurement** of cognitive, perceptual, emotional, motivational, and other factors involved in the learning process, in an attempt to determine if a student is in a position to benefit from a particular course of instruction. Readiness tests are based on the view, shared by almost all psychologists, that an individual reaches maturity in various areas only by passing through corresponding series of consecutive developmental levels, and that these series of levels are essentially similar in all normal individuals.

Reflexes

Movements or involuntary reponses initiated by an external stimulus which do not require input from the brain.

In a simple reflex, a sensory receptor initiates a **nerve** impulse in an afferent sensory nerve fiber which conducts it to the spinal cord. In the gray matter of the spinal cord, the afferent nerve impulse is fired over the synaptic gap to an efferent motor fiber which passes along the impulse to the appropriate muscle, producing the reflex.

There are other reflexes which involve neural pathways connected to the **brain.** When an ice cube is touched, cold receptors in the skin are stimulated and that afferent information is transmitted to the gray matter of the spinal cord, where it then travels via axons in the white matter to the brain. There, the sensory information is analyzed and movement such as dropping the ice cube (or keeping hold of it) may be initiated. This message is sent down the axons of the white matter to the appropriate motor nerves in the gray matter. This efferent motor information travels to the muscles which initiate the reflex.

Regression

In Freudian psychology, a defense mechanism that involves reverting to behavior characteristic of a previous stage of life.

Regression is a **defense mechanism** that was described by **Sigmund Freud.** People regress—revert to behavior characteristic of a previous stage of life—in order to gain access to the sources of gratification experienced during the earlier period. Like other defense mechanisms (such as **denial**, **repression**, or sublimation), regression is a way of coping with **anxiety** and other unpleasant feelings, such as conflict, **fear,** or frustration.

Regression may be divided into two types. In object regression, people frustrated by their current circumstances turn for comfort to a former source of gratifica-

tion (such as one's mother or a former lover); in drive regression, they turn to a drive whose satisfaction had previously been a source of pleasure (such as eating). Regression ranges from the occasional childlike overindulgence when one is upset to a full-scale return to infantile behavior by adults with severe mental disturbances. Children often regress when a younger sibling is born in an attempt to regain the gratification and security of being the favored child. They may revert to crawling or sucking their thumbs; children who are toilet trained may lose their bowel and bladder control.

Regression may be temporarily induced through **hypnosis** in order to reveal repressed traumatic experiences that are causing emotional disturbances. Persons who regress to their childhoods through hypnosis talk, act, and think very much as they did when they were children. Their handwriting even reverts to its childhood characteristics.

Further Reading
Freud, Sigmund. *New Introductory Lectures on Psychoanalysis.* New York: W. W. Norton, 1933.
Hall, Calvin S. *A Primer of Freudian Psychology.* New York: Harper and Row, 1982.
Jenson, Jean C. *Reclaiming Your Life: A Step-by-step Guide to Using Regression Therapy to Overcome the Effects of Childhood Abuse.* New York: Dutton, 1995.

Rehabilitation

A process geared toward helping persons suffering from an injury, disease, or other debilitating condition to reach their highest possible level of self-sufficiency.

Rehabilitation begins once a debilitating condition has been evaluated and treatment is either in progress or completed. Impairments are evaluated for their effects on the individual's psychological, social, and vocational functioning. Depending on the type of **disability** involved, "self-sufficiency" may mean a full-time job, employment in a sheltered workshop, or simply an independent living situation. Rehabilitation involves a combination of medicine, therapy, education, or vocational training. There are special centers for various mental and physical problems that require rehabilitation, including psychiatric disorders, **mental retardation, alcohol dependence, brain** and spinal cord injuries, stroke, burns, and other physically disabling conditions.

The goal of medical rehabilitation is the restoration of normal functioning to the greatest degree possible. Specialities involved include physical, occupational, and speech therapy, recreation, psychology, and social work. Medical rehabilitation facilities often include an "activities of daily living" (ADL) department, which offers ac-

This young athlete's rehabilitation program began after his spinal cord was injured in an automobile accident, leaving him paralyzed from the waist down.

tivities in a simulated apartment setting where patients may learn and practice tasks they will need in everyday living. Also included in the field of medical rehabilitation is a special area called rehabilitation technology (formerly rehabilitation engineering), developed during the 1970s and 1980s, that deals with prosthetics (devices attached to the body) and orthotics (equipment used by disabled people). In addition to the actual engineers who design these products, rehabilitation technology also includes professionals who serve as consultants to manufacturers on the design, production, and marketing of medical devices.

Vocational rehabilitation helps the client achieve a specific goal, which can be either a type of employment (competitive, sheltered, volunteer) or a living situation. Services include prevocational evaluation, work evaluation, work adjustment, job placement, and on-the-job training. Facilities offering vocational rehabilitation include state-supported local units in hospitals, the Veterans Administration, sheltered workshops, insurance companies, and speech and hearing clinics. Rehabilitation counseling is a relatively new field whose support personnel offer a variety of services to the disabled, par-

ticularly that of coordinating and intergrating the various types of assistance available to a particular client. The rehabilitation counselor also assists in locating job opportunities, interpreting test results, and assisting with personal problems.

Since the 1980s, supported employment (employment of the disabled through programs that provide them with ongoing support services) has become increasingly popular as a means of vocational rehabilitation. Traditionally, the most common form of supported employment has been the sheltered workshop, a nonprofit organization—often receiving government funds—that provides both services and employment to the disabled. Today, sheltered industrial employment mainstreams disabled workers into the regular workplace with jobs modified to meet their needs, especially those of the severely disabled. However, both cutbacks in funding for government support services and affirmative action provisions of the 1973 Rehabilitation Act pertaining to federal contractors led to increasing private sector participation efforts in the 1980s. Some firms became involved in career education, offering internships to disabled students, which sometimes led to permanent employment. Other recent trends include rehabilitation of persons with traumatic brain injuries and severe learning disabilities, and rehabilitation of the homebound and the elderly.

The U. S. Department of Education administers most federal programs for rehabilitation of the disabled, often through its Office of Special Education and Rehabilitative Services (OSERS). Within OSERS, the Rehabilitation Services Administration (RSA) supervises the state offices of vocational rehabilitation. Organizations involved in rehabilitation efforts include the National Rehabilitation Association, the National Association of Rehabilitation Facilities, and the President's Committee on Employment of People with Disabilities.

Further Information

American Paralysis Association
    24-hour tool-free information and referral hotline
    Telephone: 800-526-3256
National Association of Rehabilitation Facilities
    Address: P.O. Box 17675
    Washington, D.C. 20041
    Telephone: 703-648-9300
National Rehabilitation Association
    Address: 633 S. Washington St.
    Alexandria, Virginia 22314
    Telephone: 703-836-0850
National Spinal Cord Injury Association
    Telephone: 800-962-9629

Reinforcement

In either classical or operant conditioning, a stimulus that increases the probability that a particular behavior will occur.

In classical (Pavlovian) **conditioning**, where the response has no effect on whether the stimulus will occur, reinforcement produces an immediate response without any training or conditioning. When meat is offered to a hungry dog, it does not learn to salivate, the behavior occurs spontaneously. Similarly, a negative reinforcer, such as an electric shock, produces an immediate, unconditioned escape response. To produce a classically-conditioned response, the positive or negative reinforcer is paired with a neutral stimulus until the two become associated with each other. Thus, if the sound of a bell accompanies a negative stimulus such as an electric shock, the experimental subject will eventually be conditioned to produce an escape or avoidance response to the sound of the bell alone. Once conditioning has created an association between a certain behavior and a neutral stimulus, such as the bell, this stimulus itself may serve as a reinforcer to condition future behavior. When this happens, the formerly neutral stimulus is called a conditioned reinforcer, as opposed to a naturally positive or negative reinforcer, such as food or an electric shock.

In **operant conditioning** (as developed by **B. F. Skinner**), positive reinforcers are rewards that strengthen a conditioned response after it has occurred, such as feeding a hungry pigeon after it has pecked a key. Negative reinforcers are unpleasant stimuli that are removed when the desired response has been obtained. The application of negative reinforcement may be divided into two types: escape and avoidance conditioning. In escape conditioning, the subject learns to escape an unpleasant or aversive stimulus (a dog jumps over a barrier to escape electric shock). In avoidance conditioning, the subject is presented with a warning stimulus, such as a buzzer, just before the aversive stimulus occurs and learns to act on it in order to avoid the unpleasant stimulus altogether.

Reinforcement may be administered according to various schedules. A particular behavior may be reinforced every time it occurs, which is referred to as continuous reinforcement. In many cases, however, behaviors are reinforced only some of the time, which is termed partial or intermittent reinforcement. Reinforcement may also be based on the number of responses or scheduled at particular time intervals. In addition, it may be delivered in regularly or irregularly. These variables combine to produce four basic types of partial reinforcement. In fixed-ratio (FR) schedules, reinforcement is provided following a set number of responses (a factory worker is paid for every garment he assembles). With variable-ratio (VR) schedules, reinforcement is provided after a variable number of responses (a slot machine pays off after varying numbers of attempts). Fixed-interval (FI) schedules provide for reinforcement of the first response made within a given interval since the previous one (contest entrants are not eligible for a prize if they have won one within the past 30 days). Finally, with variable-interval (VI) schedules, first responses are rewarded at varying intervals from the previous one.

See also Avoidance Learning; Behavior Modification; Classical/Respondent Conditioning; Ivan Pavlov.

Further Reading

Craighead, W. Edward. *Behavior Modification: Principles, Issues, and Applications.* Boston: Houghton Mifflin, 1976.

Skinner, B.F. *About Behaviorism.* New York: Knopf, 1974.

Repression

A defense mechanism that involves forgetting uncomfortable or painful experiences.

Repression is the most basic **defense mechanism**, the selective forgetting of things associated with conflict and **stress**. Threatening events, information, or feelings are buried in the unconscious to protect the person from the **pain** they create. Repression is different from **denial** in that the material is completely unavailable to the conscious mind, whereas in denial the material is only partly buried and/or simply reinterpreted, but is still consciously available. Repression is also different from **amnesia** or from the loss of **memory** due to the normal process of forgetting, in that the mind selects information to bury.

Repressed memories can return to **consciousness** in a process called the return of the repressed. This may occur at any time given the right conditions, even years after the material was originally repressed. This theory of repressed memories and their later return has been the source of a recent phenomenon known as "the abuse excuse," in which a person has claimed repressed memories of abuse, usually of a sexual nature. Given the seriousness of the accusations and their effects on the individuals involved, debate rages over how memory, repression, and the conscious and **unconscious** mind works.

Further Reading

Firestone, Robert. *Psychological Defenses in Everyday Life.* New York: Human Sciences Press, 1989.

Goleman, Daniel. *Vital Lies, Simple Truths: The Psychology of Self-Deception.* New York : Simon and Schuster, 1985.

Miller, Alice. *Breaking Down the Wall of Silence: The Liberating Experience of Facing Painful Truths.* New York: Meridian, 1993.

Research Methods

The wide variety of strategies employed by psychologists to answer research questions.

Psychologists use a wide variety of techniques to answer research questions. The most commonly used techniques include experiments, correlational studies, observational studies, case studies, and archival research. Each approach has its own strengths and weaknesses. Psychologists have developed a diversity of research strategies because a single approach cannot answer all types of questions that psychologists ask.

Psychologists prefer to use experiments whenever possible because this approach allows them to determine whether a stimulus or an event actually causes something to happen. In an experimental approach, researchers randomly assign participants to different conditions. These conditions should be identical except for one variable that the researcher is interested in. For example, psychologists have asked whether people learn more if they study for one long period or several short periods. To study this experimentally, the psychologist would assign people into one of two groups—one group that studies for an extended period of time or to another group that studies for the same total amount of time, but in short segments.

The researcher would make sure that all the participants studied the same material, for the same total time, and were in the same study **environment**; the only thing that would differentiate the two groups is whether the learners studied for short or long segments. Thus, any difference in the amount of learning should be due only to the length of the study periods. (This kind of research has revealed that people learn better with several shorter study periods.) The experimental approach is useful when the research can establish control over the environment; this work is often done in a simple laboratory setting.

A second approach involves the correlational technique. This approach does not include control of the environment by the researcher. Instead, measurements are made as they naturally occur. For example, a group of high school students took two tests that required them to solve analogies and to recognize antonyms. The researchers discovered a correlation between students' abilities to complete analogies correctly and to identify antonyms. In general, students who were good at one task were also good at the other; students weak in one task were weak in the other. In correlational research, no attempt is made to state that one thing causes another, only that one thing is predictable from the other.

Correlational approaches are most useful when the researchers cannot control the environment or when the phenomena they want to study are complex. Instead of trying to simplify the situation, the researchers observe the complex behaviors as they naturally occur. A third approach is called naturalistic observation. This kind of research often is not highly quantitative; that is, observations are likely to be descriptive. The researcher decides on some class of behavior to observe and records the situations in which that behavior occurs and how it develops. A classic example of observational research was done by Jane Goodall in her work with chimpanzees in the wild. She spent years observing their social interactions and how the chimp "society" changed over time.

The previous techniques all involve observing a group of individuals. Sometimes, psychologists are interested in studying a single person in depth. This is called a case study. This approach is common when clinical psychologists work with a person over a long period of time. The final product in a case study is an in-depth description of a great number of different aspects of the individual's life and development. The strength of this approach is that detail is abundant; the weakness is that the psychologist cannot generalize to other people from the single individual being analyzed because that person may differ in important ways from the average person.

Finally, psychologists can use archival information to answer questions. Archival research differs considerably from the other approaches because it does not rely on direct observation or interaction with the people being studied. Rather, psychologists use records or other already existing information. For example, some psychologists were interested in whether the percentage of left-handed people in the population has remained constant throughout history. They obviously could not observe people who have died, so they decided to use existing information about the past. They recorded the percentage of left-handed people in paintings and other such renderings. After poring over paintings, they concluded that the percentage of left-handed people has not changed over the last few centuries. More commonly, archival information comes from birth and death records and other official statistics.

See also Correlation Method; Scientific Method.

Further Reading

Cozby, Paul C. *Methods in Behavioral Science.* Mountain View, CA: Mayfield Publishing Company, 1993.

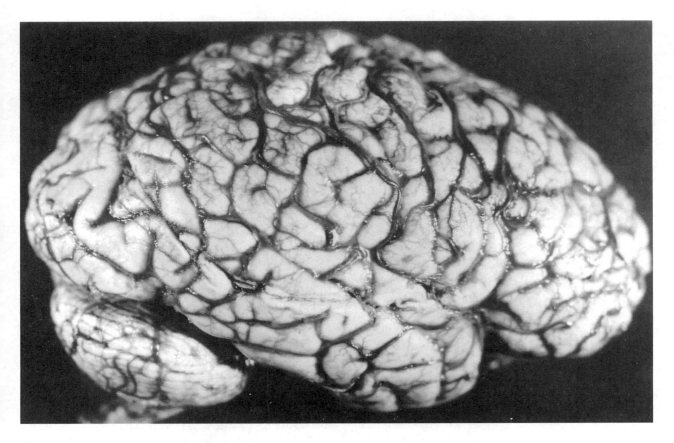

Photograph of the right hemisphere of a human brain.

Ribonucleic Acid (RNA)

A complex organic substance involved in protein synthesis in cells.

RNA consists of a five-carbon sugar (ribose), phosphate, and four nitrogenous bases (adenine, guanine, cytosine, and uracil). In an RNA molecule, the sugar and phosphate combine to form a structure to which the nitrogenous bases are attached. These molecules range in composition from fewer than 100 to several thousand nitrogenous bases, and vary in shape from helical to uncoiled. RNA is the primary agent of protein formation, and processes genetic information from **deoxyribonucleic acid (DNA)** molecules into enzymes necessary for life.

Right-Brain Hemisphere

The hemisphere of the brain that neurologically controls the left side of the body and is thought to control spatial tasks, musical and artistic endeavors, body control and awareness, and creativity and imagination.

In normal human adults, each hemisphere of the **brain**, working in concert with the other, performs cer-

tain types of functions more efficiently than the other. While the **left-brain hemisphere** is dominant in the areas of language and logic, the right-brain hemisphere is the center of nonverbal, intuitive, holistic modes of thinking. Each hemisphere mostly receives **perception**s from and controls the activities of the opposite side of the body. Scientists have been aware of the specialized functioning of the hemispheres—also known as lateralization—for over one hundred years, having discovered that language skills are controlled by the left side of the brain in approximately 95 percent of right-handed people and about two thirds of left-handed individuals. In the nineteenth century, however, this discovery led to the assumption that all higher reasoning **ability** resided in the left-brain hemisphere, which was thus regarded as dominant overall. The right brain hemisphere was thought to possess only lower-level capabilities and was considered subordinate to the left.

Research conducted in the 1950s and 1960s established that the two hemispheres of a normally functioning brain—connected by the corpus callosum, a thick cable of **nerves**—operate in a complementary fashion with both hemispheres involved in higher cognitive functioning. The primary difference between them was found to involve the *mode* rather than the level of thinking. A research group under the direction of Roger Sperry at the California Institute of Technology observed and tested patients who had undergone a surgical procedure in which the corpus callosum was severed to control epileptic seizures. In this procedure, the two hemispheres of the brain, which normally have a strong tendency to work together, were uncoupled, and each side of the brain remained ignorant of information received by the other. Thus, right-handed people had no trouble writing, which is usually governed by the left-brain hemisphere in right-handers, but were unable to draw, as the left brain was cut off from the spatial capacity of the right. When a special apparatus was used to present the image of a spoon only to a split-brain patient's left hemisphere, the subject could name it readily, but when the same image was presented to the right-brain hemisphere, the subject could not, although they were still aware of what it was.

Research on both split-brain and normal subjects since the 1960s has confirmed that both hemispheres of the brain use high-level cognitive modes. That of the left brain is verbal and analytic, while right brain thought processes are rapid, complex, whole-pattern, spatial, and specialized for visual imagery and musical ability. The right temporal lobe, in particular, governs visual and auditory imagery. People in whom this area is damaged have difficulty recognizing familiar melodies, faces, and pictures, and learning to identify new ones. The right brain hemisphere also appears to have special links to **emotion**. Right-brain damage interferes with both the ability to produce and interpret expressions of emotion. Damage to the front part of the right-brain hemisphere renders people unable to act on or express strong emotions. If the damage is further back in the brain, the person can express emotion but not recognize it in other people or in pictures.

Other general characteristics of right-brain thought processes include the tendency to synthesize rather than analyze, and to relate to things in a concrete rather than a symbolic fashion. Where left-brain thinking tends to represent wholes by abstraction (using one piece of information to represent something larger), the right brain is more likely to interpret data through analogies—seeing relationships between wholes. Right-brain functioning is nontemporal, nonrational, holistic, and intuitive, relying on leaps of insight, hunches, or visual images. Discoveries about the right- and left-brain hemispheres have led some researchers and educators to advocate educational reforms that would allow right-brain modes of thought a greater place in the current educational system, which reflects society's overall tendency to reward the verbal, analytical left-brain skills. As split-brain researcher Roger Sperry notes, our educational system "tends to neglect the nonverbal form of intellect. What it comes down to is that modern society discriminates against the right hemi-

sphere." The artistic, creative right brain is relegated to the "minor" subjects of art and music, but the main programs of study do not, as a rule, focus on developing the right-brain skills of imagination, creativity, or visualization.

See also Cerebellum; Cerebral Cortex; Handedness; Split-Brain Technique.

Right-Handedness

The tendency to use the right hand more frequently than the left for writing, manual skills, and other activities.

The dominance of the right hand is controlled by the left hemisphere of the **brain**. It is estimated that 90 percent of the world's population is right-handed. Hand preference also involves **vision** and **speech**. Approximately 95 percent of right-handed people have their speech centers in the **left-brain hemisphere.**

Some anthropologists have claimed that our primate ancestors were left-handed and that an evolutionary change to right-handedness occurred with the emergence of tools. The developmental psychologist **Arnold Gesell** noticed signs of handedness emerging in infants as early as four weeks of age, when right-handers adopt a "fencing" posture with the right hand and arm extended. By the age of one year, right-handers will perform many actions with the right hand, while the left is used for a holding grip.

See also Handedness; Left-handedness.

Rogers, Carl (1902–1987)

American psychologist who developed a nondirective, patient-centered method of psychotherapy known as humanistic psychology.

Carl Rogers was born in Oak Park, Illinois. Raised in a fundamentalist Christian home, Rogers attended the University of Wisconsin and studied for the ministry at Union Theological Seminary before deciding to pursue a doctorate in education and **clinical psychology** at Columbia University. Between 1928 and 1939, Rogers worked as a counselor at the Society for the Prevention of Cruelty to Children in Rochester. In 1940, he was appointed to the faculty of Ohio State University. By this time, he had worked out much of his new client-centered system of therapy, which was set forth in his second book, *Counseling and Psychotherapy*, published in 1942.

Rogers believed that the mental condition of virtually all patients, whom he referred to as clients, can be improved, given an appropriate psychotherapeutic environment. Central to this environment is a close personal relationship between client and therapist. Rogers's use of the term "client" rather than "patient" expresses his rejection of the traditionally authoritarian relationship between therapist and client, and his view of them as equals. The client determines the general direction of therapy, while the therapist seeks to increase the client's insightful self-understanding through informal clarifying questions. A hallmark of Rogers's method is the therapist echoing or reflecting the client's remarks, which is supposed to convey a sense of respect as well as a belief in the patient's ability to deal with his or her problems. The concept of an alliance between client and therapist has affinities with the methods of **Carl Jung.** Otto Rank (1884–1939) was also an early influence on the development of Rogers's system.

Rogerian therapy is a natural consequence of its creator's belief that a fundamental element of human nature is the drive to fully actualize one's positive potential, a concept based on an essentially positive view of humanity that contrasts with the psychoanalytic view of human beings as driven by antisocial impulses that are suppressed with difficulty and often at great cost. In Rogers's view, the primary task of therapy is to remove the client's obstacles to self-actualization. A further contrast to **psychoanalysis** lies in the fact that Rogerian therapy emphasizes the current **emotions** and **attitudes** of the client rather than early childhood experiences.

After leaving Ohio State in 1945, Rogers served on the faculties of the University of Chicago and the University of Wisconsin. Between 1956 and 1947, he served as president of the **American Psychological Association.** As Rogers gained increasing acclaim, the popularity of his method grew rapidly. Rogerian therapy was widely practiced in the 1950s and 1960s, when its tenets of anti-authoritarianism and permissiveness gave it a wide appeal to many. Rogers published *Client-Centered Therapy: Its Current Practice, Implications, and Theory* in 1951 and produced numerous of papers in the decade that followed. In 1956, the American Psychological Association awarded him its Distinguished Scientific Contribution Award. In the 1960s, Rogers was attracted to the **human potential movement** that had begun in California, and he adopted some of its principles, including its emphasis on frank and open expression of feelings and its use of **group therapy.** In 1964, he and his wife moved to La Jolla, California, where he continued to write and lecture, and served as a resident fellow at the Western Behavioral Science Institute. *On Becoming a Person*, published in 1961, became his most widely read book. In the last ten years of his life, Rogers became deeply interested in educational reform. Borrowing a central principle from his therapeutic method, he came to believe that

teachers (like therapists) should serve as facilitators rather than judges or mere conveyors of facts.

Roger's other books include *Psychotherapy and Personality Change* (1954), *Freedom to Learn: A View of What Education Might Become* (1969), *Carl Rogers on Encounter Groups* (1970), *Carl Rogers on Personal Power* (1977), and *A Way of Being* (1980).

See also Client-Centered Therapy.

Further Reading
Thorne, Brian. *Carl Rogers.* London: Sage Publications, 1992.

Role Playing/Psychodrama

A group therapy approach in which clients act out their problems to gain new insights and achieve emotional catharsis.

Role playing was developed by Jacob Moreno, a Viennese psychologist who contended that people could gain more from acting out their problems than from talking about them. This method requires a protagonist (the client whose problems are being acted out); auxiliary egos (group members who assume the roles of other people in the protagonist's life); an audience (other group members who observe and react to the drama); and a director (the therapist). The protagonist selects an event from his or her life and provides the information necessary for it to be reenacted. Although every detail of the event cannot be reproduced, the reenactment can be effective if it captures the essence of the original experience. The group members who serve as auxiliary egos impersonate significant people from the protagonist's past or present, following the protagonist's instructions as closely as possible. Techniques used in the reenactment may include role reversal, doubling, mirror technique, future projection, and dream work.

The therapist, acting as facilitator and director, assists the protagonist in orchestrating the scene, offers emotional support, enlists the audience's response, and helps the protagonist gain new insights from the experience. Immediately preceding the reenactment is a warm-up period designed to prepare all the participants for the experience by motivating them and establishing a safe and trusting atmosphere. After the reenactment, members of the audience discuss their reactions to the reenactment, including ways that it touched on their own experiences. Encouragement and support is offered to the protagonist, as well as suggestions for responding to the problems dealt within the reenactment.

Role playing is sometimes employed in a combination of techniques in other types of therapy, such as Gestalt therapy. The client may role play with the therapist

The Rorschach test, a frequently used personality test, uses ink-blots similar to this one.

in an individual treatment session or with group members in **group therapy**.

Rorschach Technique

A projective personality assessment based on the subject's reactions to a series of ten inkblot pictures.

The Rorschach test is named for Swiss psychiatrist Hermann Rorschach (1884–1922), who developed it in the 1920s. Like other **projective techniques**, it is based on the principle that subjects viewing neutral, ambiguous stimuli will project their own personalities onto them, thereby revealing a variety of **unconscious** conflicts and **motivations**. Rorschach, whose primary interest was in Jungian analysis, began experimenting with inkblots as early as 1911 as a means of determining introversion and extroversion. The Rorschach technique is administered using 10 cards, each containing a complicated inkblot pattern, five in color and five in black and white. Subjects look at the cards one at a time and describe what each inkblot resembles. After the subject has viewed all 10 cards, the examiner usually goes back over the responses for additional information. The subject may be asked to clarify some responses or to describe which features of each inkblot prompted the responses.

Test scores are based on several factors. One is location, or what part of the blot a person focuses on: the whole blot (W), sections of it (D), or only specific details (Dd). Another is whether the response is based on factors such as form, color, movement, or shading (referred to as determinants). For example, people who tend to see movement in Rorschach blots are thought to be intellectual and introspective; those who see mostly stationary objects or patterns are described as practical and action-oriented. Finally, content refers to which objects, persons, or situations the person sees in the blot (categories include humans, animals, clothing, and nature). Most examiners also assess responses based on the frequency of certain responses as given by previous test takers. Many psychologists interpret the test freely according to their subjective impressions, including their impression of the subject's demeanor while taking the test (cooperative, anxious, defensive, and so forth). Such interpretations, especially when combined with clinical observation and knowledge of a client's personal history, can help a therapist arrive at a fuller, more in-depth understanding of the client's **personality**.

While the Rorschach technique is still widely used, its popularity has decreased somewhat in recent decades. Unlike objective personality inventories, which can be administered to a group, the Rorschach test must be given individually. A skilled examiner is required, and the test can take several hours to complete and interpret. Like other projective tests, it has been criticized for lack of validity and reliability. Interpretation of responses is highly dependent on an examiner's individual judgment: two different testers may interpret the same responses quite differently. In addition, treatment procedures at mental health facilities often require more specific, objective types of personality description than those provided by the Rorschach technique.

In response to complaints about validity, a number of different scoring methods have been devised which aim at providing greater objectivity by clearly specifying certain personality variables and relating them to clinical diagnoses. The Exner Comprehensive Rorschach System, released in 1987, is a computer-based scoring system that provides score summaries and lists likely personality and adjustment descriptions for each test taker. The Holtzman Inkblot Test uses 45 inkblots and allows for only one response per card.

Further Reading

Aronow, Edward. *The Rorschach Technique: Perceptual Basics, Content Interpretation, and Applications.* Needham Heights, MA: Allyn and Bacon, 1994.

Lerner, Paul M. *Psychoanalytic Theory and the Rorschach.* Hillsdale, NJ: Analytic Press, 1991.

Rosenzweig Picture Frustration Study

A projective test administered to assess personality characteristics, in which the subject is shown scenes depicting moderately frustrating situations and asked what the frustrated person depicted would probably do, or how the subject would react in such situations.

The Rosenzweig Picture Frustration test consists of 24 cartoon pictures, each portraying two persons in a frustrating situation. Each picture contains two "speech balloons," a filled one for the "frustrator" or antagonist, and a blank one for the frustrated person, or protagonist. The subject is asked to fill in the blank balloon with his or her response to the situation, and the responses are scored in relation to a number of psychological **defense mechanism**s. For example, responses are scored as to whether, and to what degree, they indicate that the subject exhibits **aggression** toward the source of the frustration, assumes blame or guilt as the cause of the frustration, or justifies, minimizes, or denies the frustration. The score is based on a total of nine factors, derived from combinations of three types of aggression (obstacle-dominance, **ego**-defense, and **need**-persistence) and three directions of aggression (extraggression, imaggression, and intraggression). However, testers often analyze the subject's responses more informally and intuitively.

Originally developed for adults by Saul Rosenzweig, the test is now available in versions for children and adolescents. The empirical validity of the Rosenzweig Picture Frustration Study and other projective techniques is disputed by some authorities.

Further Reading

Rosenzweig, Saul. *The Rosenzweig Picture Frustration (P-F) Study*. St. Louis: Rana House, 1978.

Rush, Benjamin (1746–1813)

American physician, teacher, and statesman known as the "father of American psychiatry" for his work with the mentally ill.

Benjamin Rush was born near Philadelphia. He attended the College of New Jersey (the future Princeton University), intending to enter the ministry. Finally deciding in favor of medicine, Rush began his medical studies in Philadelphia, serving a six-year apprenticeship to a local physician. He then enrolled in the University of Edinburgh, Scotland, where many American physicians received their training at the time. Rush earned his M.D. degree in 1768, having concentrated in the study of chemistry. Returning to America, he began his own pri-

Benjamin Rush

vate practice the following year, when he was also appointed to a teaching position at the College of Philadelphia, becoming the first professor of chemistry in North America and authoring the first chemistry text by an American (*Syllabus of a Course of Lectures on Chemistry*). Rush's medical practice grew rapidly. He was known in particular for his strong endorsement of the contemporary practice of treating fevers by bloodletting and purges, as a result of his conviction that fevers resulted from arterial tension which could only be relieved by bloodletting. In severe cases, he recommended that as much as four-fifths of the patient's blood be drained.

Rush played a prominent role in the American Revolution. In 1776, he served as a member of the Continental Congress, and was also a signer of the Declaration of Independence. He also served from 1776 to 1778 as Physician General of the Continental Army. Rush was an enthusiastic supporter of the U.S. Constitution and a member of the Pennsylvania Convention that ratified it.

In 1787, Rush took charge of the treatment of mental patients at the Pennsylvania Hospital, beginning the work that eventually earned him the title "father of American psychiatry." While his treatment methods—which included bloodletting, purging, intimidation, hot and cold baths, and chair restraints—can hardly be considered clinical advances, Rush's view of mental disease represented a major advance in the understanding of that subject. He believed that insanity often has a physical cause, and that **mental illness**es, like physical illnesses, may be as treatable. Through his insistence that insanity was a disease requiring treatment rather than a crime calling for imprisonment, Rush helped bring **mental health** under the domain of medicine. He also authored the first **psychiatry** book written by an American, *Medical Inquiries and Observations upon the Diseases of the Mind*, in 1812.

In addition to his contributions to medicine and politics, Rush worked on behalf of many social issues of his day, including the establishment of public schools, education for women, prison reform, and the abolition of slavery and capital punishment. He was in the forefront of the struggle against Philadelphia's yellow-fever epidemics of the 1790s. Although he did note the apparent connection between the disease and the presence of mosquitoes, he continued to advocate bloodletting as the primary method of treatment, unfortunately influencing several generations of physicians who treated similar ep-

idemics in the nineteenth century. (He fell ill when he used his treatment method on himself in 1793.) Rush's name is also linked with physicians' rights in relation to freedom of the press. Attacked in the newspapers for his controversial medical and political views, he sued his detractors and was awarded damages by a Pennsylvania court.

In 1789, Rush gave up his chemistry professorship at the University of Pennsylvania in order to begin teaching medicine, which he continued to do for the remainder of his career, serving as a mentor to a generation of medical students. In 1797, he was appointed to the position of treasurer at the United States Mint and held that office until his death in 1813. Rush's other books include *Medical Inquiries and Observations* (1794–98) and *Essays: Literary, Moral and Philosophical* (1798).

Further Reading

Binger, Carl A. *Revolutionary Doctor: Benjamin Rush*. New York: Norton, 1966.

Weisberger, Bernard A. "The Paradoxical Doctor Benjamin Rush." *American Heritage* 27 (1975): 40-47, 98-99.

S

Sadism. See **Paraphilia.**

Sadomasochism. See **Paraphilia.**

Savant Syndrome

A condition characterized by a combination of below normal intelligence and extraordinary mental abilities in one or a few narrow areas.

Persons who display savant syndrome have traditionally been called idiot savants, a term that many currently avoid because of its negative connotations. Alternate terms include retarded savant and autistic savant, the latter referring to the fact that savant syndrome is often associated with **autism**. It is difficult to arrive at an exact figure for the incidence of savant syndrome. A 1977 study found the incidence among the institutionalized mentally handicapped in the United States to be 0.06 percent, or one in roughly 2,000. Most savants are males.

Savant skills occur in a number of different areas. Savants with musical abilities demonstrate an excellent ear for music from an early age, often including perfect pitch. They are able to reproduce melodies and even entire compositions with great accuracy and often show considerable performing talent, including both technical and interpretive skills. Others show unusual talent in the visual arts, which may include the **ability** to produce lifelike reproductions at a very young age, when most children can turn out only primitive drawings. Some savants demonstrate a computer-like ability to perform difficult mathematical calculations at lightning speeds.

Perhaps the most common area where savants show extraordinary abilities is **memory**. They may memorize historical data, sports statistics, population figures, biographical information, or even telephone directories. One savant with uncommon musical abilities could also provide biographical information about the composer of almost any piece of music as well as stating the key and opus of the piece. She could describe in detail every musical performance she had heard within a 20-year period and provide biographical information about every member of the local symphony orchestra. One particular type of memorization common to a large proportion of savants is calendar calculating, the ability to say what day of the week a particular date will fall (or has already fallen) on.

RAIN MAN

In the 1988 feature film, *Rain Man,* actor Dustin Hoffmann played Raymond Babbitt, an autistic savant. Hoffman knew virtually nothing of autism when he took the role, so he consulted with experts at the Neuropsychiatric Institute at UCLA, where he met Barnett Addis, director of the institute's Behavioral Sciences Media Laboratory. Addis had produced two documentaries about a young man with autism, Joe Sullivan. Sullivan thus became one of the two real-life prototypes for Hoffman's performance.

The first documentary Addis produced, *Infantile Autism: The Invisible Wall,* featured Joe as a boy of seven. The second, *Portrait of an Autistic Young Man,* was broadcast on public television, and featured Joe at age 25. (He was 28 at the time *Rain Man* was being produced.) Hoffman viewed the latter, together with more than 15 hours of unedited outtakes, in preparing for his role. Some of Joe's personality characteristics come through in Hoffman's portrayal. For example, both the film character Ray and the real-life Joe eat cheese puffs with toothpicks and murmur what seem to be random phrases. Both men keep fastidious notes on very specific facts of daily life and are obsessed with cleanliness. Joe is fascinated by license plate numbers, and keeps detailed records of popular music charts. Ray was adept with numerical sequences, a skill that proved to be key to his brother's success in gambling. But there are differences, too. On the screen Raymond moves rigidly, while Joe's walk is graceful. And Raymond Babbitt grew up in an institution, and Joe has always lived with his family, which included four older and two younger siblings.

Like many autistics, Joe has a compulsive need to maintain a strict routine in his daily life. His autism was diagnosed when he was about two, after he developed a pattern of withdrawal which began at about eighteen months of age. Psychiatrists knew little about autism, and Joe's mother, Ruth recounted that experts then believed that parental coldness was the cause—an idea that the Sullivan family felt sure was false. They were determined to learn more about the condition, and to help others by making accurate information accessible. Ruth Sullivan helped found the National Society for Autistic Children (later the Autism Society of America) in 1965. A high-school graduate, Joe's routine includes a part-time work schedule shelving books at the local public library. When Joe first started work at the library, he would sometimes roll up his trousers to brush the hair on his legs or pick his nose. Job coaches have helped him to abandon such habits.

Joe's co-workers find it bewildering that he cannot return their feelings of friendship. Similarly in *Rain Man,* Raymond's brother Charlie, played by Tom Cruise, expresses affection for his brother, and the audience may feel frustrated and disappointed when the sibling's emotions are not reciprocated. But the reality of autism is that interpersonal emotions do not exist.

Some savants can provide this type of information for periods covering hundreds of years.

Savants have been studied by researchers investigating such topics as the nature of human **intelligence** and the relative influence of **heredity** and **environment**.

Further Information

Autism Society of America
(formerly National Society for Autistic Children)
Address: 7910 Woodmont Avenue, Suite 650
Bethesda, MD 20814-3015
Telephone: 301-657-0881; 800-3328-8476

Further Reading

Howe, Michael J. A. *Fragments of Genius: The Strange Feats of Idiots Savants.* London: Routledge, 1989.
Obler, L.K., and D. Fein, eds. *The Exceptional Brain: Neuropsychology of Talent and Special Abilities.* New York: Guilford Press, 1988.
Treffert, D.A. *Extraordinary People.* New York: Harper and Row, 1989.

. . . .
Schizophrenia

One of the most severe and disabling mental disorders, affecting a person's thoughts, emotions, perceptions, and behavior.

The term "schizophrenia" was first used by the Swiss psychologist Eugene Bleuler (1857–1939) in 1911 to describe this disease that "splits" the mind, destroying what the National Institute of Mental Health terms its "inner unity." (However, schizophrenia is different from a "split personality," or dissociative identity disorder). Persons with schizophrenia usually require hospitalization for periods ranging from weeks to years. At any given time, schizophrenics occupy between one-fourth and one-half of the beds at long-term treatment facilities in the United States and account for 40 percent of treatment days. Between one-half and one percent of the world's population suffers from schizophrenia. Estimates place the incidence of the disorder at between one and two percent in the United States—at least 2.5 million Americans at any given time.

Currently, the most commonly held professional views on the causes of schizophrenia emphasize the interaction of physiological and **environment**al factors. It is known that certain persons are born with a greater than average vulnerability to the disorder. Children and siblings of schizophrenics are, in general, about 10 times more likely than other persons to develop the condition. Evidence of a hereditary component has been shown even more decisively by twin studies: the average risk of schizophrenia for the identical twin of a person with the disorder is 46 percent. Family members of schizophrenics are also prone to milder disorders that resemble schizophrenia, including several **personality disorders** characterized by suspiciousness, poor interpersonal skills, communication problems, and eccentric behavior.

While researchers have not identified a "schizophrenia gene," they have made some neurological observations about schizophrenia. Connections have been discovered between the functioning of several **neurotransmitters**—especially dopamine—and schizophrenic behavior. It is believed that schizophrenics may have an excess of dopamine or an oversensitivity to it, possibly due to an oversupply of receptors. In addition, several abnormalities have been found in the **brain** structure of schizophrenics, including enlarged ventricles (fluid-filled cavities in the center of the brain), smaller brain volume, and reduced blood flow to certain areas, such as the frontal lobes.

However, the fact that not all identical **twins** of schizophrenics develop the condition indicates that **heredity** is not the sole determinant of schizophrenia. Environmental factors that have been associated with the disease include **birth** complications, childhood head injuries, and viral infections during pregnancy or **infancy**. The once-popular psychological theories that attributed schizophrenia to dysfunctional family relations have been largely discredited. However, there is evidence that certain emotional dynamics within a family are related to the rates of relapse among recovered schizophrenics.

The initial symptoms of schizophrenia gradually appear in what is called the prodromal phase, which begins about a year before the disorder becomes acute. It is characterized by behavioral changes including social withdrawal, neglect of grooming and hygiene, and eccentric behavior. The acute, or active, phase is marked by the appearance of "positive" symptoms requiring medical intervention. Up to three-quarters of schizophrenics experience **delusions**—bizarre ideas that are maintained in the face of logical objections and proof. For example, they may believe that the devil or some other menacing force (such as space aliens) is putting thoughts into their heads. Also common are **hallucinations**—perceived sensory phenomena (such as voices and images) that are imaginary. The most common hallucinatory experience is hearing voices that issue commands or insults. Tactile hallucinations, such as feeling bugs crawling under one's skin, are also possible, as is unusual sensitivity to certain tastes or smells. Other symptoms typical of the acute phase of schizophrenia are incoherent thoughts, chaotic speech (including rambling, use of nonsense words, and abrupt illogical topic changes), and odd physical behavior (such as grimaces, agitated movements, pacing, or strange postures).

In one subtype of schizophrenia, listed in the **American Psychiatric Association**'s *Diagnostic and Statistical Manual of Mental Disorders (DSM)* as residual schizophrenia, positive symptoms such as delusions and hallucinations subside, and a person experiences only the low-key "negative" symptoms, so called because they are associated with the absence of certain normal characteristics. Negative symptoms include flattened or inappropriate **emotion**s, including the inability to experience pleasure (anhedonia); lack of **motivation** and logic; impaired **attention** span; and lack of interest in the outside world, accompanied by social withdrawal. Researchers have found evidence that different types of neurological abnormalities, such as varying degrees of dopamine activity, are associated with positive and negative symptoms.

The *DSM* lists four types of schizophrenia other than the residual subtype. The disorganized, or hebephrenic, type is primarily known for delusions and hallucinations. Other symptoms include rambling, incoherent speech, strange movements and facial expressions, and, in some cases, childish behavior and social withdrawal. This type of schizophrenia commonly begins in **adolescence** or young adulthood and continues for the rest of a person's life. It is often seen in the mentally ill homeless. Catatonic schizophrenics may remain in fixed positions for long periods of time, refusing to speak, assuming bizarre positions, and resisting attempts to move them by maintaining rigid postures. However, they may also exhibit wild, aimless movements. While the disorganized and catatonic types only account for, respectively, about five and eight percent of schizophrenics, about 40 percent belong to the paranoid category, whose most prominent symptoms are delusions and hallucinations focusing on a central theme of persecution. Paranoid schizophrenia, which is also accompanied by **anger,** argumentativeness, **anxiety,** and sometimes **violence,** begins relatively late in life, usually after the age of 25 or 30. The roughly 40 percent of schizophrenics whose symptoms are too diffuse for diagnosis under any other subtype are categorized as undifferentiated schizophrenics.

There is no known cure for schizophrenia, and it is one of the most difficult psychological disorders to treat. In its acute stage, schizophrenia usually requires hospitalization. Treatment generally involves a combination of medication, **psychotherapy** or counseling, and rehabilitation. Antipsychotic **drugs** are the single most important and effective factor in treating schizophrenia. They reduce or eliminate delusions and hallucinations, allow for better self-control and more coherent thought, and generally help schizophrenics function more normally. Many schizophrenics need to continue maintenance treatment—in some cases indefinitely—even after acute symptoms subside in order to prevent relapses. While not all patients respond equally to medication, they do better with it than without it in virtually all cases. However, nearly one-third of those treated with conventional antipsychotic drugs continue to experience residual negative symptoms, such as lack of emotion and social withdrawal.

A relatively new drug, clozapine, that is believed to act on serotonin as well as dopamine receptors, has been effective in relieving both positive and negative symptoms of schizophrenia. However, about one percent of people who take it are at risk for a life-threatening blood condition (agranulocytosis), so those for whom this drug is prescribed must have their blood tested regularly, which makes the cost of taking it prohibitive to many. Risperidone, a newer medication that became available in the United States in 1994, is believed to reduce both positive and negative symptoms of schizophrenia with fewer side effects and less expense than clozapine. **Electroconvulsive therapy** (ECT) has been used to relieve **depression** and catatonia in schizophrenics, especially those who do not respond to medication. However, its long-term effectiveness is not known.

While psychotherapy alone is not adequate for the treatment of schizophrenia, patients who receive therapy in combination with medication do better than those who receive only medication. Family therapy is particularly effective in reducing **stress,** educating both patients and their families about the nature of the disorder, and helping them learn to cope with it together.

Further Reading

Bernheim, Kayla F. *Schizophrenia: Symptoms, Causes, Treatments.* New York: W. W. Norton, 1979.

Lidz, Theodore. *The Origin and Treatment of Schizophrenic Disorders.* Madison, CT: International Universities Press, 1990.

Scholastic Aptitude Test. See **Scholastic Assessment Test.**

Scholastic Assessment Test

A test that measures verbal and mathematical abilities and achievement in specific subject areas.

In March 1994, the test formerly known as the Scholastic Aptitude Test became the Scholastic Assessment Test (SAT). The name change reflects the test's objectives more accurately, that is, to measure a student's scholastic **ability** and achievement rather than his or her aptitude. The format of the SAT remains basically the same, however: it is a series of tests, given to groups of students. The tests measure verbal and mathematical abilities and achievement in a variety of subject areas. It is offered on Saturday mornings seven months of the year at locations across the United States. Over 2,000 colleges and universities use the test scores as part of the college admissions process. The SAT scores provide an indicator of the student's ability to do college-level work. Intended as an objective standard for comparing the abilities of students from widely different cultural backgrounds and

types of schools, the test can also help students, their parents, and guidance counselors make decisions in the college application process.

The two major components of the test are SAT I: Reasoning Test, and SAT II: Subject Tests (formerly called Achievement Tests). All SAT test-takers complete SAT I, a three-hour multiple-choice test. The Test of Standard Written English, which prior to 1994 comprised a half-hour section of SAT I, has been eliminated. The new SAT I has three verbal reasoning and three mathematical reasoning sections. However, not all of these are half-hour sections. For both the verbal and mathematical components, two sections take 30 minutes, and the third takes only 15. This brings the total test time to 2½ hours. The remaining half hour is devoted to an experimental section called Equating, which can be either a math or a verbal section. This section is not counted in the student's score, but the test-taker does not know which one is the Equating section while taking the test.

The Verbal Reasoning section in the SAT I no longer contains antonym questions, and a greater emphasis has been placed on reading comprehension (called Critical Reading), which, in some cases, requires the student to answer questions on two different text passages instead of just one. As before, the Verbal Reasoning sections also include sentence completion and analogy questions.

The Mathematical Reasoning sections consist of multiple-choice questions covering arithmetic, algebra, and geometry; quantitative comparison (which are also multiple choice); and a section of problems requiring students to calculate their own answers (multiple-choice answers are not provided). Students are allowed (and encouraged) to use calculators for the math sections.

SAT II includes a variety of tests in subjects such as English, foreign languages, math, history and social studies, psychology, and the sciences. SAT I and II cannot be taken on the same day. Raw SAT scores are calculated based on the number of correct answers minus a fraction of a point for each wrong answer. Subtracting points for wrong answers compensates for guesses made by the test-taker, and is called the "guessing penalty." The raw score is converted using a scale ranging from 200 to 800, with separate scores provided for the verbal and math sections, and for each subject test in SAT II. Scores are reported about six weeks after the test date to students and their high schools, and to the colleges of their choice. Students may take the SAT more than once, and many do, hoping to improve upon their initial scores.

The SAT has been criticized on grounds of cultural and **gender bias,** charges that the revised version has attempted to rectify. The widespread use of test preparation

Waiting for the school bus in the morning may cause anxiety for the child experiencing school phobia.

courses and services for the SAT has also generated controversy, with detractors arguing that the test is unfair to economically disadvantaged students, who have limited access to coaching.

Further Reading

Bartl, Lisa. *10-Minute Guide to Upping Your SAT Scores.* New York: Alpha Books/ARCO, 1996.

Carris, Joan Davenport. *SAT Success.* 5th ed. Princeton, NJ: Peterson's, 1996.

Inside the SAT. New York: Princeton Review Publications, 1995. (A multimedia format including laser optical disc, reference manual, and practice test.)

Introducing the New SAT: The College Board's Official Guide. New York: College Entrance Examination Boards, 1993.

School Phobia

Occasional reluctance on the part of a child to attend school.

School phobia is a general term used to describe the occasional circumstance when a child refuses to go to school, and may also complain of symptoms that could be related to **anxiety,** such as abdominal discomfort, nau-

sea, or headache. School phobia is not a true **phobia,** but may be a symptom of an educational or social problem the child is experiencing. At its extreme, school phobia evolves into school refusal, where a child refuses to attend school on a more chronic or consistent basis. School refusal is a diagnostic criterion for separation anxiety disorder, a mental condition characterized by abnormally excessive anxiety concerning potential or actual separation from individuals (such as the parent) to whom the child is attached. In most cases, school phobia (unlike school refusal) is unrelated to separation anxiety disorder. Most children who refuse to go to school exhibit this behavior whether individuals to whom the child is attached are present or not.

When school refusal is caused by separation anxiety disorder, the child is likely to display a marked aversion to other activities, such as going away to camp, that involve separation from a major attachment figure. However, school refusal may be caused by a number of factors, and be precipitated by **stress** in the family, change of school, or other events. School refusal is fairly common, and usually first appears when the child is young. Adolescent onset of school refusal is rare.

Further Reading
Kahn, Jack. *Unwillingly To School.* New York: Pergamon Press, 1981.

School Psychology

One of the human service fields of psychology whose aim is to help students, teachers, parents, and others understand each other.

Developed in 1896 at the University of Pennsylvania in a clinic that studied and treated children considered morally or mentally defective, the field of school psychology today includes 30,000 psychologists, most of whom work in educational systems throughout the United States.

School psychologists, in various roles within the school systems they serve, focus on the development and **adjustment** of the child in his or her school setting. School psychologists minimally are required to have completed two years of training after earning a bachelor's degree; those who have earned the Ph.D. may hold administrative or supervisory positions; and are often involved in training teachers and psychologists. School psychologists play a key role in the development of school policies and procedures.

School psychologists administer and interpret tests and assist teachers with classroom-related problems and learning difficulties. School psychologists play a key role in addressing behavior issues in the classroom, and in working with parents and teachers to develop strategies to deal with behavior problems.

In some cases, the school psychologist provides teachers and parents with information about students' progress and potential while advising them how to help students increase their achievement. They also promote communication between parents, teachers, administrators, and other psychologists in the school system.

See also National Association of School Psychologists.

Scientific Method

An approach to research that relies on observation and data collection, hypothesis testing, and the falsifiability of ideas.

The scientific method involves a wide array of approaches and is better seen as an overall perspective rather than a single, specific method. The scientific method that has been adopted was initially based on the concept of positivism, which involved the search for general descriptive laws that could be used to predict natural phe-

Scientific Method

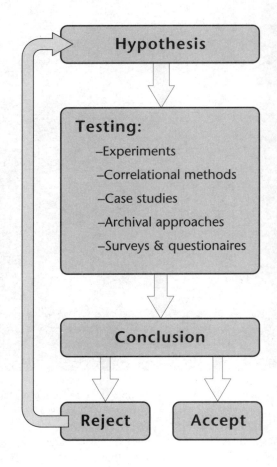

nomena. Once predictions were possible, scientists could attempt to control the occurrence of those phenomena. Subsequently, scientists developed underlying explanations and theories. In the case of psychology, the goal would be to describe, to predict, then to control behavior, with knowledge based on underlying theory.

Although the positivist approach to science has undergone change and scientists are continually redefining the philosophy of science, the premises on which it was based continue to be the mainstream of current research. One of the prime requisites of a scientific approach is falsifiability; that is, a theory is seen as scientific if it makes predictions that can be demonstrated as true or false. Another critical element of the scientific method is that it relies on **empiricism**, that is, observation and data collection.

Research often involves the hypothetico-inductive method. The scientist starts with a hypothesis based on observation, insight, or theory. A hypothesis is a tentative statement of belief based on the expert judgment of the researcher. This hypothesis must be subject to falsification; that is, the research needs to be set up in such a way that the scientist is able to conclude logically either that the hypothesis is correct or incorrect. In many cases, a research project may allow the scientist to accept or reject a hypothesis and will lead to more research questions.

Psychologists employ a diversity of scientific approaches. These include controlled experiments that allow the researcher to determine cause and effect relationships; **correlation method**s that reveal predictable relations among variables; case studies involving in-depth study of single individuals; archival approaches that make novel use of records, documents, and other existing information; and surveys and questionnaires about opinions and attitudes.

Because the scientific method deals with the approach to research rather than the content of the research, disciplines are not regarded as scientific because of their content, but rather because of their reliance on data and observation, **hypothesis testing**, and the falsifiability of their ideas. Thus, scientific research legitimately includes the study of **attitudes**, **intelligence**, and other complicated human behaviors. Although the tools that psychologists use to measure human behavior may not lead to the same degree of precision as those in some other sciences, it is not the precision that determines the scientific status of a discipline, but rather the means by which ideas are generated and tested.

See also Research Method.

Self-Actualization

A prominent term in humanistic psychology that refers to the basic human need for self-fulfillment.

The term self-actualization was used most extensively by **Abraham Maslow,** who placed it at the apex of his hierarchy of human motives, which is conceived as a pyramid ascending from the most basic biological **need**s, such as hunger and thirst, to increasingly complex ones, such as belongingness and self-esteem. The needs at each level must be at least partially satisfied before those at the next can be addressed. Thus, while Maslow considered self-actualization to be the highest **motivation** possible and the essence of **mental health**, he recognized that most people are too preoccupied with more basic needs to seek it actively.

To arrive at a detailed description of self-actualization, Maslow studied historical figures—including Thomas Jefferson (1743–1826), Jane Addams (1860–1935), Albert Einstein (1879–1955), Eleanor Roosevelt (1884–1962), and Martin Luther King, Jr. (1929–1968) whom he believed had made extraordinary use of their potential

As a child, Bill Clinton—an example of a self-actualized person—knew that he wanted to become president of the United States, a goal he achieved in the election of 1992.

and looked for common characteristics. He found that self-actualizers were creative, spontaneous, and able to tolerate uncertainty. Other common qualities included a good sense of humor, concern for the welfare of humanity, deep appreciation of the basic experiences of life, and a tendency to establish close personal relationships with a few people. Maslow also formulated a list of behaviors that he believed could lead to self-actualization. These included such directives as: experience life with the full absorption and concentration of a child; try something new; listen to your own feelings rather than the voices of others; be honest; be willing to risk unpopularity by disagreeing with others; assume responsibility; work hard at whatever you do; and identify and be willing to give up your defenses.

Carl Rogers also emphasized the importance of self-actualization in his client-centered therapeutic approach and theoretical writings. Like Maslow, he used the term to designate a universal and innate tendency toward growth and fulfillment that governs the human **personality**. Rogers believed that self-actualization is closely related to each individual's perceived reality and **self-concept**—the way one thinks of oneself. According to Rogers, one's self-concept can become distorted by the need for approval by others, which can lead to alienation from one's true beliefs and desires and suppression of one's self-actualizing tendency. Rogers' **client-centered therapy** is based on the idea that people will instinctively choose the path to self-actualization on their own once it becomes clear to them.

The Personal Orientation Inventory, a test designed to measure self-actualization, is based on Maslow's writings and consists of 12 scales, including time competence, inner directedness, spontaneity, self-acceptance, and capacity for intimate contact.

Further Reading

Maslow, Abraham. *Toward a Psychology of Being.* Princeton: Van Nostrand, 1968.

————. *Motivation and Personality.* 2d ed. New York: Harper and Row, 1970.

Rogers, Carl. *On Becoming a Person: A Therapist's View of Psychotherapy.* Boston: Houghton Mifflin, 1970.

Self-Concept

The way in which one perceives oneself.

Self-concept—the way in which one perceives oneself—can be divided into categories, such as personal self-concept (facts or one's own opinions about oneself, such as "I have brown eyes" or "I am attractive"); social self-concept (one's **perception**s about how one is regarded by others: "people think I have a great sense of humor"); and self-ideals (what or how one would like to be: "I want to be a lawyer" or "I wish I were thinner").

While a number of philosophers and psychologists have addressed the idea that behavior is influenced by the way people see themselves, investigation into the importance of self-concept is most closely associated with the writings and therapeutic practices of **Carl Rogers**. The self—and one's awareness of it—lie at the heart of Rogers' **client-centered therapy** and the philosophy behind it. According to Rogers, one's self-concept influences how one regards both oneself and one's **environment.** The self-concept of a mentally healthy person is consistent with his or her thoughts, experiences, and behavior. However, people may maintain a self-concept that is at odds with their true feelings in order to win the approval of others and "fit in," either socially or professionally. This involves repressing their true feelings and impulses, which eventually causes them to become alienated from

Self-concept includes our views about ourselves in terms of personality and appearance. It also includes how we think others view us.

themselves, distorting their own experience of the world and limiting their potential for **self-actualization**, or fulfillment. The gulf between a person's self-concept and his or her actual experiences (which Rogers called incongruence) is a chronic source of **anxiety** and can even result in mental disorders. According to Rogers, a strong self-concept is flexible and allows a person to confront new experiences and ideas without feeling threatened.

Social psychologists have pointed out that self-concept also plays an important role in social perception—the process by which we form impressions of others. **Attribution**—how we explain the causes of our own and other people's behavior—is particularly influenced by our own self-concept. **Social learning theory** is also concerned with the ways in which we view ourselves, especially in terms of our perceived impact on our environment. In the first major theory of social learning, Julian B. Rotter claimed that the expected outcome of an action and the value we place on that outcome determine much of our behavior. For example, people whose positive self-concept leads them to believe they will succeed at a task are likely to behave in ways that ultimately lead to success, while those who expect failure are much more likely to bring it about through their own actions. In a general theory of **personality** he developed subsequently with two colleagues, Rotter designated variables based on the ways that individuals habitually think about their experiences. One of the most important was I-E, which distinguished "internals," who think of themselves as controlling events, from "externals," who view events as largely outside their control. Internal-external orientation has been found to affect a variety of behaviors and **attitudes.**

Further Reading

Rogers, Carl. *Client-Centered Therapy.* Boston: Beacon Press, 1952.

Rogers, Carl, and B. Stevens. *Person to Person: The Problem of Being Human.* New York: Pocket Books, 1967.

Rotter, Julian B.; June Chance; and Jerry Phares. *Applications of a Social Learning Theory of Personality.* New York: Holt, Rinehart, and Winston, 1972.

Self-Fulfilling Prophecy

An initial expectation that is confirmed by the behavior it elicits.

One's beliefs about other people determine how one acts towards them, and thus play a role in determining the behavior that results. Experiments have demonstrated this process in a variety of settings. In one of the best-known examples, teachers were told (falsely) that certain students in their class were "bloomers" on the verge of dramatic intellectual development. When the students were tested eight months later, the "special" students outperformed their peers, fulfilling the prediction that had been made about them. During the intervening period, the teachers had apparently behaved in ways that facilitated the students' intellectual development, perhaps by giving them increased **attention** and support and setting higher goals for them.

In another experiment, a group of men became acquainted with a group of women by telephone after seeing what they thought were pictures of their "partners." The supposedly attractive women were considered more interesting and intelligent. Researchers concluded that the men's own behavior had been more engaging toward those women whom they thought were attractive, drawing livelier responses than the men who thought their partners were unattractive.

Racial and ethnic **stereotype**s can become self-fulfilling prophecies if members of disadvantaged groups are discouraged from setting ambitious goals because of other people's low expectations. The term self-fulfilling prophecy can also refer to the effect that people's beliefs about themselves have on their own behavior. Those who expect to succeed at a task, for example, tend to be more successful than those who believe they will fail.

Further Reading

Halloran, James D. *Attitude Formation and Change.* Westport, CT: Greenwood Press, 1976.

Harvey, Terri L., Ann L. Orbuch, and John H. Weber, eds. *Attributions, Accounts, and Close Relationships.* New York: Springer-Verlag, 1992.

Weary, Gifford. *Attribution.* New York: Springer-Verlag, 1989.

Wyer, R. S., and T. K. Srull, eds. *Handbook of Social Cognition.* 2d ed. Hillsdale, NJ: Erlbaum Associates, 1994.

Semantic Memory

The part of long-term memory dealing with words, their symbols, and meanings.

Semantic **memory** allows humans to communicate with language. In semantic memory, the **brain** stores information about words, what they look like and represent, and how they are used in an organized way. It is unusual for a person to forget the meaning of the word "dictionary," or to be unable to conjure up a visual image of a refrigerator when the word is heard or read. Semantic memory contrasts with episodic memory, where memories are dependent upon a relationship in time. An example of an episodic memory is "I played in a piano recital at the end of my senior year in high school."

The "tip of the tongue" phenomenon provides some insight into the way information is stored in semantic memory. Most people have experienced this situation where they are trying to recall a person's name. As the person searches through his or her memory for the name *Stern,* for example, he or she will recall other similar names—*Stone, Stein*—but not *Douglas* or *Zimmer.* Semantic memory appears to categorize information that has similar meaning (in this case, surnames), that begins with the same letter, and has the same number of syllables.

Words and other memories that are stored in semantic memory contribute to episodic memory and the two work together to function as an effective long-term memory system.

Further Reading

Bolles, Edmund Blair. *Remembering and Forgetting: Inquiries Into the Nature of Memory.* New York: Walker and Co., 1988.

Sensitivity Training

A group experience that gives people new insight into how they relate to others.

Sensitivity training began in the 1940s and 1950s with experimental studies of groups carried out by psychologist Kurt Lewin at the National Training Laboratories in Maine. Although the groups (called training or T-groups) were originally intended only to provide research data, their members requested a more active role in the project. The researchers agreed, and T-group experiments also became learning experiences for their subjects. The techniques employed by Lewin and his colleagues, collectively known as sensitivity training, were widely adopted for use in a variety of settings. Initially, they were used to train individuals in business, industry, the military, the ministry, education, and other professions. In the 1960s and 1970s, sensitivity training was adopted by the **human potential movement,** which introduced the "encounter group." Although **encounter groups** apply the basic T-group techniques, they emphasize personal growth, stressing such factors as self-expression and intense emotional experience.

Encounter groups generally consist of between 12 and 20 people and a facilitator who meet in an intensive weekend session or in a number of sessions over a period of weeks or months. The group members work on reducing defensiveness and achieving a maximum of openness and honesty. Initially, participants tend to resist expressing their feelings fully, but eventually become more open in discussing both their lives outside the group and the interactions within the group itself. Gradually, a climate of trust develops among the group members, and they increasingly abandon the defenses and facades habitually used in dealing with other people. Although the increased self-awareness resulting from sensitivity training is presumed to change a person's behavior in daily life, studies of encounter-group participants have raised doubts as to whether their training experiences actually effect long-lasting behavioral changes. In addition, the usefulness of encounter groups is limited to psychologically healthy individuals, as the intense and honest nature of the group discussions may prove harmful to persons with emotional disorders.

See also Group Therapy.

Further Reading

Kanfer, Frederick H. and Arnold P. Goldstein, eds. *Helping People Change: A Textbook of Methods,* 4th ed. New York: Pergamon Press, 1991.

Zimbardo, Philip G. *The Psychology of Attitude Change and Social Influence.* Philadelphia: Temple University Press, 1991.

Sensory Deprivation

An experimental procedure involving prolonged reduction of sensory stimuli.

Sensory deprivation experiments of the 1950s have shown that human beings need environmental stimulation in order to function normally. In a classic early experiment, college students lay on a cot in a small, empty cubicle nearly 24 hours a day, leaving only to eat and use the bathroom. They wore translucent goggles that let in light but prevented them from seeing any shapes or patterns, and they were fitted with cotton gloves and cardboard cuffs to restrict the sense of touch. The continuous hum of an air conditioner and U-shaped pillows placed around their heads blocked out auditory stimulation.

Initially, the subjects slept, but eventually they became bored, restless, and moody. They became disoriented and had difficulty concentrating, and their performance on problem-solving tests progressively deteriorated the longer they were isolated in the cubicle. Some experienced auditory or visual **hallucinations**. Although they were paid a generous sum for each day they participated in the experiment, most subjects refused to continue past the second or third day. After they left the isolation chamber, the **perception**s of many were temporarily distorted, and their **brain**-wave patterns, which had slowed down during the experiment, took several hours to return to **normal.** The intensity of the discomfort these volunteers experienced helps explain why solitary confinement is often regarded as the most severe form of **punishment** in prisons.

The deterioration in both physical and psychological functioning that occurs with sensory deprivation has been linked to the need of human beings for an optimal level of **arousal.** Too much or too little arousal can produce **stress** and impair a person's mental and physical abilities. Thus, appropriate degrees of sensory deprivation may actually have a therapeutic effect when arousal levels are too high. A form of sensory deprivation known as REST (restricted environmental stimulation), which consists of floating for several hours in a dark, sound-proof tank of water heated to body temperature, has been used to treat drug and smoking addictions, lower back pain, and other conditions associated with excessive stress.

Further Reading

Lilly, John Cunningham. *The Deep Self: Profound Relaxation and the Tank Isolation Technique.* New York: Simon and Schuster, 1977.

Solomon, Philip. *Sensory Deprivation: A Symposium Held at Harvard Medical School.* Cambridge, MA: Harvard University Press, 1961.

Serial Learning

Recalling patterns of facts or stimuli in the order in which they were presented.

In some research on **memory** for words, the learner is exposed to stimuli to be remembered and later recalls those stimuli in the same order in which they initially appeared. This procedure is called serial learning. In general, when people must recall stimuli in a particular order, they remember less material than when allowed to engage in free recall, which imposes no constraints on the order or recall.

Hermann Ebbinghaus is credited with conducting the first studies of verbal memory involving serial learning. Most serial learning studies use a procedure called serial anticipation, where one stimulus is presented at a time and the learner uses that word as a cue for the next word. The second word then serves as a cue for the third, and so on. One of the most consistent findings in research involving single words or nonsense syllables involves the serial position function or effect: learners show greatest recall for stimuli at the beginning of the list, and good but somewhat less recall for items appearing at the end of the list. Stimuli in the middle of the list fare least well. When learners must remember single words or nonsense syllables in free recall, the greatest recall usually occurs at the end of the list, with good but lower recall at the beginning. If the words to be learned are meaningfully related, such as those in a sentence, people tend to remember them by using serial anticipation, even when they are allowed to use free recall. The first seven items in a list are often the easiest to learn. This fact is consistent with the research that indicates that, regardless of the type of learning, humans can remember "the magic number seven" items without relying on rehearsal or other **mnemonic strategies.**

Serial learning occurs when students attempt to learn school-related material. For example, when trying to remember the names of the American presidents, students typically begin with Washington, Adams, and Jefferson, and continue with their serial anticipation, using each president as a cue for the next one. Somewhere in the middle of the list, though, students fail to remember names, then, toward the end of the presidents, performance improves as the students retrieve the names of more recent presidents. Quite often, people show similar patterns when attempting to memorize poems, prayers, or a short text such as the *Declaration of Independence.*

These behaviors conform with the serial position effect that is typical for most serial learning studies.

See also Free Recall Learning.

Serial Position Function

The predictable patterns of memory and forgetting of lists of stimuli.

When a person attempts to recall a set of stimuli that exceeds about seven items, there is a high likelihood that he or she will forget some of them. The generally accepted limit to memory for material that is not rehearsed is referred to as "the magic number seven" (plus or minus two items). Most studies in this area have employed lists of words or nonsense syllables, but the research results hold true for a wide range of stimuli.

As a rule, if free recall is engaged, the words that are best remembered are those from the end of the list, and they are also likely to be the first to be recalled. This tendency for the best **memory** for recently presented items is referred to as the recency effect. (The tendency for retrieving words from the beginning of a list is called the primacy effect.) Recall will be poorest for items in the middle of the list, unless a stimulus has special characteristics and stands out.

When a learner must use serial recall, or recall of the stimuli in their order of presentation, the items appearing first and last on the list still show an advantage over those in the middle, but the items at the beginning of the list are recalled more often than items at the end of the list, a reversal of the pattern in free recall.

The serial position effect occurs due to three factors: distinctiveness, constraints of short-term memory, and inhibition. First, the primacy and recency effects occur because items at the beginning and the end of the list are distinct or isolated from the other stimuli due to their positions. Second, short-term memory involves keeping some information in active, working memory; this information is likely to be the most recently presented stimuli. Third, inhibition hampers memory. Words in a list tend to interfere with one another. When they are at the beginning or at the end of the list, they are not surrounded by as many words that could interfere with them; words in the middle, on the other hand, must compete for space in working memory with more words around them.

See also Free Recall Learning.

Further Reading

Squire, Larry R. *Memory and Brain.* New York: Oxford University Press, 1989.

Most psychologists agree that gender identity is established in early childhood, but they disagree on the process by which it develops.

Sex Identity

Sex, or gender, identity refers to a person's awareness or sense of being male or female.

Human gender identity is both biological and learned. At **birth,** male children are usually larger and heavier than females, are more susceptible to disease, and display a higher level of activity and restlessness. Females demonstrate sensitivity to a greater number of stimuli. Shortly after birth, however, it is difficult to disentangle the effects of biology and **socialization.** It has been demonstrated, for example, that parents perceive their newborn babies differently depending on their sex. In Western cultures, girls are considered smaller and "softer" while boys are perceived primarily as strong and well-coordinated. Other adults also treat male and female infants differently, playing more gently and talking more to infant girls.

Gender identity is established in early childhood. Developmental psychologists employ three major approaches in accounting for this phenomenon. Those who subscribe to **psychoanalytic theory** explain the formation of gender identity in terms of the **Oedipus complex,** a crisis occurring between the ages of three and five that is resolved by children of both sexes renouncing incestuous desires for the parent of the opposite sex and identifying with the parent of the same sex. Social learning theorists stress the importance of the contrasting positive **reinforcement**s given to children of both sexes, while cognitive theorists emphasize awareness of gender permanence as the crucial point in gender identity formation.

Studies conducted in a variety of cultures have found boys of preschool age to be more aggressive than girls. As early as one year of age, boys have been found to play more vigorously than girls and prefer toys that require gross motor coordination. By age two, it is common for children to display gender-related differences in their play, including their choice of toys. By the age of three, when children generally become aware of themselves as either male or female, sex-specific behavior increases. Children begin to restrict their friendships primarily to members of their own sex, and their peers become important influences in terms of sex-appropriate behavior and dress. Between the ages of five and seven, children arrive at the realization that their gender is permanent, developing a greater interest in adults of the same sex and an even stronger preference for same-sex playmates.

Girls generally speak and write earlier than boys and excel at grammar and spelling. Boys have greater skill at manipulating objects and at spatial organization. They are noisier and more aggressive in their play, while girls are more nurturing toward others, exhibit great **anxiety,** and tend to play in a more orderly fashion. Children receive and process constant social messages about gender identity from their parents, teachers, peers, and cultural influences, such as television and film characters. Boys are encouraged to be competitive, independent, unemotional, and responsible. Girls are encouraged to be expressive, nurturing, dependent, obedient, and altruistic.

Sex identity takes on a new dimension in **adolescence** with the transition to sexual maturity. The biological and emotional changes experienced during this period have substantial effect on gender identity formation. Boys who physically mature early are admired by their peers and feel poised and confident, while girls may become self-conscious and distant from their parents, and may become sexually active early. Increased heterosexual contact during this period is important in the formation of gender identity, as adolescents begin to adopt the roles they will play as adults in relation to members of the opposite sex.

The gender identities of adults reflect behavior learned during childhood and adolescence, as well as the assumption of new roles that accompany specifically adult responsibilities, including marriage, work, and parenthood. Traditional measures of achievement have attributed greater ambition to males than females, yet it has been noted that such measures may be skewed to reflect primarily those areas of achievement where men concentrate. Studies of women have also shown a deliberate element of success avoidance that conflicts with the desire to succeed. It has been posited that some women fear success as a threat to their fulfillment of the traditional female role and a possible cause of difficulty in relating to men.

The distinction between biological sex and gender identity is especially clear in transsexuals, people who develop a gender identity inconsistent with their anatomical and genetic sex. It is estimated that about 1 in 20,000 males and 1 in 50,000 females are transsexuals. Researchers have suggested that both early socialization and prenatal **hormones** may play a role in the development of transsexuality. A number of transsexuals elect to change their sex through medical procedures that include a series of surgical operations and the administration of sex hormones to induce the secondary sex characteristics of the desired sex.

See also Gender Identity Disorder.

Sexism. See **Gender Bias.**

Sexuality

The full range of thoughts and actions that describe sexual motivation and behavior.

While sex is not necessary for an individual's survival, without it a species would cease to exist. The determinants of sexual **motivation** and behavior include an individual's physiology, learned behavior, the physical **environment,** and the social environment.

A person's sex is determined at conception by whether one out of the 23 chromosomes in the father's sperm is either X (female) or Y (male). All female eggs contain an X chromosome, so each fertilized egg, or embryo, has a genotype of either XX (female) or XY (male). Reproductive **hormones** produced by the gonads (male testes and female ovaries) determine the development of the reproductive organs and the fetal **brain,** especially the **hypothalamus.** All the human reproductive hormones are found in both sexes but in different amounts. The principal female hormones are estrogens and progesterone (of which the main ones are estradiol and progesterone); the primarily male hormones are androgens (mainly testosterone). In males, levels of testosterone remain fairly constant, regulated by a feedback loop to the brain and pituitary gland, which control hormone secretion. In females, hormone levels fluctuate within each menstrual cycle, rising at ovulation. Reproductive hormones have two types of effects on the body. Organizational effects, which occur primarily before **birth,** are irreversible and permanently govern an individual's response to further hormone secretion. Activational effects govern behavior temporarily while hormone levels are elevated.

Human females are born with about 400,000 immature eggs. Each one is contained in a sac called a follicle. When a girl reaches puberty, one or more eggs mature every month, stimulated by the release of a hormone from the pituitary gland. As the egg matures, it secretes the hormone estrogen, causing the uterine lining to thicken in anticipation of the implantation of a fertilized egg. This is followed by ovulation, as the follicle ruptures, releasing the mature egg which travels through the fallopian tube towards the uterus. If the egg is not fertilized by sperm, it disintegrates and the uterine lining leaves the body, a process called menstruation. Women remain fertile until menopause, which normally occurs around the age of fifty. Unlike the production of female eggs, the male production of sperm is not cyclical and men remain fertile throughout their lives, although they may produce fewer sperm as they age. A man produces several billion sperm each year, releasing 300 to 500 million sperm in an average ejaculation.

Unlike that of other species, human sexual behavior is not bound to the female reproductive cycle. Women may engage in or refrain from sexual intercourse at any time during the cycle. Some women have reported increased sexual interest at the time of ovulation, others around the time of menstruation, and still others experience no link at all between their sexual behavior and menstrual cycle. After their initial organizational effects at birth, hormone levels stay low until puberty when activational effects first begin, triggering the reproductive system and generating an interest in sexual behavior. Whether or not sexual activity actually occurs at this point, however, depends on the interaction of physical readiness, social skills, and opportunity. For adults, as for adolescents, sexuality is not governed solely by hormones but also by a repertoire of learned **attitudes** and behaviors. This learning begins in childhood with the development of gender roles and continues throughout the life span, and it depends on attitudes prevalent in a culture at a given time.

The laboratory research conducted by **William Masters** and Virginia Johnson in the 1950s and 1960s yielded important information about the human cycle of sexual response. This cycle has four phases for both men and women: initial excitement, a plateau stage, orgasm, and resolution, during which the person returns to a state of relaxation. Males experience a refractory period after orgasm during which they are temporarily insensitive to sexual stimulation. The same combination of physical, psychological, and social factors that govern sexuality may contribute to sexual dysfunction, any condition that inhibits the desire for or ability to have satisfying sexual experiences. In males, the most common dysfunction is impotence, or the inability to have or maintain an erection sufficient for intercourse. While impotence can have physical origins, including fatigue, diabetes, alcoholism, and the side effects of certain medications, it is usually psychological in nature. In females, a common sexual dysfunction is the inability to reach orgasm, also called **arousal** disorder, which is also associated with such psychological factors as self-consciousness, lack of self-confidence, **depression,** and dissatisfaction with the nature of the romantic relationship itself.

Although human sexual activity is primarily heterosexual, between 5 and 10 percent of males and 2 to 6 percent of females in the United States are homosexuals, individuals in whom sexual attraction and behavior are directed at members of their own sex. (Persons whose sexual behavior is directed at members of both sexes are known as bisexuals.) Researchers have found evidence of both biological and environmental origins of **homosexuality.** While no significant differences have been found in the levels of hormones that circulate in the blood of ho-

mosexuals and heterosexuals, exposure to high levels of certain reproductive hormones during fetal development has been linked to homosexuality. In addition, anatomical differences have been found between the hypothalamus of heterosexual and homosexual men, and studies of twins have found distinct evidence of a hereditary component to homosexuality. Environmental influences include early family relationships and the **modeling** of behaviors observed in the parent of the opposite sex, as well as social learning throughout the life span.

Sexual preference—the gender to which one is attracted—is only one aspect of human sexual orientation. Also involved is gender role, a general pattern of masculine or feminine behaviors that is strongly influenced by cultural factors. Distinct from this is **sex identity,** referring to whether individuals consider themselves to be male or female. Transsexualism, a condition in which a person believes he or she is of the wrong sex, occurs in approximately one in 20,000 in men and one in 50,000 in women. Today, these individuals have the option of a sex change operation that allows them to live as a member of the sex with which they identify.

See also Gender Identity Disorder; Heterosexuality.

Further Reading

Fisher, Seymour. *Sexual Images of the Self: The Psychology of Erotic Sensations and Illusions.* Hillsdale, NJ: L. Erlbaum Associates, 1989.

Levand, Rhonda. *Sexual Evolution.* Berkeley, CA: Celestial Arts, 1991.

. . . .

Shaping

Incremental change in behavior until a goal is reached.

When a psychologist attempts to change the behavior of an animal by using **operant conditioning,** that animal does not know what the psychologist wants it to do. As a result, the psychologist tries to change the animal's behavior little by little; this process is called shaping.

In shaping, each time an animal does something that vaguely approximates the desired behavior, the behavior is reinforced. The **reinforcement** can be either the presentation of something attractive to the animal (positive reinforcement) or the termination of something aversive to the animal (negative reinforcement). Over a number of trials, the researcher may become stricter in delivering reinforcements, and the animal must emit behaviors that are similar to the goal behavior before receiving another reinforcement. Gradually, the animal's behavior became closer to the desired behavior. Psychologists refer to this process as the use of successive approximations.

Although operant conditioning was developed in large part by **B. F. Skinner** using animals, the process has also been effective in changing human behavior in a wide variety of settings. In the past, patients in psychiatric facilities, for example, received positive reinforcement with tokens that could later be spent on privileges when their behaviors were appropriate. Such techniques lead to behavior that is appropriate and consistent with the treatment the patients underwent.

Further Reading

Lieberman, David A. *Learning: Behavior and Cognition.* Belmont, CA: Wadsworth Publishing Co., 1990.

Shinn, Milicent W. (1858–1940)

American child psychologist best known for her seminal systematic observational study of a child.

As the first woman to earn a Ph.D. from the University of California, Milicent Shinn is credited today for her outstanding early American study, "Notes on the Development of a Child." First published in 1898 as a doctoral dissertation, this work is still hailed as a masterpiece and a classic in its field.

A native Californian, Shinn was born in 1858 to parents who emigrated from the East and established a farming homestead in Niles, California, where she lived her entire life. In 1879, at the age of 25, she became editor of the *Overland Monthly*, a literary magazine that had fallen on hard times in post-Civil War California. Dividing her time between the family ranch and the journal, Shinn cared for her aging parents, ran the ranch with her brother and his wife, and helped care for their daughter, Ruth, who was born in 1890. Inspired by personal interest in her niece, Shinn applied her writer's skills to create a carefully recorded and minutely detailed two-year account of her niece's physical growth and **emotion**al development. Delivered as a paper entitled "The First Two Years of the Child" at the World's Columbian Exposition in Chicago in 1893, Shinn's observational study was hailed as the first of its kind in America. Convinced by others that her work represented a significant contribution to **child psychology,** Shinn resigned from the *Overland Monthly* in 1894 and enrolled as a doctoral candidate at the University of California at Berkeley, completing the degree with the publication of her dissertation in 1898.

Compelling family needs and pressures led Shinn to abandon her scholarly pursuits and return to the family ranch to care for her invalid mother and aging father. By 1913, in her mid-fifties and in ill-health herself, Shinn undertook the education of her younger brother's four children, devoting the rest of her life to her family until her death in 1940.

Further Reading

Scarborough, Elizabeth, and Laurel Furumoto. *Untold Lives: The First Generation of American Women Psychologists.* 52-69. New York: Columbia University Press, 1987.

Shyness

Uneasiness experienced when confronted by new people and new situations.

Most people, from social recluses to the rich and famous, probably have experienced feelings of shyness at various times in their lives. Physiological symptoms may include blushing, increased heart rate, sweating, and shaking. And just as these outward manifestations vary in type and intensity from person to person, so do the inner feelings. Anxious thoughts and worries, low self-esteem, self-criticism, and concern over a lack of social skills, real or imagined, are common. The causes of shyness are not known. Some researchers believe it results from a genetic predisposition. Others theorize that uncommunicative parents restrict a child's development of the social skills that compensate for discomfort caused by new experiences and people, resulting in shyness. Little research has been done on shyness as a separate and unique condition. Variously, it has been considered a symptom of social **phobia** or a simple characteristic of introversion. Learning or improving social skills through self-help courses or formal training in assertiveness and public speaking are some of the methods used to diminish the effects of shyness.

Further Reading

Cheek, Jonathan. *Conquering Shyness: The Battle Anyone Can Win.* New York: Putnam, 1989.
Shaw, Phyllis M. *Overcoming Shyness: Meeting People Is Fun.* New York: Arco, 1983.

Signal Detection Theory

A psychological theory regarding a threshold of sensory detection.

One of the early goals of **psychologist**s was to measure the sensitivity of our sensory systems. This activity led to the development of the idea of a threshold, the least intense amount of stimulation needed for a person to be able to see, hear, feel, or detect with any of the senses. Unfortunately, one of the problems with this concept was

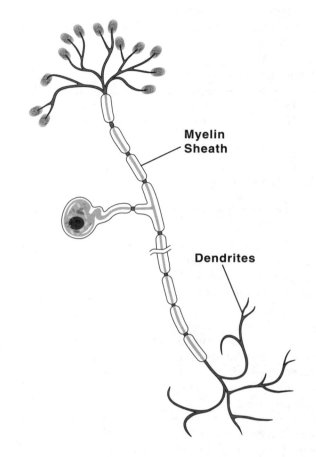

Neurons transmit messages from the sense organs to the brain. According to signal detection theorists, sensitivity to sensory stimuli is influenced by a number of factors.

Myelin Sheath

Dendrites

that even though the level of stimulation remained constant, people were inconsistent in detecting the stimulus. Factors other than the sensitivity of sense receptors influence the signal detection process. There is no single, fixed value below which a person never detects the stimulus and above which the person always detects it. In general, psychologists typically define threshold as that intensity of stimulation that a person can detect some percentage of the time, for example, 50 percent of the time.

An approach to resolving this dilemma is provided by signal detection theory. This approach abandons the idea of a threshold. Instead, the theory involves treating detection of the stimulus as a decision-making process, part of which is determined by the nature of the stimulus, by how sensitive a person is to the stimulus, and by cognitive factors. In other words, a person will be able to detect more intense sounds or lights more easily than less intense stimuli. Further, a more sensitive person requires less stimulus intensity than a less sensitive person would. Finally, when a person is quite uncertain as to whether the stimulus was present, the individual will decide based on what kind of mistake in judgment is worse: to say that

no stimulus was present when there actually was one or to say that there was a stimulus when, in reality, there was none.

An example from everyday life illustrates this point. Suppose a person is expecting an important visitor, someone that it would be unfortunate to miss. As time goes on, the person begins to "hear" the visitor and may open the door, only to find that nobody is there. This person is "detecting" a stimulus, or signal, that is not there because it would be worse to miss the person than to check to see if the individual is there, only to find that the visitor has not yet arrived.

In a typical sensory experiment that involves a large number of trials, an observer must try to detect a very faint sound or light that varies in intensity from clearly below normal detection levels to clearly above. The person responds positively (i.e., there is a stimulus) or negatively (i.e., there is no stimulus). There are two possible responses, "Yes" and "No." There are also two different possibilities for the stimulus, either present or absent. The accompanying table describes the combination of an observer's response and whether the stimulus actually there. The table refers to a task with an auditory stimulus, but it could be modified to involve stimuli for any sense.

Psychologists have established that when stimuli are difficult to detect, cognitive factors are critical in the decision an observer makes. If a person participates in an experiment and receives one dollar for each *Hit* whereas there is no penalty for a *False Alarm*, it is in the person's best interest to say that the stimulus was present whenever there is uncertainty. On the other hand, if the person loses two dollars for each False Alarm, it is better for the observer to be cautious in saying that a stimulus occurred. This combination of rewards and penalties for correct and incorrect decisions is referred to as the Payoff Matrix. If the Payoff Matrix changes, the person's pattern of responses will also change. This alteration in responses is called a criterion shift.

There is always a trade-off between the number of Hits and False Alarms. When a person is very willing to say that the signal was present, that individual will show more Hits, but will also have more False Alarms. Fewer Hits will be associated with fewer False Alarms. As such, the number of Hits is not a very revealing indicator of how sensitive a person is; if the person claims to have heard the stimulus on every single trial, the person will have said "Yes" in every instance in which the stimulus was actually there. This is not very impressive, however, because the person will also have said "Yes" on every trial on which there was no stimulus. Psychologists have used mathematical approaches to determine the sensitivity of an individual for any given pattern of Hits and False

Alarms; this index of sensitivity is called *d'* (called *d-prime*). A large value of *d'* reflects greater sensitivity.

The basic idea behind signal detection theory is that **neuron**s are constantly sending information to the **brain**, even when no stimuli are present. This is called neural noise. The level of neural noise fluctuates constantly. When a faint stimulus, or signal, occurs, it creates a neural response. The brain must decide whether the neural activity reflects noise alone, or whether there was also a signal.

For very intense signals, there is no problem in deciding if there was a stimulus because the neural effect of the signal far outweighs the neural effect of the noise. Similarly, when there is no signal, the nervous system does not respond as it does when an outside signal is present, so decisions are easy. On the other hand, for near-threshold signals, it can be difficult to know whether neural activity results from noise alone or from a signal plus noise. At this point, the observer makes a decision based on the payoff matrix.

Further Reading

Goldstein, E.B. *Sensation and Perception,* 3rd ed. Belmont, CA: Wadsworth Publishing Company, 1989.

. . . .
Significance Level

A method to describe the reliability of test results.

When researchers measure a behavior, they often compare groups to determine whether they differ on that behavior. The ultimate goal is to determine whether the difference would occur if the **measurement**s were ad-ministered a second time, or whether the difference is accidental and not likely to recur. The degree of reliability relates to the concept of significance level. The significance level refers to how likely it is that an error (that is, a wrong decision about whether the groups differ from one another) would be made. Psychologists generally accept a 5 percent error rate as reasonable. In order to decide whether differences are reliable, psychologists conduct statistical tests that provide a measure of confidence in their conclusions. This area of statistics is called inferential statistics because psychologists draw inferences, or conclusions, about what would happen if they made similar measurements with a different set of subjects.

If two similar groups are being measured, they will produce different scores even though the difference is not particularly meaningful. If a researcher measures how much time students in separate mathematics classes take to solve a similar problem, the average for those two classes is likely to differ somewhat, even if the two classes consist of students with comparable abilities

Further Reading

Berman, Simeon M. *Mathematical Statistics: An Introduction Based on the Normal Distribution.* Scranton, PA: Intext Educational Publishers, 1971.

Christensen, Larry B. *Experimental Methodology,* 5th ed. Boston: Allyn and Bacon, 1991.

D'Amato, M. R. *Experimental Psychology: Methodology, Psychophysics, and Learning.* New York: McGraw-Hill, 1970

Elmes, David G. *Research Methods in Psychology,* 4th ed. St. Paul: West Publishing Company, 1992.

Kantowitz, Barry H. *Experimental Psychology: Understanding Psychological Research,* 5th ed. St. Paul: West Publishing Company, 1994.

SIGNAL DETECTION THEORY	
Status of Stimulus	**Observer's Decision**
Stimulus is present	*Yes, there is a sound.* This is termed a HIT, because the sound is there and the observer detects it.
	No, there is no sound. This is termed a MISS, because the sound is there, but the observer fails to detect it.
Stimulus is absent	*Yes, there is a sound.* This is termed a FALSE ALARM, because the sound is present, but the observer fails to detect it.
	No, there is no sound. This is termed CORRECT REJECTION, because the sound is not there, and the observer correctly notes its absence.

Martin, David W. *Doing Psychology Experiments,* 2nd ed. Monterey, CA: Brooks/Cole, 1985.

Skinner, B. F. (1904–1990)

American psychologist and advocate of behaviorism.

B. F. (Burrhus Frederic) Skinner was born in Susquehanna, Pennsylvania. As a youth, he showed talent for music and writing, as well as mechanical aptitude. He attended Hamilton College as an English major, with the goal of becoming a professional writer. After graduation, Skinner, discouraged over his literary prospects, became interested in behavioristic psychology after reading the works of **John Watson** and **Ivan Pavlov.** He entered Harvard University as a graduate student in psychology in 1928 and received his degree three years later. Skinner remained at Harvard through 1936, by which time he was a junior fellow of the prestigious Society of Fellows. While at Harvard, he laid the foundation for a new system of behavioral analysis through his research in the field of animal learning, utilizing unique experimental equipment of his own design.

His most successful and well-known apparatus, known as the Skinner Box, was a cage in which a laboratory rat could, by pressing on a bar, activate a mechanism that would drop a food pellet into the cage. Another device recorded each press of the bar, producing a permanent record of experimental results without the presence of a tester. Skinner analyzed the rats' bar-pressing behavior by varying his patterns of **reinforcement** (feeding) to learn their responses to different schedules (including random ones). Using this box to study how rats "operated on" their **environment** led Skinner to formulate the principle of **operant conditioning**—applicable to a wide range of both human and animal behaviors—through which an experimenter can gradually shape the behavior of a subject by manipulating its responses through reinforcement or lack of it. In contrast to Pavlovian, or response, **conditioning,** which depends on an outside stimulus, Skinner's operant conditioning depends on the subject's responses themselves. Skinner introduced the concept of operant conditioning to the public in his first book, *The Behavior of Organisms* (1938).

Between 1936 and 1948 Skinner held faculty positions at the University of Minnesota and the University of Indiana, after which he returned permanently to Harvard. His ideas eventually became so influential that the **American Psychological Association** created a separate division of studies related to them (Division 25: "The Experimental Analysis of Behavior"), and four journals of

B. F. Skinner

behaviorist research were established. In the 1940s Skinner began training animals to perform complex activities by first teaching them chains of simpler ones. He was quite successful in training laboratory animals to perform apparently remarkable and complex activities. One example of this involved pigeons that learned to play table tennis.

Skinner's observation of the effectiveness of incremental training of animals led him to formulate the principles of programmed instruction for human students, in which the concept of reward, or reinforcement, is fundamental, and complex subjects such as mathematics are broken down into simple components presented in order of increasing difficulty. Presented with a set of relatively simple questions, students receive immediate reinforcement—and thus incentive to continue—by being told that their answers were correct. The **programmed learning** movement became highly influential in the United States and abroad. Although this technique eventually came under criticism by educators advocating more holistic methods of instruction, it remains a valuable teaching tool. Courses and course materials based on it have been developed for many subjects, and at levels of difficulty ranging from kindergarten through graduate school.

Skinner's work was also influential in the clinical treatment of mental and emotional disorders. In the late 1940s he began to develop the **behavior modification** method, in which subjects receive a series of small rewards for desired behavior. Considered a useful technique for psychologists and psychiatrists with deeply disturbed patients, behavior modification has also been widely used by the general population in overcoming **obesity**, shyness, speech defects, addiction to smoking, and other problems. Extending his ideas to the realm of philosophy, Skinner concluded that all behavior was the result of either positive or negative reinforcement, and thus the existence of free will was merely an illusion. To explore the social ramifications of his behaviorist principles, he wrote the novel *Walden Two* (1948), which depicted a utopian society in which all reinforcement was positive. While detractors of this controversial work regarded its vision of social control through strict positive reinforcement as totalitarian, the 1967 founding of the Twin Oaks Community in Virginia was inspired by Skinner's ideas. Skinner elaborated further on his ideas about positive social control in his book *Beyond Freedom and Dignity* (1971), which critiques the notion of human autonomy, arguing that many actions ascribed to free will are performed due to necessity.

Skinner has been listed in *The 100 Most Important People in the World*, and in a 1975 survey he was identified as the best-known scientist in the United States. Skinner's other books include *Science and Human Behavior* (1953) and *Verbal Behavior* (1957).

See also Behaviorism.

Further Reading

Carpenter, Finley. *The Skinner Primer: Behind Freedom and Dignity.* New York: Free Press, 1974.

Skinner, B.F. *Particulars of My Life.* New York: Knopf, 1976.

———. *The Shaping of a Behaviorist.* New York: Knopf, 1979.

———. *A Matter of Consequences.* New York: Knopf, 1983.

Sleep

A state that suspends the voluntary exercise of bodily functions and consciousness.

A healthy adult sleeps an average of 7.5 hours each night and most people (approximately 95 percent) sleep between 6.5 and 8.5 hours. Tracking **brain** waves with the aid of **electroencephalographs (EEGs),** researchers have identified six stages of sleep (including a pre-sleep stage), each characterized by distinctive brain-wave frequencies. Stage 0 is the prelude to sleep, which is characterized by low amplitude and fast frequency alpha waves in the brain. At this stage, a person becomes relaxed,

Father and baby enjoying a nap.

drowsy, and closes their eyes. Stages 1 through 4 are sometimes characterized as NREM (non-rapid eye movement) sleep. In *Stage 1*, the eyes begin to roll and rhythmic alpha waves give way to irregular theta waves that are lower in amplitude and slower in frequency as the person loses responsiveness to stimuli, experiences, fleeting thoughts, and images. In *Stage 2*, electroencephalogram tracings show fast frequency bursts of brain activity called sleep spindles, marked by muscle tension and accompanied by a gradual decline in heart rate, respiration, and temperature. Stages 3 and 4 normally occur 30 to 45 minutes after falling asleep. In *Stage 3*, there are fewer sleep spindles, but high amplitude and low frequency delta waves appear. When these begin to occur more than 50 percent of the time, the fourth stage of sleep has been entered. Delta waves demarcate the deepest levels of sleep, when heart rate, respiration, temperature, and blood flow to the brain are reduced and growth **hormones** are secreted. A person roused from Stage 4 sleep will be groggy and confused. Altogether, it takes about a half hour to pass through these four stages of sleep.

Rapid eye movement (REM sleep), which makes up approximately 20 percent of sleep time, is interspersed with NREM sleep every 30 to 40 minutes throughout the night. It is during REM sleep that **dreams** are experienced. In this state, the same fast frequency, low-amplitude beta waves that characterize waking states occur, and a person's physiological signs—heart rate, breathing, and blood pressure—also resemble those in a waking state. However, muscle tone decreases to the point of paralysis, with sudden twitches, especially in the face and hands. REM periods may last from 15 minutes at the beginning of a sleep cycle to one hour at the end of it. Most people complete four to six complete sleep cycles each night, with each cycle lasting about 90 minutes. These cycles vary in composition, however; early in the night most of the time is spent in Stage 3 and 4 sleep, with Stage 2 and REM sleep predominating later on. Sleep patterns also vary in the course of a person's life. On the average, an infant sleeps about 16 hours a day, in contrast to a 70-year-old who sleeps only about six hours. While REM sleep comprises about half of total sleep at **birth,** it eventually decreases to only 25 percent. Sleeping patterns also vary greatly among individuals, and even among different cultures (in terms of napping, for example).

Two theories of sleep, the repair and the adaptive theories, attempt to explain why sleep occurs. In the repair theory, sleep serves a biological **need,** replenishing key areas of the brain or body which are depleted during the day. The adaptive theory suggests that sleep as a function evolved over time because it prevented early humans from wasting energy and exposing themselves to nocturnal predators, thus aiding in survival. REM sleep in particular has been thought to serve special functions. Research subjects whose REM sleep was interrupted made up for the loss by spending extra time in the REM stage on successive nights. It has also been suggested that REM sleep aids the activity of neurons that use the **neurotransmitter** norepinephrine, thus maintaining waking alertness. Persons deprived of REM sleep have shown poorer retention of skills learned during the day, leading to the hypothesis that REM sleep helps in assimilating daytime learning experiences.

As with many other physiological processes, sleep is linked to a 24-hour circadian rhythm and affected by signals such as light and dark. The effects of disrupting the sleep-wake cycle can be seen in jet lag, which is characterized by fatigue, irritability, lack of alertness, and sleeping problems. A person affected by jet lag feels like sleeping at the wrong times of day. It has been found that the body maintains a circadian sleep-wake rhythm even in the absence of external cues like lightness and darkness, although research subjects deprived of such cues eventually adopt a 25-hour "day." The "internal clock" that maintains this pattern is a section of the brain called the supra chiasmatic nucleus (SCN), located in the **hypothalamus.**

Various disorders interfere with sleep. The most common is insomnia, the inability to fall asleep or stay asleep. Nearly one-third of all Americans are affected by some degree of insomnia. Often associated with mental distress, insomnia is treated with medication, **psychotherapy,** relaxation techniques, or a combination of these methods. The medications most commonly prescribed are benzodiazepines (Valium, Halcyon, Restoril) and barbiturates. While they alleviate insomnia in the short run, these **drugs** interfere with normal sleep patterns, and can lead to increased tolerance and dependence. Researchers and clinicians have had success treating insomnia with the hormone melatonin, a naturally occurring substance related to sleep onset and secreted by the pineal gland. Melatonin supplements first became available in American health food stores in 1993 and have become increasingly popular as a sleep aid, although their use has caused some controversy in medical circles.

Narcolepsy, a disorder characterized by sudden and uncontrollable occurrences of sleep, afflicts 100,000 people in the United States. This condition is genetically linked, and may be curable in the future. Individuals affected by narcolepsy abruptly enter REM sleep states during the daytime, collapsing and remaining immobile for a period of time after awakening. Napping and stimulants have both been used to treat this condition. Another disorder associated with sleep is sudden infant death syndrome (SIDS), in which a healthy baby stops breathing during sleep, fails to awaken, and suffocates. While the exact cause of SIDS is unknown, researchers are attempting to identify and save at-risk infants by studying the relationship between the disorder and sleeping patterns. In sleep apnea, a person repeatedly stops breathing while asleep but awakes each time. The disrupted sleep that results from these multiple awakenings leaves the sleeper fatigued and sleepy during the daytime. Night terrors are non-REM dream experiences from which the sleeper never fully awakes and which he or she does not recall upon awakening. This condition mostly occurs in children and can be treated with **hypnosis** or medication in severe cases.

See also Sleep Disorders.

....

Sleep Disorders

Chronic disturbances in the quantity or quality of sleep that interfere with a person's ability to function normally.

An estimated 15 percent of Americans have chronic sleep problems, while about 10 percent have occasional trouble sleeping. Sleep disorders are listed among the clinical syndromes in Axis I of the **American Psychiatric Association**'s *Diagnostic and Statistical Manual of Mental Disorders.* They may be either primary (unrelated to any other disorder, medical or psychological) or secondary (the result of physical illness, psychological disorders such as **depression**, drug or alcohol use, **stress**, or lifestyle factors, such as jet lag).

The Association for Sleep Disorders Centers has divided sleep problems into four categories. The first and most common is insomnia (Disorders of Initiating and Maintaining Sleep). In insomnia, sleep loss is so severe that it interferes with daytime functioning and well-being. Three types of insomnia have been identified (although a single person can have more than one): sleep-onset insomnia (difficulty falling asleep); sleep-maintenance insomnia (difficulty staying asleep); and terminal insomnia (waking early and not being able to go back to sleep). While insomnia can occur at any stage of life, it becomes increasingly common as people get older.

Some cases of insomnia are thought to be caused by abnormalities in the part of the **brain** that controls sleeping and waking. However, insomnia commonly has a wide variety of non-neurological causes, including stress, physical **pain,** irregular hours, and **psychological disorders.** Temporary acute insomnia related to a major event or crisis can turn chronic if a person becomes overly anxious about sleep itself and is unable to return to his or her normal sleep pattern. Called learned or behavioral insomnia, this problem troubles about 15 percent of people who seek professional help. In about 30 percent of cases, an underlying psychological disorder—often depression—is responsible for insomnia. Disorders that can cause insomnia include **anxiety** disorders (such as **post-traumatic stress disorder**), **obsessive-compulsive disorder**, and **schizophrenia**. Normal sleep may be disrupted by a variety of substances, including caffeine, nicotine, alcohol, appetite suppressants, and prescription medications such as steroids, thyroid medications, and certain antihypertensive **drugs.**

Many people take medications for insomnia, ranging from over-the-counter preparations (which are basically antihistamines) to prescription drugs including barbiturates and benzodiazepines. The American Sleep Disorders Association recommends benzodiazepines (a class of drugs that includes Valium and Restoril) over barbiturates and other sedatives, although only for limited use to treat temporary insomnia or as a supplement to **psychotherapy** and other treatments for chronic insomnia. Benzodiazepines can lead to tolerance and addiction, and withdrawal can actually worsen insomnia. People who take sleeping pills for two weeks or more and then quit are likely to experience a rebound effect that can disrupt their sleep for a period of up to several weeks.

A variety of behavioral treatments are available for insomnia which, when practiced consistently, can be as effective as medication without side effects or withdrawal symptoms. Different types of relaxation therapy, including progressive muscle relaxation, **hypnosis**, meditation, and **biofeedback**, can be taught through special classes, audiotapes, or individual sessions. **Cognitive therapy** focuses on deflecting anxiety-producing thoughts and behaviors at bedtime. Stimulus control therapy is based on the idea that people with learned insomnia have become conditioned to associate their beds with wakefulness. Persons involved in this type of therapy are not allowed to remain in bed at night if they can not fall asleep; they are instructed to go to another room and engage in a non-stressful activity until they become sleepy. In the morning, they must arise at a set hour no matter how much or little sleep they have had the night before. Finally, sleep restriction therapy consists of limiting one's hours in bed to the average number of hours one has generally been sleeping and then gradually increasing them.

The second category of sleep disorder is hypersomnia, or Disorders of Excessive Somnolence. People affected by any type of hypersomnia report abnormal degrees of sleepiness, either at night or in the daytime. While the most common causes are sleep apnea and narcolepsy, hypersomnia may also be caused by physical illness, medications, withdrawal from stimulants, or other psychological disorders. Sleep apnea consists of disrupted breathing which wakens a person repeatedly during the night. Though unaware of the problem while it is occurring, people with sleep apnea are unable to get a good night's sleep and feel tired and sleepy during the day. The condition is generally caused either by a physical obstruction of the upper airway or an impairment of the brain's respiration control centers. Common treatment methods include weight loss (**obesity** is a risk factor for the condition), refraining from sleeping on one's back, and medications that reduce **rapid eye movement** (REM) sleep. A technique called continuous positive airway pressure (CPAP) pushes air into the sleeper's throat all night through a small mask, preventing the airway from collapsing. In addition, a surgical procedure is available that modifies the upper airway to allow for freer breathing.

The other main type of hypersomnia is narcolepsy—sudden attacks of REM sleep during waking hours. Many narcoleptics experience additional symptoms including cataplexy (a sudden loss of muscle tone while in a conscious state), **hallucinations** and other unusual perceptual phenomena, and sleep paralysis, an inability to move for several minutes upon awakening. Between 200,000 and 500,000 Americans are affected by narcolepsy, which is caused by a physiological brain dysfunction that can be inherited or develop after trauma to the brain from disease or injury. Treatments include stimulants to combat daytime sleepiness, tricyclic antidepressants to suppress REM sleep, and other medications to control cataplexy.

Disorders of the Sleep-Wake Schedule—the third type of sleep disturbance—are also called circadian rhythm disorders because they interfere with the 24-hour biological clock that regulates many bodily processes. People with these disorders have trouble adhering to the sleep-wake schedule required by their job or **environment,** often due to shift work or jet lag. However, some persons suffer from delayed or advanced sleep onset problems with no external aggravating factor. Exposure to bright lights and chronotherapy, a technique for resetting one's biological clock, have been effective in the treatment of some circadian rhythm disorders.

Parasomnias, the final category of sleep disorder, involve unusual phenomena—nightmares, sleep terrors, and sleepwalking—that occur during sleep or during the period between sleeping and waking. Nightmare and sleep terror disorders are similar in that both occur mainly in children and involve frightening nighttime awakenings (in the case of sleep terrors, the person is awakened from non-REM sleep by feelings of agitation that can last for up to 10 minutes). Both are often outgrown but may be treated with **psychotherapy**, low-dose benzodiazepines, and, in the case of nightmare disorder, relaxation training. Sleepwalking occurs during the deep non-REM sleep of stages three and four and is also most common in children, who tend to outgrow it after the age of 12. It is also more common among males than females. The greatest danger posed by sleepwalking is injury through falls or other mishaps.

Other features of parasomnias include bruxism (teeth grinding) and enuresis (bedwetting). Both are often stress-related, although enuresis may also be caused by genitourinary disorders, neurological disturbances, or toilet training problems. Bruxism may be relieved through relaxation techniques or the use of a custom-made oral device that discourages grinding or at least prevents tooth damage. Enuresis often responds to the medication imipramine (Tofranil) and various **behavior modification** techniques. A parasomnia only identified within the past decade is REM sleep behavior disorder. Those affected by this condition—usually middle-aged or older men—engage in vigorous and bizarre physical activities during REM sleep in response to **dreams**, which are generally of a violent, intense nature. As their actions may injure themselves or their sleeping partners, this disorder, thought to be neurological in nature, has been treated with hypnosis and medications including clonazepam and carbamazepine.

Further Reading

Hales, Dianne R. *The Complete Book of Sleep: How Your Nights Affect Your Days.* Reading, MA: Addison-Wesley Longman, 1981.

Lamberg, Lynne. *The American Medical Association Guide to Better Sleep.* New York: Random House, 1984.

Smell

The sense that perceives odor by means of the nose and olfactory nerve.

Olfaction is one of the two chemical senses: smell and taste. Both arise from interaction between a chemical and receptor cells. In olfaction, the chemical is volatile, or airborne. Breathed in through the nostrils or taken in via the throat by chewing and swallowing, it passes through either the nose or an opening in the palate at the back of the mouth, and moves toward receptor cells located in the lining of the nasal passage. As the chemical moves past the receptor cells, part of it is absorbed into the uppermost surface of the nasal passages called the olfactory epithelium, located at the top of the nasal cavity. There, two one-inch-square patches of tissue covered with mucus dissolve the odor, stimulating the receptors, which lie under the mucus. The chemical molecules bind to the receptors, triggering impulses that travel to the **brain.** There are thousands of different receptors in the cells of the nasal cavity that can detect as many as 10,000 different odors. Each receptor contains hair-like structures, or cilia, which are probably the initial point of contact with olfactory stimuli. Research suggests that the sensitivity of the olfactory system is related to the number of both receptors and cilia. For example, a dog has 20 times as many receptor cells as a human and over 10 times as many cilia per receptor.

The cribriform plate forms the roof of the nasal cavity. The olfactory nerve passes through openings in this bone and ends in the olfactory bulb, a neural structure at the base of the brain. From there, olfactory signals are diffused throughout the brain to areas including the amygdala, hippocampus, pyriform cortex (located at the base of the temporal lobe), and the **hypothalamus.** Olfaction is the only sense that does not involve the **thalamus.** Olfaction messages are especially intensive in the amygdala, a part of the brain responsible for **emotion**s, which may help the unusual power of certain smells to trigger emotions and recollections based on memories from the past. Further, a person's reaction to smell is mediated by context. For example, the same smell present in body odor is responsible for the flavor of cheese. In the first case, the smell is perceived as negative, in the second, it is positive. In humans, olfaction intensifies the taste of food, warns of potentially dangerous food, as well as other dangers (such as fire), and triggers associations involving **memory** and emotion. Olfaction is an especially important sense in many animals. A predator may use it to detect prey, while prey may use it to avoid predators. It also has a role in the mating process through chemicals called pheromones, which can cause ovulation in females or signal a male that a female is in a sexually receptive state. Although the existence of human pheromones has not been verified, olfaction still plays a role in human sexual attraction, as well as in parenting. Mothers can usually identify their newborn infants by smell, and breast-feeding babies can distinguish between the smell of their mothers and that of other breast-feeding women. Researchers have also found that children are able to recognize their siblings by smell and parents can use smell to distinguish among their own children. However, as people age the sense of smell diminishes, especially for men. By age 80, many men have almost no ability to detect odors. The intensity of a particular odor is strongly affected by **adaptation.** Odors may become undetectable after only a brief period of exposure. The sense of smell also plays an important role in the discrimination of flavors, a fact demonstrated by the reduced sense of taste in people with colds. The enjoyment of food actually comes more from odors detected by the olfactory system than from the functioning of the taste system. The olfactory and gustatory (taste) pathways are known to converge in parts of the brain, although it is not known exactly how the two systems work together. While an aversion to certain flavors (such as bitter flavors) is innate, associations with odors are learned.

Social Influence

The influence of others on an individual's behavior.

Human behavior is influenced by other people in countless ways and on a variety of levels. The mere presence of others—as co-actors or spectators—can stimulate or improve one's performance of a task, a process known as social facilitation (and also observed in non-human species). However, the increased level of **arousal** responsible for this phenomenon can backfire and create social interference, impairing performance on complex, unfamiliar, and difficult tasks.

Overt, deliberate persuasion by other people can cause us to change our opinions and/or behavior. However, a great deal of social influence operates more subtly in the form of **norms**—acquired social rules that people are generally unaware of until they are violated. For example, every culture has a norm for "personal space"—the physical distance maintained between adults. Violation of this (and other) norms generally makes people uncom-

fortable, while adherence to them provides security and confidence in a variety of social situations. Norms may be classified as one of two types: descriptive and injunctive. Descriptive norms are simply based on what a majority of people do, while injunctive norms involve a value judgment about what is proper and improper behavior.

Both **conformity** and compliance are attempts to adhere to social norms—conformity occurs in response to unspoken group pressure, as opposed to compliance, which results from a direct request. Research has shown that conformity is influenced by the ambiguity of a situation (people are more apt to go along with the majority when they are uncertain about which course of action to pursue), the size of the majority, and the personal characteristics of the people involved, including their self-esteem and their status within the group. A person may conform by acting in accordance with group norms while privately disagreeing with them (public conformity) or by actually changing his or her opinions to coincide with those of the group (private acceptance).

In contrast to compliance, which characterizes behavior toward those who make direct requests but have no authority over us, obedience is elicited in response to a specific demand by an authority figure. The most famous experiment involving obedience was conducted by Stanley Milgram in the early 1960s at Yale University. Forty men and women were instructed to administer electric shocks to another person, supposedly as part of an experiment in learning. (In fact, there were actually no shocks administered, and responses were faked by the "victim," who was part of the experiment.) When the scientist in charge directed the subjects to administer increasingly severe shocks, most of them, while uncomfortable, did so in spite of the apparent **pain** and protests of the supposed victim. This experiment—which is often referred to in connection with German obedience to authority during the Nazi era—gained widespread attention as evidence of the extent to which people will forfeit their own judgment, will, and values in order to follow orders by an authority figure (65 percent of the volunteers, when asked to do so, administered the maximum level of shock possible). In variations on this experiment, Milgram found that factors affecting obedience included the reputation of the authority figure and his proximity to the subject (obedience decreased when instructions were issued by phone), as well as the presence of others who disobey (the most powerful factor in reducing the level of obedience).

Another type of social influence that can lead **normal** people to engage in cruel or antisocial behavior is participation in a crowd or mob. Being part of a crowd can allow a person's **identity** to become submerged in a group, a process known as deindividuation. Contributing factors include **anonymity,** which brings with it a reduction of accountability; a high level of **arousal;** and a shifting of attention from oneself to external events, resulting in reduced self-awareness. The so-called "herd mentality" that results weakens people's normal restraints against impulsive behavior, increases their sensitivity to environmental stimuli, and reduces their abilities to think rationally and fear censure by others.

The relatively new field of environmental psychology investigates the ways in which human behavior is affected by proximity to others in urban **environment**s, most notably the effects of noise and overcrowding. Living in high-density environments has been associated with feelings of helplessness resulting from lack of control and predictability in one's social interactions.

Further Reading

Freedman, J. L.; D. O. Sears; and J. M. Carlsmith. *Social Psychology.* 4th ed. Englewood Cliffs, NJ: Prentice-Hall, 1981.

Milgram, Stanley. *Obedience to Authority: An Experimental View.* New York: Harper and Row, 1974.

Paulus, P. B., ed. *Psychology of Group Influence.* 2nd ed. Hillsdale, NJ: Lawrence Erlbaum Associates, 1989.

Social Learning Theory

An approach to personality that emphasizes the interaction between personal traits and environment and their mediation by cognitive processes.

Social learning theory has its roots in the behaviorist notion of human behavior as being determined by learning, particularly as shaped by **reinforcement** in the form of rewards or **punishment**. Early research in behaviorism conducted by **Ivan Pavlov,** John Watson, and **B. F. Skinner** used animals in a laboratory. Subsequently, researchers became dissatisfied with the capacity of their findings to fully account for the complexities of human **personality**. Criticism centered particularly on the fact that behaviorism's focus on observable behaviors left out the role played by **cognition**.

The first major theory of social learning, that of Julian B. Rotter, argued that cognition, in the form of expectations, is a crucial factor in social learning. In his influential 1954 book, *Social Learning and Clinical Psychology,* Rotter claimed that behavior is determined by two major types of "expectancy": the expected outcome of a behavior and the value a person places on that outcome. In *Applications of a Social Learning Theory of Personality* (1972), Rotter, in collaboration with June Chance and Jerry Phares, described a general theory of personality with variables based on the ways that different individuals habitually think about their experiences.

One of the major variables was I-E, which distinguished "internals," who think of themselves as controlling events, from "externals," who view events as largely outside their control. Correlations have since been found between I-E orientations and a variety of behaviors, ranging from job performance to **attitudes** toward one's health.

The social learning theories of **Albert Bandura** emphasize the reciprocal relationship among cognition, behavior, and **environment**, for which Bandura coined the term reciprocal **determinism**. Hostile thoughts can result in hostile behavior, for example, which can effect our environment by making others hostile and evoking additional hostile thoughts. Thus, not only does our environment influence our thoughts and behavior—our thoughts and behavior also play a role in determining our environment. Bandura is especially well known for his research on the importance of **imitation** and **reinforcement** in learning. His work on **modeling** has been influential in the development of new therapeutic approaches, especially the methods used in **cognitive-behavior therapy**. Bandura also expanded on Rotter's notion of expectancy by arguing that our expectations about the outcome of situations are heavily influenced by whether or not we think we will succeed at the things we attempt. Bandura introduced the term self-efficacy for this concept, arguing that it has a high degree of influence not only on our expectations but also on our performance itself.

Most recently, Walter Mischel, building on the work of both Rotter and Bandura, has framed the determinants of human behavior in particular situations in terms of "person variables." These include competencies (those things we know we can do); perceptions (how we perceive our environment); expectations (what we expect will be the outcome of our behavior); subject values (our goals and ideals); and self-regulation and plans (our standards for ourselves and plans for reaching our goals).

Further Reading

Bandura, Albert. *Social Learning Theory.* Englewood Cliffs, NJ: Prentice-Hall, 1971.

———. *Social Foundations of Thought and Action: A Social Cognitive Theory.* Englewood Cliffs, NJ: Prentice-Hall, 1986.

Social Perception

The processes through which people form impressions of others and interpret information about them.

Researchers have confirmed the conventional wisdom that first impressions are important. Studies show that first impressions are easily formed, difficult to change, and have a long-lasting influence. Rather than absorbing each piece of new information about an individual in a vacuum, it is common for people to invoke a preexisting prototype or schema based on some aspect of the person (for example, "grandmother" or "graduate student"), modifying it with specific information about the particular individual to arrive at an overall first impression. One term for this process is schema-plus-correction. It can be dangerous because it allows people to infer many things from a very limited amount of information, which partially explains why first impressions are often wrong.

If there is no special reason to think negatively about a person, one's first impression of that person will normally be positive, as people tend to give others the benefit of the doubt. However, people are especially attentive to negative factors, and if these are present, they will outweigh the positive ones in generating impressions. One reason first impressions are so indelible is that people have a tendency to interpret new information about a person in a light that will reinforce their first impression. They also tend to remember the first impression, or overall schema, better than any subsequent corrections. Thus if a person whom one thinks of as competent makes a mistake, it will tend to be overlooked and eventually forgotten, and the original impression is the one that will prevail. Conversely, one will tend to forget or undervalue good work performed by someone initially judged to be incompetent. In addition, people often treat each other in ways that tend to elicit behavior that conforms to their impressions of each other.

Besides impression formation, the other key area focused on in the study of social perception is *attribution,* the thought processes we employ in explaining the behavior of other people and our own as well. The most fundamental observation we make about a person's behavior is whether it is due to internal or external causes (Is the behavior determined by the person's own characteristics or by the situation in which it occurs?). We tend to base this decision on a combination of three factors. *Consensus* refers to whether other people exhibit similar behavior; *consistency* refers to whether the behavior occurs repeatedly; and *distinctiveness* is concerned with whether the behavior occurs in other, similar situations.

Certain cognitive biases tend to influence whether people attribute behavior to internal or external causes. When we observe the behavior of others, our knowledge of the external factors influencing that behavior is limited, which often leads us to attribute it to internal factors (a tendency known as the fundamental attribution error). However, we are aware of numerous external factors that play a role in our own behavior. This fact, combined with a natural desire to think well of ourselves, produces actor-observer bias, a tendency to attribute our own behav-

ior (especially when inappropriate or unsuccessful) to external factors.

Further Reading
Zebrowitz, Leslie. *Social Perception.* Pacific Grove, CA: Brooks/Cole Publishing Co., 1990.

Social Psychology

The study of the psychology of interpersonal relationships.

Social psychology is the study of human interaction, including communication, cooperation, competition, leadership, and attitude development. Although the first textbooks on the subject of social psychology were published in the early 1900s, much of the foundation for social psychology studied in the 1990s is based on the work of the behavioral psychologists of the 1930s. Behavioral psychologists were among the first to call for scientific measures and analysis of human behavior, an emphasis on which social psychologists continue to focus. Social psychologists also study the way individuals behave in relationship to others, and alternatively, how groups act to shape the behavior of individuals.

As do other scientists, social psychologists develop a theory and then design experiments to test it. For example, Leon Feistinger, an American social psychologist, theorized that a person feels uncomfortable when confronted with information that contradicts something he or she already believes. He labeled this uneasiness **cognitive dissonance.** Other social psychologists subsequently conducted research to confirm Feistinger's theory by studying individuals who believed themselves to be failures. The psychologists found that such people avoid success, even when it would be easily achieved, because it would conflict with their firmly held belief that they are unsuccessful.

Social psychologists work in academic settings, teaching and conducting research. They also work with businesses and other organizations to design personnel management programs based on their knowledge of interpersonal relations. Social psychologists also contribute their expertise to market research, government agencies, and educational institutions.

Further Reading
Argyle, Michael. *The Social Psychology of Everyday Life.* New York: Routledge, 1992.
Aronson, Elliot. *The Social Animal.* New York: W.H. Freeman, 1995.
Bandura, Albert. *Social Foundations of Thought and Action: A Social and Cognitive Theory.* Englewood Cliffs, NJ: Prentice-Hall, 1986.

Key to each person's enjoyment of activities like rafting is how well the group members work together as a team. Social psychologists study the way groups influence behavior of individuals.

Baron, Robert A. *Exploring Social Psychology.* Boston, MA: Allyn and Bacon, 1989.

Socialization

The process by which a person learns to conform individual behavior and responses to the norms and values of society.

Socialization is a lifelong process that begins during **infancy** in the complex interaction between parent and child. As parents respond to a baby's physical requirements for food and shelter, they are also beginning to teach the baby what to expect from their **environment** and how to communicate their needs. The action-reaction cycle of smiling, cooing, and touching is a child's earliest interaction with "society." It is believed that these early interactions during infancy play a major role in future social **adjustment**. Consistent, responsive care helps lead to healthy relationships with others and normal personal development. Caretakers who neglect an infant's needs or otherwise stifle early attempts at communication can cause serious damage to the child's future social interactions.

The family is the most influential socialization force. Parents, grandparents, and siblings all transmit to infants and young children what they consider to be important values, behavior, skills, and **attitudes**. Household rules govern behavior, interpersonal behavior serves as a model for interactions with outside people, and socially valued qualities such as generosity and caring are learned through example within the home and in the culture. As children grow and interact more with the environment outside the family home, others begin to play important roles in the socialization process. Friends, institutions such as church and school, the media (particularly **television**) and co-workers all become important factors in shaping a person's attitudes and behavior.

Researchers have theorized that socialization is a complex process that involves both personal and environmental factors. For example, studies of aggressive tendencies in children have pointed out that certain children are more influenced than others when exposed to television **violence** or aggressive behavior by authority figures in the home. Some blind and deaf children display aggressive behavior such as stamping feet or yelling even though they have never had the opportunity to see or hear such displays of temper. Thus, it has been concluded that genetic factors must also be considered part of the socialization process.

Studies of sex-type models also point to this complex interaction between environmental and genetic factors. While many researchers believe that most of the stereotypical differences between boys and girls are invalid, some do appear significant. For example, boys tend to perform better on tests involving spatial relationships, and girls tend to score better on tests involving verbal skills. There is such an overlap among boys and girls, even on these tests, that it would be impossible to predict the scores of an individual boy or girl. It is believed, however, that perceived differences often affect the behavior of one of the most influential socialization forces of children—teachers. Some teachers reinforce the male image of dominance and independence by responding more to boys and demanding more from them in the classroom. Girls are often rewarded for passive, less demanding behavior. Similarly, some parents respond differently to sons and daughters, encouraging stereotypical behavior and traditionally male or female hobbies and careers. Media portrayals of one-dimensional characters can also perpetuate sex role **stereotype**s.

Further Reading

Clark, John, ed. *The Mind: Into the Inner World.* New York: Torstar Books, 1986.

Zimbardo, Philip G. *Psychology and Life.* Glenview, IL: Scott, Foresman, 1988.

Speech. See **Language Acquisition.**

Speech Disorders

Speech disturbances that interfere with communication.

The origins of speech disorders can vary. Those that are caused by **brain** lesions or a malfunction of the brain or **central nervous system** are referred to as *organic,* while those with no apparent physical cause are considered *functional.* Most organic speech disorders are induced by cerebral hemorrhage. Other causes include brain tumors, injuries suffered during **birth,** head wounds, and infectious diseases such as meningitis.

Speech disorders may be divided into the following four types according to symptom: rhythm, phonation, articulation, and symbolization. The main rhythm disorder is stuttering (usually used interchangeably with "stammering"), a condition in which the normal flow of speech is broken and difficulty in pronunciation is encountered at the beginning of words, with sudden breaks and spasms once the individual begins to speak. Other characteristics of stuttering include excessive pauses, repetition, self-cor-

rection, and interference with grammatical structures. No known organic cause has been found for stuttering, which, like most other rhythm disorders, is psychological in nature. Although stuttering usually disappears on its own, temporary alleviation may be obtained through distraction devices and feedback methods. Nonetheless, long-term help must address the underlying psychological causes of the problem, for example, **desensitization** to feared situations. Another speech disorder that is often confused with stuttering is cluttering, which consists of overly rapid speech; words and phrases that are omitted, run together, or even reversed; and a characteristic "flat" tone of voice. Stuttering and cluttering appear to be diametrically opposed in terms of their psychological origins; whereas stutterers tend to be introspective and shy, clutterers are generally aggressive and extroverted.

Phonation disorders involve disturbances in speech timbre, intensity, or pitch. They include guttural and falsetto (artificially high) speech, excessively nasal speech, and the disordered speech sounds associated with a cleft palate. These disorders, which are physical rather than psychological in origin, are more readily corrected by a speech therapist. Articulatory disorders are characterized by the distortion, omission, and substitution of speech sounds and the addition of extra sounds. Among these disorders are delayed speech; lalling, which involves sluggishness in the tip of the tongue; lisping; and the use of infantile sounds (baby talk) past two or three years of age.

Symbolization disorders (generally **aphasia** or dysphasia) primarily involve problems with word meanings, although they may be accompanied by pronunciation difficulties as well. The scientific investigation of these types of speech disorders has been linked to the study of speech centers in the brain since the late nineteenth century. The most well-known pioneers in this area were Paul Pierre Broca (1924–1880) and Carl Wernicke (1848–1905), each of whom gave his name to one of two areas of the brain essential to coherent speech. Two major types of aphasia can be distinguished from each other by their origin in either Broca's area in the left frontal lobe, or Wernicke's area in the left temporal lobe (both located on the side of the brain that controls speech in most of the population, including 95 percent of right-handed people).

Aphasia resulting from damage to Broca's area is characterized by the inability to combine words into a coherent sequence and, in certain cases, combining sounds into coherent words. A person who has aphasia associated with Wernicke's area experiences difficulties in choosing the correct words with which to express himself, although he has a clear idea of what he wants to say (a condition specifically known as anomia.) People with this disorder will often substitute all-purpose terms such as "thing" for the specific word or words they are unable to find. They may also use incorrect words (paraphasia), produce meaningless words, or insert incorrect sounds into words. Other organic speech disorders include dysarthria and apraxia, both involving difficulty with articulation originating from abnormalities in either the language centers in the brain or the voluntary nervous system.

Two disorders involving word comprehension are technically classified as speech disorders, specifically "disorders of input." With auditory agnosia, the listener cannot distinguish familiar speech sounds. In "pure word deafness," individual sounds are apparently recognized, but the hearer lacks the ability to combine them into comprehensible words.

Further Reading

Berger, Gilda. *Speech and Language Disorders.* New York: F. Watts, 1981.

Skinner, Paul H. *Speech, Language, and Hearing: Normal Processes and Disorders.* Reading, MA: Addison-Wesley, 1978.

Split-Brain Technique

Procedure used to study the activities of the two hemispheres of the brain separately, and independent of each other.

Psychologists have demonstrated that even simple human tasks, like thinking of a word when viewing an object, involve separate subtasks within the **brain.** These smaller tasks involve identifying the object, assessing its use, remembering what other objects are related to it, determining how many syllables are in the word associated with the object, and so on.

People do not realize the complexity of seemingly simple tasks because the brain integrates information smoothly and flawlessly almost all the time. One structure in the brain involved in the exchange and integration of information from one part to the next is the corpus callosum, a bundle of about 200 million **nerve** fibers that connect the right and left hemispheres of the brain.

Beginning in the 1940s, neurologists questioned whether the corpus callosum was involved in the development of epileptic seizures. Evidence from monkeys suggested that abnormal neural responses in one hemisphere spread to the other via the corpus callosum, resulting in major seizure activity. As such, it might be beneficial to patients suffering from **epilepsy** to sever the corpus callosum in order to prevent the spread of this abnormal neural activity. After some initial problems with the surgical procedure, neurologists documented the benefit of such surgery, called cerebral commisurotomy. This so-called split-brain surgery resulted in an increase

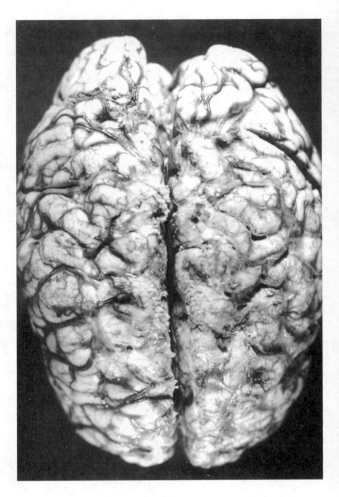

The top of the human brain. The corpus callosum lies in the fissure between the two brain hemispheres.

in split-brain research. One of the primary researchers in this area was neurosurgeon Roger Sperry (1913–1994).

Research neurosurgeons discovered that after surgery, patients often experienced a short period during which they could not speak and had difficulty controlling the left side of their bodies. This set of problems probably, called acute disconnection syndrome, reflected the trauma caused by the surgery itself. After the patient recovered from this trauma, his or her everyday behavior appeared unchanged. The two hemispheres of the brain were no longer directly connected, so information from one half of the brain should not have been able to get to the other. Researchers required subtle and sophisticated techniques to be able to differentiate people whose corpus callosum had been cut from those with intact brains.

Such techniques involve using apparatus that can present visual information so that it goes to only one side of the brain. In this case, split-brain patients may not be

344

able to label a picture that stimulates on the right side of the brain; they may have no difficulty when the left side of the brain, which normally controls language production, receives stimulation. At the same time, research in the area has been conflicting. Some work reveals considerable sophistication in language ability in the right hemisphere. Although language functions do differ across hemispheres, split-brain research has not completely resolved the issue about the nature and the degree to which the left and right hemispheres differ.

More recent research has suggested that the left hemisphere may be involved in much linguistic behavior because of its strength in dealing with analytical, structured tasks. On the other hand, the right hemisphere may be better in spatial tasks because these tasks require holistic, synthetic functioning, the strength of the right hemisphere.

When the patients were asked to point to pictures of the normal faces, they selected the normal face associated with the half of the chimeric face that stimulated the right hemisphere. When forced to respond verbally, the patients showed a preference for the picture that had stimulated the left hemisphere. Although researchers cannot specify the exact differences in the functioning of the two hemispheres, regular differences along visual and linguistic lines have emerged.

Although the research has demonstrated differences in the functioning of the two hemispheres of the brain, everyday behavior may appear completely **normal** in split-brain patients. This is true because human behavior is very flexible and adaptable. For example, a split-brain patient might turn the head when focusing on an object; thereby stimulating both hemispheres. Further, these patients use cross-cuing in which they invoke as many different modalities, like **vision,** audition, and touch, to help them make sense of their world.

See also Left-Brain Hemisphere; Psychosurgery; Right-Brain Hemisphere.

Further Reading

Springer, S. P., and G. Deutsch. *Left Brain, Right Brain.* 2d ed. New York: W. H. Freeman, 1985.

Sports Psychology

A developing subfield of psychology concerned with applying psychological theories and research to sports and other recreational activities.

Sports—which involve **emotion, competition,** cooperation, achievement, and play—provide a rich area for psychological study. People involved in sports attempt to master very difficult skills, often subjecting themselves to intense physical stress as well as social pressure. When psychologists began studying sports in the 1930s and 1940s, they focused on motor performance and the acquisition of motor skills. Sports psychology emerged as a distinct discipline in the 1960s, dominated by theories of **social psychology.** Since then, research has expanded into numerous areas such as imagery training, **hypnosis,** relaxation training, **motivation, socialization,** conflict and competition, counseling, and coaching. Specific sports and recreational specialties studied include baseball, basketball, soccer, volleyball, tennis, golf, fencing, dance, and many others.

Three primary areas of sports research are **personality,** motivation, and **social influence.** Personality studies have investigated whether there are specific traits that distinguish athletes from non-athletes. Although most of these studies failed to yield significant results, some valid connections were made between success in athletics and positive **mental health.** Research on wrestlers, runners, and oarsmen found lower levels of **depression,** tension, **hostility,** and fatigue among more successful athletes when compared with their peers and with the general population. Individual differences within a sport have also been studied. One instrument devised for this type of investigation is the Sport Competition Anxiety Test (SCAT), developed by Rainer Martens, which measures levels of **anxiety** in competitive sport. Studies of motivation have focused on optimum **arousal** levels for athletes. Mostly such studies have corroborated existing research on arousal by relating peak performance to a moderate, optimum arousal level, with performance diminishing if arousal is either increased or decreased from that level. Negative effects of excess arousal include inefficient movement patterns and loss of sensitivity to environmental cues. In successful athletes, the **ability** to control arousal and focus attention has proven to be as important as the level of arousal itself. Motivation in sports has also been approached from the angle of **behavior modification,** with attention to such issues as the effects of intrinsic versus extrinsic rewards.

Studies of social influence, which were predominant in the 1960s and 1970s, focused on such issues as the influence of spectators, teammates, and competitors. Sports psychologists have also studied specific types of behavior. For example, the origin and effect of **aggression** in sports have been investigated by researchers testing the concept of sport as a cathartic release of aggression. (It was found that aggressive sports tend to increase rather than diminish hostility and aggression.) The social dynamics of team sports have also been studied. Psychological theories from other subfields, such as social psychology and behavioral psychology, have been applied successfully to the study of sports and rec-

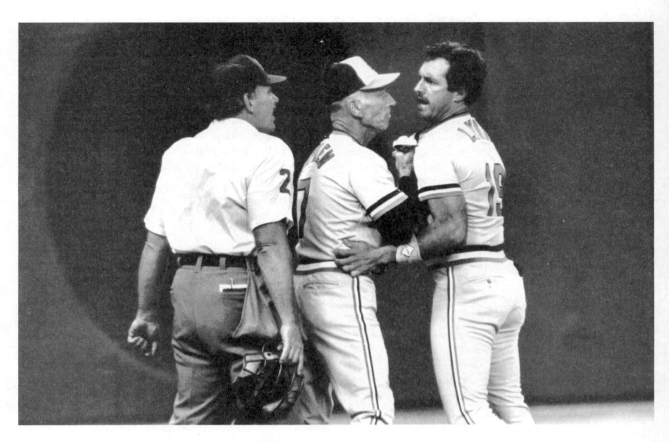

Athletes work with sports psychologists in areas as diverse as relaxation techniques, imagery training, motivation, and conflict resolution.

reation. At times, research has yielded findings which are different from those seen in these more traditional areas. Contrary to what a behavioral psychologist might predict, for instance, some studies done on coaching behaviors reveal that effective methods of instruction are not always related to high levels of praise or positive **reinforcement.** The common behavior of coaches, even successful ones, is disproportionately composed of scolding and "hustling," or urging on, rather than providing supportive feedback. Another finding that goes against conventional wisdom is that team cohesiveness in team-oriented sports does not necessarily lead to top performance.

Following the already existing practice in Europe, sports psychologists in North America now work directly with professional athletes and teams to help improve performance. Techniques applied include anxiety management, progressive relaxation, autogenic training, **biofeedback,** hypnosis, and **cognitive behavioral therapy. Mental imagery, attention** control, goal-setting, and work on interpersonal skills are also part of sports psychology programs for athletes. Positive results have been reported in enhancing performance and controlling anxiety.

As the study of sports psychology has grown, it has borrowed less from other specialties, such as **behaviorism,** making its own contributions to the field of psychology. The unique findings in this discipline have contributed to other, more conventional areas of psychology and are recognized as having significant applications to the mental health of the general population. One example can be seen in numerous research reports which have cited the benefits of jogging and other sports in alleviating depression. (Some studies have found that running is equal to **psychotherapy** in its ability to relieve depressive symptoms.) Sports psychology has also gained recognition through the popularity of such books as Thaddeus Kostrubala's *The Joy of Running,* David Kauss's *Peak Performance,* and Timothy Gallwey's "inner game" books. Psychologically-oriented instruction books such as Vic Braden's *Tennis for the Future* have also gained wide audiences. Principles developed through sports research, such as attention control training, have also been adapted for use in business and other organizational settings. Coaching and fitness models and other sports psychology concepts have been used in training managers and supervisors. Books on this topic include *Coaching for Improved Work Performance* by Ferdinand Fournies and *Coaching, Learning, and Action* by B.C. Lovin and E. Casstevens.

As medical findings continue to support the role of exercise and fitness in building and maintaining health, people are interested in learning how they can apply related information to build skills and enjoy their activities more fully. These individuals become likely subjects, along with athletes, for psychologists seeking to do research or to provide counseling in the area of sports and recreation.

While there is no specific division devoted to sports psychology within the **American Psychological Association,** those involved in the discipline may join the Academy of Sport Psychology International (ASPI), the American College of Sports Medicine, the International Society of Sports Psychology, or various other organizations. English-language journals in the field include the *Journal of Sport Psychology,* the *International Journal of Sport Psychology,* the *Journal of Sport and Social Issues,* and *Psychology of Motor Behavior and Sport.*

Further Information

Academy of Sport Psychology International (ASPI)
    Address: 6079 Northgate Rd.,
    Columbus, Ohio 43229
    Telephone: 614-846-2275
American College of Sports Medicine
    Address: P.O. Box 1440, Indianapolis,
    Indiana 46206-1440
    Telephone: 317-637-9200
International Society of Sports Psychology
    Address: Department of Kinesiology,
    University of Illinois at Urbana-Champaign,
    906 S. Goodwin Ave.,
    Urbana, Illinois 61801
    Telephone: 217- 333-6563

Further Reading

Bird, Anne Marie. *Psychology and Sport Behavior.* St. Louis: Times Mirror/Mosby College Pub., 1986.

Cratty, Bryant J. *Psychology in Contemporary Sport: Guidelines for Coaches and Athletes.* Englewood Cliffs, NJ: Prentice-Hall, 1983.

LeUnes, Arnold D. *Sport Psychology: An Introduction.* Chicago: Nelson-Hall, 1996.

Standardized Test

A test administered to a group of subjects under exactly the same experimental conditions and scored in exactly the same way.

Standardized tests are used in psychology, as well as in everyday life, to measure **intelligence**, aptitude, achievement, **personality**, **attitudes** and interests. Attempts are made to standardize tests in order to eliminate biases that may result, consciously or unconsciously, from varied administration of the test. Standardized tests are used to produce **norm**s—or statistical standards—that provide a basis for comparisons among individual members of the group of subjects. Tests must be standardized, reliable (give consistent results), and valid before they can be considered useful psychological tools.

Standardized tests are highly controversial both in psychological circles and particularly in education because true standardization is difficult to attain. Certain requirements must be rigidly enforced. For example, subjects must be given exactly the same amount of time to take the test. Directions must be given using precisely the same wording from group to group, with no embellishments, encouragement, or warnings. Scoring must be exact and consistent. Even an unwitting joke spoken by the test administrator that relaxes the subjects or giving a test in a room that is too hot or too cold could be considered violations of standardization specifications. Because of the difficulty of meeting such stringent standards, standardized tests are widely criticized.

Critics of the use of standardized tests for measuring educational achievement or classifying children are critical for other reasons as well. They say the establishment of norms does not give enough specific information about what children know. Rather, they reveal the average level of knowledge. Secondly, critics contend that such tests encourage educators and the public to focus their **attention** on groups rather than on individuals. Improving tests scores to enhance public image or achieve public funding become more of a focus than teaching individual children the skills they need to advance. Another criticism is that the tests, by nature, cannot measure knowledge of complex skills such as problem solving and critical thinking. "Teaching to the test"—drilling students in how to answer fill-in-the-blank or multiple-choice questions—takes precedence over instruction in more practical, less objective skills such as writing or logic.

Achievement tests, I.Q. tests, and the **Stanford-Binet intelligence scales** are examples of widely used standardized tests.

Further Reading

Houts, Paul L., ed. *The Myth of Measurability.* New York: Hart Publishing Co., 1977.

Wallace, Betty, and William Graves. *Poisoned Apple: The Bell-Curve Crisis and How Our Schools Create Mediocrity and Failure.* New York: St. Martin's Press, 1995.

Zimbardo, Philip G. *Psychology and Life.* Glenview, IL: Scott, Foresman, 1988.

Stanford-Binet Intelligence Scales

The oldest and most influential intelligence test, devised in 1916 by Stanford psychologist Lewis Terman.

Consisting of questions and short tasks arranged from easy to difficult, the Stanford-Binet measures a wide variety of verbal and nonverbal skills. Its fifteen tests are divided into the following four cognitive areas: 1) verbal reasoning (vocabulary, comprehension, absurdities, verbal relations); 2) quantitative reasoning (math, number series, equation building); 3) abstract/visual reasoning (pattern analysis, matrices, paper folding and cutting, copying); and 4) short-term **memory** (memory for sentences, digits, and objects, and bead memory). While the child's **attitude** and behavior during the test are noted, they are not used to determine the result, which is arrived at by converting a single raw score for the entire test to a figure indicating **"mental age"** (the average age of a child achieving that score). A formula is then used to arrive at the **intelligence quotient,** or I.Q. An I.Q. of 100 means that the child's chronological and mental ages match. Traditionally, I.Q. scores of 90–109 are considered average, scores below 70 indicate **mental retardation. Gifted children** achieve scores of 140 or above. Most recently revised in 1986, the Stanford-Binet intelligence test can be used with children from age two, as well as with adults. Although some of its concepts—such as mental age and intelligence quotient—are being questioned, the test is still widely used to assess cognitive development and often to determine placement in special education classes.

See also Terman, Lewis; Wechsler Intelligence Scales.

Statistics

A branch of mathematics devoted to the collection, compilation, display, and interpretation of numerical data.

Psychologists rely heavily on statistics to help assess the meaning of the **measurement**s they make. Sometimes the measurements involve individuals who complete psychological tests; at other times, the measurements involve statistics that describe general properties of groups of people or animals.

In psychological testing, the psychologist may interpret test results in light of norms, or the typical results, provided from previous testing. In research, psychologists use two kinds of statistics, descriptive and inferential. Descriptive statistics simply give a general picture of the scores in a given group. They include the measures of central tendency and the measures of variability. Central tendency involves different kinds of averages: the **mean, median,** and **mode.** Variability involves the standard deviation, which indicates how far scores in a group are likely to be from the average.

Inferential statistics are used to help psychologists draw inferences, or conclusions, from the data obtained from their research. The most common statistical tests include the Student's t-test and the Analysis of Variance (or F-test); these statistics help the psychologist assess whether the differences in averages across groups are due to the effects of an independent variable. Another widely used statistical test is the correlation coefficient, which describes the strength of the relationship between two variables. For example, there is a positive correlation between a student's score on the **Scholastic Assessment Test (SAT)** and his/her grades in the first year of college. Correlations involve patterns that exist in groups; individuals within those groups may not perform in the manner the correlation predicts that they will, but if large numbers of students are tested, general trends may be detected.

Further Reading

Anderson, David Ray. *Introduction to Statistics: Concepts and Applications.* St. Paul, MN: West Pub. Co., 1990.

Bluman, Allan G. *Elementary Statistics: A Step-by-Step Approach.* Dubuque, IA: Wm. C. Brown Publishers, 1995.

Freund, John E. *Statistics: A First Course.* Englewood Cliffs, NJ: Prentice Hall, 1995.

Stereotype

An unvarying view about the physical appearance, personality, or behavior of a particular group of people.

Some people believe and perpetuate stereotypes about particular ethnic groups: Italians are emotionally sensitive, loud, and talk with their hands; Irish people drink too much; Germans are serious and intelligent. While such characteristics may apply to few members of that ethnic group, some people characterize all people in a certain group to share these **traits.** Psychologists have also noted the role stereotypes play in human **memory.** When meeting a new person, for example, people sometimes combine their firsthand **perception**s of that person—appearance, **personality, intelligence**—with stereotypes they have formed about similar people. Later, when trying to describe or recall that person, the actual characteristics become distorted by the stereotypical features that often have no relation to that person.

Television has been criticized for perpetuating stereotypes, particularly regarding racial groups and women. Studies have shown that early television programs, in particular, were guilty of portraying stereotyped characters. For instance, minorities were more likely than whites to be criminals, and women were often shown in the roles of wife, mother, or sex object. Children proved to be especially vulnerable to the influence of these stereotypes. The civil rights movement of the 1960s and the women's movement of the 1970s prompted the development of "prosocial" programs such as *Sesame Street* that sought to counter racial, ethnic, and gender stereotypes.

Further Reading

Liebert, Robert M.; Joyce N. Sprafkin; and Emily S. Davidson. *The Early Window: Effects of Television on Children and Youth.* New York: Pergamon Press, 1982.

Stress

The physiological and psychological responses to situations or events that disturb the equilibrium of an organism.

While there is little consensus among psychologists about the exact definition of stress, it is agreed that stress results when demands placed on an organism cause unusual physical, psychological, or emotional responses. In humans, stress originates from a multitude of sources and causes a wide variety of responses, both positive and negative. Despite its negative connotation, many experts believe some level of stress is essential for well-being and **mental health.**

Stressors—events or situations that cause stress—can range from everyday hassles such as traffic jams to chronic sources such as the threat of nuclear war or overpopulation. Much research has studied how people respond to the stresses of major life changes. The Life Events Scale lists these events as the top ten stressors: death of spouse, divorce, marital separation, jail term, death of close family member, personal injury or illness, marriage, loss of job through firing, marital reconciliation, and retirement. It is obvious from this list that even good things—marriage, retirement, and marital reconciliation—can cause substantial stress.

When presented with a stressful event or situation, the process of cognitive appraisal determines an individual's response to it. One option—to judge the stressor as irrelevant—would cause little disturbance and thus little stress. For example, a high school student who does not plan to attend college will experience much less stress during the **Scholastic Assessment Test (SAT)** than a student who wants to attend a top university, even though both are in the same situation. Another option is recognizing the stressor as disturbing, yet positive. Retirement or marriage could fit into this category. The judgment

LIFE EVENTS SCALE: TOP TEN STRESSORS

Death of a spouse

Divorce

Marital separation

Jail term

Death of close family member

Personal injury or illness

Marriage

Loss of job through firing

Marital reconciliation

Retirement

that a situation truly is stressful would cause the most disturbance and thus the most stress. For example, few people would consider a serious traffic accident as anything less than stressful. The magnitude of resulting stress from any situation generally depends upon a person's perceived **ability** to cope with it. If the stress is predictable—a scheduled dentist appointment, for example—it usually causes less stress. A person's ability to control the stressor also can mitigate its effects. A strong network of social support undermines the magnitude of stress in most situations.

Reactions to stress, then, vary by individual and the perceived threat presented by it. Psychological responses may include cognitive impairment—as in **test anxiety**—feelings of **anxiety, anger,** apathy, **depression,** and **aggression.** Behavioral responses may include a change in eating or drinking habits. Physiological responses also vary widely. The "fight or flight" response involves a complex pattern of innate responses that occur in reaction to emergency situations. The body prepares to handle the emergency by releasing extra sugar for quick energy; heart rate, blood pressure, and breathing increase; muscles tense; infection-preventing systems activate; and **hormones** are secreted to assist in garnering energy. The **hypothalamus,** often called the stress center of the **brain,** controls these emergency responses to perceived life-threatening situations.

Research has shown that stress is a contributing factor in a majority of disease cases. A relatively new area of behavioral medicine, psychoimmunology, has been developed to study how the body's immune system is affected by psychological causes like stress. While it is widely recognized that heart disease and ulcers may result from excess stress, psychoimmunologists believe many other types of illness also result from impaired immune capabilities due to stress. Cancer, allergies, and arthritis all may result from the body's weakened ability to defend itself because of stress.

Coping with stress is a subject of great interest and is the subject of many popular books and media coverage. One method focuses on eliminating or mitigating the effects of the stressor itself. For example, people who experience extreme stress when they encounter daily traffic jams along their route to work may decide to change their route to avoid the traffic, or change their schedule to less busy hours. Instead of trying to modify their response to the stressor, they attempt to alleviate the problem itself. Generally, this problem-focused strategy is considered the most effective way to battle stress. Another method, dealing with the effects of the stressor, is used most often in cases in which the stress is serious and difficult to change. Major illnesses, deaths, and catastrophes like hurricanes or airplane crashes cannot be changed, so people use **emotion**-focused methods in their attempts to cope. Examples of emotion-focused coping include exercise, drinking, and seeking support from emotional confidants. **Defense mechanisms** are unconscious coping methods that help to bury, but not cure, the stress. **Sigmund Freud** considered **repression**—pushing the source of stress to the **unconscious**—one way of coping with stress. Rationalization and **denial** are other common emotional responses to stress.

Further Reading

Tanner, Ogden. *Stress.* New York: Time-Life Books, 1976.

Stuttering. See **Speech Disorders.**

Suicide

The act of taking one's own life voluntarily and intentionally.

The annual death toll from suicide worldwide is 120,000, and it is the eighth leading cause of death in the United States, accounting for one percent of all deaths. Between 240,000 and 600,000 people in the U.S. and Canada attempt suicide every year, and over 30,000 succeed. The suicide rate is three times higher for men than for women in the United States, although females make three times as many suicide attempts as males. Traditionally, men over 45 and living alone are the demographic group at greatest risk for suicide. However, in the past 30 years youth suicides have risen alarmingly, with rates tripling for people aged 15 to 24. The accompanying table provides statistics on the suicide rate among persons aged 10 to 24 in 1980 and 1992. Suicide among women has also increased dramatically since 1960, when the ratio of male to female suicides was 4 to 1. Suicide rates vary sig-

nificantly among different ethnic groups in the United States; Native Americans have the highest rate at 13.6 per 100,000 (although there are sizable variations among tribes), compared with 12.9 for European-Americans, and 5.7 for African-Americans.

Attitudes toward suicide have varied throughout history. The ancient Greeks considered it an offense against the state, which was deprived of contributions by potentially useful citizens. The Romans, by comparison, thought that suicide could be a noble form of death, although they legislated against persons taking their own lives before an impending criminal conviction in order to insure their families' financial inheritance. Early Christianity, which downplayed the importance of life on earth, was not critical of suicide until the fourth century, when St. Augustine condemned it as a sin because it violated the sixth commandment ("Thou shalt not kill"). Eventually, the Roman Catholic Church excommunicated and even denied funeral rites to people who killed themselves. The medieval theologian St. Thomas Aquinas condemned suicide because it usurped God's power over life and death, and in *The Divine Comedy,* the great writer Dante placed suicides in one of the lowest circles of Hell. The view of suicide as a sin prevailed in Western societies for hundreds of years, and many people are still influenced by it, either consciously or unconsciously. Suicide was a felony and attempted suicide a misdemeanor in England until 1961.

One of the greatest influences on 20th-century notions about suicide has been French sociologist Emile Durkheim's 1897 work *Le suicide.* Analyzing French statistics on suicide, Durkheim concluded that suicide is primarily a function of the strength or weakness of a person's ties to family, religion, and community. Persons with weak social ties and those for whom such ties have been disrupted (such as divorced or widowed people) are the most vulnerable to suicide. Durkheim also categorized suicide into four types. Altruistic suicide is actually mandated by society, as in the case of *suttee,* where an Indian wife commits suicide by throwing herself on her husband's funeral pyre. In egoistic suicide, individuals kill themselves because they lack the social ties that could motivate them to go on living. Anomic suicide occurs following the loss of a spouse, child, job, or other significant connection to the community, and fatalistic suicides are committed by people driven to despair by dire external circumstances from which there appears to be no escape.

Twenty years after the publication of Durkheim's work, **Sigmund Freud** provided the first theory that addressed suicide in terms of one's inner mental and emotional state. In *Mourning and Melancholia* (1917), he proposed that suicide was the result of turning **hostility** toward a loved one back on oneself. In *Man Against*

Friends of four teenagers who committed suicide together console each other outside the funeral home prior to burial services for one of the victims. Suicide among teenagers has risen dramatically since 1960.

Himself (1936), Karl Menninger extended Freud's contribution to the psychodynamic study of suicide, relating it to other forms of self-destructive behavior such as alcoholism.

Today many possible contributing factors are associated with suicide. Psychological disorders linked to suicide include **depression**, **schizophrenia**, and **panic** disorder. A variety of research studies indicate a possible physiological predisposition to suicide as well. In a study of the Amish of southeastern Pennsylvania—a population whose close-knit community structure and isolation from such influences as **drugs** and alcohol make suicide extremely infrequent—four families accounted for 73 percent of suicides between 1880 and 1980, suggesting a hereditary tendency toward self-destructive impulses. Separate studies have found a correlation between suicide and levels of the neurotransmitter serotonin in the **brain. Personality** features associated with suicide include low self-esteem, impulsiveness, and what social learning theorists call an "external locus of control"—an orientation toward believing that one's fate is determined by forces beyond one's control.

Social scientists have found that media coverage of suicides can spur imitative behavior. In the 1970s, sociologist David P. Phillips found that increased numbers of people killed themselves following front-page coverage of suicides. He also observed that such articles had a "copycat" effect, primarily in the geographic area where the original suicides took place, and that the more publicity was focused on the event, the greater the effect of the suicide. The issue of whether fictional accounts of suicide in movies or **television** influence real life behavior is more controversial and harder to document, but evidence has been found to link increases in both attempted and completed suicide to the release of televised movies featuring suicide. Probably the best-known examples of this phenomenon are the 37 deaths by "Russian roulette" linked to the movie *The Deer Hunter.*

Suicide is the third leading cause of death among all adolescents and the second leading cause among college students. (See accompanying table.) The rate of suicide is highest at the beginning of the school year and at the end of each academic term. Teenagers who contemplate or commit suicide are likely to have family problems, such as an alcoholic parent, an unwanted stepparent, or some other ongoing source of conflict. The breakup of romantic relationships is among the most common triggering factors—one study found over a third of suicidal teens were involved in the final stages of a relationship. Teen pregnancy can be another contributing factor. Drug and alcohol problems are closely related to teen suicide—one study found that drinking had preceded about a third of all suicide attempts by teenagers. In another study, almost half of all suicides between the ages of 15 and 19 in a particular geographic area were found to have alcohol in their blood.

Various harmful myths have been perpetuated about suicide. One is that people who talk about killing themselves do not actually do it—in fact, one of the main warning signs of suicide is thinking and talking about it. Another myth is the fatalistic idea that people who want to kill themselves will keep trying until they eventually succeed. For many people, the suicidal urge is related to a temporary crisis that will pass. Of all people who attempt suicide, 90 percent never try again. Yet another myth is the idea that nothing can be done to stop someone who is bent on suicide. Most people who feel suicidal are ambivalent about their intentions. Mental health profes-

sionals claim that all persons contemplating suicide give at least one warning, and 80 percent provide repeated warnings. If these warnings are heeded, potential suicides can be averted. Common warning signs include giving away prized possessions; changes in eating or sleeping habits; social withdrawal; declining performance at work or in school; and violent or rebellious behavior.

Suicide can be averted when family members or friends recognize these and other warnings and actively seek help for a loved one contemplating suicide. Suicide hotlines staffed by paraprofessional volunteers are an important source of support and assistance to people who are thinking of killing themselves. **Psychotherapy** can help a troubled person build self-esteem, frustration tolerance, and goal orientation. In cases of severe depression, antidepressant medication is an important resource; **electroconvulsive therapy** is recommended for persons who have not been helped by medication or who are so severely suicidal that it is considered too risky to wait until medication can take effect.

SUICIDE RATE* AMONG PERSONS AGES 10 TO 24			
Race, age, and sex	**1980**	**1992**	**Percent change**
White males, 10–14	1.4	2.6	+86%
White males, 15–19	15.1	18.4	+22%
White males, 20–24	27.7	26.6	-4%
White females 10–14	0.3	1.1	+233%
White females 15–19	3.3	3.7	+12%
White females 20–24	5.9	4.0	-32%
Black males, 10–14	0.5	2.0	+300%
Black males, 15–19	5.6	14.8	164%
Black males, 20–24	19.9	21.2	+7%
Black females, 10–14	0.2	0.4	+100%
Black females, 15–19	1.6	1.9	+19%
Black females, 20–24	3.1	2.4	–23%
TOTAL, MALES	14.5	15.4	+6%
TOTAL, FEMALES	3.1	2.8	-10%

Suicide rate is per 100,000 persons.
Source: Centers for Disease Control, April 1995.

Further Reading

Biskup, Michael, and Carol Wekesser, eds. *Suicide: Opposing Viewpoints.* San Diego: Greenhaven Press, 1992.

Colt, George Howe. *The Enigma of Suicide.* Fort Worth, TX: Summit Books, 1991.

Francis, Dorothy. *Suicide: A Preventable Tragedy.* New York: E. P. Dutton, 1989.

Superego

In psychoanalytic theory, the part of the human personality that represents a person's inner values and morals; also known as conscience.

The superego is one of three basic components of human **personality**, according to **Sigmund Freud**. The **id** is the most primitive, consisting of largely **unconscious** biological impulses. The **ego** uses reality and its consequences to modify the behavior being urged by the id. The superego judges actions as right or wrong based on the person's internal value system.

Freud believed that a child develops the superego by storing up the moral standards learned from experience in society and from parents and other adults. When a parent scolds a child for hitting another child, for example, the child learns that such **aggression** is unacceptable. Stored in that child's superego, or **conscience**, is that moral judgment which will be used in determining future behavior. Another component of the superego is a person's own concept of perfect behavior, which presents a second standard used to govern actions.

The complex interaction among the id, the ego, and the superego is what determines human behavior, according to Freud. A healthy balance between the more instinctual demands of the id and the moral demands of the superego, as negotiated by the ego, results in a "**normal**" or healthy personality.

Further Reading

Atkinson, Rita L.; Richard C. Atkinson; Edward E. Smith; and Ernest R. Hilgard. *Introduction to Psychology.* 9th ed. San Diego: Harcourt Brace Jovanovich, 1987.

Zimbardo, Philip G. *Psychology and Life.* 12th ed. Glenview, IL.: Scott, Foresman, 1988.

Superstition

A belief or attitude that does not correspond to what is generally believed to be true or rational.

The study of psychology generally does not include any emphasis on these seemingly irrational beliefs that motivate behavior. Nevertheless, superstitious actions are

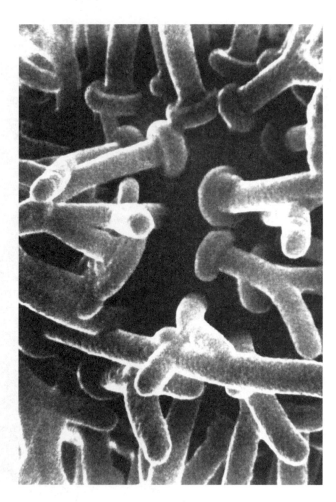

Taken in 1969 at with a scanning electron microscope at the University of California, Berkeley, this photograph is one of the first to show the small fibers and knobs that for the synapse to pass nerve impulses from one cell to another. The magnification is 5,000X.

common in our society. Avoiding walking under ladders in order to ward off disaster, crossing fingers for good luck, and knocking on wood surfaces to ensure continued prosperity or avoid tragedy are examples of commonplace superstitions that have permeated society since ancient times. **Sigmund Freud** called such superstitions "faulty actions." Some psychologists consider them expressions of inner tensions and anxieties. Others believe intense superstitious feelings indicate some sort of mental disorder. However, there has been no reliable clinical correlation between superstitious beliefs and mental illness.

Further Reading

Lorie, Peter. *Superstitions.* New York: Simon & Schuster, 1992.

Rachleff, Owen S. *The Secrets of Superstitions: How They Help, How They Hurt.* Garden City, NY: Doubleday, 1976.

Synapse

The tiny gap through which communication between two neurons takes place.

Every thought, movement, and sensation occurs due to communication between different neurons, which provide information throughout the **nervous system.** Within a single neuron, information proceeds through electrical signals, but when information must be transmitted from one neuron to a succeeding neuron, the transmission is chemical.

In order for two neurons to communicate, chemical messengers, or **neurotransmitter**s, are released into the synaptic cleft (a tiny gap about one thousandth of a millimeter between neurons), at which point they migrate to the next neuron and attach themselves to locations called receptor sites. The result is an initiation of electrical current that moves through that neuron toward the next one. After the neurotransmitter exerts its effect, it is either destroyed by other chemicals in the synaptic cleft or is reabsorbed into the original neuron. This action prevents the neurons from becoming overstimulated.

When neurons communicate, the effect can be either stimulation or inhibition of the next neuron. For example, when a person pays attention to one conversation and ignore others, the neurons in the **brain** are actively seeking out that information (stimulation) and actively ignoring the rest (inhibition). Neurons come in different shapes and sizes, affecting many other neurons, and can have different numbers of synapses. Some neurons, called Purkinje cells, may have as many as 100,000 synapses.

Taste

The chemical sense which perceives or distinguishes flavor.

Taste, or gustation, is one of the two senses triggered by chemical stimuli (the other is olfaction). A person has approximately 10,000 taste buds. Most are on the tongue, but some are located in the back of the throat. Grouped together in bumps or papillae on the surface of the tongue, the taste buds contain receptors that respond to four basic tastes: sweet, salty, sour, and bitter. (It has also been proposed that monosodium glutamate (MSG) produces a fifth taste, called "umami," that enhances other tastes.) Each receptor responds most strongly to one or two of the four basic tastes and slightly to the others. The receptors that are sensitive to bitter substances are located on the back of the tongue. Beginning at the tip of the tongue and progressing to the rear on each side are overlapping receptors for sweet, salty, and sour tastes. Although the number of basic tastes registered by human taste receptors is extremely limited when compared with the hundreds of odors that can be identified by olfactory receptors, the taste buds work together to send a unique pattern of impulses to the **brain** for each substance tasted. As any gourmet or wine taster will attest, a wide range of patterns can be created by mixing and blending the four primary tastes in different combinations.

As food is chewed, its chemicals act as the stimuli for taste, breaking down into molecules, mixing with saliva, and infiltrating the areas that contain the receptors. Activation of the taste buds triggers **nerve** impulses that travel to the brain and are there transformed into sensations of taste. Because of their relatively "toxic" environment, taste buds live short lives, being replaced about every ten days. The sense of **smell** often works in conjunction with our sense of taste by combining sensations to achieve the **perception** of flavor. In fact, the olfactory sense actually contributes more to the perception of specific flavors than does the sense of taste. This phenome-

non is commonly demonstrated in people whose sense of taste becomes dulled by colds. It has also been investigated in laboratory research, including tests in which subjects detected little taste in such strong substances as peppermint, onions, and cinnamon when their noses were congested.

When a person eats, chemical stimuli taken in through chewing and swallowing pass through an opening in the palate at the back of the mouth and move toward receptor cells located at the top of the nasal cavity, where they are converted to olfactory nerve impulses that travel to the brain, just as the impulses from olfactory stimuli taken in through the nose. The olfactory and gustatory pathways are known to converge in various parts of the brain, although it is not known exactly how the two systems work together.

Another way to regard the relationship between taste and smell is as two component parts of a perceptual function identified as the "flavor system," which also includes temperature and tactile receptors. Warm foods seem tastier because warming releases additional aromas from the mouth to the olfactory receptors. Warm foods also seem sweeter, although temperature has no effect on the perception of salty foods. A food's tactile properties (how it feels in one's mouth) influence perception of its flavor, hence distinctions such as that between smooth and crunchy peanut butter. **Pain** receptors are even included among the mouth's nerve endings involved in flavor perception, and may account for some of the appeal of hot and spicy foods. A person's nutritional state can influence perceived tastes, as well as the desire for particular foods: salt deficiency and food deprivation increase the desire for salty foods. The sweet properties of saccharin and aspartame were discovered by accident in laboratory settings, but researchers are now actively working on developing new artificial sweeteners to allow consumption of sweet foods that are low in calories.

Television

A device for transmitting images with sound using radio-frequency and microwave signals or closed-circuit connections.

For many years, behavioral and educational researchers have studied the psychological effects of television programs on viewers, particularly children. Substantial debate over television began as early as the 1960s. The term "TV **violence**" was coined in 1963 as critics accused programs of promoting antisocial violent and aggressive behavior. More contemporary discussions center on the use of rating systems to label the content of programs and the use of technology to allow parents to censor children's viewing habits.

As televisions became more economical and widely available in the 1950s and 1960s, particularly in the United States, researchers began to study television's effect on the behavior of children. Violent program content became a focus of study as concern grew over increasingly violent acts committed by children. Psychologists advanced several theories. One, the **social learning theory**, espoused the theory that children learn how to act based upon their own experiences and their interaction with parents, siblings, friends, and society in general, including television. The famous Bobo doll studies staged various experiments on a television screen using "Bobo," a knock-down doll, and characters who would act in various ways toward the doll and be rewarded or punished accordingly. The studies showed that children seeing these "performances" often learned and imitated aggressive behavior after observing it on the screen.

Another theory, the instigation theory, proposed that exposure to violent or arousing programming leads directly to an aggressive response. A final theory, the **catharsis** theory, proposed that television viewers who see violent content actually become less aggressive themselves because their innate aggressive tendencies would be diffused by viewing them secondhand. This theory, which corresponds to early drive reduction motivational theories, generally was unsupported by research. Political and public concern prompted the formation in 1969 of a national committee to study television violence and the effects of commercials, headed by the United States Surgeon General. Controversy surrounded the committee's report, however, upon its release in 1972. But while the report itself contained much ambiguity, researchers who participated in the study concluded that television violence does indeed increase aggressive behavior among certain children under certain circumstances. Children predisposed to aggressive tendencies and children who watched the most hours of violent programming were thought to be the most affected. Later studies confirmed

that this relationship between television and **aggression** is not limited to the United States.

Another concern has been that increased exposure to violence and other arousing situations through television leads to **desensitization**. Violent behavior may come to be viewed as an acceptable problem-solving alternative because it is used so often, and because consequences of violent actions are often disregarded or minimized. Emotional subject matter presented on commercial television leads to a roller-coaster of highs and lows, punctuated by advertisements every few minutes.

Television's power to influence **attitudes** has also come under scrutiny, particularly in the area of racial, ethnic, and gender **stereotype**s. As early as 1951, the subject of racial stereotypes on television sparked discussion. That year, the National Association for the Advancement of Colored People (NAACP) called for CBS to cancel *Amos and Andy* from its schedule, claiming it reinforced the image of blacks as lazy and dishonest. Through the years, there has been frequent controversy over the lack of major black characters in mainstream programming and the often violent, subservient roles they portray. Similarly, gender stereotyping in television programming has been criticized widely, particularly since the growth of the women's rights movement in the 1970s. Female characters in shows and advertisements were often portrayed as compliant housewives and mothers with typically feminine characteristics. Few women in professional occupations other than waitress or airline flight attendant were visible. Women frequently served as men's foils and sex objects rather than multidimensional human beings. Ethnic stereotypes were also perpetuated by television, critics contend. Italian characters frequently were connected to criminal behavior, for example. Those studies that have been conducted to measure the effects of such stereotyping on television viewers have confirmed that viewers, particularly children who watch many hours of television, tend to internalize the stereotypes they see on television.

However, even critics have concluded that television can serve a positive role in the areas of learning and promotion of positive social values. *Sesame Street* on public television is considered a pioneer in the "prosocial" television movement, as it seeks to educate preschool and primary school-age children through the positive portrayal of widely diverse characters. Research has shown a positive correlation between *Sesame Street* viewers and favorable attitudes toward ethnic groups. Other studies have shown that *Sesame Street* has also succeeded in teaching various academic information, such as the alphabet and counting. *Mister Rogers' Neighborhood,* also designed with prosocial lessons in mind, has also shown to have positive effects on children who watch frequently. All of these studies, however, have been subject to much criticism. For example, it is argued that children who watch such programs usually are in settings where prosocial behavior is encouraged and therefore they are predisposed to that type of behavior. Also, it is difficult to measure the validity of such studies because so many variables are involved.

Further Reading

Huesmann, L. Rowell, and Leonard D. Eron, eds. *Television and the Aggressive Child: A Cross-National Comparison.* Hillsdale, NJ: L. Erlbaum Associates, 1986.

Kelley, Michael R. *A Parent's Guide to Television: Making the Most of It.* New York: John Wiley & Sons, 1983.

Liebert, Robert M.; Joyce N. Sprafkin; and Emily S. Davidson. *The Early Window: Effects of Television on Children and Youth.* New York: Pergamon Press, 1982.

Temperament

An individual's characteristic emotional nature, including energy level, prevailing mood and sensitivity to stimulation.

Individual variations in temperament are most readily observed in newborn babies. Even immediately after **birth,** some babies are calm while others cry a lot. Some respond favorably to being held while others squirm and protest. Some are soothed by soft music and others do not stop crying long enough to hear it. Because of these immediately observable variations, temperament is often considered a biologically-based characteristic.

Hippocrates discussed variations in temperament as early as the 5th century B.C. His hypothesis that there are four basic human temperaments that correspond to various bodily characteristics—choleric, sanguine, melancholic, and phlegmatic— endured for many years before modern theories became accepted. American psychologist Gordon Allport (1897–1967), who came to dislike psychoanalytic theory and **behaviorism** because of their emphasis on seeking universal theories to explain all human behavior and disorders, believed temperament was one of three "raw materials" that distinguish individuals from one another and from other living beings. Along with **intelligence** and physique, temperament was genetically determined and unique within each person. Allport wrote that temperament includes a person's susceptibility to emotional stimulation, strength and speed of response, and **mood.** Adults as well as children display temperaments that are individually and uniquely determined by biology.

While supporting the belief that temperament is biologically based, many **personality** experts also maintain that it can develop and change over the course of a person's life in response to personal experiences and environmental conditions. Fussy babies can grow to be placid toddlers. Similarly, passive infants sometimes grow up to

Lewis Terman

be classroom troublemakers. Interaction with parents, siblings, and other social contacts as well as life experiences affect an individual's predisposition toward a particular temperament.

Terman, Lewis (1877–1956)

American psychologist whose notable work was concentrated in the areas of intelligence testing and the comprehensive study of intellectually gifted children.

Terman was born in Indiana and attended Indiana University and Clark University. He served on the faculty of Stanford University as professor of education and as professor of psychology. In 1916, Terman published the first important individual intelligence test to be used in the United States, the **Stanford-Binet Intelligence scales.** This test was an American revision and expansion of the Binet-Simon intelligence test, which had been developed in France. Along with the Stanford-Binet, Terman introduced the term **intelligence quotient,** or I.Q., and its formulation. This concept, and the Stanford-Binet test, became very widely used in the measurement of **intelligence.** Terman believed that society has a need to identify academically **gifted children** and to provide them with appropriate educational opportunities. In 1921, he began a thoroughly exhaustive and very long term study of such children. The results of this study, which are scheduled to be announced in the year 2010, may be found in *Genetic Studies of Genius* (1926). Terman's other books include: *The Measurement of Intelligence* (1916), *Sex and Personality* (1936), and *The Gifted Child Grows Up* (1947).

See also Binet, Alfred.

Further Reading
Minton, Henry L. *Lewis M. Terman.* New York: New York University Press, 1988.

Test Anxiety

Excessive worry experienced by students before and during examinations.

Students commonly experience **stress** as they anticipate taking tests. Those who experience extreme discomfort, including physical symptoms and impaired **ability** to perform well, are said to suffer from test anxiety. Physical symptoms include many of those common to people who experience other types of **anxiety**: increased heart rate, sweating, and trembling muscles and hands. Students also worry excessively about failure no matter how well prepared they are. Cognitive impairment frequently accompanies the physical symptoms. Students forget information they have learned, misinterpret questions, or fail to follow instructions. They sometimes have difficulty completing a test because they spend time worrying instead of concentrating.

A technique called "systematic desensitization" has proven successful in treating test anxiety in many patients. Students are taught progressive relaxation techniques along with accompanying visualization exercises. With practice, the patient pairs relaxation with images that correspond to test-taking situations. Often, therapy includes visits to actual exam rooms and the administration of mock exams. Specific test-taking skills are also taught.

Further Reading
Bower, Gordon H., and Ernest R. Hilgard. *Theories of Learning.* Englewood Cliffs, NJ: Prentice-Hall, 1981.

Thalamus

A collection of cell body clusters located in the middle of the forebrain.

The thalamus is a relatively large collection of cell body clusters shaped like two small footballs. It is in-

volved in receiving sensory information from the eyes and other sense organs, processing that information, and then transmitting it to primary sensory zones in the **cerebral cortex.** The thalamus also processes **pain** signals from the spinal cord as well as information from different parts of the cerebral hemispheres, and relays it to the **cerebellum** and the medulla. Together with the **hypothalamus,** the thalamus forms part of the forebrain called the diencephalon.

By registering the sensory properties of food, such as texture and temperature, the thalamus plays a role in appetite. It is also known to be involved in the control of **sleep** and wakefulness. Cognitive researchers have found that the thalamus activates or integrates language functions, plays a role in **memory,** and that a portion of the thalamus, called the pulvinar, helps in refocusing **attention.** Together with the hippocampus and parts of the cortex, it is instrumental in the formation of new memories, which are then thought to be stored in the cerebral cortex.

See also Brain.

Thorndike, Edward (1874–1949)

American educational psychologist best known for his experimentally derived theories of learning and his influence on behaviorism.

Edward Thorndike was born in Williamsburg, Massachusetts, and grew up in a succession of New England towns where his father served as a Methodist minister. After receiving his bachelor's degree from Wesleyan University, Thorndike did graduate work in psychology, first at Harvard under the guidance of **William James** and later at Columbia under **James McKeen Cattell.** His first major research project—undertaken while he was still a graduate student—involved trial-and-error learning, using first chickens and then cats. Observing the behavior of cats attempting to escape from enclosed "puzzle boxes," Thorndike noted that responses that produced satisfaction—escape from the box and subsequent feeding—were "stamped in" and more likely to be repeated in the future, while responses that led to failure, and thus dissatisfaction, tended to be "stamped out." Thorndike termed this observation the **law of effect,** one of two laws of learning he derived from his research. The other law, called the law of exercise, stated that associations that are practiced are stamped in, while others are extinguished. Applied to humans, these laws became an important foundation of both behaviorist psychology and modern **learning theory.** Thorndike based his doctoral dissertation on his research, which he also published in the form of a monograph in 1898. After earning his Ph.D., Thorndike spent a year on the faculty of Case Western Reserve University, after which he was appointed professor of **educational psychology** at Columbia's Teachers' College, where he remained until his retirement. Thorndike made many early and significant contributions to the field of experimental animal psychology, successfully arguing that his findings had relevant implications for human psychology.

Upon his return to New York, Thorndike turned his attention to a new research area—termed "transfer of training"—which was concerned with the effect of performance in one discipline on performance in others. The belief in such a connection had sustained the traditional system of instruction in formal disciplines, such as the classics, through the rationale that achievement in a given field equipped students for success in other areas. Working together with his friend and colleague, Robert Woodworth, Thorndike found that training in specific tasks produced very little improvement in the ability to perform different tasks. These findings, published in 1901, helped undermine the tradition of formal disciplines in favor of educational methods that were more specifically task-oriented.

Continuing to focus on human learning, Thorndike became a pioneer in the application of psychological principles to areas such as the teaching of reading, **language acquisition**, and mental testing. In 1903, he published *Educational Psychology*, in which he applied the learning principles he had discovered in his animal research to humans. In the following year, Thorndike's *Introduction to the Theory of Mental and Social Measurements* (1904), which provided administrators and users of **intelligence** tests access to statistical data about test results. Thorndike also devised a scale to measure children's handwriting in 1910 and a table showing the frequency of words in English (*The Teacher's Word Book of 30,000 Words*, 1944), which has been useful to researchers who rely on dictionary words. As a teacher of teachers, Thorndike was directly and indirectly responsible for a number of curricular and methodological changes in education throughout the United States. A prolific writer, Thorndike produced over 450 articles and books, including *The Elements of Psychology* (1905), *Animal Intelligence* (1911), *The Measurement of Intelligence* (1926), *The Fundamentals of Learning* (1932), *The Psychology of Wants, Interests, and Attitudes* (1935), and *Human Nature and the Social Order* (1940).

Further Reading

Clifford, G. J. *Edward L. Thorndike: The Sane Positivist*. Middletown, CT: Wesleyan University Press, 1984.

Touch

The skin sense that allows us to perceive pressure and related sensations, including temperature and pain.

The sense of touch is located in the skin, which is composed of three layers: the epidermis, dermis, and hypodermis. Different types of sensory receptors, varying in size, shape, number, and distribution within the skin, are responsible for relaying information about pressure, temperature, and **pain.** The largest touch sensor, the Pacinian corpuscle, is located in the hypodermis, the innermost thick fatty layer of skin, which responds to vibration. Free **nerve** endings—neurons that originate in the spinal cord, enter and remain in the skin—transmit information about temperature and pain from their location at the bottom of the epidermis. Hair receptors in the dermis, which are wrapped around each follicle, respond to the pressure produced when the hairs are bent. All the sensory receptors respond not to continued pressure but rather to changes in pressure, adapting quickly to each new change, so that, for example, the skin is unaware of the continual pressure produced by clothes. Once stimulated by sensation, the receptors trigger nerve impulses which travel to the somatosensory cortex in the parietal lobe of the **brain,** where they are transformed into sensations. Sensitivity to touch varies greatly among different parts of the body. Areas that are highly sensitive, such as the fingers and lips, correspond to a proportionately large area of the sensory cortex.

Sensory receptors encode various types of information about objects with which the skin comes in contact. We can tell how heavy an object is by both the firing rate of individual neurons and by the number of neurons stimulated. (Both the firing rate and the number of neurons are higher with a heavier object.) Changes in the firing rate of neurons tell us whether an object is stationary or vibrating, and the spatial organization of the neurons gives us information about its location.

The temperature of human skin is usually about 89°F (32°C). Objects or surroundings at this level—known as physiological zero—produce no sensation of temperature. Warmth is felt at higher temperatures and coldness at lower ones. Some of the sensory receptors in the skin respond specifically to changes in temperature. These receptors are further specialized, as certain ones sense warmth and increase their firing rates in temperatures of 95° to 115°F (33° to 46°C), while others sense cold. Sensations of warmth and coldness are differentiated on a skin area as small as one square centimeter. Within that area, cold will be felt at about six points and warmth at two. When cold and warm stimuli are touched at the same time, a sensation of extreme heat is felt, a phenomenon known as "paradoxical hotness." Touch and temperature interact in some sensors, producing phenomena such as the fact that warm and cold objects feel heavier than those at moderate temperatures.

With free nerve endings as receptors, pain carries information to the brain about a real or potential injury to the body. Pain from the skin is transmitted through two types of nerve fibers. A-delta fibers relay sharp, pricking types of pain, while C fibers carry dull aches and burning sensations. Pain impulses are relayed to the spinal cord, where they interact with special neurons that transmit signals to the **thalamus** and other areas of the brain. Each neuron responds to a number of different pain stimuli. Pain is carried by many types of **neurotransmitter**s, a fact that has made it possible to develop numerous types of pain-relieving medications. Many factors affect how pain is experienced. Pain thresholds vary with the individual and the occasion. Intensely concentrated activity may diminish or even eliminate the perception of pain for the duration of the activity. Natural mechanisms, including replacement by input from other senses, can block pain sensations. The brain can also block pain by signals sent through the spinal cord, a process that involves the neurotransmitter serotonin and natural painkillers known as endorphins.

Traits

Characteristics that differ from one person to another in a continuous and consistent way.

Traits include such **personality** characteristics as introversion, aggressiveness, generosity, nervousness, and creativity. Systems that address personality as a combination of qualities or dimensions are called trait theories.

The first comprehensive trait theory was that of Gordon Allport (1897–1967). Over a period of thirty years, Allport investigated over 18,000 separate traits, proposing several principles to make this lengthy list manageable for practical purposes. One was the distinction between personal dispositions, which are peculiar to a single individual, and common traits, which can be used for describing and comparing different people. While personal dispositions reflect the individual personality more accurately, one needs to use common traits to make any kind of meaningful assessment of people in relation to each other. Allport also claimed that about seven central traits dominated each individual personality (he described these as the type of characteristic that would appear in a letter of recommendation). Another concept devised by Allport was the cardinal trait—a quality so intense that it governs virtually all of a person's activities (Mother Theresa's cardinal trait would be humanitarianism, for example, while that of the fictional character

Ebenezer Scrooge would be avarice). Secondary traits, in contrast, are those that govern less of a person's behavior and are more specific to certain situations.

Using the statistical technique of factor analysis, Raymond B. Cattell reduced Allport's list of traits to a much smaller number and then proceeded to divide these into clusters that express more basic dimensions of personality (for example, the pairs talkative-silent, open-secretive, and adventurous-cautious can all be grouped under the overall source trait of extroversion). Eventually he arrived at 16 fundamental source traits and developed a questionnaire to measure them—the Sixteen Personality Factor Questionnaire (16 PF)—which uses the answers to over 100 yes-or-no questions to arrive at a personality profile.

Hans Eysenck has also proposed a factor-analytic trait model of human personality. However, Eysenck's model focuses on the following three dominant dimensions that combine various related traits: psychoticism (characterized by various types of antisocial behavior), **introversion-extroversion**, and emotionality/neuroticism-stability. Eysenck has also combined the introversion-extroversion and emotionality-stability scales into a model containing four quadrants whose groupings of traits correspond roughly to the four types of personality outlined by the physician Hippocrates over 2,000 years ago in ancient Greece—sanguine, choleric, phlegmatic, and melancholic.

Other trait-oriented theories include those of J.P. Guilford and David McClelland. Currently, a number of psychologists interested in a trait approach to personality believe that the following five factors, rather than Eysenck's three, are most useful in assessing personality: extroversion, agreeableness, conscientiousness, neuroticism, and openness to experience. A questionnaire called the NEO Personality Inventory, often called "the big five," has been developed to assess these factors.

Further Reading

Allport, Gordon W. *Personality and Social Encounter: Selected Essays.* Boston: Beacon Press, 1960.
Eysenck, Hans. *The Structure of Human Personality.* London: Methuen, 1970.

Transference

The tendency of clients to transfer to the therapist their emotional responses to significant people in their lives.

Transference is the tendency for a client in **psychotherapy**, known as the analysand, to transfer emotional responses to their therapists that reflect feelings the analysand has for other significant people in his or her life. Transference often echoes clients' relationships with their parents or with other persons who played a central role in their childhood. They may become excessively dependent on or sexually attracted to the therapist; they may develop feelings of hostility or detachment. Whatever form transference takes, it is considered to be at the heart of the therapeutic process. **Sigmund Freud** believed that clients need to relive the central emotional experiences of their lives through transference in order to become convinced of the existence and power of their own **unconscious** attachments and **motivation**s. The awareness gained through transference helps clients understand the sources of their behavior and actively aids them in working through and resolving their problems.

Sigmund Freud described the workings of transference using an analogy to chemistry. Likening the clients' symptoms to precipitates resulting from earlier emotional attachments, he compared the therapist to a catalyst and the effects of transference to a higher temperature at which the symptoms could be transformed. According to Freud, the phenomenon of transference is not unique to the psychoanalytic relationship between client and therapist—significant patterns of relationship are commonly re-enacted with "substitutes" other than psychotherapists. Psychoanalysis, however, is unique in drawing attention to this process and utilizing it for therapeutic purposes.

Further Reading

Freud, Sigmund. *New Introductory Lectures on Psychoanalysis.* New York: W. W. Norton, 1933.

Hall, Calvin S. *A Primer of Freudian Psychology.* New York: Harper and Row, 1982.

Twins

Two children or animals born at the same birth.

Identical, or monozygotic, twins are of the same sex and are genetically and physically similar because they both come from one ovum, which, after fertilization, divides in two and develops into two separate individuals. Fraternal, or dizygotic, twins occur when the mother produces two eggs in one monthly cycle and both eggs are fertilized. The conceptions may take place on two separate occasions and could involve different fathers. Fraternal twins, who are no more genetically alike than ordinary siblings, may be of the same or different sex and may bear some similarity of appearance. Twin pregnancies occur on the average in one out of every 80 to 100 births. However, the incidence of twins reflects the number of twin babies born per thousand completed pregnancies, and it is a fact that many more twins are conceived than are born.

These fraternal twins boys bear close similarity of appearance, althouh fraternal twins are no more genetically alike than ordinary siblings.

The causes of identical twinning are not fully understood. Factors affecting the frequency of twin and other multiple births include the mother's race and age, and the number of previous births. The rate of twin births in Japan is 0.7 percent, while the Yoruba of Nigeria have a rate as high as 4 percent. Dizygotic twinning appears to be a sex-linked genetic trait passed on by female relatives in the same family. The chances of having fraternal twins are increased about five times if a woman is a fraternal twin, has fraternal twin siblings or fraternal twin relatives on her side of the family, or has already given birth to fraternal twins (one in twenty chance). While the rate of identical twin births is stable for all ages of childbearing women, the chance of any mother bearing fraternal twins increases from the age of 15 to 39 and then drops after age 40. For women of all ages, the more children they have had previously, the more likely they are to bear twins. Since the 1960s, fertility drugs have also been linked to the chances of producing twins. The majority of research indicates that fathers' genes have little effect on the chances of producing twins.

There are four types of monozygotic twins, determined by the manner in which the fertilized egg, or zygote, divides and the stage at which this occurs. Two independent embryonic structures may be produced immediately at division, or the zygote may form two inner cell masses, with each developing into an embryo. A late or incomplete division may produce conjoined, or Siamese twins. As the zygote develops, it is encased in membranes, the inner of which is called the amnion, and the outer one the chorion. Among monozygotic twins, either or both of these membranes may be either separate or shared, as may the placenta. Together, the arrangement of these membranes and the placenta occurs in four possible permutations. Among dizygotic twins, each one has separate amnion and chorion membranes, although the placenta may be shared. Ascertaining zygosity, or the genetic make up of twins, can be done by analyzing the placenta(s) to determine if it is a single placenta with a single membrane or a double placenta, which account for one-third of identical twins and all fraternal twins. In the case of same-sex twins with two placentas, a **DNA** test can determine whether they share the same genes or blood groups.

The scientific study of twins, pioneered by **Sir Francis Galton** in 1876, is one effective means of determining genetic influences on human behavior. The most widely used method of comparison is comparing monozygotic and dizygotic twins for concordance and discordance of **traits.** Concordant traits are those possessed by either both or neither of a pair of twins; discordant traits are possessed by only one of the pair. Monozygotic twins who are discordant for a particular trait can be compared with each other with reference to other traits. This type of study has provided valuable information on the causes of **schizophrenia.**

Another common type of twin research compares monozygotic twins reared together with those reared apart, providing valuable information about the role of **environment** in determining behavior. In general, monozygotic twins reared apart are found to bear more similarities to each other than to their respective adoptive parents or siblings. This finding demonstrates the interaction between the effects of environment and genetic predispositions on an individual's psychological development.

See also Nature-Nurture Controversy.

Unconscious

The part of the mind whose contents people resist bringing into awareness.

Sigmund Freud assumed that the human mind was divided into three divisions: the **id, ego,** and **superego,** which, in turn, had both conscious and unconscious portions. The id, motivated by two biological drives—sex and **aggression**—operates according to the **pleasure principle,** seeking satisfaction and avoiding **pain.** Guided by the reality principle, the ego's goal is to find safe and socially acceptable ways of satisfying the id's desires without transgressing the limits imposed by the superego. Developing from the ego in childhood, the superego, or **conscience,** has as its goal to apply moral values in satisfying one's wishes. Both the ego and superego operate consciously and unconsciously, according to Freud, while the id is entirely unconscious.

In **psychoanalytic theory,** developed by Freud in the treatment of **normal** and abnormal personalities, the preconscious and unconscious minds are the repositories of secret or sexual desires that threaten our self-esteem, or ego. Once in the unconscious, these repressed desires and **fear**s give rise to **anxiety** and guilt, which influence conscious behavior and thoughts. Freud attributed the cause of many psychological disorders to the conflict between conscious and unconscious urges. In order to understand abnormal behaviors and eliminate them, he theorized, an expert was required, who, in a trusting relationship with the patient, would employ techniques such as dream analysis and **free association** to retrieve materials buried in the unconscious mind. Thus, the driving forces behind behavior could be understood, and unresolved unconscious conflicts and anxiety could become a source of insight for the patient, eliminating the primary source of abnormal behavior.

See also Repression.

Unconscious Motivation

Motivating impulses that influence behavior without conscious awareness.

Unconscious motivation plays a prominent role in **Sigmund Freud**'s theories of human behavior. According to Freud and his followers, most human behavior is the result of desires, impulses, and memories that have been repressed into an **unconscious** state, yet still influence actions. Freud believed that the human mind consists of a tiny, conscious part that is available for direct observation and a much larger subconscious portion that plays an even more important role in determining behavior.

The term "Freudian slip" refers to the manifestation of these unconscious impulses. For example, a person who responds "Bad to meet you" instead of the usual "Glad to meet you" may be revealing true feelings. The substitution of "bad" for "glad" is more than a slip of the tongue; it is an expression of the person's unconscious feelings of **fear** or dislike. Similarly, a talented athlete who plays an uncharacteristically poor game could be acting on an unconscious desire to punish overbearing or inattentive parents. Unknown to the athlete, the substandard performance actually is communicating an important message.

Freud also contended that repressed memories and desires are the origins of most mental disorders. **Psychoanalysis** was developed as a method of assisting patients in bringing their unconscious thoughts to **consciousness**. This increased awareness of the causes for behavior and feelings then would assist the patient in modifying the undesired aspects of behavior.

See also Memory; Repression.

Further Reading

Atkinson, Rita L.; Richard C. Atkinson; Edward E. Smith; and Ernest R. Hilgard. *Introduction to Psychology.* 9th ed. San Diego: Harcourt Brace Jovanovich, 1987.

Clark, David Stafford. *What Freud Really Said*. New York: Schocken Books, 1965.

······························

Underachiever

A student whose performance, usually academic, is well below estimates of his or her potential.

The underachiever is an individual whose level of actual performance on a set of (usually cognitive) tasks is consistently and significantly lower than the level predicted for that individual on the basis of relevant **ability** tests. Assuming that the tests are valid, an underachiever will perform at a level significantly below his or her level of maximum potential performance.

The specific motivational, formal, and other psychological aspects of underachievement vary considerably.

Some underachievers may be unchallenged, and need further enrichment in their academic curriculum to improve their performance; in other cases a **learning disability** may contribute to the individual's lack of achievement. Additionally, more complex issues within the family, such as issues relating to the family's relationship with the school or conflicts between family and school expectations may contribute to the student's lack of academic achievement.

So-called "late-bloomers" may also be categorized as underachievers, but are more accurately described as *latent achievers*. In such cases, the student's underachievement corrects itself with maturation.

See also Overachiever.

Further Reading

Mandel, Harvey. *The Psychology of Underachievement*. New York: Wiley, 1988.

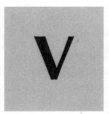

Violence

The use of unjustified physical force with the intention to injure or damage.

The high incidence of violence in the United States is of great concern to citizens, lawmakers, and law enforcement agencies alike. Between 1960 and 1991, violent crime in the U.S. rose over 370 percent, and over 600,000 Americans are victimized by handgun crimes annually. Violent acts committed by juveniles are of particular concern: the number of American adolescents arrested for homicide has increased by 85 percent between 1987 and 1991, and more juveniles are committing serious crimes at younger ages than ever before. Young African American males are particularly at risk for becoming either perpetrators or victims of violent crime. The Centers for Disease Control (CDC) has identified homicide as the leading cause of death for this demographic group, estimating that one in every 28 black males born in 1987 is likely to be murdered. For white males born in 1987, the ratio is one in 205.

The threat of violence is particularly disturbing because of new variants—including carjackings, drive-by shootings, and workplace killings—that threaten Americans in places or situations formerly considered safe. The CDC has declared workplace violence an epidemic, with the number of homicides in the workplace tripling in the last ten years. Workplace violence may be divided into two types: external and internal. External workplace violence is committed by persons unfamiliar with the employer and employees, occurring at random or as an attempt at making a symbolic statement to society at large. Internal workplace violence is generally committed by an individual involved in either a troubled spousal or personal relationship with a co-worker, or as an attempt to seek revenge against an employer, usually for being released from employment. The rising percentage of layoffs, downsizing, and impersonal management styles in many American corporations have been linked to the increase in workplace violence, nearly one-fourth of which end in the perpetrator's **suicide.**

One type of violence that has received increased attention in recent years is domestic violence, a crime for which statistics are difficult to compile because it is so heavily underreported—only about one in 270 incidents are thought to be reported to authorities. Estimates of the percentage of women who have been physically abused by a spouse or partner range from 20 percent to as high as 50 percent. According to the FBI, a woman is beaten every 18 seconds in the United States, and almost one-third of American females murdered in 1992 were killed by their husbands or boyfriends. Battering is experienced by women of all ages, races, ethnic groups, and social classes. A chronic pattern of ongoing physical violence and verbal abuse may produce a variant of **post-traumatic stress disorder** referred to as Battered Woman Syndrome, in which the victim experiences depression, guilt, passivity, **fear,** and low self-esteem.

Various explanations have been offered for the high prevalence of violence in the United States, which is by far the most violent nation in the industrialized world. Among the most prominent has been the argument that violence depicted in the mass media—including **television,** movies, rock and rap music videos, and video games—have contributed to the rise in violence in society. Quantitative studies have found that prime time television programs average 10 violent acts per hour, while children's cartoons average 32 acts of violence per hour. On-screen deaths in feature films such as *Robocop* and *Die Hard* range from 80 to 264. It has also been argued that experiencing violence vicariously in these forms is not a significant determinant of violent behavior and that it may even have a beneficial cathartic effect. However, experimental studies have found correlations between the viewing of violence and increased interpersonal **aggression,** both in childhood and, later, in **adolescence.** Viewing violence can elicit aggressive behavior through modeling, increasing the viewer's **arousal,** desensitizing viewers to violence, reducing restraints on aggressive behavior, and distorting views about **conflict resolution.**

Other causal factors that have been linked to violence include the prevalence of gangs, the introduction of crack cocaine in the mid-1980s, the increase in single-parent families, and the lack of tighter restrictions on gun ownership. In addition, scientists have found a possible link between violence and **heredity:** studies have shown that males born with an extra Y chromosome (type XYY) are more likely than normal to be inmates of prisons or **mental hospitals.** The significance of these findings has been disputed, however, as XYY males in the general population are not more violent than other males. The effects of a genetic predisposition are also tempered by interaction with a variety of **environment**al factors. Of the men who are genetically predisposed to violence, only a minority will actually commit acts of aggression.

There are a number of more credible predictors of individual violence, most of them psychological. The most reliable indicator is a history of violence: each time a person commits a violent act, the probability that he or she will commit more violent acts increases. Psychoses, including **schizophrenia,** major affective disorders, and paranoid states are also closely linked to violence, as is erotomania, or romantic obsession. This condition involves an idealized romantic love (often for someone, such as a celebrity, with whom one has no personal relationship) that becomes a fixation. Such actions as unsolicited letters and phone calls, and stalking eventually lead to violence, either out of revenge for being rejected or so that the object of the fixation may not become involved with anyone else.

Depression is also associated with violence, often in the form of suicide. Two **personality disorders** related to violence—particularly in the workplace—are antisocial personality disorder ("sociopaths") and borderline personality disorder (characterized by instability and lack of boundaries in interpersonal relationships). Chemical dependence can lead to violence by interfering with the ability to distinguish right from wrong, removing social inhibitions, and inducing **paranoia** and/or aggression. Other possible indicators of violence include neurological impairment, an excessive interest in weapons, a high level of frustration with one's environment, and the pathological blaming of others for one's problems.

In recent years, a public health approach to violence has been widely advocated. This orientation stresses outreach to those segments of the population among whom violence is most prevalent in an attempt to alter **attitudes** and behaviors that contribute to it, and to teach the skills necessary for the nonviolent resolution of conflicts. Teenagers, in particular, as well as their parents, are targeted in these efforts, especially in areas with high crime

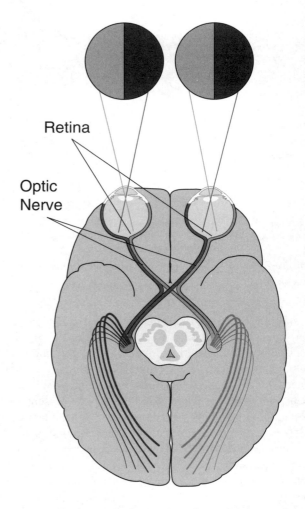

A diagram (from above) showing the retina and optic nerves.

rates. This approach has been criticized by those who believe that violence should be dealt with by addressing its underlying structural causes—including poverty, racial discrimination, and unemployment—through direct socioeconomic intervention.

Vision

The process of transforming light energy into neural impulses that can then be interpreted by the brain.

The human eye is sensitive to only a limited range of radiation, consisting of wavelengths between approximately 400 to 750 nanometers (billionths of a meter). The full spectrum of visible color is contained within this range, with violet at the low end and red at the high end. Light is converted into neural impulses by the eye, whose spherical shape is maintained by its outermost layer, the sclera. When a beam of light is reflected off an object, it first enters the eye through the cornea, a rounded transparent portion of the sclera that covers the pigmented iris. The iris constricts to control the amount of light entering the pupil, a round opening at the front of the eye. A short distance beyond the pupil, the light passes through the lens, a transparent oval structure whose curved surface bends and focuses the light wave into a narrower beam, which is received by the retina. When the retina receives an image, it is upside down because light rays from the top of the object are focused at the bottom of the retina, and vice versa. This upside-down image is interpreted by neural connections with the **brain** and the objects are seen in their proper orientation. In order for the image to be focused properly, light rays from each of its points must converge at a point on the retina, rather than in front of or behind it. Aided by the surrounding muscles, the lens of the eye adjusts its shape to focus images properly on the retina so that objects viewed at different distances can be brought into focus, a process known as *accommodation*. As people age, this process is impaired because the lens loses flexibility, and it becomes difficult to read or do close work without glasses.

The retina, lining the back of the eye, consists of ten layers of cells containing photoreceptors (rods and cones) that convert the light waves to neural impulses through a photochemical reaction. Aside from the differences in shape suggested by their names, rod and cone cells contain different light-processing chemicals (photopigments), perform different functions, and are distributed differently within the retina. Cone cells, which provide **color vision** and enable us to distinguish details, adapt quickly to light and are most useful in adequate lighting. Rod cells, which can pick up very small amounts of light but are not color-sensitive, are best suited for situations in which lighting is minimal. Because the rod cells are active at night or in dim lighting, it is difficult to distinguish colors under these circumstances. Cones are concentrated in the fovea, an area at the center of the retina, whereas rods are found only outside this area and become more numerous the farther they are from it. Thus, it is more difficult to distinguish colors when viewing objects at the periphery of one's visual field.

The photoreceptor cells of the retina generate an electrical force that triggers impulses in neighboring bipolar and ganglion cells. These impulses flow from the back layer of retinal cells to the front layer containing the fibers of the optic nerve, which leaves the eye though a part of the retina known as the optic disk. This area, which contains no receptor cells, creates a blind spot in each eye, whose effects are offset by using both eyes together and also by an illusion the brain creates to fill in this area when one eye is used alone. Branches of the optic nerve cross at a junction in the brain in front of the pi-

tuitary gland and underneath the frontal lobes called the optic chiasm and ascend into the brain itself. The nerve fibers extend to a part of the **thalamus** called the lateral geniculate nucleus (LGN), and neurons from the LGN relay their visual input to the primary visual cortex of both the left and right hemispheres of the brain, where the impulses are transformed into simple visual sensations. (Objects in the left visual field are viewed only through the **right brain hemisphere,** and vice versa.) The primary visual cortex then sends the impulses to neighboring association areas which add meaning or "associations" to them.

Further Reading
Hubel, David *Eye, Brain, and Vision.* New York: Scientific American Library, 1987.

Visual Angle

In viewing an object through one eye, the visual angle is the angle formed at the nodal point of the eye by straight lines from opposite edges of the object.

Vocational Aptitude Test

A predictive test designed to measure an individual's potential for success and satisfaction in any of various occupations and professions.

As a general example, a vocational aptitude test might consist of an instrument that assesses an individual's abilities, **personality** characteristics, and interests, and compares the individual's responses to those persons considered to be successful in their occupations and professions, with a notation of points of similarity and dissimilarity.

Vocational aptitude tests are valuable to both employers and prospective employees in a given occupation. To the prospective employee, the test results offer guidance in choosing a particular career. To the employer, they aid in the process of screening suitable employees. Vocational aptitude tests measure a wider variety of skill areas than scholastic aptitude tests. For example, the Differential Aptitude Test, one of the most widely used vocational tests, measures verbal, numerical, abstract, and mechanical reasoning; spatial relations; clerical speed and accuracy; and language usage.

Vocational aptitude tests have three primary orientations. The interactional perspective stresses the interaction between the individual and the work **environment** as the determining factor in vocational success and satisfaction. The theories of John Holland and the widely used tests based on them are an example of this approach. The central focus for Holland is congruence between an individual's personality type (realistic, investigative, artistic, social, enterprising, or conventional) and his or her vocational environment. Research has indicated that congruent person-environment interactions lead to personal and vocational stability and fulfillment.

Tests based on the person perspective emphasize the individual, rather than the work environment, as the crucial variable in vocational success. Theories associated with this orientation include Osipow's Trait Factor approach, focusing on personal characteristics linking an individual to various vocational groups, and Super's developmental **self-concept** theory, which regards vocational choice as a means of self-expression. Roe's personality theory concentrates on individuals employed in scientific fields and their relative degree of interest in people and things. Finally, the environment perspective views vocational choice and performance as primarily a function of environmental or situational factors.

Further Reading

Gale, Barry. *Discover What You're Best At.* New York: Simon & Schuster, 1990.

Voyeurism. See **Paraphilia.**

Washburn, Margaret Floy (1871–1939)

American psychologist.

Margaret Floy Washburn was the first woman ever to receive a doctorate in psychology and the second woman to be elected to the National Academy of Sciences (1931), the most eminent scientific society in the United States. The only child of Francis Washburn and Elizabeth Floy Davis, Washburn was raised in a middle class home in New York. The women in her family were exceptional and attained high levels of academic accomplishment for the era. Educated both in public and private schools, Washburn graduated from Vassar College in 1891 with a keen interest in science and philosophy. She audited graduate courses taught by **James McKeen Cattell** at Columbia University, but in spite of his full support, she was denied admission to the graduate program due to gender restrictions. Admitted as a degree candidate at Cornell University, she won the Susan Lynn Sage Fellowship in Philosophy and Ethics. In two short years, working under the noted researcher Edward B. Titchener (1886–1927) in experimental psychology, Washburn earned her Ph.D., the first woman ever to receive a doctorate in psychology. In 1894, she was elected to membership in the American Psychological Association where she eventually became a council member, establishing policy and serving on many committees.

Because women were not eligible to be hired as regular faculty in psychology or philosophy departments in any major eastern university at the close of the nineteenth century, Washburn held a series of teaching positions at women's colleges, including Wells College (1894), Sage College at Cornell University (1900) and the University of Cincinnati (1902). Although Edward Titchener had been her mentor at Cornell, he refused to admit her to the Society of Experimental Psychologists he formed in 1904. While this group was expressly designed to help young researchers, he summarily excluded all women on

Margaret Floy Washburn

the grounds that their presence would inhibit "frank discussion" among the male members. In 1903, Washburn became Assistant Professor of Philosophy at Vassar College, where she was promoted to professor in 1908, eventually becoming professor emeritus in 1937.

Washburn was known primarily for her work in animal psychology. *The Animal Mind,* which she published in 1908, was the first book by an American in this field and remained the standard comparative psychology textbook for the next 25 years. (Subsequent editions appeared in 1917, 1926, and 1936.) In *Movement and Mental Imagery* (1916), she presented her motor theory of **consciousness,** in which she attempted to mediate between the structuralist, or "introspective" tradition of Wilhelm Wundt (1832–1920) and Titchener, in which she had been schooled, and the opposing behaviorist view. These competing movements had divorced consciousness from behavior, with the structuralists studying only the former, while the behaviorists maintained that psychology should only be concerned with the latter. Washburn's theory reconciled these two perspectives by exploring the ways in which thoughts and **perception**s produce motor reaction.

In 1925 Washburn was named one of four coeditors of the *American Journal of Psychology.* She was elected president of the **American Psychological Association** in 1921 and elected to the National Academy of Sciences in 1931, the second woman ever to be chosen for that honor. Altogether, Washburn published over 200 articles and reviews, including more than 70 research articles during her 33-year tenure at Vassar. In her writings, she developed her theory of consciousness at greater length and explored such diverse topics as individual differences, **color vision** in animals, aesthetic preferences for colors and sounds, after-images, and psychology of the affective processes.

Further Reading

Scarborough, Elizabeth, and Laurel Furumoto. *Untold Lives: The First Generation of American Women Psychologists.* New York: Columbia University Press, 1987, pp. 109–29.

· ·

Watson, John Broadus (1878–1958)

Pioneering American psychologist who first formulated the principles of behaviorism.

John Broadus Watson was born in Greenville, South Carolina and, for much of his youth, he expected to enter the ministry. However, he became interested in **psychology** while an undergraduate at Greenville's Furman University and went on to do graduate work in the field at the University of Chicago, where he received his Ph.D. in 1903. Although he expected to work with **John Dewey,** who had made the university a world-renowned center for functionalist psychology, Watson was uncomfortable with Dewey's approach and instead studied animal psychology under the direction of Henry Donaldson, writing his doctoral thesis (on development in white rats) under the supervision of Donaldson and James Angell. Watson remained at Chicago as an instructor until 1908, when he was offered a full professorship by Johns Hopkins University.

Initially Watson's teaching conformed to the prevailing schools of psychology—the structuralism of Wilhelm Wundt and the functionalism of **William James** and Dewey. However, the principles he was evolving through his continuing research on animals conflicted increasingly with these approaches. Asserting his independence from them in his 1913 article "Psychology as the Behaviorist Views It," he began a process that would redefine the study of psychology. Rejecting the subjective study of inner mental states through introspection, Watson declared psychology to be a totally objective science whose goal was "the prediction and control of **behavior.**" Not surprisingly, given his research interests and background, Watson also argued for the psychological similarity of humans and animals. In 1914 he expanded his articulation of behaviorist principles in the book *Behavior: An Introduction to Comparative Psychology.* The following year he was elected president of the **American Psychological Association.**

During this period, Watson first learned of **Ivan Pavlov**'s work on conditioned reflexes in animals and performed his first experiments applying the principles of **conditioning** to humans. Eventually, he came to believe that all human behavior could be explained in terms of stimulus response. Expanding on Pavlov's work, Watson theorized that **emotion**al as well as physical reactions could be conditioned. In 1918 he began conditioning experiments on infants, arriving at the conclusion that there existed only three unconditioned, or innate, responses: **fear, anger,** and rage. All other behavior he believed to be conditioned variations on these three reactions. In 1919 Watson published his views in *Psychology from the Standpoint of a Behaviorist,* showing how animal research and behaviorist principles could be applied to human psychology. The following year he attempted for the first time to produce a conditioned emotional response in a human infant. In this famous experiment, he conditioned an infant ("Little Albert") to fear a white rat by associating the rat with a loud, frightening noise. Eventually the child came to fear not only the rat but also, to a lesser extent, other furry animals and even objects such as fur coats.

Watson's experiment with Little Albert affected both his personal and professional lives in ways that went beyond its scientific import. He and Rosalie Rayner, the graduate student with whom he had collaborated on the experiment, had an affair, which was discovered by Watson's first wife, the former Mary Ickes. After she divorced him, Watson and Rayner were married, but the scandal surrounding these events resulted in Watson's dismissal from his post at Johns Hopkins. Moving to New York, he was hired by the advertising firm J. Walter Thompson and never returned to full-time academic work, although he lectured part time at the New School for Social Research. Distinguishing himself in his new field, Watson introduced such innovations as celebrity and professional product endorsements, and his firm promoted him to the position of vice president by 1924.

In the same year, he published his New School lectures in the book *Behaviorism,* which resulted in widespread dissemination of his ideas among the general public. In this book, Watson vividly popularized his radical **environment**alist view that conditioning was overwhelmingly the dominant factor in all behavior, leaving the import of **heredity** and physiology negligible. It was here that he made his famous statement ("Give me a dozen healthy infants. . .") claiming that, given the opportunity, he could use conditioning to determine at will the **personality** and profession of any individual regardless of inborn and/or inherited characteristics. After the publication of *Behaviorism,* Watson began increasingly to write for the general public and, with the 1928 appearance of *Psychological Care of Infant and Child,* established a reputation as an authority on child rearing practices. Watson was not active in professional psychology after 1930. However by that time behaviorism had found a new champion in **B. F. Skinner,** and the approach that Watson had pioneered went on to dominate American psychology for the next three decades.

Further Reading

Buckley, Kerry W. *Mechanical Man: John Broadus Watson and the Beginnings of Behaviorism.* Guilford Press, 1989.

Cohen, David. *J. B. Watson, the Founder of Behaviourism: A Biography.* London: Routledge & Kegan Paul, 1979.

Wechsler Intelligence Scales

A widely used series of intelligence tests developed by clinical psychologist David Wechsler.

The Wechsler Intelligence Scales are divided two sections: verbal and nonverbal (or "performance"), with separate scores for each. Verbal **intelligence,** the component most often associated with academic success, implies the **ability** to think in abstract terms using either words or mathematical symbols. Performance intelligence suggests the ability to perceive relationships and fit separate parts together logically into a whole. The inclusion of the performance section in the Wechsler scales is especially helpful in assessing the cognitive ability of children with speech and **language** disorders or whose first language is not English. The test can be of particular value to **school psychologists** screening for specific **learning disabilities** because of the number of specific subtests that make up each section.

The Wechsler Preschool and Primary Scales of Intelligence (WPPSI) have traditionally been geared toward children ages four to six, although the 1989 version of the test (WPPSI-III, 1989) extends the age range down to three years and upward to seven years, three months. The Verbal section covers the following areas: general information (food, money, the body, etc.); vocabulary (definitions of increasing difficulty); comprehension (responses to questions); arithmetic (adding, subtracting, counting); sentences (repeating progressively longer sentences); and similarities (responding to questions such as "How are a pen and pencil alike?"). The Performance section includes picture completion; copying geometric designs; using blocks to reproduce designs; working through a maze; and building an "animal house" from a model.

The Wechsler Intelligence Scale for Children (WISC), now in its second revision (WISC-III, 1991), is designed for children and adolescents ages six to sixteen. The WISC differs from the WIPPSI in the following notable ways: geometric designs are replaced by assembly of three-dimensional objects; children arrange groups of pictures to tell simple stories; they are asked to remember and repeat lists of digits; a coding exercise is performed in place of the animal house; and mazes are a subtest. For all of the Wechsler scales (which also include the Wechsler Adult Intelligence Scale, or WAIS), separate verbal and performance scores, as well as a total score, are computed. These are then converted using a scale divided into categories (such as average and superior), and the final score is generally given as one of these categories rather than as a number or percentile ranking.

See also Intelligence Quotient, I.Q. test; Stanford-Binet Intelligence Scales.

Yerkes, Robert (1876–1956)

American psychologist who made important contributions to the fields of comparative animal psychology, particularly in the areas of animal intelligence and behavior.

Robert Yerkes was born in Pennsylvania, and was educated at Harvard University, where he received his doctorate in psychology in 1902. He served as professor of psychology at Harvard, the University of Minnesota, and Yale University, and as a member of the National Research Council. In 1919, Yerkes founded the Yale Laboratories of Primate Biology and served as its director from 1929 to 1941, when the lab was moved to Orange Park, Florida. A year later, it was renamed the Yerkes Laboratories of Primate Biology. A pioneer in the field of **comparative psychology,** Yerkes studied the **intelligence** and behavior of many forms of animal life, from jellyfish to humans, but he focused most of his attention on primates. Among his findings were the discovery that chimpanzees imitate both each other and human beings, and the observation that orangutans can pile boxes on top of one another to reach food after seeing this demonstrated, thus transferring this experience to other **learning** problems.

Yerkes also worked on the Yerkes-Dodson Law, which states that for every task there is an optimum level of **motivation,** and that motivation that is too strong can actually interfere with the **ability** to perform a difficult task. Yerkes also pioneered the use of monochromatic light to study **color vision** in animals. In 1911, he developed the first multiple-choice test for animals, designed to test abstraction abilities. A row of nine or fewer boxes were shown to the animal, which had to determine which of the open boxes had food in it and then remember that box in subsequent rounds of testing.

Turning his attention to human testing, Yerkes revised the **Stanford-Binet Intelligence scales** in 1915 to create a widely used point scale for the **measurement** of human mental ability. He was also a principal figure in

Robert Yerkes

the development of human multiple choice testing. During World War I, Yerkes directed a team of 40 psychologists charged with assessing the abilities of army recruits for training, assignment, and discharge purposes. Together they developed the Army Alpha test, a written intelligence test, and Army Beta, a pictorial test for the 40 percent of draftees who were functionally illiterate. By the end of the war, these tests had been used to classify some 1.75 million men. As a result of taking these tests, some 8,000 had been discharged as unfit, while the Alpha test played a role in the selection of two thirds of the 200,000 men who served as commissioned officers during the war.

In addition to its impact on the military, the wartime testing developed by Yerkes and his colleagues had a far-reaching effect on civilian life after the war. Unlike the Stanford Binet scale, which had to be individually administered by a tester, the Alpha and Beta tests were developed to be administered to groups, making them faster, simpler, and far less expensive to use. After the war, this breakthrough in mental measurement led to a dramatic expansion in intelligence testing. Yerkes and several colleagues devised one of several pencil-and-paper tests that were marketed to school administrators throughout the country. The National Research Council, the test's sponsor, described it as deriving from "the application of the army testing methods to school needs." By 1930, it had been administered to seven million schoolchildren. (The *Scholastic Aptitude Test* was developed by one of Yerkes' colleagues during this same period.) Yerkes' books include: *Introduction to Psychology* (1911), *The Mental Life of Monkeys and Apes* (1916), *The Great Apes* (1929) (coauthored with Ada Yerkes), and *Chimpanzees: A Laboratory Colony* (1943).

GLOSSARY

Ability. Skill or knowledge that can be demonstrated.

Achromatic colors. Black, white or gray.

Achievement. Demonstration of skills or knowledge.

Accuracy. Ability to get the correct (or true) result.

Afterimage. The after-effect of a sensory experience, usually used in relation to vision.

Agoraphobia. Fear of being alone, or of being vulnerable in public with no route for escape.

AIDS. Acronym for Acquired Immune Deficiency Syndrome, a condition caused by a deadly virus that attacks the body's immune system. The disease is transmitted via body fluids, especially sexual secretions and blood. Intravenous drug users risk getting AIDS from infected needles.

Alcohol. Ethanol, the intoxicating substance in distilled or fermented liquors; a drink containing ethanol.

Ambiguity. No clear-cut right or wrong answer or course of action.

Amphetamine. A chemical compound used clinically as a drug for treating hyperactive children or as an appetite suppressant; abused as a central nervous system stimulant.

Anabolism. Storage of energy, controlled by the parasympathetic nervous system, in the human body.

Anal stage. The second stage (the first is the oral stage) of psychosexual development described by the psychoanalytic theory.

Analgesic. Any drug used primarily to relieve pain. Examples of analgesics include morphine or opiates.

Anima. Term used by psychologist Carl Jung to define as a man's feminine side.

Animus. Term used by psychologist Carl Jung to define a woman's masculine side.

Aptitude. The capacity to learn.

Attention span. In psychology, the number of separate stimulus elements or the amount of stimulus material that an individual can perceive and remember after a brief presentation.

Average. A layperson's term usually used to describe the arithmetic average, or mean, calculated by adding all the scores in a set of data and dividing the sum by the number of scores.

Barbiturates. Any derivative of a synthetic crystalline acid used as a sedative or hypnotic drug, often taken illicitly.

Blood alcohol concentration (BAC). The measure of the amount of alcohol in a person's blood; given in grams per deciliter (g/dL, with 100 grams = one deciliter). The BAC given as a percentage would be equal to the g/dL. In most states, a BAC of between 0.01 and 0.09% is within the legal limit; a

BAC of greater than 0.10% would constitute intoxication.

C

Catabolism. Use of stored energy by the human body when mobilized or aroused.

Chromatography. A procedure used to identify substances, such as drugs of abuse in urine, based on separating or extracting the substances, allowing them to move or migrate along a carrier, and then identifying them.

Cocaine. A crystalline organic base derived from coca leaves, used illicitly as a euphoria-producing drug which is psychologically addictive.

Codependence. Person involved in a relationship with someone with addiction or other behavior disorders. The codependent individual exhibits personality traits such as depression, denial, isolation, and self-destructive behavior.

Community mental health center (CMCH). Includes services which are provided in a comprehensive manner in order to provide a community service. The services usually provided by CMHCs are outpatient care, inpatient care, partial hospitalization, emergency care and consultation and education.

Concentration. Amount of a drug in a unit of biological fluid, expressed as weight/volume. Urine concentrations are usually expressed either as nanograms per milliliter (ng/ml), as micrograms per milliliter (mg/ml), or milligrams per liter (mg/l). (There are 28,000,000 micrograms in an ounce, and 1,000 nanograms in a microgram.)

Consensus. Members of a group exhibit similar behaviors or ideas.

Criminal justice. Activities which include enforcement, prosecution, and sentencing to apprehend, convict, and punish drug offenders. Although thought of primarily as having supply reduction goals, criminal sanctions also have demand reduction effects by discouraging drug use.

Crisis intervention services. Activities which provide information about the availability of services and/or provide services directly to a person on an outpatient basis when he/she is in a crisis situation. A hotline could provide this service by referring a person for emergency care or to an appropriate treatment unit.

Cybernetics. The study of artificial intelligence systems and their comparison to human brain functions.

D

Depersonalization. The sense of not knowing who you are, or of questioning the truth or long-held beliefs. A factor in diagnosing dissociative disorders.

Derealization. Grossly distorted view of reality.

Detection limit. Lowest concentration of a drug that can reliably be detected.

Detoxification (drug). The period of planned withdrawal from drug dependency supported by use of a prescribed medication. If methadone is being used, detoxification cannot exceed 21 days. When methadone detoxification exceeds 21 days, the treatment modality becomes maintenance.

Detoxification (medical). The use of medication under the supervision of medical personnel to systematically reduce or eliminate the effects of alcohol in the body in a hospital or other 24-hour care facility.

Detoxification (social). To systematically reduce or eliminate the effects of alcohol in the body on a drug-free basis, in a specialized nonmedical facility by trained personnel with physician services available when required.

Diffusion of responsibility. Term used by psychologists to refer to the belief by individual members of a group that someone else in the group holds the responsibility.

Drug free. A treatment regimen that does not include any pharmacologic agent or medication as the primary part of the drug treatment including drug detoxification. Temporary medication may be prescribed in a drug free modality, e.g., short-term use of tranquilizers or clonidine for opiate withdrawal, but the primary treatment method is counseling (individual, group, family, etc.), not pharmacotherapy.

Dysfunctional family. Lay term used to describe a family where relationship support or contribute to mental disorders.

E

Early intervention services. This term is used to describe services provided soon after a problem or condition is diagnosed. Early intervention services are offered for substance abuse problems, to infants and young children with learning and developmental problems, etc. The goals include providing crisis services, educating the family members and other caregivers, and to offer appropriate support services.

Electrodes. In psychology and health sciences, electrodes are metal discs attached to the scalp or to wires connected to the skull or chest for the purpose of conducing a diagnostic test.

Estimate. A rough or approximate calculation used to find a value when there is incomplete data to ascertain the actual value.

F

Family counseling/therapy services. Services which are provided during the same session to members of a family/collateral group.

Fetal alcohol syndrome (FAS). A birth defect characterized by a variety of physical and behavioral traits that result from maternal alcohol consumption during pregnancy.

H

Halfway house/recovery home. A community-based, peer group-oriented, residential facility that provides food, shelter, and supportive services (including vocational, recreational, social services) in a supportive non-drug use, non-drinking environment for the ambulatory and mentally competent person who may be reentering the work force. It also provides or arranges for provision of appropriate treatment services.

Hallucinogen. A drug or any substance that produces hallucinations.

HIV. Acronym for human immunodeficiency virus; one of a group of retroviruses that destroy the human immune system; producing the disease known as AIDS.

Hotline. A telephone service that provides information and referral and immediate counseling, frequently in a crisis situation.

I

Immunoassay. A procedure used to identify substances, such as drugs of abuse in urine. The uncombined, tagged antigen is an indicator of the drug present in the urine specimen.

Individual counseling/therapy services. Services which are provided to a client on a one-to-one basis.

L

Licit drug. A legal drug; a prescription medication.

LSD. Lysergic acid diethylamide; an organic compound that causes psychotic symptoms, used illicitly to produce a psychedelic effect.

M

Marijuana. The dried leaves and flowers of the hemp plant, usually illicitly smoked as a cigarette for its intoxicating effect.

Metabolite. A compound produced from chemical changes of a drug in the body.

Mode. The most frequently occurring member of a set of numbers. For the set of values [2, 3, 3, 5, 6, 6, 10] there are two modes, 3 and 6, since both values occur most often.

Morphine. The principal narcotic organic base of opium, used clinically to relieve pain or as a sedative; abused as an addictive narcotic.

N

Neurosis. Outdated term for psychological disorder; formerly used to describe conditions that involved anxiety in some form.

O

Opiate. A derivative of opium, a broad term for a narcotic.

Opium. An addictive narcotic drug derived from the opium poppy.

Outpatient facility. An establishment or a distinct part of an establishment, which is primarily engaged in providing drug abuse or alcoholism services for persons who reside elsewhere.

Outpatient. Treatment/recovery/aftercare, or rehabilitation services provided by a facility where the client does not reside in a treatment facility. The client receives drug abuse or alcoholism treatment services with or without medication, including counseling and supportive services. Daycare is included in this category. This is also known as non-residential services in the alcoholism field.

Outreach services. Outreach activities involve efforts in the community for early case-finding and early intervention services to drug and alcohol abusers. These services would also include efforts to educate various groups about drug and alcohol abuse.

P

Pedophile. Person who engages in sexual abuse of children.

Persona. Term used by psychologist Carl Jung to describe a person's public image.

Pluralistic ignorance. Group behavior that influences each individual member to behave as if they were not acknowledging the significance of an event, such as an emergency.

Precision. Ability to get the same result in repeated measurements.

Psychosis. Outdated term no longer included in the American Psychiatric Association's *Diagnostic and Statistical Manual of Mental Disorders (DSM-IV)*. It was formerly used to describe condition in which the patient had lost the ability to carry on the activities of daily living.

Public welfare Medical or social service benefits or payments made available through local general assistance or general relief programs, including food stamps.

R

Random sample. A sampling from some population where each entry has an equal chance of being drawn. Random sampling is used to obtain significant statistics about groups too large to sample individually.

Reliablity. Term used in testing to describe tests that produce consistent and reproducible results.

Representative sample. A sample so large and average in composition that it can be said to accurately represent the larger group from which it was drawn.

Research services. Activities performed by unit staff to systematically collect and/or analyze empirical data based on the scientific model of developing knowledge.

Residential facility. A live-in setting where nonmedical rehabilitative drug abuse and/or alcoholism services are available to residents, e.g., foster homes, group homes, or boarding houses.

S

Self-help groups. Independent support groups or fellowships organized by and for drug abusers, alcoholics or their collaterals to help members achieve and maintain abstinence from and/or cope with the effects of licit or illicit drugs and alcohol. Examples are Alcoholics Anonymous, Narcotics Anonymous, Women for Sobriety, Al Anon or other non-professionally led groups such as Al Anon-Adult Children of Alcoholics.

Shadow. Term used by psychologist Carl Jung to describe the side of a person outside the control of the conscious personality.

Specialized hospital. Includes hospitals that emphasize the diagnosis and treatment of particular disorders, e.g., psychiatric, children, epilepsy, maternity, orthopedics, etc.

Stroke. Technically a lay term, used to refer to the loss of blook to a part of the brain and the resulting tissue damage.

Substance. A term for drugs or alcoholic beverages which are usually considered harmful and are regulated by laws.

Substance abuse. Use of a substance, such as alcohol or drugs, to excess or without medical necessity.

Symbolization. A type of inverse modeling behavior, where a person constructs an internal model of the world to provide a framework for decision-making and problem solving.

T

Teen suicide prevention services. Services for youth, family members, and peers designed to educate, prevent, or intervene in teen suicidal behavior.

Tranquilizers. Any drug that produces a calming effect without inducing sleep. Tranquilizers are used to relieve anxiety and achieve peace of mind. Although tranquilizers are useful and important drugs prescribed by doctors, they are also prone to substance abuse.

U

Unanimity. Agreement of opinion among members of a group, an extemely powerful influence in group behavior.

V

Validity. Term used in testing to describe tests that measure what they are intended to measure.

BIBLIOGRAPHY

A

Adams, Raymond. *Principles of Neurology.* New York: McGraw-Hill, 1993.

Adler, Alfred. *Co-operation Between the Sexes: Writings on Women and Men, Love and Marriage, and Sexuality.* New York: Norton, 1982.

——. *The Individual Psychology of Alfred Adler: A Systematic Presentation in Selections From His Writings.* New York: Harper & Row, 1964.

Aggression and Peacefulness in Humans and Other Primates. New York: Oxford University Press, 1992.

Aggressive Behavior: Current Perspectives. New York: Plenum Press, 1994.

Ainsworth, M., M. Blehar, E. Walters, and S. Wall. *Patterns of Attachment: A Psychological Study of the Strange Situation.* Hillsdale, NJ: Erlbaum, 1978.

Allport, G. *Pattern and Growth in Personality.* New York: Holt, Rinehart, and Winston, 1961.

Altman, Irwin. *The Environment and Social Behavior: Privacy, Personal Space, Territory, Crowding.* Monterey, CA: Brooks/Cole, 1975.

Ames, Louise Bates. *Arnold Gesell: Themes of His Work.* New York: Human Sciences Press, 1989.

Ammerman, Robert T. and Michel Hersen, eds. *Handbook of Behavior Therapy with Children and Adults: A Developmental and Longitudinal Perspective.* New York: Allyn and Bacon, 1993.

Anderson, Barry F. *Cognitive Psychology: The Study of Knowing, Learning, and Thinking.* San Diego, CA: Academic Press, 1975.

Anderson, Clifford. *The Stages of Life: A Groundbreaking Discovery: the Steps to Psychological Maturity.* New York: Atlantic Monthly Press, 1995.

Anderson, John R. *Cognitive Psychology and Its Implications.* New York: W.H. Freeman, 1985.

Andreassi, John L. *Psychophysiology: Human Behavior and Physiological Response.* New York: Oxford University Press, 1980.

Andrews, Barbara. *Dreams and Waking Visions: A Journal.* New York: St. Martin's Press, 1989.

Anonymous. *It Happened to Nancy.* New York: Avon Books, 1994.

Archer, Trevor, and Lars-Gvran Nilsson. *Aversion, Avoidance, and Anxiety: Perspective on Aversively Motivated Behavior.* Hillsdale, NJ: Lawrence Erlbaum Associates, 1989.

Ashcraft, Mark H. *Human Memory and Cognition.* New York: HarperCollins College Publishers, 1994.

Asimov, Isaac. *The Human Brain: Its Capacities and Functions.* New York: Penguin, 1994.

Atkinson, Rita L., Atkinson, Richard C., Smith, Edward E., and Hilgard, Ernest R. *Introduction to Psychology.* 9th ed. San Diego: Harcourt Brace Jovanovich, 1987.

Autism: Nature, Diagnosis, and Treatment. New York: Guilford Press, 1989.

B

Babkin, Boris P. *Pavlov: A Biography.* Chicago: University of Chicago Press, 1949.

Bajema, Carl Jay, ed. *Eugenics: Then and Now.* Stroudsburg, PA: Dowden, Hutchinson & Ross, 1976.

Bandura, Albert. *Aggression: A Social Learning Analysis.* New York: Prentice-Hall, 1973.

———. *Principles of Behavior Modification.* New York: Holt, Rinehart, and Winston, 1969.

———. *Social Foundations of Thought and Action: A Social Cognitive Theory.* Englewood Cliffs, NJ: Prentice-Hall, 1986.

———. *Social Learning Theory.* Englewood Cliffs, NJ: Prentice-Hall, 1971.

Barlow, David H. and V. Mark Durand, eds. *Abnormal Psychology.* Pacific Grove, CA: Brooks/Cole, 1995.

Barnouw, Victor. *Culture and Personality,* 4th ed. Homewood, IL: Dorsey Press, 1985.

Bartenieff, Irmgard. *Body Movement: Coping with the Environment.* New York: Gordon and Breach Science Publishers, 1980.

Bateson, Mary Catherine. *With a Daughter's Eye: A Memoir of Margaret Mead and Gregory Bateson.* New York: William Morrow, 1984.

Baumeister, Roy F. *Escaping the Self: Alcoholism, Spirituality, Masochism, and Other Flights from the Burden of Selfhood.* New York: Basic Books, 1991.

Baur, Susan. *Hypochondria.* Berkeley: University of California Press, 1988.

Beattie, Melody. *Codependent No More: How to Stop Controlling Others and Start Caring for Yourself.* San Francisco: Hazelden/HarperCollins, 1987.

Beatty, J., and H. Legewie, eds. *Biofeedback and Behavior.* New York: Plenum Press, 1977.

Beck, Robert C. *Applying Psychology: Critical and Creative Thinking,* 3rd ed. Englewood Cliffs, NJ: Prentice-Hall, 1992.

Bee, Helen L. *The Developing Child,* 5th ed. New York: Harper & Row, 1989.

Bemis, Judith. *Embracing the Fear: Learning to Manage Anxiety and Panic Attacks.* St. Paul, MN: Hazelden, 1994.

Benjamin, L. T., Jr. *A History of Psychology: Original Sources and Contemporary Research.* New York: McGraw-Hill, 1988.

Bennett, Jill. *Sight.* Morristown, NJ: Silver Burdett, 1986.

Berger, Kathleen Stassen. *The Developing Person Through the Life Span,* 2nd ed. New York: Worth Publishers, 1988.

Berk, Laura E. *Child Development.* Boston: Allyn and Bacon, 1989.

Berko-Gleason, J. *The Development of Language.* New York: Macmillan, 1993.

Berman, Simeon M. *Mathematical Statistics: An Introduction Based on the Normal Distribution.* Scranton, PA: Intext Educational Publishers, 1971.

Bernard, M. E. *Staying Alive in an Irrational World: Albert Ellis and Rational-Emotive Therapy.* South Melbourne, Australia: Carlson/Macmillan, 1986.

Berndt, Thomas J. *Child Development.* Fort Worth: Harcourt Brace Jovanovich College Publishers, 1992

Bernstein, Douglas A. *Introduction to Clinical Psychology.* New York: McGraw-Hill, 1980.

Berscheid, Ellen. *Interpersonal Attraction,* 2nd ed. Reading, MA: Addison-Wesley Pub. Co., 1978.

Biofeedback and Behavioral Medicine. New York: Aldine Pub. Co., published annually.

Bird, Anne Marie. *Psychology and Sport Behavior.* St. Louis: Times Mirror/Mosby College Pub., 1986.

Biro, J.I. and Robert W. Shahan, eds. *Mind, Brain, and Function: Essays in the Philosophy of Mind.* Norman: University of Oklahoma Press, 1982.

Biskup, Michael, and Carol Wekesser, eds. *Suicide: Opposing Viewpoints.* San Diego: Greenhaven Press, 1992.

Black, Janet K., Margaret B. Puckett, and Michael J. Bell. *The Young Child: Development from Prebirth Through Age Eight.* New York: Merrill, 1992.

Blackham, Garth J. *Modification of Child and Adolescent Behavior,* 3rd ed. Belmont, CA: Wadsworth Pub. Co., 1980.

Bluman, Allan G. *Elementary Statistics: A Step-by-Step Approach.* Dubuque, IA: Wm. C. Brown Publishers, 1995.

Bock, Philip K. *Rethinking Psychological Anthropology: Continuity and Change in the Study of Human Action.* New York: W.H. Freeman, 1988.

Bolles, Edmund Blair. *Remembering and Forgetting: An Inquiry into the Nature of Memory.* New York: Walker and Co., 1988.

Boulding, Kenneth Ewart. *Conflict and Defense: A General Theory.* Lanham, MD: University Press of America, 1988.

Bourne, Lyle Eugene. *Cognitive Processes.* New York: Prentice-Hall, 1979.

Bowe, Frank. *Equal Rights for Americans with Disabilities.* New York: Franklin Watts, 1992.

Boydston, Jo Ann. *Guide to the Works of John Dewey.* Edwardsville, IL: Southern Illinois University Press, 1972.

Brammer, Lawrence M. *Therapeutic Psychology: Fundamentals of Counseling and Psychotherapy,* 5th ed. Englewood Cliffs, NJ: Prentice Hall, 1989.

Briggs, John. *Fire in the Crucible: The Alchemy of Creative Genius.* New York: St. Martin's Press, 1988.

Broadbent, Donald E. *Perception and Communication.* New York: Oxford University Press, 1987.

Brown, Marie Scott. *Normal Development of Body Image.* New York: Wiley, 1977.

Browning, Elizabeth. *I Can't See What You're Saying.* New York: Coward, McCann & Geoghegan, 1973.

Bruner, Jerome S. *In Search of Mind: Essays in Autobiography.* New York: Harper & Row, 1983.

———. *Studies in Cognitive Growth: A Collaboration at the Center for Cognitive Studies.* New York: John Wiley & Sons, 1966.

Bruno, Frank J. *The Family Encyclopedia of Child Psychology and Development.* New York: John Wiley & Sons, 1992.

Buckley, Kerry W. *Mechanical Man: John Broadus Watson and the Beginnings of Behaviorism.* Guilford Press, 1989.

Bull, Ray. *The Social Psychology of Facial Appearance.* New York: Springer-Verlag, 1988.

Bunker, Linda K. *Motivating Kids Through Play.* West Point, NY: Leisure Press, 1982.

Burden, George. *Understanding Epilepsy,* 2nd ed., Brooklyn Heights, N Y: Beekman, 1980.

C

Cahn, Dudley, ed. *Conflict in Personal Relationships.* Hillsdale, NJ: L. Erlbaum Associates, 1994.

Candland, Douglas Keith. *Feral Children and Clever Animals: Reflections on Human Nature.* New York: Oxford University Press, 1993.

Caplan, Paula J. *The Myth of Women's Masochism.* Toronto: University of Toronto Press, 1993.

Carruthers, Peter. *Human Knowledge and Human Nature: A New Introduction to an Ancient Debate.* Oxford, Eng.: Oxford University Press,1992.

Carter, William Lee. *The Angry Teenager.* Nashville: Thomas Nelson, 1995.

Chalkley, Thomas. *Your Eyes,* 3rd ed. Springfield, IL: C.C. Thomas, 1995.

Changeux, Jean-Pierre. *Neuronal Man.* New York: Pantheon Books, 1985.

Chapman, Elwood N. *Attitude: Your Most Priceless Possession.* 2nd ed. Los Altos, CA: Crisp Publications, 1990.

Chemotherapy & You: A Guide to Self-help During Treatment. Bethesda, MD: U.S. Dept. of Health and Human Services, Public Health Service, National Institutes of Health, National Cancer Institute, 1985.

Childs, Ruth Axman. *Gender Bias and Fairness.* Washington, D.C.: ERIC Clearinghouse on Texts, Measurement, and Evaluation, 1990.

Christensen, Larry B. *Experimental Methodology,* 5th ed. Boston: Allyn and Bacon, 1991.

Cialdini, Robert B. *Influence: Science and Practice,* 3rd ed. New York: HarperCollins College Publishers, 1993.

Cicchetti, Dante and Donald J. Cohen, eds. *Developmental Psychopathology.* New York: J. Wiley, 1995.

Clark, Ronald W. *The Survival of Charles Darwin: A Biography of a Man and an Idea.* New York: Random House, 1984.

Classical Conditioning, 3rd ed. Hillsdale, NJ: L. Erlbaum Associates, 1987.

Clifford, G. J. *Edward L. Thorndike: The Sane Positivist.* Middletown, PA: Wesleyan University Press, 1984.

Cohen, David. *J. B. Watson, the Founder of Behaviorism: A Biography.* London: Routledge & Kegan Paul, 1979.

Cohen, Irving A. *Addiction: The High-Low Trap.* Santa Fe, NM: Health Press, 1995.

Coles, Robert. *Erik H. Erikson: The Growth of His Work.* Boston: Little, Brown & Co., 1970.

———. *Anna Freud: The Dream of Psychoanalysis.* Reading, MA: Addison-Wesley Publishing Company, Inc., 1992.

———. *The Moral Life of Children.* Boston: Houghton Mifflin, 1987.

Cooke, Gerald, ed. *The Role of the Forensic Psychologist.* Springfield, IL: Thomas, 1980.

Cooper, R. *EEG Technology.* New York: Butterworth, 1980.

Corballis, Michael C. *The Lopsided Ape: Evolution of the Generative Mind.* New York: Oxford University Press, 1991.

Coren, Stanley. *The Left-Hander Syndrome: The Causes and Consequences of Left-Handedness.* New York: Vintage Books, 1993.

Craighead, Linda W. *Cognitive and Behavioral Interventions: An Empirical Approach to Mental Health Problems.* Boston: Allyn and Bacon, 1994.

Cunninghame, Karen. *Autism: A World Apart.* Fanlight Productions, 1988.

D

D'Agostino, F. *Chomsky's System of Ideas.* Oxford: Oxford University Press, 1986.

Dalton, Katharina. *PMS: The Essential Guide to Treatment Options.* London, Eng.: Thorsons, 1994.

D'Amato, M. R. *Experimental Psychology: Methodology, Psychophysics, and Learning.* New York: McGraw-Hill, 1970

Darwin, Charles. *The Autobiography of Charles Darwin, 1809–1882.* Edited by Nora Barlow. New York: Norton, 1969.

Davis, Lennard J. *Enforcing Normalcy: Disability, Deafness, and the Body.* New York: Verso, 1995.

De Beer, Gavin. *Charles Darwin: Evolution by Natural Selection.* London: Doubleday, 1963.

Deikman, Arthur J. *The Wrong Way Home: Uncovering Patterns of Cult Behavior in American Society.* Boston: Beacon Press, 1990.

Dembo, Myron H. *Applying Educational Psychology,* 5th ed. New York: Longman, 1994.

Diagnostic and Statistical Manual of Mental Disorders. 4th ed. Washington, D.C.: American Psychiatric Association, 1994.

Dix, Albert S. *Humor: the Bright Side of Pain.* New York, NY: Carlton Press, 1989.

Dockrell, Julie. *Children's Learning Difficulties: A Cognitive Approach.* Cambridge, MA: Blackwell, 1993.

Dolinar, Kathleen J. *Learning Through Play: Curriculum and Activities for the Inclusive Classroom.* Albany, NY: Delmar, 1994.

Doob, Leonard William. *Inevitability: Determinism, Fatalism, and Destiny.* New York: Greenwood Press, 1988.

Darwin, Leonard. *What Is Eugenics?* London: Watts, 1928.

Davis, Lennard J. *Enforcing Normalcy: Disability, Deafness, and the Body.* New York: Verso, 1995.

Decker, Philip J. *Behavior Modeling Training.* New York: Praeger, 1985.

Dennett, D.C. *Brainstorms.* Cambridge, MA: Bradford Books, 1980.

Dentemaro, Christine. *Straight Talk About Anger.* New York: Facts on File, 1995.

Dix, Albert S. *Humor: the Bright Side of Pain.* New York, NY: Carlton Press, 1989.

Duke, Patty. *Call Me Anna.* New York: Bantam, 1987.

Dworetzky, John. *Introduction to Child Development,* 5th ed. Minneapolis: West Publishing Co., 1993

E

East, Edward Murray. *Mankind at the Crossroads.* New York: C. Scribner's Sons, 1923.

Edmonston, William E. *The Induction of Hypnosis.* New York: Wiley, 1986.

Edwards, Allen. *When Memory Fails.* New York: Plenum, 1994.

Eiser, J. Richard *Social Psychology: Attitudes, Cognition, and Social Behavior.* New York: Cambridge University Press, 1986.

Electroconvulsive Therapy: Theory and Practice. New York: Raven Press, 1979.

Elkins, James. *The Object Stares Back: On the Nature of Seeing.* New York: Simon & Schuster, 1996.

Ellis, Albert. *Anger: How to Live With and Without It.* New York: Citadel Press, 1977.

———. *Humanistic Psychotherapy: The Rational-Emotive Approach.* New York: Julian Press, 1973.

——— and W. Dryden. *The Essential Albert Ellis.* New York: Springer, 1990.

Ellis Jeffrey W., ed. *Miracle of Birth.* New York: Beekman House, 1989.

Elmes, David G. *Research Methods in Psychology,* 4th ed. St. Paul: West Publishing Company, 1992.

Endocrine System: Miraculous Messengers. New York: Torstar Books, 1985.

Engel, Joel. *Addicted: In Their Own Words. Kids Talk About Drugs.* New York: Tom Doherty Associates, 1990.

Epling, W. Rank. *Solving the Anorexia Puzzle.* Toronto: Hogrefe and Hubers, 1991.

Epstein, Joseph. *Ambition: The Secret Passion.* New York: E.P. Dutton, 1980.

Erikson, Erik. *Identity, Youth, and Crisis.* New York: W. W. Norton, 1968.

———. *Childhood and Society.* New York: W. W. Norton, 1950.

Eysenck, Michael W. *Individual Differences: Normal and Abnormal.* Hillsdale, NJ: L. Erlbaum Associates, 1994.

F

Farnham-Diggory, Sylvia. *Cognitive Processes in Education,* 2nd ed. New York: HarperCollins, 1992.

Festinger, Leon. *A Theory of Cognitive Dissonance.* Stanford, CA: Stanford University Press, 1957.

Firestone, Robert. *Psychological Defenses in Everyday Life.* New York: Human Sciences Press, 1989.

Fisher, Helen E. *Anatomy of Love: The Natural History of Monogamy, Adultery, and Divorce.* New York: W. W. Norton, 1992

Fisher, Ronald J. *The Social Psychology of Intergroup and International Conflict Resolution.* New York: Springer-Verlag, 1990.

Fisher, Seymour. *Sexual Images of the Self: the Psychology of Erotic Sensations and Illusions.* Hillsdale, NJ: L. Erlbaum Associates, 1989.

Foerstel, Lenora, and Angela Gilliam, eds. *Confronting the Margaret Mead Legacy: Scholarship, Empire, and the South Pacific.* Philadelphia: Temple University Press, 1992.

Forbes, H. D. *Nationalism, Ethnocentrism, and Personality.* Chicago: University of Chicago Press, 1985.

Forer, Lucille. *The Birth Order Factor.* New York: D. McKay Co., 1976.

Forgione, Albert G. *Fear: Learning to Cope.* New York: Van Nostrand Reinhold, 1977.

Forrest, D.W. *Francis Galton: The Life and Work of a Victorian Genius.* London: Elek, 1974

Foster, Carol, et al., eds. *AIDS.* Wylie, TX: Information Plus, 1992.

Freud, Anna. *The Writings of Anna Freud.* Vol. 6, *Normality and Pathology in Childhood: Assessments of Development.* International Universities Press, 1965.

Freud, Sigmund. *Dora: An Analysis of a Case of Hysteria.* New York: Collier, 1963.

———. *Introductory Lectures on Psycho-Analysis.* New York: W.W. Norton & Co., 1966.

———. *An Outline of Psychoanalysis.* New York: W.W. Norton, 1989.

———. *The Standard Edition of the Complete Psychological Works of Sigmund Freud.* London: Hogarth Press, 1962.

Freund, John E. *Statistics: A First Course.* Englewood Cliffs, NJ: Prentice Hall, 1995

Friedman, William H. *Practical Group Therapy: A Guide for Clinicians.* San Francisco: Jossey-Bass, 1989.

Frith, Uta. *Autism: Explaining the Enigma.* Basil Blackwell, 1989.

Fromm, Erich. *Sigmund Freud's Mission.* New York: Grove Press, 1959.

Funk, Rainer. *Erich Fromm: The Courage to be Human.* New York: Human Sciences Press, 1989.

G

Galanter, Marc. *Cults: Faith, Healing and Coercion.* Oxford: Oxford University Press, 1989.

Gale, Barry. *Discover What You're Best At.* New York: Simon & Schuster, 1990.

Gay, Kathleen. *Rights and Respect: What You Need to Know About Gender Bias.* Brookfield, CT: Millbrook Press, 1995.

Gay, Peter. *Freud: A Life for Our Time.* New York: Norton, 1988.

Gilligan, Carol. *In a Different Voice: Psychological Theory and Women's Development.* Cambridge, MA: Harvard University Press, 1982.

Ginsburg, Herbert, and Sylvia Opper. *Piaget's Theory of Intellectual Development.* Englewood Cliffs, NJ: Prentice-Hall, 1988.

Goddard, Henry Herbert. *The Kallikak Family: A Study in the Heredity of Feeble-Mindedness.* New York: Macmillan, 1927.

Goleman, Daniel. *Vital Lies, Simple Truths: the Psychology of Self-Deception.* New York: Simon and Schuster, 1985.

Goodluck, H. *Language Acquisition: A Linguistic Introduction.* Cambridge, MA: Blackwell Publishers, 1991

Goodwin, Donald W. *Anxiety.* New York: Oxford University Press, 1986.

Gray, Jeffrey Alan. *The Psychology of Fear and Stress,* 2nd ed. New York: Cambridge University Press, 1988.

Green, Lila. *Making Sense of Humor: How to Add Joy to Your Life.* Glen Rock, NJ: Knowledge, Ideas, and Trends, 1994.

Gregg, Daphna. *Alzheimer's Disease.* Boston: Harvard Medical School Health Publications, 1994.

Gribbin, John. *In Search of the Double Helix.* New York: McGraw-Hill, 1985.

Grinney, Ellen Heath. *Delinquency and Criminal Behavior.* New York: Chelsea House Publishers, 1992.

Grossmann, Reinhardt. *The Fourth Way: A Theory of Knowledge.* Bloomington: Indiana University Press, 1990.

Gruber, Howard E. *Darwin on Man: A Psychological Study of Scientific Creativity.* London: Wildwood House, 1974.

Guiley, Rosemary. *The Encyclopedia of Dreams: Symbols and Interpretations.* New York: Crossroad, 1993.

Guilford, J. P. *The Nature of Human Intelligence.* New York: McGraw-Hill, 1967.

Guinness, Alma, ed. *ABCs of the Human Mind.* Pleasantville, NY: Reader's Digest Association, 1990.

H–I

Hales, Dianne. *Depression.* New York: Chelsea House Publishers, 1989.

Hall, Calvin S. *A Primer of Freudian Psychology.* New York: Harper and Row, 1982.

——— and Vernon J. Nordby. *A Primer of Jungian Psychology.* New York: Mentor, 1973.

Halpern, Diane F. *Sex Differences in Cognitive Abilities.* Hillsdale, NJ: L. Erlbaum Associates, 1992.

Handbook of Psychological Assessment. New York: Wiley, 1990.

Hans, James. *The Mysteries of Attention.* Albany: SUNY Press, 1993.

Harris, Judith Rich and Robert M. Lieber. *The Child: A Contemporary View of Development,* 3rd ed. Englewood Cliffs, NJ: Prentice Hall, 1991.

Hartmann, Ernest. *Boundaries in the Mind: A New Psychology of Personality Difference.* New York: BasicBooks, 1991.

Harvey, Terri L., Ann L. Orbuch, and John H. Weber, eds. *Attributions, Accounts, and Close Relationships.* New York: Springer-Verlag, 1992.

Helmering, Doris Wild. *Group Therapy—Who Needs It?* Millbrae, CA: Celestial Arts, 1976.

Herman, Judith Lewis. *Trauma and Recovery.* New York: BasicBooks, 1992.

Hibbs, Euthymia, ed. *Adoption.* Madison, CT: International Universities Press, 1991.

Hoffman, Edward. *The Right to be Human: A Biography of Abraham Maslow.* Los Angeles: Tarcher, 1988.

Holmes, Lowell D. *Quest for the Real Samoa: The Mead/Freeman Controversy and Beyond.* South Hadley, MA: Bergin & Garvey, 1987.

Holtzman, Wayne. *Inkblot Perception and Personality.* Austin: University of Texas Press, 1961.

Hook, Sidney. *John Dewey: An Intellectual Portrait.* New York: John Day Co., 1939.

Hopcke, Robert. *A Guided Tour of the Collected Works of C. G. Jung.* Shambhala; distributed in the U.S. by Random House, 1989.

Hotchner, Tracy. *Pregnancy and Childbirth: The Complete Guide for a New Life,* 2nd ed. New York: Avon, 1990

Houts, Paul L., ed. *The Myth of Measurability.* New York: Hart Publishing Co., 1977.

Howard, David. *Aphasia Therapy: Historical and Contemporary Issues.* Hillsdale, NJ: Erlbaum, 1987.

Howe, Michael J. A. *Fragments of Genius: The Strange Feats of Idiots Savants.* London: Routledge, 1989.

———. *The Origins of Exceptional Abilities.* Cambridge, MA: B. Blackwell, 1990.

Huesmann, L. Rowell, and Leonard D. Eron, eds. *Television and the Aggressive Child: A Cross-National Comparison.* Hillsdale, NJ: L. Erlbaum Associates, 1986.

Hughes, Fergus P. *Children, Play, and Development.* Boston: Allyn and Bacon, 1991.

Hunter, Ian. *On Pornography.* New York: St. Martin's Press, 1993.

Hyde, Margaret. *Brainwashing and Other Forms of Thought Control.* New York: McGraw-Hill, 1977.

Inglehart, Marita Rosc. *Reactions to Critical Life Events: A Social Psychological Analysis.* New York: Praeger, 1991.

J

Jackson, Stanley W. *Melancholia and Depression: From Hippocratic Times to the Present.* New Haven: Yale University Press, 1986.

Jamison, Kay. *Touched with Fire: Manic-Depressive Illness and the Artistic Temperament.* New York: Free Press, 1993.

Jenson, Jean C. *Reclaiming Your Life: A Step-by-step Guide to Using Regression Therapy to Overcome the Effects of Childhood Abuse.* New York: Dutton, 1995

Johnson, Sonia. *Wildfire: Igniting the She/Volution.* Albuquerque, NM: Wildfire Books, 1989.

Johnson-Laird, Philip N. *The Computer and the Mind: An Introduction to Cognitive Science.* Cambridge, MA: Harvard University Press, 1988.

Jordan, Rita. *Understanding and Teaching Children with Autism.* New York: Wiley, 1995.

K

Kahn, Ada, and Jan Fawcett, eds. *The Encyclopedia of Mental Health.* New York: Facts on File, 1993.

Kahn, Jack. *Unwillingly to School.* New York: Pergamon Press, 1981.

Kanfer, Frederick H. and Arnold P. Goldstein, eds. *Helping People Change: A Textbook of Methods,* 4th ed. New York: Pergamon Press, 1991.

Kantowitz, Barry H. *Experimental Psychology: Understanding Psychological Research,* 5th ed. St. Paul: West Publishing Company, 1994.

Kappeler, Susanne. *The Will to Violence: The Politics of Personal Behavior.* New York: Teachers College Press, 1995.

Katz, Dr. Stan J., and Eimee E. Liu. *The Codependency Conspiracy: How to Break the Recovery Habit and Take Charge of Your Life.* New York: Warner Books, 1991.

Kernberg, Paulina F. *Children with Conduct Disorders: A Psychotherapy Manual.* New York: Basic Books, 1991.

Klatzky, Roberta L. *Memory and Awareness: An Information-processing Perspective.* New York: W.H. Freeman, 1984.

Klinger, Eric. *Daydreaming: Using Waking Fantasy and Imagery for Self-Knowledge and Creativity.* Los Angeles, CA: J. P. Tarcher, 1990.

Kohlberg, Lawrence. *Child Psychology and Childhood Education: A Cognitive-Developmental View.* New York: Longman, 1987.

————. *The Psychology of Moral Development: The Nature and Validity of Moral Stages.* New York: Harper and Row, 1984.

Köhler, Wolfgang. *The Task of Gestalt Psychology.* Princeton, NJ: Princeton University Press, 1972.

Kohn, Alfie. *No Contest: The Case Against Competition.* Boston: Houghton Mifflin, 1986.

Kuiken, Don, ed. *Mood and Memory.* Newbury Park, CA: Sage Publications, 1991.

Kupperman, Joel. *Character.* New York: Oxford University Press, 1991.

L

Lacks, Patricia. *Bender Gestalt Screening for Brain Dysfunction.* New York: Wiley, 1984.

Lamberg, Lynne. *The American Medical Association Guide to Better Sleep.* New York: Random House, 1984.

Latani, Bibb. The *Unresponsive Bystander: Why Doesn't He Help?* New York: Appleton-Century Crofts, 1970.

Leahey, T. H. *A History of Modern Psychology.* 2nd ed. Englewood Cliffs, NJ: Prentice-Hall, 1994.

Lerner, Harriet Goldhor. *The Dance of Anger: A Woman's Guide to Changing the Patterns of Intimate Relationships.* New York: Perennial Library, Harper & Row, 1989.

Letting Go of Anger: The 10 Most Common Anger Styles and What To Do About Them. Oakland, CA: New Harbinger Publications, 1995.

Levand, Rhonda. *Sexual Evolution.* Berkeley, CA: Celestial Arts, 1991.

Levenkron, Steven. *Obsessive-Compulsive Disorders: Treating and Understanding Crippling Habits.* New York: Warner Books, 1991.

Ley, Ronald. *A Whisper of Espionage.* Garden City Park, NY: Avery Publishing Group, 1990.

Licata, Renora. *Everything You Need to Know About Anger.* New York: Rosen Publishing Group, 1994.

Lidz, Theodore. *The Origin and Treatment of Schizophrenic Disorders.* Madison, CT: International Universities Press, 1990.

Lieberman, David A. *Learning: Behavior and Cognition.* Belmont, CA: Wadsworth Publishing Co., 1990.

Liebert, Robert M., Joyce N. Sprafkin, and Emily S. Davidson. *The Early Window: Effects of Television on Children and Youth.* New York: Pergamon Press, 1982.

Lilienfeld, Scott O. *Seeing Both Sides: Classic Controversies in Abnormal Psychology.* Pacific Grove, CA: Brooks/Cole, 1995.

Lilly, John Cunningham. *The Deep Self: Profound Relaxation and the Tank Isolation Technique.* New York: Simon and Schuster, 1977.

Locke, John. *An Essay Concerning Human Understanding.* Buffalo: Prometheus Books, 1995.

Lorenz, Konrad. *The Foundations of Ethology.* New York: Springer-Verlag, 1981.

Lorie, Peter. *Superstitions.* New York: Simon & Schuster, 1992.

Luhn, Rebecca R. *Managing Anger: Methods for a Happier and Healthier Life.* Los Altos, CA: Crisp Publications, 1992.

M

McCann, Lisa. *Psychological Trauma and the Adult Survivor: Theory, Therapy, and Transformation.* New York: Brunner/Mazel, 1990.

McConville, Mark. *Adolescence: Psychotherapy and the Emergent Self.* San Francisco: Jossey-Bass Publishers, 1995.

McGoon, Dwight. *The Parkinson's Handbook.* New York: Norton, 1990

McKinney, William T. *Models of Mental Disorders: A New Comparative Psychiatry.* New York: Plenum, 1988.

Mackintosh, N. J. *Conditioning and Associative Learning.* New York: Oxford University Press, 1983.

Maloney, Michael. *Straight Talk About Eating Disorders.* New York: Facts on File, 1991.

Mandel, Harvey. *The Psychology of Underachievement.* New York: Wiley, 1988.

Marcus, Irwin M. and John J. Francis, eds. *Masturbation: From Infancy to Senescence.* New York: International Universities Press, 1975.

Martin, David W. *Doing Psychology Experiments,* 2nd ed. Monterey, CA: Brooks/Cole, 1985.

Martin, Margaret. *The Illustrated Book of Pregnancy and Childbirth.* New York: Facts on File, 1991.

Martini, Frederic. *Fundamentals of Anatomy and Physiology.* Englewood Cliffs, NJ: Prentice-Hall, 1995.

Maslow, Abraham. *Toward a Psychology of Being.* Princeton: Van Nostrand, 1962.

———. *Motivation and Personality.* 2nd ed. New York: Harper and Row, 1970.

May, Rollo. *Power and Innocence: A Search for the Sources of Violence.* New York: W. W. Norton, 1972.

Meinhold, Patricia. *Child Psychology: Development and Behavior Analysis.* Dubuque, IA: Kendall/Hunt Publishing Co., 1993.

Miles, T.R. *Dyslexia.* Philadelphia: Open University Press, 1990.

Mind and Brain: Readings from Scientific American Magazine. New York: W.H. Freeman, 1993.

Minton, Henry L. *Lewis M. Terman.* New York: New York University Press, 1988.

Minuchin, Salvador. *Family Therapy Techniques.* Cambridge, MA: Harvard University Press, 1981.

Moore, Bert S. and Alice M. Isen eds. *Affect and Social Behavior.* New York: Cambridge University Press, 1990.

Morrison, James. *DSM-IV Made Easy: The Clinician's Guide to Diagnosis.* New York: The Guilford Press, 1995.

Moyles, Janet R. *The Excellence of Play.* Philadelphia: Open University Press, 1994.

Moynihan, Martin. *The New World Primates: Adaptive Radiation and the Evolution of Social Behavior, Languages, and Intelligence.* Princeton, NJ: Princeton University Press, 1976.

N

Nardo, Don. *Anxiety and Phobias.* New York: Chelsea House, 1991.

Nathaniels, Peter. *Life Before Birth and a Time to Be Born.* Ithaca, NY: Promethean Press, 1992.

Nicholi, Armand, ed. *The New Harvard Guide to Psychiatry.* Cambridge, MA: Harvard University Press, 1988.

Nietzel, Michael T. *Introduction to Clinical Psychology,* 3rd ed. Englewood Cliffs, NJ: Prentice Hall, 1991.

O

Obler, L.K., and D. Fein, eds. *The Exceptional Brain: Neuropsychology of Talent and Special Abilities.* New York: Guilford Press, 1988.

Of Mice and Women: Aspects of Female Aggression. New York: Academic Press, 1992.

Oldham, John M. *The New Personality Self-Portrait.* New York: Bantam, 1995.

O'Leary, K. Daniel and G. Terence Wilson. *Behavior Therapy: Application and Outcome.* Englewood Cliffs, NJ: Prentice-Hall, 1975.

Ostow, Mortimer. *The Psychology of Melancholy.* New York: Harper & Row, 1970.

Owens, Karen. *The World of the Child.* New York: Holt, Rinehart, and Winston, 1987.

P

Packard, Vance Oakley. *The People Shapers.* Boston: Little, Brown, 1977.

Palma, Giuseppe. *Apathy and Participation: Mass Politics in Western Societies.* New York: Free Press, 1970.

Papalia, Diane E. *A Child's World: Infancy through Adolescence,* 5th ed. New York: McGraw-Hill, 1990.

Papolos, Demitri, M.D., and Janice Papolos. *Overcoming Depression.* New York: Harper and Row, 1987.

Paulus, Paul B., ed. *Psychology of Group Influence,* 2nd ed. Hillsdale, NJ: L. Erlbaum, 1989.

Peavy, J. Virgil. *Descriptive Statistics: Measures of Central Tendency and Dispersion.* Atlanta, GA: U.S. Dept. of Health and Human Services/Public Health Service, Centers for Disease Control, 1981.

Perry, Ralph B. *The Thought and Character of William James.* Cambridge, MA: Harvard University Press, 1948.

Personality and Ability: The Personality Assessment System. Lanham, MD: University Press of America, 1994.

Personality Disorders and the Five-Factor Model of Personality. Washington, DC: American Psychological Association, 1994.

Peterson, Christopher. *Learned Helplessness.* New York: Oxford University Press, 1993.

Piaget, Jean, and Bärbel Inhelder. *The Psychology of the Child.* New York: Basic Books, 1969.

Porterfield, Kay Marie. *Focus on Addictions: A Reference Handbook.* Santa Barbara: ABC-CLIO, 1992.

———. *Straight Talk About Post-traumatic Stress Disorder: Coping With the Aftermath of Trauma.* New York: Facts on File, 1996.

Powell, Barbara. *The Complete Guide to Your Child's Emotional Health.* Danbury, CT: F. Watts, 1984.

Putnam, Hilary. *Representation and Reality.* Cambridge, MA: MIT Press, 1988.

R

Ridley, Mark. *The Darwin Reader.* New York: Norton, 1987.

Rodgers, Joann Ellison. *Psychosurgery: Damaging the Brain to Save the Mind.* New York: HarperCollins Publishers, 1992.

Rogers, Carl. *Client-Centered Therapy.* Boston: Houghton Mifflin, 1951.

———. *On Becoming a Person.* Boston: Houghton Mifflin, 1961.

———. *A Way of Being.* Boston: Houghton Mifflin, 1980

Ronch, Judah L, William van Ornum, and Nicholas C. Stilwell, eds. *The Counseling Sourcebook: A Practical Reference on Contemporary Issues.* New York: Crossroad, 1994.

Rotter, Julian B. *The Development and Applications of a Social Learning Theory of Personality.* New York: Praeger, 1982.

Ruben, Douglas H. *Avoidance Syndrome: Doing Things Out of Fear.* St. Louis, MO: W.H. Green, 1993.

Russell, Bertrand. *A History of Western Philosophy.* New York: Simon and Schuster, 1945.

S

Salkind, Neil J.and Sueann Robinson Ambron. *Child Development,* 5th ed. New York: Holt, Rinehart and Winston 1987.

Satir, Virginia. *Conjoint Family Therapy.* Palo Alto, CA: Science and Behavior Books, 1983.

Sayers, Janet. *Mothers of Psychoanalysis.* New York: W.W. Norton, 1991

Scarborough, Elizabeth and Laurel Furumoto. *Untold Lives: The First Generation of American Women Psychologists.* New York: Columbia University Press, 1987.

Schultz, D. P. *A History of Modern Psychology,* 3rd ed. New York: Academic Press, 1981.

Schwitzgebel, Robert L., and R. Kirkland Schwitzgebel. *Law and Psychological Practice.* New York: Wiley, 1980.

Selye, Hans. *The Stress of Life.* New York: McGraw-Hill, 1978.

Siegel, Larry. *AIDS: The Drug and Alcohol Connection.* Center City, MN: Hazelden, 1989.

Singh, Joseph. *Wolf Children and Feral Man.* Hamden, CT: Archon Books, 1966

Sizemore, Chris Costner. *I'm Eve.* Garden City, NY: Doubleday, 1977.

Skinner, B.F. *About Behaviorism.* New York: Knopf, 1974.

———. *A Matter of Consequences.* New York: Knopf, 1983.

———. *Particulars of My Life.* New York: Knopf, 1976.

———. *The Shaping of a Behaviorist.* New York: Knopf, 1979.

Smith, Anthony. *The Mind.* New York: Viking Press, 1984.

Smith, Norman Kemp. *New Studies in the Philosophy of Descartes.* New York: Russell and Russell, 1963.

Stern, Richard. *The Practice of Behavioural and Cognitive Psychotherapy.* New York: Cambridge University Press, 1991.

Stone, William F., Gerda Lederer, and Richard Christie. eds. *Strength and Weakness: the Authoritarian Personality Today.* New York: Springer-Verlag, 1993.

Stress, Risk, and Resilience in Children and Adolescence. New York: Cambridge University Press, 1994.

Sutton, Nina. *Bettelheim, A Life and a Legacy.* New York: Basic Books, 1996.

T

Teplitz, Charles J. *The Learning Curve Deskbook: A Reference Guide to Theory, Calculations, and Applications.* New York: Quorum Books, 1991.

Thayer, Robert. *The Biophysiology of Mood and Arousal.* New York: Oxford University Press, 1989.

Thayer, S. *The Origin of Everyday Moods.* New York Oxford University Press, 1995.

Thigpen, Corbett H. *The Three Faces of Eve.* New York: Popular Library, 1957.

Thomas, R. Murray. *Comparing Theories of Child Development,* 3rd ed. Belmont, CA: Wadsworth Publishing Company, 1992.

Toth, Michele. *Understanding and Treating Conduct Disorders.* Austin, TX: Pro-Ed, 1990.

Tuttle, Frederick B. *Characteristics and Identification of Gifted and Talented Students.* Washington, D.C.: National Education Association, 1988.

V

Valenstein, Elliott S. *The Psychosurgery Debate: Scientific, Legal, and Ethical Perspectives.* San Francisco: W. H. Freeman, 1980.

Vernon, Ann, ed. *Counseling Children and Adolescents.* Denver, CO: Love, 1993.

Vrooman, J. R. *Rene Descartes: A Biography.* New York: Putnam, 1970.

W

Waites, Elizabeth A. *Trauma and Survival: Posttraumatic and Dissociative Disorders in Women.* New York: Norton, 1993.

Wallace, Betty, and William Graves. *Poisoned Apple: The Bell-Curve Crisis and How Schools Create Mediocrity and Failure.* New York: St. Martin's Press, 1995.

Weary, Gifford. *Attribution.* New York: Springer-Verlag,1989.

Weigert, Andrew. *Mixed Emotions.* Albany: SUNY Press, 1991.

White, Gregory. *Jealousy.* New York: Guilford Press, 1989.

Williams, Redford, M.D., and Virginia Williams, Ph.D. *Anger Kills: Seventeen Strategies for Controlling the Hostility that Can Harm Your Health.* New York: HarperPerennial, 1993.

Wise, Paula Sachs. *The Use of Assessment Techniques by Applied Psychologists.* Belmont, CA: Wadsworth Publishing Co., 1989.

Wolf, Theta Holmes. *Alfred Binet.* Chicago: University of Chicago Press, 1973.

Wolpe, Joseph. *The Practice of Behavior Therapy.* Tarrytown, NY: Pergamon Press, 1990.

Wyer, Robert S., Jr., ed. *Knowledge and Memory: the Real Story.* Hillsdale, NJ: Lawrence Erlbaum, 1995.

——— and T. K. Srull, eds. *Handbook of Social Cognition,* 2nd ed., Hillsdale, NJ: Erlbaum Associates, 1994.

Y

Your Child's Emotional Health: Adolescence. New York: Macmillan, 1994

Z

Zebrowitz, Leslie. *Social Perception.* Pacific Grove, CA: Brooks/Cole Publishing Co., 1990

Zigler, Edward. *Understanding Mental Retardation.* Cambridge, Eng.: Cambridge University Press, 1986

Zimbardo, Philip G. *Psychology and Life,* 12th ed. Glenview, IL: Scott, Foresman, 1988

———. *The Psychology of Attitude Change and Social Influence.* Philadelphia: Temple University Press, 1991.

Videorecordings

A Conversation With Magic. Lucky Duck Productions, 1992.

Epilepsy: An Overview. Cleveland, OH: Cleveland Clinic Foundation, 1993.

Moving Parts. Princeton, NJ: Films for the Humanities, 1985.

PMS: It's Not in Your Head. Omaha, NB: Envision Communications, 1993.

The Three Faces of Eve. Beverly Hills, CA: Fox-Video, 1993.

ORGANIZATIONS

Alcoholics Anonymous World Services (AA)
Address: P. O. Box 459, Grand Central Station
New York, NY 10163
Telephone: 212-870-3400

American Academy of Pediatrics
Address: 141 Northwest Point Blvd.
P. O. Box 927
Elk Grove Village, IL 40009-0927
Telephone: 708-228-5005

Academy of Sport Psychology International (ASPI)
Address: 6079 Northgate Rd.,
Columbus, Ohio 43229
Telephone: 614-846-2275

American Academy of Child and Adolescent Psychiatry (AACAP)
Address: 3615 Wisconsin Avenue, NW
Washington, DC 20016
Telephone: 202-996-7300

American Anorexia and Bulimia Association (AA-BA)
Address: 418 E. 78th Street,
New York, NY 10021
Telephone: 212-734-1114

American Association of Psychiatric Services for Children (AAPSC)
Address: 1133 15th Street, NW, Suite 1000
Washington, DC 20005
Telephone: 202-429-9440

American Association for Correctional Psychology (Formerly American Association of Correctional Psychologists)
Address: West Virginia University
College of Graduate Studies Institute
Morgantown, West Virginia 25112
Telephone: (304) 766-1929

American Association of Mental Retardation (AAMR)
Address: 444 North Capitol St. NW, Suite 846,
Washington, DC 20001
Telephone: 202-387-1968

American College of Sports Medicine
Address: P.O. Box 1440, Indianapolis,
Indiana 46206-1440
Telephone: 317-637-9200

American Dietetic Association (ADA)
NCDC-Eating Disorders
Address: 216 W. Jackson Blvd.,
Chicago, Illinois 60606
Telephone: 800-366-1655

American Paralysis Association
  24-hour tool-free information and referral hotline
  Telephone: 800-526-3256

American Psychiatric Association
  Address: 1400 K Street, NW
  Washington, D.C. 20005
  Telephone: 202-682-6000

American Psychological Association
  Address: 1200 Seventeenth Street NW
  Washington, D.C. 20036
  Telephone: 202-336-5500

American Psychological Society
  Address: 1010 Vermont Avenue, Suite 1100
  Washington, D.C. 20005
  Telephone: 202-783-2077

American Psychology-Law Society
  Address: University of Massachusetts Medical Center
   Department of Psychology
   55 Lake Avenue N.
  Worcester, Massachusetts 01655
  Telephone: (508) 856-3625

American Society for Adolescent Psychiatry (ASAP)
  Address: 24 Green Valley Road
  Wallingford, PA 19086
  Telephone: 215-566-1054

American Society of Clinical Hypnosis
  Address: 2200 East Devon Avenue, Suite 291
  Des Plaines, Illinois 60018
  Telephone: (847) 297-3317

Anxiety Disorder Association of America (ADAA)
  Address: 6000 Executive Blvd.
  Rockville, MD 20852
  Telephone: 301-231-9350

Association of Sleep Disorders Centers
  Address: 604 2nd St., SW
  Rochester, MN 55902
  Telephone: 507-287-6006

Autism Society of America
  (formerly National Society for Autistic Children)
  Address: 7910 Woodmont Avenue, Suite 650
  Bethesda, MD 20814-3015
  Telephone: 301-657-0881; 800-3328-8476

The College Board
  Address: 45 Columbus Avenue
  New York, NY 10023
  Telephone: 212-713-8000

Council for Learning Disabilities
  Address: P. O. Box 40303
  Overland Park, KS 66204
  Telephone:913-492-8755

International Society for Traumatic Stress Studies
  Address: 435 North Michigan Ave., Suite 1717,
  Chicago, IL 60611
  Telephone: 312-644-0828.

International Society of Sports Psychology
  Address: Department of Kinesiology,
  University of Illinois at Urbana-Champaign,
  906 S. Goodwin Ave.,
  Urbana, Illinois 61801
  Telephone: 217- 333-6563

Mental Disability Legal Resource Center (MDLRD)
  Address: c/o American Bar Association
  1800 M Street, NW
  Washington, DC 20036
  Telephone: 202-331-2240

National Alliance for the Mentally Ill (NAMI)
    Address: 1901 Fort Myer Drive, Suite 500
    Arlington, VA 22209
    Telephone: 703-524-7600

National Anoretic Aid Society
    Address: 445 E. Dublin-Granville Road,
    Worthington, Ohio 43229
    Telephone: 614-436-1112

National Association of Anorexia Nervosa and
Associated Disorders (ANAD)
    Address: Box 7, Highland Park, Illinois 60035
    Telephone: 708-831-3438

National Association of Rehabilitation Facilities
    Address: P.O. Box 17675
    Washington, D.C. 20041
    Telephone: 703-648-9300

National Association of School Psychologists
    Address: 4340 East-West Highway, Suite 402
    Bethesda, MD 20814-4411
    Telephone: 301/657-0270

National Clearinghouse for Alcohol and Drug
Abuse Information
    Address: P. O. Box 2345
    Rockville, MD 20857
    Telephone: 301-443-6500

National Council on Alcoholism and Drug Dependency
    Address: 12 West 21st St., 7th Floor
    New York, NY 10010
    Telephone: 212-206-6770;
    Toll-free: 800-NCA-CALL (622-2255)

National Down Syndrome Congress
    Address: 1800 Dempster Street
    Park Ridge, Illinois 60068-1146
    Telephone: 708-823-7550; (800) 232-NDSC

National Down Syndrome Society
    Address: 666 Broadway
    New York, New York 10012
    Telephone: 212-460-9330; (800) 221-4602

National Institute of Child Health and Human Development, Office of Research Reporting
    Adddress: Building 31, Room 2A32
    Bethesda, MD 20892
    Telephone: 301-496-5133

National Institute of Mental Health, Information
Resources and Inquiries Branch (IRIB)
    Adddress: 5600 Fishers Lane, Room 7C-02
    Rockville, MD 20857
    Telephone: 301-443-4513

National Rehabilitation Association
    Address: 633 S. Washington St.
    Alexandria, Virginia 22314
    Telephone: 703-836-0850

National Spinal Cord Injury Association
    Telephone: 800-962-9629

Society for Clinical and Experimental Hypnosis
    Address: 3905 Vincennes Road, Suite 304
    Indianapolis, Indiana 46268
    Telephone: (800) 214-1738

World Health Organization
    Address: 20 Avenue Appia
    CH-1211
    Geneva 27, Switzerland
    Telephone: 41-22-791-21 11

INDEX

BY SUBFIELD

Abnormal Psychology

Abnormal Psychology *(continued)*

Psychotic Disorders

Pyromania

Reaction Formation

Savant Syndrome

Schizophrenia

Sodomy

Transference

Behavior

Aggression

Ambivalence

Anger

Arousal

Attachment

Autoeroticism

Avoidance Learning

Behavior Disorder

Behavior Modification

Behavior Therapy

Behaviorism

Biofeedback

Birth Order

Birth Trauma

Bystander Effect

Classical/Respondent Conditioning

Compensation

Conditioned Response

Conditioned Stimulus

Conditioning

Darwin, Charles

Desensitization

Diagnostic and Statistical Manual of Mental Disorders (DSM-IV)

Extinction

Fear

Heterosexuality

Homosexuality

Hostility

Imprinting

Instinct

Jealousy

Law of Effect

Learned Helplessness

Melancholia

Motivation

Narcissism

Nature/Nurture Controversy

Obsessive-Compulsive Disorder (OCD)

Operant Conditioning

Paraphilia

Placebo Effect

Psychological Abstracts

Psychosexual Development

Punishment

Reflexes

Reinforcement

Sexuality

Shaping

Shyness

Superstition

Biographical Profiles

Adler, Alfred (1870–1937)

Bandura, Albert (1925–)

Beers, Clifford (1876–1943)

Bettleheim, Bruno (1903–1990)

Binet, Alfred (1857–1911)

Bruner, Jerome S. (1915-)

Calkins, Mary Whiton (1863–1930)

Cattell, James McKeen (1860–1944)

Chomsky, Noam (1928–)

Darwin, Charles Robert (1809-1882)

Descartes, René (1596-1650)

Dewey, John (1859-1952)

Ebbinghaus, Hermann (1850–1909)

Ellis, Albert (1913–)

Erikson, Erik (1902–1994)

Freud, Anna (1895–1982)

Freud, Sigmund (1856–1939)

Fromm, Erich (1900–1980)

Galton, Sir Francis (1822-1911)

Gesell, Arnold (1880–1961)

Horney, Karen (1885–1952)

James, William (1842–1910)

Jensen, Arthur R. (1923–)

Jung, Carl (1875-1961)

Kohlberg, Lawrence (1927–1987)

Köhler, Wolfgang (1887–1967)

Ladd-Franklin, Christine (1847–1930)

Maslow, Abraham (1908–1970)

Masters, William (1915–)

Mead, Margaret (1901–1978)

Meyer, Adolf (1866–1950)

Otis, Arthur (1886–1964)

Pavlov, Ivan (1849–1936)

Piaget, Jean (1896–1980)

Pinel, Philippe (1745–1826)

Puffer, Ethel Dench (1872–1950)

Rogers, Carl (1902–1987)

Rush, Benjamin (1746–1813)

Shinn, Milicent W. (1858–1940)

Skinner, B. F. (1904–1990)

Terman, Lewis (1877–1956)

Thorndike, Edward (1874–1949)

Washburn, Margaret Floy (1871–1939)

Watson, John Broadus (1878–1958)

Yerkes, Robert (1876–1956)

Biological

Action Potential

Addiction/Addictive Personality

Aging

Alcohol Dependence And Abuse

Alcoholism

Alzheimer's Disease

Apgar Score

Aphasia

Autoeroticism

Autonomic Nervous System

Biofeedback

Bipolar Disorder

Birth

Brain

Central Nervous System

Codependence

Color Vision

Coma

Delirium

Dendrite

Denial

Deoxyribonucleic Acid (DNA)

Biological *(continued)*

Diagnostic and Statistical Manual of Mental Disorders (DSM-IV)

Disability

Down Syndrome

Drugs

Dyslexia

Electrical Stimulation of the Brain (ESB)

Electroencephalograph (EEG)

Endocrine Glands

Epilepsy

Equilibrium Sense

Experimental Design

Hallucinations

Hearing

Heterosexuality

Homosexuality

Hormone

Hypothalamus

Left-Brain Hemisphere

Left-Handedness

Marijuana

Neocortex

Nerve

Nervous System

Neuron

Neurotransmitter

Obesity

Organic Disorder

Parkinson's Disease

Premenstrual Syndrome (PMS)

Psychological Abstracts

Psychosomatic Disorders

Psychotic Disorders

Rapid Eye Movement (REM)

Reflexes

Ribonucleic Acid (RNA)

Right-Brain Hemisphere

Right-Handedness

Signal Detection Theory

Sleep

Sleep Disorders

Smell

Split-Brain Technique

Taste

Thalamus

Touch

Twins

Unconscious

Vision

Cognitive Development

Amnesia

Artificial Intelligence

Assimilation

Attention

Cognition

Cognitive Behavior Therapy

Cognitive Dissonance

Cognitive Psychology

Consciousness

Diagnostic and Statistical Manual of Mental Disorders (DSM-IV)

Forgetting Curve

Free-Recall Learning

Information-Processing Approach

Instrumental Behavior

Language Acquisition

Learning Theory

Memory

Cognitive Development *(continued)*

Mental Imagery

Mnemonic Strategies

Neuron

Paired-Associate Learning

Psychological Abstracts

Psychotic Disorders

Role Playing/Psychodrama

Semantic Memory

Serial Learning

Serial Position Function

Sex Identity

Synapse

Developmental Psychology

Achievement Tests

Adaptation

Adolescence

Aggression

Aging

Arousal

Assimilation

Child Development

Classical/Respondent Conditioning

Cognitive Development Theory

Concept Learning

Critical Period

Cross-Sectional Study

Defense Mechanism

Depression

Developmental Stages, Theories of

Diagnostic and Statistical Manual of Mental Disorders (DSM-IV)

Ego

Emotion

Empiricism

Ethology

Experimental Design

Heredity

Identity

Imitation

Imprinting

Infancy

Intelligence

Intelligence Quotient, I.Q. Test

Interpersonal Attraction

Jukes Family

Kallikak Family

Longitudinal Study

Mental Age

Mental Retardation

Middle Years

Modeling

Moral Development

Nature/Nurture Controversy

Oedipus Complex

Paired-Associate Learning

Personality

Play

Programmed Learning

Psychoanalysis

Psychological Abstracts

Psychosexual Development

Puberty

Repression

Schizophrenia

Self-Actualization

Self-Concept

Sex Identity

Social Influence

Social Learning Theory

Socialization

Developmental Psychology *(continued)*

Speech Disorders
Stress
Test Anxiety
Traits

Twins
Unconscious
Wechsler Intelligence Scales

History of Psychology

Absolute Threshold
Applied Psychology
Associationism
Child Psychiatrist
Child Psychologist
Child Psychology
Classical/Respondent Conditioning
Client-Centered Therapy
Clinical Psychology
Cognitive Psychology
Comparative Psychology
Conditioned Response
Consciousness
Counseling Psychology
Determinism
Developmental Psychology
Diagnostic and Statistical Manual of Mental Disorders (DSM-IV)
Differential Psychology
Electroconvulsive Therapy (ECT)
Empiricism
Encounter Group
Ethology
Eugenics
Experimental Psychology
Figure-Ground Perception
Forgetting Curve
Functionalism
Gestalt Principles of Organization
Gestalt Psychology

Group Therapy
Hypnosis
Hypothesis Testing
Industrial Psychology
Instinct
Intelligence Quotient, I.Q. Test
Learning Theory
Localization (Brain Function)
Mental Health
Parapsychology
Philosphical Psychology
Phrenology
Physiological Psychology
Pleasure Principle
Projective Techniques
Psychiatry/Psychiatrist
Psychoanalysis
Psychological Abstracts
Psychology/Psychologist
Psychophysics
Psychotherapy
Reinforcement
Rorschach Technique
Rosenzweig Picture Frustration Study
Scholastic Assessment Test
Scientific Method
Sensitivity Training
Social Learning Theory
Social Psychology
Sports Psychology

Methodology and Statistics

Achievement Tests

Assessment, Psychological

Bender-Gestalt Test

Brainwashing

Classical/Respondent Conditioning

Client-Centered Therapy

Conditioned Stimulus

Control Group

Correlation Method

Cross-Sectional Study Method

Dependent Variable

Diagnostic and Statistical Manual of Mental Disorders (DSM-IV)

Draw-A-Person Test

Experimental Design

Forensic Psychology

Frequency Distribution

Health Psychology

Holtzman Inkblot Test

Hypothesis Testing

Learning Curve

Learning-to-Learn

Longitudinal Study

Mean

Measurement

Median

Metapsychology

Mnemonic Strategies

Mode

Norm

Normal Distribution

Psychological Abstracts

Psychosurgery

Rating Scale

Readiness Test

Regression

Rehabilitation

Research Methods

School Psychology

Scientific Method

Signal Detection Theory

Significance Level

Stanford-Binet Intelligence Scales

Statistics

Vocational Aptitude Test

Wechsler Intelligence Scales

Organizations

American Psychiatric Association

American Psychological Association (APA)

American Psychological Society (APS)

National Association of School Psychologists

National Institute of Mental Health

Perception

Absolute Threshold

Alienation

Binocular Depth Cues

Catharsis

Color Vision

Conscience

▌Perception *(continued)*

Contrast

Daydreaming

Delayed Response

Depth Perception

Diagnostic and Statistical Manual of Mental Disorders (DSM-IV)

Dreams

Fantasy

Figure-Ground Perception

Frequency (Audition)

Gestalt Principles Of Organization

Hallucinations

Handedness

Insight

Just-Noticeable Difference

Kinesthetic Sense

Localization

Pain

Perception

Preconscious

Psychological Abstracts

Psychophysics

Psychosomatic Disorders

Self-Actualization

Self-Concept

Sensory Deprivation

Signal Detection Theory

Sleep Disorders

Social Perception

Stress

Visual Angle

▌Personality

Ability

Achievement Tests

Anonymity

Archetype

Attitudes and Attitude Change

Attribution

Authoritarian Personality

Body Image

Catharsis

Character

Conduct Disorder

Creativity

Defense Mechanism

Depression

Desensitization

Diagnostic and Statistical Manual of Mental Disorders (DSM-IV)

Dissociation/Dissociative Disorder

Dissociative Identity Disorder

Ego

Emotion

Experimental Design

Free Association

Id

Identity

Imagination

Inferiority Complex

Instinct

Intelligence

Intelligence Quotient, I.Q. Test

Interest Inventory

Interpersonal Attraction

Introversion/Extroversion

Jukes Family

Kallikak Family

Personality (continued)

Libido

Modeling

Mood

Moral Development

Motivation

Nature/Nurture Controversy

Oedipus Complex

Overachiever

Personality

Personality Disorders

Personality Inventory

Pleasure Principle

Power

Projective Techniques

Psychoanalysis

Psychological Abstracts

Psychosexual Development

Reaction Formation

Regression

Schizophrenia

Self-Actualization

Self-Concept

Social Learning Theory

Socialization

Standardized Test

Stanford-Binet Intelligence Scales

Superego

Temperament

Traits

Transference

Twins

Unconscious

Unconscious Motivation

Underachiever

Social Psychology

Adaptation

Adjustment Disorders

Adoption

Affect

Affiliation

Americans with Disabilities Act (ADA)

Arousal

Assimilation

Attitudes and Attitude Change

Birth Order

Bystander Effect

Child Abuse

Cognitive Dissonance

Competition

Conduct Disorder

Conflict Resolution

Conformity

Conversion Reaction

Correlation Method

Cross Cultural Psychology

Cults

Depression

Desensitization

Diagnostic and Statistical Manual of Mental Disorders (DSM-IV)

Divorce

Drive Reduction Theory

Effectors

Emotion

Empathy

Environment

Ethnocentrism

Family Size

Family Therapy

Social Psychology *(continued)*

Fixation
Functional Fixedness
Gender Bias
General Adaptation Syndrome
Gifted Children
Halo Effect
Human Potential Movement
Humor
Identity
Incest
Internal-External Control (I-E)
Interpersonal Attraction
Juvenile Delinquency
Learned Helplessness
Mania
Marriage Counseling
Mental Hospitals
Milgram's Obedience Experiment
Modeling
Need
Normal
Panic

Personality
Placebo Effect
Pornography
Prejudice
Psychiatric Institution
Psychological Abstracts
Punishment
Racism
Rape
Role Playing (Psychodrama)
School Phobia
Self-Concept
Self-Fulfilling Prophecy
Sex Identity
Social Influence
Social Learning Theory
Social Perception
Socialization
Stereotype
Suicide
Television
Violence

SUBJECT INDEX

C

D

influence on Arthur R. Jensen 207
theory of personality 272
views on introversion/extroversion 203

F

Family size 147
Family therapy 147–148
Fantasy 148–149,
Fear 133, 149, 275, 286
    and motivation 246
    avoidance learning 39
Fechner, Gustav 127, 144, 275, 295
    experimental psychology and 144
    Elements of Psychology 144
Feminism and psychoanalysis 290
Feral children 36, 150
Festinger, Leon 341
    theory of cognitive dissonance 34, 75–77
Fetal alcohol syndrome 15
"Fight or flight" response 5, 149, 265, 284
Figure-ground perception 151
Firestone, Shulamith 290
First-born children 50
Fixation 151–152
Fixed action patterns in ethology theory 141
Flight or fight. *See* "Fight or flight" response
Flood 284
Forebrain 52, 62
Forensic psychology 27, 152–153, 295
Forgetting curve 153
Formal operations stage 66, 75
Foulkes, David 121
Fournies, Ferdinand 346
Fowler, Lorenzo 277
Fowler, Orson 277
Free association 60, 153–154, 156, 285, 291
    unconscious 363
Free-recall learning 154
Frequency (audition) 154–155, 270
Frequency distribution 155
Freud, Anna 155–156, 292

childhood amnesia 21
influence on Erik Erikson 139
Freud, Sigmund 8, 24, 60, 66, 67, 79, 97, 130,
        156–158, 196, 233, 243, 259, 271, 291,
        294, 296, 307, 349, 352, 360, 363
    aggression 12
    conscience 85
    consciousness 285
    daydream and fantasy 97
    definition of conversion reaction 88
    determinism 107
    dreams 120
    environment 136
    father of Anna 155
    fixation 151
    free association 153
    humor 183
    incest 193
    influence on Adolph Meyer 240
    influence on Carl Jung 208
    influence on Erich Fromm 158
    influence on Karen Horney 181
    influence on William James 206
    instinct 197
    homosexuality 180
    libido 225
    narcissism 247
    personality development 272
    post-traumatic stress disorder 283
    psychosexual development 296–297
    psychotherapy 298
    reaction formation 306
    regression 307
    unconscious motivation 363
    views on the id 190
Fritsch, Gustav 226
Fromm, Erich 158, 272, 292
    influence on Abraham Maslow 231
Frustration-aggression hypothesis 12
Functional disorder 159
    controversy over use of term 159
Functional fixedness 159
Functionalism 159–160
Fuzzy logic 29

G

H

I

J

K

L

M

N

O

P

T